PEGGY

PEGGY

THE
WAYWARD
GUGGENHEIM

JACQUELINE
BOGRAD
WELD

E. P. DUTTON | NEW YORK

*Published in the United States by
E. P. Dutton, a division of Penguin Books USA Inc.,
2 Park Avenue, New York, N.Y. 10016*

*Library of Congress Cataloging-in-Publication Data
Weld, Jacqueline Bograd.*
    Peggy, the wayward Guggenheim.
    *1. Gugenheim, Peggy.   2. Art patrons—
United States—Biography.   I. Title.*
N5220.G886W4 1986   709'.04'00750924 [B]   85-13162
ISBN 0-525-48431-0

*Published simultaneously in Canada
by Fitzhenry & Whiteside Limited, Toronto*

Designed by Steven N. Stathakis

10 9 8 7 6 5 4 3 2

For **My** *Crowd and for Matt*

CONTENTS

Photographic inserts follow pages 174 and 398.

With a tiny oval landscape by Tanguy dangling from one earlobe and a small Calder mobile from the other, Peggy Guggenheim opened her museum-gallery Art of This Century in wartime New York. Her hair dyed a shoe-polish black, her startled cerulean eyes staring relentlessly above a large and bulbous nose, her lipstick running and always out of place, Peggy, said a friend, looked more like one of de Kooning's women than a doyenne of modern art. Well over forty, and an avowed art addict, she was back in New York after a self-imposed exile of twenty years in Europe spent at the heart of bohemia, and she was just beginning her biggest adventure.

In 1940, with the Germans about to march through Paris, Peggy had scrambled around the city, frantically buying up pictures by the great modern masters, carefully checking off each one against a master list. Then, with the Nazis at her heels, Peggy escaped to America with her former husband, their children, his wife, *their* children, her own husband-to-be, and her paintings, eager to show New York what she had acquired.

"Isms rampant!" screeched the press, and the public agreed. Not only was the art revolutionary, but the gallery space that Frederick Kiesler had created for Peggy's collection caused a sensation. Curved gumwood walls, ultramarine canvas sails, turquoise floors, pictures mounted on what looked like baseball bats or suspended from ropes, paintings whirling on a Ferris wheel, Surrealist creations viewed through a peephole—these and more innovations thrilled gallery-goers, painters, and museum directors alike. It was a carnival of the *outré,* a theater for painting, a world away from the neighboring galleries up and down Fifty-seventh Street, all discreetly covered in dark velvet and tastefully displaying their pictures in baroque gilded frames. Peggy was interviewed and photographed; reporters pondered the astonishing phenomenon on West Fifty-seventh Street; and the woman at the center gloried in every attention-grabbing moment.

At first Peggy exhibited her own collection of European avant-garde art, but soon she began showing little-known and unrecognized American artists such as Robert Motherwell, Mark Rothko, Clyfford Still, William Baziotes, Hans Hofmann, and the most sensational of all, Jackson Pollock—a generation of artists who would radically change the course of art in America. Intrepid and even reckless, Peggy was giving a chance to those embryonic Abstract Expressionists—painters other dealers wouldn't touch. A revolution in painting was going on, and she was its impresario.

Peggy's gallery and the artists and intellectuals around her were an extraordinary addition to New York during the 1940s. As thousands of European émigrés sought refuge from Hitler's advancing armies, in her gallery and in her house overlooking the East River on Beekman Place Peggy played hostess to the most dazzling salon of the war era. Young American painters could come and meet the European giants they had until then only read about: Mondrian, Léger, Breton, Tanguy, and Peggy's then husband Max Ernst.

Peggy had traveled a long way. And whether she was, as it was always disputed, monstrous or angelic, horrific or gracious, she was nevertheless a Guggenheim heiress. Born in 1898 at the outer edge of the Victorian era into one of the stuffiest families of New York's Jewish elite, popularly known as "Our Crowd," Peggy grew up with the twentieth century. Leaving behind her gilded childhood with its nannies and German governesses and grand tours of Europe, Peggy made her way through the bohemian world of the 1920s, furiously rebelling against her family and its mores, to seize her moment and make of herself a Guggenheim legend.

This glamorous woman lived her life surrounded by brilliant people. In a time when women found value through their husbands, Peggy sought it through association with the great and the famous. She had an uncanny instinct for stars, and above all, for talent. By ignoring the day-to-day problems that distract other people, Peggy was able to create a historic art collection with relatively little money and to promote along the way the breakthrough artists of her era.

Peggy belonged to a generation that was out to stun. Like the generation of the 1960s, Peggy's contemporaries reacted to an unpopular war by turning inward and smashing all accepted notions of taste, decorum, and convention. Dada and Surrealism were spawned by this collective nihilism and it was with Surrealism that Peggy became most closely associated. Surrealism was not just a hermetic art movement (in fact it gave little importance to aesthetics), but a social and political movement that strove for nothing less than to change the world. Scandal was its weapon, newsprint was its ally. With appetites for self-promotion worthy of rock stars, the Surrealists became early "media personalities," created by a press eager for titillation who saw in their wild antics a threat to the very heart of the established order. (Peggy, too, learned how to turn publicity to her own advantage.)

In the 1930s and 1940s Surrealism offered an alternative to the dehumanizing forces of guns and dictators. Then in the 1960s Dada and Surrealism returned as Happenings, performance art, Pop Art, and Andy Warhol's soup cans. And today, artists are turning once again to the jarring content, total environments, and inward-searching perspective of the Surrealists. Dada and Surrealism continue to fascinate, although it is no longer shocking when an artist pins a stuffed monkey to a wall, dances nude to a cello, or encloses the remains of his dinner in Plexiglas. In advertisements, rock videos, and plate-shard "paintings" we are bombarded with the fruits of the Surrealist revolution: originality for its own sake, the notion that life itself—pure, raw, and naked—is an art form, and that the "idea" is more important than its execution.

When I met Peggy Guggenheim she was nearing eighty, a frail woman with an astonishing nose, a fringe of white bangs, and huge, wistful, almost pleading blue eyes. She looked rather grandmotherly. In contrast to this meek demeanor, the references I had heard to her were often violent and bitter. How was I to reconcile this shy, plaintive presence with the flamboyant Peggy Guggenheim of the wild escapades and a thousand lovers? How had it happened that while other far richer heiresses had spent their time buying dresses and marrying playboys this woman collected the greatest art and artists of her day? These became the questions I set out to answer in this book.

ACKNOWLEDGMENTS

A book such as mine could never have been written without the kind and generous participation of Peggy's friends, relatives, and associates who were willing to share their memories and time. I am grateful to Peggy Guggenheim herself, who spent hours and days with me and who made available to me her scrapbooks, photographs, and letters. I am deeply grateful to Sindbad and Peggy Vail for their kindness and encouragement; to John Hohnsbeen for his help and hospitality; to Clover Vail, Apple Vail, Sharon and John Cowling; to Jean and Jacqueline Hélion, Fabrice, David, and Nicolas Hélion, Sandro Rumney, Jimmy Ernst; and to Alan Ansen, Rupert Barneby, Paolo Barozzi, Ethel Baziotes, Roloff Beny, Paul Bowles, Robert Brady, Elizabeth Broadhurst, Joel Carmichael, Eleanor Castle-Stewart, Brian Coffey, John Coleman, Jenifer Cosgrieff, Malcolm Cowley, Joan Lewisohn Crowell, Eileen Geist Finletter, Robert Fizdale, Ruth Ford, Audrey Fowler, Christina Franchetti, Mark Glazebrook, Silas Glossop, Arthur Gold, Mary Jayne Gold, John Goodwin, Clement Greenberg, Yvonne Hagen, David Hare, Nigel Henderson, Sidney Janis, Buffie Johnson, Maria Jolas, David Kalstone, Ormond de Kay, Lillian Kiesler, Guitou Knoop, Lee Krasner, Jacqueline Lamba, Peter Lawson-Johnston, Julien and Jean Levy, Audrey (Mrs. Cornelius Ruxton) Love, Iris Love, Joe Martin, Paul Matisse, Pierre Matisse, Mary

McCarthy, Hazel McKinley, Taylor Mead, Thomas Messer, Dorothy Miller, Susan Miller, Henry Moore, John Bernard Myers, Betty Parsons, Flavia Paulon, Roland Penrose, Eleanor Perenyi, Guido Perocco, Benedict Read, Sir Norman Reid, Rebecca Reis, John Richardson, May Tabak Rosenberg, Maria Theresa Rubin, Jane and Philip Rylands, Giuseppe Santomaso, Ethel Schwabacher, Charles Seliger, Maude Seligman, George Smith, Theodoros Stamos, Jimmy and Tanya Stern, Marietta Stern, Hedda Sterne, Roger Straus, Jane Bouché Strong, James Johnson Sweeney, Bridget Tichenor, Christina Thoresby, Peter Tunnard, Emilio Vedova, Catherine Viviano, Lorna Wishart, and Michael Wishart.

I am grateful to Peggy Guggenheim for permission to quote from her unpublished letters; to Sindbad Vail for permission to quote from his unpublished letters and for permission to quote from the unpublished memoirs and letters of his father, Laurence Vail; to Aube Breton for permission to quote from the unpublished letters of André Breton; to Lillian Kiesler for permission to quote from the unpublished letters of Frederick Kiesler; to Dorothy Miller for permission to quote from Holger Cahill's statements at the Columbia University Oral History Archives; to Benedict Read for permission to quote from the unpublished letters of Herbert Read.

I am grateful to the following libraries and archives: The Archives of American Art, Smithsonian Institution, Washington, D.C.; Helen Harrison and the Guild Hall Museum, East Hampton, Long Island; The Museum of Modern Art Library; Frederick Kiesler Archives at The Museum of Modern Art; The University of Maryland, McKeldin Library, Djuna Barnes Archives; The University of Victoria Library, Special Collections, Herbert Read Archives; The New-York Historical Society; The New York Society Library; The New York Public Library; The Columbia University Oral History Archives; Carl White and Paula Grey at the J. & W. Seligman Archives; George Fountaine and the Solomon R. Guggenheim Foundation; Ward Jackson and Regina O'Brien at the Solomon R. Guggenheim Museum Archives.

I am also indebted to Steven M. L. Aronson, who helped me and encouraged me when this book was just an idea; to Dr. William G. Niederland for his views on German child-rearing practices; to Dr. Nathaniel Ross for his insights into the mental illnesses of Peggy's world; to Martha Bograd Lubowski for her help with the notes and citations; to Pat Hackett for her valuable contributions; to Dr. Barbara Welt Bernheim for her help with the manuscript and notes and expertise on "Our Crowd"; to my agents, Pat Berens and Philippa Brophy, for their efforts on my behalf; to Thomas Lee Jones for his suggestions; to Bill Murray for his help; to Susan Wells for her research assistance; to Ronald A. and Pamela Dwight and Elaine Dedekian for their help in Washington, D.C.; to Kerry Roland for keeping my body together; to Elizabeth Burke for her help with the manuscript; to John Whethers for getting me my Victor 9000 Computer.

I am especially indebted for her valuable suggestions and dedication to my editor, Jennifer Josephy, who has guided me and been enthusiastic, unstintingly supportive, and delightful to work with; to Jean Rawitt, who has likewise been enthusiastically supportive; I am also grateful to my loving family, who put up with me through years of obsessive absorption in the life of Peggy Guggenheim: Miguel and Beatriz Bograd; Mercedes, Joel, Rachel, and Peter Levin; Martha, Ruben, and Alicia Lubowski; Estrellita, Dan, Alexander, Katy, and Thomas Brodsky; to Jane, Jonathan, Elizabeth, Eric, and Penelope Weld, Sally and Grant Webb; and to my dear friends Jane and Billy Hitchcock, Alfredo Ortiz-Murias, Jeannette and Alexander Sanger; and to my husband Matt.

PART I

A GILDED CAGE

FROM SELLING RAGS TO RICHES

When Peggy's mother Florette Seligman married Ben Guggenheim in 1894, noses went up—especially Seligman noses—and it was widely believed among Florette's relations that she was making a *mésalliance.* In the cloistered world of New York's Jewish elite the Seligmans reigned supreme. Educated, cultivated, and wealthy, they had been respected international bankers for thirty years and had lived in America for nearly twice that long. The aristocrats of "Our Crowd," "they set the tone of German Jewish society in New York for many years," wrote Stephen Birmingham, occupying "an anchoring position" without which "there might have been no crowd at all."

The Guggenheims were rich but they were parvenus. Although the first Guggenheims had arrived in America in 1848, they had not made it to New York until 1888, and by then the Seligmans had been in ascendancy for more than forty years. To the members of "Our Crowd" the Guggenheims appeared unpolished, boorish, even stupid, though no one could deny that they were rich. Indeed, they were very, very rich, having amassed one of the largest mining fortunes this country had ever produced. With two notable exceptions, the seven Guggenheim brothers each ultimately left between six and sixteen million in prewar, pretax dollars. The Seligmans, on the other hand, were well off, but as the family historian, Geoffrey T. Hellman, pointed out, "Most of the Seligman brothers . . . left between two and five million dollars apiece. This isn't hay, but it isn't John Hay Whitney, either."

Nevertheless, the Seligmans never wearied of pointing out that the Guggenheims were beneath them. To convey, in exasperation, that their Florette was marrying into the mining, smelting family of Guggenheims, the Seligmans dashed off a cable to their cousins abroad that inadvertently misread: "Florette Engaged Guggenheim Smelt Her."

Why the "Googs" should have been considered so alien by the Seligmans is difficult to say, since in truth the two families had a great deal in common. Both of Peggy's grandfathers had started humbly enough as foot peddlers and went on to accumulate huge fortunes with a dedication and single-mindedness still breathtaking to contemplate a century later. By the time Peggy was born, each was worth millions.

A dark and studious boy with silky hair, Joseph Seligman was the first of Peggy's direct ancestors to leave Europe for America. With one hundred dollars that his mother, Fanny, had sewn into the seat of his pants, he left Baiersdorf, Bavaria, a village of two thousand people. In a cart with eighteen others, he rolled down a rutted road that led to Bremen and the sea, stopping along the way to camp and to forage for food. Bavaria held few opportunities for Jewish boys, no matter how gifted, since their lives were constricted with legal limits and regulations. It was difficult for Jews to own land, study, enter the professions, or even to marry and have a family. Joseph was convinced that only by emigrating to America could he find a solution to his predicament.

When he reached Castle Garden, New York, in 1837, at the age of eighteen, he set out on foot for Mauch Chunk, Pennsylvania, along the Delaware River, where he had a cousin, Lewis Seligman. There, Joseph went to work as a clerk for Asa Packer, who was later named president of the Lehigh Valley Railroad. Joseph rose to the level of cashier and finally became Packer's private secretary at the highly respectable salary of four hundred dollars a year.

Joseph wanted to make enough money to send for the ten brothers and sisters he had left behind in Germany. At the end of a year, he had saved two hundred dollars, enough to start out on his own. He turned to an age-old trade for Jews in Europe, one of the few open to them that did not require the ownership of property or a university degree: peddling. He invested his small savings in merchandise that he felt would appeal to the housewives and farm folk of rural Pennsylvania and set off, once again, on foot.

By the spring of 1839, Joseph had made five hundred dollars, enough to send for his brothers William and James and to repay his mother, Fanny, that hundred dollars. James Seligman was Peggy's grandfather. Years later, he recalled: "In the Spring of 1839 two wagon loads of peasants again left the little village. My brother William and myself among them. I was then 15 years old. We each had $40 from our mother sewed in a bag around our waists." William and James arrived in America on the Fourth of July.

James started out as a carpenter's apprentice in Bethlehem, Pennsylvania, working on a roof in a cemetery for room and board. He intensely disliked his job, largely because he "had to work long after nightfall." After ten months of this, James begged his brothers to let him join them at peddling. (As George S. Hellman, another family historiographer, observed: "He wanted to nail customers, not shingles.") Joseph staked James to three hundred dollars' worth of "rings, bracelets, and watches —some gold plated, others German silver," and sent him on his way.

James turned out to be a successful and charming salesman, on his first day selling one hundred dollars' worth of trinkets. He then sold Joseph on letting him buy a cart and horse so that he could cover a larger territory, and set off with his wares through the South. In his absence, his brothers opened a small store in Lancaster, in Pennsylvania Dutch country.

By the time James returned from his peregrinations the next brother, Jesse, had arrived from Bavaria. All the brothers were so impressed by James's success in the South—he had netted one thousand dollars—that they decided to relocate there. The Lancaster store was dismantled, and the boys left on a schooner from New York that took six weeks to reach Mobile, Alabama. The brothers had a pooled capital of five thousand dollars; although this was not bad, Joseph calculated it to be too small to allow them to stay in Mobile. They chose to settle in the less competitive town of Selma, and between 1841 and 1847 the Seligman brothers set up stores throughout the state, with James making periodic trips to New York for supplies and the brothers continuing to peddle their wares in the countryside.

By 1843 all eleven Seligman siblings had arrived in America, along with their father, David. Poor Fanny had died in Bavaria and did not live to see the grand success of her brood. The Seligmans prospered, and James came back north in 1846 to establish a small dry-goods store, J. (for Joseph) Seligman & Brothers, Merchants, on William Street in New York. The Seligman boys from Baiersdorf were on their way to becoming millionaires, each and every one.

In 1848, another young and eager immigrant, Meyer Guggenheim, was wending his way to these shores from the village of Lengnau, one of Switzerland's restrictive Jewish ghettos. He arrived with his entire immediate family: his father, Simon, a tailor; his stepmother, Rachel

Meyer; her children; and his stepsister, Barbara, who later became his wife.

Twenty-year-old Meyer and his family settled in Philadelphia where, like Joseph Seligman, Meyer started out peddling with a pack on his back. He would set out on Mondays and come back at the end of the week to share his earnings with his father and family, while Simon did daily tours door-to-door within the city. Peddling required strength and stamina to walk great distances, shoulder heavy packs, and survive camping in the open air. Meyer and his father sold needles and thread, bits of lace, and stove and furniture polish.

Meyer noticed that one of his best-selling products, a stove polish, looked simple enough to make. Two-thirds of his profit on every sale was payable to its manufacturer, so Meyer took it to a German friend in Bethlehem, Pennsylvania, and asked if he could copy it but leave out an ingredient that housewives complained was blackening their hands. Soon Meyer was out peddling an improved stove polish that his father, Simon, concocted at home and now even supplied to other peddlers.

Meyer married his stepsister, Barbara, in 1852 in downtown Philadelphia. The couple moved to Roxbury where they started to produce a brood of children at the rate of one every two years—eleven in all. These were to be Meyer's greatest assets, seven (an eighth died in childhood) talented and industrious sons, as well as three daughters (Jeannette, Rose, and Cora). The names of the Guggenheim brothers— Isaac, Daniel, Murry, Solomon, Benjamin, Simon, and William—were one day to become synonymous with enlightened philanthropy, the arts, dentistry, metallurgy, and aeronautics.

From his successful stove-polish operation, Meyer moved on to spices and lye, to selling coffee extract to Union troops during the Civil War, and to establishing himself in the lace-importing trade. As his youngest son, Will, observed, "He had shifted from business to business without hesitation and with an unerring instinct for profit." As the boys grew up they joined their father. What schooling they received was geared toward business and by 1880 the four eldest sons were lace merchants with the firm of Guggenheim and Pulaski in Philadelphia. Meyer once remarked, "I didn't make my money with my head. I made it by getting hold of good things and sitting on them. So you see, I do not owe my prosperity to my head at all, but to another extremity entirely."

The Guggenheims had become comfortable businessmen, changing addresses to bigger and better houses. Yet had they remained lace merchants, in all likelihood no more would have been heard of them. But in 1879 Meyer jumped into yet another business, one that would make for the Guggenheims one of the largest fortunes in American history.

In 1879, Meyer was approached by Charles H. Graham, a fellow Philadelphian and friend, for a loan to finance the operation of two lead and silver mines in California Gulch near Leadville, Colorado. Leadville had once been a gold town, but the discovery of silver in 1878 changed that. Graham was convinced that the mines he owned, the A. Y. and the Minnie, situated next to a proven rich lode of silver, could not fail to produce that precious metal. (Graham had acquired the mines from A. Y. Corman, a gold prospector, who had staked out the A. Y. for himself, and the Minnie for his wife. Even after years of living hand-to-mouth, in debt to everyone, he was loath to give up his grubstake. But his wife persuaded him to accept Graham's offer of four thousand dollars, and Corman died a poor man at the foot of the Rockies.)

By the end of Graham's visit Meyer had become a one-third owner of the mines. He told Graham that rather than lend him the money, he would give it to him in return for a partnership interest. It is unclear whether Meyer bought his way in for five thousand dollars or twenty-five thousand, but the results have never been in doubt. Soon thereafter, Meyer went out to Colorado to inspect his new investment, taking with him a few yards of lace and other goods, just in case he could do a little business on the side.

Leadville was rough and wild, the streets rutted dirt canals with what sidewalks existed built high enough to avoid the filth. The main diversions in this town full of miners were the saloons and the whore-houses, but alcohol and women were not on Meyer's mind.

He realized immediately when he saw the mines that there was a problem: they were waterlogged. Returning to Philadelphia he bought pumping machines and shipped them to Leadville. The investment paid off, and by 1887 the A. Y. and the Minnie were producing nine million ounces of silver and eighty-six thousand tons of lead, and they were valued at $14,556,000.

Benjamin, Peggy's father, was sent out west to supervise the mines. Ben had enrolled at New York's Columbia College in 1882, but had not liked it and dropped out. He became his father's agent in Colorado. Fair and slight, the good-looking Ben, not yet twenty, found himself living in a roominghouse high in the Colorado mountains where brawling men fell out of saloons and lady "artistes" sauntered about the town. For a boy brought up in a stern and authoritarian household where the Sabbath was observed on Friday nights, life in the Rockies offered an eye-opening panorama.

Having studied mining when he was at Columbia, Ben realized that the great problem in mining silver was the huge cost of refining the ore after it had been painstakingly extracted from the mines. Along with a high level of pure silver, the ore from the A.Y. and the Minnie had a large percentage of zinc oxide, making its refining expensive. If a process could be found that would minimize the cost of reducing the ore, and if the Guggenheims were to do their own refining, then that much more profit would be theirs. Also, a new refinery would be attractive to the other operators then shipping ore all the way to the Holden Smelting Company in Denver at great inconvenience and expense.

Ben had become friendly with Edward Holden, who proposed a new smelter in partnership with the Guggenheims, and Ben went east to discuss the project with Meyer. In December 1888 the new Philadelphia Smelter, costing five hundred thousand dollars, was inaugurated in Pueblo, Colorado, with much fanfare and local attention.

Meyer perceived that the smelter would open a huge new field of endeavor for his sons. Meyer was a millionaire, but he had seven sons, and he was determined that each one of them would also have his own million. He proposed to turn over his controlling interest in the smelter to M. Guggenheim's Sons, the lace business that the four oldest brothers had run since Meyer retired from it in 1881. The condition, however, was that M. Guggenheim's Sons admit their three younger brothers— Ben, Simon, and Will—as equal partners. The older brothers—Isaac, Daniel, Murry, and Solomon—were not enthusiastic. They felt they had done most of the work in the lean years of their father's business while the younger ones got a free ride. To heal the split between the brothers, Meyer promoted the parable of the twigs. "My sons," he would say, "you are like seven sticks which, singly, can very easily be broken. Bound together, you can resist whatever force may be brought to bear against you. It is my desire and my resolution to see you so united as to insure your invincibility."

With the establishment of the Philadelphia Smelter came the eventual takeover of the American Smelting and Refining Company and the acquisition of a vast mining empire with enterprises in Chile, Mexico, and the Congo. Following the creation of M. Guggenheim's Sons, in 1888, Meyer had retired from active participation in the business. In turning over his smelter interest to his sons, Meyer brought to a close more than forty years of striving to give his family a place in this country free from the prejudices and privations of his own early life.

With Meyer's retirement, it was Daniel, the second-oldest son, who was to expand Meyer's vision into the next generation of Guggenheims. He shared his father's boldness and shrewdness in business. Daniel guided the brothers, masterminding the subtle stock transaction that allowed the Guggenheims to take control of American Smelting and Refining Company and at the same time earn more than forty million dollars.

In 1888, Meyer and his gentle wife of thirty-six years, Barbara Guggenheim, moved to 36 West Seventy-seventh Street in New York City, and the brothers soon followed. Meyer, his side-whiskers long since white, devoted himself to the stock market and touring in his electric brougham through Central Park and up Seventh Avenue. Peggy remembered him then as "an old man, driving around New York in a sleigh with two horses and a sealskin cape with a sealskin collar, all alone in the sleigh." Bernard Baruch, who became an agent for the Guggenheims and whose father, a doctor, treated Meyer, saw him from time to time, "always smoking a cigar, indifferent to the ashes which spilled down his coat."

Friday nights, the Sabbath eve, were family nights for Meyer and Barbara. All the brothers and their wives would converge on their parents' house. Like her husband's, Barbara's whole existence was centered on her family, but where he was stern she was soft and motherly, and all the brothers were devoted to her. Peggy was less than two years old when Barbara died and those Friday night gatherings came to an end. Meyer survived his wife another five years. He died in Palm Beach, Florida, on March 16, 1905, where he had gone to recover from a cold. *The New York Times* reported:

> He had succeeded in imparting to his sons, Isaac, Daniel, Murry, Solomon, Benjamin, Simon and William, the secret of his personal success, enthusiasm, close attention and eagerness to understand all the details of the business, a willingness to learn from others, coupled with unflagging industry and unyielding courage.

Ben Guggenheim had come back east from Colorado to supervise another refinery for the Guggenheims at Perth Amboy, New Jersey, which he managed for several years. In New York, he became engaged to Florette Seligman, the youngest daughter of James Seligman, the onetime carpenter's apprentice. By then James was no longer a peddler but a partner of thirty years' standing in the prestigious international banking house of J. & W. Seligman, with offices in London, Paris, and Frankfurt as well as New York.

Like the Guggenheims, the Seligman brothers had risen through hard work and dedication. With the establishment by James of J. Seligman and Bros., Merchants, in 1848 the brothers moved back north to New York. Jesse and another brother, the newly arrived Henry, opened a dry-goods store in Watertown, New York, where they befriended Ulysses S. Grant, who liked to while away his leisure hours in the store playing whist and poker.

But news of the Gold Rush inspired Jesse to head for San Francisco —or Yerba Buena as it was then called. In 1850 he and his brother Leopold left with twenty thousand dollars' worth of merchandise in packs and boxes. At the typically inflated prices of a California gold town, where tin cups sold for five dollars, whiskey for thirty dollars a quart, and ordinary blankets for forty dollars, anything could be sold for two or three times its value in the East.

Jesse had the prescience to open his little shop, J. Seligman and Co., General Importers, in one of the few brick buildings in San Francisco, right next door to a famous house of "entertainment." Thus, in May 1851, when fire wiped out most of the city, Jesse was left with one of the only standing (and therefore thriving) businesses in town.

Jesse had begun to consign gold to his brothers in New York, who in turn reshipped it abroad and made a profit on the "float"—a form of arbitrage. At a time when banking rules and laws were in a state of flux, just about every merchant acted as a banker, too—lending money, extending credit, dealing in acceptances and currencies, and paying third parties on written orders—so that the Seligman leap from merchandising to banking was not a quantum one.

Joseph urged his brothers to follow him in the direction of banking, which he had begun to realize was where his future lay. During the Civil War the Seligmans made a fortune by supplying the Union army with uniforms, for which the brothers were eventually paid nearly one and a half million dollars. And Joseph had been instrumental in placing Union bonds in Germany and Europe at a time when no one would touch them. He understood that the percentage to be made from brokering millions of dollars of paper bonds and securities was dramatically greater than what the brothers could earn from a mere merchandising or importing operation.

On May 1, 1864, a Sunday, the firm of J. & W. (for William) Seligman, bankers, officially opened for business at 59 Exchange Place in New York. By 1873 the partners had a combined capital of six million dollars and in the next decade were to exceed that tenfold, selling government securities for their friend Ulysses S. Grant, as the movers behind the Panama Canal, and as participants in the great American industrial revolution. Joseph was even asked to be secretary of the Treasury, an honor he declined.

With wealth came social prestige, and the boys who had arrived in steerage from Bavaria dined with Harrimans, Whitneys, and U. S. presidents. The three brothers remaining in New York (the others had left to open offices in London, Paris, and Frankfurt), Joseph, James, and Jesse, moved into ever grander residences on the fashionable streets of Manhattan. They arrived at the office wearing Prince Albert frock coats and tall silk hats, in horse-drawn carriages with liveried servants. They belonged to exclusive clubs and gave lavish parties with the best foods, wines, and champagnes served in the most delicate crystal and on the most exquisite china.

The Seligmans were grateful to their new country for the bounty it had yielded them. Joseph named his offspring after patriots and dignitaries: George Washington, Edwin Robert Anderson, Alfred Lincoln (Abraham seeming too Semitic), Isaac Newton. The other brothers had sons named DeWitt, Washington, and Jefferson. In fact, the brothers themselves had already anglicized their names from the original German: James from Jacob, Jesse from Isaias, Leopold from Lippmann, William from Wolf, Henry from Hermann. George Hellman tells the story of how when William called on his brother Joseph to suggest that now that they were respected bankers they should change their name from Seligman to something a little less Jewish and more "American," Joseph agreed: "for you I suggest the name Schlemiel."

Joseph's love affair with America underwent a severe test when in 1877 he was refused admission to the Grand Union Hotel in Saratoga Springs because he was Jewish. Joseph could not understand this snub by a hotel where he and his family had stayed many times before. He had grown to believe that in America, unlike his native Bavaria, people were judged by their achievements and not by their religion. Disheartened and disillusioned, he returned to New York in his plush private railway car to a furor of publicity. Because of Joseph's standing, the episode received widespread attention, but ironically, rather than diffusing anti-Semitic sentiments it served to focus them. Americans as a people were relatively ignorant of what it meant to be a Jew—many even guessed it was a form of Lutheranism—but the rise of the great Jewish fortunes brought with it an increased awareness of the Jews as a force and a people apart. The Grand Union affair proved to be a preview of anti-Semitism in clubs, hotels, and resorts where little had existed before.

The Saratoga incident was a blow from which Joseph never truly recovered. He died in his bedroom at his daughter's house after dinner on April 25, 1880. Similarly, in 1894, Jesse also died shortly after an anti-Semitic incident. His son had been denied admission to the Union Club in New York City—a club of which Jesse himself had been a founding member. Jesse resigned immediately as vice-president and never again set foot in the club. A delegation of sixty Union Club members nevertheless attended Jesse's elaborate funeral.

ECCENTRICS

James Seligman, Peggy's grandfather, was the longest-lived of the Seligman brothers. He survived well into his nineties, a white-haired and respected old man, affable and elegant. In December 1851 James had married Peggy's grandmother, Rosa Content, a seventeen-year-old girl who came from one of New York's oldest Dutch-Jewish families. Rosa was related by blood or marriage to numerous other Jewish families in New York. Either because there were too few other Jews to marry or because the established families felt it was beneath them to marry more recent immigrants, New York's Jewish elite inbred to an inordinate degree. Cousins married cousins, whose offspring married their cousins; brothers from one family married sisters in another. The dizzying inter-relationships produced a chilling number of emotional and mental casualties, suicides, and schizophrenics.

James and his bride moved in with his brother Joseph at 102 Rivington Street. It did not take long for James to discover that his handsome bride was disturbingly erratic. Rosa Content was very beautiful, with a "highly bred, olive skinned Modigliani face and huge dark flashing eyes." But she was also a "strongly tempestuous unaccountable woman." She spent extravagantly, and James, who was miserly, suffered enormously as he watched her in action. Rosa was fond of reminding James that she came from a far superior family, whose forebears went back to Revolutionary times, and she mockingly referred to the Seligmans as peddlers. She delighted in calling her English butler James and her husband Jim. Rosa would go up to shopkeepers and ask them confidentially to guess, "When do you think my husband last slept with me?" "Imagine!" said Peggy. Believing that other children were a source of germs and contagion, she isolated her own unfortunate offspring and refused to allow their little friends to visit the house, which she went around disinfecting at every opportunity. In fact, she did not like children at all—sanitized or otherwise—and would exclaim in their presence, "Oh! Children make me so nervous! Take that child away."

To Peggy, Rosa was her "crazy grandmother," who had "sort of very curly or frizzy white hair. She must have been very objectionable," Peggy mused, "as her husband left her in the end. He couldn't stand it anymore." When Florette, their youngest child, was married—a wonder, given the fact that every time she invited young men to her house her mother made a scene—James sought sanctuary from his wife in the Hotel Netherland, leaving her and her tantrums behind on Fifty-seventh Street. In December 1907, Rosa died of pneumonia at her apartment in the Hotel Savoy.

The blue-eyed James had a more pleasing personality. The best-looking of the brothers, with strong, elegant features, he was likable but ineffectual. His partners in the firm would cross their fingers every time he made a loan, because he couldn't say no. When the telephone became an instrument of convenience in the 1890s, James was so wary of it that he made his assistant place all his calls for him. On his eighty-eighth birthday, in 1912, he was interviewed for *The New York Times,* and the reporter found him on the eleventh floor of the Hotel Netherland, at Fifty-ninth Street and Fifth Avenue, an "old gentleman clad in black, with snow-white, flowing locks and long, spare, white beard, deeply immersed in the contents of a newspaper, his slippered feet extended before him upon a velvet hassock. Perched upon his shoulder was a bright yellow canary bird, which sang at intervals, and it fluttered between its open cage and its master."

When James died in 1916 at the age of ninety-two, he was the oldest member of the New York Stock Exchange. He had been president of New York's most prestigious Reform synagogue, Temple Emanu-el, for more than twenty years, an honor he received by virtue of having been the vice-president when the president died.

During their marriage Rosa and James Seligman produced, not surprisingly, a line of extremely eccentric offspring. There were eight children in all, DeWitt, Samuel, Washington, Eugene, Jefferson, Adeline, Frances, and Florette, Peggy's mother. When they were children, the boys were educated along with Joseph's sons by a meek and frail professor named Horatio Alger, who was so impressed by the family that he later patterned his heroes after Joseph's rise to fame and riches.

DeWitt, Peggy's favorite uncle (named after DeWitt Clinton), wrote plays that were never produced and published a weekly magazine, *Epoch*, even though he held a law degree and was a partner at J. & W. Seligman.

His brother, Washington, "a family name no doubt," quipped one wag, to relieve his perennial indigestion, ate charcoal from a handy chunk he carried in a specially designed zinc-lined pocket. Even with blue-black teeth, he managed to find himself a mistress and kept her in his room by threatening to commit suicide if she were evicted—a not entirely idle threat since once before he had tried to take his life by slashing his throat from ear to ear with a safety razor. To Peggy, "he looked emaciated and very thin . . . like a ghost, with white hair and a sort of thin wrinkled face." At age fifty-six, still a bachelor, he shot a .38 into the roof of his mouth at the Hotel Gerard on West Forty-fourth Street. On two hotel envelopes he had written, "I am tired of being sick all my life," and left it at that. His father, James, then an octogenarian, shocked one and all when he walked down the aisle at Washington's funeral service with his son's mistress.

Washington's was not the only Seligman suicide. Three years later, in December 1915, his cousin Jesse came home with a severe headache and went up to his room. His wife followed him. While their three-year-old daughter sat helping her grandmother wrap candy for her forthcoming birthday party in a nearby room, Jesse shot first his wife and then himself. They were found, she in an evening dress and he in shirtsleeves, by her mother. A note left on a piece of furniture read: "This is the only way. Please bury us together. The baby is to receive all we have, including the stock. Let mother Seligman have little Mary. If she does not want her give her to mother Maxwell. Good-bye and forgive."

Peggy's uncle Eugene practiced law with two of his cousins. He was known as "the stingy one," which, in a family not renowned for its openhandedness, was praise indeed. A niece recalled that "he would come to visit in the country and bring a sandwich in his pocket," to avoid the expense of eating out. To further save money at meals, he would arrive unannounced "just for a minute" and devour everything in sight. An infant prodigy, ready for college at eleven, he waited until he was fourteen to enroll, graduating from Columbia College with the highest honors at eighteen.

Samuel Seligman, like his mother Rosa, was a fanatic about cleanliness and bathed several times a day. Jefferson Seligman married Julia Wormser, who often took Peggy to the opera. Separating from his wife, Jefferson moved into an apartment in the same building as the Copacabana nightclub at 14 East Sixtieth Street. "He was so stingy," remembered a cousin by marriage, Maude Seligman, that "he wanted to see the floor show, and he had them put a chair on a landing going down into the Copa so he could see the show without paying for it." He collected dresses from S. Klein's Department Store and all sorts of feminine apparel for his stable of "chippies," or *"nafkas,"* as his sister-in-law, Mrs. DeWitt Seligman, called them. Jefferson's closets were bursting with women's clothes, and when his nieces came to visit, he would say, "Go look in the closet and take what you want." Peggy's mother, Florette, arrived one day and went straight to the closet. Putting her arms around a bundle of clothes, she remarked, "I don't see why I shouldn't have some, too." When Peggy grew up, she sent Margaret Anderson, co-founder of the *Little Review,* to her uncle Jeff in the hope that she would get at least a fur coat out of him, if not a contribution.

Jefferson, like DeWitt, was made a partner in J. & W. Seligman. When his father, James, died in 1916, he inherited a considerable share of the firm, which "helped subdue any desire he might have had to take on daily responsibilities." The impression he made there was not for his contributions to the world of high finance, but for his varying enthusiasms. Convinced that fruit and ginger would help to reduce fatigue and increase productivity, Mister Jeff, as he was called, would begin the day by distributing a piece of fruit and ginger to each partner—"where the brains were supposed to be"—and then on down to every employee of the firm, all from a large basket he kept for that purpose.

When the stock market crashed in 1929, he went to the floor of the exchange, where he had not been seen in years, if ever, "wearing a flower in the buttonhole of his Prince Albert," and striped pants, to watch the frenzied havoc with curious interest. Like his mother and Samuel, Jefferson shared a concern over unsanitary practices. He believed, for example, that shaking hands was a terrible germ spreader and so he preferred kissing as a social greeting.

Jefferson died in 1937, at age seventy-eight, leaving, according to the Seligman family chronicler, Geoffrey Hellman, "a somewhat diminished estate, which consisted, in part, of a rather large remainder of ginger and Klein's dresses. This was handled gingerly by Walter Seligman and one of the partners in Cravath, de Gersdorff, Swaine & Wood . . . who is said to have been astonished at the claimants who trooped into his office, many of them nattily dressed out of the deceased's closets."

Of Peggy's two aunts, Angeline was a well-known catatonic, and her sister, Frances Seligman Nathan—Aunt Fanny—never spoke, but instead sang her conversation. DeWitt Seligman's granddaughter, Susan Miller, recalls that when Fanny visited Susan's mother, Alma, "she would call 'ALLLLmaaa, I'm HEEErrre,' and my mother would go hide in the bathroom. Fanny would go into the kitchen and ask the cook for a recipe, which is what she had come for, and then she'd call: 'Good-byeeee ALLLLMaaaa!' '' This same aunt Fanny, always wrapped in a feather boa and with a rose in her hair, would burst into arias at bus stops, to the despair of all passersby. "Oh. She was absolutely mad," said Peggy. "She had hat pins [which] instead of being in the hat, there they were sticking out of her hair!" Fanny's husband, Robert Nathan, after thirty years with her, tried to kill his wife by hitting her with a baseball bat; failing at that, he drowned himself in the Central Park Reservoir with lead weights attached to his feet. Their surviving son renamed himself Bobby Norton, and collected stray dogs in his Sea Bright, New Jersey, home, and for a time sold vacuum cleaners.

Florette Seligman, Peggy's mother, was a handsome woman with the striking, heavy-lidded blue eyes that were the Seligman trademark. "Whether she was stupid, or what," no one quite knew, but she never seemed to get anything straight. Maude Seligman took a first-aid course with her and remembered that Florette couldn't even learn how to make beds. But Florette, after all, had been brought up in a home where servants were always about, and neither the lady of the house nor her children were expected to know how to do anything. As an adult, rather than cook on the maid's day off, Peggy would eat her meat raw. And another member of the Seligman family surmised, "I would probably starve, if I had to do any cooking for myself."

Florette was "dizzy." People called her Floretty and joked about her because she repeated things—three times. At the milliner's, Florette would order a hat with a "feather, feather, feather," and when it was ready to be called for, would be genuinely surprised to receive a hat with three feathers on it. She would start the day saying, "Good morning, good morning, good morning." The father of the archaeologist Iris Love, who married a Guggenheim himself, told her, "Florette used to drive Ben mad. She'd say: 'Ben, Ben, Ben, don't forget your rubbers, rubbers, rubbers,' or 'We're having lunch, lunch, lunch with many, many, many.' ''

Her nephew, Harold Loeb, remarked that "Florette repeated most of her phrases so often that her speech resembled a piece from Gertrude Stein." As far back as Peggy could remember, her mother not only re-repeated words but also dressed in triplicate—three watches, three wraps, three sweaters.

It was well known that Florette's husband didn't pay much attention to her. "Right away, as soon as he married her, he knew he'd made a mistake," recalled Peggy about her parents. "I guess she didn't attract him and other women attracted him more, probably." Ben had a series of mistresses (which caused Florette considerable agony), "ranging in glitter from a red-headed registered nurse, employed in his own household, to a marquise of Paris."

To Harry Guggenheim, one of his nephews, Ben gave the measured advice: "Never . . . make love to a woman before breakfast for two reasons. One, it's wearing. Two, in the course of the day you may meet somebody you like better."

Ben was not alone within the Guggenheim family in his amorous adventuring. Old Meyer was not so feeble as to avoid a lawsuit brought shortly after his wife's death by one Hannah McNamara, age forty-five, who claimed she had been intimate with Meyer for twenty-five years while retained in the family's employ as a domestic. She sued Meyer for twenty-five thousand dollars, alleging there had been an implied contract between herself and the elder Guggenheim. Meyer hotly denied the affair and went so far as to offer ten thousand dollars to anyone who would swear he had seen the pair together. When no one came forward, the suit was dropped, but Peggy noted in her memoirs that after her grandmother died, Meyer was "looked after by his cook. She must have been his mistress, I remember seeing her weep copious tears because my grandfather vomited."

Most of Meyer Guggenheim's sons kept mistresses as well. It was said that Meyer himself arranged each one's introduction to sex by taking the boys to a prostitute when they reached bar-mitzvah age, or thirteen. Ben and Will were the most excessive and public in their escapades, perhaps because they were the most attractive. Discreet Victorian liaisons were more to the taste of the older brothers, who kept their women quietly and safely out of sight.

Solomon's heart was conquered by the indomitable Baroness Hilla Rebay, who introduced him to the world of art and whose efforts culminated in the Solomon R. Guggenheim Museum on Fifth Avenue and Eighty-eighth Street. No one knew for sure whether she was actually his mistress, but everyone assumed she was. "She poisoned my aunt's life. She was always staying there and living there and bossing everybody about. My aunt hated her," Peggy said. Peter Lawson-Johnston, Solomon's grandson, remarked that for years as he was growing up he heard his mother and grandmother talking about "the B," and assumed they were talking about "the Baroness." To his surprise he discovered he was wrong; they were referring to "the Bitch." "The baroness was a fiend," added Peggy. And even after Solomon's death, the baroness was a presence to be reckoned with. "She went on in the museum for a while," Peggy said, "until they put her out of the museum, got rid of her. . . . She got away with a lot of money, and she had pictures and a house in Connecticut. I think they had to sue her for pictures that they thought belonged to them, but that she had stolen, and in order to get them out of her, they had to pay a million dollars. . . . Well, I think they really didn't belong to her at all."

Will Guggenheim had been impetuous enough to marry a divorcée, Grace Herbert Brown, who was identified on sight by his older brother, Daniel, as the kept "lady" of another prominent New Yorker. After the intercession of all his brothers, Will was shipped off to Europe with Ben and a divorce decree obtained in Chicago, where it was hoped that the whole affair would not surface. Grace, however, ran through the money the Guggenheims gave her as an inducement to divorce Will, and even though she remarried, she sued Will in 1908, alleging the divorce was illegal because neither party had been a legal resident of Chicago. The newspapers had a good time with the story, but the judge decided against Grace on the grounds that she was no innocent.

Into this group of eccentric personalities and mad aunts and uncles, Peggy Guggenheim was born.

THE TORMENTS
OF THE DAMNED

When Peggy was born on August 26, 1898, and named Marguerite, the New York telephone directory listed the family as living at the Hotel Majestic, on East Sixty-ninth Street. A year later, they had moved to a spacious and stately town house, which Ben had had remodeled, at 15 East Seventy-second Street, off Fifth Avenue, near the entrance to Central Park. In this house Peggy shared her miserable childhood years with her sisters, Benita, born in 1895, and Barbara Hazel, born in 1903. Like most Victorian houses, it was big but gloomy. A sweeping staircase led from a large marble foyer up to the parlor floor. A huge eagle, which Ben had illegally shot in the Adirondacks, dominated the entrance. Animal skins decorated the premises, and a bear with a graphic red tongue, which fell out on occasion, was a sight Peggy always remembered. Her parents occupied the third floor, and their pink bedroom was just beyond a sitting room where enclosed bookcases held all the classics, unread, and where somber portraits of family members hung. In this room, while staring glumly at her grandparents, Peggy was force-fed by her nurse until she would throw up in protest. It was only at dusk, when her mother's hair was being combed out, that Peggy was allowed to play in her parents' lace-curtained room.

The three little girls had the fourth floor to themselves, a standard arrangement in most New York town houses, so the children would be neatly out of their parents' way. Peggy lamented her childhood as "excessively lonely and sad." Growing up in isolation, separate from playmates their own age, the Guggenheim girls were intensely alone. "I had no other friends . . . because I didn't go to school. If you don't go to school, you don't have friends, I guess," Peggy recalled. Florette never invited other children over to the house to play with Peggy or her sisters. Peggy continued, "I don't think there were any good mothers in those days. I think we were all left to governesses and nurses."

And what nurses they were! Peggy's wretched childhood was shared by others in the snobbish German-Jewish community, which looked to their country of origin for their manners and culture. The German nanny was ubiquitous in these households. Stern disciplinarians, more often than not they carried under their arms the books of Professor Daniel Schreber, the German variant on Dr. Spock, whose sadistic views on child rearing from the cradle to adolescence had been popular for generations. Schreber recommended coercion and discipline, cold baths, rigid sleeping positions—preferably balanced between two hard chairs —mechanical contrivances including head belts and body harnesses to keep the children's eyes on their homework, and other restraining devices to force them to follow the straight-and-narrow path away from their supposedly bestial inner nature. The illustrations in his books looked like scenes of medieval tortures. Only later did it turn out that Schreber's own son, after subjection to his father's teachings and contraptions, became a notorious psychotic, immortalized in a classic case study by Sigmund Freud.

In addition to Herr Schreber, children were weaned on German fairy tales, generally far more horrific and violent than their counterparts from other European countries. Witches decapitate their own daughters, whose blood then drip, drip, drips down the stairs, or a lover, as in the German version of Rapunzel, falls face-first on a thorn bush and is blinded. Bad little girls burst into flames. Bad little boys shrivel up and die for not eating their suppers, or are blown away by the wind. Listening to these stories or seeing the graphic and grisly pictures that accompanied them gave children nightmares and made them pray that they would never, never be disobedient again.

Cleanliness, order, and toilet training were obsessions. Humiliation and cruelty were favorite disciplinary tactics, and often at dinner a child would be forced to recite his or her faults and excesses, then stand in a corner while the family ate. Many adults later recalled the mortifying shame they felt as children when they faced these dinner gatherings and the terrible cruelties they suffered at the hands of the "governesses" imported with all good intentions to rear them. No wonder Peggy's contemporaries shuddered looking back on their "privileged" childhoods.

Peggy's cousin, Harold Loeb, was never able to forget his terrifying governess. She would push him into a dark laundry closet, then taunt him about the Guggenheims, saying mean things about them. "As a child," said his onetime girl friend, Jenifer Cosgrieff, marveling that he could even look at a woman after his early experiences, "Harold loathed the sight of blood. The governess would leave her dirty Kotex for him to see. And she had one of those folding beds and he was terrified she would close it on him." Peggy described suffering the tortures of the damned at the hands of a running stream of nurses—nurses who threatened to cut out her tongue or cut off her hair; nurses who gave her enemas that brought on appendicitis.

Moreover, Peggy and her sisters had no one to turn to. Their parents approved of the upbringing they were receiving from the various governesses and rarely saw the children, who were relegated to the top-floor nursery, connected directly with the servants' quarters by a flight of steep, dark stairs. Florette, who had also been handed over to servants as a girl, did not involve herself very much in the routine of her children's lives, and the girls were deprived of a great deal in the way of maternal affection. Hazel lamented, "I had no connection with my mother, who never read me a book or told me a story." Hazel was sure that the reason she hardly ever saw her mother was that she was too busy with Peggy, but Peggy rarely was with her either. The girls felt rejected as, in effect, they were, by their parents, who had placed them in the hands of caretakers who often brought to their jobs little education or enthusiasm and sometimes outright hostility. These women passed on to their charges their own inhibitions, sexual frustrations, and outlooks, so that the children were brought up in two distinct worlds—the wealthy, civilized one of their parents and the superstitious, ignorant one of their nursemaids. "I have no pleasant memories of any kind," wrote Peggy of her childhood. "It seems to me now that it was one long protracted agony."

The love of Peggy's childhood was her sister Benita. Three years older, Benita served as a substitute for a mother, as well as for friends and companions. "Peggy was so possessive of her," complained Hazel. "Benita was an angel, most beautiful. She looked like Anaïs Nin. Benita was dominated by Peggy." By the time Hazel was born Peggy was five and Benita eight, and Hazel was excluded from the world that the older two had created. Hazel was kept "completely out of it, poor thing," said Peggy, and she grew up separate from the other girls and even had different nurses. "She gave me a miserable childhood. She was terrible to me," said Hazel of Peggy. "I got Peggy's old clothes, old toys. When

I was born, Peggy was terribly jealous and someone told her, 'Don't worry, make believe it's just a dear little doll.' 'Oh!' Peggy answered, 'then it's all right to stick pins in her.' " Peggy's earliest memory was of the time Hazel was born, and of the intense envy she felt. And Hazel, who so wanted Peggy to like her and be her friend, felt pushed aside and overshadowed.

Peggy was a pretty child, with smiling blue eyes, brown curls, and a pleasing oval face. Hazel, with her heavy-lidded Seligman eyes and long face, looked like her mother. Both Benita and Hazel were thought of as beautiful, but Peggy was animated. Her memories of childhood revolved around Central Park, where she went for rides with her mother in her electric brougham or pedaled in a toy automobile around the Mall. In winter, their nurses forced the girls to ice-skate on the frozen lake—a torture for Peggy whose ankles were perpetually turning and whose toes got painfully cold. The park, indeed, held only unpleasant memories, and when she returned to New York in the 1940s she shunned it.

The three Guggenheim sisters grew up in an atmosphere of immense anxiety and misery. Ben, married to a woman he clearly did not love, made no secret of his womanizing. He withdrew from his family into his business—for which he had little talent—and spent longer and longer periods in Europe. "I adored my father because he was fascinating and handsome," wrote Peggy, "and because he loved me. But I suffered very much, as he made my mother unhappy, and I sometimes fought with him over it." Florette, publicly humiliated, and angered by Ben's divagations, devoted herself to the typical life of an upper-class Jewish matron—tea parties, dinners, and tours of Europe.

The issue of divorce did not come up until Ben fell in love with his brother-in-law's sister, Amy Goldsmith. The Guggenheims, however, swiftly stepped in to avoid scandal, and the brothers begged Florette not to divorce Ben. They came entreating "all day long, they came in streams, and she didn't divorce him," Peggy remembered. The Guggenheims paid Amy off and she then married a croupier in Menton, France, with whom she enjoyed her spoils. And part of Peggy's inheritance was diverted to Amy on a regular basis right up to her death when, said Peggy, "she was about a hundred."

Peggy, Benita, and Hazel lived in a household with no limits. "The understanding was that both [Ben and Florette] were absolutely nuts," recalled Joan Lewisohn Crowell, a Seligman relation. As children, "we were told that branch was crazy and we were never to speak to them. . . . Peggy's father chased her mother around the dining room table with a kitchen knife. There were no rules, no lines. As my father would say: They weren't housebroken."

In this ambience Peggy developed into a precocious child, learning early that by saying an outrageous thing she could be guaranteed attention, even if it was of a negative sort. "I remember once I said something all wrong," Peggy related. "My mother had some friends for dinner and I said to a lady, 'Where's your husband?' and she said something and I said, 'No, that's not true. He ran away from you.' " Once when René Gimpel, a friend of the family whose command of English was not fluent, came to visit, Peggy asked him impudently, "Why don't you learn to speak English?" According to Hazel, Florette would gush, "Isn't my daughter clever?"

Peggy's behavior was all the more astonishing in this German-Jewish world where children were literally to be seen but not heard. During meals, for example, children were strictly forbidden to talk—especially with each other. They were to respond only to direct questions from their parents or nanny, and when they talked out of turn were punished by criticism, censorship, being made to stand in the corner, and, in recalcitrant cases, by swift blows with a large and specially constructed stick, an *Ausklopfer,* administered by the father in front of the whole family.

When she was seven or eight, Peggy actually confronted her father at dinner one night and speculated, "You must have a mistress because you go out every night." Banished from the table, she hid "in the sitting room under the piano and wept." But she insisted, "I just knew it."

In all likelihood, Peggy had heard the endless and indiscreet squabbles of her parents over Ben's philandering or the well-informed running commentary of her nannies. Furthermore, Ben conducted some of his escapades at home. He hired a registered nurse to massage away his headaches, who, Florette was afraid, massaged more than his neck. But once she was sent away, the incorrigible Ben simply went on to other mistresses. When the girls accompanied their parents to Paris, the family ran into one of them at tea in Rumpelmayer's, and then again, shopping at Lanvin's, Peggy noticed a woman who "had the same agreeable quality . . . of his trained nurse." She turned out to be Ben's latest diversion, the Countess Taverny. Later on when a girl friend of Peggy was boasting of her mother's lovers, Peggy could chime in, "I can't say much for my mother, but my father has lots of mistresses."

Summers, the girls were taken to Europe. Peggy was a year-and-a-half old when she made her first recorded transatlantic crossing. But no sooner had they landed than they got word that Barbara Guggenheim, Ben's mother, had died, so they all turned around and went back. In 1902, Ben and his family went to Monte Carlo and Paris. In Vienna they paused long enough to have a portrait of Peggy and Benita painted by

Franz von Lenbach, who fancifully gave Peggy golden hair. The picture hung in Peggy's bedroom until her death—the greatest treasure of her childhood.

Florette had countless Seligman relatives in Europe and she "went always to Frankfurt and London and Paris to see her cousins. She had about a hundred Seligman cousins and we would always do that, and then we used to go to Marienbad, Trouville, those are the only places I remember," said Peggy. "We had a very limited program, I think."

In 1909, the Ben Guggenheims took a four-month tour on which a hapless Miss Hartman was brought along to instruct Peggy, Benita, and Hazel. Peggy was more interested, however, in sending passionate love letters to a friend of her father.

Peggy detested the New Jersey shore, where the girls spent those summers when they did not go to Europe. The Seligmans as well as the Guggenheims had homes there. Long Branch, Elberon, West End, Deal —many members of "Our Crowd" owned huge, Victorian houses planted amid the flat, graceless sands of that area. Peggy hated it so much that she couldn't bear the sight of the rambler roses, hydrangeas, and nasturtiums that grew so prolifically on that coast. For Peggy, the great thrill of one summer was when a notoriously anti-Semitic hotel in Allenhurst burned down.

Other summers would be spent in the Adirondacks with still more little Jewish boys and girls, and of this experience Peggy could only remember a little boy named Charles Blumenthal who bashed her over the head with a mallet and a girl called Ellie Stein. Isaac Newton Seligman kept a large "camp," a rambling, dark, wooden lodge on Saranac Lake called Fish Rock, which served as the focal point for family activities.

Back in New York Benita, Peggy, and Hazel had lessons at home in geography, history, arithmetic, spelling—Peggy sharing the lessons with another child, Dulcey Sulzberger of *The New York Times* family. But Peggy's home was not a cultivated environment. Books were rarely read, and the pictures that hung on the walls were not very good. The girls took lessons in riding, dancing, and all the other activities it was deemed suitable for young women to know.

Once a week, Florette entertained the ladies on her "at home" day for tea, and Peggy was forced to participate. "Oh, they were just very boring," Peggy ventured of her mother's tea parties held in the living room. "She sat under that wonderful tapestry of Alexander the Great entering Rome, and before an enormous tea table with a silver tea set on it, and entertained the ladies of the *haute bourgeoisie.*" The women discussed the latest gossip, fashions, decor, children, and, of course, the difficulty of finding reliable servants. It was a hermetic world, dark, fussy, and draped with red damask, in which Florette was very much at home.

Florette held elaborate children's parties, and Hazel had a costume party for her eighth birthday at the St. Regis at which Peggy was dressed as Little Bopeep and the birthday girl came as a gypsy. Little Florence Leopold came in Oriental dress and Susan Seligman came as Buster Brown. Peggy's cousin, Eleanor Guggenheim, the future Countess Castle-Stewart, remembers these kiddie parties fondly; there was "a lot of candy," and a great many primly dressed and wide-eyed little girls.

By 1911, Florette and the girls were living at the St. Regis Hotel. They had rented their house on East Seventy-second Street to Ben's sister, Cora Rothschild, the year before, and Ben was leading his own life elsewhere. "I guess my mother didn't want to be bothered housekeeping anymore," Peggy sighed. The Daniel Guggenheims had an enormous suite of apartments at the St. Regis—"miles and miles"—so that the hotel was somewhat of a Guggenheim enclave. It was at the hotel that Florette undertook that baffling first-aid course with Maude Seligman. Florette practiced making beds at the hotel, where she had rows and rows of them to learn on.

THE *TITANIC*

Ben was spending a great deal of time in Europe, where he was expanding the operations of the International Steampump Company, the concern that built the elevators for the Eiffel Tower. In 1912, while in Paris on business, he ran into his nephew, Harry Guggenheim, and took him to lunch on April 9. Ben spent the long lunch talking about his plans and activities. He was on his way to Cherbourg to board a ship back to New York. Because of a stokers' strike, the liner he had originally booked passage on was delayed, and he had decided to join the maiden voyage of the new ocean liner just recently completed by the White Star Line. The *Titanic* was reputed to be the fastest, safest, and most luxurious ship ever built. Seven stories high, with miles of decks, a swimming pool, gymnasiums, elegant staterooms, and excellent dining rooms, it was the ship that "God himself could not sink."

On April 10, 1912, Ben Guggenheim boarded the enormous liner with his secretary, Victor Giglio, and his chauffeur, René Pernot. Along for the maiden voyage of the White Star Line's prize vessel were the president of the company, Bruce Ismay, the architect of the ship, and many of New York's most distinguished and wealthiest citizens, including John Jacob Astor. One-way passage in first class cost one thousand five hundred and twenty dollars.

The captain, Edward J. Smith, had been with the line for thirty-eight years, and the officers had been culled from the best the fleet offered. "Each day, as the voyage went on, everybody's admiration of the ship increased," wrote the second officer, Commander Charles Herbert Lightoller, "for the way she behaved, for the total absence of vibration, for her steadiness even with the ever-increasing speed, as she warmed up to her work." But there had been iceberg warnings in the north Atlantic; an unusually mild winter had sent ice floes drifting down from the Arctic cap.

On Sunday evening, April 14, the ship received a wireless message warning that there were icebergs ahead, but the operator, deluged with the souvenir cables and communications his passengers were asking to send, put the message aside under a paperweight. "It was pitch dark and dead cold. Not a cloud in the sky, and the sea like glass," continued Lightoller. "The very smoothness of the sea was, again, another unfortunate circumstance. . . . If there had been either wind or swell, the outline of the berg would have been rendered visible, through the water breaking at the base." At 11:40 P.M. the *Titanic* struck a tremendous iceberg on its starboard side. The ship had been designed to float with any two of its sixteen watertight compartments flooded, but the iceberg rent a hole in six consecutive compartments; "nothing could have saved her."

The steam let off a deafening din the minute the engines died, so the silence when it stopped seemed all the more horrible. The band, led by Wallace Hartley, struck up some music to raise spirits, and all through the night they could be heard in the background. Lifeboats had been provided that would accommodate 1,178 people, but there were more than 2,000 persons on board. At first, passengers collected on the decks more out of curiosity than fear. No one could believe that the unsinkable ship could actually sink.

Women and children were allowed into the lifeboats. The *Titanic* sent off rocket flares, but those were misunderstood by the only ship close enough to come quickly to the rescue. The *Californian's* wireless operator had gone to sleep, and the *Titanic's* frantic pleas for help went unheeded.

Ben Guggenheim, in his stateroom, B-84, was awakened and given a life jacket by the first-class steward, Henry Samuel Etches. It hurt him in the back and the steward obligingly adjusted it. Etches pulled a heavy sweater over Ben's life jacket and told him to report to the deck.

The *Titanic* was sinking rapidly. Commander Lightoller eerily recalled: "That cold, green water, crawling its ghostly way up that staircase, was a sight that stamped itself indelibly on my memory. Step by step, it made its way up, covering the electric lights, one after the other, which, for a time, shone under the surface with a horribly weird effect."

Distress signals kept flashing until 12:27 A.M. The giant ship kept listing and shifting in the waters, until at the end it made a ninety-degree angle with the sea and went under, creating a vortex that sucked everything around it down into the icy twenty-degree waters. From the lifeboats women watched in horror as their husbands disappeared.

A sister ship, the *Carpathia,* fifty-eight miles away, heard the distress signals and rushed to the scene to pick up what survivors could be found drifting in lifeboats through the landscape of mountainous icebergs. Only 651 people were saved: more than 1,500 people drowned.

That tragic Sunday night, Peggy and her sisters were returning from their grandfather James Seligman's birthday party, where the girls had recited verses and performed. On the way home, about four or five hours before the ship went down Benita had a strange premonition. Hearing a vendor shout *"Extra! Extra!"* hawking the usual evening news, she turned to her mother and begged, "Mama, please buy that newspaper. I *know* something happened to that ship!" "Nonsense," answered Florette, "they couldn't sink that boat."

Ben's brother Solomon was part of the crowd coming out of a Broadway theater on April 15, when he heard the frenzied shouts of *"Extra! Extra!* The *Titanic* sinks in North Atlantic!"* He hurried to the White Star offices, where they would get no more information than that 675 people were on board the rescue ship *Carpathia.* It was impossible to learn if Ben had been saved. The *Carpathia'*s wireless had only a hundred-mile range and until the ship docked the survivors could not be identified.

The White Star Line's offices on lower Broadway were mobbed by eight o'clock the following morning with relatives of the unfortunate passengers, eager for information. Florette, accompanied by her brother DeWitt Seligman and his wife, was photographed by *The New York Times* outside the White Star offices, where she had arrived at about 10 A.M. suffering "great mental agitation. Although she bore up bravely, it was apparent that the terrible suspense was threatening a complete breakdown." Florette searched the list of passengers the company supplied and collapsed on a bench, declaring, "If so many were lost then the White Star Line did not have enough boats. . . . There should have been more boats." *The New York Times* reported: "Then she suddenly drew back in her seat and sat for some minutes staring quietly ahead of her at the line of weeping women and broken men who were passing by, but giving no indication that she saw them at all." She left an hour later, returning to the St. Regis with no word of her husband.

When Daniel's family went to the dock to meet the survivors on board the *Carpathia,* hoping against hope to see Ben come down the gangplank, they saw instead the blond singer who was reputed to be Ben's mistress. Peggy believed that to avoid scandal this woman was paid by the Guggenheims to return immediately and discreetly to Europe. *The New*

York Times reported early on that "Mr. & Mrs. Guggenheim" were on the ship. With Florette in New York, this story naturally gave rise to speculation that the "Mrs. Guggenheim" in question was the blond.

Once it was certain that Ben had not survived, Florette gave in to inconsolable sorrow. How horrible to imagine Ben going down, swimming about in the dark icy waters! When Henry Etches, the first-class steward who had taken care of Ben, arrived at the St. Regis and asked to see her, Florette was "prostrated with grief."

"The steward produced a piece of paper. He had written a message on it, he said, to be certain it would be correct," reported the *Times* on April 20. It read: "If anything should happen to me, tell my wife in New York, that I've done my best in doing my duty."

Etches then gave a description of Ben's final moments to Ben's brother Daniel: Ben and his secretary

> stayed together, and I could see what they were doing. They were going from one lifeboat to another, helping the women and children. Mr. Guggenheim would shout out, "Women first" and he was of great assistance to the officers.
>
> Things weren't so bad at first but when I saw Mr. Guggenheim and his secretary three quarters of an hour after the crash there was great excitement. What surprised me was that both Mr. Guggenheim and his secretary were dressed in their evening clothes. They had deliberately taken off their sweaters, and as nearly as I can remember there were no lifebelts at all.
>
> "What's that for I asked." "We've dressed up in our best," replied Mr. Guggenheim, "and are prepared to go down like gentlemen." It was then that he told me about the message to his wife, and that is what I have come here for. . . . I waved goodbye to Mr. Guggenheim and that was the last I saw of him and his Armenian secretary.

Peggy never really believed the story. She suspected that the steward had come forward with the Guggenheim fortune in mind and had concocted a tale they would be grateful to hear; but if it was true she felt it was "very nice."

"The *Titanic* more than any other single event marks the end of the old days, and the beginning of a new, uneasy era," wrote Walter Lord in *A Night to Remember.* For Ben Guggenheim's family, too, it was a debilitating shock and the beginning of a different life.

When Ben died, Florette did not yet know that her husband had forfeited nearly eight million dollars at the time he and Will separated themselves from the operations of the older brothers in 1900. The break had occurred over the inclusion of nonfamily members in the newly formed Guggenheim Exploration Company, Guggenex, which expanded until at one point it controlled eighty percent of the world's mining industry and assets of about two billion dollars, making the Guggenheim brothers as a family among the richest in America.

The split between the brothers had been widening for years, exacerbated by the resentment the older brothers still felt at the inclusion of the younger ones as full partners in M. Guggenheim's Sons. Simon, the sixth brother, gradually drifted into his senior brothers' camp. He had become a senator from Colorado and contributed his prestige to the brothers. But Ben and Will, their mother's spoiled darlings, reserved their best talents for womanizing. Floundering on their own, the objects of scandal, neither Ben nor Will managed successful lives in the eyes of their judgmental brothers.

The handsome, blue-eyed Ben had had no great organizational talents. He had not enjoyed school very much, preferring the freedom he found in the Rockies. Will, too, had spent time in Leadville, much preferring its saloons and whorehouses to his studies. Later Will, who fancied a literary career, wrote his autobiography, relating his experiences in Colorado under the pseudonym of Gattenby Williams. He prided himself on not looking Jewish, on being the only one of the brothers who had enjoyed college, and on being of a finer nature than his rough-hewn siblings. Indeed, Will, recalled his niece Peggy, "was very beautiful and rather distinguished, you know, not at all like the others. He looked as though he'd come from a different mold."

After separating from his brothers, Ben devoted himself to the manufacture of mining machinery. In 1903, he built a plant in Milwaukee, which later merged with the International Steampump Corporation. Yet things did not go well with Ben's ventures; when the *Titanic* went down, International Steampump was near bankruptcy.

Ben's executors, Daniel, Isaac, and Murry, sorted through the muddled affairs of International Steampump. "It took seven years to settle my father's estate," Peggy said, "when we had no money at all, and the Guggenheims advanced us money without our knowing it. When my mother found out she nearly had a fit. She sold her jewelry and her paintings, and moved into a cheaper apartment, and when her father died she paid them back."

But it came as a rude awakening to Florette and the girls that they were no longer as rich as they had thought they were. Florette moved her family to less expensive quarters at 763 Fifth Avenue, on the corner of Fifty-eighth Street, and began to spend her own money, a measure Victorian ladies resorted to only when pressed. Hazel, telling a friend how poor they became after Ben died, said, "My mother made eggs by the hot water from the faucet."

In the end, Ben's net estate was valued at $2,639,597. Florette received almost $800,000. Peggy and each of her sisters would come into an inheritance of close to $450,000 each, which their uncles suggested be kept in trust until each girl reached the age of twenty-five, when she could receive half of the principal outright. When that time came for Peggy, her uncles wisely urged her to keep all of the money in trust. Peggy agreed. Ben acted generously in also leaving money in trust for his unconventional sisters-in-law, the soprano aunt Fanny and the catatonic Angie.

While $450,000 was a far cry from the millions Peggy was believed to have inherited, nearly half a million dollars could go a long way when five cents bought a movie ticket and ninety cents a fine silk scarf. Yet, Peggy said, "I didn't ever consider myself a real Guggenheim anymore, after that, because I was very poor compared to my uncles and . . . only to my uncles. . . . It was natural to feel it. They were so madly, madly rich and I only had $450,000."

By contrast, Isaac Guggenheim, who owned a Renaissance mansion on Sands Point, Long Island, with a private boat landing and formal gardens, left ten million dollars; Murry, sixteen million; and Dan, more than six million. Peggy's cousins Edmond and Lucille, Murry's children, inherited eight million each. And another cousin, Robert Guggenheim ("Colonel Bob"), who boasted two estates, a 180-foot yacht with thirty-one man crew, and a racing stable announced that since every wealthy family "supports at least one gentleman in leisure. I have elected to assume that position in mine."

The disparity in wealth of the two sets of Guggenheims was such that Will decided to sue his brothers for ten million dollars. In 1916, he started legal proceedings, claiming that he had been illegally excluded from the profits of the Guggenheims' Chilean mines. He alleged that in January 1912, when he and Ben had signed an agreement waiving participation in the mines, they had been misinformed as to their prospects. Will's suing his brothers when his funds were low colored the merits of his claim, but he did succeed in extracting a six-million-dollar settlement from them.

Florette would have nothing to do with Will's suit. "She loved the Guggenheims. She wouldn't have done such a thing . . . she was so loyal and so nice," said Peggy. But Will enjoyed his windfall to the fullest, investing it on Wall Street where he was known as "Willie the Plunger," maintaining a house where 833 Fifth Avenue now stands, with nineteen in help, two chauffeurs, and his and hers Rolls-Royces, as well as a mansion in Sands Point. By the time he died in 1941 at the age of seventy-two, bequeathing his fortune to four former show girls including Miss Connecticut of 1930 and Miss America of 1929, the grand sum of five dollars was all that was left.

ADOLESCENCE

Peggy was not yet fourteen years old when she lost the father she adored. In the disordered household in which she lived, Ben had been a beguiling presence. He called Peggy "Maggie" and bought her jewelry designed like daisies in honor of her name, Marguerite. Peggy listened for his whistle as he climbed the stairs and ran to greet him when he came home. She blamed her mother for driving him away and never quite recovered from the trauma of his death. Peggy escaped into books, reading the same novels over and over again.

Until she began school, Peggy had few, if any, friends. All the Seligman girls attended the Jacoby School on Manhattan's West Side, and at age fifteen Peggy was also sent there. Painfully shy, she would walk across Central Park to join her classmates who came from other rich and snobbish Jewish families. Jacoby was more of a finishing school than a real academy, since women were not expected to need much in the way of education.

Soon after beginning school, however, Peggy developed whooping cough and bronchitis, and was forced to spend the rest of the semester in bed, doing her homework alone and reading to pass the time. Her second semester at the Jacoby School was more felicitous, with much of it spent planning and rehearsing the school play, *Little Women*. Peggy did not care for the school itself, but for the first time in her life she was making friends with girls her own age. She organized a dance club that sponsored once-a-month parties and she gave her first kiss to Bobby Wormser. Peggy graduated in 1915, and Benita dissuaded her from going to college. "I have no idea what she said to me," remarked Peggy. "She just talked me out of it. . . . I do regret it, yes, [but] I don't care anymore. I consider myself self-educated."

Peggy's homelife remained chaotic. Florette and Ben had battled constantly over Ben's extramarital sex life. When Ben died, Florette assigned all her energies to her daughters, overinvolving herself in their lives. A friend said, "She drove the girls crazy about sex, about douches, about Lysol—she was always wiping everything with that disinfectant. And when they traveled they had a whole trunkload of medicine." Florette was "mad about hygiene. We would laugh," recalled their cousin, Eleanor Guggenheim, "because she made Peggy and Benita peel everything, apples, fruit. . . . I felt very sorry for poor Benita, Hazel, and Peggy."

Florette shuttled Peggy from one doctor to another, and when Benita developed whooping cough one winter, she was quarantined and Peggy sent to a hotel with Hazel. At the first sign of a sniffle, Florette would thrust a thermometer in the girl's mouth. "She was frightfully interested in our temperatures," Hazel once said, "but she could never get down the mercury in the thermometer, shaking it about like mad."

Florette's life was circumscribed by family obligations. Peggy resented this family that produced "sick sons and sick daughters, " said a Seligman cousin, Susan Miller. "There was no social life except the family and the people they brought around. . . . They were all of a group . . . too intertwined. They never saw anybody else. Wall Street was acceptable. The rabbi came every Sunday for lunch. . . . Once, we had a man over who said he was thinking of leaving Wall Street to go into merchandising. My parents were very nice, but appalled. . . . Those times made people like that."

Peggy lashed out against her mother and her family—"those stupid, staid, bourgeois people." She became increasingly rebellious, shaving her eyebrows and painting the toilet seat red. But it remained what she said and how she said it that caused a stir. Despite a refined demeanor and a voice that rarely rose past a well-mannered whisper, she was just as apt to ask, "Does your mother have a lover?" as "Would you like to come for tea?"

The world in which Peggy grew up was a rigid grid of do's and don'ts, largely the result of the peculiar and ambivalent attitude German-Jewish society had toward its own religion. Although its members socialized only with each other, they also wanted to blend into the larger

Gentile society around them, to become "Americanized." With riches and grandeur had come a desire to move in the highest levels of American aristocracy—with Morgans and Vanderbilts, whose wealth their own fortunes rivaled.

With Joseph Seligman's abrupt rejection by the Grand Union Hotel in 1877, the Seligmans and the other established Jewish families were awakened to the reality of prejudice. They were rich, cultivated, and intelligent, yet they were meeting a wall of resistance in their relations outside their insular world.

They reacted by trying not to appear too "different." At Temple Emanu-el, the large and exclusive synagogue on Fifth Avenue where the Seligmans were influential as past presidents and members of the congregation, bar mitzvahs were frowned on and a rabbi was imported from England to intone his sermons with an impeccable British accent. As Stephen Birmingham points out, "New York's German Jews began, in the 1870's, to say to one another, 'We are really more German than Jewish.' " They absorbed from the German culture its anti-Semitism and self-hatred and strove to acquire the manners and customs of their Christian counterparts, accepting the notion that to appear Jewish was somehow not as desirable as to appear Episcopalian. Isaac Newton Seligman was quite proud of the fact that he was the only Jew admitted to the Saranac Club; another Jew might have been too offended to join. Young girls were admonished not to appear too "ethnic" by wearing garish clothes or inappropriate accessories. One member of "Our Crowd," coming from the almost spartan appointments of the Century Club, was surprised to see at its Christian counterpart, the Piping Rock Club, lavish and sumptuous facilities.

As masses of poor Eastern European and Russian Jews began arriving in New York in the late nineteenth century, the older German-Jewish families looked on in embarrassment and blamed these unwashed hordes for causing anti-Semitism. Provincial, Yiddish-speaking, and clinging tenaciously to their faith, the new arrivals were everything the elite were seeking to escape. In families that had risen not only from rags to riches but from selling rags to riches in one generation, snobbish attitudes developed toward their "co-religionists." As the newcomers were rejected and excluded, appearances and proper behavior became even more important among the established families. Senator and Mrs. Simon Guggenheim were members of St. Thomas Church and Will Guggenheim's son went every Sunday to the Church of the Heavenly Rest.

The threat of a *mésalliance* was very real—to marry outside the acceptable group of Jewish families was abhorrent. When Alva Bernheimer married Bernard Gimbel of the department store family, it was generally felt she had married beneath her into a family of shopkeepers.

Peggy remembered her teacher at the Jacoby School, Martha Orenstein, weeping copiously and nervously breaking countless pencils over Alva's disgrace. On the other hand, it was considered highly desirable to marry into a non-Jewish family. When Peggy's cousin Eleanor, Solomon's daughter, married the Earl of Castle-Stewart's son and heir, approving tongues wagged, "Now *there* is a son-in-law!" Unlike the Eastern European arrivals, for whom to marry outside the faith was to die in the eyes of the community, a transatlantic marriage to a wealthy nobleman was the dream of many a young girl of Peggy's world.

The self-loathing generated by this ambivalent attitude toward their own Jewishness caused great psychological tension in many families. By Peggy's generation, anti-Semitism in clubs and schools was commonplace. Anyone with social aspirations outside Jewish society quickly learned to hide, to compensate, almost to apologize for this heritage.

Peggy's cousin Harold Loeb was immortalized by Ernest Hemingway in *The Sun Also Rises* as Robert Cohn, a self-deprecating Jew who tries too hard to be liked. Hemingway opened the book with the following observation:

> Robert Cohn was once the middle-weight boxing champion of Princeton. Do not think that I am very much impressed by that as a boxing title, but it meant a lot to Cohn. He cared nothing for boxing, in fact he disliked it but he learned it painfully and thoroughly to counteract the feeling of inferiority and shyness he had felt on being treated as a Jew at Princeton. There was a certain inner comfort in knowing he could knock down anybody who was snooty to him, although, being very shy and a thoroughly nice boy, he never fought except in the gym.

The archaeologist Iris Love did not even know she was Jewish until she was a boarder at the Madeira School. "I was brought up," she said, "as an Episcopalian. I sang in the choir at St. James, so I went to church three times a week." Iris, who was rarely allowed to entertain, invited a friend, Eugenie Hess, for Thanksgiving lunch. "My grandmother was there," she continued, "and asked about the Anheuser-Busches from St. Louis. It was established that they were related in some way. . . . When I came back to school I found a sort of kangaroo court and I was asked, 'What is your religion?' I didn't know what they were driving at. . . . Finally, they said, 'You're Jewish' and left." Iris was perplexed. She asked her nanny, "Am I Jewish?" "Of course not. Whatever gave you that idea?" Then Iris asked her father, who reacted with, "Don't ever ask me such a thing again." She asked her sister, Noel, who said, "Jesus! What did you think the Guggenheims were?" Finally, Iris approached her grandmother. "So, you found out."

Iris had stumbled upon the family secret and was put in the discomfiting position of living a lie. She did not know what to say at a club, once, when the mother of a school chum proudly told her, "No Jew has ever set foot here."

Iris Love was not, of course, the only one to have suffered in this fashion among the progeny of New York's old Jewish families, who were sent off to restrictive boarding schools, frequently to be the only Jew in the class and to suffer because they were considered different and unacceptable.

It is not surprising to find in the fourth generation of Guggenheims such stridently non-Jewish names as Lawson-Johnston, McNeil, King-Farlow, and Tassie.

Peggy certainly absorbed the snobberies and distinctions made by "Our Crowd" Jews, claiming to feel not at all Jewish herself. "It never crosses my mind." Indeed, it rankled to be reminded of her religion. Peggy generally preferred the company of non-Jews, and was more than once accused of being anti-Semitic herself. Joel Carmichael confided that after his brief affair with Peggy in the 1950s she announced that he was the only Jew she had ever slept with.

THE SUNWISE TURN

After graduation from the Jacoby School, Peggy was a young woman adrift. The parameters of her social and family life bored her. When Peggy's grandfather, James Seligman, died the following year, Florette received a sizable inheritance that ended her financial difficulties. The little family moved once again, this time to 270 Park Avenue, near the corner of Forty-eighth Street.

Peggy was ready to make her debut into what she called *haute* Jewish society. Florette gave her a Leap Year party, where Peggy wore a white dress trimmed in then fashionable kolinsky fur. The eighteen-year-old Peggy had lost the open piquancy of her girlish face, and in its stead pensive blue eyes stared from under very dark brows. A slender, delicate young woman, with thin arms and stemlike legs, she wore her thick, wavy chestnut hair pulled back from a center part. Julien Levy, who knew Peggy as a young woman, thought that "she was the ugly duckling of the family and upset about her looks. She had no bosom, was skinny. Hazel was a beauty, but scatterbrained. Benita was the family's favorite beauty, but Peggy was the most interesting—the one with the brains." Peggy felt accursed by her nose. "She had a terrible nose," said her sister Hazel, "like a potato." Maude Seligman felt that "she was always pretty ugly." Even if her contemporaries found Peggy less than perfect, she appears in surviving photographs to have been, by today's more liberal standards, quite attractive.

To pass the time, along with Italian, history, and economics lessons, Peggy began to take instruction from Lucille Kohn, a radical socialist and reformer. Kohn made Peggy feel "I had to give a lot of money away to causes."

America had entered World War I, and Peggy decided to get a job somehow related to the war effort. Having few marketable skills, she enrolled in business school to learn typing and stenography, but, hopelessly inept, Peggy soon quit. She did learn to type, after a fashion, and continued to use this half-mastered skill all her life in personal correspondence that was full of typographical errors.

In 1918, Peggy was hired to sit at a desk and dispense discount cards to newly inducted soldiers. As part of her duties she had to help the recruits fill out forms so they could buy uniforms and other goods at a reduced rate. For the first time Peggy began to meet non-Jews. "I never saw anybody else except Jews until the war," Peggy said, "then, of course, I met all these army officers, and they weren't Jewish." The work was far from strenuous, but Peggy, unaccustomed to work of any kind, soon was at the point of a nervous breakdown. She would not eat and could not sleep. "I just went around worrying all the time . . . crazy." Peggy sought out a psychologist who, when asked if she were losing her mind, replied: "Are you sure you have a mind to lose?" With the help of the trained nurse who once had taken care of her grandfather James, Peggy slowly recovered.

When Peggy turned twenty-one in August 1919, she finally came into her inheritance from her father. The trust fund of four hundred and fifty thousand dollars generated an income of close to twenty-two thousand a year, then a considerable sum. Although Peggy continued to feel very much a poor Guggenheim, having her own money allowed her to free herself somewhat from her mother, who tried hard to control her but rarely succeeded. Peggy set out to tour the United States with a chaperone, traveling mostly in trains and buses.

That winter Peggy decided to do something about her nose and went to Cincinnati, where she knew of a plastic surgeon. She requested a nose "tip-tilted like a flower," but in the middle of the operation the doctor threw up his hands when he could not transform Peggy's tuber of a proboscis into anything remotely resembling a flower. Peggy, racked by the pain and discomfort, ordered him to stop. Her nose remained huge, more a blob than a lily, and seemed to have a life of its own. Her nose was the first feature people saw and remembered about her, and Peggy blamed this failed operation for a large part of the problem. But given that her son's nose was a replica of hers, one wonders if she did not exaggerate the negative effect of an operation which, even into her seventies, she actually considered having done again.

Back in New York, nursing her bruised and swollen nose, Peggy's unhappiness increased when she found herself the sole object of her mother's effusions. Hazel was away at boarding school, and the beautiful twenty-two-year-old Benita had impetuously wed a pilot, Edward Mayer, the previous spring. Peggy, who romanticized Benita and hoped she would marry a prince or a Russian baron, rejected Mayer as "completely unworthy of her. He was handsome in a flashy way, but superficial with no depths of passion." And Peggy resented his taking Benita away.

Desperate for something interesting to do—a temporary job as a substitute dental nurse was not a solution—Peggy approached Harold Loeb, who had recently become involved in a bookstore. He obliged Peggy by allowing her to work at the Sunwise Turn for no salary. This lucky development changed Peggy's life and opened the door to a world she would soon embrace as her own.

The Sunwise Turn was a cozy little bookshop started by Mary Mowbray Clarke and Madge Jenison at Thirty-eighth Street and Fifth Avenue. Harold Loeb had been in the habit of stopping by the shop every day on his way home from his duties as a desk sergeant with the army. Soon after the Armistice, it became apparent to Harold that the two women were losing money and that the store was in desperate financial shape. He decided to invest about five thousand dollars in the operation and to become a partner in the shop he loved.

By the time Peggy came to work for the Sunwise Turn, Harold had succeeded in improving the store's finances, and the bookshop was more than covering its costs. It had moved to larger quarters in the Yale Club building, on Forty-fourth Street across from Grand Central Station. The new Sunwise Turn had high ceilings, "walls painted a rich orange and the light bulbs swathed in fluff." A wide balcony, where Peggy worked, housed two desks.

Peggy had no idea of what was expected of a volunteer clerk in an avant-garde bookshop. She later wrote, "Though I was only a clerk, I swept into the bookshop daily, highly perfumed, and wearing little pearls and a magnificent taupe coat." In his memoirs Harold Loeb described Peggy: "Awkward as a young magpie in her furs and jewelry, she captivated us all by her willingness to go through with the dullest clerical work, and by her joy in being around. Coming under Mary Clarke's spell, Peggy gradually discarded many traditional taboos and adopted a whole set of new ones."

From her perch on the balcony, Peggy observed Mary Mowbray Clarke in action. She was a woman different from any Peggy had ever known. Mary could be seen cornering a potential customer and lecturing him about the merits of a particular book. Unlike most booksellers, Mary would only sell the books she loved and relegated those she didn't believe in to the stockpile in the storeroom. Mary loved ideas and conversation, and her stone farmhouse in Rockland County, New York, was a haven for writers, poets, sculptors, and creative people. Peggy absorbed as much as she could of this alien creature, whose conversation was not about children and servants but about art and books. "Oh she was wonderful," said Peggy. "I was very much impressed with her. I don't know about her influence, but I was certainly impressed. She was sort of like a saint. She was so serious and so good and so wonderful about her work, idealistic, absolutely devoted to what she was doing. She was a very superior person. I suppose she thought she was educating the world."

Mary was not the only person Peggy could observe from her perch. The bookshop sponsored readings and exhibitions, and writers and intellectuals of all sorts had begun making the Sunwise Turn a port of call. Ananda Coomaraswamy, a great friend of Mary Clarke, Gilbert Cannan, who had run off with James Barrie's wife, F. Scott Fitzgerald, the painters Charles Burchfield and Marsden Hartley, and the poets Lola Ridge, Alfred Kreymborg, and Babette Deutsch all stopped at the shop. These were people who regarded writing and the arts as the most important things in the world. To be one of these people, to be part of a more exciting and interesting world, was an idea that took hold of Peggy at the Sunwise Turn.

But Florette was disconcertingly nearby at 270 Park Avenue and she was horrified that a well-to-do girl should work, so Peggy's reveries would be interrupted when her mother would barge in with a pair of galoshes for her, or when one of the Guggenheim aunts would come in to buy books by the yard, wielding a measuring stick across stacks of novels to fit the dimensions of her bookshelves.

Peggy was not allowed down from the balcony except at lunchtime. Then she was permitted to sell books, but only if everyone else was out. It was a "slight which she never forgot," wrote Loeb. "She complained about it till Gilbert Cannan told her, 'Never mind, my dear, Lady Hamilton started out as kitchen maid.' "

Peggy managed to make friends with Helen and Leon Fleischman. Leon then worked for Liveright and Boni, the publishing house. Helen, née Kastor, came from a prominent Jewish family and eventually married James Joyce's son, Giorgio. The couple took Peggy to visit Alfred Stieglitz's gallery, 291, on Fifth Avenue and Thirty-first Street. Here she had her first glimpse at a modern painting, a landscape by Stieglitz's lover, Georgia O'Keeffe. It was so incomprehensible to Peggy that she kept turning it around to see which side was up. The Fleischmans also introduced Peggy to a handsome young man from Paris, in America to oversee the production of his one-act play *What Do You Want?* by the Provincetown Players. With his brilliantly blond hair hanging almost to his shoulders, Laurence Vail fascinated Peggy. When she first met him, Vail was worried about what he should do with his life. Edna St. Vincent Millay reported that he had said, "I'm almost as old as Christ was when he died. And yet Christ really did a very remarkable thing.—But I don't think I have much talent for that sort of thing."

Vail was staying in Greenwich Village, a part of New York about which Peggy knew little, since she was living a "very bourgeois" life with her mother. But during the years 1919–1920, the Village teemed with young writers and radical intellectuals attracted to the cheap rents, like Malcolm Cowley, Djuna Barnes, E. E. Cummings, who, among many others, warmed themselves by the steam pipes of tiny studios on Hudson or Bank streets, waiting for the call that would take them, en masse, to Europe and particularly Paris. These idealistic writers and creative young people would become Peggy's boon companions.

PART II

LOST IN THE TWENTIES

OVER THERE

Peggy spent six months at the Sunwise Turn. However wondrous the people she encountered during the day seemed to her, she returned every afternoon to Florette and Park Avenue. Her social life consisted of dates with other young women her age or white-glove tea dances with formal young men. When Harold Loeb left for Paris in 1920, Peggy began to think of Europe as the place for her, too. She had always much preferred her summers there to the miserable ones on the Jersey shore, surrounded by family. Ever since her father's death Peggy had longed to return to Europe, but while the war persisted it had been impossible to go.

Peggy sailed for Europe in 1920. She was twenty-two years old, an heiress, still awkwardly wrapped in furs, but full of energy and plans. Peggy induced her mother, Florette, to come to Europe with her, as Peggy was conventional enough to believe that young ladies needed chaperones. So mother and daughter set out with another young woman, Valerie Dreyfus, Peggy's cousin. The trio traveled from the English Lake District to the château country in France. Leaving Florette in Paris, Valerie and Peggy continued on to Holland, Belgium, and finally, Italy. Peggy was able to fill leather-bound scrapbooks with hundreds of tiny black-and-white pictures of all she had seen.

Eventually, weary of frantically going from place to place, Peggy returned to Paris, at that time a paradise for the rich. At the first-class hotels where she and her mother stayed, such as the Crillon or the Plaza-Athénée, a guest's mailbox would be filled with announcements and invitations to the couturiers—Poiret, Chanel, Molyneux, Worth. An afternoon could pass pleasantly in the fitting of tulle, voile, and crêpe-de-chine confections. American guidebooks of the time suggested that a woman wear only her best lingerie when visiting the haute couture establishments and that she leave her frayed and mended culottes at home. Peggy certainly had the time and the money to entertain herself in this way, and she went, as she put it, to "only the best."

Fashions in the 1920s were "an intoxication," and Peggy's thin figure looked wonderful in them. The flapper had done away with the corseted styles of the Edwardians, and dresses with loose-fitting torsos began to inch up, until by the middle of the decade they exposed the knee. Legs were shaved, tattooed, and given an attention they had never before received. Fabrics of oriental lushness—brocades, lamés of silver and gold, shimmering beads—made colorful costumes with fringed skirts perfect for dancing, that swayed from the hips. Imaginative head-dresses of peacock feathers and rhinestones were worn low on the fore-head and satin shoes were buckled with beaded straps. Hair was pomaded and slicked back into a short cap. Eyebrows disappeared. Peggy had caused a scandal in New York when she, too, shaved off her eyebrows and painted in their stead big, black half-moons. A friend, Arthur Jeffress, once called Peggy the eternal twenties girl and her face bore its stamp all her life. Her small mouth was always brightly rouged, the upper and lower lips done in one fast stroke with the whittled point of a lipstick, called, in the manner of the 1920s, "Eternal Wound."

Headquartered at the Crillon in the Place de la Concorde, Peggy and a friend, Fira Benenson, gaily set about collecting suitors. Florette had a wide network of Seligman cousins and relations in Paris, and Peggy saw the same kind of men she would have been courted by in New York, all well-to-do and Jewish. There was Armand Lowenguard, a nephew of the art dealer Joseph Duveen, who introduced Peggy to the writings of Bernard Berenson. But, Peggy said, "He couldn't keep up with me." In addition, there were Boris Dembo, Marion Sulzberger, and Pierre Weinstein. Peggy was leading the "most expensive sort of life" and never strayed far from the confines of her luxury hotel and social set. Categorizing herself and Fira Benenson years later, Peggy wrote, "We dressed in the most elegant French fashions and I am sure we were idiotic."

Peggy cut short her Parisian spree to return to New York for Hazel's marriage—the first of many—to Sigmund Marshall Kempner, a graduate of Columbia and Harvard. It took place at the then-fashionable

Ritz-Carlton on June 2, 1921. "Siggy," as the groom was called, was still a virgin and very worried. Finally, in desperation, he asked Benita's husband, Edward Mayer, "How far shall I put it in, and how long shall I keep it there?" "Isn't that marvelous?" demanded Peggy. "How can you ask such a question. Imagine getting married asking such a stupid question." Florette heaved a sigh of relief in the mistaken notion that she had married off Hazel who, like Peggy, had turned out to be quite a handful. But little over a year later the couple divorced, and Hazel went on to marry the journalist Milton Waldman, a popular twenty-five-year-old Yale man, in Paris.

One result of Peggy's return to New York for the wedding was that she persuaded Helen and Leon Fleischman to sail back with her to Paris, where a new age was beginning.

THE KING
OF BOHEMIA

Shiploads of Americans had started arriving in France escaping from Prohibition, parents, and provincialism in a giant wave of expatriation. In France, Americans could get a "decent alcoholic drink that would not digestively kill, maim, or blind them." Ernest Hemingway had arrived in 1921. Malcolm Cowley, John Dos Passos, E. E. Cummings, Virgil Thomson, Djuna Barnes, Robert McAlmon, the acerbic writer from Clifton, Kansas, and Man Ray, the bug-eyed photographer from Philadelphia and Brooklyn, were joining James Joyce, Ezra Pound, Ford Madox Ford, and F. Scott Fitzgerald in a mad spree. Paris had become a magnet for the talented and restless youth of Peggy's era and for many of the greatest artists of the time—Matisse, Stravinsky, Picasso—a place where the seamy and the spiritual promised magical opportunity.

At one point just two cents bought a franc, so a few American dollars went a long way toward buying a baguette, a bottle of Bordeaux, and a room for the night. An American could live on a hundred dollars a month, and many found easy jobs to make ends meet. Since most writers and artists in the United States could count on little support from institutions or regular writing jobs, the possibility of life on the cheap in Europe held infinite allure.

World War I had introduced many young Americans to the glories of Europe. Those who had seen service overseas might spend a weekend in Paris and then go off to the trenches by train on Sunday. The war had been exciting, and Malcolm Cowley noted that for many Americans it ended too soon. "They would spend the next ten years looking for another stage on which they could re-enact the dangers and recapture the winey taste of war."

There were nightclubs where the writer Willy Seabrooke insisted human flesh could be consumed. At the Gypsy Bar women dressed in tails and monocles and danced with one another. Josephine Baker would become the talk of Paris, clad in a bunch of bananas at the Folies Bergères. Les Copeland, a former cowboy, played the piano at the Jockey, where Marcel Duchamp or Man Ray or Jean Cocteau was likely to turn up.

Old-style restaurants were changing to accommodate the rage for *le dancing*—tango, fox-trot, and Charleston. Women smoked cigars. Nancy Cunard wore ivory bracelets up to her elbows. Kiki, the artist's model, appeared in exotic makeup, white-faced with great swirls of color about the eyes. Tristan Tzara sported a monocle. Eccentricity of every sort was encouraged.

It seemed as if a whole generation was in revolt, breaking the rules and creating none. This was a far cry from Temple Emanu-el and the Jacoby School, from teas under Florette's tapestries and croissants at the Ritz. It was a dreamworld Peggy had glimpsed at the Sunwise Turn but had not yet entered. And it was almost by accident that she ever entered it at all. Had Peggy never met Laurence Vail she might well have ended up in a Park Avenue drawing room, writing checks for the Firemen's Auxiliary Fund and the Jewish Guild for the Blind.

Peggy's friend Helen Fleischman had begun having an affair with Laurence Vail, the handsome young man Peggy had met in New York. Fleischman encouraged his wife's liaisons with other men, and one evening the couple invited Peggy to dinner with Laurence. Laurence was thirty years old, seven years Peggy's senior. An American born in France in 1891, "the year the Seine froze over," he was in many ways more French than expatriate. He had been educated at Oxford and at French schools and he spoke English with a mixture of those accents.

If Peggy's homelife had been confused, in Laurence she at last met a man whose childhood miseries matched her own. Laurence's mother, Gertrude Moran, a well-to-do Wasp from Providence, Rhode Island, was cold and distant. "She had no problem about her identity at all." An avid mountaineer, Mrs. Vail had been the first woman to climb Mont Blanc, which she did in blackface to protect her skin. Laurence loved mountains as well, and had climbed the Matterhorn when he was eight years old and Mont Blanc when he was nine.

Laurence's father, Eugene Vail, himself the son of a New Yorker who had married a fifteen-year-old French girl when he was forty, was a painter given to *crises de nerfs.* He spent much of his time in and out of sanitoriums, and when he wanted attention he would simply have a tantrum—a device he passed on to his son. Eugene could be morbid and "had suicidal tendencies," Laurence's stepdaughter, Bobbie, once said. "He used to put himself on train rails." For his paintings he was known as the *Maître noir.* Laurence always said he caught his pessimism and gloom from his father.

Eugene had a brother, George Vail, Uncle George to Laurence, who was a great lover. To commemorate his conquests he garnered pubic hairs from each of his ladies and kept them pressed between the pages of a book like so many flowers. One day his unsuspecting great-niece, looking for something to read, chanced to open this loving repository only to put aside all thoughts of literature when its contents spilled over her lap.

Uncle George was also a passionate roller-skater—so much so that he died on wheels, suffering his fatal collapse while indulging in his favorite stunt—hanging on to the back of a big truck as it barreled through Paris, his big white moustaches flapping in the breeze.

Just as Peggy had clung to her sister Benita, Laurence passionately adored his younger sister Clotilde. She was very much like Laurence, blond, angular, artistic. With streaming golden hair and identical beaky noses, together they would haunt the Parisian cafés and Bohemian hangouts. A perfectly matched pair of *Wunderkinder,* it was often said that they were made for incest. After William Carlos Williams met the pair, he patterned the brother and sister of his novel *A Voyage to Pagany* on Laurence and Clotilde. In that book the sister tells her brother: "I shall never love anyone as I love you."

When Peggy met Laurence, he was living in his mother's apartment near the Bois de Boulogne with Clotilde. Mrs. Vail kept Laurence on a tight rein, giving him an allowance of about a hundred dollars a month out of her ten-thousand-a-year income. Compared to the hungry writers and artists whose company he preferred, Laurence was rich. "A few Byronic figures loomed among us," wrote Matthew Josephson, who spent a great deal of time in the Parisian cafés of those days; "they owned private incomes and showed no great urge or haste to fill many volumes with their written words. Laurence Vail was such a one, who wrote and also painted a little, but more often and more seriously seemed bent on painting the Left Bank of the River Seine red."

Laurence had written a play, dabbled at prose and verse, been published in little magazines, but what he really did best was sit in cafés and collect people. In the Paris of the 1920s cafés were the core around which all social life revolved. On the corner of the Boulevard Montparnasse and the Boulevard Raspail could be found a glittering selection of cafés, originally bistros and workingmen's hangouts, expanded to meet the influx of American men and women and their need for American-style cocktails. Starting in the morning, the denizens of the demimonde, the *poules,* pimps, artists, and writers, would sit at the tiny round tables of the cafés on cane-backed chairs over strong coffee. As the day progressed, the little clusters of talking and gesticulating patrons would begin spilling out into the streets and the circles around the tables would widen until the boundaries between one group and another merged.

One of the distinguishing features of Montparnasse was that artists and prostitutes mixed effortlessly. When the composer Erik Satie, a man who had spent a considerable amount of time at the bar of the Stryx, died, "there was a remarkable procession at his funeral. All or most of the *poules* of the Quarter turned up, as well as quantities of people from the French art world. I think only in Paris could such a procession have followed an artist to his grave."

For the most part, people just sat and watched each other. Occasionally, a game of dominoes was played. The *poules* went on their nightly rounds, the unsuccessful ones sadly writing letters from the back of the cafés; bicycle *gendarmes* rode in pairs; mink-draped ladies from the Ritz arrived in Hispano-Suizas the size of horse vans; taxi drivers snarled traffic on the cobblestone streets, hurled obscenities, and tooted madly on their horns. Talk was of sex and personal indiscretions, although Matthew Josephson concluded, "Surely nothing can be more boring than hearing the accounts of *other* people's fornications."

All heads turned when Hemingway, already recognized as a new kind of writer, would shadowbox on his way to breakfast at the Closerie des Lilas. A nearly blind James Joyce, with his hat on the back of his head and his sneakers none too clean, would twirl his ash cane coming from Sylvia Beach's bookstore, Shakespeare and Co., and Gertrude Stein would appear "wearing sandals with toes like a prow of a gondola . . . driving around Paris on the high seat of her antiquated Ford."

In this world Laurence Vail was a familiar fixture. He loved to sit in the cafés with Clotilde for hours and hours, drinking, talking, observing, and being seen. "With his long mane of yellow hair always uncovered, his red or pink shirts, his trousers of blue sailcloth, he made an eye-filling figure in the Quarter," wrote Matthew Josephson. "Moreover, he was young, handsome, and for all his wild talk, a prince of a fellow; whenever he came riding in, usually with a flock of charming women in his train, he would set all the cafés of Montparnasse agog."

Not surprisingly, Peggy labeled Laurence the "King of Bohemia," which to her bright and eager eyes he was. The extraordinarily charming Laurence was utterly different from any man Peggy had ever known. For one thing, he was the descendant of a New England minister. For another, he was in constant rebellion against the values of people like Peggy's family. For the impressionable girl from New York, Laurence held the promise of a life totally and forever at odds with the one she had left behind.

In turn, Laurence was attracted to the young magpie Peggy then was. Shy, soft-spoken, and totally naïve, Peggy presented Laurence with a vacuum he could fill. He would teach her about art, life, and literature. Her chestnut hair and astonishing blue eyes, her tiny laugh and offhand manner of speaking intrigued him—as did her money. "Let's say," observed Laurence's great friend Malcolm Cowley, "had Peggy been a poor girl he would not have married her."

The affair with Helen Fleischman came to an end, and Laurence courted Peggy. "I guess I took him away," Peggy boasted. For their first date, Peggy appeared in an elaborate outfit she had designed for herself, edged in kolinsky fur, for a walk along the Seine. She was so awkward she didn't know what to order in the small French bistro he took her to, and asked for a "porto flip." Her life at the Plaza-Athénée had not included much sightseeing in the less chic areas of town. Nevertheless, she and Laurence hit it off.

At age twenty-three Peggy felt accursed by her virginity. She had experimented with her less exciting suitors, letting one thing lead to another, but she had not slept with any of them. When Laurence made advances to Peggy in her hotel room, she acquiesced so eagerly that he was taken aback. "I was ahead of my time," Peggy explained. Rising quickly, she put on her coat and hat to follow him to his new room on the rue de Verneuil, where her initiation could be completed without interruption from Florette, who was due back at any minute. Peggy had seen a book of Pompeiian frescoes showing lovers in a series of positions, and she enthusiastically made Laurence go through each one.

This was the beginning of a long and celebrated career for Peggy. It has been said that she had a thousand lovers, to which she herself snapped, "That's ridiculous." On the other hand, she once confided that she had been to bed with practically every man she had ever met—a point not all of them conceded.

9 — THE ROYAL WEDDING

Peggy played an increasingly important role in Laurence Vail's life. He loved the company of writers and painters and people of all sorts. In the community of Montparnasse he knew everyone, "and even if he didn't, would buy him a drink." Laurence would cruise the streets asking people to parties at his mother's apartment. He would as likely invite the corner tobacconist as he would an old and dear friend. The first such party Peggy went to was a wild and fulminous affair: young boys weeping in each others' arms in the toilet; Thelma Wood, the Robin of Djuna Barnes's *Nightwood,* declaring undying passion on her knees; Flossie Martin, the former Follies girl, declaiming loudly and drunkenly; and, for good measure, Laurence's father having one of his tantrums. Peggy, not knowing what else to do, sat on a man's lap all evening.

Laurence pursued Peggy somewhat conventionally, and eventually got around to proposing to her at the top of the Eiffel Tower. Peggy said yes instantly, but almost immediately Laurence wavered, wondering if he had made a dreadful mistake. "Every time I saw him look as though he were trying to swallow his Adam's apple I knew he was regretting his proposal," wrote Peggy. He ran away to Rouen to deliberate, and his mother, in the hope of deflecting him from Peggy, paid for his former girl friend, Mary Reynolds, to go there with him.

Until the last minute Peggy could not be sure that Laurence would go through with the marriage, so when Mrs. Vail called up to say, "He's off," Peggy assumed she meant he'd bolted. But he did, in fact, arrive at the Plaza-Athénée to pick her up. Peggy had not even bought a wedding dress, so uncertain was she that Laurence would go through with the wedding. Instead, since pink (shades from "flesh" to "begonia") was the color of the 1920s, she had purchased a hat of "antique rose" with a feather in it and a very chic dress with a skirt that matched the color of the hat and a white top embroidered in gold.

The couple arrived via tram car at the *mairie* of the Sixth Arrondissement on the avenue Henri Martin to be married in a civil ceremony on March 10, 1922. An unlikely crew of well-wishers had been hastily assembled.

Later on, Florette, so flustered and distraught over Peggy's choice of husband that she had wanted him investigated, gave the young couple a wedding reception at the Plaza-Athénée where there was lots of champagne and dancing. And Peggy and Laurence continued the celebration with a second party at the Boeuf sur le Toit, Cocteau's favorite restaurant on the rue Boissy d'Anglais, to which Laurence asked even more of his friends (including James Joyce, who wrote to Robert McAlmon: "I scarcely know him though I think they [my family] met him or her somewhere."). Peggy's former suitors rounded out the party—Boris Dembo, who wept over his loss, and Marion Sulzberger, who had begged her to come and live with him as a sister. Maria Jolas, whose husband Eugène edited one of the best-known reviews of the time, *transition,* remembered that when she first came to Paris, "the whole place was buzzing that Laurence had married Peggy—it was a quick marriage." There was tremendous excitement and speculation about Peggy's money and about Laurence's fickle affections, as most people thought he had been engaged to Mary Reynolds. Florette was so madly curious about Peggy's initiation into the ways of love that she pointedly and euphemistically asked her daughter how many times she had "used the Lysol" (an apparently *all*-purpose product) the night before.

Three days after the wedding the newlyweds started out for Rome and Capri, Florette dashing to get Peggy a passport with her new name, Marguerite Vail, on it, in case she should want to run away. In Rome the Vails paid a visit to Peggy's cousin, Harold Loeb, who was there publishing a magazine called *Broom,* to which Laurence had previously contributed his *"Marche funèbre."* Peggy showed up at the editorial offices "barelegged and be-sandaled," Harold recalled, and "Vail's pink face and bright blue eyes were framed by a pale, open-necked shirt and hair to match." Loeb was eager to have another piece by Laurence for his magazine, and before moving on, Laurence composed "Little Birds and Old Men":

Old men and little birds
Too early in the morning
Make squeaks,

Little birds are more brazen;
Primly, they dip feet in puddles.
Old men have delicate feet.

Old men have weak bowels,
Little birds are careless,
Near love of neither
Is sweet.

Little birds chirp, chirp, chirp, chirup;
Old men tell stories, tell stories;
Both die too late.

The poem appeared in the September 1922 issue of *Broom*. Soon thereafter Loeb received a letter from Edmond Guggenheim, another cousin, who was, with Harry Guggenheim, in charge of the Chilean copper mine, Chuquimata. Edmond wanted to ask Harold his "candid opinion and judgment on two poems written by Laurence Vail." "Little Birds and Old Men" particularly troubled Edmond, who wondered if it should be taken as a slur on the Guggenheim uncles whom Laurence had met in Paris. Loeb calmed Edmond down, drawing his attention to logical reasons for "a comparison between senile men and juvenile sparrows," and "pointing out similarities [between the two] such as lax intestinal control and excess vocal expressiveness." Satisfied with the response, Edmond sent off copies to Harry, Simon, and all of Peggy's uncles.

From Rome, Laurence and Peggy went on to Capri, where they had rented a villa. All too soon, Peggy's idyllic honeymoon of swimming and walking alone with Laurence was interrupted by the arrival of Clotilde. Together the brother and sister, locked arm in arm, sought out Capri's social life. "My brother" this, "my brother" that, "everything was 'my brother' with Clotilde." Peggy complained, "She did not relinquish one inch of him to me." Peggy felt like an unnecessary and useless presence on her own honeymoon.

The honeymoon trio ended up in St. Moritz in late summer 1922, where they were joined by Mrs. Vail and a few old friends. After a short trip to New York so Peggy could see Benita, the young couple were settled and back in Paris for the winter. Laurence took up the steady round of cafés, bistros, and parties that he adored. He could go for days without sleeping, throwing off ideas and discoveries with boundless energy. Peggy, who was already pregnant and sick most of the time, would stay home in bed waiting for Laurence—apt to be drunk and in trouble—to come home. "He brought me into an entirely new world and taught me a completely new way of life," Peggy wrote. "It was thrilling, often too thrilling."

"Laurence was in the center of things," recalled Malcolm Cowley. "If you knew *anyone,* you knew Laurence." "I met so many people," Peggy said, "I didn't know whether I was coming or going." Early on she met Djuna Barnes and Mary Reynolds, who formed part of Laurence's entourage. Both had been mistresses of Laurence and were among the most outstanding beauties of Montparnasse. "They had the kind of nose I had gone all the way to Cincinnati for in vain," Peggy wailed.

Not all of Laurence's friends were women. Vail was devoted to Robert Coates, the *New Yorker* art critic. Both loved plays on words, parables, non sequiturs, turning around a sentence, "a kind of Surrealist thing." Coates would insist Peggy share her morning-sickness medicine with him, and guzzled down a considerable amount to ease his own stomach troubles. Robert McAlmon (nicknamed Robert McAlimony because he had made a Cinderella marriage in reverse to a shipping heiress) would often join the Vails in the small hours. At an all-night bistro near the Gare Montparnasse they would have onion soup, fling their glasses at the mirrored walls, pay for the destruction along with their check, and walk out. Kay Boyle described McAlmon as having thin lips closed like a wallet, but as the publisher of the Contact Press, McAlmon helped those writers he believed in, including Ernest Hemingway.

From the beginning Laurence would have violent and frightening fights with Peggy. Laurence had made a scene at the Plaza-Athénée "even before we were married," said Peggy. "I should have taken this as a sample, but I didn't realize." Laurence when drunk loved dramatic rows, throwing things around in restaurants, "breaking crockery and smashing mirrors and attacking chandeliers." He knocked Peggy over, walked on her stomach, threw her downstairs, and rubbed jam in her hair. Once he put her head under water in the bathtub. He had an odd obsession with shoes—in shoe shops he went wild and bolted for the door, and at home he threw Peggy's out the window.

Peggy's response to Laurence's outbursts was either "little agonized screams" that drew even more attention, or weeping. Neither did much good. "Someone should have told him not to be such an ass," she concluded years too late.

Laurence drew attention to himself not only by his tyrannical behavior: he also loved to dress up in fantastic costumes. He had shirts made from unexpected fabrics—upholstery weaves, sailcloth—and liked nothing better than to find an extraordinary use for an otherwise ordinary fabric. He would turn up at shirtmakers with armfuls of the odd textiles that he had found, insisting they be made into shirts. Laurence had overcoats in white and bright blue and wore the most conspicuously colorful trousers he could find. His daughter Clover recalled walking with him one day during her sixteenth year: "He wore a suit of Venetian wool, turquoise top, canary yellow pants, up to [the knee] and then turquoise again at the bottom, a red Russian cape with fur dragging along the ground." The mortified Clover trailed behind.

Outrageous behavior was commonplace in the Paris of the 1920s. At the round tables of the cafés, one heard of the latest antics of a new movement called Dada. A young Romanian dandy, Tristan Tzara, had attracted the attention of certain French intellectuals for his brand of postwar anti-art. Born in Zurich, Dada was a furious rejection of all art that had gone before, indeed of art itself. After World War I conventions had broken down—the corset was thrown away, knees were bared, armpits were shaved, and sex was pulled out of the closet. It seemed that almost overnight a whole generation had progressed from the strict Victorian morality of their parents to a new permissiveness of anything goes. Youth was searching for new values. Dada's nihilism existed because "it spat in the eye of the world."

André Breton, then a square-jawed young intellectual, had eagerly invited Tzara to Paris. When he arrived in January 1920, a band of Dadaists set out to shock the city. Hiring the Salle des Fêtes of the Grand Palais, they decorated it with Dada poetry and posters and invited an audience for a serious literary reading. The Dadas all shouted at once to the sound of clanging bells and beating drums. Tzara presented a play made up of disconnected phrases cut from newspapers and pulled at random from a bag. Performers appeared in knee-length cardboard costumes and stovepipe hats. Breton announced to the audience: "You are all ASSES."

A sententious press reported these goings-on in full detail, so for the next big festival, May 26, the audience came well equipped. During the intermission of *Vous M'Oublierez (You'll Forget Me),* a play in which the actors attacked balloons with knives and hatchets (informing the specta-tors that before tearing out their sex organs they would all take an antiseptic bath), there was "let loose a great volley of rotten eggs and tomatoes, overwhelming the performers." And Tzara wrote ecstatically, "For the first time in the history of the world . . . people threw at us not only eggs, salads and pennies, but beefsteaks as well. . . . The audience were extremely Dadaist." What had begun as a Dada play had ended up a free-for-all with the performers hurling back wilted produce at the spectators.

With serious intellectuals receiving chopped meat in the face and calling it "art," provocation itself became an artistic statement. One of Vail's earliest brawls, according to Peggy, was a Dada confrontation. Raymond Roussel, an obscure writer much admired by Breton, had written a play called *Locus Solus* in 1914, but the war interrupted its production. Full of odd images and mechanical contraptions, including an enormous aquarium with a mermaid and underwater flora, it was finally being produced in late 1922. Roussel's work was to be presented on a double bill with another, more conventional play in order to lure an audience to the theater. One night Breton led a band of Dadaists to the performance for the purpose of hissing the hackneyed drama and cheering the Roussel.

In keeping with Breton's spirit, Laurence also attended the Roussel play with Peggy on a subsequent night and initiated a ruckus of his own. Shouting insults, Laurence was pinned down to the floor by outraged patrons while the pregnant Peggy cautiously stood to the side until the *commissaire de police* rescued Laurence, and Peggy and Vail could reclaim their seats in safety.

By the end of April 1923, Peggy was advanced enough in her pregnancy to go to England for the birth of her baby. Neither Peggy nor Laurence wanted a child born in France, for if it were a boy, he would be forced to do military service. Looking, she said, "as if Brancusi's egg had been superimposed on my slender person," Peggy rented a house in the Kensington section of London for her accouchement.

Benita arrived from New York to be with Peggy. She had suffered through a succession of miscarriages and looked to her sister to fulfill vicariously her desire for children.

Florette was not told about the impending birth. Her flutterings made everyone so nervous that it was agreed to keep her in ignorance as long as possible. Florette had continued to spend a great deal of time in Europe and for most of Peggy's early married life had been an ubiquitous presence. Herself a rich widow of fifty-three, Florette had her share of suitors. Peggy recalled that "when she got to Europe she got several beaux, people who wanted to marry her, but she lived her life fussing about her daughters, most of the time driving us all crazy."

Florette was overprotective, overpossessive, and intrusive. With her maddening habit of repeating everything three times unabated, she called Peggy to tell her to wear "a warm coat, coat, coat," because it was "cold, cold, cold" outside, and she visited as often as she could wedge her foot in the door. She was the type of mother who would waltz into an occupied bathroom unannounced.

Laurence, who disliked Peggy's family and teased her about them, flirted with Florette to soften her up. One night at dinner he tickled her under the table. "Shush," she exclaimed. "Peggy will see. Peggy will see. Peggy will see." In his novel *Murder! Murder!* (an impulse he felt quite often around his mother-in-law), Laurence describes a visit by Florette, whom he calls Flurry, to her daughter, Poll, and her son-in-law, Martin:

> Knock, Knock, Knock Without waiting for outside encouragement the door caves in. Is it the mistral, The police? No, it's Flurry my mother-in-law, paying an informal morning call. . . .
> Her eyes snap gaily, girlishly, "Love little Poll, Martin? Love little Poll-Poll? Mad about her, aren't you? Mad, mad, mad . . .?
> Agitatedly, Flurry proceeds to make herself at home. Having flung one of her two extra cloaks on a chair, she places the other one on the bed. Then, having removed the cloak she wore she puts on the lighter of the two extra cloaks, then, having found the lighter one too light. . . .

In the book the Peggy character complains, "It's only when there's nothing to worry about that she drives one mad," to which Flurry replies, "I don't drive people mad, I don't drive people mad, I don't drive people mad."

With this group in attendance and into this unsettled atmosphere was born on May 15, 1923, a red-faced, black-haired little baby, to be named Michael Cedric Sindbad Vail. Florette called him "Cedy boy, Cedy boy, Cedy boy." He called himself Michael for formal occasions when he grew up, but his parents always called him Sindbad. The combination of "sin" and "bad" was not an easy name to live with.

Peggy gushed love for the infant, and Laurence seemed quite pleased with himself. Peggy always adored babies; children were another matter. She promised to give Laurence a baby girl, as well. Meanwhile, Sindbad was given over to the care of a nurse, bundled up, and whisked off to Paris so that Laurence could celebrate the Fourteenth of July.

The Vails arrived in Montparnasse "still with their toes on view," wrote Harold Loeb, referring to their bare legs and open sandals. The Bastille Day celebration of 1923 began as a three-day weekend and evolved into a three-month bacchanal. Dissipations had "mass velocity. . . . Chinese lanterns hung in rows among the trees; bands played at every corner" while people danced on the cobblestones. The celebration was always a "vast plebeian carnival," since anyone who could afford to usually fled Paris for the summer.

Various friends gathered on the Fourteenth of July, looking for a good time. Laurence and Peggy, Malcolm Cowley, Robert Coates, and Harold Loeb formed one band. Periodically joining the group were Harold Stearns, "Harvey Stone" in *The Sun Also Rises,* and Louis Aragon, Clotilde's boyfriend, whom Robert McAlmon characterized as the type of man "who would get out of bed early, shave and leave the only towel in the place wet and full of bloodstains from his decapitated pimples."

At the Café du Dôme, Laurence and Malcolm Cowley focused their increasingly inebriated attention on the Café Rotonde across the way: its proprietor was rumored to be a police informer. They worked themselves up into a fever of indignant certitude: "An informer," decreed Cowley, "should not be permitted to serve decent people." Suddenly, Laurence exhorted those around him to go over "and assault the proprietor of the Rotonde!"

About a dozen men and women dressed in evening clothes crossed the street from the Dôme to the Rotonde. Aragon rallied the crowd at the bar with a stirring speech about the despicability of stoolpigeons, *"mouchards."* The waiters, sensing imminent trouble, surrounded the owner. Laurence, wearing "a raincoat which he never removed in the course of the hot starlit night," pushed his way through and started a harangue in rapid French. "Harold Loeb, looking on, was a pair of spectacles, a chin, a jutting pipe and an embarrassed smile," while Malcolm Cowley straggled in, spotted the *patron* "with his look of a dog caught stealing chickens and trying to sneak off," and hurled himself past the circle of waiters to land a punch square on the man's jaw.

"I wanted some action," Cowley explained; "the others were just bantering back insults in French." Cowley was herded out the door by the crowd before he could do any more damage, but later on he could not resist one last stand. He walked by the Rotonde with Tzara and shouted, *"Quel salaud! Ah, quel petit mouchard!"* Quite pleased with himself, he crossed the street and was promptly seized by two *flics,* who dragged him to the *préfecture* and charged him with unprovoked assault and forcibly resisting an officer.

Near the Dôme, McAlmon ran into an extremely agitated group led by Laurence and Peggy, who told him of Cowley's arrest. Then all rushed to the station and swore that it was the owner and not Cowley who had started the fight. Cowley, nevertheless, passed the night in jail.

The next morning Clotilde telephoned around town, trying to muster witnesses to testify for Cowley. Peggy and eight or ten others went back to the police station, as imposingly dressed as possible, to testify on their honor that Cowley had not been at the Rotonde the night before. Impressed by the elegant ladies, the magistrate decided against the *patron,* who had only his waiters to testify for him and who was disliked anyway for his nasty disposition.

From the night of his *significant gesture*—a Dada term for an action that was without self-interest or relevance—Cowley was something of a celebrity—lionized by the Dadaists, profiled in the press, and asked for contributions to Surrealist reviews. "In any case, Cowley soon went back to America," acidly remarked McAlmon, "and joined the staff of *The New Republic*, where he could be duly ponderous, the young intellectual fairly slow on the uptake." Cowley, for his part never did like McAlmon, saying he "would take one Laurence Vail, any day, over ten Robert McAlmons."

After three nights of celebrating Bastille Day on the streets of Montparnasse, Peggy and Laurence went to Normandy, where they had rented a villa at Villerville for the rest of the summer. Then, joined by Clotilde and Mary Reynolds, they went on to Capri, where Vail flew at an Italian officer for treating Clotilde too cavalierly and broke the man's thumb.

Once Laurence was released from jail, the couple drifted on to Amalfi and Egypt, dragging Sindbad and his nurse along. Laurence had a reputation as a philanderer, but he never really strayed far from the hearth. In a Cairo brothel he went to bed with a Nubian girl because, as Sindbad once explained, "mother wanted to see how they did it." During the day, Laurence bought himself suits in the brightest of Egyptian cottons and Peggy collected earrings—much in vogue in the 1920s —an idea she had copied from Clotilde and Mary.

PROMISCUOUS

In the fall, Laurence and Peggy returned to Paris and moved into an apartment on the boulevard St. Germain for six months. As always, Laurence could not wait to drop by the cafés, filled to bursting with young Americans come to find *la vie bohème.* At times, noted the journalist Harold Stearns, "you could have sworn you were only in a transplanted Greenwich Village . . . except for the fact [that] some people still stubbornly persisted in talking French."

In Paris the weather was generally mild, the sun shone on the wide tree-lined boulevards, and the clack of horse-drawn wagons could be heard on the cobblestone streets. Fruit and vegetable stalls lined avenues in the early mornings as housewives haggled over what to pay for oranges. "Paris had a quality in those days," recalled the photographer Berenice Abbott who had sailed for Paris with six dollars in her pocket, "that you can't have in an overcrowded place. People were more *people.*"

On Sundays Laurence and Peggy were "at home," and anyone was likely to turn up for the free drinks and excited talk. Still the proper young New Yorker, Peggy was appalled by the lack of manners of the multifarious throng and always worried that someone might run off with the silver or worse. "I hated people being sick in my house, and I especially hated people making love on my bed." When the guests left,

Peggy, in some ways very much her mother's daughter, wiped all the furniture clean with cotton balls soaked in Lysol. That way, she believed, she would not get a venereal disease. "I was so naïve and stupid and I supposed everybody had syphilis. Crazy wasn't it?"

Florette overcame her scruples and came to Peggy's parties and even appeared to enjoy them. True, she was outraged when Kiki called Man Ray a "dirty Jew," but otherwise the eccentric personalities (none of whom she would think of inviting to her own stuffier festivities at the Ritz) amused her. Whenever she could, however, she vented her negative views on the life Peggy led to her daughter and referred to anyone without a substantial trust fund—presumably including Laurence— as a "beggar." Then, to underline Laurence's inadequacies, Florette sent Peggy furs and a car.

Peggy usually presided over her "at homes" in an outfit designed for her by Paul Poiret, then renowned in Paris for his exotic Diaghilev-inspired clothes in oriental colors and brocades. Her dress had a long, tight-fitting bodice in Chinese colors of blue and pink and a skirt made of gold lamé. Peggy so adored the Poiret that she wore it over and over again, and gave one to Mary Reynolds as well. Harold Loeb remembers seeing Peggy, Mary, and Djuna Barnes all dressed like birds of paradise. To complement her Poiret dress, Peggy affected a long cigarette holder and wore an Egyptian-style headdress made by Stravinsky's wife, Vera, a snug double band of gold. As Julien Levy observed, "Everyone walked around with something or another in Paris."

Man Ray, who had started out photographing Poiret's fashion models, was taking pictures of all the better-known denizens of the Quarter and he photographed Peggy in her Poiret ensemble. It was her most beloved portrait and she never ceased to exclaim every time she saw it, "Isn't it beautiful? Isn't it marvelous?"

In the spring, the Comte de Beaumont started the Soirées de Paris. The count was famous for his masquerade balls, at which could be seen a masked Nancy Cunard in a man's tailcoat made of silver lamé and her father's top hat. Or Pablo Picasso could show up in a toreador's bolero and Man Ray in a black dinner jacket, black shirt and tie, with wired red light bulbs for studs. The Comte de Beaumont intended to produce evenings to rival Diaghilev's dazzling Ballets Russes and its stars, Nijinsky and Pavlova. Artists were eager to contribute, and Erik Satie and Les Six as well as Stravinsky composed scores; Joan Miró, Max Ernst, Giorgio de Chirico, and Picasso designed sets. Beaumont's ballet became chic and people went as much to be seen as to see the marvelous costumes and the elaborate mise-en-scènes. And the Dadas—now metamorphosed into Surrealists—went too, to protest the sellout of art to commerciality.

The ballet proved a welcome change for Peggy, who hitherto spent every night with Laurence lounging in cafés. "If I were to add up the hours," she wrote, "I have whiled away at the Café du Dôme, La Coupole, the Sélect, the Dingo, and the Deux Magots (in the Saint Germain quarter) and the Boeuf sur le Toit, I am sure it would amount to years."

The young Vails had been married two years and were still transients, shuttling from one hotel to another rather than establishing a permanent home. They left Paris in the summer of 1924 and spent most of the next year traveling, from the Tyrol to Venice, where Peggy bought a fifteenth-century oak buffet and a thirteenth-century chest. They spent New Year's Eve in Rapallo, fighting: Laurence called Benita a bore, Peggy called Clotilde a whore; Laurence rushed into the ocean fully dressed, and then sat the rest of the night shivering and wet in a movie theater. By March the Vails were in New York. Peggy brought with her some flower collages done by Laurence's friend Mina Loy, and she tried merchandising them up and down Madison Avenue.

With the birth of their second child imminent, the couple sailed back across the Atlantic. They decided to have this baby in Switzerland and went to Ouchy, on Lake Geneva, where Sergei Diaghilev had stayed during World War I with members of his troupe—Igor Stravinsky, Léonide Massine, and the painters Léon Bakst and Natalia Goncharova. At the Beau Rivage Palace Hotel on August 18, 1925, Peggy gave birth to a girl, who was named Pegeen Jezebel Vail, the "first name for fertility," explained the proud father, and "the second for use."

Laurence and Peggy were parents once again, but this role did little to tame their undomesticated spirits. Back in Paris during the winter Peggy was unfaithful to Laurence for the first time with a man she was too drunk to remember. In a jealous frenzy, Laurence threw Peggy's shoes out a window, piled her clothes in the middle of their room, and ran through the streets clutching clumps of the hair Peggy had bobbed and then saved the year before.

One evening, Peggy waited at a bistro called Pirelli's for Laurence, Clotilde, and some others. In her shimmering turquoise-and-gold Poiret, Peggy sat at one of the small round tables reading a red-leather volume of Dostoevsky's *The Idiot*. From time to time she took a distracted drag through her long cigarette holder as she turned the pages. When Laurence spotted Peggy calmly engrossed in her book, he was seized with an uncontrollable fury and barely was the group assembled when Laurence started smashing wine bottles on the walls and mirrors of the bistro. Peggy rose and yelped excitedly for him to stop, but already a stray bottle had grazed one of a group of French army officers who were trying to enjoy a meal amid the fracas. Vail was seized, beaten, handcuffed, and dragged off to jail, yet again. Clotilde pleaded with one of the officers to drop the complaint. The officer, Captain Alain Le Merdie, had little sympathy for Laurence's tantrum, but he was so smitten with Clotilde that Laurence was released the next morning, bruised but barely penitent. The captain, "a great, big, blustering sort of a fellow," persisted for years in his quest to marry Clotilde and eventually succeeded. Even so, Clotilde was reluctant to take on Le Merdie's name, which sounded unpleasantly close to the popular French expletive.

Laurence's rage did not subside. When Peggy typically would ask to be taken home after dining, Laurence returned to the cabarets on his own. One night, Laurence chanced upon Peggy at the Sélect, dancing on a table, very shrill and very drunk, two red lipstick crosses painted on her cheeks and a circle on her forehead. Grabbing her roughly, Laurence barked, "Let's go home to the Lutetia," whereupon he hauled Peggy off to a brothel to be greeted by fifteen nude women.

Even in exceptional circumstances like these, Peggy had a mental makeup that let her remain curiously dispassionate. She went about her daily routine like an actor who performs on stage impervious to chairs hurtling through the air and bottles crashing against the set. Laurence told his daughter Apple, "The one thing I couldn't stand about Peggy was her total unconcern . . . like when she came to visit me in jail. I'd be upset about something and she'd be reading a book—Dostoevsky—doing a list." Peggy herself conceded, "I whirled through life in a kind of dream. I never quite realized what was happening."

Nothing reached Peggy. She lost her temper "only once in twenty thousand years." She could make abrasive remarks and not give a thought to their effect on the feelings of others. Laurence, too, with his street brawls, his posturing, and his wild costumes, "was in constant and furious rebellion against his mother, his father, his family," without ever understanding why. Laurence and Peggy "had very much in common, a total disregard for *convenances*. They didn't care," observed Maria Jolas. "That was Laurence's philosophy to the very end."

Although "there was a blankness" in Peggy that was extreme, she was not alone among her contemporaries in flaunting this quality. On a visit to Paris, William Carlos Williams was moved to remark on the indifference of the women he found there. Of Nancy Cunard, the thin, aristocratic daughter of the hostess Lady Emerald Cunard, who lived with a black man to defy convention and went mad at the end of her life, and of Iris Tree, another English expatriate, he wrote:

> They were completely empty, and yet they were young, appealing and unassailable. No one could touch them to harm them in any way or be deeply moved by them. They were as quiet in their moods and as profligate in their actions (it was said) as figures cut from chalk.

Sherwood Anderson also noticed the apathy of the women of Paris:

The younger folk seem to feel nothing. Now if you or I, sitting by a girl in our youth, had placed an arm around her waist, she would either have responded coyly, or have smacked our face. I believe that today the same girl would not even be aware that an arm was around her waist. She would go on smoking her cigarette and sipping her brandy.

By their frenetic activities and parties it seemed as if a whole generation were trying desperately to *feel* something, at any cost. "It was a more frivolous, less psychoanalytic group," observed Maria Jolas of her contemporaries, "looking for one thing—titillation. There was a tremendous amount of Lesbianism, the beginning, you might say, the first rivulets, of the wave of sexuality." Rules were to be flouted, and the body abused.

The wanton manners of her contemporaries appealed strongly to Peggy. They fulfilled a need to rebel against the stuffy, emotionless background of her childhood and to feel, whatever the price. They were a glittering reproach to Florette with her fussy ways, to the prim, rejecting world of wealthy New York Jewry, where her family strove for grandeur and acceptance. What had at first shocked the innocent and naïve Peggy, now offered her a comradery of similar souls and a sense of belonging she had lacked all her life.

What had begun as a trickle ended up a deluge, as Americans flocked to France and expatriate life became more and more of a tourist spectacle and sideshow. Buses would regularly pull up in front of the Dôme or the Rotonde and the "bohemian" artists and writers seated at the tables would be pointed out. Those expatriates that could escaped the crowds to "runaway" colonies in the south. The Gerald Murphys, wearing the striped jerseys and jaunty nautical caps of French fishermen, proselytized for the off-season splendors of the Riviera, first discovered by the Americans in the 1920s. To their villa came Picasso, John Dos Passos, and those golden darlings of the Jazz Age, Zelda and Scott Fitzgerald, from whose lives of wealth and madness came the myths that fed the times.

Peggy and Laurence had fallen in love with an old inn in Pramousquier, between St. Raphael and Toulon. Cocteau had stayed there with his lover Raymond Radiguet, and Laurence urged Peggy to buy it. Situated in a densely wooded area carpeted with wild flowers, Pramousquier (which Florette insisted on mispronouncing "Promiscuous") boasted clear green water and dramatic sandy beaches so remote one could bathe in the nude. The house had no electricity (an old-fashioned icebox required block ice) and no telephone, but its very rusticity charmed Laurence and after the birth of Pegeen the couple spent more and more time there. At least in Pramousquier Peggy's life had some routine. In the morning she picked up the block of ice that was thrown off on the railway line, and then, as all good French housewives do, she attended to the daily shopping in the nearby town of Le Lavandou. She had just enough time for sun and a swim before lunch. The rest of the day Peggy spent reading, relegating Sindbad and Pegeen to the care of a nurse. It was a languorous life, punctuated by visitors from Paris: Clotilde, Mina Loy, Mary Reynolds, Harold Loeb, and the painter André Masson.

Peggy kept scrupulous household accounts, entering receipts and expenditures in minute detail in a battered notebook. She loved checking the sums and fretted if there was a discrepancy of a few francs. She was ever alert for the unscrupulous vendor or the careless maid, endlessly contriving to save money and get things for less. It infuriated Laurence to rush home in an amorous mood, only to discover Peggy absorbed by her accounts, or to propose running away somewhere and be rejected with: "No thank you. Today is laundry day." It drove him mad to see her crosschecking, rechecking, comparing her lists.

Neither Peggy nor Laurence was exactly poor. Peggy had the income from her trust, and Laurence enjoyed an allowance from his mother until the day he would inherit her blue-chip stocks and bonds. Compared to their artist friends, for whom anyone who had three meals a day was rich, the Vails were positively regal. Still, the incessant concern over money and how it was spent persisted—a preoccupation most often found, ironically, in the very rich and the very poor.

" 'Stingy' was her middle name," declared the Irish writer Jimmy Stern of Peggy. Peggy's sister Hazel readily agreed. "Peggy was very stingy, just like my mother," she said. Indeed, Florette was so niggardly that the porters of one hotel would forewarn others in hotels to come by chalking big white crosses on her luggage. And Peggy's grandfather, James Seligman, was said to have been so stingy that he managed to arrive at a variation on "biting the hand that feeds"—he starved his own nurse—while rumors abounded that Peggy likewise starved her husbands and her servants. Peggy agonized if a butler ate more than his share of apples and went to great lengths to ascertain the price of the fruit so she could deduct it from his wages. She kept almost no food in the house—half a slice of boiled ham, for example—and insisted that all the fruit, however rotten, be consumed before any fresh could be served.

Peggy nagged Laurence about the money they spent on trips. She would deny him small indulgences and she never let him forget she had more money than he. Vail "hated the pettiness, the tremendous economic pettiness, all the time," said his friend Yvonne Hagen. When she once asked Laurence why he had divorced Peggy, he replied, "We lived in a house with orange crates. We had no furniture. She'd be sending off checks to some foundation and say we didn't have the money for furniture." Peggy used her money, said Hagen, "to torture people." Peggy never said good night to Laurence without asking if he'd remembered to turn out the lights. "I think that drove him crazy," Peggy confided.

Laurence, for all his braggadocio, was a weak man, anxious himself about money, always complaining that he didn't have enough, that he was losing capital and wasn't going to have any left. "He never really worked," said his daughter Clover, "never knew if he could make money." When he was drunk he was either violent, knocking Peggy around, or sickeningly maudlin. Sober, he could be cruel and taunting. "He was a wildly difficult man. He would pick on your weakest possible spot and put his finger in it," said Jimmy Stern of his friend, twisting his own finger for added emphasis. He loved stirring up trouble. "When you walk into a room," he used to say, *"always* disagree, especially if you don't know what you are talking about." Jacqueline Hélion, who was once married to Sindbad, said,

> Peggy was very hurt and disappointed by Laurence Vail. After her meeting and marriage to Vail she hardened herself to things. He was utterly selfish, always made fun of people. He was sort of a monster. He was sadistic, destructive, turning everything around into ridicule, laughing at things. If you showed any interest in something he would run it down. I imagine when Peggy first knew him she was quite innocent and unworldly and plunged into bohemian life abroad, far removed from the milieu in which she grew up, and I think she was serious about marriage and he wrecked it.

"He hated himself for marrying her," said Jimmy Stern. He was snobbish toward Peggy's family of "rich Jews" and made fun of the "mad Guggenheim women." He found them ridiculously pretentious and bourgeois. Episcopalian himself, he never let Peggy forget she was a Jew. And he never took Peggy seriously intellectually, telling her in no uncertain terms that she was stupid. "Oh, you bloody idiot," he would exclaim, "you don't know anything about anything." Said Sindbad of his parents' relationship, "She was not literary, whereas my father was. She was tolerated by my father, just about tolerated." Laurence saw Peggy as a charge. "She was more a pupil than a wife and companion," he wrote in his unpublished memoirs. "She knew nothing when I met her and doesn't know much now. I'm always explaining things to her and trying to convince her about something."

Nonetheless, Laurence persevered in teaching Peggy about literature and art. He had a "marvelous way of making you interested in reading." While sitting around the fire after dinner, he'd jump up in midsentence to go pull out a magazine or a book from his extensive library to illustrate a point. He worshiped writers. Kay Boyle, Laurence's second wife, was incensed when she read in a magazine Peggy's account of life with Laurence, in which she described his jumping on her stomach. "Can you imagine?" Kay said to Apple, her daughter by Vail. "That's all she has to say about Laurence! He introduced her to the arts. He introduced her to books. He introduced her to authors. She knew nothing. She was an ignorant woman." And Hazel once concluded, "If it hadn't been for the bookshop and Laurence, she'd be playing golf at the Westchester Country Club."

A ROLLS-ROYCE ON THE BLINK

Although Peggy was miserly by nature, she was also capable of what Mary McCarthy labeled a "neat, precise generosity," sending out monthly checks with the same single-mindedness with which she did her accounts. Peggy came from a Jewish tradition of giving to charity. Her father, Ben, had left countless bequests to organizations ranging from the Manhattan Trade School to the Home for Colored Orphans. Peggy dispatched checks to her former teacher, Lucille Kohn, for her socialist causes, and Peggy believed herself to be a leftist politically, saying with conviction, "I don't believe in privileges, or inherited money." She donated to the Katonah Labor College, and in 1926, contributed ten thousand dollars, the last of her inheritance from her Seligman grandfather, to the relief fund for the British general strike. As is often the case with penny-pinchers, Peggy could spend larger sums because they were abstract.

Laurence recommended that as Peggy had no brains and no talent, she should give her money away to those writers, poets, and artists who did. Peggy lent Berenice Abbott five hundred francs to buy a camera, and in return Abbott photographed Peggy and her children. Peggy gave Jane Heap the same sum for the *Little Review*. And she began to subsidize the redheaded writer from Cornwall-on-Hudson, New York, Djuna Barnes.

Djuna had had a brief affair with Laurence when they were both in New York's Greenwich Village writing plays for the Provincetown Players. Even before Peggy's marriage to Laurence, Leon Fleischman had approached Peggy for one hundred dollars to bring Djuna to Paris. Helen Fleischman coaxed Peggy into sending the newly arrived Djuna some underwear. Without giving it much thought, Peggy sent over some of her used and darned lingerie; this Djuna found insulting. Ashamed, Peggy dispatched some brand-new underclothes, and a truce was called. Subsequently, Peggy surprised the writer when she happened to drop by as Djuna was working at her typewriter clad in nothing but one of her new teddies and thoroughly embarrassed after all the fuss she had made about them.

Dutifully, Peggy sent Djuna a monthly check that grew to three hundred dollars in the 1970s. Mina Loy, who was a great friend of Djuna, lived in the same apartment compound on the Avenue San Roman and was also once Julien Levy's mother-in-law. "Mina could see every month," he recalled, "Djuna was in agony because she expected a check every first of the month. She'd staved off the grocer, the landlord with promises of the check, and Peggy's check always came late. It never came until the 25th of the month. Mina asked Peggy why she did it, when it caused Djuna so much hardship. Peggy said that 'Somehow, the only pleasure I get while I give is when I withhold for a while to give them pain. That's the only way I can feel good about it, know they'll appreciate it.' She admitted, 'I don't know why I do it, I can't help it.'"

Mina Loy was another beneficiary of Peggy's zeal to make up for her feeling of stupidity by helping out creative people. Mina, like Djuna, possessed great beauty and style, as well as a most cerebral wit. She wrote, but try as she might she never seemed able to make enough money to meet her needs. She dreamed up all sorts of ideas to make a few pennies here or there and "had a distinct talent for inventing fantasies," according to Robert McAlmon. Among her projects, "she transferred archaic pictures and maps upon glass globes and bottles, and she inserted lights inside them, and marketed these as table lamps." Her apartment was a veritable fairyland out of the Marché aux Puces—rooms divided by wirework cages, walls a patchwork of multicolored metallic papers, "wrappings of countless bonbons pasted together in floral collages," colored cellophane everywhere.

"Mina," said Julien Levy, "unlike Djuna, wouldn't take money from Peggy. So, Peggy put up the money for Mina to go into business."

In due course a shop was opened on the rue de Colisée, near the Champs Élysées, to sell Mina's lamps and bric-a-brac. The rent was high, but Peggy insisted Mina needed a chic address for a chic clientele. The potential profits of Mina's lamp bases delighted Peggy, because the raw materials—empty wine bottles—were free and the finished product could be sold for twenty-five dollars. In her zeal to make the store a financial success, Peggy invited her mother's *lingère* to display underwear at the opening, which so incensed Mina that she refused to attend. In addition, Peggy had the store selling slippers hand-painted by Clotilde and the occasional picture by Laurence.

The boutique prospered, but rather than liberating Mina, it shackled her with orders to fill and all the minutiae of running a small business. And Peggy's obsession with sums, ledgers, and detailed accountings of every cent drove Mina to distraction. At one time a dozen women were employed by the lamp shop. Joella, Mina's daughter, worked as a salesgirl by day and a forewoman at night. Peggy ran the shop and Mina the workroom. "Mina blamed Peggy because she got into it too deep," explained Julien Levy. Mina had become enslaved to a business she was dying to drop, but she continued in this scheme gone sour until Julien's father offered to pay Peggy back and free Mina.

But before the venture ended, when Peggy went to New York for a visit with her sister Benita, she brought with her fifty of Mina's lamps and shades and she gleefully canvassed as many shops as she could, taking orders and mounting the shades herself. In the Guggenheim tradition, Peggy was still peddling, but, unlike her grandfather, Peggy had no need to travel with her wares on her back—she kept her merchandise beside her on the seat of Benita's chauffeured limousine.

The Vails, who by 1927 were living in Paris at the Lutetia for the winter and entertaining in Laurence's studio, were the undisputed, unofficial host and hostess of Montparnasse. Julien Levy was whisked off to a party chez Vail on his arrival, and saw Laurence's studio crowded with the famous personalities he had heard about in New York: Hemingway, Ezra Pound, Cocteau, Janet Flanner, and Isadora Duncan (she insisted Peggy never call herself "wife" and nicknamed her "Guggie Peggleheim"), who was dressed in plum-colored silks and draped on a couch. Julien overheard someone saying: "Try some of this, my dear. It's prohibition gin, imported from the States. It gets you drunk *rapidly,*" and Marcel Duchamp responding, *"Il faut de l'eau fort, pas trop d'effort."*

"In those days," wrote Matthew Josephson, "Peggy was very much a young matron, somewhat shy in manner and plain in appearance." She was skeletally thin, her hair slicked back in a skullcap, her arms and legs like reeds, and fragile enough to snap in two. Her nose remained the first thing one saw, but a lovely smile made up for it. Jimmy Stern's wife, Tanya, remembered Peggy coming through Montparnasse in a little gray fur coat and matching toque. "She had an elegant figure and the money to dress well."

To the people who saw Peggy, "she represented extraordinary license, for anything and everything, and plenty of money," said Maria Jolas. "Everyone went with her. There was always plenty to eat, plenty to drink and plenty of places to go to bed with each other."

For all the fun Paris represented, at the first sign of spring Peggy and Laurence were back in Pramousquier, where life essentially bored Peggy. "She was always a city girl," wrote Laurence, "she enjoys bustle, people, intriguing, and excitement, and some business—buying and peddling. Oh she can tolerate the country sometimes, but she likes her country pretty dainty, intimate, thatch cottages and English hedges."

It was in Pramousquier that word reached them that Benita, Peggy's much beloved sister, had died in childbirth on July 21, 1927. Peggy cried and cried for weeks. She berated herself for not having been with Benita, as if then she might have prevented her death, and she blamed Benita's husband, Edward Mayer, for making her pregnant. Looking at her own children filled Peggy with remorse. "I felt I had no right to have any."

Laurence despaired of ever consoling her, and narcissist that he was, soon grew jealous of all the attention Peggy was lavishing on her sister's memory, exploding in fits of violence. He ripped up Benita's photographs, which Peggy had morbidly placed about the house, and Peggy claimed she never felt the same way about Laurence again.

Florette, who had not liked Benita's husband from the first, never forgave him for her daughter's death. She arrived in Europe in the fall and Peggy drove to Cherbourg to greet her, but she was no consolation, either. "She bored me so," said Peggy, who remained depressed and despondent.

Tired of country living, she moaned she was being buried alive. The man who had once appeared to her to be the "King of Bohemia" now more closely resembled a weak and colicky child. Laurence remained a charming dilettante. "Don't take yourself seriously," was his motto. Peggy tried writing her memoirs but got no farther than the opening paragraph. A painting she undertook with a group of others came to nothing. What was she to do?

During the summer of 1928, Emma Goldman, the American anarchist, was established in a little villa in St. Tropez, financed by Peggy, laboriously writing her memoirs, *Living My Life*. Goldman had been a fixture in the cafés of Montparnasse—most usually on the terrace of the Sélect—where she sat for hours, disheartened and disillusioned. Short, "squat, with feet turned outwards like a web-footed bird, and the famous red hair . . . streaked with grey" she talked about her experiences. She bore little resemblance to the woman who had panicked Americans into deporting her to Russia; she appeared almost motherly. More or less an outcast, she had become disgusted with the Soviets, who she felt had "cynically betrayed all anarchist principles." She "had become a bitter old woman whose one purpose in life, it seemed, was to hate—to hate and to forget." Weekly, Emma would go dancing with Alexander Berkman, the man who had emptied his revolver into Henry Clay Frick. She had been deported with him and he was now hungry and ill, barely making ends meet.

Peggy was immediately taken with Goldman. "I began by worshiping her," she said. Emma's anarchy and Berkman's activism were immensely appealing to Peggy, who transferred to them her old affection for her socialist tutor Lucille Kohn. "What was happening," observed Maria Jolas, "was that a total absorption in money and what it could buy had been questioned by the Russian revolution and the people she, Peggy, associated with. There was social defiance in helping Emma Goldman" who, "in a sort of, how shall I say, closely compressed form, lived the whole gamut of illusion and disillusion. . . . It was attractive to even the rich and poor alike, particularly to the idle rich who were psychologically most on their guard."

Eventually, Peggy decided, "Emma Goldman was an awful fake, a terribly, terribly vain woman," and Laurence repeatedly said that Emma was "horrible." Consequently, Goldman left Peggy out of the very memoirs Peggy had helped underwrite. (And close to twenty years later, when Aaron Bohrod reviewed Peggy's own autobiography, *Out of This Century,* he wagered that most of the people Peggy had included in her "informal memoirs" wished that they had been similarly slighted.)

But that summer Laurence and Peggy were still in the thrall of the aging anarchist. With Laurence at the wheel of their Hispano-Suiza, they would career dangerously from Pramousquier over to St. Tropez to visit Emma. Emma would treat them to dinner cooked in a "Jewish cordon bleu" style, of which her gefilte fish was the "pièce de résistance." Laurence joked that she would do better writing a cookbook instead of her memoirs.

As writing did not come easily to Emma Goldman, she hired to help her a Wellesley graduate from Oakland, California, named Emily Holmes Coleman. Emily had married a man she had met as a "pen pal," Deke Coleman, and had given birth to a son, Johnny. Soon after giving birth, Emily suffered a nervous breakdown and spent two months in an insane asylum, subsequently turning her brush with madness into poetry and a novel, *The Shutter of Snow* (published in 1930). She arrived in Paris in 1925 and joined expatriate life, contributing pieces to Eugène Jolas's avant-garde literary review, *transition.* (She had been fired from her job on the Paris edition of the Chicago *Tribune* for hitting her editor over the head with a dictionary.)

Emily was an enthusiastic reader and an energetic talker, a trait, thought Djuna Barnes, who became her friend in Paris, most acceptable in the very young; Djuna, however, was quick to point out that Emily was nearing thirty. Indeed, Emily was wildly enthusiastic about everything. Arriving for the weekend with a bag full of books, she would mark them up with scribbled notations and observations—regardless of to whom they belonged—and follow up with long, intense conversations about literature. With her blue-eyed, blond-haired, all-American college-girl looks, Emily was striking, if not beautiful, and with a son near Sindbad's age, she became one of Peggy's closest friends.

Emily had left her husband behind in England and, though technically still married, had fallen in love with John Ferrar Holms, a redheaded Englishman who lived in St. Tropez with an equally redheaded Englishwoman—his girl friend of many years, named Dorothy. He shared Emily's enthusiasm for endless conversation, and was much admired for his brilliance. He thought of himself as a writer but, consumed with guilt and bemoaning the loss of his gifts, he wrote nothing at all and drank a great deal instead. "He was," said Emily's son, Johnny Coleman, "like a Rolls-Royce on the blink. Perfectly remarkable but not quite making it." With his thin, tall body, his sparse red beard, and pink, sunburned skin, John Holms looked more like a lanky Jesus Christ than a lady-killer. But it turned out to be Peggy, not Emily, with whom Holms would become involved, and Laurence immediately sniffed him out as trouble, snidely referring to him as "Pink Whiskers."

On the anniversary of Benita's death, July 21, 1928, Peggy would have preferred to sit home and weep, but she reluctantly agreed to go dancing in St. Tropez with Laurence, Emily, Dorothy, and John Holms. Peggy made a fool of herself, drinking too much, dancing wantonly on the table, and flirting outrageously with John, who obligingly pulled her aside and kissed her.

Peggy was so taken with Holms, whose English accent thrilled her, that she began to think about leaving Laurence for him. The fact that Holms had a woman living with him did not overly concern her. Subsequently, Peggy invited John and Dorothy to Pramousquier, where under a moonlit sky, Peggy seduced Holms by luring him away for a nude swim in the ocean.

Peggy insisted that John and Dorothy move into an unused cottage on the property at Pramousquier. Proximity made it easy for Peggy and Holms to resume their affair, and the two would slip off into the woods or down to the rocks by the shore and make love. It wasn't the sex that delighted Peggy so much as the fact that Holms took her seriously. She was barely alive, he said. She needed to be set free from that mad husband of hers who flung bottles about cafés and had tantrums at the drop of a hat.

Indeed, one night the Vails spent at a bistro in St. Tropez with Emma Goldman, Alexander Berkman, and Laurence's sister Clotilde, Clotilde made "a spectacle of herself dancing with her skirts up to her thighs" and Laurence, suspecting that Peggy was up to something, grabbed at Peggy's blouse and ripped it open. Peggy was used to being Laurence's "whipping boy," but although they had plenty of arguments at home, this scene, played out in front of the open-mouthed Goldman and Berkman, was too embarrassing; it was the final straw, and her irresolution over leaving Laurence evaporated.

Peggy pushed Papi Le Merdie, Clotilde's sister-in-law, who was visiting them for Thanksgiving, at Laurence, hoping to distract him. Laurence, who had never trusted John Holms ("He is a man who feeds on other people's emotions and on intrigues," he wrote to a friend), now could not help but notice that Peggy and John spent all day together, supposedly out "driving." Later on, they would all have dinner or talk into the night. It was too cozy. One evening, while the group was assembled in the large sitting room and Dorothy was taking a bath, Peggy artlessly said she was going upstairs, and John announced that he, too, was retiring to his cottage. As Laurence later wrote in describing the incident, "Suddenly, I surprise a queer intimate glance. I know—though I think it is ridiculous— that there is a rendezvous."

Laurence went upstairs to check the bedroom. Peggy wasn't there, so he walked to the cottage, where he discovered Peggy and John Holms embracing and kissing. Laurence exploded with rage, attacking John Holms, swinging wildly, swearing through gritted teeth, "I'll kill you. I'll kill you." Dodging Laurence's punches, Holms pleaded with him to be sensible, to be a "mature man." Peggy screamed and rushed out for help. She came back with the gardener, who separated the two men and held Laurence down long enough for Holms to escape. Shaking off the gardener, Laurence ran to the big house, where he came upon John, Dorothy, and Peggy conferring in the misty bathroom where Dorothy had been taking her bath. In front of Laurence, Peggy asked Holms and Dorothy to leave. Laurence, appeased, calmed down, happy that he had won the round and that the pair would shortly be out of his life. Or so he thought.

The following morning, Laurence awoke with a hangover aggravated by a painfully tender black eye. He watched Peggy "dressing briskly, as she always did: pull up panties, into frock, right shoe, left shoe, couple tugs at the hair, two strenuous and misplaced dashes of lipstick." She started her busywork, sorting the wash, making lists, adding up bank accounts, questioning servants. An expression "would come over her face when she was ruminating the details of some domestic problem, the same one little problem, over and over again and always exactly the same angle." Suddenly, Peggy asked Laurence if she could go to London to visit a friend. When, he wondered, today or tomorrow? "No," Peggy said, shaking her head, "I can't go today. I have to take the wash to Le Lavandou."

That afternoon, before Laurence went off on an errand concocted by Peggy, she kissed him good-bye. Leaving Laurence a note on his pillow: "Don't know if I'll come back. Life too hellish. I'll write you," she drove straight to the train station at Fréjus and boarded the *rapide,* meeting up with both the Holmses in Avignon.

Returning home, Laurence went crazy. In his own way he adored Peggy. "He was absolutely mad about me," she claimed. Laurence liked having a wife to come back to and snuggle with. "He was a strangely domestic sort of fellow," noted his friend Malcolm Cowley. Had Peggy gone off with that unthinkable Englishman? Papi Le Merdie consoled him by pointing out that Peggy could not possibly have left without her two children, and furthermore: "No one could fall for the red beard. You've felt his hands like a dead fish, cold and clammy. And that pink flesh of his is a little disgusting. . . . And you're forgetting Dorothy. I can imagine a woman running off with any man," she added sagely, "even a horror, a monster. But one does not go off with a couple."

Hearing no word from Peggy, Laurence went to Paris to find sympathy from his mother and Clotilde, taking Sindbad along with him. Pegeen had a cold, so he left her behind with her nurse to rejoin him when her sniffles were better. He could do nothing but wait.

MEDEA

Earlier in the fall of 1928, when Peggy was just contemplating leaving Laurence, her sister Hazel was undergoing similar problems of her own. She had married Milton Waldman after her first marriage to Sigmund Kempner ended. Now, after five years, Waldman wanted a divorce. He was tired of Hazel's erratic temperament, but Hazel could not bear the idea that he wanted to leave her. Fuming bitterly, she packed herself up and took their two children with her to New York, leaving Milton in Paris.

Once in New York, Hazel moved into the Plaza Hotel and called her cousin, the newly married Mrs. Cornelius Ruxton Love. Audrey Love was living in a luxurious penthouse at the Hotel Surrey on Manhattan's East Seventy-sixth Street, and was surprised to hear from Hazel, with whom she had never been particularly close. Hazel wanted to come over right away. Mrs. Love tried to persuade her to postpone her visit until another day, but Hazel was not to be deterred. Reluctantly, Mrs. Love resigned herself to the impromptu visit and went out to buy some ice cream for the children.

Hazel arrived an hour early, while Mrs. Love was still out. She was let in by the Irish cook, Nellie McCormack, who asked if she might be of help, to which Hazel replied, "No, I'll be all right." With that Nellie left Hazel to make herself at home until Mrs. Love returned. Hazel had arrived with her two little boys, Terrence, aged four, and Benjamin, aged one. For some reason she decided not to wait inside the apartment but to go out onto the terrace. The Loves had decorated and surrounded their terrace with a picket pole fence, but Hazel decided to go through the gate and walk onto the roof of the building. "There was no need for her to go around the back," said Mrs. Love. "She could have sat in the front . . . it was sturdy."

On October 20, 1928, *The New York Times* reported on its first page the deaths of Terrence and Benjamin Waldman, Hazel's two sons, in a thirteen-story fall. The facts appeared unclear. The paper stated that Hazel, while waiting for Mrs. Love, felt fatigued and sat down on the foot-high parapet surrounding the hotel roof. Mrs. Love remembers the parapet as being higher, at least high enough to sit on. Hazel had the baby in her lap, with Terrence scrambling near her. Hazel later explained to the authorities investigating the deaths that the older boy, jealous of his baby brother, had tried to climb into her lap. Somehow, she lost control of the children and in the melée they both went over the sides of the parapet. Dazed and shrieking, Hazel saw the bodies of her two babies on the roof of the neighboring hotel.

Mrs. Love arrived home to be greeted by her husband with the dreadful news. "You musn't be upset," he told her. "It had nothing to do with you." Later on Audrey Love would cry, "Why would she choose me? I was just married." All anyone knew for sure was that the Waldman children were dead. Neither of the witnesses to the event, a painter working on the adjacent building and Nellie, the cook, came forth with any details that would incriminate Hazel. No one, it seemed, had actually seen the children fall off the roof.

Nevertheless, it was widely believed in New York that Hazel, in a fit of rage over her husband's desertion, had flung the boys off the roof herself. Behind her back she was called "the murderess." Iris Love, Mrs. Love's daughter, likened Hazel to Medea who killed her and Jason's children as "the only way left to her to revenge herself " after he abandoned her for another. Another cousin, Susan Miller, believed "she was so jealous of her husband, she thought she would teach him a lesson. Some lesson." And Laurence, when facing his own custody battle with Peggy over their children, wrote, "I shall have to prove the family is insane etc. Take the Hazel episode. Hazel told people here she would rather kill the children than let Milton have them."

At dinner, Julien Levy recalled, family conversation turned to the fact that Hazel got tired of having children and got rid of them. A friend once said: "No one could believe she did it until they met her." The Lewisohn girls were admonished about this crazy cousin of theirs, who threw her babies off the roof, and advised to stay away from that entire family, including Peggy. Cornelius Love referred to the incident as the day "Hazel killed her children." Milton Waldman, the children's father, had nightmares until the day he died in which Hazel, poised on the roof, waited until he arrived on the scene before hurling the boys off. And Hazel, who "looked like her mother, but . . . was fat and sloppy," added fuel to the speculation by behaving in unpredictable and unattractive ways. Julien Levy recalled Hazel as very disagreeable and mean. He remembered an incident that occurred while he was visiting Hazel in the country. "She was all frumped up, very made up, trying to look like a streetwalker of sixteen." Her then-boyfriend walked into the house with a turtle and she "began to kick it from one end of the kitchen to the other until the poor thing had a cracked shell." She said, "It won't live long now."

No one will ever know for sure whether Hazel, enraged at her husband, threw her babies off the roof of the Hotel Surrey, or whether it was a frightful accident. Not even Hazel appeared to know what happened. She could talk about it up to a point and then would shrink back, referring only to a "nervous breakdown." The episode was investigated by the New York police and declared an accident. "She was sent to a sanatorium immediately and then shipped to Europe," according to Susan Miller.

Many preferred to believe that the powerful Guggenheim family had bought off the witnesses and suppressed the investigation. "The painter was paid off," said Susan Miller. "In those days it was still possible to pay people off. . . . The Guggenheims bought lots of people off." Iris Love remembers, "My father came home to find all the Guggenheims there. They had all come together to protect Hazel." The lawyer who handled the case is now dead; his papers and the answers to the mystery are in the files of the New York law firm of Coudert Brothers, accessible only with Hazel's permission and that of the firm. Today's Guggenheims do not admit that there was a payoff, but probably they do not know. "Had she been Hazel Smith," wondered Malcolm Cowley, "who knows what would have happened."

The day after the children died, Florette sent the Ruxton Loves a huge crystal candelabra, to thank them for their trouble. The incident left an indelible mark on Peggy's family and on Peggy as well. Hazel's ways were imputed to Peggy, and which sister was which became fuzzy in the minds of many. What lingered was a certainty that "those people" were insane. To the members of "Our Crowd" the episode was intensely alarming. "There was enough craziness in our family," said Joan Lewisohn Crowell. "I had two uncles who committed suicide. . . . The Guggenheim thing was very threatening. The nuts had intermarried."

Of all the things Peggy would talk about—lovers, abortions, scandals of all kinds—she would absolutely never discuss the death of Hazel's children. "It has nothing to do with me. It was completely out of my life," she insisted, whether out of indifference or because she was too prudent to accuse her sister of murder. Peggy was always embarrassed by Hazel, and discouraged her friends from seeking her out. The secrecy with which the event is shrouded only adds to the mystery and suspicion.

Hazel went on to remarry several more times and have two more children, a son and a daughter. After her divorce from the anguished and bereaved Milton Waldman, Hazel married an Englishman, Denys King-Farlow. Before the marriage, Florette, concerned lest news of her daughter's unfortunate "accident" spoil her chances with the groom-to-be, went over and "spoke to the Englishman's family and said there was a great deal of scandal, and they said they had met Hazel and liked her, and that was the important thing." Their son, John King-Farlow, always wondered if his mother had done it and asked of her close friends, "Did mother ever tell you?" According to Maria Jolas, Hazel's friends "were only too glad to let the waters close and forget."

FINIS

The first news Laurence had about Peggy and her whereabouts was a telephone call from her lawyer two days after his arrival in Paris. The attorney informed him of her intention to seek a divorce as well as custody of the two children. He then discovered that Peggy was back in Pramousquier and had Pegeen with her.

Although Laurence strongly suspected that Peggy had run away with John Holms, he did not know this for certain until several weeks had passed and he received a frantic telephone call from Dorothy in Paris. "Something dreadful is happening," she wailed. "John and Peggy are living together."

Rejected and miserable, Dorothy had left John and Peggy to live out their passion for a trial period of six months. She fervently hoped that in the end she would be reunited with Holms, although lust could certainly be ruled out as her motivation, because, as Laurence wrote to a friend, "His woman told Clotilde he only makes love to her once a year."

Laurence's mother snickered when Laurence told her the story. "She was always a fool about anything in trousers. Disgusting!"

Before the divorce papers could be filed at all, there was the tricky matter of the children. Emma Goldman took it upon herself to intervene in this delicate matter and wrote Laurence begging him to be generous and let Peggy have both children.

After several weeks of legal wranglings and deliberations, it was decided that Laurence would retain custody of Sindbad and that Peggy would have custody of Pegeen. Sindbad would visit Peggy sixty days a year. Peggy thought "it was only fair."

The custody issue resolved, Peggy and John Holms were free to go on a "honeymoon," as Laurence snidely called it. They went to Vienna, where it was so cold that the Danube froze, and they visited the Porquerolles Islands near Pramousquier. Peggy and John kept Pramousquier as their home base, but were frequently away on trips, indolently spending as much time in bed as possible between sights. The much-contested Pegeen, a flaxen-haired, peach-skinned baby with a sad expression, was left with her nurse, even though the child would cling to Peggy, frightened of being left behind.

By the spring of 1929, Dorothy had been on her own in Paris for more than six months, and John showed no inclination to leave Peggy and return to her. Defeated, Dorothy saw only one possibility. She had been lying over the years to family and friends that she and John were married. It would be too humiliating to admit the truth at this point after being "most unceremoniously" ditched, as Laurence observed. Now Dorothy pleaded with John to marry her. How could she get a divorce without having been married first? She would return to England, but she would not go back unmarried. Secretly, Peggy suspected, Dorothy "thought he'd go back to her if he married her." Astonishingly, John agreed to Dorothy's wild proposal and went up to Paris to marry her. Peggy was in no position to object, as her own divorce from Laurence was far from final. "I was the bridesmaid," Peggy remarked bitterly. "If I had been divorced, he would have married me instead of her. I should think so. It would have been more natural, wouldn't it? It was crazy. The whole thing was so crazy."

To complicate matters, Peggy was pregnant by John but decided to have an abortion. "I had so many abortions," Peggy confessed teary-eyed. "I think I had seven abortions. . . . I had most of them with Holms. . . . I didn't want to have a child, because I wasn't married to him. It was stupid, I think now, but in those days it meant more."

Peggy was soon replaced in Laurence Vail's affections by Kay Boyle, a talented writer from St. Paul, Minnesota. Kay had made a reputation for herself writing for the literary reviews such as *transition* that proliferated in Paris. At one point she had assisted the poet-editor of *This Quarter,* Ernest Walsh, with whom she had a daughter. With one failed marriage, an infant to take care of, and no money, in 1928 Kay went to work for the Dayang Muda, or princess, as she preferred to be called, of Sarawak, the sister of the English "White Rajah" of a small country in the north of Borneo, who was in the process of writing her "memoirs." Kay spent much of her time inventing dialogue to attribute to celebrities the princess was eager to have appear in her book.

Ensconced at the Dayang Muda's, Kay met Isadora Duncan's brother, Raymond, a notably thin man in his fifties, who was then running a sort of pastoral commune, patterned on the ancient Greeks, in Neuilly, on the outskirts of Paris. Raymond affected Grecian-style tunics that he alleged were loomed in his village, and sturdy thong sandals made from leather he claimed he had tanned himself. A pair of Raymond's upturned sandals adorned the mighty feet of Gertrude Stein, who had known Raymond in his pretunic period, when he had worn a carnation in the buttonhole of his pin-striped suit. Now Raymond sported two waist-length braids that he coiled about his head like a crown. On "ceremonial occasions" he would add a thin wreath of bay leaves.

Duncan spoke long and earnestly to Kay in his flat, midwestern twang of the joys of his colony, where everyone—children and adults—dressed alike in tunics and sandals. There, he said, children grew strong eating fresh goat-milk yogurt and cheese, and the sound of tinkling bells could be heard as the goats passed by in the early morning. The simple pleasures—weaving and crafts—soothed the tensions of the spirit, while eurythmic exercises fulfilled the needs of the body.

Consequently, when Kay finished her work on the princess's memoirs and found herself with nothing to do and nowhere to go, she headed for Duncan's colony. Duncan welcomed her with a large party—strictly nonalcoholic—for which he mixed a heady punch flavored with herbs and spices. But behind Raymond's back, Kay's friends merrily poured bottles of gin, whiskey, and brandy into his tame brew.

Soon, however, Kay was introduced to the realities of living at the Duncan center. Six days a week, she was expected to mind one or the other of Raymond's two shops in Paris—on the faubourg St. Honoré and on the boulevard St. Germain. There Kay sold sandals and, among other items manufactured at the colony, batik-dyed fabrics produced in the two large bathtubs Duncan had expropriated from his sister Elizabeth's bathroom. For her labor, Kay was provided with three hundred francs, or about twelve dollars, a month for her "of-the-world expenses" and a meager lunch of goat cheese and yogurt, which she was to eat as quickly as possible in the back of the store so as not to miss any customers. Robert McAlmon remarked sarcastically on the skimpiness of Kay's remuneration: "but then Raymond Duncan was never a practical man. What could money mean to him when it was Kay who needed it?" On Sundays, Kay could look forward to cooking spartan vegetarian meals for the colony.

Kay and her baby, Sharon, affectionately called Bobbie, slept on the floor of the Duncan center "rolled in a blanket on a kind of pallet," while the other children in the group lay on sheepskins. Soon the group took Bobbie with them to Nice, leaving Kay behind to look after the stores. In the six months she spent at Raymond Duncan's colony, Kay saw the fabled goat procession only once; she discovered that the tunics said to be woven at the center were imports from Greece; and she learned that the sandals were put together from soles and thongs bought at a small Parisian shoe shop. The final straw came, as far as Kay was concerned, when Duncan, who had always vowed that life for everyone at the commune would improve if only he had more money, received a windfall for his designs and spent it all on a new car for himself.

One evening around Christmas 1928, Kay wandered into La Coupole with its neon lights, red-leather seats, and basement for dancing, carrying with her a sprig of mistletoe. She spotted Robert McAlmon seated with Clotilde and Laurence Vail, whom she had never met. Laurence beckoned her to join them and, rising, took the mistletoe from her hand, raised it above her head, and kissed her eyes, nose, and mouth. "I'll sit between you and my brother," said Clotilde, as she hastily pulled Kay down beside her, "so he won't eat the mistletoe."

Kay escaped from the Duncan center on Christmas Eve and by January 1929, she and Laurence were always together. Harry Crosby, Kay's publisher, reported seeing them at the Dayang Muda's, Kay recumbent on a divan. To Harry's wife, Caresse, Kay appeared a Seminole maiden, her hair black, "her eyes silver green, the color of moss." Excruciatingly thin, "built like a blade" with an aquiline nose, Kay stood as "neat as a needle."

After the vexations of the Duncan colony, life with Laurence seemed blissfully serene. Grateful for the opportunity to eat more than goat curds and settle down, Kay created a home for herself and her daughter, as well as for Laurence and Sindbad. The family began to expand, as Kay was soon pregnant and, married or not, proposed to have the baby. Kay hoped "I would be a girl for Poppa," said Apple, who was born in December 1929. "He had lost Pegeen and she was the big love of his life. When I was born, he transferred his love to me. Pegeen never forgave me."

Kay dominated Laurence with a firmness Peggy never possessed. "Whenever she felt Laurence was going to make a scene," Peggy sneered, "Kay made a scene instead. My mother said to me, you should have done that." When Peggy told Florette that Laurence was frightened of Kay, Florette said regretfully, "Too bad he wasn't frightened of you, frightened of you, frightened of you."

Kay limited contact with Laurence's sister, Clotilde—who had been such a thorn in the side for Peggy—to the degree that Bobbie barely remembers "Aunt Coco." But Kay did write a short story, "Wedding Day," in which she idealized a nearly incestuous brother and sister. *Short Stories,* Kay's first book of many, was published by the Crosbys' Black Sun Press in March 1929 and dedicated to Laurence.

Under Kay's tutelage, Laurence dedicated himself to writing. The couple worked opposite each other at a big desk on various projects, at one time collecting newspaper clippings to use for journalistic fiction.

At their home one awoke to the "clicking of a busy Underwood and the aroma of chicorized coffee . . . Kay tapping the keys with one hand while with the other she bathed the baby in the kitchen sink and scrambled eggs on a driftwood-burning stove."

Kay's daughter, Bobbie, believed that "Laurence and my mother were very much in love. . . . His relationship with Peggy Guggenheim was . . . sort of an insane absurd thing. . . . With my mother he led an *équilibrée* life. . . . She's a creator which Peggy wasn't." Yet Peggy insisted that Laurence "didn't love Kay Boyle as much as he loved me."

In truth, Laurence often said, "I would have stayed with any one of them." "Laurence was dependent. Women somehow set the pace for him," said Clover Vail of her father and Kay. "The fantasy Peggy projects about him, the King of Bohemia, is misleading. He was much more vulnerable than that."

Between Peggy and Kay there was instant, irreversible animosity. "I loathed her and she loathed me. Oh my God! How she loathes me!" Peggy exclaimed. Kay envied Peggy her money and her freedom but thought her frivolous and spoiled. Peggy was amazed and disappointed that Laurence had replaced her so quickly. Unfortunately the two women had to deal with each other for the next twelve years, as Kay was now involved in making the arrangements for Peggy to see Sindbad.

After her flight with John Holms, six months passed before Peggy saw Sindbad again. In that time, he had grown into a spindly-legged, knob-kneed six-year-old, with huge, wistful blue eyes. He arrived to meet her in Paris, all dressed up in a sailor suit, and he barely knew her. Laurence hovered about protectively as mother and son sat on a park bench. Thereafter, Laurence allowed Peggy to see him once a week.

It appeared that Kay liked to stir up trouble. "Kay Boyle is the falsest person I ever met," said the artist Jean Hélion. "Bitchy. The minute she starts talking, she manages to say something bitchy." Malcolm Cowley recalled that his friend "Laurence Vail said about Kay Boyle, as if to sum up—'She was always a liar.' " Kay irritated Hart Crane so much at a lunch party that he threw a copy of the *American Caravan* into the fireplace because it contained a short story of hers, despite the fact that it also included a poem of his.

Kay fanned the flames of distrust between Peggy and Laurence. She pointed out how easy it would be for Peggy to kidnap Sindbad and encouraged Laurence in ideas of moving far away—to Russia, even—so that Peggy could not get at Laurence's son. When Peggy called to make arrangements to pick up Sindbad, Laurence would pretend he did not recognize her voice and hang up. Sindbad was bombarded with admonitions from his father and soon-to-be stepmother to be wary of Peggy. "I always saw Sindbad," said Peggy ruefully, "but, you know, under awful circumstances, with Laurence standing around as a spy. Laurence was afraid I was going to steal him, always. And Laurence told him I was going to steal him and frightened him so . . . crazy, crazy."

Peggy was awkward with her own son, and when she picked him up for daylong excursions she did not know what to do with him. "My mother took me for long walks and fed me a lot of ice creams," recalled Sindbad of those meetings. He felt he probably suffered from the same "problems of those movie kids," alternately experiencing moments of lavish attention and long pulls of neglect. As a grown man Sindbad resented Peggy: "She was a lousy mother."

Peggy was petrified that she had lost Sindbad to Kay, who was "a very good stepmother. I saw her now and then. We really hated each other. . . . She was jealous of me, and I suppose I hated her because of the way she acted about my children. She always treated me like a sort of idiot and acted as if she was the only person who knew how to bring up children. And then she used to say how poor they were all the time, when I was giving Laurence three hundred dollars a month, and they never admitted it. They never told Sindbad. They were always saying how poor they were and how rich I was. Horrible."

Sindbad settled the issue of who was the "good" mother by classifying both Peggy and Kay as "perfect bitches." And his half-sister Clover concluded, "They were *all* terrible—my father, Peggy, my mother."

PART III

THE BRIDE STRIPPED BARE BY HER BACHELORS, EVEN

HANGOVER HALL

When the New York stock market crashed in October 1929, Peggy and John Holms were in Paris, staying at the Hôtel de Bourgogne et Montana. Although Peggy's life continued unchanged, for other Americans living abroad, surviving as they had been on dollars from home, the crash had immediate repercussions. Desperate letters from America arrived daily to be read aloud in the cafés of Montparnasse from mothers and fathers ruined in the aftermath of the collapse. For young people whose only concern but a few months before had been the mad verses of Lautréamont, these letters meant only one thing—a one-way ticket back home.

By the mid-1930s most of the American expatriates had repatriated themselves, and once home, nostalgia gnawed at their souls. "That enchanted country of drink that was the world one had been young in, in the twenties!" wrote Edmund Wilson.

One drank to go back there, where one's friends were, where life was irresponsible and daring, where it was passionate, amusing and frank. One got homesick under the grind of the depression and one could not help slipping away. But then one did not find what one had come for: one's friends were no more their old selves than one was one's old self; one could pick up one's cues for the old clever play, but a moment of alcoholic revelation would show up its essential banality, its superficiality, its falsity, and one would walk out with indignation and rudeness.

Peggy was lucky to have escaped the fate of most of her contemporaries. Her uncles in New York had prudently avoided the worst of the debacle of 1929 and Peggy could still rely on roughly twenty-two thousand dollars a year. The exchange rate, which contributed to the sense of release and abandon of the 1920s, continued high—twenty-five francs to the dollar—and those who had dollars still found Paris a haven. Peggy was one of the few expatriates who could afford to stay on, and stay on she did, having found independence and a way of life she could never give up. Peggy sold the house at Pramousquier, which she considered Laurence's anyway, and she and Holms moved to Paris.

Some of Peggy's friends were still around. Peggy introduced John Holms to Helen Fleischman, now separated from her husband, Leon, and seeing James Joyce's son, Giorgio. Together the two couples would visit Giorgio's parents. At these gatherings Giorgio might burst out singing with a slight Irish brogue, "Il Mio Tesoro." Or his father would accompany himself at the piano for an evening of Irish songs. Eugène Jolas and his wife, Maria, were also constant guests at the Joyces'. Maria would delight them with her rendition of "Farewell the Titanic." Peggy could entertain only with crazy stories of antics in Paris before the crash.

Other nights were spent in cabarets, which were considerably emptier now without the Americans. Dawn would frequently find John Holms still drinking and without Peggy, who had long since left him to carry on without her. Peggy's mother, Florette, ever the formidable dowager, stormed through Paris wrapped in furs—Depression or no—and was horrified to discover Peggy "living in sin" with a dubious Englishman. Florette finally had adjusted to Laurence, difficult as that was, but Holms was beyond her capacity.

Peggy's divorce from Laurence became final in the summer of 1930, and although marriage between Peggy and John was out of the question, since John had married Dorothy, the couple could now at least live together openly. John found a house in a working-class district of Paris. Located on the avenue Reille near the Porte d'Orleans, it had been built by Picasso's collaborator in Analytic Cubism, Georges Braque. Five stories high with just one or two rooms to a floor, the house was dubbed the "little skyscraper" by Peggy. John was quite content to let Peggy provide him with a nest. As his friend the writer Alec Waugh observed, Holms's "fortunes may be said to have risen and fallen in accordance with the financial status of the particular woman of whom he was the consort."

For most of his life John Holms had been searching for the right place and the right time (and the right room and the right chair and the right robe) in which he would, finally, write. He read voraciously and was overly critical of what other people produced, always preparing to write himself but never quite getting around to doing it. Said Peggy, "I never knew why, exactly, it got worse and worse, 'cause he should have been a brilliant writer. He was a very brilliant philosopher."

What John was was a great talker, concentrating all his thwarted talents on the art of conversation. "With him you felt in the presence of an extraordinary genius," said Johnny Coleman. "He was a very extraordinary person—a rare bird." Peggy often found herself dozing during his interminable monologues peppered with quotations from Donne and Wordsworth, but she was completely convinced she was living with a genius. "Everyone," recalled a friend, Silas Glossop, "always assumed he was writing a great book of criticism or philosophy, but when he died he left not one page."

As his guilt and misery grew over his inability to write, Holms's drinking worsened. Ever more despondent and melancholy, tormented by nightmares, he compared himself to Bramwell Brontë, the gifted, alcoholic brother of the Brontë sisters, and felt his life was worthless. Night after night he drank to stupefaction. "Alcohol," points out Maria Jolas, who herself found Holms fascinating, "was a constant" in the story of Peggy's life. Mrs. Vail once remarked to her son Laurence, "You drink, Peggy drinks. And that redheaded Englishman—I saw him at St. Tropez drinking like a fish. It's drinking that has made all this trouble." Mostly Holms sat on a sofa all day and drank. Often he just stayed in bed, nursing his hangover, until six o'clock, when he would rouse himself to begin yet another night of steady drinking and talking.

Faced with John Holms's relentless patter, Peggy became passive and obedient. She was still rail-thin, her chestnut hair wavier and longer than it had been in the 1920s when the slick bob of the flapper was in vogue. To protect her weak ankles she wore ankle socks and strapped shoes, which accentuated the slimness of her legs. Peggy found it endlessly reassuring to have John make all her decisions. "He instructed her, daily, hourly," wrote his friend the novelist William Gerhardie,

without stinting himself or sparing her, how to spend her money to the best cultural advantage. She had grown strangely listless, rarely disputed now, while he explained to her indefatigably, in soft, tender, caressing tones, why she could not, having regard to the circumstances of her birth, surroundings, education, appraise the points in their purchases which he, given his special opportunities and advantages, could not help knowing. . . . Everything he approved was eighteenth century, seventeenth century . . . always something she could not know.

Peggy had long been convinced that she was inept. "I think I'm rather stupid to begin with. Yes, I do. I have no memory, I don't remember anything. That's very bad for an intellectual," she averred. Like Laurence Vail before him, John Holms enjoyed building himself up at Peggy's expense and fed her insecurities. Peggy was "very uneducated," observed Mary McCarthy. She had an "uneven development. There were so many things she had not heard of. There were huge areas of ignorance. She never had any formal education." Although Peggy loved to read, she felt totally unprepared when John talked about avant-garde writers, and she certainly had no quotations—modern or classical—at her disposal for ready use in conversation.

In this atmosphere of alcoholic literary criticism, Peggy's children were merely onlookers. To them Holms appeared a benign presence sprawled on the sofa with a "headache." Pegeen was driven every morning by her nurse, Doris, to Maria Jolas's newly opened École Bilinguée an hour away in Neuilly. The girl rarely saw Peggy, except for a few brief moments in the evenings before her dinner and bedtime. If Peggy and John had to leave Paris, Pegeen would be left behind with her nurse in a rooming house. Jacqueline Ventadour remembered meeting Pegeen in 1931 when they were both pupils at Mme. Jolas's school. "We were six," said Jacqueline. "She never talked about her mother, or father. . . . [For a time] Pegeen was living in a *pension-famille* with a governess, Doris, who was the only adult I ever saw around her. She was frightened to death of her." When Florette called for Pegeen, "She arrived at four o'clock after school with a tremendous long car with a chauffeur and fur rugs, and we'd go to Rumpelmayer's. It didn't do much for Pegeen. I never saw Peggy during this period."

Laurence finally felt secure enough to let Sindbad visit Peggy more often—a month in the summer and two weeks at Easter and Christmas. It was only to please Sindbad that Peggy attended Laurence and Kay's wedding in April 1932. "It was so stupid," said Peggy. "They all wanted to be so friendly about nothing." This was the second wedding Sindbad attended that year, as Alain Le Merdie had finally succeeded in marrying Clotilde. In the photographs of "Aunt Coco's" wedding, a scrawny Sindbad clutches his father's hand and his enormous blue eyes stare straight at the camera.

John Holms had not been back to England in years. When he and Peggy visited for a few days in the spring of 1932, they decided to stay for the summer. Perhaps in England, immersed in his own culture, surrounded by his own people, John could begin to write. Luck brought them to a commodious gray stone house about a hundred years old, baronially called Hayford Hall. The manor had eleven bedrooms, which quickly became the most popular spots, as the public areas were gloomy and unattractive. The large central hall was especially unappealing, paneled in raw-looking wood and lined with forbidding ancestral portraits.

To Hayford Hall, Peggy and her ménage retired for two months. John's harem of female friends—Emily Coleman and Djuna Barnes—"worshippers, not mistresses," Peggy was quick to point out—arrived. Peggy gave Djuna a "rather rococo" bedroom that reminded her of Djuna, but Djuna complained she got it because no one else wanted it.

In striking contrast to the lethargy of his soul, John Holms's body was wonderfully athletic. He played tennis, rode, and took Sindbad hiking and swimming. Johnny Coleman still remembers John diving over and over, "leaping out repeatedly from the water." The children loved to follow him. Peggy enjoyed the occasional game of tennis or horseback ride, but she was never much of an athlete. Her ankles twisted constantly, and she was much more at home in the drawing room than outdoors.

Predictably, John Holms wrote not one word during his summer retreat to Hayford Hall, but one of his guests created a masterpiece. Locked in her bedroom all day, emerging only at mealtimes and for her daily ten-minute constitutional, Djuna Barnes worked on her evocative and disquieting novel *Nightwood.* She wandered about in a nightgown, later to explain, "I spent all summer looking for a night to go with that nightgown."

Djuna was insufferably self-absorbed; but even in the best of times the relationship between Peggy and Djuna was never easy. Six years older than Peggy, Djuna could be haughty and had an acerbic tongue. Although Djuna accepted money from Peggy, she treated her with contempt, joining the chorus of her detractors who said she was dull-witted and even insulting Peggy to her face. Johnny Coleman recalled "Djuna, having *un caractère du chien,* saying, 'You bitch, you got the dough,' and all the time having the hand out." Djuna's rude remarks were wounding and Peggy was terribly hurt when Djuna turned to her and stated, "You've got the money, but I've got the brains." Nevertheless, Peggy continued to subsidize Djuna, all the while suspecting that Djuna's own family could have done more. Peggy so longed to be loved and needed by creative people that even if the price was sometimes steep, she was often willing to pay it.

When *Nightwood* was published in 1936, it was dedicated to Peggy Guggenheim and John Ferrar Holms, without whom, indeed, it might never have been written. Peggy was touched that Djuna included John in the dedication and wrote Djuna years later, "I never felt that you really liked him too much and that you dedicated *Nightwood* to him to please me."

Was Peggy a character in the novel? Some believed she was Robin, the elusive heroine. But Robin was based on Thelma Wood, a woman for whom Djuna Barnes held a passionate love. Others believed Peggy was Jenny Petheridge—a rich American woman, nearing middle age, who impulsively had to get what she wanted—and they may have been closer to the truth.

The strong lesbian theme in *Nightwood* made it avant-garde and scandalous for its time, and the novel is still disturbing today. Naturally, there was speculation about a lesbian relationship between Peggy and Djuna, but Djuna, according to Johnny Coleman, "never, so far as I am aware, never, played the field. She had this passionate, all engrossing affair on which *Nightwood* was based. It went to the very limits of her own experience there, so that, curiously enough, even in translation it comes out. . . . Djuna had a large number of men lovers, but I'm not aware of a single woman other than the one in *Nightwood*. . . . People just had some restraint in that field." Peggy herself denied that she had an affair with Djuna.

Nightwood had no greater admirer than Emily Coleman (she badgered T. S. Eliot for years to get it published), yet between her and its author there was a great rivalry. Emily's own novel, *The Shutter of Snow*, based on her experience in the asylum, never received the acclaim accorded *Nightwood*. It annoyed Djuna that Emily monopolized John, whose critical acumen she valued, barely leaving her a minute of his time, launching into hours of unprovoked conversation. Djuna always felt Emily talked too much altogether and joked that she would make marvelous company if "slightly stunned." The tension between Djuna and Emily escalated to the degree that Djuna hid her manuscript from Emily, fearing the latter would burn it.

Indeed, Emily behaved like a spoiled little girl. Her table manners were terrible, she had tantrums if she did not get what she wanted, and once even punched Peggy in the eye. "Emily was very strange," recalled Sindbad of his mother's friend, "though I did not know it at the time. She was probably in love with John Holms. She was not an attractive woman physically; later she became very Catholic and lived in a convent. She might have been a lay sister. I know she had a young man whom she made sleep on a carpet at the foot of her bed. She was quite batty in the end. I guess she was jealous of my mother, of Djuna, who was so beautiful and clever, and frustrated about Holms." For years afterward, Djuna and Peggy would use Emily's erratic behavior as a point of reference—to say someone was "even worse than Emily" explained it all between them.

To add symmetry to the complicated emotions in the air, Pegeen and Sindbad carried on their own rivalry. They fought constantly, each one vying for their mother's attention, but Peggy was too self-involved to notice.

In the fall, Djuna left for Tangiers, her unfinished manuscript under her arm. There she shocked the locals with her makeup of bright "blue, purple, and green in a day when no one used such colors."

Peggy and John returned to Paris and the avenue Reille. By the spring of 1933, however, they were back in England, waiting for another summer to begin at Hayford Hall.

Jane Bouché Strong remembered visiting Hayford Hall that summer with her parents. The Bouchés and John drank so much that Jane dubbed the place "Hangover Hall." There was "steady, steady drinking." To Jane, "Emily Coleman looked like an old college girl. She looked funny to me," and Doris, Pegeen's nurse, "was pretty, not terribly much a servant type." Emily was very difficult and carried on so much that by the end of the season when Emily announced, "I had such a happy summer," Peggy replied tartly, "You're the only one who has." Jane Bouché spent most of her time with Johnny Coleman, who was ten, with Pegeen who was eight, and with Sindbad who was then ten and had a crush on her.

When summer was over, Peggy and Holms decided to sublet the house on the avenue Reille and look for a permanent place in London. They found a flat at 12 Woburn Square in the heart of London, an eighteenth-century house, which Peggy made less dreary by her simple and spartan furnishings.

Jane Strong remembered Peggy at this time sporting a "modernistic gray coat with two big buttons. She wore it with a conical hat. I said, 'You look like a clown.' " Her face was always animated and she wore bright-red lipstick to set off her very white teeth. "She had an awfully pretty smile," Jane said, and "she was very interested in what other people had to say." Peggy always asked questions and appeared to be listening attentively to the responses, which she punctuated with lively "No, she did?"s and "She didn't?"s and "Really?"s. But this was merely a social technique, not an indication of deep interest, since she eventually admitted, "I've spent all my life asking questions I didn't hear the answers to."

John Holms spent only six weeks in the flat on Woburn Square. He had dislocated his wrist in a riding accident the preceding August and was advised that the best thing to do was to have the wrist reset. He celebrated his forthcoming operation by drinking all night and waking up with a hangover. When the doctors arrived, Peggy hesitated to tell them about John's drinking the night before. She had canceled the operation once when John had the flu and was embarrassed to do so again. With misgivings, she allowed the doctors to proceed. "If I had had any sense of responsibility," she wrote, "I would not have allowed the operation to take place."

Since the wrist had to be broken, the excess growth on it removed and the bones reset, the operation required anesthesia. Holms consented to chloroform, though he hated it, and Peggy held his hand until he fell asleep, at which time she was gently waved from the room.

The entire procedure should have lasted only a half hour, but Peggy began to worry as time went by and there was still no word from the doctors upstairs. She listened outside the door for a clue, but heard nothing. The doctors were busy trying to revive Holms, whose system was so weakened by alcohol that his heart gave way under the anesthesia. The doctors finally opened his chest and massaged his heart, but it was hopeless. The combination of those two drugs proved lethal. John Holms died on the operating table on January 19, 1934, at the age of thirty-six. He had never gotten around to writing a book—any book, let alone the longed-for masterpiece. But Peggy mourned him as the man who taught her everything she knew, the love of her life, crying, "Everyone I love dies."

YEW TREE COTTAGE

For seven weeks Peggy gave herself up to despair, weeping quietly, her blue eyes filling with tears. Emily Coleman moved in with her, even sleeping in the same room.

At the end of that time the "widowed" Peggy—for she had considered herself to be John's wife spiritually, if not legally—remembered Douglas Garman. John had introduced Peggy to Garman, who had edited *The Calendar of Modern Letters* in which Holms's only published story had appeared. Handsome and five years younger than Peggy, the brown-haired Douglas Garman had visited Peggy and Holms and had flattered his hostess with so many compliments that Peggy, in those moments when John was morose and drunk, began to daydream of the dashing publisher. After John's death, Garman had sent her a letter of condolence asking if he could help in any way, and Peggy decided to put his offer to the test.

The son of a country doctor, Garman had been supporting his severe, churchgoing mother, the illegitimate daughter of Earl Grey, and seven eccentric sisters since his student days at Cambridge. Garman's youngest and favorite sister, Lorna, married his closest friend from Cambridge, Ernest Wishart, known as Wish. Uncomfortable with his wealth, Wishart was swayed by Garman's leftist ideas. (Yet "his idea of Communism," said the writer John Richardson, "was you still had four servants, but they sat down to dinner with you and the family.") Wishart appeared like an "old tweed suit with a storm cloud where the head should be" to his son Michael (who as a schoolboy intoned, "Our father Wishart in Heaven" and wondered why *his* was the only father in Heaven). Together the two friends established the publishing firm of Wishart and Company (later Lawrence and Wishart), which would one day be the largest Marxist publisher outside of Russia, with Garman as the chief reader and adviser.

The affair between Peggy and Garman had not progressed very far when Peggy abruptly left for the Austrian Tyrol to spend Easter with Laurence, Kay, Pegeen, and Sindbad. Laurence was now living in Kitzbühel. An avid skier, he had learned the sport when the Norwegians first introduced it at St. Moritz. With the news of Holms's death, Laurence decided to "forgive" Peggy for leaving him. Yet he could barely hide his satisfaction over the sad demise of "Pink Whiskers" and he reveled in making Peggy cry over John Holms, tucking her in bed every night so he could watch her tears. Soon Peggy had had enough. She hated the cold, the ice, the snow, the skiing, and Kay, who made her feel unwanted and unnecessary.

Back in England, Peggy resumed her affair with Garman, renting a place for the summer of 1934 in South Harting, near where Garman had bought a house for his mother. And when at the end of the summer the lease was up, Peggy opted to buy a neighboring cottage.

Yew Tree Cottage was named for a giant tree that grew just outside it. The Elizabethan house was set among rolling meadows and from its tiny windows cows could be seen placidly grazing. Although the acreage was small, the lawn opened out onto a lovely vista of the downs and valley of South Harting—just the kind of manicured countryside Peggy liked.

Garman, along with his daughter Debbie, moved in with Peggy in the winter of 1935. Peggy discovered that the virile Garman was very different from the aesthetic Holms. Of the four men she called "husbands" Peggy asserted that Garman was the least suitable for her. Although she hastened to add about Garman, "he was a great sexual attraction. . . . He was very handsome." Nonetheless, his comparative youth made Peggy, whose hair was beginning to gray, feel insecure and self-conscious. She could dye her hair, but the insecurities were another matter.

Young Pegeen had been "very unhappy," according to Sindbad, shunted from place to place and school to school, losing first one father and then the next, and finally losing even her nurse, Doris. When Garman and his daughter moved in, she brightened. Garman was kind to her, and her school chum Jacqueline Ventadour observed that "there was a period when Pegeen was happier in England, at Yew Tree Cottage, due to Garman. He was a charming, good-looking character, an unusual character, a country gentleman and a communist."

At least with Garman, the house had a semblance of order. Peggy had shown neither a great interest in nor a great talent for housekeeping, being naturally rather sloppy and too much of a child at heart to care. She was good at ensuring that the servants returned the empties to the local grocery, squabbling over discrepancies in bottle counts, and pennies here and there, but she was not very good at the larger picture. Garman criticized Peggy as too messy and also disapproved of the haphazard way that she dressed. Peggy literally pulled on whatever was at hand in the morning, flattering or otherwise, and was ready for the day after she swiped her mouth with two slashes of bright-red lipstick and tossed the various keys to the closets where she hid the cash or the wine into the same battered purse she took with her everywhere.

Yew Tree Cottage had no central heating and it was so cold that Peggy carried a few oil burners from room to room. (Years later when she went to visit the newly married Jackson Pollocks at the Springs, Long Island, Lee Krasner remembered, "In our Hampton House she came to visit; it was so cold there was ice in the toilet. We gave her an oil stove for warmth and she carried it around with her. She came down in one of her negligees with the oil stove and said: 'This reminds me of the castles in England.'") It was so uncomfortable that Silas Glossop recalled, "She retired for several weeks reading Proust in bed with woolen gloves on." Rats invaded the premises periodically, and Garman would exterminate them by making believe they were Fascists and knocking them out with a large stick. As to the quality of the entertainments proffered chez Garman-Guggenheim, Glossop said: "Food, you never quite knew. The standard of cooking was not high. You might get a marvelous Château Haut-Brion and the next time something ghastly."

Garman took it upon himself to remodel the downstairs, which was charming with exposed rafters and an enormous fireplace, but small. The Communist also added gravel tennis courts, a pool, and a cricket pitch, planted seeds, and landscaped the property—all at Peggy's expense.

Occasionally, Garman would go to London, to a little flat that Peggy kept on Guilford Place, but Peggy could not often bear to return to the city where Holms had died. She preferred to spend her time on her pet project, a collection of John Holms's correspondence with Hugh Kingsmill, which she hoped could be published and make up for the book Holms never wrote. Peggy retyped the letters and interested Kingsmill and Peter Hoare in editing them. Edwin Muir wrote a touching introduction, which he later incorporated into his own *The Story and the Fable* and which Peggy included in her memoirs. The correspondence, however, was not very interesting, and Peggy was still hoping to find a publisher for the letters as late as 1979.

Peggy generally enjoyed provoking Garman. She drank to displease him, whereupon Garman became somber, "a gloomy sort of chap. When I met him," said Silas Glossop, "I thought him miserable." Michael Wishart felt that it could not have been easy for Peggy. Nevertheless, the purely physical aspect of the relationship continued to thrive. As Peggy effusively put it, "We were fighting all day and fucking all night."

In the fall of 1936, Sindbad was sent as a boarder to the Bedales School, quite near Yew Tree Cottage, and Laurence and Kay moved to Devonshire to be near him. It was a miserable year for Laurence, the end of a series of tragedies and losses. Clotilde, his beloved sister, had died in November 1935. She had been admitted at the American Hospital at Neuilly-sur-Seine for an appendix operation and had never woken up. Laurence repelled any expression of condolence from Peggy, who he claimed had hated Clotilde, and for years afterward he would get drunk and cry for his sister. "He would go into a big act," said Jacqueline Ventadour of these crying jags. "He wept about her—his poor sister! There was only one photo in his studio and that was of his sister."

Laurence's father, the neurasthenic Eugene, and his Uncle George, the roller-skater and collector of errant hairs, both died shortly after Clotilde. The silver lining in this cloud of disasters was that Uncle George left Laurence a legacy enabling him to buy a châlet in Mégève, in the French Alps. He fancifully called it "Le Châlet des Six Enfants," for, soon, in addition to Kay Boyle's Bobbie and Laurence's Sindbad and Pegeen, there were Apple, Kathe, and Clover Vail, the three little girls Laurence had with Kay.

Pegeen and Sindbad regularly spent holidays with their father and Kay in Mégève learning to ski, forming part of an extended family. After seeing Pegeen perennially alone, Jacqueline Ventadour visited the Vails one Easter when her brother was at boarding school in Mégève and was surprised to discover that "Pegeen had all these brothers and sisters." When Pegeen visited her father, she experienced a very different type of life from the one she had with Peggy. Kay fussed over her tiny brood, all identically turned out in long blond curls to resemble Laurence and Clotilde as children. "Kay was very motherly," recalled Jacqueline. "I was very fond of her. Life with Kay was fun. It was *Saturday Evening Post* with mother, clean children. . . . In Mégève she created an atmosphere. She was affectionate to everybody. She worried about you, if you had a cold or didn't look well." Pegeen once wrote to Kay that she had taught her how to love.

Kay would have herself photographed with her neat and prim little girls surrounding her for magazine articles. To Clover it was all a dreadful sham. "I always had the feeling that we were being blown apart. My mother did create some family thing," Clover said, "but to me it was a facade. We were displayed like mannequins." "Nobody ever communicated in my family. My mother likes to say there was a terrific closeness between my mother, Sindbad, and Pegeen," Apple recalled; then she shrugged her shoulders as if to say, "Who knows?"

"I think of my mother and father as coming out of a Victorian age," said Clover. "They loved hypo-drama, had a Victorian mentality with no understanding of how people really work or function or how children feel. There was a tremendous amount of neglect. We tagged along wherever the adults had to be . . . there was no sense of a life around children. We were ruled by the grown-ups' lives. There was no such thing as families."

Garman had become a fanatical Communist, traveling about the country, recruiting new members for the party. He was in a fever pitch of excitement over the Spanish Civil War, and Peggy was terrified that he would run off and join the International Brigade. "He was like Sir Galahad after he had seen the Holy Grail." Garman tried to convert Peggy, but Peggy just bristled whenever he started lecturing her. "I got terribly bored with it," Peggy complained. "I went almost mad, I got so bored with it." Rather than call her a whore when he was angered, Peggy joked, Garman would call her a Trotskyite!

Instead of the writers and intellectuals who had come around when she was with Laurence or Holms, now only dour party members and workers called at the house. Nevertheless, Peggy wanted to marry Garman. She had been named as co-respondent in his divorce, "which annoyed me terribly," Peggy said. "I didn't think it was fair, because his wife had left him long before he knew me." But she agreed, at Garman's insistence, to be found in bed with him by hired detectives. "He said I had to do it and I did it." Peggy assumed that when Garman's divorce was final he would marry her. Garman made a bet with Peggy: if Edward VIII married Wallis Simpson then he would marry her. But when the "American Victory" finally came, he welshed and there was no parallel victory for Peggy. Douglas Garman simply refused to marry her and he moved back to London.

By Easter 1937, Garman, who "got more and more Communist," had found a proletarian woman who he felt was better suited than Peggy to share his dedicated life. Yet, added Peggy, "he was awful to her, because he was always bringing up the fact that she was working class and he was, what d'you call it, gentle-folk."

Eventually, Peggy and Garman worked out a separation as if they had been married. Since Peggy had impulsively put Yew Tree Cottage in his name, she now proposed to let him keep it but to lease it from him. "Isn't that crazy?" she asked. "I used to give him a hundred dollars a month, which he used to give to the Communist party and I didn't care," she declared. "People say I'm stingy!" Peggy magnanimously let him keep her bedsheets, which came in handy, as he and his future wife were very poor. (Some twenty-five years later, Peggy remembered the sheets and decided to reclaim them.) Peggy still maintained her small flat on London's Guilford Place.

Florette arrived to see her daughter in the summer of 1937. She had disapproved of Peggy's life in and out of wedlock with each of her choices—none of whom had detectable professions or fortunes—and was not at all shocked to learn of the latest breakup. But Peggy was stunned by the news that her mother had only six months to live.

Florette had been living in New York at the Hotel Plaza in a two-bedroom suite with a family retainer, Mlle. Anna Hoffman. Florette had developed lung cancer and, although she was a relatively young woman, had aged grievously. Her whole face seemed to have fallen and there were deep circles under her eyes. She had undergone several operations in New York, for which Peggy had not had the time to be with her. "My grandmother was a fussy old woman," Sindbad recalled, and yet "my mother behaved terribly with her, wouldn't go back to see her." Peggy acted as if her mother had the plague. On one occasion Peggy became hysterical because Sindbad took a bath in his grand-mother's bathtub. "She had cancer and she thought it was dirty," said Sindbad. "She thought [the cancer] was contagious," added his wife Peggy Angela. But, as Sindbad noted, it's not hard to understand Peggy's fear of contagion when one remembers that in her family, "they went around rubbing things with those cotton balls soaked in Lysol all the time."

Peggy insisted that Florette was a dreadful bore, as if being dull warranted exclusion from the human race. Peggy's children grew up thinking that to be boring, that is, conventional, was the worst sin in the world. Since Florette was certified a bore by Peggy, she therefore had no right to any consideration, and was left to spend her final years in the company of her brother DeWitt Seligman's family. She visited them in summer on the Jersey shore, wrapped in three scarves against the cold. "She wanted to go in swimming," recollected her niece Susan Miller, "but she had to be wrapped and wrapped. She had a small head, a figure you couldn't tell quite what-was-what. She was beautifully dressed, wore lovely clothes, . . . her hair was blondish-reddish . . . her make up was well done. . . . She was eccentric sometimes, but not to those who loved her." Florette could also be funny: "She had beautiful feet and legs, and she said, 'There is only one thing for me to do—I'll just have to walk on my hands!'"

"Florette had gone through a lot," Mrs. Miller pointed out. "She lost the child I think she loved the best; her husband was unfaithful to her; Peggy was something to put up with; and there was Hazel's *problem.*"

Peggy, disoriented over her own life and facing the imminent loss of her mother, confided to Emily, "I think my life is over." To which Emily replied, "If you feel that way, perhaps it is."

16 ———— A CHANGE OF LIFE

Peggy at thirty-nine faced a number of crises. Her mother was dying; her lover had moved on; her children were away at boarding school. Peggy had done nothing for the last fifteen years but follow around her "husbands," first Laurence Vail, then John Holms, and finally Douglas Garman, and what had it brought her? She had tried to play the dutiful wife, mother, and confidante, all without much success. It was clear, if not to Peggy, that she had no talent for domestic life. Even the sense of style or decor in her homes came from her husbands. Now, alone, bereft, and bored, she had to do something.

Milton Waldman's wife, Peggy, an old friend from New York, came to visit and seeing Peggy's despondency tried to interest her in starting a business. She suggested a publishing house or an art gallery. With Peggy's money and connections either should be simple enough and would get Peggy out of the house and involved with new people and activities. Peggy was instantly taken with the idea of an art gallery: it had to be cheaper to run than a publishing house, with its printing costs and writers to support; and anyway, the writers she knew never seemed quite grateful enough. Without much deliberation, Peggy embraced the world of art.

Heretofore, Peggy had displayed little if any interest in the visual arts. Indeed, some of her friends were surprised and not a little skeptical when she announced her new venture. "I never knew," remarked one acquaintance, "how Peggy, who had never shown any special tendencies about art matters, went into the galleries."

In fact, many of the people Peggy knew and associated with did not give her credit for much at all. Peggy was simply considered Mrs. Moneybags, a free meal ticket, a summer joyride. "My mother never got over it," said Johnny Coleman, "but the mail Peggy got, day to day, were requests for money, not to mention the beady eyes on her all the time." There has always been an uneasy alliance between money and art—an unspoken understanding that the rich exist to benefit those who create —and so the artists who benefited from Peggy's largess frequently repaid her by not taking her seriously as a person or as a friend. And Peggy's generosity was mingled with an equally compelling desire to economize, a stinginess that made people uncomfortable. The fare at her dinner table was generally spartan, and all during the meal she would monitor closely how much was being eaten; if a guest did not finish his portion, Peggy would dash over and scrape it right back into the serving bowl, excusing herself with, "It's too good to waste." Houseguests heard her endless complaints over how much this or that cost, and saw her constantly writing her accounts and tallying them. She did not create around her an atmosphere of easy giving. It was difficult not to feel ambivalent about Peggy, even if—especially if—one were on the receiving end of her generosity.

Peggy made it easy for people to underestimate and criticize her. Johnny Coleman once pointed out, "Peggy made herself pretty hated by a number of people by presenting herself aggressively, the worst possible side of her. . . . She put her worst foot forward, so that people who hate her guts have no trouble at all in supporting their case." And yet there was something touching about Peggy, a little-girl frailty and naïveté that made it difficult to judge her harshly. "She has a quality," said Sindbad's wife, Peggy Vail, "which makes you feel compassion, regardless of the stories." At her own parties Peggy often sat back and watched, seemingly out of place.

"We liked Peggy," reminisced Silas Glossop. "We were fond of her. . . . She was almost naïve in some ways and in other ways extra shrewd. She was too underestimated for her intelligence. . . . She was an original. All the intelligentsia made the foolish mistake of assuming she wasn't smart." Glossop included both Djuna Barnes, whose lover he had been, and Emily Coleman among those who misjudged Peggy.

An art gallery held enormous appeal for Peggy. If she herself was not talented, then she would do as Laurence had suggested long ago and help those who were. She could become a patroness of the arts, spend her money in an orderly fashion, and command the respect of those who had once scorned her as stupid or silly.

Peggy had been attracted to the world of artists ever since she caught her first glimpse of it from the balcony of the Sunwise Turn bookshop in New York as a young woman. Thrown headlong into the heady society of writers and painters with Laurence, she never recovered. Moreover, the idea of selling art was pleasing. Like her grandfather Meyer, she always liked to peddle things, carting Mina Loy's collages through New York, selling the lampshades. With an art gallery, she could help artists and make a profit, too.

But what kind of art should she represent? Old Masters were far too expensive. She knew little about modern painting, but in all those long hours spent with Laurence in café after café, listening to the discussions of those around her, she could not have helped but absorb the excitement of the new art. "She was far from stupid," observed Maria Jolas, who added, comparing Peggy's experience to her own, "she was probably very quick to learn. I came here [Paris] in 1919; I met an extremely gifted aesthetician [Eugène Jolas]. He gathered painters, sculptors; I heard people talking about painting and sculpture, the cubist movement for hours. . . . You *do* learn."

Peggy learned enough to know that modern art carried with it the power to scandalize, and at an early age she had realized that being outrageous was a guaranteed attention-getter. Peggy enjoyed the uneasiness her bohemian life-style provoked in her mother and even in her sister Benita. She so loathed her staid, bourgeois family background that anything rebellious delighted her. Peggy had a total disregard for convention, and what was modern art if not a break with past values? Dangerous, irreligious, immoral—modern art was called all this and more. Peggy knew from firsthand experience the delirium with which the Dada antics had been met by the press and her fellows. The ruckus and publicity, all in the name of high art, greatly appealed to her.

Peggy had been preceded into the art world by two of her uncles, Solomon and Simon. Simon, who was the sixth eldest of the Guggenheim brothers, established the John Simon Guggenheim Foundation in 1925, in memory of his younger son, who collapsed and died after a track meet at the age of eighteen. He endowed the foundation with three million dollars to provide scholarships and grants-in-aid to men and women, regardless of race or religion, in all the Americas, to "promote the advancement and diffusion of knowledge and understanding, and the appreciation of beauty." The requirements were purposely worded in a vague way to encourage talent in any area, and thousands received Guggenheim fellowships in an era when serious patronage of the arts was always left to individuals. Indeed, many of Peggy's contemporaries had arrived in Europe on Guggenheim fellowships. By 1937, according to the Guggenheims' biographer, Harvey O'Connor, Simon had succeeded in giving away half his fortune. (Simon's other son, George Denver, named in honor of the city in which Simon had spent so much of his youth, committed suicide in 1939, in a hotel room in New York City. He was barely thirty-two years old.)

Solomon R. Guggenheim, another of Peggy's uncles, from his personal appearance, demeanor, and mild-mannered outlook, seemed the least likely person one would associate with modern art. Yet, with his beautiful wife, Irene Rothschild, "S.R.," as he was called, had collected Old Master paintings for years, and since 1926 his attention had been directed to the acquisition of avant-garde and modern art. In that year the "grand old man" of the Guggenheims, aged sixty-five, met Baroness Hilla Rebay von Ehrenweisen, some thirty years his junior. The daughter of a German army officer, born and raised in Strasbourg, Hilla Rebay had dedicated herself to painting. Despite the opposition of her father, she studied art in Düsseldorf and in Berlin, eventually traveling all over Europe exhibiting her canvases. She painted first in an academic style, then in an expressionist one, and so on through the twentieth-century movements, until she became convinced that the only, true art was *non-objective,* Wassily Kandinsky's term for an art reduced to its essential elements—in the case of painting, to color, form, and line.

Hearing that the baroness was a painter, Solomon insisted that she do his portrait. During the sittings, he had ample time to observe her vitality and charm, her pert good looks, and to listen to her messianic fervor about modern art in general and non-objective art in particular. She believed that only through art could man be elevated and she ascribed to art spiritual powers. Solomon's portrait was not very flattering (the baroness's poor use of perspective made it appear as if he had legs like two huge hams on pegs), but he was nevertheless enchanted by the painter as well as the painting. He was so pleased that the baroness began to accompany Solomon and his wife on their art-buying tours of Europe.

Hilla Rebay took Solomon to the studios and ateliers of all the artists she admired, and under her spell Solomon began to buy the work of Kandinsky, László Moholy-Nagy, and not a few pieces by the much less-well-known Rudolf Bauer. The baroness had a passion for Bauer, a Polish-born painter, who "like a lazy echo, copied each Kandinsky period ten years after it was over." Rebay had met Bauer in 1917 as an art student in Germany and, convinced that he was an unsung genius, had fallen "crazily in love," in the words of Kandinsky's wife, Nina, no great admirer of the baroness. "Always Bauer," said Mme. Kandinsky.

Hilla urged Solomon to buy up Bauer's pictures ("a genius, the greatest of all painters"), often at prices inflated by the artist, who knew a good thing when he saw it. If Bauer discovered that Solomon coveted a Kandinsky, Bauer would go to that painter's house and wrangle one out of him at a reduced price, reselling it later to Solomon for a tidy profit. Bauer's circumstances gradually improved until he was able to afford a grandly furnished home and the servants to staff if. Over the threshold was written, "The Home of the Spiritual in Art," a phrase derived, like his art, from Kandinsky.

Solomon's docility prompted evil tongues to wag. And Peggy was convinced that Hilla Rebay was Solomon's mistress. "She must have been," she said. The baroness herself always denied such rumors. "Rubbish!" she exclaimed to an interviewer. "Why, when I knew him first, he was an old man; old enough to be my father, and this he was exactly to the end."

Solomon indulged the baroness in every whim. He bought her an estate in Bridgeport, Connecticut, and lined the house with pictures by the masters of modern art. He brought her beloved Bauer to America during World War II and gave him a house in New Jersey. There Bauer fell in love with and married his housekeeper, incurring the everlasting wrath of Hilla Rebay. Lawsuits and counterlawsuits for libel followed when the baroness wrote in a letter that Mrs. Bauer was a "streetwalker and a spy." Soon thereafter, undoubtedly led there by Bauer, the FBI arrested the baroness in 1942 on suspicion of being a Nazi sympathizer and agent, and charged that she was stockpiling rationed commodities. (They found fourteen hundred pounds of sugar and five hundred pounds of coffee along with cases of tea in her garage.) "Heil Hilla," started one account of the incident that kept Rebay in custody for two months. Solomon came to the rescue and secured her release, but years later she was once again in trouble with federal agents when she incorrectly reported the market value of eight pictures that she had donated to various colleges.

Long before her troubles with the law, however, Hilla Rebay dreamed of a great museum to house non-objective art and to promote the work of Rudolf Bauer. Solomon was quite susceptible to this suggestion: "to be blunt about it," said one observer, "because he liked sleeping with Hilla. It's as simple as that." And partly because, of late, the Guggenheims gloried in making of themselves "public benefactors." Not only had Simon established his foundation, but Murry Guggenheim and his wife, Leoni, had funded a dental clinic for poor children and all the brothers had contributed toward the creation of the Guggenheim Pavilion at Mount Sinai Hospital. To a younger generation of Americans who had no knowledge of the Guggenheims as mining and smelting magnates, they were becoming known as philanthropists and patrons of the arts, following the pattern of other great industrialists—Rockefeller,

Morgan, and Mellon—who tried to win social acceptance for their methods of collecting wealth by giving some of it away.

Thomas Messer, the current director of the Solomon R. Guggenheim Museum, observed, "Solomon had never heard about this kind of art before he met Hilla. He was no collector. The Guggenheims were not close to culture. They were close to philanthropy. They feel it to be partly duty—a perpetuation of the name. No Guggenheim I have ever met did it out of a passion for art. It was highly remote. So Hilla brought passion to it."

Solomon Guggenheim, as well as his niece Peggy, had been exposed from an early age to the German-Jewish emphasis on *Kultur.* The Seligmans based their superiority in large measure on being "plausible pedants." Joseph Seligman was a classical Greek scholar and spoke several languages; Isaac Newton Seligman sketched and drew; Edwin Robert Anderson Seligman taught economics at Columbia University for forty-five years and was an expert on public finance; Peggy's uncle Eugene Seligman had a huge library that he donated to Columbia. The wealthy German-Jewish Americans had boxes at the opera, took grand tours of Europe's cultural shrines, talked knowledgeably about painting, and in some cases amassed fabulous collections of priceless Old Masters.

By now embracing the world of modern art, both Solomon and his niece Peggy could feel in the forefront of a movement that was special, demanding, and vital. By becoming patrons of the avant-garde, both could assert in the face of their detractors not only that they were cultured but that they were *so* cultured that others could not even understand their art. In any event, Solomon never could say no to Hilla. His museum would be his Taj Mahal to the baroness—a museum for the public welfare bearing his name as an enlightened Medici of a new and spiritual art.

In June 1937, just before Peggy first thought of establishing an art gallery of her own, Solomon announced to the world the creation of the Solomon Guggenheim Foundation. Within two years, the Museum of Non-Objective Art opened its doors in a rented town house at 24 East Fifty-fourth Street in New York City, around the corner from the Museum of Modern Art.

The Baroness Rebay became its first director, making herself slightly ridiculous by organizing exhibitions dominated "in a somewhat immodest fashion by the baroness' own canvases and by those of her great friend of many years, Mr. Bauer." The painter Max Ernst, when he came to New York some years later, after a tour of the Museum of Modern Art, which was then under the directorship of Alfred Barr, Jr., the Guggenheim Museum, and the Albert Gallatin collection at New York University, referred to the three respectively as the Barr house, the

Bauer house, and the Bore house. Furthermore, many art lovers and painters were embarrassed and repelled by the ecstatic paeans to modern art, written by the baroness to accompany the exhibitions. (One critic labeled them "mystic double-talk.") Still, at the time Peggy conceived the idea of becoming a gallery owner, the Guggenheim name was well known in the world of art. It had become synonymous with money, patronage, and not a little absurdity.

Peggy knew nothing about starting an art gallery. She began by having an affair with a young English intellectual by the name of Humphrey Jennings. Peggy had been introduced to Jennings by Emily Coleman, who was tired of him and passed him on to Peggy in much the same way as one would pass on a well-read book. For some reason his extremely boyish face reminded Peggy of Donald Duck.

Jennings, a writer, painter, photographer, and filmmaker, formed part of the then minuscule English art world. He was very excited at the prospect of a gallery for modern art in London and he encouraged Peggy with her idea, promising to work with her and help in the new gallery.

Until this point Peggy had had relatively few lovers. "Very few," she recalled. "Almost none. Just John Holms, Laurence, my husband, Garman, and one other person, once. I think that was all. And Humphrey Jennings, of course." Nonetheless, Peggy always had sex on the brain; she had been obsessed by the idea of lovers and mistresses ever since she was a little girl. Any masculine attention pleased her, but it was not until after her three-year relationship with Garman ended that Peggy, newly liberated, began her sexual explorations in earnest. "After the death of John Holms," explained Johnny Coleman, "Peggy was with a charming chap . . . Douglas Garman. It fell apart for many reasons. He really was devoured by his Communism and Peggy just began sleeping around as though her life depended on it . . . including some women."

When Peggy went to Paris to be with her mother, Jennings followed. Peggy soon wearied of his amorous advances, but he took Peggy to see the "Pope of Surrealism," André Breton, whom Peggy had not met before. She told Breton that she was about to open an avant-garde gallery in London. Breton could only encourage this American woman, even though he doubted she was a serious person. Jennings also took Peggy to see Yves Tanguy, the Surrealist painter, and together they persuaded him to come to London and show his remarkable landscapes. However, by the time they returned to London Peggy was bored with Jennings, whom she discarded at the first opportunity, and the gallery itself was still more an idea than a reality.

THE GALLERY
AND THE BACHELOR

Florette had returned to New York and did not last until Christmas 1937, which was when her daughter Peggy intended to visit her. She died at the age of sixty-six on November 15, in her suite at the Plaza, attended by her faithful companion, Mlle. Hoffman, and a paid nurse. Peggy could not, or would not, attend the funeral, which was held at Temple Emanu-el. Florette's mourners were her Seligman relatives—DeWitt Seligman's grandchildren—who filed past Florette's body at the hotel, where it lay in state.

Even in death Florette was the object of a joke—a macabre one. "She had a trained nurse," her niece Susan Miller said,

at the end, at the Plaza, and Charles of the Ritz had a hairdressing salon downstairs where Florette used to go to. . . . And the hairdresser was so mean to the nurse that the nurse had it in for him. . . . Aunt Florette died in bed and in those days the body wasn't removed immediately, so the nurse called down to the hairdresser and told him Mrs. Guggenheim wanted her hair done and would he come up? When he did the nurse directed him into the bedroom where Florette's body was. She closed the door and left him alone in there. When he realized Florette was dead, he fell down in horror and hit his head. Later, he sued the estate. I heard it from Mamselle.

Now, with her inheritance from Florette forthcoming (roughly another five hundred thousand dollars), Peggy lost no time in getting the gallery started. She hired—at a nominal salary—Wyn Henderson, an energetic, Rubensesque redhead whom she had met through Emily Coleman, to manage the new gallery and be her secretary. Together the two women searched for a suitable location until the ideal one materialized on a tiny street parallel to Bond Street, which, like Bond, was lined with tailors' shops. Peggy signed a lease for two square rooms on the second floor of 30 Cork Street and hoped for the best. Wyn suggested she call the gallery Guggenheim Jeune, a name imitative of Bernheim Jeune in Paris, which showed Matisse and the Futurists. Wyn promptly started decorating the rooms to make them ready, but what to hang *in* these rooms was another matter.

Peggy admittedly knew nothing about modern art. The last book Peggy had read on art had been Bernard Berenson on the Italian masters of the Quattrocento, and she knew nothing of the movements beyond Impressionism. Yet she was committed to the idea of a modern art gallery and she needed help in order to effectuate her dream. Consequently, when she was confronted by the real business of running a gallery, it was to the enigmatic master of the avant-garde that Peggy turned.

Marcel Duchamp was the friend and lover of the American beauty Mary Reynolds, one of Laurence Vail's closest friends. Mary's husband had been killed in World War I and, a rich widow, she continued to stay on comfortably in Paris, where she became a great favorite among the Americans as well as the French, who knew she could always be relied on for a coffee or a snifter of brandy. Mary loved to visit the night spots in Montparnasse, and went every evening to the Boeuf sur le Toit. She was devoted to Duchamp, whom she had met in 1923, and they had, until the end of her life, what Duchamp called "a true liaison." Peggy would often go with John Holms to Mary's house, where Marcel had papered the walls with maps and put up curtains made of strings. There Mary would hold open house, her guests sitting for hours after dinner in her quiet garden, and there Peggy would see Marcel, whom she came to know as just another witty friend.

In Duchamp, Peggy recognized someone who was revered by the people who mattered to her, even though she would later still insist, "I didn't realize then that he was so important or so anything. I thought John Holms was so much more important, and so much more everything. Afterwards, Marcel became a sort of god in America and then one began to realize how important he was, *if* he was."

Wherever Duchamp went, his presence was commanding. He enjoyed typically Gallic good looks, thin, long-nosed, easily elegant. "He was classically an extremely attractive person," said his stepson Paul Matisse. "Walking into a room, you felt he was there—so self-contained, so on his own. Marcel had that radiance . . . his handsomeness was in the bearing, as much as in the actual features." Maria Jolas exclaimed: "No one had a more civilized head than Marcel had. He was extraordinarily courteous and gentle and just." Peggy remembered him smoking his pipe, meditating his next move on the chessboard, "mad about chess." One observer said of Duchamp, "I liked that face . . . that kind of haughty dandyism . . . and that silent laugh that cut the ground from under pedants."

Although it was not until the mid-1950s that critics took notice of Duchamp as a major figure in twentieth-century art, in the 1930s in Paris he was already a legend. He mystified and intrigued his fellows when in 1923 at the age of thirty-six, having completed (or rather *in*completed) his masterpiece, *The Bride Stripped Bare by Her Bachelors, Even,* he abruptly abandoned a successful career as a painter to take up chess. In a Paris where Dada acts and Dada gestures were highly prized, this illogical about-face aroused enormous admiration. Breton had often exhorted his disciples to give up writing, painting, jobs, families—their bourgeois lives—so Duchamp represented the bravest flowering of the Dada spirit. He was held in awe. "It is characteristic of the guilty conscience of our age," wrote Duchamp's friend and biographer, Robert Lebel, "that such curious prestige should be enjoyed by a man who gave proof of his talents and then suddenly declined to use them. He soon became a sort of living reproach; even the mention of his name was embarrassing."

Duchamp agreed to lay the foundation for Peggy's gallery. In doing so, he laid the foundation as well for Peggy's education not only in art but in the art of fashioning a life into a legend.

To understand Peggy's gallery and the collection she would one day have, it is necessary to understand the philosophy and personal history of her guide. In 1905 at the age of eighteen, Marcel Duchamp decided to become a painter and followed his two older brothers to Paris, where the leading artists of the day converged. With astounding virtuosity, Duchamp taught himself one modern movement and then another—moving from Impressionism through Fauvism and arriving at "not exactly Cubism, but the dissection of a subject." It was typical of Duchamp's impatient imagination that Cubism, the most advanced "ism" of his day, began to bore him, in fact, all art movements bored him. The expression *bête comme un peintre* (dumb like a painter) held a literal meaning for him—he tired of glorifying the talent of the hand and aspired to an art that was more cerebral than visual.

A breakthrough came when his brother Raymond asked several of his artist friends to paint something for his kitchen in Puteaux, just outside of Paris, and Duchamp, then twenty-four, decided to paint a coffee grinder. It was the first of a series of paintings in which he would equate the machine with the organic and use machine images as metaphors for human, visceral functions.

Then, in a frenzy of creative activity, Duchamp completed a number of pictures, all of them masterpieces, between 1911 and 1912, introducing idiosyncratic themes—chess, sex, metamorphosis, evanescence—considered "heresies" in Cubist avant-garde art. Painted in a Cubist mold, these pictures in fleshy pink tones were decidedly un-Cubist. What made them different was the movement with which Duchamp imbued each one. In a magazine Duchamp had come across Jules Étienne Marey's "chronographs"—a series of photographs of a man and of a woman that when flipped in sequence gave the impression of moving pictures. Duchamp decided to apply this technique on canvas and the most famous result was the *Nude Descending a Staircase,* in which both the nude as she moves down and through a somber, sepia-toned ambience and the staircase are virtually unrecognizable. He completed a second version of it in January 1912.

Duchamp decided to exhibit the *Nude Descending a Staircase, No. 2* at the Salon de la Section d'Or, formed by his brothers and the painters at Puteaux to show their works. Although the picture was provocative, Duchamp was unprepared for the reaction of this supposedly avant-garde group. The hanging committee was horrified by the picture. It seemed to them an affront to Cubist principles. "At that time," Duchamp recalled, "in 1912, it was not considered proper to call a painting anything but Landscape, Still Life, Portrait, or Number Such and Such." Duchamp's brothers were called on to intervene. "On the day before the opening," remembered Duchamp, the painter "Gleizes asked my brothers to go and ask me at least to change the title. . . . So I said nothing. I said all right, all right, and I took a taxi to the show and took my painting and took it away. So it never was shown at the Indépendants of 1912, although it's in the catalog."

Embittered by this experience, Duchamp would thereafter keep aloof from any formal art movement. Occasionally he would allow himself to be "borrowed" by people like André Breton, but he was always careful to get right back on the unique shelf he came from. "I was through with the world of the artists, *through,"* he said. If Duchamp had chafed under the dogmatic formalism of the so-called reasonable Cubists, the violence of their rejection of him merely served to emphasize what he had been feeling all along—a need to strike out in new and innovative directions, independent of formulas (and Cubists).

Duchamp refused to repeat himself or draw or paint another conventional picture. "I always had a horror," he admitted, "of being a 'professional' painter. The minute you become that, you are lost. Besides," he added, "I was never passionate about painting. I never had the olfactory sensation of most artists. They paint because they love the smell of turpentine. Personally, I used to paint for two or three hours a day, and I couldn't get away fast enough."

Duchamp found a soul mate in the artist Francis Martinez Picabia, the wealthy son of a Cuban diplomat and a French mother. They were introduced to each other at the Salon d'Automne in October 1911, where Picabia had submitted a painting of a machine, a subject calculated to jar the hard-line Cubists. Like Duchamp, Picabia had been a precocious talent, who as a child had sold his father's Old Master pictures and replaced them with his own precise forgeries in order to buy more stamps for his collection. Working his way through Impressionism, Futurism, and Cubism, Picabia arrived, bored, on the threshold of more challenging possibilities.

Wildly extravagant in his spending and drinking habits, Picabia had an irreverent sense of humor that strongly appealed to Duchamp's own quieter spirit of rebellion. Picabia was well known as a practical joker who took nothing at all seriously. Always the dandy, Picabia could be observed from the terraces of the cafés behind the wheel of a long, racy car, scarf trailing in the wind, the very image of the dark Latin lover. When he died, in 1957, he had gone through 127 cars and seven yachts. For the young man from Blainville, meeting Picabia was an introduction to a whole new world, "a social milieu," as he once said, "I knew nothing about, being a notary's son!" Picabia was, in 1911, already going to opium dens every night, and even if Duchamp did not accompany him, he saw in his friend a totally new breed of iconoclast. Along with Guillaume Apollinaire the two friends went to see Raymond Roussel's play *Impressions d'Afrique.* Its nonsensical painting machines and illogical dialogue greatly impressed Duchamp.

A huge exhibition of modern painting and sculpture was about to take place in New York's Sixty-ninth Regiment Armory, on Lexington Avenue and Twenty-fifth Street. Sponsored by the Association of American Painters and Sculptors, it was to be a survey of modern art beginning with Ingres, going through the art of Degas, Renoir, Cézanne, and on to the Cubists and the latest examples of radical avant-garde art. From New York the exhibition was to travel to Chicago and Boston. Two of the organizers, Walt Kuhn and Arthur B. Davies, were in Europe in the fall of 1912 to select pieces for the show. In France, Walter Pach, an

American exile, introduced them to leading artists, dealers, and collectors, among them Duchamp and his brothers, Jacques Villon and Raymond Duchamp-Villon. Duchamp submitted four works to the organizers—*Portrait of Chess Players* (a Cubist work), *The King and Queen Surrounded by Swift Nudes,* the ill-received *Nude Descending a Staircase, No. 2,* and a watercolor sketch titled *Nude.* When the Armory Show, as it came to be called, finally opened in February 1913, it caused a sensation. Royal Cortissoz in the *New York Tribune* was outraged by "some of the most stupidly ugly pictures in the world and . . . sculpture to match." A schoolteacher was quoted as suggesting that children not be allowed to see the show, because it was immoral, nasty, lewd, and indecent.

Needless to say, New Yorkers could not stay away. Some seventy-five thousand waited on line to see the new and scandalous works, including Duchamp's *Nude Descending a Staircase,* the biggest hit of the show. But where was the nude? people wanted to know. Or the staircase? One cartoonist created his own version, titled *The Rude Descending a Staircase,* depicting a frantic New York subway crowd at rush hour, and an incredulous reporter called it "an explosion in a lumber yard." Almost overnight, Duchamp's picture became the "most famous 'woman' painting in America . . . sharing the honor with only one other painting, the *Arrangement in Black and Grey,* more commonly known as 'Whistler's Mother.' " Yet, for all its avant-garde appearance, the work was actually more accessible than many of the other paintings in the show. An outline, a depiction of movement, could be grasped by even the most obtuse observers; clearly, *something* was descending *something.*

Despite the scandal surrounding the Armory Show, or perhaps because of it, the European paintings sold very well to American collectors. Duchamp sold all four of his works for the sum of $970, including the now famous *Nude Descending a Staircase* for $324 to a San Francisco art dealer, Frederic C. Torrey. Jacques Villon did equally well, selling all his contributions. All the exhibitors sold pictures and sculptures that had been ignored in Europe, but that now, in America, were well received by an enthusiastic albeit small number of collectors—John Quinn, Arthur Davies, Walter Arensberg, Alfred Stieglitz, Arthur Jerome Eddy —and many famous American collections date from this exhibition.

One day in 1913, Duchamp had the "happy idea" of taking a discarded bicycle wheel and mounting it on a kitchen stool in order to watch it rotate. He took an inexpensive reproduction lithograph and placed one red and one yellow dot on it and labeled it *Pharmacy.* A wine-bottle drying rack, found in many French households, became, when wrenched out of its everyday context, a work of art by the simple act of signature. These were the first of many works Duchamp would later label "Readymades."

On June 15, 1915, when Peggy was just graduating from the Jacoby

School, Duchamp was coming down the gangplank of the *Rochambeau* to the docks of New York, a momentous event he referred to as his "Columbus Day." War had broken out in Europe—a war that would claim Marcel's brother Raymond—but Duchamp, who supposedly had a weak heart and had served a year in 1906, was declared unfit for military service. Simply walking down the street in France became a problem for him. Jeers and insults greeted a healthy-seeming young man out of uniform. Consequently, when Walter Pach suggested that he go to New York, Duchamp leaped at the chance.

On his arrival, Duchamp was surprised to find himself something of a celebrity. A throng of reporters awaited him when the ship docked. They were amazed to see that the creator of the infamous *Nude Descending a Staircase* was a soft-spoken and dignified young man of "smiling composure." He announced to the rapt journalists that he had "nothing but antipathy for the accepted sense of any of the terms of art."

In New York, Duchamp found himself readily accepted in avant-garde circles, always introduced as the man who painted the *Nude Descending a Staircase*. Remarkably, he seemed to be considered an "artist." He met a small but important nucleus of artists and intellectuals centered on Alfred Stieglitz and his gray-walled, sky-lit gallery, barely fifteen feet square, at 291 Fifth Avenue, a "tiny peephole through which America could look at the rest of the art world."

Picabia, who had been inducted into the French army, showed up in New York en route to a military assignment in Cuba. A few days with his old friend Duchamp convinced him the war could go on without him. Duchamp and Picabia became the "brightest stars" in the Stieglitz firmament, quickly absorbed into a round of gatherings and parties.

Duchamp supported himself by giving French lessons for two dollars an hour to two young and wealthy sisters, Florine and Ettie Stettheimer (distant cousins of Peggy), from whom he learned more English than they learned French. For a time, Duchamp even worked as a secretary for a French army captain, earning thirty dollars a week. Everywhere, Duchamp's good looks and elegant manners, in addition to his mysterious personality, made him a great favorite, especially with women, whom he drove to a frenzy by responding to their advances at first and then ignoring them.

On a visit to an artists' colony in Ridgefield, New Jersey, Duchamp met a Philadelphia-born painter and photographer with a thick Brooklyn accent called Man Ray. Man Ray had been greatly impressed by the Armory Show and had begun experimenting with new shapes and ideas on canvas. A French girl friend predisposed him to all things French and he was eager to befriend Duchamp. Under Duchamp's influence, Man Ray experimented more boldly with new techniques. He painted a trompe-l'oeil picture of a collage, based on cutouts of colored paper that had fallen on his studio floor, called *The Rope Dancer Accompanies Herself with Her Shadows.* He sprayed paint around a silhouette with an air gun to produce what he labeled Aerograms and began to create photographs by placing hands and tools directly on a negative—he called these Rayograms.

Man Ray, along with Duchamp and Picabia, who did not stay long in New York, embarked on an ever-escalating, anti-art campaign. Picabia sketched a picture of a spark plug and baptized it *Young American Girl in a State of Nudity.* He painted a large, purposeless machine, giving it brass cylinders and silver pipes and calling it *A Very Rare Picture upon This Earth.*

Duchamp continued to take objects out of one context and place them in another. By contrast with his personal fastidiousness, his apartment was littered with discarded objects, crumpled newspapers, and layers of dust, so that it looked, said Man Ray, "as if he had been moving out and leaving some unwanted debris lying around." In 1917, Duchamp bought an ordinary porcelain urinal, such as those commonly found in men's rooms, at a plumbing supply store. He signed it "R. Mutt" and sent it, along with a six-dollar entrance fee, to the newly formed Society of Independent Artists for inclusion in their group show, under the title *Fountain*—not altogether surprising from the man who once said, "The only works of art America has given [us] are her plumbing and her bridges."

Even the Society of Independent Artists, which had been established to provide an impartial and nonjuried forum for artists, and of which Duchamp was a founder, could not see its way clear to exhibiting an ordinary urinal as a work of art. In those days, it should be remembered, "one did not discuss functional plumbing, much less functions—least of all, the functions of the artist." It was decided to accept *Fountain* but to keep it out of sight, hidden behind a partition. Duchamp resigned in protest over the hypocrisy of the society, and rumors quickly flew that it was Duchamp who had signed himself R. Mutt, an astonishing revelation to all those who expected Duchamp to come up with another masterpiece along the lines of the *Nude Descending a Staircase.*

The proffering of a urinal as a work of art was a violent act in 1917. It rivaled in aggression the Dada acts and demonstrations taking place in Europe. Without knowing it, the New York group of Man Ray, Picabia, and Duchamp was behaving very much like its counterpart across the ocean, possessed of a Dada spirit, intensely nihilistic, anti-war, anti-art, anti-everything.

After the Americans entered the war in 1917, Duchamp left for Buenos Aires, where the only people he knew ran a brothel. "I'd be taken for a pacifist," he once said, speaking of his flight to Argentina, "a dreadful revolutionary. And it's not true: I really couldn't give a damn." In Buenos Aires he devoted himself to chess, searching out chess books, and writing the Stettheimer sisters: "my attention is so completely absorbed by chess. . . . I like painting less and less." He stayed in Buenos Aires only nine months, and after a trip to Paris, where he came in contact with the French Dadaists, he was back in New York in 1920, playing chess every night at the Marshall Chess Club.

Around this time, Duchamp created an alter ego, a sort of human Readymade. At first he searched for a Jewish name, but when one did not materialize to his satisfaction, he joyfully fell upon Rrose Sélavy ("Marvelous! Much better than to change religion"), which when pronounced in French sounded like *Eros c'est la vie*—Eros is life. Made up like Rrose, dressed in women's clothes, Duchamp posed for Man Ray's camera and signed as Rrose Sélavy the Readymades he continued to produce, including a birdcage filled with marble "sugar cubes," not all of which had the spectacular effect of "R. Mutt's" *Fountain.*

In 1923, Duchamp finally "incompleted" *The Bride Stripped Bare by Her Bachelors, Even,* or the *Large Glass,* an enigmatic love machine (in which the bachelors continuously fail to satisfy the bride) etched in lead wire, colored in dust, and sandwiched between two clear panes of glass —at once visible and invisible—for which Duchamp calculated every detail as if "he had been designing an aeroplane or a space-capsule," and turned his attention—or so he claimed—to chess.

Duchamp lived frugally, doing without a telephone, for example, so that people had to fetch him or send a telegram if they needed him. He liked to say, "My capital is my time, not money." "I remember," said Man Ray, "having dinner with Knoedler, the art dealer, who regretted that Duchamp wasn't painting anymore. He asked me to try and rouse some enthusiasm in Duchamp by informing him that he [Knoedler] was prepared to pay Duchamp an annual sum of ten thousand dollars if only he would agree to painting one picture a year." But Duchamp simply smiled in response and said no, he did not care to repeat himself. As Duchamp put it, "I sensed the danger right away"—the danger of being trapped in a role he was ready to discard, of becoming the professional painter, producing pleasing, "original" works of art to be sold like stocks or bonds.

While money meant little to Duchamp, personally, he had a gift (some would say a predilection) for getting along with those who had it. His "disarming courtesy and polished charm" made it easy for Duchamp to find and keep wealthy patrons. As a young arrival in New York, he was taken to the home of Walter Arensberg, a rich Harvard-educated collector, little older than Duchamp, who wanted to meet him. Duchamp and Arensberg became great friends and the two spent long hours playing chess and inventing word games and puns. Arensberg provided Duchamp with a studio on Sixty-sixth Street (where he worked at night by the light of a single bulb on his *Large Glass*) and started buying and tracking down everything he could get his hands on by the artist, including the *Nude Descending a Staircase.* Unofficially, Duchamp began to advise Arensberg on his collection, weeding out lesser works, generally steering him to the newer school of Paris artists and finding pictures for Arensberg on his trips to Europe—even rounding up many of his own pieces. (When the Society of Independent Artists was hatched in Arensberg's apartment, Duchamp was present to contribute his ideas. He helped install the "miles and miles" of paintings, before shattering the group with that anonymously sent urinal.)

Arensberg remained Duchamp's lifelong admirer and champion, but he was not the only wealthy American patron Duchamp succeeded in winning over. A large, reddish-blond Teuton of a woman named Katherine Dreier became another avid Duchamp supporter and friend. The daughter of a successful German importer-exporter, Dreier pursued artists and intellectuals. In this way she met Marcel, who treated her with respect and kindness—in a world not always charitable to the slow-but-steady—bringing her along to the gatherings at Arensberg's house. Dreier was delighted to feel "one of the gang," even though she was somewhat lost amid the fast-talking, nimble talents gathered there. Her host, Arensberg, did not take to her, snubbing her with open disdain, yet Katherine Dreier proved herself an invaluable and indefatigable sponsor of the new art, championing it with a missionary vigor.

When the Society of Independent Artists split apart, Katherine Dreier decided to start a museum exclusively for modern art that would serve as an information center, presenting exhibitions, concerts, and lectures to the public in an informal setting, and that would build a permanent collection of its own. Duchamp encouraged her and enlisted Man Ray's participation. It was Man Ray who came up with the idea for the museum's name, which he had come across by chance in a French magazine, "Société Anonyme—which I thought meant Anonymous Society. Duchamp laughed and explained that it was an expression used in connection with certain large firms of limited responsibility—the equivalent of incorporated. He further added that he thought it was perfect as a name for a modern museum."

Within a month the Société Anonyme opened its doors in a dilapidated brownstone off Fifth Avenue at Forty-seventh Street. Not everyone involved was equally ready for modern art. On the morning before the gallery's opening, Katherine Dreier discovered that although everything else seemed to be in place, one item listed in the catalogue was missing—an object by Man Ray, *The Lampshade.* In a panic she pointed to the corner where the support for the piece stood, but no spiral object. Man Ray insisted he had already delivered *The Lampshade* when, finally, the janitor was called in to see if he knew what had happened. "Oh, the paper wrapping for the stand, he said; he'd crumpled it up and removed it with the other rubbish." Man Ray assured Dreier he could duplicate it and the museum opened without further incident.

By the time Peggy asked him to help with Guggenheim Jeune, Duchamp had counseled Walter Arensberg, planned and organized shows for the Société Anonyme, and advised Katherine Dreier on purchases of Joan Miró, Constantin Brancusi, Paul Klee, Wassily Kandinsky, Kurt Schwitters, and his own brothers, Jacques Villon and Raymond Duchamp-Villon. Duchamp was criticized for being Dreier's lackey (Dreier was condemned as an early Fascist and anti-Semite who visited Hitler), but when asked if his role as museum curator wasn't rather anti-Duchampian, he replied, "I was doing it for friendship."

Duchamp acted as guardian angel to both Katherine Dreier and Peggy. Both women were relatively untutored but eager and willing converts to modern art, armed with the money to accomplish much good. Whereas others might not—and did not—take either woman seriously Duchamp was happy to help, and introduced the wealthy women to his friends in the art world. He often remarked that the only way to be truly anti-art was to be indifferent to it, and believed that if anyone could create art, then anyone could disseminate it.

Duchamp kept alive the flame of his myth, to which he was not totally indifferent. Much like an actor, from time to time he would make an enigmatic gesture—refuse to go to an opening or float a bond issue to finance his system at the Monte Carlo casino—and then retreat once again into silence. "The artist exists only if he is known," he once said, and added on another occasion, "The game is never over for the artist. Despite the scandal and the publicity which surrounded the *Nude Descending a Staircase,* had I died in 1912, no one would talk about me anymore. But I replenished the *Nude* with the Readymade, then the Readymade with the *Large Glass.* Success is just a brush fire, and one has to find the wood to feed it."

Since 1924, Duchamp had been living in Paris and making frequent visits to New York. Except for a brief marriage to a French heiress he hardly knew (who, exasperated by her husband's constant chess playing even on their honeymoon, glued the chessmen to the board and divorced him within six months), Duchamp had maintained his comfortable relationship with Mary Reynolds. At the age of fifty, he had managed to elude classification. "It would have suited them nicely to have shut me up in some category or formula," he said. "But that's not my style. If they're dissatisfied, *Je m'en fous.* One mustn't give a F——— *et merde,* ha ha."

A GREEN-EYED
OBLOMOV

Peggy went to see Marcel Duchamp to assemble a first exhibition for her new gallery just before Christmas 1937, leaving Wyn Henderson to put the finishing touches on the decoration of Guggenheim Jeune. Duchamp was engaged in designing the theatrical installation of coal sacks and fallen leaves for the International Surrealist Exhibition to be held in January 1938, immediately before Peggy's gallery was to open in London, but he agreed to help her and charted a course for her to follow. Together they decided that Peggy's gallery should exhibit Surrealist and Abstract art, the two most avant-garde tendencies of the day. Duchamp recommended that Peggy see a number of artists in and around Paris, whom he felt she should consider showing. But to begin with he had to teach her something about the modern movements. "He had to educate me completely," Peggy admitted. Without him, "God knows!" she exclaimed. "I wouldn't have got any idea what to do at all."

Peggy praised her mentor as "so spiritual, human, good." Duchamp taught her everything she needed to know "naturally, in conversation, very simply," she said. He did not overwhelm her with facts and dates; as a teacher Duchamp's touch was as lighthearted as his approach to art. "There are people," said his stepson Paul Matisse, "who when you are with them enlighten you by the way they say or do things. The power of the teaching is almost in its invisibility." And Peggy was eager to learn, boundlessly enthusiastic about this new venture of hers, and unintimidated by the names of artists she had only just heard. To some degree, her ignorance of art and artists served her well. She was willing to forge ahead, oblivious to the petty jealousies of the art world, content to think of art as a simple business.

"Duchamp really influenced her," observed Maria Jolas. "He was a man of tremendous authority, but also a *copain*, a witty friend. He brought to the advice he was giving her the break with old painting and what was valuable in the new." Unlike many artists, Duchamp could be fair and detached about what was good in the work of others. "The meeting of Peggy and Marcel Duchamp was divine," said Maria Jolas. "Peggy would spend and Marcel had the know-how."

Without Duchamp's willingness to help, Peggy would doubtless not have been able to open (or run) Guggenheim Jeune, yet Duchamp was content to stay behind the scenes. "He had the kind of effect," said Paul Matisse, "that was always greater than he let on. He would never push himself forward."

Peggy certainly never paid for his labors. Duchamp did not ask Peggy for money, and Peggy, who always waited to be asked, never offered any. "That's the way she was," remarked Pierre Matisse. "She took." Paul Matisse believed, "He would be doing it because it was there to be done. The opportunity presented itself, and he liked to do things . . . and disappear. He had the capacity and personal solidity to not really want anything for himself."

Peggy had originally come to Paris with the idea of giving the first exhibition at Guggenheim Jeune over to Constantin Brancusi, because he was the only artist she could think of, having met the sculptor in her early Paris days. When Brancusi could not be located, Duchamp and Mary Reynolds introduced Peggy to Jean Cocteau, the poet-aesthete, who had been scandalizing Paris for years, and it was decided to open the gallery with a Cocteau show.

Peggy visited Cocteau in his hotel room on the rue Cambon, where Cocteau often received in the manner of a royal *levée,* dressed in silk pajamas, before or after his breakfast or luncheon opium pipe. There was usually enough smoke in the room to make anyone dizzy, and it was entirely possible for a visitor to have a waking dream.

Peggy found Cocteau in bed, smoking opium, his exquisite hands and long, tapering fingers, of which he was inordinately vain, fondling the pipe. "The odor was extremely pleasant, though this seemed a rather odd way of doing our business," recalled Peggy. Subsequently, Cocteau invited her to dinner, but he spent the entire night admiring himself in a nearby mirror. Peggy was mesmerized by such exaggerated narcissism. Cocteau agreed to send Peggy drawings and furniture for her show, but she could not get him to agree to come to London for the opening, as his health was too frail. Still, Peggy had her first show lined up.

Peggy's days in Paris now were filled with a delicious expectancy and stimulating conversations with Duchamp about plans for future shows. Quite by accident Peggy ran into her old friend Helen Fleischman, now married to Giorgio Joyce. Helen was leaving for America to visit her ailing father, and she invited Peggy to dinner the day after Christmas for a farewell party.

Helen's father-in-law, James Joyce, had in recent years reduced his social circle to fewer and fewer friends. His old friendships, most notably with Sylvia Beach, who had published *Ulysses,* and Adrienne Monnier, her lover, had turned sour. Robert McAlmon had returned to Paris with his manuscript for *Being Geniuses Together,* a chatty memoir of the 1920s, in which he remembered Joyce mostly for his drinking. Disliking the portrait of himself, Joyce referred to McAlmon's book as "the office boy's revenge," thereby cooling relations between the two men considerably. Now Joyce saw Paul Léon, his secretary of sorts, and Léon's wife, Lucy, Stuart Gilbert and his wife, Maria and Eugène Jolas, and a quiet young writer by the name of Samuel Beckett.

Joyce liked Beckett, who perplexed him, and he wrote to his daughter-in-law, Helen, "He has talent, I think." Joyce and Beckett frequently sat, their legs tightly crossed and, according to Richard Ellmann, "engaged in conversations which consisted often of silences directed towards each other, both suffused with sadness, Beckett mostly for the world, Joyce mostly for himself."

Nevertheless, Joyce kept Beckett at an emotional distance, telling the younger man pointedly, "I don't love anyone except my family." Not so Joyce's daughter, Lucia. She was wildly attracted to the brooding Beckett, who occasionally took her out to dinner or to a movie. When her feelings for him intensified, Beckett bluntly informed her that he came to the Joyce apartment essentially to see her father.

Beckett appeared to be so close to Joyce that many mistakenly believed that he was the elder man's secretary, but that honor belonged to Paul Léon, who painstakingly did Joyce's typing and wrote his letters for no greater remuneration than the opportunity of working with his idol. (Joyce enlisted all his friends in the often tiresome research for his "work in progress," *Finnegans Wake,* sending off books to be read and underlined, such as the copy of *Huckleberry Finn* that he sent his grandson, Stephen. From Beckett, who was a linguist and scholar from Trinity College, Dublin, he asked for help in the translation of *Anna Livia Plurabelle* and the names of all the rivers in Europe.)

On December 26, Joyce took a little party, including Beckett, to Fouquet's, his new favorite restaurant, where he was then dining "almost always." Peggy had been invited by Helen. Joyce was expansive; he loved to entertain and to spend money, even if he did not have much of it. As Sylvia Beach observed, he "enjoyed spending the way some people enjoy hoarding." At dinner Joyce, wearing an Irish waistcoat that had belonged to his grandfather, was talkative and charming. Even though he was worried about his daughter Lucia's worsening mental condition (she eventually did go mad) and Helen's departure, Joyce was interested in the news of Peggy's forthcoming gallery and thought it very exciting.

Peggy, however, was far more interested in the young man seated opposite her with the huge blue-green eyes that stared straight ahead with "pinpoint precision." She had met Beckett once before and had often heard about him in London from her neighbor, George Reavey. Beckett could not help squirming under her direct and insistent gaze, which he was careful to avoid.

Beckett was "very tall and slim to leanness, of handsome aquiline features," wrote Nancy Cunard, who first published his poem "Whoroscope," and there was something "in his face of the fierce austerity of a Mexican eagle." Peggy found Beckett terribly shy, young (he was thirty-one years old to her thirty-nine), and awkwardly dressed in ill-fitting clothes. His melancholy air reminded Peggy of John Holms, although Holms had had red hair and Beckett's was dark. After dinner the party repaired to Helen Joyce's apartment in the Villa Scheffer, and Beckett asked Peggy if he could take her home.

Beckett was never able to forget what happened next, because Peggy talked and wrote about it at every opportunity. He took her arm and walked her to her borrowed apartment on the rue de Lille. Once inside, Beckett asked her sheepishly if she would lie down on the sofa next to him. "We soon found ourselves in bed," Peggy recounted, "where we remained until the next evening at dinner time. We might be there still," she continued optimistically, "but I had to go to dine with Arp [the sculptor Duchamp had recommended to her], who unfortunately had no telephone." When Beckett finally left, after having dashed out to buy champagne, which the two polished off in bed, he said, "Thank you. It was nice while it lasted."

A few days later she bumped into him on a traffic island in the boulevard Montparnasse and some sort of combustion must have taken place, for the two went off to Mary Reynolds's house (which Peggy was using while Mary was away) and stayed there for the next twelve days, during which—according to Peggy—they talked, drank, and made love. Delighted that she had discovered someone new with whom she could explore the life of the mind, Peggy talked with Beckett about books and art. "It was wonderful for me to have someone I could talk to again, because I couldn't talk to Garman," Peggy said. "So, it was wonderful for me to have Beckett who spoke my own language." Beckett fascinated her. He gave her his books to read, some of which she understood, some not. "He said he wanted to write like Céline," she recalled, but when she asked him about Joyce, it was as if she had invoked the spirit of a jealous and wrathful god. Beckett insisted that Joyce was the master, all other writers belonging to a lesser, secondary place, in which the darkly misanthropic Louis Céline was supreme.

Peggy discussed her gallery with Beckett. Although she was about to open a showcase for modern art, she confessed that she much preferred Old Masters. Beckett encouraged her to accept the art of "our day as it was a living thing." He spoke to her of an artist by the name of Geer van Velde, whom he greatly admired, and strongly urged her to give him a show. Peggy agreed, to please him.

Peggy soon discovered that Beckett was extremely passive and eccentric. He spent mornings in bed, was barely able to rise in the afternoon, drank much of the time, and was habitually dazed and withdrawn. He was addicted to long silences and tormented by memories of life in his mother's womb. Peggy presented him with a copy of the famous Russian novel whose hero is so helplessly neurotic that he cannot even think about getting out of bed, and she nicknamed him after it "Oblomov," a name he merely shrugged at. He would leave her abruptly during the days they spent together and she never knew if he would return, but Peggy was sure this was love. She insisted for years that she was in love with Beckett and that at least for that brief period he was in love with her.

Their idyll did not last long, for Beckett slept with another woman and when Peggy confronted him he did not deny it, but said that "making love without being in love was like taking coffee without brandy." From this remark Peggy was free to infer that she was the brandy in his life. Still, she was furious and refused to see him, even after he telephoned her the next evening.

When Peggy would not see him, Beckett went back to his hotel, the Liberia, and found an invitation there from some friends to go to the movies. Having nothing better to do, he went. On the way home after the standard stop in a café, Beckett and his two friends, Alan and Belinda Duncan, ran into a pimp named Prudent who worked on the avenue d'Orléans. Prudent fell into step beside Beckett, asking for money, which Beckett insisted quite honestly that he did not have. Prudent persevered, offering the services of one of his *poules* in return for a small loan. Beckett tried to move away, but Prudent simply grew louder and grabbed him by the arm, whereupon Beckett flung the man away, knocking him to the ground. Enraged, the pimp got up, stabbed Beckett in the chest with a clasp knife, and fled. The knife barely missed Beckett's heart —his heavy overcoat deflected the thrust—but the knife penetrated the left side of his chest. Realizing what had happened, the Duncans began frantically shouting for help. A young pianist on her way home after a late-night concert, Suzanne Deschevaux-Dumesnil, chanced upon the scene. She stopped and briskly wrapped the wounded Beckett in Duncan's coat, placing a makeshift pillow under his head, until an ambulance could arrive to take him to the Hôpital Broussias.

Peggy, who had no idea of the incident, started calling Beckett the morning of January 7—she was leaving for London to open her gallery and wanted to say good-bye. She finally learned what had happened from the owner of Beckett's hotel and rushed to the hospital. She left flowers and a note, telling Beckett that she loved him and forgave him all. The next day she went back, this time with Joyce and Paul Léon. Joyce's eyes had deteriorated so badly that he had to be led through the hospital corridors by Léon, searching for Beckett from one ward to another. Joyce, who was extremely solicitous of his friends when they were ill, was appalled that Beckett was in a public ward and insisted that he be moved immediately into a private room at his expense. In contrast with Joyce's generosity, Peggy, who had far more money than Joyce, was prepared to let Beckett stay where he was. Beckett was quite surprised and, by her account, quite happy to see her, but she had to return to London to prepare for her gallery opening so she said good-bye, leaving him in the care of his friends.

Once the pain subsided, Beckett was able to enjoy the fuss and attention around him. He wrote a short poem from his hospital bed and agreed to translate Cocteau's introduction to his catalogue for Peggy. Although Beckett's injuries were serious enough to keep him hospitalized for quite some time, when he finally recovered and appeared before the magistrate and Prudent the pimp apologized, Beckett was broadminded enough to reply, *"Je vous en pris"* ("Think nothing of it").

"LA JEUNE"

Peggy arrived in London just three weeks before the scheduled opening of Guggenheim Jeune. Duchamp appeared shortly afterward to help with the installation. The gallery had been decorated under Wyn Henderson's steady eye and all that remained was for Cocteau's works to arrive from Paris.

Peggy began to receive the drawings Cocteau had made for the scenery of his play *Les Chevaliers de la Table Ronde,* as well as furniture he had designed for that production. Additionally, Cocteau sent other drawings and two large linen bedsheets. One of the sheets contained an ink likeness of his protégé the actor Jean Marais with two other figures. All three had precisely rendered pubic hair over which Cocteau had, in Vatican fashion, pinned a few leaves. This mocking attempt at modesty did nothing to mollify the outraged sensibilities of the British customs inspectors, who refused to let the sheet into the country. Duchamp and Peggy dashed to Croydon, where the work was being detained. Peggy asked the irate inspectors why they objected to nudity in art, and they responded that it was not nudity but pubic hairs that offended them.

The sheet was finally released on the condition that it not be exhibited to the public. Consequently, the offending dirty linen was hung in Peggy's private office, available only to her friends. (Peggy became quite fond of it and finally bought it. Later she passed it on to Pegeen, who as a teenager tacked it up in her bedroom and used it to write telephone messages and numbers on in lipstick.)

Wyn Henderson's eighteen-year-old son, Nigel, was enlisted to help Duchamp with the work of installing the show. Nigel recalled, "I was mesmerized by Duchamp's charismatic personality. He was disinterested in a marvelous way. It was a show of Cocteau's. He didn't like it very much—drawings of hands and fingers." Nevertheless, Duchamp hung the exhibition with care and attention.

When Guggenheim Jeune finally opened on January 24, 1938, with a crowded and lively party, Duchamp was nowhere to be seen. "He never went to openings," said Peggy. "That was part of his myth." Duchamp himself remarked, "I have a horror of openings. Exhibitions are frightful." Nevertheless, word had spread about an exciting new gallery in which the acknowledged master of the avant-garde had had a hand.

Announcements of Peggy's opening were linked to wild reports of the opening in Paris of the huge 1938 International Exhibition of Surrealism, for which Duchamp had just done his madcap installation, a total environment more like the Happenings of a later decade than the traditional salons and exhibitions of French artists.

At the Paris exhibition the opening-night guests, arriving in evening gowns and formal dress, stumbled upon Salvador Dali's *Rainy Taxi,* a dilapidated vehicle with vines growing out of it, in which two "passengers"—mannequins—sitting amid lettuce leaves and scores of live crawling snails were constantly drenched by an artificial rain. More wax dummies lined the long hallway, each one bizarrely dressed by the individual contributors to the show. One wore a cage on her head and a G-string with glass eyes on it. To dress his dummy, Duchamp simply gave it his own hat and coat so that it would attract the least attention. The mannequins peopled a "Surrealist Street," which led into a large hall where guests were met by Hélène Vanel, an actress dressed in a torn nightgown, writhing on one of four beds and periodically arising to splash in a lily pond. To see in the darkness, visitors needed flashlights, which they could then point at the Surrealist pictures adorning the walls. Duchamp had hung twelve hundred coal sacks from the ceiling and spread leaves, twigs, moss, and other arboreal material over the uneven floor, "to try and get a bit of gaiety into it."

Peggy herself had not even seen the Paris show, but Surrealism, modern art, Cubism, Futurism, Constructivism were all the same to the general public. Peggy and her gallery were confused with the publicity-generating activities of the Surrealists. Peggy did nothing to dispel the illusion. Her flamboyant personality and lifelong desire to shock fostered that image. At her opening-night party—a great success—nearly everyone remarked on Peggy's long, dangling earrings—mobiles by Alexander Calder—and on the engaging and sometimes awkward manner of the hostess. "The jeune concerned is Peggy," wrote Noel Thompson in the *Daily Sketch.* "At the cocktail party which opened her gallery in Cork-street she wore earrings made up of half-a-dozen curtain-hooks apiece. Brass curtain-hooks, too. It seemed rather ungrateful to copper." "She wore fairly crazy dresses," recalled Wyn Henderson's son, Nigel. "I think she was out to stun. She resembled W. C. Fields. Her brittle wrists and ankles were charming. She had very warm, slightly piggy eyes." Her smile was "very disarming."

Peggy was thrilled with the publicity that the gallery engendered, much of which centered on her person, but she did not stay in London long enough to enjoy the acclaim for Guggenheim Jeune. She was too obsessed with Beckett.

Days after the opening, Peggy went back to Paris with Duchamp and Mary Reynolds, leaving the gallery in the capable hands of the cherubic, titian-haired Wyn Henderson.

Beckett had sent Peggy a good-luck cable for her opening. He was out of the hospital and back in his hotel. Peggy wanted to take a room there to be near him, but Beckett was apprehensive that his mother, who was staying with him, might encounter Peggy, or that Peggy might run into Suzanne Deschevaux-Dumesnil, the woman who had come upon Beckett the night he was stabbed and taken care of him. Practical and down to earth, Suzanne appealed to Beckett's need to be mothered, and slowly she edged Peggy out of whatever tiny place she had occupied in his heart.

Disappointed, Peggy borrowed her sister Hazel's apartment on the Île St. Louis. Hazel was now living in Paris. She had left Denys King-Farlow and was seeing Paul Léon's brother-in-law, Alexander Ponisovsky, who had once been engaged to Joyce's unfortunate daughter, Lucia. Joyce wrote disdainfully to Helen Joyce:

> I really know nothing about Mrs K-F except the two versions of her children's death (neither of which seems to trouble her overmuch) and the fact that she asked the pleasure of our company at dinner. . . . It is rather curious that the two men in whom poor Lucia tried to see whatever she or any other woman or girl is looking for should now be going around with two sisters.

Beckett seemed less and less interested in going to bed with Peggy, if indeed he ever had been interested at all. Peggy found him "very peculiar," but continued to try to prod him into making love to her. She taunted him with stories of other men's interest, hinting broadly that Brian Coffey, a friend of Beckett, frequently flirted with her.

Peggy continued to needle Beckett and complain about his apathetic sex drive, until, finally exasperated, Beckett boldly announced that he would never make love to her again. He suggested that she console herself with Coffey, who at least might satisfy her. Peggy proceeded to follow Beckett's advice. "I don't know why I did it," Peggy said of this affair. "I didn't want to, but I guess in those days I had a sort of devilry —I had to go to bed with every man I saw. After I did it, Brian Coffey realized I belonged to Beckett and told him he didn't want to interfere in our relationship, but Beckett said, 'You can have her.'"

Her sexual relationship with Beckett, whatever it had been, seemed to be over. Yet Peggy continued to pine and sigh over him. Peggy never seemed to learn that certain men would not or could not return her favors, and before long she would resume her pursuit.

While Peggy worried about Beckett, Marcel Duchamp worried about her gallery. He wanted Guggenheim Jeune to show the work of Wassily Kandinsky, who in 1938 was still virtually unknown in England. Although the painter enjoyed a reputation in America—he had exhibited in the infamous Armory Show of 1913 in New York and had had a one-man exhibition at the Société Anonyme in 1923—his work had never had much exposure in Britain.

In 1910, Kandinsky had painted a watercolor with no recognizable subject matter and consequently he became known as the father of abstract art. Until then, even the Cubists had started with an object that they then fragmented and distorted. Kandinsky, on the other hand, believed that painting should imitate music, a "pure art," where notes and sounds do not mimic nature. However, if painting were not to degenerate into mere decoration, like the folk art he had known in his native Russia, he felt art needed to be *about* something—an experience or a spiritual knowledge. In 1911, he published a treatise called "On the Spiritual in Art," in which triangles, circles, and squares symbolized Kandinsky's mystical views of the cosmos, where nothing was solid, all was in flux, and matter consisted of infinitesimal particles orbiting each other. To an observer, Kandinsky's profoundly emotional, even religious, paintings of swirling pure color looked like "stream-of-consciousness symphonies." Ironically, Kandinsky never liked the term *abstract* as applied to his paintings; he found it confusing and imprecise. He preferred *concrete* or *non-objective.*

Since 1933, Kandinsky, a naturally reserved and aloof man, had been living in Boulogne-sur-Seine just outside of Paris. He had fled Germany when the Nazis closed the Bauhaus School, where he had been teaching. Although seventy-two years old, his creative powers were undiminished and he had accomplished some of his most lyrical and colorful work in recent years. At Duchamp's urging, Peggy went to meet the painter and his much younger Russian wife, Nina Andreevskaya, to discuss the possibility of an exhibition at Guggenheim Jeune.

The Kandinskys were well acquainted with Peggy's uncle Solomon and his "art consultant" the Baroness Hilla Rebay. Peggy was warmly greeted by the painter and found him "so jolly and charming." Peggy was astonished to discover that Kandinsky wore immaculate pinstriped suits, rimless glasses, and spoke and acted more like a Wall Street lawyer than an avant-garde painter—not altogether surprising considering that Kandinsky, who turned to painting in his thirties, had once taught juris-prudence in Russia. But Kandinsky was merely illuminating the maxim "that men with the most daringly original minds are rarely eccentric in their clothes and their living quarters."

Kandinsky and his wife—whom Peggy thought horrid, claiming that "everybody adored him and detested her"—were delighted at the prospect of a London show. As the artist had no dealer, who would ordinarily take on the practical responsibilities, the Kandinskys offered to arrange and select the entire exhibition themselves. They even asked André Breton to write an introduction for the catalogue. All Peggy had to do was send over the floor plans, so that the efficient Kandinskys could decide where in the gallery each picture should hang.

The exhibition, which opened on February 18, 1938, and ran until March 12, included thirty-eight paintings, watercolors, and gouaches spanning the period 1909–1937. It proved a great success, and Peggy was hailed in the press for bringing Kandinsky's important paintings before an English public which hitherto had seen the artist's work only piecemeal.

Sales, however, were another matter. "No," Peggy sighed, "I didn't sell a Kandinsky. . . . Maybe I sold a few gouaches. But nothing but fifteen guineas, something ridiculous like that." To keep from upset-ting Kandinsky, Peggy bought a 1936 oil, *Dominant Curb,* for fifteen hundred dollars herself (and years later regretted she had not bought all the other pictures in the show). Peggy continued this tactful practice of buying a painting from each exhibition to bolster the morale of artists who otherwise sold little of what they showed. In this way, quite inad-vertently, Peggy began to build her collection.

Despite the lack of sales, Kandinsky was pleased with his introduc-tion to the British public. "I think he was very grateful to me," Peggy said, " 'cause later on I wanted to buy a painting from him, an earlier one, and he wanted to make me a very special price, but his wife was such a bitch, she wouldn't let him." Unfortunately for Peggy, it was Nina who handled money matters, and whereas he just "looked like a busi-nessman," Nina was truly "businesslike."

During the Kandinsky show, Peggy had a curious correspondence with her uncle Solomon. Kandinsky was hurt that Hilla Rebay had bought so many paintings by Rudolf Bauer (a man he considered a second-rate counterfeit of himself) for Solomon's Museum of Non-Objective Art and had ceased in the process to buy Kandinskys. "Kandinsky claimed," Peggy wrote, "that though he had encouraged my uncle to buy Bauer, Bauer never encouraged my uncle to buy Kandinsky." Kandinsky asked Peggy to intercede on his behalf. Dutifully, she wrote her uncle Solomon a note explaining that a particular Kandinsky picture was now available and asking if he would be interested in buying it.

The Baroness Rebay, to whom Solomon referred the matter, was indignant. She disapproved of Peggy's gallery and was incensed that she would sully the name of Guggenheim, "known for great art," by using it "for commerce" to promote "some small shop." In a perfervid letter to Peggy, the baroness offered a number of unsolicited and insulting suggestions—in between misspellings—including this bit of advice: "You will soon find you are propagating mediocrity; if not trash. If you are interested in non-objective art you can well afford to buy it and start a collection. This way . . . you can leave a fine collection to your country if you know how to chose [sic]." Peggy was taken aback by the intensity of the letter, but she managed to shrug it off with a laugh. (Yet its message so impressed her that she did not destroy it and years later she quoted it in its entirety in her memoirs.)

Left to her own devices for the next exhibition at Guggenheim Jeune, Peggy came up with a series of fifty caricatures done over an eighteen-year period by a friend of Wyn Henderson, Cedric Morris. A farmer, Morris was best known for his paintings of flowers, birds, and landscapes, but spectators were titillated by his unkind ferocious treatment of overwhelming personalities and curious to see precisely how Morris treated his victims.

The biggest excitement caused by this exhibition—which even Peggy admitted had no business "in any Surrealist and Abstract gallery" —came when an irate guest at the opening-night party put a match to the stack of catalogues. Morris, a former lumberjack, sent blood splattering onto the walls of the gallery when he punched his upstart critic.

Fortunately for Peggy, Marcel Duchamp continued arranging shows and shipping them from Paris to her in London. For April 1938 he organized and selected a show of sculpture that was to include works by the contemporary masters of the art, including Duchamp's friend Constantin Brancusi, Jean Arp and his wife Sophie Täuber-Arp, Alexander Calder, Raymond Duchamp-Villon, Antoine Pevsner, Henri Laurens, and, from England, a young sculptor named Henry Moore. Many were already established artists, but their works had not been seen before in England. Much of the sculpture had to be sent from Paris, and at British customs there was trouble once again.

Since 1932, there had existed an obscure law designed to protect British stonecutters against the importation of cheap Italian tombstones. Under its provisions, stone and wood engravings, mass-produced Italian wood trinkets and sculptures, holy statues, and the like coming into the British Isles were subject to stiff import duties. They were treated as raw materials—wood, stone, bronze, or whatever—unless they fell within the exception made for artworks. In cases of doubt, it was left up to the director of London's prestigious Tate Gallery to decide what was or was not "art." When the works for Peggy's sculpture show began arriving, befuddled customs inspectors called in the Tate's director, James Bolivar Manson, a white-haired Impressionist painter of sorts. (He enjoyed the dubious distinction of having rejected a Cézanne painting as a gift for the Tate. Manson was still recovering from the damage done to his reputation by a libel suit brought against both him and the Tate by the painter Maurice Utrillo. Utrillo had been incorrectly listed in a Tate catalogue as dead from alcoholism when he was in fact alive and sober.)

Manson walked in, surveyed the pieces, and decreed that no, these were "not art." Indeed, he gleefully dismissed Brancusi's *Sculpture for the Blind,* a large egglike marble, as "quite idiotic" and pronounced that "they were all the sort of stuff I should like to keep out." "We do not consider intention," Manson pontificated. "It's difficult to know what intention is. We consider results."

Suddenly Manson found himself at the center of a huge controversy. A lively debate broke out in various newspapers about "What is art?" and "Who is Manson to decide what it is not?" "He is not a dictator of taste," declared the *Daily Express.* The *Manchester Guardian* reminded Manson that Brancusi had passed a similar test coming into the United States. Others pointed out that most of the barred sculpture was familiar stuff and the work of men already middle-aged. Henry Moore wrote heatedly in defense of Brancusi and one St. John Hutchinson wrote in the *Daily Telegraph:*

> We know that Mr. J. B. Manson is an artist himself, but we also know that Herr Hitler painted water-colours, and the fact that the latter has announced that Cézanne and van Gogh are degenerate lunatics and can only be exhibited as a warning to others, shakes our complete trust in the artist as best judge of what works we should be allowed to see.

Peggy remarked, "I think it is a disgraceful thing that we should be under the dictatorship of Mr. Manson," and privately said, "I thought it was ridiculous."

Wyn Henderson was so incensed that she circulated a petition that was eventually signed by all the leading art critics against Manson's action. Manson resigned his post as director of the Tate Gallery soon after his fateful decision, his nerves strained past the breaking point. (Subsequently, he startled the assembled guests at an official luncheon in Paris with a trick he had of "crowing like a rooster, like a French cock, when he'd had something to drink.") Finally, the case was brought before the House of Commons as the final arbiter, where it was decided to let the sculpture in. (Decades later, Peggy came up against the same law when she tried to bring into England the glass sculptures of her Venetian protégé Edigio Constantini. Once again the director of the Tate was brought in to decide the question, "Is it art?" and once again the answer was no.)

PART IV

NEW VICES

MY HEART BELONGS TO DADA

Duchamp thought that Peggy needed help installing the "Contemporary Sculpture Exhibition," which was scheduled to open at Guggenheim Jeune on April 8, 1938, and he suggested that the Alsatian-born artist Jean Arp, who had assisted in the selection and was exhibiting in the show, go to London.

Arp had an enormous reputation in modern art circles. Multitalented—a painter, sculptor, writer, and poet—he had turned to modern art in exasperation after copying "stuffed birds and withered flowers" in art school. The son of a German mother and French father, young Arp was eligible for induction into both the French and the German armies, a situation that he recognized "was no good for me." In 1915, Arp had fled to neutral Zurich to escape World War I, changing his name from Hans to Jean to avoid any association with things German.

Arp was not alone in fleeing to Zurich. During the war the city crawled with all sorts of young men seeking to evade something: revolutionaries (Lenin could be seen playing checkers in the cafés), pacifists, anarchists, conscientious objectors. Looking around, one saw grim-faced German prisoners of war marching by, brought to Zurich by the Red Cross. In addition, thousands of students from all over Europe flocked to Zurich's still-functioning university, carrying on as if there were no war raging beyond Switzerland's borders.

It was easy to connect with like-minded souls in the cafés swirling with tense and spirited youth, and Arp had no trouble making the acquaintance of a young Romanian poet, philosophy student, and dandy hiding behind a monocle, Tristan Tzara. Bursting with nervous energy, the dark-haired little man was full of ideas. Tzara introduced Arp to a fellow Romanian, the elegant Marcel Janco, enlarging their circle with Richard Hülsenbeck, a medical student, and Hugo Ball, a conscientious objector from Germany, and his wife, Emmy Hennings. The friends talked about art and the state of literature and poetry. Arp knew a great deal about the developments in Paris and spoke to his friends about Kandinsky and Klee. Ball hit upon the idea of starting a literary nightclub. Having some experience with stagecraft, Hugo Ball convinced a retired Dutchman to rent him one large room on a narrow street at No. 1 Spiegelgasse to establish a cabaret that Ball hoped would serve as a forum for his friends and for other young artists and intellectuals who found themselves in Zurich. Fancifully called the Cabaret Voltaire, the nightclub opened on February 5, 1916.

At the beginning, the mostly student clientele that frequented the Cabaret Voltaire was treated to a little piano playing and some poetry readings. Occasionally, a balalaika orchestra played. Soon, however, what had started out as tepid performances became a startling assault on the complacency of the audience. Ball allowed his friend Tzara to stage recitals. Borrowing an idea from the Futurists, who declaimed simultaneously, Tzara and his friends read their work aloud at the same time, so that no one could be understood. Accompanied by deafening "music" made by clanging pots, jangling keys, and striking typewriters, Arp recited his poems and Hülsenbeck screamed his verses at the top of his lungs.

Fired by the nihilism in the air and the futility and frustration that had seized so many young people during the war, Tzara and his cronies began to indulge in chaotic farces, as much out of rage as out of a desire to shock. The initial response of indignant delight on the part of the beery audience prompted ever greater efforts. Tzara piled up chairs with words on their backs as a form of "silent" poetry. Characters did weird dances, in hideous, pinned-together paper costumes made by Janco. Ball harangued the students with jibes and "sound" poems—his recent invention—of nonsense syllables. A not atypical recitation at the Cabaret Voltaire began: "manhattan there are tubs of excrement before you / mbaze mbaze bazebaze mleganga garoo." Around the room were hung pictures by Kandinsky, Picasso, Klee, and, of course, Arp. The audience did not know what to make of these strange goings-on and the evening's events were often topped off with a fist-fight, but mostly the patrons had fun.

Realizing that what they had begun was greater than themselves, the group at the Cabaret Voltaire needed a name for what they were doing. Ball, so the story goes, stuck a paper knife at random in a French and German dictionary and, coming across the word *dada* (French for hobby horse), christened the new movement. Not content to let this explanation lie, Arp insisted that it was Tzara who one evening in February 1916 invented the name Dada. "I was there," he persisted, in typical Dada hyperbolic fashion,

> with my twelve children when Tzara pronounced for the first time this word, which aroused a legitimate enthusiasm in all of us. This took place at the Terrace Café in Zurich, and I had a roll of bread up my left nostril. I am persuaded that only imbeciles and Spanish professors can be interested in dates. What interests us is the dada spirit, and we were all dada before Dada began.

Hans Richter recalled hearing Tzara and Janco saying dada, da da, or yes, yes in Romanian.

Armed with a name, the newly baptized Dadas declared their own war on convention, respectability, art, literature, and tradition. Dada's aim was "to be subversive and . . . exasperating to the public." Nothing held any meaning. "Logic is always false," said Tzara; " 'literature' is a dossier of human imbecility for the guidance of future professors." Tzara exhorted his followers to "ring up your family on the telephone and piss down the hole designed for musical, gastronomic and sacred nonsense."

Art could be made of anything—rusty nails found in the gutter, burlap sacks, discarded matchboxes, anything at all. Picabia took a stuffed monkey and called it *Portrait of Cézanne.* Arp made collages by placing cutouts, by chance, on paper. Tzara wrote "poetry" by cutting up newspaper articles. Dada was all and all was Dada. Life was Dada. Dada was a state of mind, a way of living, frenetic and unreasoning, a life "with neither bedroom slippers nor parallels."

The Dadas, with their bizarre performances and pronouncements centered on the Cabaret Voltaire, began to draw a following. The press reported with undisguised contempt and resentment the activities of this group of young people hell-bent on the destruction of their elders' values. Elated with their success in shocking and scandalizing the public, the Dadas moved out to various halls around Zurich to stage Dada Nights, gaining increasing notoriety with each fresh outrage. On Bastille Day 1916, Tzara proclaimed the First Dada Manifesto at the Salle Waag. "We spit on humanity," he declared.

DADA remains within the framework of European weaknesses, it's still shit, but from now on we want to shit in different colours so as to adorn the zoo of art with all the flags of all the consulates. . . . This is Dada's balcony, I assure you. From there you can hear all the military marches, and come down cleaving the air like a seraph landing in a public bath to piss and understand the parable.

Dada fever "spread like a spot of oil," from Zurich to Hanover, Berlin, Cologne, and Paris. In New York Dada was already "in the air," and Duchamp, Picabia, and Man Ray were engaging in proto-Dada activities. The gospel was preached through the circulation of a Dada review, the *Cabaret Voltaire,* in which appeared the crazed poetry of Tzara and company—Arp, Hülsenbeck, Janco, Ball, Emmy Hennings, Apollinaire, and Blaise Cendrars. More reviews followed called *Dada I, II, III,* and so on, carrying the message of the Dada revolt.

When the fifty seats at the Cabaret Voltaire could no longer contain the curious, the Dadas moved to a larger space at the newly christened Galerie Dada, where they put on performances and decorated the walls with pictures and the work of artists they admired, including Kandinsky, de Chirico, Ernst, and Klee. The Dadas continued in a frenzy of destruction, sweeping aside masses of accumulated cultural prejudices.

As the war drew to a close, the Dada spirit grew ever more frantic, as thousands returned home from what was to them a meaningless slaughter, what the painter Max Ernst called "the whole immense *Sweinerei* of that imbecilic war. We young people came back from the war in a state of stupefaction, and our rage had to find expression somehow or other." Dada exhibitions, demonstrations, and provocations assaulted an unsuspecting public, charging it with lethargy and complacence. As Georges Hugnet wrote, "Dada was born from what it hated. . . . Dada was the sickness of the world."

The publicity and fanfare surrounding Dada was repugnant to Jean Arp, who was shy and sensitive by nature, but he was powerfully attracted to its sense of fun. Childlike and playful, with a shaved head and blue eyes, Arp was always ready for a good laugh. Matthew Josephson, who met the young Arp, said he was "one of the most lovable and fantastically comic companions I have ever had," who told the "best stories with a dead pan expression, but with a slightly mad glint in his eyes that had a devastating effect." Josephson likened him to a Mack Sennett clown.

Arp gladly participated in the Dada performances and demonstrations, declaiming his own poetry and hanging his creations on the walls of the Cabaret Voltaire. He once remarked, "They may call us by any names they please: Surrealists or something else . . . but they will find that underneath my skin I am always and forever a dyed-in-the-wool Dadaist."

The irreverence of Dada and its clean sweep of the past liberated Arp's imagination. He began to use new materials—cloth and paper. He spilled ink on paper, letting his mind freely associate forms. He worked in collaboration with his future wife, Sophie Täuber. He used everyday objects—bottles, forks, shirts, shoes, eggs—as inspiration for his forms in wood reliefs and collages. Even the homeliest objects caught Arp's eye. Something of a fetishist about shoes (he designed his own), he could walk for hours simply to get a better look at the cut of a heel or the contour of a sole glimpsed ahead of him, which would then appear in bas-reliefs, such as one Peggy was to buy called *Overturned Blue Shoe with Two Heels Under a Black Vault.* "In nature," he once said, "a broken twig has exactly the same beauty, the same importance, as the stars."

In time, Arp's shapes grew increasingly abstract and biomorphic, so that his creations resembled living, breathing things. Arp's garden in Meudon, outside of Paris, where Peggy visited him in late 1937, seemed to be a living jungle, littered with organic sculpture. By this time, Dada as a movement was long since dead, and Arp was working with sculpture in the round, in bronze or stone, which he had taken up seven years before at the age of forty-three.

Peggy fell in love with one piece, which had recently been cast. It was so round and undulating it looked like a writhing baby and begged to be held. Once Peggy touched it, she had to have it, and the small bronze, *Shell and Head,* just under eight inches high, became the first modern sculpture Peggy bought.

Peggy was distressed that Arp pressed upon her the work of his wife. "He was always trying to push Sophie," Peggy declared. Sophie created fanciful marionettes and masks for the performances at the Cabaret Voltaire as well as tapestries, and she worked on projects jointly with Arp, such as the *Sculpture Conjugale,* which was to be exhibited in Peggy's show. Peggy was in Meudon to see Arp, not his wife. But then, Peggy never liked the wives of the painters and artists she exhibited—not even the talented ones.

When Arp came to England to help with Peggy's contemporary sculpture show, he stayed in Peggy's tiny flat, cooking breakfast for her and doing the dishes. His only word in English, *candlesticks,* had to go a long way. (He was once delighted to see everywhere around him posters "bearing his name ARP, which impressed him no end until he discovered that the letters meant Air-Raid Protection," and indicated the location of bomb shelters.) Arp's presence in London was a great event for young English artists. His reputation in art circles as a co-founder of Dada and for his "creative abstraction" was enormous. Now fifty years old, Arp was a sort of elder statesman of the modern movement. Henry Moore, who also was exhibiting in Peggy's sculpture show at Duchamp's suggestion, was terribly excited to be included. "It was an important period for me," he said, "to see one's work alongside other European sculptors."

Moore, who was close to forty at the time, was working with massive wooden forms, re-creating a small child's experience of rubbing his mother's monumental back. He was not finding much of a climate for modern sculpture in England at the time and to make ends meet he was teaching. He was grateful to Peggy for the opportunity to exhibit in illustrious company and he found her "very lively, very attractive." A large reclining figure of his was chosen to sit in the center of the gallery.

Peggy liked Moore and his sculptures and wanted to own a piece by him, but she found "the sculpture I had exhibited in that exhibition was much too big, an enormous, wooden thing. So, I said, I was sorry I couldn't buy it, but . . . I would have liked something smaller. So, he came in one day with a little suitcase with these two small sculptures," miniature versions of his large-scale work, a lead figure and one in bronze. Peggy immediately bought the bronze (the lead went eventually to the Museum of Modern Art) and was convinced that it was she who inspired Moore to create his miniature pieces.

(Peggy's tiny sculpture met a foul end in 1945. Peggy was in New York and reluctantly agreed to lend the work to an exhibition given in the Armory for which ten critics chose ten pieces each. "Unfortunately," Peggy wrote to a friend, "the editor of the Magazine of Art had better taste than some of the others, and borrowed my little Henry Moore bronze figure, which I gave him reluctantly. Quite rightly so as a truck driver threw it away in a garbage heap. It seems to be irretrievably lost, and the people responsible most reluctant about reimbursing me. I wonder if Henry Moore will make me another one some day. I feel its loss greatly as I doted on the little thing." Peggy had to have a second bronze cast from the Museum of Modern Art's lead version.)

Moore went to the opening of the sculpture show, which was a big event, and found Djuna Barnes there. "Djuna Barnes was pretty famous then," he remembered, "I didn't care for her much. Was she a lesbian?" he asked. "I didn't take to her at all. I remember something unpleasant." The publicity the customs dispute had occasioned brought in record numbers of visitors to the gallery for almost a month—everyone wanted to see what the director of the Tate called "not art."

"The art world was entirely different then. In those days," Henry Moore observed,

there were only three or four contemporary painters and sculptors who could make a living. America had a depression, Roosevelt had an art program. This was the period between the wars when certainly in England I wasn't able to earn my living until after the shelter drawings. . . . The Academicians, and Epstein, Augustus John made their living because they did portraiture. Peggy Guggenheim's gallery helped. Any encouragement for so-called contemporary art helped.

A NEW VICE: SURREALISM

Little was known about modern art in London when Peggy began Guggenheim Jeune. In fact, there was little in the way of artistic activity at all in England—a few painters and sculptors struggling, a few critics trying to be heard. In general, young Englishmen of literary or artistic ambitions crossed the Channel to France. "The atmosphere in London was so different from Paris," said Nigel Henderson of those days. "London was hopelessly asleep."

In the late 1930s, however, London began to change, in part because of world forces that would soon tear Europe asunder and move the center of the art world to New York, and in part as a result of what has been called the last great European movement—Surrealism. Surrealism captured the imagination of a generation around the world, and its ideas gave Peggy a persona. She became identified with Surrealism, which provided her with a context for her heretofore vague notions of style and art.

Surrealism was born in Paris, where a small Dada band of young intellectuals, writers, and poets, led by André Breton, breathlessly awaited the arrival of Tristan Tzara in January 1920. Almost immediately upon Tzara's messianic arrival, a Dada matinee was planned at the Grand Palais's Salle des Fêtes. There Cocteau declaimed the poems of

Max Jacob. Breton dragged onstage a blackboard on which appeared a machine drawn by Picabia and summarily began to erase it. He then introduced a cheap reproduction of the *Mona Lisa* on which Duchamp had drawn a moustache and inscribed the inflammatory initials *L.H.O.O.Q.,* which in French read, *"Elle a chaud au cul"* (she has hot pants) and in English *"Look."* Tzara proclaimed the Dada manifesto and then began to read a newspaper article while bells clanged. As always with Dada provocations, the audience had been led to expect one thing, in this case a personal appearance by Charlie Chaplin, but was given something wholly different. It was predictably infuriated.

With Tzara in Paris, the self-styled "enemies of order" continued to stage Dada demonstrations and performances with ever-increasing vigor, to the jeers and insults of the press, which they manipulated with finesse. In no time Dada festivals and pranks became fashionable and Dada soirées were held at the Université Populaire. Well armed with tomatoes and wilted produce, audiences began to enjoy the Dada skits. What was intended to shock the public became fun for all, to the annoyance of the *provocateurs,* particularly Breton, who had quickly elbowed Tzara aside to become the leader of the Dada movement in France.

Like others of his disaffected generation, Breton had seized on Dada as the only solution to a ridiculous world, because Dada cultivated insanity and illogic. It illustrated the stupidity of traditions and "wished to destroy the hoaxes of reason." "We were intentionally irrational," said Man Ray of those Dada years, "but what IS logic? To me 2 and 2 equals 22; not 4." Yet by 1921 Dada was burning itself out and the Dada festivals, nonsensical trouble-making excursions, and "organized pranks" seemed meaningless. Not much was left to destroy. Tzara wrote a poem that consisted of the word *roar* repeated 147 times. Cubism, André Gide, and Anatole France had all been roundly insulted. What else was there to do? "The work of destruction of values completed," wrote Julien Levy, "the need was felt for new values." Or as Duchamp phrased it, "Dada was very serviceable as a purgative."

Breton had been a medical student and during the war, while working in several neurological units, had developed an interest in psychology—a science then in its infancy, the creation largely of Sigmund Freud —and tried psychoanalysis on some of his patients. In 1921, together with the poet Philippe Soupault, Breton sat down to write "automatically" whatever drifted into his head, in much the same way as a patient on an analyst's couch reveals his thoughts through free association. In this manner the two friends produced *Les Champs Magnétiques,* a plotless stream-of-consciousness work. Delighted with its fantastical imagery and "extraordinary verve," Breton went on to more experiments with the unconscious, even dabbling in the occult and attending séances. For too long, it struck Breton, society had denied man access to this inner realm, buffering him from his true self. Constricting reality, as opposed to the world of dreams, fantasies, and visions, kept man's imagination in chains.

The "First Surrealist Manifesto," published by André Breton in 1924, heralded the official beginning of a new movement. "A new vice has just been born," Louis Aragon declared, "one madness more has been given to man: *surrealism,* son of frenzy and darkness. Step right up, here is where the kingdoms of the instantaneous begin." As a word, *Surrealism* was inadvertently invented by Guillaume Apollinaire when he subtitled his 1917 play *Les Mamelles des Tiresias, "un drame surréaliste."* Breton seized upon it and defined it as "psychic automatism in its pure state." Most of the Dadaists eagerly followed Breton's lead. Poets and writers, men like Paul Éluard, Philippe Soupault, Louis Aragon, Pierre Naville, and Robert Desnos were quick to abandon the world of summary reality —of logic, analysis, and reason—to embrace the hidden world of super-reality, an absolute reality of dreams and myths and marvels. "Let us not mince words," wrote Breton, "the marvelous is always beautiful, any-thing marvelous is beautiful, in fact only the marvelous is beautiful."

Every evening a band of a dozen or so young Surrealists met at the Café Certa, the Tabac, or the Cyrano on the Place Blanche, or at Breton's apartment at 42 rue Fontaine, filled with curious artifacts, pictures, docu-ments, and rare books. Encircled by a redolent haze of cigarette smoke competing with the aroma of fruity liqueurs, Breton directed the "work" of Surrealism: the rediscovery of "life under the thick carapace of centu-ries of culture—life pure, naked, raw, lacerated." Its purpose—"to ex-plode the social order, to transform life itself."

After some debate, the group would set off to see Charlie Chaplin or Buster Keaton films. They walked the streets of Montmartre encoun-tering prostitutes and pimps, frequenting bordellos, and talking to the *poules.* They attended the circus and befriended aerialists and clowns. They rode on merry-go-rounds and on bumper cars in amusement parks.

Writers who had long since been committed to the ashcan of literary history were unearthed, reread, and defended as precursors of Surreal-ism. The self-styled Comte de Lautréamont's feverish *Chants de Maldoror* (originally published in 1869), composed of bizarre images and juxtapo-sitions, the most famous being the chance meeting of an umbrella and a sewing machine on a dissecting table, was rediscovered and acclaimed. The Marquis de Sade, once dismissed as a pervert, was lauded as the man who "set free the imagination of love" and reclaimed his primitive instincts. The dramatist and novelist Raymond Roussel, who spent his life wandering in a luxurious motorized caravan recording his impres-sions and playing chess, was suddenly revered. They were all applauded as "the first to indicate in their works the existence of the enormous illogical world that the Surrealist movement has subsequently brought to light."

In October 1924, the Surrealist Bureau of Investigation was officially opened at 24 rue Grenelle (open every day except Sunday for two hours), to collect, from all who cared, material for the Surrealist investigation into the modern epoch and the collective unconscious. Soon thereafter, in December, the first issue of *La Révolution Surréaliste* appeared, announcing the following inquiry: Is Suicide a Solution? Among the many answers printed in the subsequent issue was Pierre Reverdy's observation, "Suicide is an act in which the gesture takes place in one world and the consequence in an other." The magazine featured accounts of dreams, chronicles of suicides, Surrealist writings, pictures, and open letters, such as the one that exploded: "OPEN THE PRISONS RETIRE THE ARMY." The format of *La Révolution Surréaliste* was simple, straightforward, and "scientific," in an effort to impart to the Surrealist experiments a serious veneer.

The work of Surrealism did not stop there. The Surrealists had Surrealist wives and ate Surrealist meals—chocolate chicken, one of Breton's favorites and later one of Peggy's specialties, or roast beef with oysters, after Leonora Carrington's recipe. They dressed in Surrealist clothes. Breton could be seen in his jade-green suit and round, green-tinted lenses at the Surrealist Bureau of Investigation. Costume parties were very popular where people appeared in various states of dress and undress, wearing feathered and tinseled headgear, huge masks, or streaming multicolored ribbon garters. The painter Leonor Fini kept throughout her apartment floor tiny heaps of excrement "sprayed with perfume." At gatherings, which were frequent—the Surrealists did everything together—a Surrealist truth game, La Vérité, would be played; a moderator, most often Breton, went around a circle asking embarrassing questions, preferably about sexual or intensely personal matters, and a forfeit was called if a player refused to answer or seemed evasive. Breton led the group in another Surrealist game, the "exquisite corpse," during which a drawing or a phrase was composed by several people, each one adding something to a piece of paper, folded so that the prior entry was obscured, resulting in bizarre nonsense. Breton held Surrealist discussions, reprinted in *La Révolution Surréaliste,* where he would ask questions about love, orgasm, or masturbation, which in those days, recalled the Surrealist filmmaker Luis Buñuel, seemed incredible.

In their war on convention, scandal remained the Surrealists' greatest weapon. At a literary banquet in 1924, Breton shot up to interrupt the speaker in the middle of some impromptu remarks crying "Enough! Enough!" while Robert Desnos added, "For twenty-five years now she's bored the shit out of us, but no one's had the nerve to tell her." Paul Claudel, a noted critic, accused the group of outright perversion in July 1925. "Neither dadaism nor surrealism," he said, "have anything but a single meaning: pederastic." In retaliation, the Surrealists distributed an open letter, printed on red paper, calling Claudel a prig and a scoundrel and placing a copy under each of the napkins set out for another literary banquet. Pandemonium broke out at the affair when the poet Rachilde felt compelled to say that a Frenchwoman should never marry a German. At this, Breton rose, announced it was an insult to his friend, Max Ernst, a German, seated nearby and flung his napkin at Mme. Rachilde. Within seconds fruit was flying through the air and cries of *"Vive l'Allemagne! Vive l'Allemagne!"* sprang from the Surrealists, as Soupault grabbed the chandelier and swung himself over the accumulated china and glassware on the table.

Seated at the head of the table at the Certa, or in an armchair at home, surrounded by his disciples, it was Breton who gave Surrealism its cohesiveness, fired by a sense of mission so intense that he gave the movement an almost mystical quality. The sheer force of Breton's mesmeric personality drove people to him and made men love him, in the words of Jacques Prévert, "like a woman."

Matthew Josephson remembers Breton at twenty-five as "an imposing *chef d'école*. He had a huge head, like one of the old Jacobin leaders, a mass of wavy brown hair, pale blue eyes, regular—though heavy—features, and jaws of granite."

Breton's personal tastes and dislikes pervaded Surrealism. What Breton hated, Surrealists had to shun, and what Breton said, Surrealism became. "Now, *there* was a governess," declared one observer, who knew Breton and his ways, "and not a very high-class one." He disapproved of music, thinking it "confusional," and would not tolerate it or any discussion of it at Surrealist meetings. Work, in the traditional sense of earning a living, Breton dismissed as a bourgeois activity, making it difficult for some of the Surrealists to survive. He loathed homosexuals; Cocteau he abhorred, writing to Tristan Tzara, "He is the most hateful being of our time." If Breton spied a homosexual in a room, he would turn and say disdainfully, *"Qu'est-ce que c'est ce pédé?"* Behind his back, Breton was called "the Pope" for the severity of his pronouncements, disapproving as he did of any Surrealist's visits to whorehouses for other than strictly scientific purposes.

André Breton declared the modern era to be "the age of Lautréamont, of Freud, and of Trotsky," and joined the French Communist party, taking his disciples with him. But the French party looked on these new converts as a mixed blessing, and in the end, Breton was expelled from the party for nonconformist behavior. Unlike Marcel Duchamp, who preferred to remain in the background, Breton propelled himself to the fore. "Breton was so totally different from Marcel," said Paul Matisse. "There was a man with an *ego* radiating around him, filling rooms and rooms."

From its inception, Surrealism attracted a great many artists and painters, who felt adrift in the wake of Dada's frenzied attack on all traditions and were searching for new values. The camera had usurped the traditional role of art by reproducing more exactly than the brush the physical world; and both Cubism and abstract art seemed to many younger painters sterile and dehumanizing. Surrealism, however, provided a new subject matter—the unconscious—as well as the novel attitude, inherited from Dada, whereby the value of a work of art lay in its conception rather than its execution. Talent, skill, technique—all the attributes valued in Western art—were made secondary to fantasy, spontaneity, and Dada's lighthearted passion for the irrational and accidental. What was important was the revelation of the psyche. Surrealism brought back, said Marcel Duchamp, "things that were taboo," like lust and sexual longing; "subject was absolutely unimportant. All you had to do was paint an apple on a chair—that was enough."

Breton supervised and helped organize the first exhibition of Surrealist painting at the Galerie Pierre in 1925. The artists represented included Max Ernst, Man Ray, Jean Arp, Joan Miró, André Masson, and artists the Surrealists liked to claim for their own—Picasso, de Chirico, and Klee. From the beginning, two strains appeared in Surrealist painting, the "abstract" and the "dreamlike." Painters such as Masson and Miró worked in a shallow Cubist space, but took from Surrealism its subject matter and its technique of automatism or free association to force inspiration. Miró, for example, experimented with colors and techniques to pull from his psyche a childish, whimsical, fantastical iconography. He poured blue wash on canvas and spread it with rags and when he accidentally spilled some blackberry jam it inspired a picture.

But it was through the paintings of artists like the Spaniard Salvador Dali and the Belgian René Magritte that Surrealism became most widely known. The dream painters depicted what the eye could not see in a highly realistic and illusionistic fashion. Taking their cues from nightmares or paranoiac visions, these painters gave expression to strange images and oneiric visions of melting watches, desertscapes of fantasy and desire, or men with barbells for faces.

Without the language barriers that limited the impact of Surrealist writing, Surrealist painting traveled well. Thus a movement started by poets became most closely associated with its painters and in particular with one—Salvador Dali.

Dali was discovered wading on the beach at Cadaqués, Spain, by Paul Éluard's fiery Russian-born wife Gala—who soon left her husband to navigate for her tempestuous find. Dali's obsessive fascination with masturbation, cunnilingus, paranoia, and hallucinatory phenomena titillated the public's imagination. His visual games rendered in a precise, almost photographic technique, could be appreciated by a large audience. Dali's posturing, pranks, and self-serving stunts made him and his waxed and exaggerated moustaches even more renowned—if tarnished —in the eyes of his Surrealist friends with whom he became aligned around 1930.

The years of Dali's preeminence in the Surrealist movement coincide with what has been called the Golden Age of Surrealist painting. Surrealist groups sprang up everywhere—in Czechoslovakia, Hungary, Belgium, Switzerland, Romania, and even in Japan and Egypt. Surrealist books and periodicals spread the movement to many more countries. International expositions of Surrealist paintings and objects were mounted and set off scandals wherever they opened.

Throughout the 1930s André Breton made royal visitations to the offshoot groups, lecturing, organizing, breathing life into his own creation. Dali, too, did his share to spread the intoxication of Surrealism. When he first arrived in New York, very much the peasant from Catalonia, he was attached by strings to all his pictures. The press went wild when they discovered that in a portrait of Gala, by then his wife, he had painted two lamb chops as her shoulders. A later visit to New York resulted in a highly publicized free fall from a window at Bonwit Teller's department store, when Dali realized to his dismay that a carefully plotted display of his creation, incorporating a clothed mannequin in a bathtub, had been disturbed by a windowdresser who took the dummy *out* of the tub so its clothes could be seen to better advantage. In the ensuing fracas, the bathtub and Dali slid out the window onto Fifth Avenue and into the newspapers across the country.

In time, Dali's publicity-provoking activities and fascistic leanings displeased Breton, and he was officially excommunicated by the Surrealists. Dismissing Dali, so recently hailed as an "immense carnivorous flower blooming in the Surrealist sun," Breton gave him credit for an "undeniable ingenuity in staging."

Surrealism arrived in England largely through the efforts of two young Englishmen, David Gascoyne and Roland Penrose. Penrose, a wealthy, Cambridge-educated painter and writer, had been living in France since 1922. When he went to investigate a studio in Montmartre he met the Surrealist painter Max Ernst, who introduced him to his next-door neighbor, Joan Miró, as well as to André Breton, Paul Éluard, and the rest of the Surrealist crew. Penrose also met the poet David Gascoyne and they decided to carry the flame of Surrealism with them to England. "It was the encounter of two explorers," wrote Penrose, "who had discovered independently the same glittering treasure."

In 1935 Gascoyne wrote the first work to appear in English on the subject—*A Short Survey of Surrealism*—and Penrose traveled back and forth to Paris to talk with Man Ray, Breton, Éluard, and Surrealist writer

Georges Hugnet about the possibility of a large-scale Surrealist exhibition in London. As the idea slowly became a reality, excitement was generated on both sides of the Channel.

On June 11, 1936 (one of the hottest days of that year), the "International Surrealist Exhibition" opened at London's New Burlington Galleries. Breton and Éluard came to London, and Breton inaugurated the show with "a passionate speech in French to a sweating and bewildered crowd of art lovers and journalists" while standing next to Penrose's *Last Voyage of Captain Cook,* a mannequin's torso painted in broad stripes of green, black, and ochre and encased in a wire globe. Salvador Dali also arrived for the exhibition and masterminded a number of eye-catching events. He gave a lecture on his favorite subject, paranoia, dressed in a bubble-headed diver's suit, accompanied by a pair of large and mangy dogs. The heat was so intense, however, that Dali "had to be brought to the surface and the headpiece unscrewed before his discourse from the depths of the subconscious left him completely unconscious." It was Dali's idea to advertise the show by having a woman, wearing a mask of red roses, parade around Trafalgar Square feeding the pigeons.

The exhibition was a succès de scandale. Sixty artists from fourteen different countries exhibited close to four hundred of the most bizarre and provocative works their imaginations could bring forth. Paintings like Man Ray's *The Lovers,* two giant, thin lips floating spectrally above the horizon, or Max Ernst's *Elephant of Celebes,* an evocative, robotlike mastodon, hung side by side with primitive art from Oceania, Africa, and the two Americas. Objects—found, familiar, and natural, including two walking sticks—were interspersed with Surrealist objects by Breton, Gala Dali, and even by the art critic Herbert Read. Salvador Dali draped his *Aphrodisiac Jacket* on a clothes hanger—a man's dinner jacket on which were affixed countless shot glasses in neat rows. Meret Oppenheim exhibited her now-famous *Fur-Covered Cup, Saucer and Spoon.* The art of children and the insane was used as a counterpoint to the Surrealist pictures, and works by Duchamp, Picasso, and Klee were also shown. "Do not judge this movement kindly," wrote Herbert Read in his catalogue introduction. "It is not just another amusing stunt. It is defiant —the desperate act of men too profoundly convinced of the rottenness of our civilization to want to save a shred of its respectability."

The public and the press took Read's advice and did not judge the Surrealists and their show kindly. The organizers were reviled—called disgusting, decrepit, dowdy, and seedy. The public did not know what to make of the pictures or the objects, many of which they knew they could find in their own backyards, probably in the rubbish heap, exhibited now with all the trappings of art; or what to think of Dali's accessible but disturbing images of paranoiac visions and erotic desires. Was the whole thing a giant hoax? A critic concluded that "the most that can be said of them is that their pettiness and ignorance are in good faith." Delighted with the outraged press reaction, the Surrealists were only too glad to catalogue some of the finer calumnies in their own *Bulletin International du Surréalisme.*

In spite of the terrible reviews, or perhaps because of them, the international exhibition of Surrealism was a sensation. Twenty thousand visitors gawked at the show hailed by Breton as the "highest point in the graph of the *influence* of our movement."

Although Peggy was in England living at Yew Tree Cottage at the time of all this commotion, she was indifferent to the art of the Surrealists, save for reading about them in the press along with many other housewives. When someone invited her to see the show, she demurred, preferring to stay home. "I wasn't interested in Surrealism," she explained, "until I got my gallery." Yet it was the "International Surrealist Exhibition" that created the artistic ferment in which Peggy's gallery some eighteen months later would thrive.

The 1936 exhibition galvanized the English art world, somnolent for so long. From it emerged a hard core of Surrealist enthusiasts, eager to promote the movement and dedicated to twentieth-century art, a group that included Penrose and Gascoyne, Herbert Read, Julian Trevelyan, Henry Moore, Humphrey Jennings, and the transplanted Belgian E. L. T. Mesens, among many others.

With the new interest in Surrealism came English-language editions of Éluard, Le Comte de Lautréamont, the Marquis de Sade, and Breton's *What Is Surrealism?* as England began to emerge from the cultural isolation of past decades. "The Surrealist exposition of 1936," said Roland Penrose, "was a breakthrough."

When Peggy opened Guggenheim Jeune at 30 Cork Street in January 1938, the gallery joined two neighbors in being among the handful of London galleries showing avant-garde art. Cork Street had once been a street of moneylenders and, later, a sort of Savile Row of tailor's shops. But three galleries, next door to one another—the Mayor Gallery and the London Gallery being the other two—made tiny Cork Street into the center of London's minuscule art world.

Freddy Mayor started with a cigar shop that evolved into an art gallery at Number 19 Cork Street. Mayor gave Miró his first one-man show in England in 1933 and subsequently brought over Paul Klee in 1934.

The London Gallery, which opened at 28 Cork Street, was next door to Guggenheim Jeune. It was started in 1936 by Lady Norton, the wife of a diplomat, Sir Clifford Norton. Lady Norton showed Edvard Munch and had had some exhibitions of abstract art before her husband was posted abroad. When the opportunity arose to take over Lady Norton's lease on the gallery, Roland Penrose, after discussing the idea of starting a gallery for Surrealist art with Humphrey Jennings and others, went ahead. The London Gallery reopened as a showcase for Surrealist art in 1937, shortly before Guggenheim Jeune. It immediately caused a stir in the Surrealist group and among young artists and intellectuals of all persuasions. "It was a very new thing," recalled Nigel Henderson, "and it attracted a lot of us." Penrose hired as its manager the enterprising Belgian Surrealist E. L. T. Mesens. Overweight, pink-faced, and given to heavy drinking, Mesens guided the London gallery with a mixture of panache and commercialism not always popular with English artists and intellectuals, who criticized him as "vulgar" or "very Belgian."

The London Gallery became the headquarters not only for Surrealist art, but for all avant-garde art, at a time when the boundaries between one school of art and another were hazy. In addition, the gallery became an information center, disseminating Surrealist ideas through its periodical loosely based on French models, the *London Bulletin,* which first appeared in April 1938. The *London Bulletin* ran poems and essays by Breton, Éluard, Read, Jennings, George Reavey, and Samuel Beckett, as well as Peggy's friends Djuna Barnes and Antonia White. Surrealist activities, symposiums, lectures, and publications were faithfully reported, and illustrations of Surrealist works appeared in every issue.

By the end of its first year the *London Bulletin* could announce that it had become the only avant-garde publication in England concerned with contemporary poetry and art. By then, too, it had acquired a U.S. representative in the person of Charles Henri Ford, a "New York Letter" contributed by Parker Tyler, and a readership across the Atlantic. The three Cork Street galleries all advertised in the *London Bulletin.* In return, the magazine ran copies of their catalogues, saving everyone printing costs, and reviewed their shows, providing provocative material on the artists and placing the exhibitions on Cork Street within the context of mainstream European art.

It "was rather good," Peggy said about the *London Bulletin,* "but, like Mesens himself, a little too commercial. The paper advertised everything Mesens sold in his gallery." It also advertised Guggenheim Jeune, so that when Peggy came to America some years later, her reputation as an avant-garde art dealer had already been established.

"We had a united front," Peggy wrote of the three Cork Street galleries, which the London *Times* labeled three little bethels "devoted to 'fancy religions' in art." "She was part of a movement," declared Roland Penrose of Peggy and her gallery. "It only lasted eighteen months, a little group on our own." Quite naturally, the Cork Street gallery owners "were very friendly," said Peggy, " 'cause we were neighbors." On occasion, Peggy even bought pictures from her competitors, such as a Paul Delvaux, *The Break of Day*, one of her favorites, in which four full-breasted women emerge from tree trunks like woodland mermaids. "I was so fascinated by the picture they wanted me to buy, so I bought it."

The members of the Surrealist group, centered on the London Gallery, went to Peggy's Guggenheim Jeune to see the art and to her openings—usually afternoon sherry parties—to meet pretty girls. Roland Penrose recalled, "Guggenheim Jeune was very lively. Her openings were always very crowded with lots of nice young people." Nigel Henderson, who went to nearly all of Peggy's openings, concurred. "They were very crowded; there was good food, masses to drink." Peggy stood out in the crowd, gotten up in wild, extravagant, and often grotesque jewelry and dramatic, if not always flattering, outfits. "She is very slim," said a reporter for the *Daily Express*, "with a rather attractively jerky way of talking and a collection of about eighty pairs of earrings." Roland Penrose found her "difficult to describe. One always saw the nose first. She was immensely alive and amusing, and she knew lots of one's friends."

The press adored Peggy and faithfully covered her vernissages. She had so effortlessly absorbed Surrealism's flair for self-promotion that she gave journalists plenty to write about. As Peggy's tastes grew ever more flamboyant and exaggerated (and her earrings spikier), journalists found her ever more newsworthy and amusing. Peggy could always be relied on for a quip or one-liner and from the moment she started Guggenheim Jeune, Peggy Guggenheim was the subject of endless anecdotes. "She had the sort of personality columnists dote on exploiting and the kind of fortune artists dream of in a patron."

After openings at Guggenheim Jeune Peggy would take "lots of people to the Café Royal for dinner." She loved to gather people around her, and Julien Levy once observed that "Peggy liked the *salon* life, and she made her life into one. She created the gallery perhaps dreaming that it would pay for itself. If you're going to have people in for cocktails, you may as well do it professionally."

Peggy also continued entertaining at Yew Tree Cottage, which she had leased from Douglas Garman under their unusual separation arrangement. "Week-ending was much in the air then," said Nigel Henderson. "I remember arriving at four in the morning, penniless, thinking someone would pay for me. I'd ring Peggy, and she'd say, 'Hold it. I'll be there.' She was some kind of angelic person, very touching and very warming. I'd like to have joined the many who bedded her, but I can't say I did."

Much of the Surrealist circle could, in fact, claim the honor. Penrose, Mesens, and their friends were young, filled with idealism, and to the newly liberated Peggy immensely attractive. "She had a sort of liking for the glassy-eyed, cold English type," said Henderson. In due time Peggy went to bed with all of them—Penrose, Jennings, and even Mesens, whom she described as a "gay little Flamand, quite vulgar, but really very nice and warm." Not one of them took her seriously, although she liked to believe otherwise. To the crowd at the London Gallery, Peggy seemed an easy conquest, and they were quite happy to oblige.

Peggy ran her gallery as she did her home—casually. What did a few cigarette ashes on the floor matter? The adjustment from housewife to gallery owner and impresario was easy. "I'm very adaptable," Peggy said. In those days, however, standards were relaxed and amateurs could prosper. Galleries were not then streamlined business machines. "None of us were taken seriously," explained Roland Penrose. "Little was thought of twentieth-century art. In London we were a small band of pioneers."

A SAILOR
FROM BRITTANY

No matter how engaging the English art world proved to be, Peggy could not shake her fixation with Samuel Beckett, and she frequently left the operations of Guggenheim Jeune to her secretary, Wyn Henderson, while she took the car ferry to Paris to pursue him in vain.

Fat, zestful, with red hair and voluptuous curves, Wyn seemed to Peggy a faded Venetian portrait with a bawdy sense of humor. Wyn had managed the Hours Press for Nancy Cunard and before that had been co-founder of a small press, the Aquila, where she did everything from licking envelopes to making tea to setting type. Her experience as a typographer came in handy at Guggenheim Jeune where she designed the first catalogue—bold capital letters spelling Guggenheim Jeune running at right angles to the page like a giant L. (Peggy liked Wyn's design so much that she continued to use the same basic logo on all her catalogues and stationery, not only at Guggenheim Jeune but later on at her gallery in New York and at her museum in Venice.) Wyn Henderson ran the everyday machinery of the gallery, helped set up exhibitions, soothed ruffled feathers, and, with a great deal more tact than Peggy, wooed clients. She did all this efficiently and well in return for a nominal salary—another precedent that Peggy saw no need to break in her relations with subsequent secretaries. Wyn constantly encouraged Peggy and bolstered her ego. "She seemed to know just what people were made of," said her son Nigel.

Peggy had promised Beckett that she would give a show for Geer van Velde, Beckett's friend. Peggy soon realized he was a second-rate imitator of Picasso, but she hoped that through this favor Beckett would pay attention to her once again.

The van Velde show was duly scheduled to succeed the sculpture exhibition on May 5 and to run through May 26, 1938. Beckett wrote the introduction to the catalogue—the text of which appeared in its entirety in the *London Bulletin.* In it he pointed out that van Velde had started out as a house painter. "Like at least one other eminent man," one reviewer observed dryly, referring to Adolf Hitler.

The van Velde show met with a large, disappointed critical yawn from an art public that had been so excited by the controversial sculpture show. But van Velde was thrilled; his paintings were bought up by Peggy under assumed names: "all because I loved Beckett so much and he loved van Velde," wrote Peggy.

Beckett accompanied his friend to London for the opening and Peggy invited Beckett, van Velde and his wife, and Beckett's friend George Reavey and his wife for a weekend at Yew Tree Cottage. Beckett dreaded telling Peggy of her rival Suzanne Deschevaux-Dumesnil, who was now his mistress. But he did break the news, describing Suzanne to Peggy and chronicling her organizational and domestic talents —finding him an apartment on the rue des Favorites and helping him to decorate it. Peggy recalled that Beckett "asked me if I minded, and I said, no, I couldn't mind, because she wasn't attractive enough, and she made curtains for him and she didn't sound like a mistress. She sounded more like a mother." Peggy often repeated, "She made curtains and I made scenes." And in any event, "He needed someone like her to take care of him and be a devoted slave and I wouldn't be like that."

Peggy disregarded Beckett's admission and decided to follow him back to Paris soon after the van Velde opening. She wired Beckett that she was coming, but he made no effort to meet her car at Calais and waited for her, she remembered, "listlessly in his apartment and seemed bored with me." Indeed, he seemed hopelessly bored with everything.

One afternoon, Peggy chanced to witness a strange scene between Beckett and van Velde. The two men began to undress in front of each other and exchange clothes, each one finally dressing like the other. It reminded Peggy of the homosexual scene from *Women in Love.* At that moment it became obvious to her that Beckett only really loved van Velde.

After the clothes-swapping episode, the three went to a restaurant where Peggy gave vent to her suspicions and taunted Beckett on not being a real man. Beckett stalked out and left her with the startled van

Velde. After this, Beckett and Peggy got on even less well until Beckett began to avoid her altogether. Yet he was loath to lose Peggy as a valuable connection for his friend, van Velde, so he agreed to a farewell drive with her and the van Veldes in Peggy's car to the south of France, where the van Veldes planned to live.

Beckett made up some excuse to Suzanne, with whom he now habitually spent his weekends, so he could leave on a Sunday. "God knows where she was," said Peggy. But from the beginning, the trip was ill-conceived. Beckett behaved very peculiarly and the van Veldes, who believed that Peggy and Beckett were finished as a couple, could not stop looking at each other and wondering what was going on. Once the van Veldes were deposited in Marseilles, Peggy could not wait to get back to England. She realized, somewhat belatedly, that her relationship with Beckett was hopeless.

Nevertheless, on the way back to Paris, they stopped at a hotel in Dijon for the night. To Peggy's delighted surprise, Beckett asked for a double room. Naturally, she assumed, he wanted to sleep with her, so she crept into his bed: "but he said no, that he didn't want to sleep with me and I asked him, 'Then why did you take the double room?' and he said, 'It was cheaper.' Isn't that disgusting?"

Although her affair with Beckett was brief, Peggy could not resist making much of it and talked about it to anyone who cared to listen. Beckett, on the other hand, recoiled from any such association. "I don't think he wants to remember me, anyway," Peggy admitted. "He's furious his name crops up all the time in connection with me"—largely, one might add, because Peggy made sure that it did. "He probably thinks it was a very unimportant affair. To me it was terribly important, but to him it wasn't."

If Peggy magnified her relationship with Beckett, Johnny Coleman suggested it was "because she looked at it in hindsight and she saw she'd hit the celebrity jackpot." Sindbad was not even sure it ever happened. "I don't think Beckett thought it happened." Julien Levy had his special theory. "As far as I know," he said, "Peggy had no lovers. People giggled at her. She had hot pants for everybody, but famous lovers were a great fantasy. What she really had were paid—taxi drivers, gondoliers. She was a popular roll in the hay. These men," he added, referring to the great men she claimed as lovers, "were not easy to get into bed—unless they were very drunk, which is probably what happened with Beckett."

Peggy lost no time in finding another object for her affections. Dropping off Beckett on the rue des Favorites in Paris, Peggy rushed to pick up the painter Yves Tanguy and his wife to take them to England for the July 5 private opening of his show at Guggenheim Jeune. Peggy had already met Tanguy the previous fall through Humphrey Jennings, who had convinced her to give Tanguy his first one-man exhibition in London.

Tanguy was born in Gustave Courbet's bed in the Ministry of the Marine on the place de la Concorde in 1900, where his father, a retired sea captain, was then an administrative official. What Courbet's bed was doing there or what Tanguy's mother was doing in it is a matter of some mystery. His boyhood summers were spent on the coast of Brittany, where he was deeply impressed by its landscape of tall prehistoric stones and monuments. There, too, he watched for hours as the local artist named Touché set up his easel and painted dusky landscapes, squinting at his subject through a dark glass. While still a teenager, Tanguy went to sea as an apprentice officer in the French merchant marine, visiting Africa and South America. But he was soon drafted into the French army, where, depressed and miserable, he met Jacques Prévert, an intellectual, poet, and future filmmaker who introduced the young Tanguy to the world of art.

Tanguy was released from the army and joined Prévert in Paris. There the two discovered the Comte de Lautréamont's *Les Chants de Maldoror,* and Tanguy toyed with the idea of becoming a painter. "I took a pencil," he said, "and started to draw on a napkin." (He meant this quite literally, as he sketched on the paper tablecloths of various cafés.) While riding on a bus, Tanguy happened to spot a painting by Giorgio de Chirico in a gallery window. He bounded off to get a closer look and it was at that moment, he later said, that he resolved to become a painter.

Methodically and thoughtfully, Tanguy taught himself to paint. When he showed his sketches and drawings to André Breton the latter was very encouraging. Breton liked their naïve and intuitive style and set about converting Tanguy to Surrealism. In 1926, *La Révolution Surréaliste* published its first Tanguy illustration and thereafter Tanguy aligned himself with the Surrealist group. The following year, he had his first one-man show at the Galerie Surréaliste in Paris. (He spent an entire afternoon with Breton looking through psychiatric manuals thinking up titles for his paintings.) If the Surrealists could not meet at Breton's house or at one of their favorite cafés they went to 54 rue du Château, where Tanguy shared an apartment with Jacques Prévert and Marcel Duhamel—who paid the bills.

Moved by the sharp contrasts of light and dark and the large mineral forms that he had seen on a trip to North Africa in 1930–1931, Tanguy began to paint strangely evocative landscapes, peopled with lonely, unidentifiable, bonelike structures—an odd and quiet world that "belongs to the domain of travelers' tales, those imaginary ocean voyages in which the helmsman of a ship of dreams watches for the faint faraway signals that will orient him to long-lost-lands," at once intensely real yet surreal.

To Breton it appeared possible to decompose Tanguy's "light into nasturtium, coq de roche, poplar leaf, rusty well chain, cut sodium, slate, jellyfish and cinnamon." "What is Surrealism?" Breton once asked. "It is the appearance of Yves Tanguy, crowned with the big emerald bird of Paradise."

Peggy found Tanguy, who was a year younger than she, "adorable." He had an engaging childlike manner, a chortle of a laugh, and a giggle that sounded like a strangled "tchk-tchk tk." If he'd had just a little too much to drink his hair stood up on end like an Iroquois warrior. "He was such fun," remembered his friend Roland Penrose, "an extraordinary character. He was very simple among the other Surrealists, especially with Breton—he was so simple and instinctive. He was devoted to Breton; he followed his steps everywhere. The bottle was important to him and he would get so drunk, he would eat spiders. He was strange-looking, always a tuft of hair coming out of his head." Pierre Matisse, his friend and schoolmate, recalled that "he would put a piece of sugar in the country on the grass, and when it was covered with ants, he would eat it. What he really liked was white wine." The poet John Goodwin, a relative by marriage, found Tanguy a "clown-child," and having heard that he ate spiders put him to the test, sampling some himself in the process. "They tasted like pimentos." Tanguy had a fat, peasant wife named Jeannette, who Peggy thought "awful looking" and who watched her charming husband like a hawk. She didn't watch him carefully enough, though, for without much difficulty Peggy insinuated herself into his embraces.

Peggy deposited the Tanguys in London with Peter Dawson, an English Surrealist, leaving Dawson and Tanguy to install the exhibition at Guggenheim Jeune. She sped off to Yew Tree Cottage to see Pegeen. Hazel, who had been living in England working as a watercolorist, was now ensconced in Yew Tree Cottage, acting as a surrogate mother when Pegeen would spend weekends away from school. Like Sindbad, Pegeen was at boarding school, and "Mama," as both children called Peggy, was terribly busy pursuing her own life and having what she considered "discreet" affairs. Even if Peggy noticed how troubled and melancholy Pegeen was, there was little she imagined she could do about it.

What Peggy did do was create an intensely sexual atmosphere about herself, which even an adolescent girl (Pegeen was almost thirteen) could not help but observe. She saw her mother light up at the sight of a man and girlishly flirt with anyone who came her way, even if she hid the actual affair from her. Often Pegeen could overhear Peggy talking about lovers and "millions" of them at that. "She talked quite a lot," recalled Nigel Henderson, "certainly at the time I was closest to her."

Peggy's stay at Yew Tree Cottage was brief. She soon returned to London for the Tanguy opening. The show was to be a major retrospective, and not only were both the Tanguys terribly excited at the prospect of the exhibition, but the English Surrealist group was keyed up for an important event. Peggy's main interest was in Tanguy, to whom she made her wishes quite clear. She had to wait, however, until one day in the gallery when they both decided to go back to Peggy's apartment and consummate their lust. Tanguy spent the night with Peggy, to the great chagrin of his wife, who thereafter redoubled her useless surveillance of her husband. Wyn Henderson, having once counted over a hundred lovers of her own, knew all too well the demands of passion and fended off Mme. Tanguy as best she could, inviting her to lunch and entertaining her, so that at least on one other afternoon Peggy and Tanguy could indulge themselves. Not for a moment did either one believe their affair more than a passing fancy.

Peggy invited the Tanguys for a weekend at Yew Tree Cottage. Hazel was still there and Tanguy mischievously dubbed her "La Noisette," French for "the hazelnut." Mme. Tanguy, overweight, unattractive, speaking only French, found herself adrift in an atmosphere of utter confusion. Things got so bad that one afternoon she wound up in the local pub, weeping in her cups for so long that the desperate pub keeper finally called Peggy's house and asked if anyone there knew the lady.

The Tanguy show ran from July 6 through 16 and met with tremendous enthusiasm. The English Surrealist group considered Tanguy one of the most important among those Surrealist painters who fixed dream images on canvas in a traditional style, borrowing from the Old Masters their deep spatial perspective and chiaroscuro modeling to create a metaphor for the unconscious. ("Tanguy," wrote David Gascoyne, was the "creator of the most tragic landscapes that the eye has never seen.") These illusionists whose "astonished reality," said Georges Hugnet, "seems more convincing than the reality of a photograph," became popular in the late 1930s and Surrealism came almost exclusively to be identified with them.

Some twenty-five of Tanguy's works were in his exhibition at Guggenheim Jeune, including Tanguy pictures lent by Breton, Penrose, Man Ray, Mesens, and Peter Dawson. The *London Bulletin* devoted half its July issue to the show, printing a piece by Breton in the original French, praising his *"adorable ami"* Tanguy and reproducing pages torn out from the *T* section of a dictionary, superimposed with realistic sketches of people by Tanguy. Wyn Henderson came up with the idea of a rafting party down the Thames in honor of Tanguy, during which everyone got roaring drunk.

The English press called Tanguy a "sailor" and categorized his landscapes as "weird," but this show was the first of Peggy's exhibitions to sell well—"because he was so good, I guess," said Peggy. Tanguy's exquisite draftsmanship and technique, his realistic rendering of a world that could not be, found an enthusiastic public. As he was fond of saying, "I expect nothing from my reflections but I am sure of my reflexes." "Suddenly," Peggy wrote, "Tanguy found himself rich for the first time in his life."

The Tanguy show marked the end of Peggy's first season as a gallery owner and dealer. She had learned a great deal about painting and painters, flinging herself wholeheartedly into her new career. As far as the press was concerned, Peggy was a Surrealist phenomenon. Captivated by modern art, she became "more and more so" as time went on and warned others to be careful when they looked at modern pictures or "you'll become an art addict." Peggy had found her niche—in the art world—where she could follow her fantasies and leave the dull day-to-day work to someone else.

STRANGE ILLUSIONS

When the Tanguys left for France, Mme. Tanguy cried, presumably for joy, but Peggy resolved to see Tanguy again before long. It was summer; the gallery was closed. Peggy had to be in Paris anyway, because Mlle. Hoffman, Florette's companion, had made the trip to France to bring Peggy her deceased mother's pearls.

Once in Paris, Peggy met Tanguy at a café, but both were terrified that Jeannette Tanguy might somehow stumble on them and make a scene. They decided to take the train to Rouen. But even there they feared Mme. Tanguy would find them and the next day made their way to Dieppe and boarded the ferry back to England. So far the only person who had spotted them was Nancy Cunard, and she was not the type to contact Tanguy's wife.

Sindbad, who was spending the summer at Yew Tree Cottage with his mother, could not understand what Tanguy was doing back in England with her but without his wife. As far as the boy could tell, Tanguy "never looked at all awake. I saw him around, but I was too innocent to know what was going on."

Tanguy amused himself by doing a great many drawings in green ink, with the meticulous care for which he was known. One of these, which had a feather sticking out of it, Peggy felt looked so much like her that she insisted he give it to her, and Tanguy obligingly dedicated it to her in his precise little scrawl. He also designed a tiny phallic motif, which he had engraved on her cigarette lighter, and painted a miniature set of landscapes for Peggy to wear as earrings. She was so eager to wear the oval pictures, dangling from a chain, that she smudged one, and Tanguy was forced to replace it with another in a different color. So Peggy had a blue Tanguy landscape for one ear and a pink scene for the other.

Soon, however, Tanguy grew bored with English country life, long walks, and reading Proust and longed to return to Paris, where his idol, André Breton, was expected back from an extended lecture tour of Mexico. Peggy had no recourse but to take Tanguy to Newhaven, where he took the ferry to France.

It was not long before Peggy decided to follow Tanguy. She had the facility of believing herself madly in love with any man she made love to, and better yet, the happiness of believing that these men took her seriously. In Paris she put Sindbad on a train to Laurence in Mégève, and met Tanguy at the same station. Beckett had lent Peggy his apartment, while he went off in Peggy's car to Brittany with Suzanne.

Ever fearful that Tanguy's wife would find them and make trouble, Tanguy and Peggy felt safe only within the confines of Beckett's apartment. In addition, a feud in the Surrealist camp made it even more difficult to appear in public. Feuds were not exactly new to the Surrealist group, which was periodically sundered by petty rivalries and dissensions. Breton's single-mindedness and the overpowering personalities of some of his disciples made such schisms inevitable. Ernst and Miró had been condemned in 1926 for selling out to commerce by accepting a commission from Sergei Diaghilev to design costumes for his *Romeo and Juliet.* Soupault had been expelled for spending too much time writing novels. De Chirico had been declared dead long before his time for abandoning his early dream-piazza style in favor of a more classical academism. Dali, the once-shining flower of Surrealism, had been dropped for his vulgarity and avarice.

In summer 1938 Breton had returned from Mexico, where the painter Diego Rivera had introduced him to the exiled Leon Trotsky. The two men spent a great deal of time together at Rivera's home where, in July 1938, they evolved a manifesto called *Towards an Independent Revolutionary Art.* The manifesto condemned Stalin's totalitarian regime, calling it an apology for crime and a twilight of mud, and appealed to their readers to resist its police spirit. The document was signed by Breton and Rivera but was in fact largely written by Trotsky. (In New York, at least, Parker Tyler was moved to observe, the manifesto "seems to have failed to spark in the soggy minds of most of our cultural representatives.")

Once Breton had come out against Stalin and his brand of Communism, he expected all the Surrealists to follow his lead. Consequently, he was furious to learn, while still in Mexico, that his long-time friend and collaborator, Paul Éluard, continued to submit poems to the Communist review *Commune*. Breton was incensed at this betrayal and no sooner had he returned to Paris in August than he chastised Éluard. Éluard reacted by breaking with the Surrealists and taking with him his close friends and supporters.

In the shifting game of alliances and recriminations, Tanguy was squeezed in the middle. He much admired the expelled men, but he was too in awe of Breton to take a stand against him. As Breton had characteristically forbidden any communication between the Surrealists and the insurgents, Tanguy found it extremely difficult to perambulate around Paris as he was bound to run into his former friends.

As the result of all these intrigues, Tanguy spent most of his time watching out for any excommunicated Surrealists and Peggy spent her time watching out for Tanguy's wife. One afternoon, Peggy passed a café with Mary Reynolds in which the Tanguys could be seen having a meal. Mary insisted that the polite thing for Peggy to do was say hello. Gamely, Peggy walked up to the couple and said, *"Bonjour."* Mme. Tanguy said nothing. She merely raised her knife and fork and neatly shot three pieces of fish at Peggy. "I must say, I don't blame her," Peggy admitted.

The idea of marriage to Tanguy rattled through Peggy's head, although it does not appear that he ever breathed a word to her on the subject. This despite the fact that Tanguy had a penchant for rich women, and, as Pierre Matisse said, "He always had them around. He got two sisters to lend him money to break the Monte Carlo bank." But Peggy concluded that "I needed a father and not another son." What was Yves Tanguy's attitude toward Peggy? Julien Levy remembered Tanguy once remarking to him, "When a girl doesn't want to go to bed with you she can tell you, 'I have the curse.' But I don't know what to tell Peggy." Levy's comment on the matter was, "Well, she *thought* she had an affair with him." Pierre Matisse, another great friend of Tanguy, when hearing of Levy's skepticism, said with a chuckle, "Julien Levy wasn't *everywhere.* Tanguy had an affair with Peggy Guggenheim. It took place."

THE SECOND SEASON

Peggy lingered in Paris through September. Hitler had annexed Austria in March 1938, and now at the end of September Chamberlain was meeting with Mussolini, Daladier, and the German leader in Munich, to stave off a full-scale invasion of Czechoslovakia. The anxiety in Paris was great: the Munich meetings could very well lead to war, as both France and the Soviet Union had treaties in which they promised to aid Czechoslovakia. The British had made it clear that they would not step in to help France. Consequently, the British and the French preferred appeasing Hitler to fighting him, and Neville Chamberlain returned a hero from Munich where Germany was given the Sudetenland—nearly one-third of Czechoslovakia. "I believe it is peace in our time . . . peace with honor," said Chamberlain in a speech he delivered back in England, to the relief of those whose memories of war were still painfully fresh. "Neither your war nor peace," cried the Surrealists, attacking both the Communists and the Fascists. But for Peggy these developments were merely distant distractions about which she was not even curious. For the moment, her world was circumscribed by Tanguy and his wife, her children, her gallery, and her self.

The painter Buffie Johnson, then a wide-eyed young woman exploring Paris, remembered meeting Peggy at a cocktail party. "She was not a very attractive person . . . rather given to dramatic pose . . . that manner of hers. I know that she was very insecure. Nevertheless, she acted as if she was very important . . . a little bit arrogant."

Eventually, Peggy had to return to London to launch the second season of Guggenheim Jeune with an exhibition of children's drawings and paintings.

Peggy got the idea from the Surrealist exhibitions where the paintings of the major Surrealist artists—Arp, Ernst, Tanguy—and Old Masters like Brueghel and Bosch were exhibited alongside the work of children and the insane. Maria Jolas sent up from her school in Neuilly some of her students' works; Laurence's daughters contributed their pictures; and Pegeen, who had taken up painting at her school in Wimbledon, was a featured artist. (Over the years Peggy would be frequently criticized for including the works of her daughter, her former husband Laurence Vail, her sister Hazel, and her friends Djuna Barnes and Gypsy Rose Lee, among the works of other, more serious artists. But in those days no one had any special claims to seriousness.)

The show, which opened on October 14, 1938, attracted little attention and Peggy's second season was off to a slow start. There were better exhibitions elsewhere. Most of the excitement of the moment was generated by Pablo Picasso's antiwar picture *Guernica.* The painting had been brought to London by Penrose and a committee formed expressly for that purpose and was exhibited, not long after Chamberlain's return from Munich, at the New Burlington galleries alongside the studies and sketches that Picasso had done in preparation for it.

On the heels of the children's show, Peggy scheduled an exhibition, "Collages, Papiers-Collés, and Photo-Montages," for November. *Collage* is technically a pasting of extraneous elements to a surface, but Surrealists preferred to label *papiers collés* those compositions, such as Picasso's Cubist pictures, wherein scraps of paper or bits of string are incorporated into a formal structure or design. In contrast, for the Surrealists collage was yet another avenue of experimentation leading to hidden psychological content without regard to a picture's aesthetic quality. Max Ernst, for example, cut out engravings, advertisements, and odds and ends from newspapers or magazines and put them together arbitrarily to create enigmatic and disturbing images. Jean Arp cut out papers colored on one side and put them all face down. He then shuffled them about to come up with a composition dictated by chance. Kurt Schwitters, a master of collage, collected string, matches, and refuse from the streets and incorporated them into *Merz,* a meaningless word with which he labeled all his collages. In Peggy's exhibition there were collages by Breton and Ernst, Picasso and Gris, as well as by Roland Penrose, whose work the *New English Weekly* said was "very excitingly far beyond the kindergarten stage."

Penrose was one of the foremost collectors of Surrealist art in England, in addition to being the owner of Peggy's neighbor the London Gallery. Peggy had a Tanguy painting left from her July show that she wanted very much for Penrose to buy. When Penrose came to the gallery to see the Tanguy he was immediately taken with the painting but Peggy was even more taken with him. Dashingly dark and handsome, young and rich, Penrose was just the stuff Peggy's dreams of English country idylls were made of.

Penrose's house near Yew Tree Cottage in Hampstead was crammed with Surrealist pictures. It was easy enough for Peggy, on the pretext of wanting to see the collection, to repair to Penrose's country retreat and pounce on him. She discovered, and then wrote in her memoirs for all the world to know, that "He had one eccentricity: when he slept with women he tied up their wrists with anything that was handy. Once he used my belt, but another time in his house he brought out a pair of ivory bracelets from the Sudan. They were attached with a chain and Penrose had a key to lock them. It was extremely uncomfortable to spend the night this way, but if you spent it with Penrose it was the only way."

Oddly enough, what upset Penrose the most about Peggy's indiscretion was that she had also written that he "was a painter, he wasn't a good painter, but he was a painter," and had gratuitously added, "He looked like a man made of straw and he really seemed quite empty. His ex-wife had once said of him, 'He is a barn to which one could never set fire.'" When Peggy's memoirs were reissued in 1979, with all the transparent pseudonyms she had used in the original to protect herself changed to real names, Penrose gave his consent on condition that she delete these two offensive remarks. The references to ivory bracelets, chains, and belts did not bother him at all. "I thought it was a lot of nonsense," he said, "but if she wanted to write about it that was up to her. I objected when she said Wrenclose [her pseudonym for Penrose] was a bad painter and I don't know where she got that absurd thing about Valentine saying I had no passion. Valentine would never have said that. Until we separated we had a very passionate relationship."

Was Penrose's relationship with Peggy serious? "It was never very serious," Penrose admitted. "How could it be serious when she went to bed with everyone she met? She was very much in heat, one might say, anyone could jump into bed with her." Peggy intimated in her memoirs that their "affair" was more than just a passing fancy, but Penrose insisted, "There was never any sensation that it would last. Peggy knew I was passionately in love with Lee Miller who was then [married and] in Egypt. She had spent two summers with me and I moaned about her and Peggy said, 'Why the hell don't you just go there?' And so I did and she came back the next summer and stayed." Peggy liked to claim that she had "arranged" Penrose's marriage to Lee, and indeed she had fanned Penrose's desire to convince Lee to return to England.

In December 1938, Peggy scheduled a show of leather portrait dolls and masks done by one Marie Wassilieff. Peggy had met her in Montparnasse, where she ran a canteen as well as an art school, and was something of an institution. Greta Garbo, Marlene Dietrich, and Josephine Baker were among the stars portrayed by the tiny Russian, who was the life of many a party with her impromptu Cossack dancing. Along with the dolls and masks, Wassilieff showed celluloid hats and head-dresses, guaranteed washable and rainproof. One onlooker remarked that "pink ones, such as the one Miss Guggenheim wore at the private view, cast a becoming rosy blush over one's features." At least one newspaper reporter suggested that people go buy their Christmas presents at Guggenheim Jeune. Along with the Russian's fanciful headwear, Peggy, with an eye, no doubt, to filling many a Christmas stocking, had an exhibition of pottery by a woman called Jill Salaman.

Nineteen thirty-nine was to be an uneasy year; people were increasingly frightened, following Germany's annexation of Austria and the Sudetenland. By March Hitler had started on a series of new aggressions, forcing the president of Czechoslovakia to yield Bohemia and Moravia —what was left of Czechoslovakia—and taking Memel, a strip of land above East Prussia on the Baltic Sea. Shortly after, Hitler announced his intended annexation of Danzig in Poland, and Britain and France became greatly alarmed. "Appeasement" was dead.

Peggy appeared unperturbed. It had not yet occurred to her that these ominous developments in Europe would in any way affect her. She rang in the New Year with a show advertised as an "exhibition of works forming part of a unique scientific research" by Dr. Grace W. Pailthorpe and Reuben Mednikoff. Dr. Pailthorpe, a psychiatrist and surgeon, founder of the Scientific Institute for Delinquency, was fascinated by Surrealist ideas. Together with Mednikoff, an artist, she explored and studied the unconscious through a series of automatic paintings designed to expose the hidden infantile or unconscious side of personality. The show aroused widespread interest. Pailthorpe provided an explanatory text revealing the meaning of the various pictures. "With few exceptions," observed the *London Bulletin,* "the visitors to this show expressed the opinion that the works were the most authentic Surrealist art yet exhibited."

Guggenheim Jeune attracted a great many visitors. The gallery was an ideal place to meet new people. Anyone who wandered in was likely to find its winsome proprietor dressed in a simple suit, giving her book-keeping a once-over, jotting down calculations, or just leaning in the

.doorway, her hand at her throat clutching a handkerchief, remarkably accessible and open to new friendships. She might grumble a bit if a stranger approached her, but if the stranger were persistent, within a few minutes Peggy would be chatting affably and peppering their conversation with her "Reallys?"

When the neighboring galleries brought illustrious visitors to London, they would stop into Guggenheim Jeune and introduce themselves to its owner. In this fashion she met Piet Mondrian, who had created controversy in the world of art with his strictly geometrical, two-dimensional paintings. Like Kandinsky, Mondrian looked like a well-heeled banker, arriving nattily dressed and carrying a briefcase. He was known to set to work restoring his own pictures on the spot if he found one in need of attention, aided by the contents of this handy accouterment. With Peggy, Mondrian talked about places to go dancing and nightclubs, even though she found his English difficult to understand, his French peculiar, and hoped—for his sake—that he did better with his native Dutch. Together they went dancing and Peggy, who loved to fox-trot, jitterbug, and tango and often had friends over to listen to records, was surprised to discover how lively and spry Mondrian, a septuagenarian, proved to be.

Mondrian was in London for a large exhibition held at the London Gallery, called "Living Art in England," which included sculptors Barbara Hepworth and Henry Moore, Surrealist painters Eileen Agar, Rita Kernn-Larsen, and the team of Pailthorpe and Mednikoff, Roland Penrose, Mondrian, and several others. In the group were a number of Continental artists who, like Mondrian, had come to England to escape the growing agitation in Europe. With the Germans advancing on their homelands, artists from Germany and occupied Austria and Czechoslovakia had begun trickling into the country.

Thus, included in the exhibition "Living Art in England" were such artists as Naum Gabo, Henghes, and Oskar Kokoschka, the Expressionist painter, whose works had been highly influential in Germany, Austria, and Czechoslovakia. Ultimately, the war would make it impossible to seek a refuge in England, and America would become the next haven for artists. In the meanwhile, Peggy benefited from the tragic turn of world events. The anxious exodus toward England created a ferment of intellectual and artistic activity in London that would not have existed without "the bangs of the dictators and the pirouettes of Mr. Chamberlain."

One of the artists presented in the "Living Art in England" show was a fair-haired young Englishman called John Tunnard. He walked into Guggenheim Jeune one afternoon dressed in a loud coat, paused to scan the room through round glasses until he spotted Peggy, and introduced himself. He asked permission to show her his gouaches, which,

(ABOVE, LEFT) *Peggy's maternal grandfather, James Seligman.*

(ABOVE, RIGHT) *Jefferson Seligman, a member of the Early Riser's Club,
and one of Peggy's most memorable uncles. (Courtesy J. & W. Seligman)*

(BELOW) *Meyer Guggenheim surrounded by his seven sons (left to right):
Benjamin (Peggy's father), Murry, Isaac, Meyer, Daniel, Solomon, Simon, and William.
(Courtesy the Nassau County Museum)*

(OPPOSITE, TOP) *A five-year-old Peggy (right) and her adored older sister Benita in 1904.*

(OPPOSITE, BOTTOM) *The elegant Ben Guggenheim shortly before his death on the* Titanic.

(ABOVE) *Peggy (top row center) surrounded by the graduating class of the Jacoby School in* Little Women, *1915.*

(BELOW) *A bright-eyed ten-year-old Peggy posing for the camera.*

Benita, the beauty of the family.

Hazel as a young woman, 1919.

Peggy in Paris, 1920.

(LEFT) *Laurence Vail,*
the King of Bohemia.

(BELOW) *Peggy as a young*
society girl out on the town
with Boris Dembo,
Paris, 1922.

A newly wed Peggy photographed by Man Ray, Paris, 1922.

(ABOVE) *Peggy with Mina Loy in their Paris shop, 1927. (Bettmann Archive)*

(BELOW, LEFT) *Sindbad photographed by Berenice Abbott, 1926.*

(BELOW, RIGHT) *Pegeen pouting.*

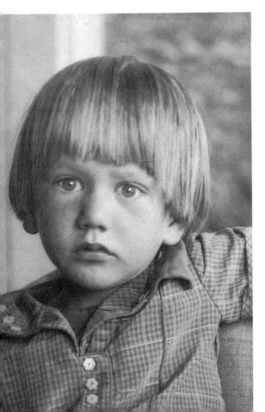

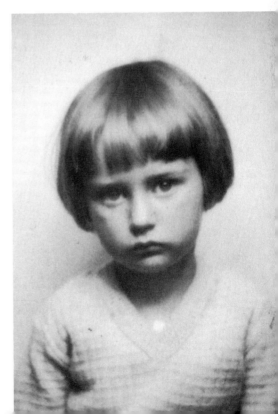

Peggy and the love of her life, John Ferrar Holms, standing with Sindbad and Pegeen in front of Hangover Hall, 1933.

Peggy and Douglas Garman, 1935.

Florette visiting Peggy and Pegeen at Yew Tree Cottage, 1935.

Yew Tree Cottage.

(OPPOSITE, TOP) *Peggy with Laurence Vail and Kay Boyle, exchanging Pegeen and Sindbad, 1936.*

(OPPOSITE, BOTTOM) *Peggy's uncle Solomon Guggenheim seated before one of his many Rudolf Bauers. (AP/Wide World Photos)*

(LEFT, TOP) *Peggy on the lawn at Yew Tree Cottage seated next to Samuel Beckett and a reclining Geer van Velde, while Debbie Garman looks on.*

(LEFT, MIDDLE) *Peggy and Yves Tanguy during their affair, 1938.*

(LEFT, BOTTOM) *Peggy and Herbert Read, seated in front of Yves Tanguy's* The Sun in Its Jewel Case, *discuss plans for their museum, 1939. (Gisèle Freund; courtesy The Solomon R. Guggenheim Museum)*

(OPPOSITE) *Peggy in Paris, 1939,*
posing with a construction
by Antoine Pevsner.

(OPPOSITE, INSET) *The earrings*
Tanguy designed for Peggy.

(ABOVE) *The adolescent Sindbad.*

(LEFT) *Pegeen in Mégève,*
where she spent the early days
of World War II with her
father at the Chalet des Six
Enfants, 1940.

(RIGHT) *Max Ernst enthroned at Hale House in his Victorian chair. (Berenice Abbott)*

(BELOW) *The artists in exile, each seated next to the one he most disliked. From left to right (first row): Roberto Matta Echaurren, Ossip Zadkine, Yves Tanguy, Max Ernst, Marc Chagall, Fernand Léger; (second row): André Breton, Piet Mondrian, André Masson, Amédée Ozenfant, Jacques Lipchitz, Pavel Tchelitchew; (third row): Kurt Seligmann, Eugene Berman. (George Platt Lynes; courtesy The Museum of Modern Art, New York)*

though of excellent quality, he had not yet been able to sell. To Peggy the painter resembled Groucho Marx, but she was impressed by the lyrical colors of his work and his lively manner and decided then and there to give him an exhibition. Tunnard was delighted. He was so accustomed to rejection that he came close to looking over his shoulder and asking, "Who, me?" When someone admired his work, he would shrug and insist, "Don't be silly, don't be silly." "Tunnard was a great jazz enthusiast, a good painter," said Roland Penrose. "He also showed at the London Gallery and I was glad when she took him on." Before the Tunnard show could proceed, Peggy had scheduled an exhibition of the works of Wolfgang Paalen, from February 15 to March 11. Paalen had turned to Surrealism in 1935 and in his search for new techniques invented *fumage,* by which the painter used trails of smoke left on the surface from a burning candle to improvise images dictated by the unconscious. In Paalen's case, these images were often morbid—skeletons, knives, and birds of prey—products of his troubled imagination. What caught the public's eye was an umbrella made entirely of sponge titled *Nuage Articule.*

When the Tunnard show opened, the curly-haired artist excited as much attention for the eccentric manner of his dress—a startling blue checked suit, light blue pullover, and bright pink tie—as for his pictures. An elderly man walking around the exhibit of musical instruments and images rendered in a surrealistic fashion remarked that obviously, "the man who did them isn't healthy." Whereupon, "like lightning, Mr. Tunnard turned a complete somersault, landing before the carping critic with extended hand saying:—'I'm *perfectly* healthy—could I do this if I weren't?' "

The Museum of Modern Art had opened in New York in 1929. Its forward-looking director, Alfred Barr, Jr., organized a series of exhibitions to acquaint the American people with the major currents in modern European art, such as Cubism and Surrealism. The MOMA, as it came to be known, had departments dealing with film, architecture, and design—areas into which no museum had ventured before. Consequently, people in London began talking about an art center based on the model of the MOMA in New York. Roland Penrose and E. L. T. Mesens had discussed with Helena Rubinstein the possibility of forming an arts council. But it was Peggy who seized on the idea and appropriated the project for her own.

Guggenheim Jeune had created a stir, yet had not sold all that many pictures and the overhead was considerable. In the first year the gallery lost six hundred pounds, and Peggy did not much like to lose money. She wondered if there were not another way she might be involved with art without the commercial uncertainties. "I felt," she wrote, "that if I was losing that money I might as well lose a lot more and do something worthwhile." She decided to close the gallery and start a real museum for modern art. Peggy had disregarded Hilla Rebay's offensive letter when the baroness wrote to her that she should start a collection and avoid being "in trade," yet the idea had taken root. With her usual single-mindedness, Peggy approached the man to help her make her dream a reality, Herbert Read, and asked him to be the director.

A shy, reserved man who looked like a well-scrubbed farm boy, Read was the outstanding art scholar of the time and a well-known personality in art circles. He had a reputation for brilliance as the "arch highbrow of modern art critics." In countless articles and books, including his *Surrealism* and the highly influential *Art Now,* Read had proselytized for avant-garde art. He had been a professor of fine arts at the University of Edinburgh and a lecturer at the University of Liverpool. In addition, he was a prime organizer of the English Surrealist exhibition in 1936 and had written the introduction to the catalogue. Despite his natural shyness, Read was always ready to speak out in panels, symposiums, and meetings on the superiority and merits of modern art, and in particular Surrealism.

At first Read was resistant to taking Peggy's idea seriously. The son of a Yorkshire farmer who died when Read was nine, he was always worried about money. Since 1933 he had been an editor of the *Burlington Magazine* and was reluctant to give up his security on the whim of a rich American woman known as much for her affairs with artists as for her seriousness about their art. Yet Read was apostolic about modern art and if Peggy really wanted to establish a museum for its appreciation, said Penrose, he "wouldn't let an opportunity like that pass."

Read left his job with *Burlington Magazine* and agreed to become the director of Peggy's proposed museum. He signed a five-year contract with her, voluntarily offering not to accept any money until the museum began operations. He did borrow a year's salary in advance, so that he could buy into Routledge's publishing house. Wyn Henderson was to be the "registrar" of the museum and Peggy's exact title was left up in the air.

It was a strange combination, the highbrow scholar and the flighty American. With his distinguished air and easy manners, "he looked like a prime minister," Peggy admiringly wrote. He symbolized to her a father figure, a man with authority and purpose. Behind his back she called him "Papa," although he was not much older than herself. Peggy had him autograph all his books for her and gushed, "He treated me the way Disraeli treated Queen Victoria, adding, "I suppose I was rather in love with him, spiritually." Read was flattered by Peggy's schoolgirl affection and wide-eyed admiration. "He had fairly close, warm relationships with women," explained Read's son Benedict. "I suspect if things got too close he would shy off. He was a very reserved man." This type of relationship, he went on, "has happened with my father and other women. He may have been terrified of my mother," and not let them progress too far. Peggy flirted, but Read resisted her sexual advances and became a lifelong friend instead of another brief affair. "I think that was one of the sources of their friendship: that he never did," observed Read's son Piers Paul Read. "Probably he was too busy." And there was Read's wife, Ludo, who "would have been on her guard."

The news of Peggy's and Read's proposed museum was met in some quarters with less than total enthusiasm. The London Gallery group was quite resentful that the idea they had bandied about had been expropriated by Peggy. Mesens was particularly annoyed that there was to be no part for him in the fledgling venture, and engaged in intrigues against it. Djuna Barnes made it clear to Peggy that she thought the whole project misguided. Soon, she said, Peggy would be merely signing checks while Herbert Read ran the show.

As Peggy told the press, the plan was to create a museum that would be more than simply a place to hang pictures. Artists would be able to interrelate with the public and with other artists and like-minded souls. The collection that Peggy had slowly begun to amass from her own gallery shows and from the neighboring galleries was to form the nucleus of the permanent collection. The idea was to secure donations and to borrow as many of the works for the museum as possible, as Peggy was convinced that she could not afford to buy all the pieces. Read suggested that their opening exhibition should be a pictorial survey of the period they were hoping to cover. Herbert Read sat down and wrote out a list of all the nonrealistic movements in art beginning with Picasso and Cubism in 1910, including the names of all the artists he felt should be represented in the museum. It was meant to be a comprehensive historical list covering Constructivism, Suprematism, *Merz,* de Stijl, Surrealism, and Futurism in addition to Cubism. Neither Cézanne nor Matisse was included, because Peggy did not feel that they "fit in." It was to be Peggy's function to go to Paris and try to borrow representative works from Read's list for their first exhibition, which was scheduled for the fall of 1939.

In the meantime Guggenheim Jeune continued to function until the end of the season in June. A large exhibition of "Abstract and Concrete Art" was due to arrive from Paris in May. The abstract and concrete was an opposing trend to the Surrealism Peggy had shown almost exclusively. Indeed, the *London Bulletin,* when it ran the preface Wassily Kandinsky had written for the show in French in which he likened painting to music for which one must "open the eyes," felt obliged to disclaim its views. Abstract art was concerned not with the rendering of dream images and unconscious content, but rather with form and design.

In the late 1930s, abstract art was considered suspect by many in the avant-garde. Indeed, it was thought that abstract painting, which evolved from Cézanne, Matisse, and Picasso, divorced painting from realism but impoverished it by eliminating meaning, history, humanity. It was accused of "byzantism, escapism, absolutism, transcendentalism," and there was a sharp division between the Surrealists and those who believed in abstraction.

A DARWINIAN DILEMMA

Flirting outrageously with any man who came her way, Peggy began to pursue sex as a parallel career to her gallery. She chased men totally uninterested in her, men she barely knew. Not a few were outright homosexuals, flattered to be asked and too gentlemanly to say no. Frequent sexual encounters made Peggy feel alluring, desirable, wanted. Picking up the scent of sex, Peggy would light up girlishly with eyes sparkling, lips smiling, hands fidgeting at her neck. It was quite clear that she would not rebuff any advances.

But Peggy was confused when it came to love. An afternoon of groping on the sofa could in her mind become an "affair," a one-night stand a "lover." It was easier for Peggy to perform the sexual act than to arrive at any true intimacy. She did not like kissing, just the bare essentials. Hopping from one bed to another in the tiny art community of London, Peggy was considered a nymphomaniac, to be had for the asking. She preferred to remember her famous lovers like Tanguy and Beckett, but there were many less illustrious whose names were not as cherished. In a Surrealist world, where Peggy neither sculpted nor painted nor wrote, she used sex to defy convention.

"Llewelyn" was Peggy's pseudonym for an English sculptor, well known in the Surrealist group, which he joined in 1935 at age twenty-four. Passionately concerned about the Spanish Civil War, Llewelyn organized, along with his fellow Surrealists, a three-day auction of paintings to benefit the Spanish relief. Peggy met Llewelyn when she was asked to help collect pictures for the project. Soon a show of Llewelyn's work was scheduled at Guggenheim Jeune in June. Llewelyn's etchings were declared "skillful in technique, disquieting in intention, excremental, testicular, vaginal"—just the sort of subjects Peggy had on her mind.

Lanky and shaggy-haired, Llewelyn was happily married to a member of the Darwin family. Nevertheless, while his wife was ill and he was feeling depressed, Llewelyn succumbed to Peggy's habitual flirtations during a weekend house party in Dieppe. "He slept with me and no one was supposed to know, of course," said Peggy. "It was very stupid." Full of remorse, Llewelyn was terrified lest anyone find out and tell his sick wife. After two days of Llewelyn's nerves, Peggy left the party to return to London. Llewelyn heaved a sigh of relief. "I think he was very happy when I left," Peggy candidly admitted. "Because it was a worry to him, we'd be found out. He saw me off, and gave me a little bottle of brandy."

Sometime later Peggy discovered, much to her surprise, that nearly forty-one, she was pregnant. Ironically, at this time Llewelyn invited Peggy to his house to see his wife's pottery work. "The minute I went into the room, I knew we were *both* pregnant," recalled Peggy. Later, Mrs. Llewelyn suffered a miscarriage, confirming Peggy's suspicions. Peggy decided to offer her unborn baby to Llewelyn and his disappointed wife. "His wife's baby had died," Peggy reasoned, "and I had one I didn't know what to do with it. So, I thought to give it to them. It was a crazy idea anyhow." Llewelyn was less than overjoyed at Peggy's offer, and declined. To begin with, there would be the business of explaining to his wife where the baby had come from.

Peggy was left with only one alternative, and was terribly annoyed at Llewelyn because "he never offered to pay anything for the abortion. I suppose he thought I could afford it, which I could, but he never came to see me in the hospital or anything."

Peggy was still pregnant at the closing-night party at Guggenheim Jeune, and felt sick and queasy through most of the affair. As guests arrived they looked forward to projections of Gisèle Freund's color photographs of artists and intellectuals—James Joyce, André Breton, Vita Sackville-West, T. S. Eliot. But Freund and her projector were soon forgotten as a huge crush of people, some invited, many not, arrived and headed for the well-stocked open bar. John Tunnard again turned heads in his peacock-blue suit, a green-and-red scarf, and a large red carnation in his buttonhole. Another guest, Leon Underwood, boasted to as many women as were interested that his ribbed velvet suit was made out of the same cloth Welsh miners reserved for their Sunday waistcoats. The eighteen-year-old Anne Goossens, a self-proclaimed "hot swing" and jitterbug addict, was adjudged the prettiest girl in the room in her mauve turban, high-heeled cork sandals, and theatrical wrist-length net gloves, while an enraptured onlooker labeled her a "baby Marlene Dietrich."

Mrs. Llewelyn, noticing how pale and ill Peggy looked, asked innocently what the matter was. Peggy said she had a sprained ankle, for it was true that she could barely walk. "It was peculiar, I couldn't walk. I don't know. And she said to her husband, 'Take her over your shoulder and bring her around.' Can you imagine?" Peggy recounted. So Llewelyn carried Peggy—pregnant with his baby—from party to party at the suggestion of his considerate, and blissfully unaware, wife.

Guggenheim Jeune had been put to rest, to be supplanted by a more brilliant achievement, a permanent modern art museum. But for many observers, Peggy would "always be jeune, for her approach to life and art is romantic, wayward, capricious, adventurous and disarmingly candid." Peggy emerged from her experience with Guggenheim Jeune staunchly committed to modern art, wildly enthusiastic about her new mission, and delighted with the "madly egotistical" artists she had met. "They're full of wonderful ideas and fantasies, they are so much more alive than stockbrokers and lawyers," she said. She was now, irrevocably, one of their world.

Immediately after the closing of Guggenheim Jeune, on June 22, Peggy retired to a nursing home to have her abortion. She then repaired to Yew Tree Cottage to convalesce and spent most of July rereading Proust. From her sickbed Peggy feverishly continued making plans for the new museum, writing lists, and balancing budgets. She did not delude herself: the new venture was going to be expensive, and since she never felt she had enough money, she decided to take some cost-cutting measures. She sold her Delage car and replaced it with a smaller, less costly Talbot. New clothes she would simply do without. And although Peggy was reluctant to cut back on her obligations to her friends or her former husband, she nevertheless suggested to the able-bodied Djuna Barnes that she might go out and get a job. This threw Djuna, whose art was always paramount, into a panic and a frenzy of letter-writing to friends about Peggy's treachery. But Peggy calmly insisted that money had to be saved somewhere.

Read called to tell her that he had found the perfect place for the museum, Sir Kenneth Clark's house on Portland Place. Feeble and wobbly, Peggy left her bed to see it. It was so large, Peggy thought that it would be cheaper if she moved in and lived there alongside the museum. Mrs. Read had the same idea and almost instantly arguments started as to which floor each would have. Fortunately, as matters turned out,

Peggy did not sign the lease on the place, because her lawyers were out of town.

The year before, an imperious, fashionably made-up woman had walked into Guggenheim Jeune and introduced herself as Nellie van Doesburg, the widow of Theo van Doesburg, the painter and theoretician who with Piet Mondrian had founded the influential review *De Stijl*. Peggy had become reacquainted with Nellie during the "Abstract and Concrete Art" show in May, in which Theo van Doesburg's work had been exhibited. Huge brass Calder bracelets jangling and a large brass wire concoction pinned on her dress, Nellie cornered one gallery-goer after another to show them the abstract picture that had nearly sent her husband to jail more than twenty years earlier. Blue eyed, red-haired, and very pretty, Nellie enchanted Peggy with her warm vitality and good humor. Soon Nellie became Peggy's "most adorable, dearest friend for years. She was very chic and marvelously vivacious, full of energy, absolutely bursting with vitality."

In Nellie, Peggy found a friend who shared wholeheartedly her enthusiasm for modern art. Indeed, Nellie felt herself to be the sacred guardian of her husband's reputation, just as Peggy felt herself to be the messiah of the avant-garde.

Generally, Peggy did not much like women: "Women are so boring." Yet she adored Nellie, who was very much like her, only an improved version, charming where Peggy could be abrasive, pulled together where Peggy was slapdash, and well made up where Peggy was always smeared and smudged.

Nellie was excited about Peggy's plans for a modern art museum and promised to help her locate paintings and sculptures for it. As a "de Stijl baby," Nellie had a great many contacts in the art world, and was extremely knowledgeable about twentieth-century art. First, she went over the list Read had given Peggy of artists and art movements that should be represented, and made changes where she felt Read had erred. Later, Marcel Duchamp in Paris also revised the list and put his stamp on it. In the meantime, Nellie suggested that Peggy should come with her to France, where Nellie had a house outside of Meudon, and that they should travel around the Midi a bit before the serious business of collecting art began.

PART V

WAR CLOUDS

THE PHONY WAR

Peggy and Nellie van Doesburg set off in August from Yew Tree Cottage for the south of France, with Sindbad jammed into the back seat of his mother's Talbot. The sixteen-year-old Sindbad was allowed to steer the car through Normandy, but once in Paris, he was dispatched via train to his father in Mégève. Peggy had planned to visit the Surrealist painter Gordon Onslow-Ford, who was ensconced in a château in the south of France that was overrun with other Surrealists, such as Breton and Tanguy. Tanguy had once suggested that Peggy meet him there. These last several months, however, after their escapade in Paris, Tanguy's letters to Peggy had grown rarer and vaguer, to the point where Peggy was sure that he had another love interest, as was in fact the case. Tanguy had forgotten Peggy and begun romancing the American painter and heiress Kay Sage to whom Peggy had sent Tanguy in the hope of selling her a picture. As Kay was still married to an Italian nobleman, the Prince of San Faustino, Peggy snidely referred to her as the "Princess." Even with Tanguy out of the romantic picture, Peggy hoped to extract a Surrealist painting or two from Onslow-Ford for her museum.

Gaily, Peggy and Nellie traveled south, plans for the future museum in their heads, chatting about everyone they knew, comparing lovers, past and present, eating at small inns and restaurants by the side of the road, and staying, wherever possible, at the cheapest hotels. The war hanging ominously over the European Continent during that summer of 1939 seemed a matter of no concern for either of them.

Peggy decided to visit Laurence in Mégève. She had often promised to do so, but now with Nellie in tow, Peggy could stay at a hotel and use Nellie as a buffer to Kay Boyle's insufferable needling.

Forgetting about Onslow-Ford and his Surrealists, Peggy and Nellie arrived in the charming little village in the French Alps, near the Swiss border, to find Laurence surrounded by Sindbad and his girls, Bobbie, Pegeen, Apple, Kathe, and Clover. Peggy and Kay still loathed each other, but Peggy could get along with Laurence quite nicely. She referred to him as her "eternal husband," who became, she said, "one of my best friends, afterwards—when he stopped beating me up." The children stared in awe at Nellie with her flamboyant dress and bangles, and Peggy with her irreverent and offbeat remarks.

Although the visit went smoothly enough, after a week Peggy and Nellie went on to Grasse, high in the hills above the Riviera, not far from Mégève. There Nellie had a friend for whom she had once organized an abstract art show in Paris, a certain Mr. Sides, at whose house Peggy and Nellie made themselves at home, enjoying the wonderful meals and wines of France.

Every day Peggy would drive Nellie to the seashore for a swim and sun in one of the many inlets and rocks along the coast. Peggy was eager to show Nellie all the places she had lived in with Laurence and with John Holms. Occasionally they paused to weep over dead "husbands," Nellie for hers and Peggy for John. In Pramousquier, Peggy was stunned to see her former home occupied by a middle-class couple and stripped of any bohemian allure.

Nina and Wassily Kandinsky were vacationing in Le Canadel and Peggy and Nellie went to visit them. Characteristically, Peggy chose a run-down, cheap hotel over the grand, comfortable hotel where the Kandinskys were staying. Kandinsky, with barely any money himself, could hardly hide his astonishment that a rich woman would choose to stay in such a dump. But Peggy, always looking to prolong her association with each dollar, did not mind going from door to door in the hope of finding a cheaper hostelry just up the street.

It was in Le Canadel that Peggy first learned of the general mobilization for war. Hitler's foreign minister, the aristocratic Joachim von Ribbentrop, had signed in Moscow a mutual nonaggression pact with Stalin. To every thinking person it could mean only one thing: war. It had long been assumed that any eastward advance of Germany would be checked by the Russian colossus. But now, with Stalin neutralized and a secret agreement arrived at for the partition of Poland, there was no power to halt Hitler's ambitions to the east. Already in March 1939, while Peggy was making plans for her museum with Read, Germany's annexation of those parts of Czechoslovakia not ceded by the Munich pact of the previous September (a plot, James Joyce was convinced, to distract the world from his recently completed *Finnegans Wake*) had provoked a pledge on the part of England and France to come to the aid of Poland should Hitler's eye fall on it, too.

The news of the Russo-Nazi pact sent frissons of anxiety down the spines of Frenchmen. In Paris the prime minister, Édouard Daladier, ordered a general alert and mobilization. Thousands volunteered for the army as monuments along the Champs Élysées were sandbagged in case of air attack, and treasures from the Louvre and the cathedrals of Rouen and Chartres were packed up and sent off to hiding places. Gas masks were issued for fear of chemical attack and cars ran at night with only one blue-painted headlight, as streetlights glowed phantasmically under coats of navy paint.

On September 1, 1939, barely a week after the signing of the pact with Stalin, Hitler sent his meticulously trained and equipped army, Luftwaffe, and tanks into Poland, realizing everyone's worst fears. By evening, twenty Polish towns had been destroyed. On September 3 the Germans sank a U-boat off the coast of Ireland, and on the same day war was declared on Germany by England and France for the second time in twenty-five years. Australia, Canada, South Africa, and New Zealand joined their mother country and World War II was officially begun.

News bulletins carried daily reports of the German war machine's efficiency and ruthlessness, which in little over two weeks brought most of Poland to collapse. Hitler's minister of information labeled it a *Blitzkrieg,* or lightning war, and people believed it. By the end of September only Warsaw, with its citizens starving and twenty-five thousand dead bodies rotting in the rubble, resisted the Nazi onslaught. Each morning, a Chopin polonaise was broadcast over the radio to hearten a defiant Polish people, but finally, on September 28, after days of heavy bombing, Warsaw fell, and a funeral dirge was heard in its stead.

At first no one could believe that the war could go on for more than a few weeks. Surely the Allies with their superior arsenals and enormous armies could crush Hitler. Mr. Sides, to whose house Nellie and Peggy returned, kept his radio on day and night for news of unfolding events and reassured Peggy that the war could not last. Why, only last July in Paris there had been the most formidable display of war machinery ever assembled, representing hundreds of thousands of troops. French, Indochinese, Senegalese, Irish, Scottish, English, Foreign Legionnaires, Grenadier Guards, and even Alpine chasers on skis had paraded around the Place de l'Etoile, while French Blochs and British Wellingtons and Spitfires thundered in the air. (No one wanted to remember Hitler's own demonstration in Berlin the previous April of German military might—tanks, artillery, guns, and squadrons of bombers roaring above cheering crowds.) Peggy was crazy to worry about the war, Sides concluded optimistically.

But Peggy was worried now. Her children, Sindbad and Pegeen, were in Mégève with Laurence, fortunately not too far away. What would happen to all of them? How could she return to England and start her museum if there was a war going on? Would there be bombings and catastrophes? Until now, she had not thought much about the possibility of war, let alone the ramifications; she had been too preoccupied with plans for her museum. Like millions of other people, Peggy had assumed the Munich pact would keep Hitler at bay. It only now dawned on her that perhaps the reason Kenneth Clark had been so willing to rent his house for her museum was that he saw a war coming. What should she do?

Laurence, who had reclaimed his position as head of the family, calmed Peggy down. Returning to England, he declared, was out of the question, proposed museum or not. Bombing might start there at any time. In any event, it would be preferable for all of them to be in the same country. Sindbad would be placed in boarding school in France and Pegeen could stay with Laurence in Mégève. Everything would be all right. "I did not know what to do about the future," Peggy remembered, "but Laurence kept very calm and decided everything for me."

Peggy reluctantly wrote Herbert Read of her decision to remain in France and abandon the museum for the moment. It was ridiculous to persist with such a project in wartime and expose valuable paintings and works of art to German air raids. In addition, who would be able to find the time to organize or want to attend exhibitions, encumbered by steel helmets and gas masks? Read was bitterly disappointed and believed, on the contrary, that London would be an ideal place for a museum in wartime. Nevertheless, his dream would have to wait. "The war made all the plans crash," said Henry Moore. Peggy did advance Read half of his expected salary, about twenty-five hundred pounds.

With the museum shelved for the time being, there was not much for Peggy to do but worry. That autumn of 1939, most Frenchmen were convinced, along with Sides, that the war could not possibly last more than a couple of weeks. The Allied superiority in arms and men would surely crush the upstart Hun. Yet everyone felt anxious and Peggy was terrified. In Grasse, where Peggy and Nellie were, lines of inexperienced and ill-equipped young soldiers were being marched to who-knew-where. Many were billeted in and around Grasse. Rumors spread unchecked and unheeded. "One day," Peggy wrote, "we were told that Cannes would be bombed in two hours. It didn't seem to make much impression on anyone."

Peggy was restless and still drove to the beach and her old haunts even though the roads were crowded with cars heading home. Gas lines seemed a minor inconvenience as long as Peggy could continue to get about. She spent a great deal of time in Cannes dispatching telegrams to Laurence or to England, waiting on interminable lines with other equally tense and depressed people.

Her hopes for the future scrambled, her life in suspension, Peggy needed something to distract her. It occurred to her to set up an artists' colony for the duration of the war, a place for painters and sculptors to work in safety. Artists would come to this oasis and, in exchange for a small allowance from Peggy, would give her the pictures they produced. Nellie thought it was a good idea and agreed to be the colony's secretary. Peggy, never happier than when she was making plans, sent enthusiastic postcards to friends in England outlining her new project. Peter Hoare spent an evening amusing himself by imagining the strange bedfellows Peggy's colony would attract. It made an ironic contrast to the ever-darkening streets of London, where blackouts had already started and people carried their gas masks around with them in cardboard boxes. Most evenings rang with the shriek of air raid alarms.

In the south of France, Peggy and Nellie drove around looking for a château or hotel that would make a suitable artists' retreat, but by the time they made it up to Paris and "met a few of the people we had thought of inviting, I realized," said Peggy, "what a hell life would have been. They not only could not have lived together, but did not even want to come to dinner with each other." With a sigh, Peggy scuttled the misbegotten idea of an artists' colony and she and Nellie moved into Nellie's house in Meudon, near Paris.

In Paris, Peggy found most of her old friends preoccupied with the war. The five thousand or so expatriate Americans who had not left France during the Depression were now trying desperately to get back to the country they had abandoned twenty years earlier. Bookings were practically impossible to get and the trains leaving Paris for Bordeaux, from where the United States Line sailed, were so jammed that people stood even in the baggage cars.

Those still in Paris were waiting for the time when they, too, would be sailing from Bordeaux. Yves Tanguy was living in Kay Sage's apartment on the Île St. Louis, waiting for his travel documents to come through in order to follow Sage to New York. He spent his last days in France with his wife, beseeching Peggy to take care of the loyal Jeannette when he was gone. Peggy made friends with Jeannette, now that they were no longer rivals, and even bought a Tanguy from her, paying in monthly installments so that she would have something to live on. Djuna Barnes, disgusted with Peggy's earlier ultimatum that she go out and get a job, waited for her brothers in America to send her passage money to return. In the meantime she sat, draped in Peggy's maribou blanket, on Peggy's bed and sipped champagne. "If we're all going to die," she kept saying, "at least it should be in style." In mid-September, late one night, Peggy drove Djuna, her nails bitten to the quick, her nerves frazzled, to the Gare d'Austerlitz and put her "in a complete state of collapse" on board a train to the port of Cherbourg. Coincidentally, Tanguy was departing on the same boat and, as Peggy saw him off, she entreated him to take care of Djuna, who was too fragile to look after herself, a responsibility he forgot the moment the ship left the dock.

Peggy settled in at Mary Reynolds's house on the rue Hallé. Mary had spent the first part of September waiting on long lines to get her French safe-conduct visa and be fingerprinted and then had fled with Marcel Duchamp and the Salvador Dalis for Arcachon, outside of Paris.

In Paris, there were fewer parties and blackouts began. Strips of paper could be seen across shop windows—still full of seasonal furs and fashions—to keep the glass from shattering in case of air attack. Gas masks were issued to the general public and women were warned against the use of mascara, which would burn under the masks and make the temptation to remove them irresistible. Pictures appeared in the newspapers of shopgirls wearing their masks with neat silk bows attached for chic. People expected the worst at any minute and devoured the news from Poland in the eighteen daily newspapers.

Sixteen thousand Parisian children were evacuated to the countryside, as were the rarest animals in the zoo. Trains headed for the Maginot Line from the Gare de l'Est were crammed with troops. Air-raid shelters were set up in basements and periodic alarms took on the gaiety of a party as people arrived in their bathrobes and politely shook hands with one another. Some concierges served soup or coffee until the all clear sounded.

By late September Warsaw had surrendered. The rape of Poland was complete and von Ribbentrop, in Moscow, toasted Stalin and the new partition. "Take a look around Warsaw," boasted Hitler to reporters on a tour of that devastated town. "That is how I can deal with any European city." Parisians shuddered at the use of the word *any*. The Germans beheaded civilians, burned men and women alive, and prepared the first death camp, Auschwitz, for the elimination of Jews and other undesirables. The complete collapse of Poland stunned the French, as it did all Europe; the defeat was so fast and so brutal. Feelings ran high as rumors of German repressions and executions spread. Some, staggered by the effectiveness of the German onslaught, wondered where it would end. Others were convinced it had ended in Poland.

Indeed, with the fall of Poland, a new, disquieting phase of the war began. No attempt had been made by the Allies to open a front behind Germany and Hitler did not move anywhere else. An unreal stillness pervaded the boulevards. German radio propaganda heard in Paris was conciliatory. ("I have no war aims against Britain and France," said Hitler.) Many took comfort in the idea of the Maginot Line, a supposedly impregnable line of men and fortifications along the eastern perimeter of France and the Low Countries designed to arrest any German advance before it reached Paris. "We were all safe behind the Maginot Line" was a soothing balm to most Frenchmen. "This vain guarantee," wrote Mary Jayne Gold, a young American woman living in Paris, "colored our thoughts. For example, my masseur, having given me a hard workout, once exclaimed in despair, *'Mademoiselle, votre derrière est comme la ligne Maginot: infranchissable.'* "

By October the Germans were nowhere to be seen, disaster had not struck, and the feeling of dread so pervasive in September began to lift. Could it be that the war was over? The Gallic spirit reasserted itself. Little had really changed, if one thought about it—fishermen still angled along the Seine, wine and food were still plentiful, and uniformed soldiers were rarely seen. The older *poilus,* or foot soldiers, at the front were given leaves to drive taxis. There were gardens to tend, films to see, sidewalk cafés to linger at. It was a "phony war," what the French called the *drôle de guerre* and the Germans, the *Sitzkrieg.* Nothing seemed to happen. After the frenzy of earlier days, "people were tentatively picking up the threads of ordinary existence—tentatively and a little sheepishly, as if ashamed of their initial agitation."

Some of Peggy's friends and acquaintances, who had rushed out of Paris when war was declared, began to reappear. James Joyce came back with his family, including Giorgio and his wife, Helen, who was on the brink of a nervous breakdown. Like Joyce's daughter, Lucia, Helen was showing signs of insanity. Giorgio sought out Peggy as she had been a friend of Helen ever since they were both young girls in New York. Peggy listened to Giorgio and tried to reassure him, urging that Helen be allowed to remain "free" no matter how much trouble she was causing running around Paris spending money like mad and denouncing people she knew to the police. In the interim, Peggy and Giorgio whiled away the time together in bed. Their affair did not mean much to her and when Giorgio suggested that Peggy move into the same hotel, along with all the Joyces, she declined.

Beckett returned to Paris from London, and he and Peggy saw each other, although there was no hope of resuming their liaison. Peggy fell down the stairs at Mary Reynolds's house, dislocating her knee, and for several weeks she lay in bed, incapacitated, while air-raid sirens shrilled. Giorgio visited to give her news of Helen, and Nellie van Doesburg was ever present.

As the Christmas season approached, Peggy's leg improved. Windows in Paris were bedecked with the usual Yuletide displays and bells

rang on the street corners. It was an extremely cold and early winter—
the coldest in nearly half a century—and people bundled up as they went
about their Christmas shopping. As A. J. Liebling, the correspondent for
The New Yorker, observed:

> You cannot keep your mind indefinitely on a war that does not
> begin. Toward the end of the year many of the people who three
> months before had been ready to pop into their cellars like prairie
> dogs at the first purring of an airplane motor, expecting Paris to be
> expunged between dark and dawn, were complaining because res-
> taurants did not serve beefsteak on Mondays, Tuesdays, and Fri-
> days, and because the season had produced no new plays worth
> seeing.

Things seemed calm enough so that Marcel Duchamp and, with
him, Mary Reynolds, decided to return to Paris, where Duchamp could
continue collecting miniatures for his *Bôite-en-Valise,* a complete repre-
sentation of his life's work, including a tiny porcelain urinal. This meant
that Peggy had to move out of Mary's house, and she made arrangements
to rent Kay Sage's penthouse apartment on the Île St. Louis, left vacant
now by Tanguy.

Peggy began 1940 in her new apartment, on the Quai d'Orléans
just behind Nôtre Dame. The penthouse had a large studio under the
eaves, with a charming view of the Seine, and a small bedroom covered
in silver paper. Nellie complained that it did not have enough wall space
to hang paintings. Consequently, when Peggy unpacked her pictures and
sculptures, which had arrived from London unharmed, she could only
display the small works and had to store the rest. The penthouse was the
perfect setting for small dinner parties for which Peggy cooked. When
Helen Joyce was finally sent home to America, Peggy inherited Helen's
two large long-haired Persian cats, Giorgio and Sans Lendemain. Peggy
liked to tell visitors to her apartment that the cats were pederasts. She
found herself very content, happy to watch the river traffic go by and the
sunsets over Nôtre Dame, stroking the two purring Persians.

The war seemed far away, barely audible. Peggy joined other Parisians in feeling secure behind the Maginot Line. Sindbad was in a French
boarding school and Pegeen with her father in Mégève. There appeared
no reason for Peggy to leave Paris and so she settled in, she believed,
for the duration of the war.

A PICTURE A DAY

When she was forced to abandon the idea of a modern art museum in London, Peggy was left with Herbert Read's list and a tidy sum of cash. Why not, it dawned on Peggy, buy the pictures and artworks on the list and make a museum anyway, if not in London, then in Paris or somewhere else? Artists who, with the uncertainty of the war, were reluctant to lend pictures to a fledgling museum, would be delighted to sell them. In this way, Peggy would build up a historically accurate collection of modern art and have her museum someday.

Nellie van Doesburg was excited. With her vast connections in the art world, she would help Peggy locate the artists and their work. Marcel Duchamp could secure the works of his brothers, Raymond Duchamp-Villon and Jacques Villon, as well as advise her about other artists. Peggy set out to buy paintings and sculptures at the rate of a "picture a day," her working motto.

An invaluable helpmate appeared in the form of Howard Putzel, a pudgy, red-faced art dealer from California, who had corresponded with Peggy in 1938 on the occasion of the opening of Guggenheim Jeune. He was a great fan of Tanguy and sent Peggy some of his own Tanguys for her London show. Putzel, the son of a lace manufacturer, was born in New Jersey in the same year and month as Peggy, August 1898, and grew up in San Francisco. When his father died, he tried his hand unsuccessfully at the family business, but soon became a music and art critic for the San Francisco papers. He opened an art gallery in the back of the Gelber Lilienthal bookstore on Post Street, where he showed modern European art; it soon became a charming stop for conversation if not an enormous financial success. In 1935, with the aid of the ever helpful Marcel Duchamp, Putzel mounted an exhibition of Kandinsky's watercolors. Moving his gallery to Hollywood Boulevard in Los Angeles, he sold Tanguy, Miró, and the Surrealists to "movie people," and met Mark Rothko before closing shop and heading for Europe in 1938. There he finally met Duchamp, Tanguy, and Ernst. Peggy ran into him at Mary Reynolds's house and, with a passion for modern art in common, the two became friends. He was, recalled Buffie Johnson, who knew him in 1939, "thrilled about meeting her." Putzel was delighted with Peggy's plan to create a major collection of modern art and was eager to help her find what she needed. Putzel was mad about paintings; he loved them with a near-visceral passion. Modern art was his chief joy and he talked endlessly, and often incomprehensibly, about Marcel Duchamp and Max Ernst. Always on the lookout for new ideas and faces, Putzel joined in Peggy's plan with single-minded intensity. He lost no time in ferreting out pictures for her and would arrive cheerfully at her house early in the morning with various finds tucked under his arm. Each one was a treasure, he pleaded, she must not pass up.

One of the first artists to whom Putzel introduced Peggy was the Surrealist painter Max Ernst. Ernst had made a name for himself with his inventiveness and originality. At the time Peggy first met him, he was alienated from André Breton over Paul Éluard's expulsion from the movement. In disgust, Ernst had resigned from the Surrealists and removed himself to St.-Martin-d'Ardèche, some thirty miles north of Avignon, with the enchantingly beautiful English painter Leonora Carrington. There he bought an ancient farmhouse and decorated it with reliefs of fabulous animals indigenous only to his imagination. He kept a studio in Paris on the tenth floor of a building at 26 rue des Plants, where Peggy once had gone hunting for a studio for John Holms and where Putzel took her to meet Ernst.

At first glance Peggy was more impressed with Leonora's good looks than with Ernst's. Leonora sat serenely at her beloved's feet, while Max looked like a startled bird, delicate and fine-boned, with a beaklike nose and stunning blue eyes. His hair, white for years, surrounded his head in a wispy halo. After looking around the studio, Peggy came away with an oil painting by Leonora, *The Horses of Lord Candlestick,* and thought no more of Ernst.

Peggy's approach to the Romanian-born sculptor Constantin Brancusi was somewhat more direct. She had known him since the 1920s when Brancusi's great bearded face and white Samoyed dog, Polaire, were fixtures of expatriate life. Brancusi had a weakness for American women, who came frequently to his studio, but he "generally," said William Carlos Williams, "no more than observed them; they *'déraillent'* too easily, he said, jump the track, go into the ditch too easily for the most part, want to play but do not 'take the pin.' " Peggy, of course, was different. Peggy was all too happy to "take the pin" and jump into bed with Brancusi, especially as she hoped he might give her a discount on his *Bird in Space,* a soaring bronze he envisioned as a "project for a Bird, which if enlarged, would fill the sky." Much influenced by the eleventh-century Tibetan monk Milarepa, Brancusi felt "a true form ought to suggest infinity. The surfaces ought to look as though they went on forever, as though they proceeded out from the mass into some perfect and complete existence."

Brancusi loved to entertain and Peggy liked to drop by his atelier and bring friends. At the end of an alleyway, Brancusi's narrow, top-lit studio on the impasse Ronsin was covered in fine white plaster dust, filled with slabs of stone and marble, tree trunks, and sculptures in various states of completion. Brancusi, streaked with dust, stood out like a bohemian Santa Claus among his elves. In the middle was a huge stone furnace made by the sculptor in which he fired his works and also cooked his well-known dinners, following "his own famous cuisine." "Like a gnome in a grotto," Brancusi danced to jazz as he served Romanian hors d'oeuvres, steak or chicken left to broil to a crisp in his furnace, and great amounts of liqueurs and wine. A cylindrical plaster hunk made do as a dining table, which he "shaved after each meal in order to save the labor of cleaning a table."

His dark eyes twinkling with mischief, Brancusi had the amiable manners of a peasant. Dressed like one, in a blue smock and sabots, he would arrive at the best restaurants and order the most expensive things on the menu, watching with delight as the head waiter squirmed with worry about the bill to come. "Pegitza," he would say, "have a little more of this." He was so attentive, Peggy thought, surely she would be able to get a good price for the *Bird in Space* she coveted for her collection. Laurence suggested she go so far as to marry Brancusi so she could inherit his sculpture when he died. Brancusi was not so tractable. "He loved me very much," wrote Peggy in her memoirs, "but I never could get anything out of him." In fact, Brancusi did not like to part with his sculptures under any circumstances (death included), as they formed too much a part of the display. His works were carefully arranged, "every one was wrapped in a thick piece of flannel with a metal ring at the top. They were like cloaked figures," observed the art dealer Sidney Janis, "shrouded in mystery." To show the sculpture, Brancusi reached for a long pole with a hook at the end. "Slowly he fitted the hook to the ring.

More slowly still he raised the cloak, inch by inch, thereby revealing the gleaming body of the sculpture beneath. The whole performance was erotic in the extreme, like the gradual undressing of a beautiful young woman."

Brancusi would not sell *Bird in Space* for less than four thousand dollars, and Peggy got into a terrible argument with him over the price. Considering their relationship, she said, it was astonishing that he would ask so much. But Brancusi's first love was his work, not Peggy. With hindsight, it was a laughably inexpensive price for a major Brancusi bronze, but Peggy nevertheless stopped seeing him on account of it. She turned around and bought another *Bird,* the 1912 *Maiastra,* from the dress designer, Paul Poiret's sister, paying only one thousand dollars, a much better price.

In this regard, it should be borne in mind that no one was thinking about buying art on the eve of the Battle of France. For a decade, since the Depression, painters and artists had resigned themselves to slow sales or no sales. Kandinsky barely sold a picture during the 1930s; Max Ernst was frightfully poor. The news that Peggy Guggenheim, the copper heiress and owner of Guggenheim Jeune, was going about buying up pictures, spread like wildfire. (René Magritte tracked down his own *Voice of the Winds* so he could sell it to Peggy and leave.) She was "buying extensively in Paris at a time when nobody else was buying and she was able to pick out things directly with the artist, so you can imagine how popular she was," said Pierre Matisse. Peggy herself recollected, "Nothing could have been easier. The Parisians were expecting a German invasion and [were] delighted to sell everything and flee. . . . everyone pursued me mercilessly. My 'phone rang all day and people even brought me paintings in the morning to bed, before I rose."

Peggy was able to pick up masterpieces for very little money. She bought Picabia's *Very Rare Picture upon This Earth* for three hundred thirty dollars, Braque's *The Waltz* for fifteen hundred dollars and a Fernand Léger, *Men in the Town,* for one thousand dollars. "My initial investment, which bought half the most important pictures," Peggy said, "was $40,000.00. The whole collection cost about $250,000." (Four decades later, the collection was conservatively estimated to be worth forty million.)

At the time, however, Peggy had no idea of what the pictures and sculpture would one day be worth. No one had. Art was not yet purchased as an investment, as it is today. It was only thought of as something to hang on the wall or place in the garden. It did not occur to anyone to buy paintings and sculpture and store them away for the future. "You know," Peggy said, "I didn't even realize then that I was buying things cheap because of the war, and everyone since then has accused me of taking advantage of the situation, but I didn't even realize it. I didn't know anything about the prices of things. I just paid what people told me."

Dutifully, Peggy went off to Alberto Giacometti's tiny studio near the avenue du Maine in search of one of his sculptures for her collection. For a time, Giacometti allied himself with the Surrealists and created sexually charged "objects" that delighted André Breton. One in particular, which Breton owned, provoked the looker to slide a suspended ball along a crescentlike shape, in a game that was meant to be both erotic and frustrating, akin to masturbation. By 1935, however, Giacometti had left Surrealism and returned to an oeuvre based on the model, carrying "little Greek heads . . . in his pocket." Along with Giorgio de Chirico, who abandoned his metaphysical paintings in favor of a more academic style, Giacometti was dismissed by the Surrealists from the ranks of living artists.

To Peggy, Giacometti looked "like an imprisoned lion, with his lionesque head and an enormous shock of hair. His conversation and behaviour were extremely Surrealist and whimsical." Giacometti was so poor he could be seen for a time holding up his trousers by means of a rope tied around his waist. Peggy had found a damaged plaster cast in an art gallery and asked the chain-smoking sculptor if he would fix it for her if she brought it to him. Giacometti replied that he had a much better one, *Woman with Her Throat Cut,* done in 1932 when he was still under the sway of the Surrealists. It appeared to be a "vaguely crustacean female anatomy," cracked like a lobster in a number of places, spread over the floor, where Giacometti displayed it. It seems that, "from earliest childhood, the obsession with a sexual murder provoked [him]. . . . With chance acquaintances or friends, especially women, he could not refrain from imagining how he might kill them." This fascination found its way into *Woman with Her Throat Cut,* and Giacometti promised to have it cast for Peggy in bronze. When he arrived on Peggy's terrace on the Île St. Louis excitedly bringing her his work, she thought he appeared "exactly like a painting by Carpaccio . . . of St. George leading in the captive dragon."

Even though Peggy toed the Surrealist line and decided she disapproved of Salvador Dali's stunts, she still wanted one of his pictures. She was accompanied on her search by none other than Dali's muse, Gala, who Peggy insisted was too artificial to be likable. Gala in turn thought Peggy misguided. Peggy should do as she did and dedicate her life to one great genius. Gala chose *The Birth of Liquid Desires* for Peggy's collection.

One painter, however, from whom Peggy got nothing "but rude remarks" was Pablo Picasso. When Peggy arrived at his studio with her shopping list, hoping to buy one of his most recent pictures, the painter arrogantly ignored her, pointedly talking instead to some other guests. Then, ambling over to Peggy, he said contemptuously, "Lingerie is on the next floor."

Peggy's activities were met with a considerable amount of disapproval from Hilla Rebay's representative in Paris, Yvanhoë Rambosson, who was entrusted with the establishment of the Centre d'Études Artistiques Solomon R. Guggenheim in Paris. Preparing for an exhibition of the Guggenheim collection there, he saw in Peggy a threat to the dissemination of non-objective art. He feared Peggy's name would confuse and "deviate the movement on a wrong way" and he sent impassioned letters to New York warning Rebay of Peggy's encroachments. "I think Peggy Guggenheim is trying to ride on our fame," replied the baroness to Rambosson's repeated warnings. "However, I believe it can do only good if she buys lots of paintings of the poor starving painters in times like this."

Between visits to artists' studios, Peggy entertained in her apartment or went to dinner with friends, chatting gaily about her future museum, her paintings, her plans. She visited Mary Reynolds and Marcel Duchamp those icy winter months and exchanged ideas for her collection. With her new beau, Bill Whidney, she spent afternoons at the Dôme or the Coupole.

As spring approached, the tenor of life in Paris began to change. American Under Secretary of State Sumner Welles found Paris in March "full of pessimism." Food restrictions had been extended to restaurants and cafés, which annoyed the Parisians, but as yet "the war effort seemed wholly inert." The war that Hitler's ally, Stalin, had been waging against the Finns ended with the Russo-Finnish Treaty on March 13, and nothing more happened. "The first year," commented Mary Jayne Gold, "which was called the 'phony war,' was rather a bore. Nothing much happened on the military fronts and there was nothing much to do in the rear. Except that you knew it couldn't last, and a vague anxiety kept inching ever closer."

When spring arrived, the weather was cool and crisp like those first days of September when the war began. Along with the change of season came fresh rumors of a German invasion. Intelligence reports of German activity increased: boats, troops, parachutists were aimed at Norway and Denmark. In the early morning of April 9, 1940, Germany finally invaded those two countries. The planning for the invasion proved so meticulous that King Christian X surrendered Denmark in two hours—with their morning coffee the Danes discovered they were the newest citizens of Hitler's Reich.

With British help, the Norwegians were able to battle the German forces for some time longer. The superficial calm of the "phony war" had masked preparations on both sides for a mass offensive. Paris was abuzz with the news of the German invasion of Norway and Denmark; fears long buried were beginning to surface in all their horror. Rumors of a fifth column, a Trojan horse, a lightning war chilled French men and women. But Peggy kept buying pictures. "The day Hitler walked into Norway," she was fond of repeating, "I walked into Léger's studio and bought a wonderful 1919 painting from him for one thousand dollars. He never got over the fact that I should be buying paintings on such a day."

Peggy's main concern was for the pictures that she had accumulated during the first winter of the war. She now had, in addition to the Léger, paintings by Picabia, Klee, Gleizes, Kandinsky, Gris, Severini, Balla, Mondrian, and Van Doesburg, as well as Miró, Ernst, de Chirico, Tanguy, Dali, Magritte, Man Ray, and Brauner. And she was the proud owner of sculpture by Brancusi, Lipchitz, Giacometti, Arp, Moore, and Pevsner. Optimistically, Peggy rented the apartment on the Place Vendôme where Chopin died and began to have it remodeled by the architect Georges Vantongerloo against the landlord's suggestions that she think it over first. Like others there, Peggy had convinced herself that the Germans would be stopped by the Maginot Line long before they reached Paris.

On May 10, Hitler commenced his long-feared and well-prepared invasion, postponed nineteen times over six months, code-named "Danzig." As German Stuka bombers attacked and immobilized airfields in Holland and Belgium, crack parachutists dropped into the Low Countries and Panzers rolled ferociously over everything in their way. Within hours, the Germans had reached the Albert Canal, the most strongly defended point in Belgium. The outcome of the fighting was a forgone conclusion. Visions of *Blitzkrieg* panicked and demoralized the Belgians even though they held out for eighteen days. Parisians awoke that morning to air-raid sirens and antiaircraft guns, the first in months, and the shattering news of the German advance on Holland and Belgium. Furloughs were canceled and citizens lined up in the chilly morning air at newspaper kiosks to get the latest bulletins. Strangely, it was almost with relief that people accepted that the "phony war" had ended. *"Finie la drôle de guerre,"* they said. "So much the better! It will be like bursting an abscess." As of yet, the French were not overly concerned. After all, the Germans had not come up against any French or British troops, the finest in Europe, or even the Maginot Line. Nevertheless, "The Germans gained their victories so easily. It gave one a queasy feeling in the pit of the stomach when one thought about it."

Hitler's plan counted on the French and Allied forces moving north, in the mistaken belief that the main German offensive would come from that direction, as it had in World War I. The armored Panzer divisions of Rommel, Guderian, and von Rundstedt would then be free to thrust through the Ardennes forest east of Paris, believed by the French high command to be unbroachable. It, therefore, was undefended and the weakest link in the Maginot Line. If the plan succeeded, the Panzers could roll over the plains uninterrupted into the heart of Allied territory, trapping the bulk of the Allied forces in the north, cut off by the German army. Hitler wept with joy when he heard that the French troops were indeed moving northward in accordance with his audacious master plan. By May 13, three days after the offensive began, German tanks broke through the Ardennes and were preparing to cross the Meuse River. The next day, Queen Wilhelmina of the Netherlands was on her way to London with her government, and on May 15 the Dutch surrendered.

Prime Minister Winston Churchill was awakened by a desperate telephone call from Paul Reynaud, the new French premier: "We have been defeated. We are beaten; we have lost the battle." The Germans had crossed the Meuse, broken the front at Sedan, and were pouring through. Churchill asked in astonishment, "So soon?" and tried to reassure the French leader that matters could still change. The next day, in Paris, when Churchill asked about the strategic French reserves, which surely were kept behind the Maginot Line in the event it was penetrated, General Gamelin of the French high command answered: *"Aucune"*— none. On May 21, the Germans were at Arras, and on May 28, King Leopold III of the Belgians surrendered.

Hordes of Belgian and Dutch refugees clogged the roads—making it difficult to move troops—and began to stream into Paris. At the beginning came the luxurious sedans of the rich; they were soon followed by humbler vehicles, bicycles and farm wagons piled high with blankets, pots, mattresses, and flaxen-haired children and drawn by massive gray draft horses. Trains brought in exhausted, disheveled people who had no vehicles of their own. Others made their way on foot, pushing baby carriages, wheelbarrows, anything that rolled, stacked with what had filled their homes. What to do with the refugees was uppermost in everyone's mind, but Peggy could only think of her collection and how to protect it. Mary Reynolds, disgusted, told her it was "indecent to think of anything except the refugees," and snidely suggested that Peggy hire a truck, fill it with her pictures, and run over the homeless people on the roads.

It was becoming obvious to even the most obtuse that France was in grave danger. The German advance had been swift and deadly. Hundreds of thousands of British and French troops were trapped at Dunkirk. It was only a matter of time before the Germans reached Paris itself. Many of Peggy's friends made plans to leave. Howard Putzel was going to New York. The James Joyces were on their way to Switzerland.

Duchamp was quietly planning to go to America, Mary Reynolds to Arcachon.

Those who remained "seemed to concentrate on the boulevards. It gave them comfort to look at one another. They were not yet consciously afraid, however," noted *The New Yorker*'s A. J. Liebling. "There were long queues in front of the movie houses, especially those that showed double features. You could get a table at a sidewalk café only with difficulty, and the ones that had girl orchestras did particularly well." As May drew to a close, there was antiaircraft fire every night, and although food was still plentiful, "People got thin worrying. . . . The cheekbones, the noses, and the jaws of all Paris were becoming more prominent."

On June 3, the Germans bombed factories on the outskirts of Paris. Peggy was with Brancusi having lunch and making plans to pick up her much coveted *Bird in Space,* which Brancusi had been painstakingly polishing by hand. Nellie van Doesburg had interceded and patched up the fight, settling on a price in francs, so that Peggy could save a thousand dollars on the exchange rate. Inured to sirens, Peggy refused to hurry her lunch in any way. When she finally came back to pick up the *Bird,* the Germans were even closer, but Peggy was still collecting art. Brancusi wept when he saw his treasure depart, and Peggy didn't know if it was for her and the uncertainty of whether he would see her again, or because he would miss his favorite *Bird.*

Peggy was obsessed with saving the collection that she had so avidly amassed in the months since the beginning of the year. The Louvre was evacuating its rarest treasures, wrapped in flannel and asbestos, to hiding places in the countryside. Fernand Léger suggested that the Louvre might give Peggy a cubic meter of space for her pictures, and Peggy frantically began taking them off stretchers and wrapping them up. The Louvre, however, did not feel Peggy's pictures worth saving. The sculptures they did not even consider. "I asked everyone I met," said Peggy, "if they would store my collection for me." Finally, Alex Ponisovsky, Hazel's one-time suitor, asked Maria Jolas, who had evacuated her bilingual school to a château outside of Vichy, if she would hide Peggy's artworks. When she agreed, they were trucked to Vichy in "two or three great, big crates," recounted Mme. Jolas, "and were put in the garage," where the modern masterpieces remained safe for the moment.

On June 5, the Germans began their attack on France, pushing south toward the Somme. The situation was becoming ever more bleak. Telephone service was suspended in the hotels; taxis were nowhere to be seen. "Every day somebody said good-bye to me," wrote Liebling. Antiaircraft guns left little clouds of white smoke on the horizon. Another stream of cars began coming in at the east gate, crossing Paris along the boulevard Saint Michel and the Luxembourg Gardens—where some refugees allowed their livestock to graze before moving on—and out through the portes d'Italie and Orléans. People slept in the railroad stations in the hope of getting a train out.

In this widening nightmare, Peggy just sat with Bill Whidney at the Dôme sipping champagne on those days when hard liquor was not available. "It is really incomprehensible now to think of our idiotic life, when there was so much misery surrounding us. Trains kept pouring into Paris with refugees in the direst misery," she wrote, "and with bodies that had been machine-gunned en route. I can't imagine why I didn't go to the aid of all these unfortunate people. But I just didn't; instead I drank champagne with Bill." After the war, an unofficial committee of journalists—apparently no fans of honesty—awarded Peggy, by unanimous vote, a sprig of poison ivy as a mock Pulitzer Prize for this candid passage in her memoirs.

By June 8, Rommel's Panzers were forty miles outside of Paris, along the Seine. It was clear that the situation was desperate. The government made plans to evacuate Paris and declare it a free city to spare its treasures from German bombs, and on June 10 the government left Paris for Tours. That same day, Mussolini declared war on France. Anyone who had access to transportation left Paris that evening or the next day. Peggy was no exception. All her friends had left, except for Whidney, who was staying behind with his ailing wife, and Brancusi, who could not bear to part from his sculptures.

On Tuesday, June 11, Nellie, Peggy, and the two Persian cats inherited from Helen Joyce piled into Peggy's tiny Talbot automobile, for which Peggy had saved gas in cans on the terrace of her penthouse, and set off for Mégève. Peggy's traveling permit had expired, but the need for papers was forgotten in the crush of people fleeing on the roads. A cloud of black smoke, probably a smoke cover used by the Germans on the Seine, spread over the city and blanketed the travelers with soot. The roads were clogged, gorged with

> possibly the strangest assortment of vehicles in history . . . from fiacres of the Second Empire to a farm tractor hitched to a vast trailer displaying the American flag. . . . A few men rode horses along the grassy edge of the road, making better progress than the automobiles. During the first few kilometers cars stood still for from five minutes to an hour at a time, moving forward only a few yards to stop again with grinding brakes. . . . The Paris autobuses . . . carried the personnel of government offices and major industrial establishments.

People slept in their cars or on benches outside of brasseries. Troops moving north added to the congestion. Peggy exclaimed, "It was terrific."

Some miles outside of Paris the traffic let up and it was easier to move. Peggy managed to leave the main auto routes and travel east on side roads. Most of the homeless were headed toward Bordeaux, where the government had decided to move, finding Tours too small and too close to danger. Consequently, the roads east to Mégève were comparatively empty. On the way, Peggy and Nellie heard the tragic news of the fall of Paris and the triumphant German entry on June 14. "There wasn't much left of France," Peggy observed, "but what there was we clung to desperately." Overcome by the speed of the defeat, the French wept with rage, observed Kay Boyle. "In every shop, in every mouth, in every face there is the one thing heard, or said, or written out: 'We have been betrayed.'" The last issue of the *London Bulletin* declared: "No dream is worse than the reality in which we live."

THE *BOCHES*

Some ten million refugees fled home, jobs, friends, and neighbors in a panic before the conquering Germans. They formed an uneasy, ragged mass, descending on the sun-soaked villages of the south of France, spreading disorder and depleting stores. "The intruders," wrote Mary Jayne Gold, "had occupied every hotel bed; they slept at the side of the road in their parked cars, or worse, in your own garden, your own hayloft. In some towns the mayor had taken the precaution of converting the local movie theater into a refugee center."

In Mégève, Peggy found her children happy to see her but Laurence and Kay firm in their resolve not to leave France, and especially not to join the miserable throngs on the road. By the terms of the armistice signed on June 22, the Germans were to occupy two-thirds of France, leaving the rest to be governed in Vichy by that relic of World War I, the ancient Marshal Pétain. Fortunately, Mégève and the south of France were in the Unoccupied Zone.

Once the armistice was signed and the shattered French government reverted to the hands of Pétain, people began to calm down. The *Boches,* as the Germans were called, let France keep its colonies abroad, its fleet, and its government at Vichy. As they had during the "phony war," the French resigned themselves to a situation over which they had little control. The refugees began to go home: buses came from Holland to pick up the Dutch; French men and women returned to their villages and shops; even some Jews went back. Yet thousands of expatriates from Czechoslovakia, Germany, and Poland settled in the Unoccupied Zone for an indeterminate time. The Jews, for the most part, chose to stay behind. The influx of foreigners, and especially foreign intellectuals, caused an "extraordinary run on the public libraries."

Life seemed to return to normal, except that German officers could be seen alighting from sleek black cars, straight-backed and resplendent in the gray uniforms and polished swastikas of the Reich, and once-thick newspapers, reduced to two, possibly four, pages, were filled with ads of the most heartrending kind: "Mother seeks baby daughter, age two, lost on the road between Tours and Poitiers in the retreat," or, "Generous reward for information leading to the recovery of my son, Jacques, age ten, last seen at Bordeaux, June 17th." There were otherwise few indications, that first summer of the Occupation, of war. Food was still abundant—the French barometer for good times—and the only real shortages were of razor blades, soap, and gasoline.

Peggy rented a house at Le Veyrier, on the Lac d'Annecy, a huge, glistening lake surrounded by Alps. Boating languidly in the sun, it was easy to forget the war. Nellie van Doesburg joined Peggy, as did Jean and Sophie Arp, who had fled their little Parisian suburb. Arp was miserable at having left his sculptures behind and loathed the Germans. He, along with his generation, had lived through two wars started by them and could barely stand to hear Beethoven on the radio. Arp and Laurence had long and animated conversations about the war and the course of events on those occasions when Laurence came down from nearby Mégève with his girls.

Peggy had Sindbad and Pegeen for the summer, whom she had not seen since the previous Easter. At this point in their lives, the two teenagers were more interested in sex than in the problems with the *Boches.* Sindbad at seventeen was an awkward young man, all huge blue eyes and nose. And Pegeen, nearly fifteen, was a lithe, attractive girl with her father's mournful Vail face, sad eyes, and masses of wavy blond hair. She had a marvelous figure and long slender legs. Since the beginning of the war, Pegeen had been living with her father and Kay Boyle in Mégève. From being a lonely, solitary child with Peggy, she went to being one of five girls, with Bobbie, Kay's daughter, and the Vail girls Apple, Kathe, and Clover, the new baby.

Pegeen and Sindbad had breathed an air of sexual precocity into the lives of the Vail children. They brought talk of sex, boys, kissing, and suicide to Mégève. "They were very hung up on sex, those kids," said Apple. "Bobbie and I never talked about sex until the Guggenheim kids, Sindbad and Pegeen, came along. I guess it's what they heard at home."

At first, Apple was wary of Pegeen. "I was scared of her. She was very sophisticated. . . . Her influence on Bobbie was terribly great. Bobbie was in the throes of trying to be de-virginized. To be a virgin was the most horrible thing to be."

Peter Lawson-Johnston, Peggy's cousin, recounted how Peggy once asked a fifteen-year-old girl at Harry's Bar in Venice, "Are you a virgin?" It was the kind of interrogation Peggy passed on to her children. Sindbad would never fail to ask Apple, not yet eleven in 1940, "Are you *still* a virgin?" "It was painful as hell," winced Apple. "Then he'd say: 'There is nothing more disgusting than a nun. They don't go to bed with anyone.'" Years later, when they were all grown up, Apple went to see Sindbad, who soon asked her, "Isn't life boring?" and then asked about her young son, Benjamin, "Is he still a virgin?" Apple stayed away from Sindbad. "He scared me too much. Like Peggy, he was very sarcastic; he would make fun of you. I couldn't cope with the ridicule."

Bobbie and Pegeen, who were about the same age, became great friends. "Pegeen came and Bobbie dropped me," said Apple, "and proceeded to grow up and talk about boys. I was a very solitary kid, and I went to the ravine behind the house. . . . Pegeen and Bobbie forbade me to go there. . . . There was a *cachette des trois enfants* where they were experimenting with kissing. Pegeen, Bobbie, and the neighbor boy. I was a nuisance." Bobbie remembered that "Pegeen and I were like twins, extremely close in Mégève. She was always madly in love—like all unhappy children." Bobbie adored Pegeen and would do anything for her, including, one day, letting Pegeen swallow twelve aspirins so that she could "commit suicide."

That summer on Lac d'Annecy, Pegeen and Sindbad spent long hours swimming, playing, and chasing after a brother and sister also summering in Annecy with their family, Yvonne and Edgar Kuhn. Sindbad had a mad crush on Yvonne, which went totally unrequited, and Pegeen was smitten with Edgar, to whom she finally lost her much bewailed virginity.

With her children off romancing the locals, Peggy had plenty of time to herself. She went to the local beauty parlor and developed a passion for her hairdresser. In order to keep going back to him, she began dyeing her hair different colors: first chestnut, the closest to her natural color, and then a garish red. "It was the brightest red, quite artificial," recalled Jacqueline Ventadour. Sindbad laughed when he saw his mother, but Pegeen was mortified by Peggy's outlandish carrot top and insisted that she do something about it. Finally, Peggy settled on a deep blue-black, the color of shoe polish. It did little to flatter her features; in fact, it made Peggy's nose seem all the more prominent, her complexion the more florid. She seemed to be wearing an aviator's helmet of shiny patent leather. Along with the large pendulous earring that Peggy liked to wear, the hair gave her a distinctly Surrealist look. The earrings, the peony nose, and ebony hair became Peggy's trademarks.

When Peggy had no need to touch up her roots, or ran out of things for her hairdresser to do, she dragged Pegeen along to have her daughter's hair combed and brushed. Pegeen suffered as she saw her mother flirting with the hairdresser. Her mother's insistent sexuality depressed and disturbed her. Sex is something other people do, not one's parents, and Peggy was so terribly obvious. Everyone knew she was in love with the man.

Indeed, Peggy chased after every man she could find. As Kay's daughter, Bobbie, observed, "She did sort of rape every man in sight." With Nellie egging her on, Peggy plotted her escapades. She tried to seduce a fisherman, in addition to the hairdresser, and when Mrs. Kuhn's brother arrived, freshly escaped from the deprivations of a French detention camp, Peggy stealthily invited him to "dinner."

Meanwhile, forty-five-year-old Nellie van Doesburg was carrying on her own affair with a black African student aged twenty-five. "She was terribly lively and *sympathique*," observed Bobbie. "She had an affair with one of my boyfriends I had never had an affair with." Peggy herself was an object of similar wonderment. Apple recalled, "You could have fun with Peggy. She was very outspoken. She was the grown-up who said extraordinary things. I enjoyed her as a kid, although my mother didn't like her. . . . She was slightly evil, very fascinating. . . . She said extraordinary things, shocking things, such as 'Are you a homosexual?' " (a question Peggy asked with almost as much frequency as she did, "Are you a virgin?").

At the end of the summer, Peggy moved into a hotel in Mégève, and Pegeen and Sindbad returned to their schoolday routines. At this time Laurence's marriage to Kay was coming apart. Kay had fallen in love with a handsome Austrian baron, Josef Frankenstein, who came to give the girls German lessons. Kay enjoyed the role of the femme fatale and let her girls know of her flirtations and conquests. Still she did not talk about them in quite the same way as Peggy did. With Baron Frankenstein, Kay carried on a "sultry love affair, more discreet than passionate," in the words of Jacqueline Ventadour. Bobbie simply adored Josef. "He was extremely handsome, extremely kind, extremely gentle. I didn't know very much about him; he gave us German lessons and would melt whenever my mother appeared. He was a darling. He was a great, great hero. He trained for the OSS. He was a great Catholic," and he was greatly in love with Kay Boyle.

Josef was "in a state of *traumatisme,* stung with misery," over his relationship with Kay, when Peggy came along and seduced him under Kay's aquiline nose. "I went off one night," said Peggy, delighted with herself, "and slept with her new boyfriend, her future husband, and it was very funny. I didn't realize that it was her boyfriend, and then, of course, I never was allowed to see him again after that. And then, I guess, finally, I was told he was her boyfriend, and that's why I couldn't see him anymore." Sindbad got a kick out of the whole affair. "Mother hated Kay Boyle, because she was father's second wife, and her kids liked her better than her some of the time. Mother got at Kay Boyle by sleeping with Frankenstein, seducing her lily-white prince. Kay called him a baron, but Austrian barons were a dime a dozen."

Kay proposed to go off with Frankenstein and her youngest daughters, leaving Laurence to fend for himself with the older girls in Mégève. When it came to wives, Laurence did not have much luck. In the end they all left him.

As autumn progressed, it was clear that Peggy could not return to Paris. After the initial sun-filled days of the Occupation, when it appeared that the *Boches* would not be bearing down too hard, the new, repressive order asserted itself. The first German ordinance for the Occupied Zone of September 27, 1940, forbade all Jews who had fled before the German advance to return to the zone. Even before this ordinance, German border guards were turning back Jews. In addition, all Jews who remained in the Occupied Zone were required to register with the police and to carry identification papers labeled *Juif.*

The Vichy government promulgated a series of edicts and proclamations preparing the way for a police state and, without direct orders from the Germans, launched its own vigorous campaign of anti-Semitism. To begin with, Vichy announced that it would reexamine all naturalizations granted since 1927 and strip all "undesirables" of their citizenship. Entry into the civil service, the doctors' guild, and the bar was limited to those born of French fathers—edicts that applied with special rigor to the Jews. The law forbidding press attacks on persons or groups because of race or religion was revoked. At the beginning of September, a law was passed making it possible for prefects to intern individuals deemed dangerous to the public safety without trial. In October, Vichy passed a statute on the Jews which barred all Jews from holding public office or jobs in journalism, radio, films, and teaching. On October 4, it was determined that all foreign Jews could be arrested by prefects and sent to special camps or *residences forcées* in faraway villages without right of appeal or explanation. All foreign men between the ages of eighteen and fifty-five were liable to be rounded up into labor gangs.

It was best for a Jew in Vichy France to tread extremely cautiously. Since Peggy carried an expired safe-conduct visa (one of several ways in which foreigners were restricted in France) on which she had forged a date, it was important for her not to travel too much. If she were caught with a forged visa she could be sent to a detention camp. She was safest near Mégève, where she could keep an eye on her children and be near Laurence. Consequently, Nellie van Doesburg suggested that Peggy go to Grenoble, from where she could travel in and out of Mégève with ease. There Nellie had a friend, André Farcy, who was the director of the local museum. Farcy said he would let Peggy keep her pictures in the museum—a risky business, since many of Peggy's artists, including Max Ernst, had been labeled "degenerate" by the Nazis. Given the policy of cooperation with the conquerors of the Vichy regime, Farcy was reluctant to commit himself to showing Peggy's collection, as Peggy hoped, but he would let her uncrate and store her works and show them informally. This was far better than letting the collection sit under tarpaulins on the Quai d'Annecy, where it had been parked for several weeks. Peggy soon had her pictures shipped to Grenoble and followed with Nellie.

In Grenoble, Peggy settled into a hotel that as a result of the war was poorly heated and barely stocked. For breakfast, there was only stale bread—the sale of the fresh item was inexplicably forbidden by Vichy —ersatz coffee, tasting of burned wheat, and jelly made from the dregs of grapes pressed for wine. Soap became a luxury and everyone saved the thinnest slivers.

When winter arrived, rationing began in earnest. Ration books were issued, printed on cheap paper ruled into squares; on each square was written the number of grams of a food allowed the recipient. Portions were far from extravagant. A half pound of pasta and rice had to last a month and only ten ounces of meat and four ounces of cheese could be consumed a week. Even in those cases where the allotment was generous, for example, sugar at one pound a month, the actual stuff was difficult to find and long lines formed early in the morning for those foods that were still available. Cooking oil was nonexistent and people had to use water to prepare their meals. Whereas at the beginning of the war Peggy could still get a good meal at a restaurant or a decent pastry at a café, now, listed alongside the menu were figures representing grams. A waiter, equipped with scissors, would snip out the corresponding coupons with a diner's order. Only in a black-market restaurant could one still hope to get a meal vaguely resembling those of pre-Vichy France. To the French, nothing spoke more eloquently of the disaster that had befallen them. They were furious to think of their Brie and Camembert being consumed in Berlin.

A British blockade was succeeding, and fuel, rubber, and tropical foodstuffs were hard to get. Peggy's Talbot remained in the garage for want of gasoline. Heating oil was scarce, and she sat indoors wearing her coat or bundled up in sweaters and socks, her two fat Persian cats warming her lap. Only men were allowed to buy cigarettes, and Peggy had no choice but to cut back on her smoking. For a while, red wine helped pass the time, but that, too, gave out.

Peggy spent her days cataloguing the treasures that she had accumulated since the war began. Hunched over the same portable typewriter on which she had copied John Holms's letters, wearing fingerless woolen gloves, Peggy worked for the day when she could again show her collection. She was desperate to display it, but André Farcy would not allow it, because of his fear of being dragged off to a detention camp. Nevertheless, he gave Peggy an entire room in which she stacked her paintings and held casual viewings and where the pictures could be photographed for her catalogue.

There was pitifully little in the way of distraction in Grenoble. Occasionally, Farcy would come to dinner with Peggy and Nellie and entertain them with stories of his youth as a cyclist in the Tour de France. The painter Robert Delaunay came up to Grenoble from his temporary home in the south of France to sell Peggy a picture and left with Giorgio, one of the Persian cats, as Peggy could no longer stand the two huge furry creatures in her small hotel room.

For the most part, Peggy and Nellie had each other. They were inseparable friends. Peggy imitated Nellie's fashion and makeup, her extravagant style and Surrealist jewelry. Nellie, in turn, encouraged Peggy in her aspirations to one day have a great modern art museum and helped her in every way to meet artists.

But Peggy's relationship with Nellie went beyond mere friendship. Peggy had strong lesbian feelings and Nellie reciprocated them. Although Peggy dismissed their intimacies as "nothing that ever meant anything, nothing that ever existed, hardly," Peggy's feverish pursuit of men had something false about it. It was as if she were trying to prove something, if not to herself then to the world at large. It was terribly important to Peggy to perpetuate the myth of her sexuality and seductiveness. She needed to be thought of as a temptress of talented and famous men, and her relationships with women were intensely embarrassing to her. She admitted to their existing "just for a minute, you know. Now and then. Just a little sex or something. Just one or twice. But nothing that meant anything at all. . . . No love affair at all, for a second. Maybe I had sex once or twice with women."

Peggy had a history of intense emotional relationships with women: Emily Coleman, Djuna Barnes, Nellie van Doesburg. But the truth was that Peggy could not be close to anyone, male or female. No sooner did Peggy begin to feel close to someone, as she did to Nellie, than she chafed. With Nellie she argued furiously and quarreled over trivialities; but always at the heart of the matter was an attraction that made Peggy uncomfortable. Even Laurence noticed how heated things had become between the two women. Matters boiled so that Peggy asked Nellie to move to Lyons, from which distance they could remain friends.

Spring came early in 1941; by February the worst chills had passed, and even if Peggy still went to bed hungry, at least it was not in an overcoat. Laurence decided that he, Kay Boyle, Peggy, and the children should all return to America. He loathed it as much as Peggy did, if not more, but it was evident that life in Vichy France was dangerous as well as unpleasant.

Every day there were fresh rumors of a German occupation of the Unoccupied Zone. It was common knowledge that the Gestapo prowled the south of France and that it had access to French police files. No one felt truly safe. Anti-Semitism, which had existed in France before the Occupation, was encouraged. In the Occupied Zone Jews had to post signs saying "Jewish Enterprise," which destroyed business. Everywhere shopkeepers in unoccupied France displayed signs: "French Enterprise," meaning that they were not Jewish, to show their solidarity with Vichy's policies. In some cases, Vichy confiscated Jewish property outright.

As of yet, the Reich respected American citizens, but who could guarantee that would last? If the United States came into the war, then Americans would become enemy aliens, subject to the same humiliations as other nationalities. The American consulate in Lyons had been encouraging all Americans to go home. How long would it be safe for Peggy, as a Jew, to remain in France? No one had the answers. As times grew worse, food scarcer, the amenities of life more limited, and the threat of detention camps more menacing, there was little reason to remain in Vichy France.

Laurence's decision coincided with the arrival in Grenoble of René Lefebvre-Foinet, the shipper who had consigned pictures to Peggy from Paris to London for Guggenheim Jeune. He helped Peggy resolve the one obstacle to her returning to America: the collection. She would not leave without it. Peggy was frantic trying to think how to send the pictures ahead to New York. Why, nothing could be simpler, insisted Lefebvre-Foinet. She was moving, wasn't she? It would be easy to pack all the paintings and sculptures in with the blankets, pots and pans, and other domestic effects—even put some into her car, which was collecting dust in a local garage—and send the whole lot off as "household goods." René and Peggy spent two months packing the collection, jamming it into cases between sheets and plates. In addition, Peggy added M. Lefebvre-Foinet to her personal collection, finding in his embraces solace for the moment.

THE EMERGENCY
RESCUE COMMITTEE

The situation of the refugees in France was desperate. As part of the armistice with Hitler, the French government agreed to "surrender on demand" all citizens of the Reich named by the Germans. This included citizens of Czechoslovakia, Poland, Austria, as well as Germany, and eventually grew to mean anybody, regardless of nationality, whom the Germans wanted in custody. France was full of such refugees who had escaped the Nazis. Many were already languishing in the filthy French internment camps created at the outset of the war. A few who through luck, connections, or currency managed to escape the camps lived in perpetual fear of being picked up and interned. Without proper papers a refugee was in constant danger of being stopped and sent to a concentration camp. In gravest peril were the political anti-Fascists such as Fritz Lam, the German socialist, who ran the risk of being sent back to Germany by the Gestapo and its Kundt Commission operating in France. Trapped in this way were Thomas Mann's brother, Heinrich, and son, Golo; the writer Franz Werfel and his wife, Alma Mahler; the social scientist Hannah Arendt; the painters Marc Chagall and Max Ernst; and the sculptor Jacques Lipchitz. Even French intellectuals were in grave danger; still in France were the Surrealists André Breton, Benjamin

Péret, André Masson, and their fellow traveler, Marcel Duchamp. Their antiestablishment stance and active anti-Fascist proclamations would not stand them in good stead with the new regime.

In New York, an Emergency Rescue Committee was formed with the sole purpose of getting out of France those artists, intellectuals, and political activists in greatest danger from the Nazis and their cohorts, the Spanish, French, and Italian Fascists. In conjunction with the American Federation of Labor, the Museum of Modern Art, and representatives from various émigré groups already in America, a list was drawn up of two hundred or so anti-Fascist artists, politicians, and intellectuals believed to be in France and in danger of internment by the Nazis. The obvious solution lay in securing American visas for the refugees, which required affidavits of support from American citizens and political bona fides. With the cooperation of Eleanor Roosevelt, the committee was able to bypass the quota system and get more visas than was strictly allowed. The biggest problem would be actually getting these people out of France.

To help as many exiles as possible, legally or illegally, the committee sent Varian Fry, a young classics scholar from Harvard, complete with horn-rimmed glasses and pinstriped suit, to Marseilles in August 1940. Word quickly spread that Fry was armed with a suitcase full of money and those tickets to heaven: American visas.

Once in Marseilles, Fry faced a grim reality. To begin with, there were far more people in serious danger from the Nazis—shattered, frightened rank-and-file workers and lesser-known artists—than on his original list. These men and women needed money to live and places to stay, if only to keep out of the way of intermittent roundups by the French police and the Gestapo. Then Fry learned that many of the people on his list were already dead or in the hands of Vichy. Fortunately, the AFL had already sent to Marseilles its own man, Dr. Frank Bohn, who had started sending refugees to America. He and Fry decided to divide their labor; Bohn would take over the political refugees and Fry would concentrate on the artists and intellectuals.

To hide his covert operations, Fry set up the Secours Américain as an American relief office and hired a staff. He learned in short order the business of false exit visas (expert forgeries by an artist whose brushstrokes resembled a government stamp), Czech passports, Chinese visas, and safe, walkable paths to the Spanish border. Eventually, Fry managed to smuggle hundreds of refugees out of France before the Vichy government and the American consulate brought pressure on him to leave. Until then, Fry and his staff kept countless desperate men and women alive with the promise of freedom and money.

Money, however, was soon a problem. Fry had arrived in Marseilles with several thousand dollars, but he quickly found the need to be more than he could cover. The committee in New York was busy raising contributions, but immediate funds were necessary.

One day, Peggy received a telegram from Kay Sage, Tanguy's new American wife, asking Peggy if she would pay the passage to America of certain distinguished European artists. When Peggy cabled back for a clarification, Kay enumerated: André Breton, his wife, Jacqueline Lamba, and five-year-old daughter, Aube; Max Ernst; and Dr. Pierre Mabille, the doctor to the Surrealists. Peggy objected that Dr. Mabille was not a distinguished artist, and neither, for that matter, were Jacqueline Lamba and Aube Breton. Peggy flatly refused to pay for Dr. Mabille, but did commit herself to taking care of the Breton family and Ernst.

Breton was then living in a large, dilapidated bourgeois villa half an hour from Marseilles called the Air-Bel. Originally rented as a haven from gloomy and poorly heated hotel rooms by Mary Jayne Gold, a young American woman who assisted Fry, it had haphazardly evolved into a halfway house for refugees awaiting passage or papers. Breton and his family, as well as the Bolshevik writer Victor Serge, were invited by Gold to stay there when she discovered that they had nowhere else to go. Varian Fry and members of the Secours Américain staff also lived at the villa, which was renamed by Victor Serge the "Villa Espèrevisa."

With Breton's presence, the villa quickly took on a Surrealist atmosphere. To pass the time, Breton collected butterflies and sea glass. One day, Mary Jayne Gold came upon him arranging a bouquet of green leaves as a centerpiece in the dining room. Puzzled at this display of domesticity, she stepped up to take a closer look and saw, to her amazement, two praying mantises making love. The female, observed Breton gleefully, was already eating the neck of her lover.

On Sundays, the terraces and huge living rooms of the old house filled with the roar of Breton's voice and the chatter of other Surrealists living nearby who came to pay homage: Victor Brauner, Oscar Dominguez, Wilfredo Lam, Benjamin Péret. Breton would bring out all his paraphernalia: "old magazines, colored paper, pastel chalks, scissors and pastepots, and everybody would make montages," said Varian Fry, "draw, or cut out paper dolls. At the end of the evening André would decide who had done the best work, crying, *'Formidable!' 'Sensationnel!'* or, *'Invraisemblable!'*"

One day, when the police came to search the villa for suspected Communist activity prior to Marshal Pétain's visit to Marseilles, they found what they took to be a damning bit of evidence, a Surrealist drawing. On it was a Gallic cock and underneath was inscribed, *"Le terrible crétin Pétain."*

"Revolutionary propaganda," declared the *commissaire,* and Breton,

Fry, Mary Jayne Gold, and Victor Serge were taken to a boat in the middle of Marseilles Harbor, along with other undesirables, to cool their heels during Pétain's visit.

Shortly after their release, Peggy decided to pay a visit to Marseilles and the Emergency Rescue Committee. Independently, she had heard from Victor Brauner, the Romanian-born Surrealist painter, who had lost an eye as a bystander at a Surrealist party, asking her to help him; he was living in hiding near Marseilles and was in constant fear of being picked up and interned as a foreigner and a Jew. Wanting to help Brauner, Peggy thought she should consolidate her activities with the committee.

She met Brauner in Marseilles and went to see Fry. Fry was eager to return to New York and speak to the Emergency Rescue Committee people in person. His communications from France had to be circumspect and it was hard for him to get news of the refugees who had already left. In addition, he was under increasing pressure from the French police to leave, and the American consulate, embarrassed by the committee's illegal activities in a country toward which they were supposedly friendly, would not back his operations. He was loath to leave, however, even for a short time, without having someone to take his place, preferably an American who would be relatively immune from Vichy. If he left, he feared that his European staff would quickly land in Vichy prisons. Fry asked Peggy if she would work with the committee. She was an American, had money, and was committed to art and artists. This would be an opportunity for her to help many to safety. Would Peggy take his place while he went to New York for a short time?

Peggy knew little of what the committee did or represented, and Marseilles, with its narrow streets, clandestine activity by smugglers and black-market profiteers, demobilized soldiers, and hungry refugees frightened her. As she later wrote, "Living in Grenoble and thinking only about art I was completely unconscious of the underground and had no idea what all this was about." She went to the American consul for advice, but he, who had been hoping Fry would leave and cease embarrassing the U.S. State Department, only told Peggy to stay away from any involvement with the Emergency Rescue Committee. Terrified, Peggy gave Fry some money and a promise to pay for Max Ernst's voyage as well as funds to Breton for his trip, then returned to Grenoble.

Soon thereafter, toward the end of March 1941, Breton with his wife and child boarded a steamer for Martinique. That way, Fry had discovered, it was possible to avoid the problem of crossing Spain, a Fascist country. From Martinique, it was easy to get to New York. Breton was always grateful to Peggy. "She was a generous woman," recounted Jacqueline Lamba, "She paid for the voyage, took care of us, and gave us some money until André found work in New York."

Twenty-five years later, Breton wrote Peggy: "I have not, meanwhile, forgot NY, nor that Marseilles at the turn of 1940 from which I was able to escape in time, thanks to you. It is evidently one of the greatest landmarks of my life and I can never think without emotion that all depended then on your generous intervention."

Countless people passed through Marseilles and the offices of the Emergency Rescue Committee that spring of 1941 on their way to Lisbon and from there to America, among them Marc Chagall, Jacques Lipchitz, André Masson, and Consuelo de St. Exupéry, the widow of the writer. Kay Boyle came trying to secure the necessary papers for her Austrian lover, Baron Frankenstein, to go to the United States. Fry remembered her as like her books: "intense, emotional and very finely wrought," always wearing flower-shaped, white bone earrings, reminiscent of the edelweiss, her cold blue eyes, the color of lapis lazuli. And Max Ernst arrived in a white sheepskin coat, under his arm a roll of paintings which he tacked up over the ersatz leather wall covering in the dining room of the Villa Air-Bel. Like others before him, Ernst settled in to wait.

Once back in Grenoble, Peggy continued with her plans to return to America. René Lefebvre-Foinet, who was helping her pack her collection by day and sleeping with her at night, suggested, as did Laurence, that as long as she was paying for Max Ernst's trip to America, she should at least get a picture or two out of it. Perking up at the thought, Peggy wrote Ernst at the Villa Air-Bel. Why of course, Ernst answered graciously, and sent a photo of a painting he thought would be suitable. She did not like the particular picture he sent, but perhaps she could choose another one? Peggy decided to return to Marseilles and see for herself.

Peggy had not seen Max Ernst since the day when Howard Putzel took her to Max's Paris studio. Since then the German-born Ernst had had a difficult time. At the outbreak of the war, he was rounded up and interned as an enemy alien at Largentière, an abominably filthy, crowded former prison with narrow cells and execrable food. At the end of six weeks, he was moved to another French internment camp, Les Milles, near Aix, which was a converted brick factory full of Austrians, Czechs, Foreign Legionnaires, Jews, and *apatrides*—men without a country. "One slept on bricks, one saw only bricks, one even breathed bricks!" said Ernst later of his experience. There he ran into Hans Bellmer, a fellow Surrealist famous for his life-size dolls. As a souvenir of these grim times, Bellmer did a portrait of Ernst, outlined entirely in trompe-l'oeil bricks.

Through the desperate intercession of Leonora Carrington, who pounded on every door she could think of, and of Paul Éluard, his longtime friend, Ernst was released around Christmas 1939, only to be reinterned when the Germans began their western offensive in May. Shuffled to more camps, he wound up at St. Nicolas, an isolated farm where the inmates slept in tents, with no sanitation and plenty of lice. Max managed to escape and made his way on foot by night to his home in St.-Martin-d'Ardèche.

He found the house deserted. Leonora had broken down under the emotional strain of seeing Max taken away for the second time. She described her experience in the Surrealist magazine *VVV:* "I wept for several hours, down in the village; then I went up again to my house where, for twenty-four hours, I indulged in voluntary vomitings induced by drinking orange blossom water and interrupted by a short nap. I hoped that my sorrow would be allayed by those violent spasms which tore my stomach apart like so many earthquakes." Leonora sold the house for a bottle of brandy, and made her way to Spain, where she ended up in an insane asylum. Max found his paintings still in the house and made off with them in the middle of the night; but his friezes and sculptures he would have to rescue more directly from the new owner. Hungry, poor, and alone, Max lived in hiding until he was anonymously denounced to the authorities and wound up again in St. Nicolas. Finally, he was released when it was discovered that he had been married to a Frenchwoman, from whom, he neglected to add, he had also been divorced. In December 1940, he went to Marseilles to begin making arrangements to go to America, where he had a son, Ulrich, known as Jimmy, from his first marriage.

When Peggy made her return visit to Marseilles, Victor Brauner met her at the train station. Brauner was in terrible shape. A Romanian Jew, he could not get a visa to emigrate to the United States, as the tiny quota had been filled. Moreover, as a foreign Jew whose papers were anything but in order he was liable to be picked up and summarily interned in a concentration camp or placed in a work gang. Peggy promised to see what she could do, but aside from giving him some money, making inquiries at the American consulate, and involving Varian Fry, she had very little power to do anything. She did, however, console him with her caresses, and Brauner could not help being a little in love with her.

That evening at a café, Brauner and Peggy met Max Ernst, who was still living at the Villa Air-Bel waiting for his papers for America. Peggy was astonished when she saw Max, who had aged considerably since she had last seen him. The vicissitudes of war had given his delicate good looks a pale-faced intensity. As he came over to them, white-haired and angelic, draped in a black cape, she thought him utterly romantic, reminiscent of Laurence Vail. Ernst appeared happy to see Peggy again and delighted to have a chance to show her his paintings.

The next day, Peggy and Brauner went out to the Villa Air-Bel to see Max's works. Proudly, he brought out his latest paintings, which he had worked on in moments snatched between concentration camps. These eerie canvases, with their earthy, porous forms squashed or rubbed on with wet paint, evoked images of decay—once-great cities in ruin and civilizations at their end. Ernst showed Peggy pictures like *Europe After the Rain II* and the *Fascinating Cypresses,* but Peggy dismissed these. She much preferred his earlier work. Max was crestfallen that his recent work failed to interest her, especially since Peggy took no pains to hide her views. As to the earlier work, Peggy proposed to buy the whole lot for two thousand dollars, minus the money that she had already advanced toward Ernst's trip to America.

Max was frankly displeased with the idea, but he had little choice. Ernst's dealer of many years, Julien Levy, said, "Max resented terrifically her buying all his paintings." Nevertheless, Peggy was helping him to get to America at a time when Max's own resources were close to nil. Since 1935, the painter had suffered a period of intense financial insecurity. His paintings did not sell and his last show had been at Roland Penrose's London Gallery before the war. Ernst often had not had the money to eat or pay his bills. Julien Levy recalled that once he bought two hundred dollars' worth of pictures from Ernst "when he was very poor and desperately needed money. Max was so happy he threw a huge party and invited the whole block. There was champagne for everybody. When I asked if he had enough money left to pay the rent, Max pointed to a woman with two champagne bottles poised like dunce caps on either breast, and said 'Don't worry, that is my landlady.' " Ernst's son Jimmy remembered a time in Paris when he went to visit his father who, not wanting to admit his terrible poverty, took Jimmy to a restaurant and freely ordered from the menu. When it came time to pay the bill, he gently suggested to Jimmy, "Take a walk for thirty minutes, will you?" Pressing his nose to the window, Jimmy could see his father telling the waiter that he had no money to pay. Ernst spent an entire day visiting galleries trying to collect the money for Jimmy's fare back home to Germany. In despair, he turned to his son and snapped, "Why couldn't you have had your return fare, too?" When Peggy offered that two thousand dollars, Max was surviving thanks to the generosity of his friend the poet Joe Bousquet, who periodically sent Max modest subsidies. Ernst could not pass up Peggy's offer.

Max let Peggy, with Brauner's help, pick out whatever she wanted. Brauner, as a Surrealist painter, had a greater sense of Ernst's historical importance than did Peggy, and kept finding more and more exciting works, which Ernst generously included in the bargain. In this fashion Peggy acquired some of the jewels of her collection: Ernst's 1919 mechanical drawing/gouache *Little Machine Constructed by Minimax Dadamax in Person, Aeroplane Trap,* the 1932 collage *The Postman Horse,* and several others. To consummate the transaction, Ernst took out a bottle of wine that he had rescued from his vineyard at St.-Martin-d'Ardèche and invited Peggy and Brauner to celebrate his fiftieth birthday, which was the following day, April 2.

During the process of selection, Peggy had time to observe Max and was, in the words of Ernst's biographer, Patrick Waldberg, "seduced by the painter as well as his art." Ernst had quite a reputation as a lady-killer. His cool, Germanic looks were irresistible to women; his round, blazing blue eyes seemed to take in everything. He had the type of looks that Peggy loved—aristocratic, fine-featured, and thin-lipped. He was, Peggy pronounced, "wonderful."

DADAMAX ERNST

For many, Max Ernst was the supreme Surrealist painter. Unquestionably, he was one of the most remarkable artists of his era. His career, in its diversity and impact, resembled that of Marcel Duchamp, who, like Ernst, spent his life searching for new means of expression. Interestingly, they shared a childhood experience of deafness: Duchamp had a partially deaf mother; Ernst's father, though not deaf himself, ran a Catholic school for the deaf in the little town of Brühl, near Cologne. Both artists grew up in a silent world in which their inner fantasies gave rise to violent but mute expression, where gestures spoke louder than words. These silent worlds also nurtured in each an idiosyncratic use of language, a love of puns and double meanings.

As a young boy, Ernst watched his father, an accomplished Sunday painter, work on realistic canvases. Philipp Ernst was so literal, however, that once, when he painted their garden and omitted from his composition a tree that stood in its center, he chopped down the tree. The second of seven children, Max was cowed by this authoritarian, sadistic man and grew up a moody, isolated child subject to fits of depression and nightmares, alternating with insane extremes of joy. He tried to run away when he was five—a little blond urchin dressed in his red nightshirt—

only to be returned by a band of religious pilgrims who mistook him for the infant Jesus.

Max painted from the age he could hold a brush and retreated into a world of fantasy, German fairy tales, and legends. *"Seeing,"* he said, "was my chief preoccupation. My eyes were greedy not only for the amazing world which assaulted them from without, but also for that other, mysterious, disturbing world which surged up and melted away in my dreams." In later years, Ernst mythologized his youth and exaggerated episodes of which he nurtured unsettling memories. He gave great importance to the death of his pet pink cockatoo, Hornebom, on the eve of his sister Loni's birth. From that time, a "dangerous confusion between birds and humans became encrusted in his mind," wrote Max Ernst to explain his obsessive preoccupation and identification with birds and in particular with "Loplop," the Bird Superior, his alter ego, similar to Duchamp's "Rrose Sélavy." Max identified with "the bird as a phallic symbol." He fancied himself and, indeed, looked like a bird.

He retained and later used vivid impressions of the forest near Brühl, where his father often went to draw, accompanied by young Max. The forest was so dense that it was dark at high noon, kept still by a carpet of leaves. Max had the feeling every time he went there that he was crossing a threshold into a world of magical if frightening possibilities. The image of the enchanted forest, along with the bird, haunted his art.

His parents sent Max to the University of Bonn to study philosophy, hoping that their son would become a doctor or a lawyer. But, by his own admission, Ernst avoided "all forms of study which might degenerate into gainful employment." Instead, he was particularly fascinated by abnormal psychology, read the works of Sigmund Freud, and visited with great interest the local insane asylum, where he noticed the strange conjunction of words and symbols in the drawings of schizophrenics. Riveted by the disquieting art of the insane, Max hoped—long before the Surrealists made it chic—to one day write a book about it. By this time, it was clear that painting was Max's first love. In 1913 he went to Paris, fell madly in love with the city, and vowed to return and live there forever.

Max found a mentor in August Macke, an older painter, well acquainted with developments in French painting and with its practitioners. Through him, Ernst met the Delaunays and soon thereafter the jovial Jean Arp. Arp and Ernst became great friends, but their friendship was cut short by World War I, which Arp chose to sit out in Zurich, while Ernst was drafted into the German artillery. Put to work marking positions on maps, Ernst was able to wander and paint in his free time. After eight months, he was sent to the Russian front where he suffered two injuries, both in the head: one from the recoil of a gun, the other from the kick of a feisty mule, earning him the nickname "Ironhead."

When Ernst was discharged in 1918, he felt reborn, resuming his art activities with relish. Dada madness had spread like influenza and Ernst was not immune to its anarchic charms.

Together with Arp, who had returned to Cologne from Zurich, and Johannes Baargeld (the name used by Alfred Grünwald, the iconoclastic son of one of the Rhineland's leading financiers), Ernst formed a Cologne Dada group called the Zentrale W/3. The W/3 stood for West-stupidien/3, a play on a postal address that translates as The West Stupid Three. This tiny Dada band managed to break up a production of a patriotic drama and publish Dada periodicals, including the highly political *Der Ventilator*, which was distributed on the streets and outside factory gates. Ernst experimented with mechanical drawings and published an album of them called *Fiat Modes* in 1919. Arp, Baargeld, and Ernst participated in *Fatagaga—Fabrications des tableaux garantis gazometriques*— a series of collages made from magazine and book cutouts, signed by the three partners but all executed by Ernst.

The highlight of Cologne Dada, however, was the splendid provocation at the Brasserie Winter, a beer hall, in 1920. In order to reach the exhibition, patrons were routed across the beer hall and through its lavatory—urinals and all—to arrive at a glass-enclosed, sky-lit courtyard. There a young girl dressed in her First Communion gown loudly recited obscene poetry to the beery visitors. Baargeld's *Fluidoskeptrick of Rotzwitha von Gondersheim,* an ordinary fish tank, was filled with a blood-red liquid in which floated a woman's wig and an alarm clock, and out of which protruded a mannequin's wooden hand. This item caused such a furor that before long it was reduced to a hill of glass shards and wet red goo by an enraged spectator who had decided to manifest his disapproval. Indeed, viewers were invited to vent their fury with an ax chained to a wooden sculpture exhibited by Max Ernst for that exclusive purpose. Many of the patrons, already drunk from the beer hall, were glad to oblige, and the exhibition was a huge "triumph of Dada."

The greatest indignation was directed at a composite work by Ernst. The police were sent to investigate charges that the exhibition was a fraud against the public, an obscenity, and a front for a male homosexual brothel. Suspicious, they seized a highly offensive etching, only to determine later that it was in fact a reproduction of Albrecht Dürer's *Adam and Eve.* The police shut down the exhibition, but allowed it to reopen after interrogating Ernst and Baargeld and being satisfied that, whatever else this exhibition might be, it was not a fraud. As Max pointed out, it was merely Dada.

The scandal that resulted from the Dada exhibition prompted Ernst's father to write him: "My curse upon you. You have dishonoured our name," severing forever the ties between them. But if Max had lost one family, he had gained another, for André Breton wrote him from Paris, delirious at the success of Cologne Dada, and invited Ernst to show his works in the City of Light. He organized an exhibition under the slogan *"Au delà de la Peinture"* (Beyond Painting), at the Galerie au Sans Pareil (without equal), to which Max, who was unable to get a passport to enter France, sent fifty-two watercolors, collages, and drawings wrapped in plain brown paper. Attended by all the Paris Dadaists, tieless but white-gloved, the exhibit was a Dada event. Louis Aragon hopped about like a kangaroo, Philippe Soupault ran after Tristan Tzara, and the latter, ever scatological, climbed up on a chair to announce that one glass of wine had been adulterated with a powerful laxative as a sort of booby prize for an unlucky partygoer. Breton was delighted to welcome to the fold an artist whose talent could rival Francis Picabia's, since that painter's irascibility had been annoying him. Breton gleefully told a friend that Max Ernst's collages had "driven Picabia crazy with resentment."

However, Dada was coming to an end, and Ernst, too, was affected by a desire for a more systematic movement in art. For some time he had been perfecting his unique brand of collage, snipping out pictures from nineteenth-century illustrated novels and catalogues, placing them in incongruous contexts—two girls bicycling in the clouds, sides of beef hanging in a Victorian parlor, a girl all wired up lying on a divan—and giving them such romantic titles as *The Chinese Nightingale, Above the Clouds Midnight Passes,* and *The Massacre of the Innocents.* By keeping the cutting-and-pasting to a minimum, Max achieved a unified image in which it was difficult to tell where the cutout ended and the work of his own hand began. In Ernst's collages one saw a lace ball with a dancer's high-heeled legs, a man's head on a female body, a boxer with chicken feet.

The images in Ernst's collages were important for what they revealed of the unconscious, charged as they were with humor, sex, puns, and double meanings. The art critic Lucy Lippard suggests that for density of association Max Ernst is rivaled only by James Joyce. For example, in *The Hat Makes the Man,* an image taken from a hat advertisement, bowlers seem to spring up in accordionlike pillars. At the time Max's father-in-law owned a hat factory and Ernst used the hat as a phallic symbol as well as one for his own father, who frequently sported a bowler.

One day quite by accident, Ernst came across a pamphlet on the painter Giorgio de Chirico with reproductions of his recent work. De Chirico's deadpan renderings of everyday objects, rearranged in situations that could only have reality in dreams or obscure memories, transfixed Max Ernst. He was staggered by de Chirico's sun-seared piazzas traversed by menacing shadows, a girl running with a hoop, a rubber glove tacked on a wall, classical columns. Much of the power of de Chirico's canvases came from his use of a deep, illusionistic perspective, idiosyncratically foreshortened. Banal objects took on great significance, as though seen through the eyes of a child, who perceives as enormous those things that fascinate him—a ball, a slice of bacon sizzling in a pan, a dressmaker's dummy. "If it is to be really immortal," wrote the painter, "a work of art must go far beyond human limits. Good sense and logic will have no part in it, and it will be near to the state of dreams, and to the mentality of children." Moreover, in these early metaphysical landscapes of de Chirico there prevails a sense of profound stillness, which was terribly appealing to Ernst. It was the silence of dreams, but "a pregnant rather than a calm silence, charged with elusive, nightmarish foreboding."

Max recognized in de Chirico's paintings what he had been doing in his collages—juxtaposing images taken out of their usual context. De Chirico pointed the way to Surrealism for Ernst, as he did for Tanguy in the years 1921–1924, just before Surrealism officially declared itself.

Immediately, Ernst responded with a series of paintings akin to painted collages. He borrowed de Chirico's use of perspective and idiosyncratic placement of highly personal elements. In *Aquis Submersus,* a boy dives headlong into a pool illuminated by a sun with the face of a clock while menacing shadows reach out at him. In *The Equivocal Woman,* a maiden floats in the air, her wavy hair on end, connected through her eyes to a fantastical machine. In contrast to de Chirico's use of commonplace objects, Ernst's images were fantastical. Painted in a droll, unemotional manner, his canvases bear a heightened sense of other-reality, of dreams and memories. The important thing in these pictures is not the design; their value lies in their power to disquiet.

By 1925, Ernst was a full-scale Surrealist, living in Paris and thrown headlong into Surrealist gatherings, séances, and life. When he first arrived, the Surrealists were experimenting with *sommeils,* or waking dreams, induced by self-hypnosis, in which they spoke directly from the unconscious. From "automatic" writing they had gone on to "automatic" talking, which some of them did to perfection, spontaneously spilling out elaborate and violent stories of wandering hordes and conquering armies.

Under the influence of Breton and his friends, and intrigued by the idea of "automatic" painting, Ernst began thinking about tapping his own unconscious more directly. One rainy day in 1925, he later wrote in *Beyond Painting,* he was drawn by a childhood memory to stare at the worn floorboards of an old inn in Brittany in which he was staying. Seized with inspiration, he hurled himself on the floor armed with paper and a lead pencil. Dropping the paper at random over the floor, he began to rub. As in a dream or a state of erotic anticipation, he said, forms strange and wonderful appeared to him—birds, horsemen, forests. He was so excited by his discovery that he made rubbings of bits of thread, linen, and fallen leaves and turned them into pictures. It seemed to Max that here was the pictorial equivalent of Breton's *automatisme,* and of stories spilled forth at Surrealist séances. *Frottage,* as this new method was called, was hailed by Breton and Aragon and *frottages* were exhibited at the Galerie Surréaliste, which opened that fall.

Ernst plunged into the pursuit of innovative techniques or, as he put it, forced inspiration. He became more and more obsessed with birds, and they appeared over and over in his work, especially his alter ego, Loplop, the bird superior. Ernst applied layers of paint and then scraped them off in *grattage;* he dropped strings wet with paint on canvas, using accident and chance. His paintings charged with sexual images to which he gave fanciful titles were evocative on many levels.

Ernst tried his hand at sculpture, at set design, at collage "novels." His invention was dazzling. Even during the war, interned in detention camps, he continued experimenting with *décalcomie,* rubbing wet paint on canvas. By the time Peggy caught up with him in 1941, Max Ernst had logged twenty-five years at the center of European avant-garde art. He was a celebrity of major proportions in the art world, a man whose talent seemingly had no bounds.

Ernst's Surrealism, Peggy knew, did not end with his art. He enjoyed a tempestuous love life. For many years he lived with the poet Paul Éluard and his wife, Gala Diakonova (the future wife of Salvador Dali), in a well-known ménage à trois. At a 1922 Dada meeting in the Austrian Tyrol, Ernst had left his wife, Louise, and infant son in their ramshackle house and had moved in with Gala and Paul next door. Éluard tried to accommodate himself to the situation by shrugging his shoulders and announcing: "Well, I love Max Ernst much more than I do Gala." He fooled no one, but as it was bad form to subscribe to convention, and especially the worn-out convention of marriage, Éluard was condemned to look on as his wife conducted a stormy affair with Ernst. Clad in well-worn lederhosen and sandals, his athletic legs a perfect golden tan, Ernst, wrote Matthew Josephson, "was altogether of an extraordinary male beauty—that of a 'fallen angel,' the women used to say."

Leaving his wife and young son, Jimmy, in Cologne, Max moved to France in 1922, entering illegally on a passport lent him by Éluard. He moved in with the couple in Eubonne, a suburb of Paris, decorating their house with fantastical landscapes of animals and plants, covering doors and walls; even the bathroom was transformed into one huge strawberry. "Love," wrote Ernst, "is the great enemy of Christian morality . . . sexuality has been enfeebled by the suppression of pleasure and the duty of procreation, and . . . passionate impulses have been tamed by the necessity of praying to a Virgin. . . . Love—as Rimbaud said—must be reinvented."

Because he had entered France illegally, Ernst spent the next five years clandestinely. He invented aliases and took odd jobs. He could not sell his paintings; in fact, until 1926, Éluard was the only person who bought his work. For two years Ernst worked in a souvenir factory producing trinkets, bracelets, cigarette holders. Occasionally he got work as a film extra, a career cut short when he decided to remove his wig during a take. This impecunious chapter came to an end when Ernst met and seduced pretty Marie-Berthe Aurenche, the seventeen-year-old daughter of the registrar general of the Commercial Court. The girl's father was outraged, but eventually relented and consented to the marriage, if only to save his daughter's honor. Ironically, Ernst, who so recently had been a factory worker, now found himself related to a family with pretensions to the throne of France. His new father-in-law used his influence to get him a legal residence permit. It seemed, scoffed an observer, that every time Ernst had immigration problems, a woman came to the rescue.

After Marie-Berthe, there was a series of affairs, always with beautiful and tempestuous women who fell in love with Ernst's reserve and cool, astonishing white-blond looks. In 1933 he had a fling with Meret Oppenheim, the inventor of the fur-lined teacup, the scandal of various Surrealist exhibitions. Later, Max took up with Leonor Fini, another Surrealist, a "crazy little darling" who lived in a velvet-draped apartment and had a penchant for fancy masquerades, boots, hats, masks, and "stage-jeweled coronets." She owned one dress made entirely of black feathers and wore clothes designed by Max with little pictures of himself. As his old friend the dealer Julien Levy recalled, "Max had a strong visual fantasy. He dressed up all his girls to match, like all the painters with their models—Picasso/Jacqueline." For an evening at Tristan Tzara's, the rule was that guests be nude from chest to thigh. Leonor Fini wore knee-length white leatherette boots and a matching feather cape. "Blue feathers and tinsel dust were sprinkled in the curls of her hair." Ernst, who also adored dressing up, wore a spiked belt, winged sandals, and a headdress and breastplate made of scouring pads.

The writer and concert pianist Arthur Gold recalled seeing Ernst show up at a reception perfectly dressed—ostensibly—in a white suit. Looking closer, however, he noticed that Max's fly was open and that cascading out of it were long curly hairs. Similarly, his partner had a deep décolletage and "made a startling effect, which looked perfectly normal until you looked closely and saw she had hair coming out of her cleavage."

At the time Peggy first met Max Ernst, he was involved with

Leonora Carrington, an English Surrealist painter and great beauty. Meeting Leonora at his show at Roland Penrose's London Gallery in 1937, Ernst whisked the willing artist, many years his junior, off to Paris. "She was simply the most beautiful creature," said the artist Hedda Sterne of Leonora. "She went around in jodhpurs and boots—nobody was doing that. I remember a show, a Surrealist show . . . and at the opening again Leonora Carrington, when people didn't do that, came in a dress from a thrift shop, a high-necked lace dress. She looked absolutely beautiful." Peggy herself admired Leonora's looks. "Marvelous! Alabaster skin, wavy black hair, and big, brown eyes. She was marvelous looking. Wonderful."

In a Surrealist vein, Leonora nurtured her instabilities. "Carrington was too wacky," observed Ernst's friend Julien Levy. "She had an impossible temperament: impetuous, tempestuous, you never knew when you were going to hurt her feelings. She was oversensitive." But such shortcomings did little to alleviate the jealousy Peggy felt over Leonora's delicate beauty (that tip-tilted nose), and her talent as a Surrealist painter: Peggy would have loved to have either.

THE UGLY DUCKLING
AND THE SWAN

Max Ernst invited Peggy to help him celebrate his fiftieth birthday on April 2, 1941, with a seafood dinner at Marseilles' Vieux Port. In addition to Peggy he took Victor Brauner, who followed Peggy around like a lapdog, and René Lefebvre-Foinet, who had just arrived from Grenoble. Varian Fry joined them at a black-market restaurant—the only kind that served decent food in a city where people congregated in front of a *rôtisserie* to watch a lone chicken revolve on a spit.

Peggy could not keep her eyes off Ernst and flirted girlishly with him. Ernst was not averse to Peggy's carrying on, although ordinarily he preferred much younger and prettier women. She did have a charming smile, lovely figure, and seductive manner, and Max was lonely and in need of feminine companionship. He had not seen Carrington since the spring of 1940, when he was taken by the French police. Moreover, the thought of Peggy's money was intoxicating. After years of privation and real suffering, unable to make a living selling paintings, shunned as a German alien in his beloved France, Ernst was ready to be taken care of, if only for a while.

Peggy was vivacious, full of fun, and intensely Surrealist: that coal-black hair, those outrageous earrings dangling as she spoke, and the impertinent things she said! "Do you like sex?" She was making it possible for him to leave France, and what, after all, would be the point of resisting the tenacious Peggy Guggenheim?

Max bent over and whispered in her ear, "When, where, and why shall I meet you?" To which Peggy, unabashedly slipping him her hotel key, replied, "Tomorrow at four in the Café de la Paix and you know why."

Peggy was delighted that the fifty-year-old Ernst made love to her three times in succession on their first night together. "That was pretty good, wasn't it?" she asked happily. For ten days she chased after him in Marseilles until she had to leave, reluctantly, for Mégève, where she had promised Laurence and her children she would spend Easter. As he saw Peggy off at the old train station, Ernst cried and gave her a book that he had previously inscribed, "To Leonora real, beautiful, and naked."

When she reached Mégève, Peggy found Laurence despondent. Kay Boyle had finally gone off with her Austrian lover to Cassis, taking the babies with her and leaving the older girls, Bobbie, Pegeen, and Apple. Kay wanted no more to do with Laurence, was tired of his tantrums and childishness, and wanted a divorce. Laurence moaned that all his wives left him and grew frankly incestuous with his daughters, Apple in particular. He would lie in bed with her, lamenting his fate, or would take baths with her. Apple, guilty and frightened, would take care not to look at "that thing." "My father," said Clover Vail, "was very seductive with his children. I think it was because he came from a very Victorian age, tremendously rigid, very afraid of sex. He used to say he wanted to marry his daughters, because his daughters could never leave him. Until I was three or four they used to keep me nude. He loved to go to nudist colonies." When Peggy arrived, Bobbie's natural conclusion was that Peggy was there to replace her mother, and Bobbie was terrified. "Peggy came and lived with us for a while. I was such a closed-in little girl," she said, "to think that she was replacing my mother —I couldn't bear. There was a great ritual about who should serve the soup, Laurence, Peggy, or us girls."

Peggy and Laurence were quite oblivious to the girls' sufferings, preoccupied as they were with themselves. Peggy was obsessed with Max, who had not tried to reach her in Mégève, and Laurence was distressed over the loss of Kay, who had been directing his life for twelve years. Returning to America seemed the best thing to do, so Peggy and Laurence went to Lyons to straighten out their travel papers. There they met Marcel Duchamp, who had made his way south from occupied Paris (where he had left Mary Reynolds doing resistance work). Duchamp, too, was anxious to get to New York.

No sooner had Peggy arrived in Lyons than she heard that Ernst was in Mégève, beguiling the girls. "Max Ernst—a fascinating creature," pronounced Bobbie, "arrived one night in a black cape and told us these marvelous stories and showed us photographs of his paintings and told us about his affection for Leonora Carrington." The young girls, who themselves had love perpetually on their minds, were delighted. Peggy could not wait to get back to Mégève.

In Mégève, Peggy and Max resumed their affair, to the chagrin of the girls, who wanted him all to themselves, and who had subscribed wholeheartedly to his profession of undying devotion to Leonora. Moreover, Pegeen and Bobbie were made all too aware of what was going on. One night "he came into the wrong room on all fours," remembered Bobbie, who shared a room with Pegeen. "He said he was looking for his pyjamas. We all looked at this very cynically."

After a week Peggy followed Max to Marseilles. As hotel rooms were scarce, Peggy accompanied him to the Villa Air-Bel, where she impressed Varian Fry by wearing the earrings Tanguy had designed for her. Mary Jayne Gold remembered Peggy as quite a character: "In the early days when she was having trouble with Max Ernst, she complained: 'Oh! this new insult—*bourgeoise*. Why doesn't he call me a whore like all the other men in my life?' "

Gold, then a lovely young blonde, noticed that Max "kept staring at me, and I would look back. He was a remarkable-looking man. His eyes kept coming back to me. Later, when I got to know him better, I asked him what that had been all about, and he said: 'You look very much like a woman who ran away with a woman I was in love with.' " Peggy found life at the villa a little too close for comfort. She loved the idea of having an affair, but staying in the same cramped room with someone was no fun. At the first opportunity, she moved back to the De Noailles, a large hotel on the water.

Marseilles, as the largest city in Vichy France, was the center of visa and passport activity. Consequently, it was in Marseilles that all efforts were to be made to get travel documents in order for the Vail family, for Peggy and her children, and for Max Ernst as well. Laurence arrived, to be whisked out of the Gare St. Charles through the restaurant, as he had no safe-conduct visa. Kay, having deposited her lover on a boat sailing from Marseilles, showed up to turn her attention wholeheartedly to her family's plans. Duchamp, trying to get his emigration papers in order, joined the group, as did Brauner, who clung to a slight hope of overcoming the Romanian quota for immigration to the United States.

As they sat together at dinner, Kay wickedly announced that she had just heard that the ship carrying Peggy's collection to New York had been sunk. An argument broke out when Laurence complained that Kay had not considered going to Mégève to pack up the family until Frankenstein was safely off. Laurence began throwing plates about and screaming. Duchamp and Peggy ignored Laurence's antics, as for them it was old hat, but Max, who preferred to be the center of attention himself, was astonished.

The amount of paperwork required to leave Vichy was enormous, and the procedure was complicated by the circuitous route that people were forced to take. Most refugees headed for the Spanish border. If one were lucky and escaped detection by the French authorities before reaching that border, the Spanish would look the other way if French exit visas were not altogether in order. Once in Spain, it was fairly safe to cross into Portugal, where Pan American Clippers left Lisbon for the long flight to New York. Kay Boyle took matters in hand and made ten reservations on one of the planes. (Initially, Kay had had the effrontery to want the Baron Frankenstein included on the Clipper, but Laurence put his foot down and said absolutely not. "I must say," Peggy remarked —as she so often did when it was she herself who had caused trouble— "I don't blame him.")

Peggy had been traveling within France on her expired French safe-conduct visa; Laurence did not even have such a visa; and all of their passports had expired (or were otherwise invalid) during their many years in Europe.

After Brauner, Ernst was in the worst shape. Before any foreigner would be allowed to leave France, he needed a French exit visa. In many cases this could be more difficult to secure than an American visa, because for German nationals, permission had to be requested via the Reich. All decisions came from Berlin, giving the Nazis a dual opportunity to prevent the departure of their enemies and to pinpoint precisely where they were. If a person was on Hitler's wanted list, the chances of obtaining a permit to leave were slim. Furthermore, the longer Ernst waited in France without the proper papers, the greater were his chances of being seized in a roundup or sent back to Germany. He had already been interned in French detention camps, and he was a known enemy of the Reich. His 1923 picture *The Fair Gardener* had been confiscated by the Nazis and toured in an exhibition of "degenerate" art under the heading "Insult to German Womanhood." There was no knowing when Max might land in another concentration camp, or if he could be sent back to Germany.

Max was frightfully nervous lest his American visa (initiated in New York by the Museum of Modern Art in collaboration with Varian Fry and the Emergency Rescue Committee) should expire before his exit visa came through. This was precisely what happened. Consequently, Ernst paid many visits to the American consulate, a large brick house half an hour's trolley ride from the center of town. There was always a mob of tired refugees milling around the entrance, and Peggy flashed her American passport to get through with Max in tow. Despite the consul's sympathy, it was difficult to renew the artist's entry visa into the United States; it would take time.

Jacqueline Ventadour, Pegeen's childhood chum, recalled sitting around with Peggy and discussing at great length Ernst's problems. "Peggy once said, 'I'll marry him,' but nothing came of that. Finally, I had a preference visa, and it was discovered that if Max were to marry me, he could come in. But I was fifteen and a half years old. They decided it was not necessary. But one whole evening was spent considering it."

By April, the French police began to take a more menacing attitude toward the refugees hiding or waiting in Marseilles. All the Jews staying in the hotels were rounded up and brought to the police station. The artist Marc Chagall was taken from his room in the Hôtel Moderne, along with anyone who looked Jewish. Max had warned Peggy, if she were ever questioned by the police, not to admit to being Jewish but to say simply that she was an American.

Early one morning Peggy was disturbed in her hotel room by a plainclothes policeman combing the hotel for Jews. He examined her documents and noticed the changed dates on her safe-conduct. Peggy had the presence of mind to insist that it had been done by the officials in Grenoble. He then observed that she had not registered, as was required, with the Marseilles police. When he suggested that her name was Jewish, Peggy countered that it was Swiss, from St. Gallen. After searching her room to see if she was concealing anyone under the bed or in the cupboard, he told her to accompany him to the police station. Peggy asked him to wait in the hall while she dressed. Fortunately, when she emerged the policeman's superior had arrived and he decided, said Peggy, that she looked too nice and told his man to leave her alone. In all likelihood, Peggy was spared because she was an American. She was requested to register with the Marseilles police and was given directions. Greatly relieved, yet still frightened, Peggy was told by the concierge, "Oh, that is nothing, madam. They were just rounding up the Jews."

EXIT MARSEILLES

Finally, word came that Ernst would be allowed an emergency visa to enter the United States. This time, Max decided that he would not wait for his French exit permit to arrive, but would try to leave without one. There were risks involved, to be sure, but staying in France presented still greater risks.

On May 1, 1941, Max packed his canvases and said his good-byes to Peggy and Brauner, promising to see Peggy again in Lisbon, where they would all be reunited. To avoid the French police checkpoint, Ernst entered the train station through the *buffet*. In the crowded train, all went well until he reached the French border station at Campfranc.

Max was traveling without a valid exit visa or even a good forgery, so he was nervous as he handed his documents to the French officials who came through the train. He was asked to open his suitcases, in which the French inspectors were surprised to find Ernst's rolled-up paintings. As the compartment filled with more and more of his works, they questioned the painter about his ideas and methods. Realizing that he was talking for his life, Max fired all his energies and charms into making his explanations delightful, wonderful. "I spoke that day about painting," he later said, "as I had never spoken before, and in a way it would be impossible for me to speak again. . . . I had the feeling of playing for my life, and it was true!"

One of the inspectors took him aside and said, "You know your papers are not in order, don't you?" Max, trembling, answered, "Yes." "If your papers were in order," the inspector went on, "you could get on that train to Madrid over there"—he pointed purposefully to a train on the adjacent track. *"Hélas!* my duty obliges me to ask you to take that train, that is going to Pau," he continued, gesturing toward a train on the opposite track. "Above all, monsieur, do not make a mistake. I adore talent."

Max took the inspector's hint and climbed aboard the train to Madrid, petrified lest a misstep land him once again in an internment camp. A few moments later the train crossed the Spanish border, and he was free. From Spain, Max sent Peggy a hasty note letting her know that he was safe and would wait for her in Portugal. He had no trouble getting to Lisbon, unburdening himself on the way of his large canvas, *Europe After the Rain II,* which he wrapped in plain paper and addressed: "Max Ernst c/o the Museum of Modern Art, N.Y." Miraculously, the picture arrived at the museum without incident. In Lisbon, Ernst moved into a cheap pension and waited for the Vails and Peggy to arrive.

Laurence had returned to Mégève, joined by Kay Boyle, and he and his family had been packing since Easter for their departure. The Vails —Laurence, Kay, five girls, and Sindbad—left Mégève on May 13, boarding a train for Spain. Peggy could not go with them as she had to wait in Marseilles for the money to pay the air fare to New York for all of them. The red tape involved in getting the cash out of France was cumbersome, and it took three weeks for the Banc de France to come through with the money. Secretly, Peggy was just as glad that Laurence had left first. "I didn't want to travel with all those children!"

The children were apprehensive, Kay fussed all the time about her boyfriend, and Laurence was utterly miserable, but they had no trouble crossing the French border into Spain. They spent some time in the Pyrenees before continuing on to Lisbon to wait for Peggy.

Alone in Marseilles, Peggy read Rousseau's *Confessions* in her high-ceilinged hotel room. Victor Brauner, dejected because neither he nor Peggy had been able to do anything to bypass the State Department's Romanian quota, kept Peggy company. They sat in the cafés that lined the port of Marseilles, and occasionally he would accompany her back to her room at night. Nellie van Doesburg came down to see Peggy when she heard that Peggy was leaving for America, and the two friends forgot their trifling arguments and differences and were reconciled. In these last days Peggy did what she could to get Nellie to New York, but in the end, Peggy had to leave Nellie behind to arrange her own emigration.

Peggy was joined by Jacqueline Ventadour, Pegeen's fifteen-year-old friend. Her mother, Fanny, whom Peggy had known since her days in Paris with John Holms, wanted to send the girl to a boarding school in Cassis, but Peggy insisted that Jacqueline would be far better off with her relatives in New Orleans and offered to take Jacqueline with her to the United States—although she always suspected Fanny of manipulating this outcome.

After nearly a month of waiting in Marseilles, Peggy set off with the adolescent Jacqueline at her side. They boarded a through-train to Spain, sneaking into the station by way of the restaurant, as had Ernst before them. Once underway, seated on the raffia-covered seats, the herringbone patterns playing tricks with their vision, Peggy succumbed to the mesmerizing rhythm of the wheels. The lush Mediterranean flashed by, its aquamarine waters and swaying date palms recalling a youth and ease now vanished. Peggy's years in France as a young woman, full of dreams and expectations, first with Laurence and then with John Holms, dissolved. How life had changed in those twenty years! France, the country of freedom for an entire generation, was in the hands of the Gestapo. As eager as Peggy had once been to arrive in France, she was now even more eager to be gone.

At the border, Peggy had trouble with the French police. Made suspicious by her Jewish name, they gave her a body search, hoping to find smuggled currency. Finding none, they permitted her to continue into Spain. In Lisbon, Laurence, Max, Sindbad, and Pegeen met Peggy and Jacqueline at the train station. What a relief for Peggy to see her children, and Max, whom she had missed terribly.

But almost immediately, Peggy was deflated. Ernst took her aside and holding her by the arm, whispered, "I have found Leonora. She is in Lisbon." Shaken, Peggy could only reply: "I am very happy for you." Catching wind of this development, Sindbad and Pegeen were quite upset for their mother, and Sindbad thought that Peggy was "getting a dirty deal." Later, while walking through the congested streets of wartime Lisbon, Ernst told Peggy that Leonora was recovered from her madness and was in Lisbon living with a new lover—a Mexican journalist —whom she proposed to marry and accompany to America. Max took Peggy to see Leonora and she listened without enthusiasm as Leonora discussed her situation. Peggy returned by herself to Laurence and the children, joining them for an endless and excruciating dinner with Kay Boyle. She was shattered by the obvious attachment Ernst still felt for Leonora.

For the next two weeks in Lisbon, Peggy was depressed. The Vails had moved to the same cheap pension where Ernst was staying, and Peggy, with Jacqueline, Sindbad, and Pegeen, was lodged at the Frank-fort-Rocio Hotel. Peggy saw little of Max, who spent his days with Leonora and his evenings wandering about town with Laurence, going to fado establishments and cafés. Occasionally, Ernst and Laurence would invite Peggy along to go walking or dancing with a group of former spouses and lovers including Leonora, her Mexican, and Kay.

It was dreadful for Peggy to watch Max moon so wretchedly for Leonora, while he paid so little attention to her. When Leonora was temporarily hospitalized for a minor operation on her breast, he went every day to the clinic, staying by her side for hours, blissfully content. Kay, sent to the same clinic for a sinus problem, encouraged Leonora to stay with the Mexican and leave Max. It enraged Ernst to think of Kay's giving Leonora this advice. "Well," said Peggy, "it wasn't such a bad idea for Leonora to leave Max, because she was too much in his power, his slave and under this thumb and she had enough of it." Even so, Ernst still hoped that Leonora would go with him to America, undeterred by the fact that Leonora had actually married the Mexican. For Max, marital technicalities were never an obstacle.

As the days passed, it became apparent that there was going to be a wait before anyone boarded the Pan American Clipper to New York. Lisbon was full of refugees hoping to get a seat on a flight. Peggy and company were placed on a waiting list and it was simply a matter of checking every few days to see when they would finally leave. Laurence moved with the children to Monte Estoril, a beach resort just outside of Lisbon. Max, faced with Leonora's refusal to abandon the Mexican and run off with him, decided to join Laurence there, and Peggy followed. Two weeks were plenty in Lisbon with its swelling crowd of anxious refugees and the smell of oily sardines grilling on every corner.

In Monte Estoril they formed one big unusual family: Peggy, Laurence, the children—Bobbie, Apple, Kathe, Clover, Pegeen, and Sindbad—and Jacqueline Ventadour and Ernst. They all stayed in the same hotel. Jacqueline recalled it as a "big, nineteenth-century, old-fashioned hotel, where we had almost the whole floor. We sat at a great big table in the middle of the dining room. There were people there from all over the world, people who looked like spies, English spinsters."

"We ate like pigs," Sindbad declared, "went swimming all day long, and had eight-course meals." Peggy sat at the head of the table, with Max and Laurence on either side. The children faced each other along the length of the table. Kay, who had remained in Lisbon nursing her sinus condition and her grievances, would arrive on Sundays for the day. Occasionally, Leonora would stop by to be with Ernst. The hotel staff was in a state of utter confusion. "No one knew whose wife I was," wrote Peggy, "or what connection Kay and Leonora had with us." Or to whom, precisely, all those children belonged.

Days were spent at the beach. Peggy was content to lie inert for hours in the sand, turning as dark a brown as she could. (The Portuguese police, however, were on a constant vigil against indecent bathing suits, and Peggy and her family were harassed for wearing the skimpy suits sold to them only minutes before in the Monte Estoril shops.) In the evenings, she went for walks with Laurence and Ernst to the nearby fishing village of Cascais, where they could watch the boats bring in the day's catch. Returning one night, Max, Peggy, and Laurence encountered a prostitute on the road, dressed in a garish salmon-colored satin dress.

"La jolie robe," said Max sarcastically.

"Et la belle moustache," added Laurence.

"Why don't you talk to her, Laurence," exclaimed Peggy, always ready for excitement. Laurence obediently exchanged a few pleasantries with the woman.

From that point on, Concepção (Conception as she was dubbed), was devoted to Laurence and his family. Every morning, "like some mute and faithful animal," when the Vail entourage descended to the beach, Conception would be waiting, still in her evening's uniform of salmon satin. "When we went swimming," Laurence wrote, "she watched over our clothes and property. And later, when we came in from the breakers, she would enter the tent where we were removing our bathing suits and vigorously rub our backs with a towel." Conception, it seemed, had never been befriended by anyone before, and Laurence, who had a penchant for whores, enjoyed flirting with her. Apple was left very confused. On the one hand her father was complaining piteously because Kay Boyle had left him, and on the other, he was encouraging the attentions of this nice but strange woman in the salmon dress.

Every few days, Laurence would take the train into Lisbon and inquire at the Pan American offices as to their progress on the waiting list. As the days became weeks, they all began to despair of ever getting to America. Peggy sat in an English tearoom overlooking the sea and wondered if she would stay in Monte Estoril forever.

Ernst could always be counted on to liven things up. One night, for the fun of it, Max, whose hair "was totally white and quite beautiful," recalled Jacqueline, "put his head in a basin full of methylene, and he came down with a head of turquoise blue hair." The other diners could only look on with quizzical expressions, but the children, naturally, loved it. "Max was very humorous, quite fascinating," observed Jacqueline. "He was an extraordinary raconteur; he could go on all evening.

He was very imaginative, like his paintings; to us he only talked about himself." Peggy added, "In a very Surrealist way he told funny stories. . . . Oh, he wouldn't let anybody talk about anything except himself. He always got the conversation around to himself—whatever anybody was talking about. He used to say very, very funny things." (Later, when his son told him he had received a Guggenheim Foundation grant, Ernst remarked, "I used to have a Guggenheim, too, but it was not a fellowship.")

Ernst would occasionally take the children on excursions. "He took us around to museums to see Bosch," said Jacqueline, "the only painter he considered a painter. When we came out into the street there was a cart drawn by an old horse and a little man alongside. The horse had all his bones sticking out, and the man took a long bone and began beating the horse's back. We said: 'For God's sake! Do something!' and Max replied: 'Not at all. I'm enjoying it.'"

For the children it was a very unsettling time. Kay Boyle remained in Lisbon. Two-year-old Clover, suffering from boils, and seven-year-old Kathe were looked after by Bobbie and Pegeen. Everyone knew that Kay was not coming back to resume her former life. The children felt abandoned. They could only assume that their future included an extended family of which Peggy was the head and Max and Laurence her co-consorts, and would take place in a country the adults hated.

The atmosphere was charged with sex. Peggy was openly pursuing Max, who resumed their sexual relationship in Monte Estoril, even though he would still wait eagerly for Leonora's telephone calls and visits. The children knew they could anticipate any discussion between Max and Peggy ending up in a bitter argument over Leonora. "It was horribly obvious, horribly sordid," said Bobbie of Peggy's chase after Ernst. "Pegeen didn't enjoy that situation."

Apple, who was then eleven, remembers that time in Monte Estoril as "very traumatic." One evening she chanced to see "Max Ernst in the nude. . . . All us children were without supervision. It was so hot we slept on the roof. . . . I was walking along the balustrade when I saw him reflected in a mirror; those closets had mirrors on the doors. He was nude and looked good, putting a little blue in his hair, standing in front of the mirror, the door to his room open."

Sindbad became obsessed with losing his virginity. He had heard it often enough referred to as a curse, saw his mother liven up at the mention of sex, his father moan about it, and knew that Pegeen had been deflowered by Edgar Kuhn. There were family discussions about whether he should dispose of it, like an unwanted shoe, in Portugal, a country where he could easily catch a venereal disease, or wait until he got to New York. But as his mother sympathized, "He was ashamed to arrive in America with it." Wide-eyed, Sindbad asked his father question after question about the date and tenor of his first sexual experience.

Jacqueline Ventadour developed a terrific crush on Sindbad, a sensitive-looking young man with enormous, sadly inquisitive blue eyes—and his mother's nose. But Sindbad pined for the Kuhn girl he had met on the shores of Lac d'Annecy. Indeed, they all were on a merry-go-round of affection. Peggy was obsessed with Max; Max was obsessed with Leonora; Laurence was obsessed with Kay; and Kay was obsessed with Baron Frankenstein. No one was obsessed with the children. Their lives had the structure of a comic opera.

PART VI

NEW YORK, NEW YORK

ELLIS ISLAND

After five weeks of limbo, word came that there was room for the Vail/Guggenheim/Ernst ménage on the Pan American Clipper leaving Lisbon for New York July 13. They had all practically despaired of ever leaving Portugal, especially Max. Pan American refused to sell him a ticket until he obtained a visa for Trinidad, which was just a stopover on the voyage to New York, but a potential problem because of Ernst's German nationality. Finally, impossibly, everything and everyone was ready. Cables were sent to New York to inform the artist's son, Jimmy Ernst, Howard Putzel, already in New York, and Laurence's mother that the group would arrive on July 14.

The Pan American Clippers making the voyage from Lisbon to New York looked more like distended whales than flying machines. They traveled at one hundred and ninety miles an hour and took thirty-six noisy, queasy airborne hours to land at the LaGuardia Air Terminal in New York City, with several stops to refuel en route. The ride to New York was rocky, the plane bumping on patches of air turbulence and gyrating to the vibration of the propeller engines. It was impossible for passengers not to grow irritable and grumpy. While the adults read, drank Scotch, or argued (particularly Max with Kay Boyle, whom he detested for her interference with Leonora), the children got airsick and "kept vomiting into paper bags." To make the long trip easier, the Clippers were provided with Pullman-style sleeping berths and state-rooms and in the evening Ernst got into a heated argument with Pegeen over the last berth. He refused to sleep sitting up, so Peggy shared her berth with Pegeen to solve the problem.

At last, tired and crumpled, the passengers saw from their tiny porthole windows the Long Island beaches and the Statue of Liberty. Jimmy Ernst was waiting at the airport, as were Howard Putzel and Gordon Onslow-Ford and his wife. The Surrealist painter had been invited to New York by the Society for the Preservation of European Culture—organized by Kay Sage. Howard Putzel had organized some exhibitions to accompany his lectures at the New School for Social Research. In this way, Onslow-Ford introduced many New Yorkers to the works of de Chirico, Giacometti, Delvaux, Hayter, Brauner, Matta, Ernst, and Magritte. Putzel announced that Peggy's pictures had all arrived safely before her. The metropolitan press besieged the arrivals with questions about the war and their escape to America. Peggy loved the attention and posed repeatedly, tanned and smiling in an enormous outlandish straw hat (purchased at a refueling stop in the Azores), for an article announcing "American family of nine arrived." Peggy told reporters about her collection, and one journalist observed: "Peggy Guggenheim, while old cities crumble, is saving art treasures for a post-war world."

Jimmy Ernst, unable to find his father amid the strange cast of characters, went to the Immigration Room to see what was holding him up. He found Max, badly frightened, stammering to a group of report-ers, while three officers studied his passport at a nearby table. Why, they wanted to know, was he traveling on a German passport when he had spent so many years in France? Jimmy's explanation that he had tried to gain French citizenship but to no avail made no impression on them, and Ernst was refused admission into the country. He would have to be cleared by immigration officials on Ellis Island. As the last boat to the island had already left, he was to be placed under surveillance by a detective for the night and sent out to Ellis Island the next day. Up to this point, Ernst had only managed a few words to his son, in English: "Hello, Jimmy, how are you?"

Peggy came toward him. "You must be Jimmy." He recognized her name and quickly realized that she was the "and party" in the telegram he had received announcing his father's arrival. She seemed even more awkward to him than he was himself, a shy, faltering young man barely out of his teens who looked a great deal like his famous father. "The anxiety-ridden eyes were warm and almost pleading," he wrote of this first meeting with Peggy, "and the bony hands, at a loss where to go, moved like ends of broken windmills around an undisciplined coiffure of dark hair. There was something about her that wanted me to reach out to her, even before she spoke." He found her face "childlike," the features of it "intent on wanting to draw attention away from an unnaturally bulbous nose."

Max was allowed to spend his first night in America at the Belmont-Plaza hotel under the watchful eyes of a Pan American detective and of Peggy, who followed him there. Sindbad and Pegeen went with Laurence to the Hotel Great Northern, where Laurence's mother had made reservations for the entire family. The detective proved kindhearted and let Ernst and Peggy have dinner with Howard Putzel, even suggesting a little restaurant in Chinatown, but the next morning, faithful to his duty, he delivered Max to the immigration officials.

Along with countless other refugees waiting for an immigration hearing, Max was hauled off to Ellis Island to be processed and interned. Used to the stench and vermin of the French camps, he was impressed, albeit sardonically, by the spotless facilities on Ellis Island. Peggy was frantic with worry that they would send her lover back to France or, worse, Germany, and she hired a launch to ferry her to Ellis Island, where she was only allowed to see Max for an hour. Peggy asked Julien Levy, the art dealer who first showed Ernst in America, to join her, in case there was need for him to testify on Ernst's behalf, and Levy waited in the tiny boat while Peggy consoled the dejected painter. For three days, Peggy set out faithfully each morning for Ellis Island to wait for Max. "We just had to wait," said Peggy. "There was nothing to do. A ship had come in just before Max with 80 passengers on [board]. They all had to be examined before Max was." Peggy kept a loyal vigil, sending Ernst little notes to cheer him up, telephoning whomever she could, hoping to provide for the artist some "visible means of support." She had already determined to marry him and had informed Julien Levy, as they sat in the ferry, that since Max was to be her future husband, and since she was planning to open her own gallery, he would be having no further use for Levy's services as a dealer. "From hearing this," wrote Levy in his memoirs, "and the turbulent boat ride, I began to feel a little sick."

In the meantime, the Museum of Modern Art mobilized its forces, securing the support of its patrons Nelson Rockefeller and John Hay Whitney and other influential personages. Alfred Barr wrote a letter of recommendation outlining Ernst's importance as a painter and urging his admission into this country, which he entrusted Jimmy to deliver to Ellis Island. Jimmy, who had been in America since June 1938, was working in the mail room of the museum for fifteen dollars a week, a job Julien Levy secured for him.

When Jimmy arrived on the island, he found his father's immigration hearing about to begin. Various lawyers, Peggy, representatives of

American Smelting and Refining, Julien Levy, and museum trustees were waiting in a forbidding chamber to testify on Ernst's behalf as Jimmy was ushered in. Three black-robed and stern-faced commissioners questioned Jimmy Ernst as to his job, lodgings, and ability to support his father on his small salary—an irony in view of the distinguished company waiting to lend their prestige to Ernst's application. But the commissioners were satisfied with young Jimmy's candid answers and released Ernst to his custody. Peggy, relieved it was all over, asked Jimmy, "Will you let me share the custody with you?"

In the congratulatory brouhaha that followed Ernst's release, Peggy was forgotten and shared a cab with Jimmy to the hotel, while Max was whisked off in a sleek limousine. Listening to Peggy's nervous chatter, her repeated questions about whether Max had ever spoken of her, her short quick breaths, Jimmy thought to himself, "Sophisticated . . . people were not supposed to be so insecure." At the hotel a slew of well-wishers were waiting to welcome Ernst—André Breton, who had arrived in New York some months earlier, Yves Tanguy, Kay Sage, and Howard Putzel, among others.

As Jimmy was leaving, Peggy offered him a job as her secretary. She would have a great deal to do, she said, sorting her collection, preparing a catalogue, and writing letters. She offered him twenty-five dollars a week to quit his job at the museum. She was trying to please Max, who was horrified when he heard about his son's meager existence in a tiny rented room. Jimmy was pleased but anxious. He had seen his father leave too many women. First his mother, then Marie-Berthe, and Leonora. And Peggy was so shy, so different from the other women in Ernst's life that Jimmy wondered just how much his father had changed.

Peggy and Max moved into the Shelton Hotel and began to roam about New York, making the rounds of all the museums. The Museum of Modern Art, whose director, Alfred Barr, was a great admirer of Ernst, was having a Picasso show, including many of Roland Penrose's paintings. The Museum of Non-Objective Art, full of Bauers in huge silver frames, with Bach wafting through the halls, was a major disappointment. The best paintings were reserved for uncle Solomon's suite at the Plaza. Like a schoolboy on holiday, Max adored the Museum of Natural History, with its dinosaurs and animal dioramas, and the Museum of the American Indian, replete with masks, totem poles, and kachinas.

There were many people in New York for Max and Peggy to see. Even while Ernst was on Ellis Island, Peggy had visited André Breton in Greenwich Village, where he was living with his beautiful young wife. Glad to see his benefactress again, Breton filled Peggy in on his adventures since leaving France the previous March. His trip had not been altogether smooth. In Martinique, where French detention camps existed, he had been detained and questioned. He quizzed Peggy about Ernst and wanted to know the gossip about Leonora. He told Peggy that people in New York believed that Peggy had been delayed in Lisbon because Max would not leave Leonora. Having no idea that Peggy had aspirations toward replacing Leonora in Ernst's affections, Breton went blithely on talking about Max's love for Leonora.

In New York, Breton was totally out of his element. He hoped to re-create a Surrealist group, but for the moment he did not know a word of English and steadfastly refused to learn the first one. At the suggestion of Kay Sage, Peggy promised to give Breton two hundred dollars a month for a year so that he could get back on his feet.

Laurence Vail and the children were living at the Great Northern, a large, old-fashioned hotel on West Fifty-seventh Street. Laurence was morosely brooding about where to set up home with Apple and Kathe in view of the fact that Kay was going off to join the Baron Frankenstein and taking Clover, the baby, with her. Bobbie was in shock at the belated realization that Laurence was not her real father. The aged Mrs. Vail had a sense of déjà vu about the whole affair.

Laurence retired to a guest house on Matunuck Beach, Rhode Island, to get away from the heat, with Apple and Kathe. It was cool and pleasant, but he wrote Djuna Barnes, "I don't think I'm likely to be thrilled about any place in this country so might as well stay here as anywhere. . . . This place I live in is a sort of boarding house mad house —old women fighting for toilets and children yelling in the stairs. The best moment for shaving is 6 A.M. My mother has come down for 5 days to help—which means endless conversations, then she weeps and has to be cajoled." To another friend, he described himself as "deep in domestic smash up—so have to take decisions quickly. . . . I'm hardly glorious, but far above the chronic dumps."

From his retreat, Laurence asked Djuna Barnes, who had preceded their arrival in New York, to see what she could do about getting Sindbad into Columbia College for the fall semester. The war had interrupted Sindbad's plans to take the College Boards in Geneva, making it difficult to apply to school. Laurence pointed out all of Sindbad's talents to Djuna, but Djuna did nothing. Sindbad managed to get into Columbia on his own, and proposed to go on a bicycle tour for the duration of the summer.

Quite by accident, Jimmy Ernst ran into Leonora Carrington at Columbus Circle. Ernst was thrilled to hear this, as he had entrusted his paintings to Leonora and "that Mexican" to bring to America when he was in Lisbon. Ernst prevailed upon Julien Levy to hang the canvases in his gallery, where a few of his New York friends, including Breton, Putzel, and Laurence, came to see them.

Peggy's sister Hazel was now living in Santa Monica, California, with yet another, recently acquired husband, Charles McKinley. She invited Peggy to visit her and Peggy accepted with alacrity. She was eager to see the West, so rhapsodically described by Jimmy, who had taken a trip there himself when he first arrived in this country, and most of all to leave New York, where Max was longing so palpably for Leonora. Possibly, Peggy thought, she could find a home in California for her museum. In addition, it would be a nice trip for Jimmy and Pegeen, and a good opportunity for Max to renew his acquaintance with Jimmy, with whom he had not spent any time in several years.

It had been with mixed emotions that Jimmy greeted the father who had abandoned him at the age of two to live in a ménage à trois with the Éluards. His earliest memory was a nightmare image of Ernst in the Tyrol standing waist-high in a lake, the water very calm, and holding out his arms to Jimmy, who was being handed to him. "I noticed," said Jimmy, "scary insects on his palm, and I screamed, 'I don't want to be handed to him,' and then I read, I heard about my mother and father's life . . . I found out that day they went to the mountain lake . . . and on the way back, my father told my mother that tomorrow morning he was leaving with Éluard and Gala."

Jimmy and his father were awkward in each other's presence. Neither quite knew what to do with the other, or what to say, or in what language—French, German, or English. "Max was a stranger to him, they had never had a normal relationship, I don't think," observed Peggy, "from the beginning." Nevertheless, Jimmy worshiped his mercurial father and to inch a little closer, allied himself to Peggy.

Peggy, Max, Jimmy, and Pegeen decided to fly to California and then drive back across the country from there. At the last minute Hazel wired that she was having a nose job and couldn't entertain them. Rather than postpone the trip, Peggy and Max decided to explore San Francisco and then drive down to Los Angeles. In San Francisco, the foursome toured the city, went to Chinese restaurants, and ate seafood by the bay. Sidney Janis, the art dealer, met Peggy and Ernst at an exhibition of primitive American art that he had organized for the San Francisco Museum. "They came in and Max said [the primitives] were the best American artists he'd seen," causing a furor in the art press, which took Ernst's remarks as an arrogant insult.

In Santa Monica, Peggy found Hazel recovering from the nose job, happy with her latest husband, a handsome young aviator working toward his pilot's license. Over the bed in the guest room hung a sign warning: "Nothing to Excess." To keep Hazel's Irish maid happy, Max and Peggy were given separate accommodations. This arrangement ("Max had to get up and sleep on a cot," laughed Hazel) and the motto over the bed occasioned many jokes and much ribald dinner party conversation, to the embarrassment of Pegeen and Jimmy. Ernst took over Hazel's front porch as a studio and managed to finish *Napoleon in the Wilderness,* a picture he had begun in France, letting his son, who also painted, have Hazel's studio. Ernst gave Hazel, who fancied herself an artist, some lessons, finding his pupil far more surrealistic than any picture.

Tearful scenes, however, punctuated the California visit. From the beginning, Pegeen, Peggy, and Max were constantly quarreling, dragging in the frightened Jimmy as referee. Peggy had gotten the idea that Kay Boyle had turned Pegeen against her, and Pegeen steadfastly defended Kay against Peggy and Max, who, like Peggy, made no secret of his dislike of Kay.

In Beverly Hills, Max and Peggy saw Man Ray, the Dada and Surrealist photographer, who reportedly hated America as much as Peggy. At a cocktail party that Hazel gave, the three pointedly insulted the American painter George Biddle, while Hazel distinguished herself by denying admission to some other friends because they brought along their half-Japanese houseguest, the sculptor Isamu Noguchi.

In Hollywood, Peggy went to see Walter Arensberg's collection. Arensberg, Duchamp's patron, welcomed Peggy and Ernst warmly, but she found him a rather sad old man, surrounded by his lovely Duchamps, Kandinskys, and Picassos. On his bedside table, she noticed a copy of Djuna Barnes's book *Nightwood* and begged to borrow it so that Ernst, who could barely speak let alone read English, could admire the dedication to herself and John Holms.

To Jimmy's delight, Peggy bought a sleek gray Buick convertible. On the way back across America, Peggy, Max, and the children stopped to explore the sights—the sand dunes of Death Valley, the cliffs of Big Sur, the snow-capped peaks of the Sierra Nevadas. In Santa Fe, New Mexico, they again met Hazel, who had taken her children, Barbara and John, there for vacation. Ernst and Jimmy entertained themselves buying kachinas, weavings, and other Indian artifacts.

Peggy took a side trip to visit Emily Coleman, who had once been so ubiquitous in her life. Emily now lived in Arizona with a cattleman named Jake Scarborough, whom she met at a dude ranch. "She was capable of anything," said Peggy of Emily's situation. Dressed in blue jeans and cowboy boots, Emily was intrigued by Peggy's liaison with Ernst.

While there, Max fell in love with the dry, red-baked desert landscapes of Arizona, so much like his paintings. Jimmy recalled,

> driving back across Arizona, it must have been in the vicinity of Flagstaff, or Gallup, he stopped the car because a rattlesnake was going across the road—for a European that's rather unusual. . . .

Then after looking at the snake he looked up at the landscape, and he sort of stiffened. He was studying one of his own landscapes. There was absolutely no doubt about it. The landscape he was looking at—he had been painting it years ago in Europe. There was, in particular, a mountaintop made magenta by light reflection.

As they traveled, Peggy relentlessly pressured Max to marry her. In each state, Peggy sent Jimmy to scout out the local marriage laws. Peggy recalled, "Pegeen said to me: 'Oh, poor thing. Don't make him marry you. Look how miserable he looks,' and Max said he wasn't miserable because of that. Probably he was miserable, but I don't know if he was miserable because he was going to marry me or some other reason." Jimmy noticed that each foray to inquire after the local statutes was followed by a new chill between Max and Peggy.

En route to New Orleans, where they were to see Jacqueline Ventadour, who was living there with her grandmother, Pegeen fell ill. They stopped in Wichita Falls, Texas, until Pegeen felt better, and Peggy took the opportunity to jot down the wonders of the place for Djuna: "At night it is very gay," she wrote, "when the bugs come out of the desert over everything. In the cinema they climb down your dresses and up your legs and get into your hair. In the day time the people think about oil. She couldn't have chosen a worse place to stick us in. It's marvelous."

HALE HOUSE

Peggy, Max, Pegeen, and Jimmy returned to New York in late September. To Max's great relief, New York still seemed the best place to live. Although he loved the wildness of California and Arizona, he heard in New York the "echo of people appreciating." In New York, there was the Museum of Modern Art, a growing population of European émigrés, including many old friends, his dealer, Julien Levy, and, of course, the beautiful, albeit married, Leonora Carrington.

Peggy was determined to establish her museum, to uncrate her treasures and show them at last. When traveling through California, she had indulged a momentary fantasy that perhaps she could locate her collection there. Scouting for a suitable site, she dragged Ernst and the children around as she investigated bowling alleys, an abandoned castle, and Ramon Navarro's home. But Peggy realized that to create a true center for art and artists it was necessary for there to be an art public, even if only a small one, and California, while dramatic with its cliffs and ocean, lacked that requisite public.

Max and Peggy moved into the Great Northern, where Laurence had been living, near Carnegie Hall and the old Metropolitan Opera, with its Alameda Room jammed nightly with men and women dancing to upbeat Latin rhythms. While they began to look for a permanent place to live, their small two-room suite became office, command station, and temporary home. Every day Jimmy walked over from his furnished room to help with the correspondence, endless telephone calls, and the many inconveniences of setting up life anew in New York. One of the things Jimmy noticed was the remarkable number of solicitations for money from perfect strangers that Peggy received with each day's mail. Through the suite paraded a steady stream of visitors—André Breton, Alfred Barr, Howard Putzel, Laurence Vail, Guggenheim cousins, art dealers, real estate brokers.

While Sindbad studied at Columbia, Pegeen was enrolled as a boarder at the Lenox School on New York's East Seventieth Street, a two-year preparatory school for Finch College, then known as a finishing school for socially elite young women.

At first, Peggy thought that she would move near Laurence, recently settled in Connecticut on the advice of his friend Malcolm Cowley, and commute to New York when necessary. Cowley and his wife, Muriel, influenced many European émigrés to set up house around their Sherman farm, re-creating in the Connecticut hills the halcyon atmosphere of their days at the Dôme and the Coupole. Unfortunately for Cowley, Laurence wound up seducing Muriel and "wanted her to leave Malcolm and live with him," said Sindbad. "It was lucky for her, she didn't." Peggy looked at two houses there, but when neither proved acceptable, continued her search in Manhattan. Housing was scarce, but just when she was ready to give up, Peggy found a magnificent town house for rent at 440 East Fifty-first Street.

At the end of a quiet residential cul-de-sac, Hale House, so named after the patriot Nathan Hale, who was hanged on the site, looked over the East River, with its endless procession of tugboats and slow-moving barges. It had a view of the Fifty-ninth Street Bridge to the north and the Brooklyn and Manhattan bridges to the south. On the first floor the house boasted a baronial, double-height living room that opened out onto a terrace facing the river. Peggy labeled this room the chapel, because she could imagine white-robed choirboys chanting in the balcony that overhung the main room. A dramatic bay window of thick mullioned panes overhung Fifty-first Street and an enormous chimneypiece dominated the room. Down a narrow steep flight of stairs were a large kitchen and several maids' rooms, which Peggy planned to convert into guest quarters. There were two more floors of bedrooms. One was reserved for Pegeen, who was miserable boarding at Lenox. The other, the third floor, had a master bedroom suite, with a studio on the river for Ernst. Clifford Odets rented the top floor of the house and occasionally Peggy would hear the clatter of his typewriter above her head. The house had a modern look and only one real problem—the zoning ordinances would not permit Peggy to use it as a museum. It was so perfect in every other respect, however, that she could not resist it.

"It was a fabulous house," said Hedda Sterne, the artist, who was received by Peggy one morning in a pink satin negligee trimmed with matching marabou feathers. "Architecturally it was very unusual. . . . At the time people had conventional homes: living room, dining room, library. . . . No one had huge spaces; people had old-fashioned houses."

The tall, bare walls and blue-white light from the river made a dazzling backdrop for Peggy's Surrealist and abstract pictures. In the living room, Peggy installed Léger's *Men in the Town,* Kandinsky's *Landscape with a Red Spot,* Miró's *Seated Woman,* and Brancusi's resplendent *Bird in Space.* On the coffee table rested Giacometti's *Woman with Her Throat Cut.* In the entrance foyer were Ernsts and Kandinskys. From time to time paintings on approval would be propped up casually against any wall. "At dinner, once," said Jane Bouché Strong, "my parents had brought a large Picasso; it was just leaning against the wall. I was so afraid someone might step into it." In her bedroom Peggy hung her collection of zany earrings—a glittering frieze. (Julien Levy was convinced that Jackson Pollock got his idea for "allover" painting from Peggy's jangling, shimmering jewelry displayed on the walls.)

Interspersed throughout the house were totem poles from the Pacific Northwest, Navajo rugs, Hopi kachinas, and peace pipes, which Ernst had begun collecting on the trip out west. Indian art soon became his passion. (The Surrealists had always held in high esteem the art of the primitive as a manifestation of the unconscious, and in Paris Breton crammed into his apartment on the rue Fontaine primitive art from Oceania and Africa between the Tanguys and de Chiricos.) Whatever money Ernst got from the sale of a picture, or from the money Peggy advanced him (and Peggy never gave him a cent unless he gave her a picture in exchange), he spent on Indian artifacts. He would scout out prizes at Julius Carlebach's antiquarian gallery, competing there for an Eskimo mask or Hopi doll with Breton or the anthropologist Claude Lévi-Strauss. Carlebach would, to Peggy's chagrin, extend Ernst liberal credit and phone him the minute something new or interesting arrived.

Max also roamed the antiques shops lining Third Avenue near University Place. One day he found a thronelike, ornately carved Victorian chair, probably a discarded stage prop, upholstered in red velvet. Its back stood nearly ten feet high and after Ernst bought it, he loved to sit in it, even for dinner, in front of the bay window. Buffie Johnson found Ernst's chair the most striking thing in an already striking house. "Sitting in it, he looked Mephistophelean."

Max also "loved clothes," Peggy stated. "He wanted to dress up always. He had the beautiful black cape. I bought a fur coat once. He was so jealous I had to buy him one also." Ernst adored walking around New York in his sheepskin coat.

Occasionally, Max would wink at Jimmy and say that he was going on a "treasure hunt," which Jimmy understood as a quest for booty of the female variety. Sometimes while Peggy was absent he would bring his finds—usually young and beautiful—back to see the collection. On these occasions, Jimmy wished he were somewhere else.

Peggy herself was very generous about showing her collection. Whereas she was not allowed openly to show her art to the public from Hale House, she did make her collection available to just about anyone who was interested. One had only to call her and ask to come over. Putzel brought people to the house; Alfred Barr, the director of the Museum of Modern Art, came to see Ernst's work along with James Thrall Soby, his aide-de-camp. James Johnson Sweeney, an influential art critic and former secretary to James Joyce, came. Anyone who cared about modern art quickly learned that Peggy was in town.

As the war continued, many of the Surrealists arrived in New York. Breton and his latest nemesis, Salvador Dali, were already settled there. Tanguy was in Connecticut with his wife, Kay Sage. André Masson and Kurt Seligmann joined the exodus, as did artists the Surrealists would have liked to convert: Amédée Ozenfant, Fernand Léger, and Piet Mondrian. Josef Albers was in America, as were Jacques Lipchitz, Marc Chagall, and Pavel Tchelitchew. In their escape from Nazi oppression, European intellectuals and artists of every stripe made wartime New York a kinetic center for the world's creative geniuses.

At the beginning New York seemed a magical place to the new arrivals. Fernand Léger had an earthy, peasant style and he loved herding people around in big gangs to obscure restaurants in Chinatown or to Armenian bistros on Twenty-eighth Street. The beefy artist was thrilled with the city's skyscrapers and chromium-filled car showrooms. Bathroom fixtures and central heating gave him goose bumps. He stopped dead in his tracks for any billboard. "I think," wrote Julien Levy, "he believed all the advertisements." Everything seemed so surreal. Hedda Sterne said, "When I came to America, I lost interest [in Surrealism], because America was Surrealist. America had the kind of freedom the Surrealists wanted to show the European bourgeois. I remember my European friends were so enchanted with those . . . [Band-Aids] where you could peel off this plastic strip. It was Surrealist. They were enchanted by all those kinds of thing."

Peggy's house on the river seemed a natural meeting ground for the displaced Europeans. Almost from the moment Peggy moved into Hale House, she began to give parties. "Very often we went to Peggy's house," said Jacqueline Lamba Breton. "Everyone met there. We were sort of a colony of refugees. She received everybody. She was a fantastic collector. She knew how to find people." Peggy invited people in the art world, old friends from earlier times, Seligman or Guggenheim cousins, even Leonora Carrington, because she was so beautiful, to huge cocktail parties where anything went and the guests were offered potato chips and cheap whiskey. "Peggy threw the best art parties the New York art world ever had," exclaimed Ethel Baziotes, the widow of the painter William Baziotes. "She had a genius for people. She was a catalyst. She would bring so many interesting people together." And Sidney Janis remembered that the guests were "rarely under a hundred people. People came and went, artists, collectors, parties went on and on." There was a great crossover from other worlds. Peggy even had a lot of baseball players at one party. The painter Theodoros Stamos noted that "in the forties the art world also involved theater people—there was lots of sex going on—that sort of sex," he said with a knowing seesaw of the hand, "actors, actresses—Zachary Scott, Ona Munson (Eugene Berman's wife), also the *Partisan Review* crowd." Gypsy Rose Lee, one of Ernst's few paying collectors, became a frequent guest at Hale House.

Nudity, bare breasts, strange costumes were taken for granted. Jacqueline Lamba appeared in Mexican dresses and Navajo necklaces or beaded Indian slippers with mirrors in her hair or a collar made of yellow horse teeth. Other women wore unusual chunky jewelry designed by Alexander Calder or perhaps a silver lorgnette. They wanted heads to turn, eyebrows to raise—and never, ever, to appear conventional. At a hat party Peggy gave, costumes were required from the neck up. Among the guests was a very attractive black singer who wore her hair in a braid wound high around her head. Her costume was a quivering little white mouse peering out from the top of the conical braid.

Peggy, too, presented herself in an extremely exaggerated fashion. Her hair got blacker and blacker, her lips redder and redder. At her ears dangled her trademark oversize, bizarre earrings made of brass, steel, silver, or glass. She affected a jaunty, challenging stance, resting her hands on her hips, and sported shocking clothes—transparent or with well-placed rips to reveal she was wearing nothing underneath. Hedda Sterne described Peggy at one of her big parties: "Her daughter, Pegeen, had made her dress. It had a big pink cummerbund and two pieces of fabric coming up her shoulders. [The fit was eccentric] since the dress was not made by a professional, and half the time Peggy would walk around like an Amazon, absentmindedly pulling the dress back up, because it kept slipping off. She had nice breasts—self-supporting."

Overheard at Peggy's house were heated conversations in French, as men stood arguing face to face and shaking their fingers. "She did preside over the French," observed the botanist Rupert Barneby, who met Peggy and Max around this time. "All those nasty French, just complaining because it was not *la belle France,* the food was bad.... They just didn't want to go back and watch the Germans drink their champagne." "As I recall," said Ormond deKay, then a French-speaking young man in sailor's uniform, "New York was full of refugees then, mostly French, and you could hear them in the back of the bus, loudly complaining about the barbarism of America."

Peggy circulated among her guests, her eyes vibrant, making sexual allusions or asking personal questions without listening to the answers. She liked nothing better than to make a surprising, shocking statement and drift on to wherever there was new excitement or an argument. At one party, Peggy got into a disagreement with Henry McBride, a friend of Gertrude Stein. As Pierre Matisse told it, "perhaps he made some remarks, and they were drinking champagne, and she threw her champagne all over on him *à la Surréaliste, provocateur.* . . . She liked to be provoked and she liked to provoke and she liked to fight."

If Peggy had a disingenuous, spirited quality that made her fun, she also had " the disconcerting habit, where you'd be sitting talking to her," said Rupert Barneby, "and suddenly, she would say something under her breath intensely disagreeable, dropped just as an aside in a play, directed toward the person. For example, 'Why is this man boring me so?' It was like a dagger in the heart. She was capable of doing very cruel things, especially to those in a position of servitude—pulling rank, making it clear who was paying the piper, in front of other people." And Buffie Johnson added, "Peggy had . . . almost a mannerism of making it clear to others that they really didn't count for much."

Ofttimes, Peggy could appear curt or thoughtless. Jacqueline Lamba observed, "She was never beautiful, and when I knew her, she was becoming old. She wasn't pretty all her life. She liked people, needed them around her, but she was very timid. Sometimes, if she appeared very arrogant, very brusque, I believe, it was her timidity." Jimmy Ernst saw her as a tentative and fragile person, "whose lack of affectation, whose shyness suggested a painful past."

Occasionally, Max prepared elaborate salads or curries with the precision of a surgeon, or Peggy concocted chocolate chicken, a recipe Breton brought back from Mexico. But "Peggy's parties were memorable," said Barneby, "mostly for the cheapness of the physical entertainment. She was very mean. There would be six people to dinner and one bottle of wine—a cross between vinegar and ethyl." The artists Robert Motherwell and William Baziotes complained that they always got a hangover from the Golden Wedding whiskey Peggy liked to serve.

With the anxieties of the war and a sense of displacement came a frenetic round of social activity, a celebration of life in the shadow of death and devastation abroad. Peggy's was not the only house people congregated in. Louise Nevelson, the sculptor, observed, "During that time we were partying all the time. . . . You were at parties three or four times a week, and good parties in the sense that there was plenty of opening up, liquor and food. I think that the point was the tensions of the outside world and the war and all demanded that people get together somehow."

Bernard Reis was an accountant who often traded his professional services for paintings by artists who could not otherwise afford his fees. In this way he and his wife, Rebecca, collected a great many valuable works. They were also collectors of people, and to their house went many of the same crowd who frequented Peggy's, the exiled Surrealists, André Breton, Max Ernst, Leonora Carrington.

At the Reises', there was "always good food, an easy atmosphere, good wines, and framboise to follow." There Breton held court in a way he did not feel comfortable doing at Peggy's, with whom he had very little real rapport. "We had fun," said Becky Reis, "sitting in the drawing room and playing Surrealist games." Breton moderated La Verité, the Surrealist truth game Peggy found "awful," as its object was the revelation of the most devastating psychological truth, preferably sexual, about one's neighbor. Breton took these games very seriously and was severe about calling his middle-aged friends to order. "It was amazing the respect all these grown men gave Breton. It was ingrained in them that he was superior."

In this life of artists, musicians, writers, actors, and strippers Peggy belonged, as James Johnson Sweeney observed, "not so much to the world outside, as to the world inside. She had a center, a bohemian life. She lived in a rather fantastic world in New York during the war years when New York had the immigrants." And, he might have added, a good part of that "rather fantastic world" was created by Peggy.

MARRIAGE

The tensely anticipated American entry into World War II became a fact on December 7, 1941, when the Japanese attacked the U.S. naval base at Pearl Harbor. Soon thereafter, Congress declared war on Japan; then Germany and Italy declared war on the United States. American boys made ready to fight the Axis, and Sindbad Vail and Jimmy Ernst, both draft-age young men, were eligible to be called up for service.

Max Ernst was frightened on his own behalf. He dreaded that he might be deported or interned. Peggy "did not like the idea of living in sin with an enemy alien," but it was Ernst who, when faced with having to be fingerprinted and registered (he was especially disturbed not to be permitted to own a shortwave radio or travel without restriction), opted to change their arrangement. "Ernst always married a girl from the country he was involved with," observed Sidney Janis. "Louise: Germany; Marie-Berthe: France; Peggy: U.S.A."

New York State required a waiting period of several days after the blood test results before a couple could legally marry. Furthermore, in New York the marriage might be picked up by the newspapers and, for once, Peggy and Max wanted privacy. They decided to drive to Washington, D.C., where Peggy's cousin Harold Loeb was living, in order to be married as soon as possible. Peggy feared that if she gave Ernst too much leeway in the matter, he might reassess the situation and change his mind.

Peggy's children were not overjoyed when they heard the news that Max would soon be "Daddy." The children were jealous of Ernst—Peggy had never remarried after the dissolution of her marriage to their father some twelve years earlier. Both Sindbad and Pegeen felt disoriented in New York. They were French-speaking foreigners whose British accents made them different from their peers. "They didn't know," said Jane Bouché Strong, who dated Sindbad, "whether they belonged here, in England, or in France." Peggy certainly did not provide them with a counterbalancing sense of home, but, said Strong, surrounded the children with "all this sex and drunkenness—so bohemian and so wild." Sindbad was living uptown at Columbia. On Monday nights, his mother allowed him to use the gray Buick convertible and he would take Jane Bouché out to Enrico and Paglieri, a restaurant that he loved. Peggy still lived with the memory of the privations of Vichy, Muriel Cowley recalled, and when Sindbad visited his mother, he was asked to bring his own soap.

Teenage Pegeen had a crush on Max, who called her "honeychild," and she competed with Peggy for his attention—and with *him* for Peggy's. "I think," said her mother, "she was quite annoyed by him, 'cause he was so selfish, always, 'cause he always wanted the best studios and the best everything and she had to fight for her own rights." Pegeen was forever making pointed remarks, ridiculing the possibility of a marriage between Peggy and the artist. "Oh, marriage is so bourgeois! Don't you think?" she would ask him. Or, "Mama, why do you have to marry? Why don't you live together?" On the eve of the couple's elopement, Pegeen inveighed against the idea. "Pegeen told me not to marry him, that he didn't want to marry me, and that he looked so miserable because he was going to marry me," said Peggy. "He was just miserable because we'd had a fight the night before. . . . It was jealousy, but she was quite right, of course, I shouldn't have married him, it was ridiculous, absurd."

Sindbad, too, made his views known. "I liked Ernst. They should never have gotten married." Sindbad "knew it would be fatal," Peggy said. "Neither child wanted me to marry him. . . . They probably thought they knew more than I did."

Jimmy Ernst had lived through too many of his father's relationships not to be nervous about this latest one. He liked Peggy, but working with her, he felt too close to a situation he knew could very well explode. Visions of his mother, Louise Straus, a Jew, first abandoned by Ernst in Cologne and now languishing somewhere near Marseilles, powerless to leave, made him despondent. Peggy, in one of her generous impulses, offered to adopt him, if that would help in getting his mother to America, but Jimmy declined.

Peggy rationalized her marriage to Max. "I guess he must have been rather fond of me. After all, how could he live with me if he didn't like me? I'm such an extraordinary person. He couldn't not like me, if I may say so. How could he not have some feeling for me. He must have, don't you think? I don't think he especially wanted to get married, but I don't think he minded that much."

From Washington, Peggy and Max went on to Maryland, where they attempted to be married, but discovered it was not so simple. Neither one had divorce papers written in English, and Ernst had no proof whatever that his first divorce was valid. Consequently, they continued on to Virginia, where, with only a valid blood test, anyone over the age of eighteen could be married with ease. Having secured their marriage license at the county clerk's office in rural Fairfax, Peggy and Max were married on December 30, 1941, by a local justice of the peace. Harold Loeb and his wife, Vera, served as witnesses, and the entire affair took less than half an hour.

Peggy soon discovered the truth of Oscar Wilde's famous observation that the only thing worse than not having what you want is having it. Max had married her, but he did not love her. He looked forward to spending his afternoons with Leonora and leaped at every opportunity to tour the city with his former mistress. Or he might cruise amorously around town on his daylong "treasure hunts." Otherwise, he spent his days painting in the studio Peggy provided for him.

Avid for the company of other painters, Max would wander on the Lower East Side and the Bowery where artists had poorly heated and barely habitable lofts in abandoned warehouses. He missed Europe and the easy comradery of the local café. "In Paris at six-o'clock," he once said, "any evening you knew on what café terrace you could find Giacometti or Éluard. [In New York] you would have to phone and make an appointment in advance. And the pleasures of a meeting had worn off before it took place." Max spoke very little English; his conversations with Peggy were therefore always in French and, given her accent, enough to depress anyone. As Sidney Janis commented, whereas "Ernst spoke beautiful . . . French, German, Spanish—he had a gift for language—Peggy's gift was abominable. She spoke French with a perfect American accent." "Fundamentally," observed John Russell, "he was like a radio that had been wired for the wrong voltage." All in all, Peggy offered little compensation for the life he had lost.

With her he was reserved, often sadistically so. This manner was an element of his success with women. By his own account women found him "a difficult character, hopelessly complex, obstinate and with an impenetrable mind." But Peggy loved beautiful people and found in beauty its own reward. And even in his fifties "Ernst was very beautiful," said Becky Reis. "Everything he did had an elegant look and feel." Max had that same charismatic quality Marcel Duchamp possessed—something that made people take notice when he entered a room. "The way he moved, too," observed Paul Matisse, "slowly—just slowly moving and comfortable with himself, like Marcel." He also danced exaggerating his movements, according to Dorothy Miller, Alfred Barr's assistant at MOMA. "Fascinating, a super charmer, about five foot five or six."

Max was not only beautiful, he was also intellectual—cultured, well read, a student of philosophy. Becky Reis was surprised to observe that during an afternoon game of *boules* in Rheims some years later, "when Ernst wearied, he sat down at a small table to read a book. I looked over to see what it was, and he was reading a book on philosophy by Hegel."

Peggy once told Emily Coleman (living by then near Hartford with her ailing father, having left the cowboy for Catholicism), "There are three reasons why I love Max: because he is so beautiful, because he is such a good painter, and because he is so famous." Peggy watched, enraptured, as Max was sought out by reporters and photographed by magazines, always in his Victorian chair and always with "ferocious glee" in his eye. "Max assumed extraordinarily photogenic aspects the moment the camera was trained on him," wrote Julien Levy. "He composed himself perfectly in every imaginary frame, and projected an unerring image of a Max Ernst possessed. . . . Seemingly unaware of the most candid camera, they both, Ernst and Dali, fell into their pose as instantly as the shutter could snap." Peggy basked in Max's reflected glory, hoping some of it would rub off on her.

Max treated Peggy like a cordial acquaintance, addressing her in French in the formal *vous.* He once inscribed a book to her "À Peggy, son ami Max Ernst." But Peggy longed in vain to be his muse, his inspiration—to be adored like Leonora, painted in picture after picture —to share in his fame.

"I liked Max, but not the way he handled women," said the sculptor David Hare.

> Peggy was a rich woman, a Guggenheim. She liked art and Max wanted to get here. Perhaps he was afraid if he didn't marry her, he couldn't stay. He probably felt, "Why not?" Max wasn't a gentle person. He wasn't so much reserved as cold. He was Germanic, sadistic. . . . He gave Leonora a rough time and Peggy, too. I don't think he was ever in love with Peggy.
>
> Max was cold-blooded about using her. But he did a lot for her too. She wanted to be bohemian. With Vail, Peggy was the boss. Vail was a ne'er-do-well, a hanger on; with Max, she was no longer

the boss, and Peggy worried about toeing the line. Max was frightened about being here in America with no cash.

Yet Hare concluded, "Max is a nasty thing."

Since she could not get at Max in any other way, Peggy used money, just as she had with Laurence Vail, in petty ways. She complained that he did not contribute to the household expenses but instead bought Indian artifacts. She reminded him constantly that it was her money that was paying the bills. Too proud to accept such a situation, Max insisted she take his paintings as payment for his share of the household expenses. Every other month Peggy would sit down with a minute list of the household outlays and study it carefully, alert to an extra lamb chop or Indian totem, and settle his share for the market value of his newest painting.

Peggy had endless arguments with Max over Leonora. She had arguments with him over almost everything. She needled him about trivialities. She complained that he could not speak English well, that he paid no attention to her, that he only saw her in passing on his way to his studio. "They had public quarrels," according to David Hare. "They yelled and screamed a lot." Peggy concurred. "I used to get furious all the time with him about nothing. I think I made scenes all the time. He couldn't stand it. I made scenes because I was so unhappy. I suppose because I knew he wasn't in love with me, and I suppose I couldn't stand it, I guess he couldn't stand the scenes." All Peggy really wanted was attention, and the only way she had ever gotten it, as a child and as an adult, was negatively, by making a fuss or a crazy remark. With Max such behavior did not work and Peggy became so difficult and argumentative that he would complain to his friends, "Ugh! Peggy. I don't want to go home tonight."

Even in this dissonant atmosphere, Max continued to paint. For several hours a day he could forget Peggy's shrill recriminations, her stinginess, and the sensation of being a foreigner—a man without a country. Henry Miller wrote of him, "I felt that he was born *dépaysé,* a fugitive bird in human guise, always straining to soar 'beyond the exterior world with its wolf dens, cemeteries and lightning conductors.' I hoped forlornly to hear him say: 'I am wasting time here.' " Perhaps it was because he had always been an exile that Max was one of the few expatriate painters who found in America the ability to change and go forward in new artistic directions. His restless imagination roamed over odd objects or everyday implements, turning them in his mind's eye into art with a "magic ingenuity." Julien Levy remembered him suddenly grabbing a spoon and looking at it "with that abstracted, distant sharpness one finds in the eyes of poets, artists and aviators."

Max finished some canvases begun in Europe, such as *Day and Night.* He worked on a large one that he called *Le Surréalisme et la Peinture,* in which a monstrous bird, his alter ego, Loplop, is orchestrating a painting, surrounded by all the tools of the trade, including a trowel, an instrument Max discovered for the first time in America. *La Planète Affolée* incorporated a maze of cylindrical dripped lines that he created by swinging from a string (over a canvas spread on the floor) a can of liquid paint with a hole punched in its bottom—a form of tin-can *automatisme.* Various American painters saw these works, including the very young Robert Motherwell (advised by his art history professor at Columbia, Meyer Schapiro, to get to know some artists), and a little-known painter pal of his, Jackson Pollock, who inquired of the elder painter just how he achieved his effects. Max himself ultimately abandoned the technique, but he always called it his "present" to Pollock.

Peggy longed to appear, as Leonora had, in one of Max's paintings. She was thrilled to discover herself in a small study she called *The Mystic Marriage,* which evolved into the *Anti-Pope,* completed in March 1942. This picture was painted in an illusionistic style, using Old Master techniques of perspective and modeling alongside distinctly Surrealist techniques, like *décalcomie,* to create unsettling images. Peggy liked to call it a family portrait because she saw Max, herself, and Pegeen in the monster figures of the painting. (Lucy Flint in her handbook to Peggy's collection suggests that the painting more accurately depicts Max's broken relationship with Leonora, who stands in the form of a double-headed horse-owl-female figure to the left forlornly gazing at the other protagonists representing Max, Peggy, and Pegeen, separated irrevocably from her by a spear that bisects the canvas.)

In the spring of 1942, Max had enough new work for a show. Peggy wanted to sell his works herself from the museum gallery that she hoped to establish. But as the gallery was not yet a reality and Julien Levy, Max's dealer, had been called up for military duty, Max had his first American exhibition at the Valentine Gallery in March and April. Ernst was proud of having produced some of his best work and the exhibition was enormously successful from the point of view of quality. Yet these otherworldly *décalcomies* and *frottages* did not sell well, and he was greatly disheartened.

Peggy did better than did the Valentine Gallery by merchandising Max's pictures from her home with the help of Howard Putzel. Peggy loved selling her husband's work, counting dollars and imagining herself the partner of a great artist. If Max disposed of his works himself, if he made a disadvantageous trade or, even worse, if he gave anything away, she became extremely jealous. One day he appeared with a tiny, fluffy white Tibetan Lhasa Apso, which he had received from Bridget Tichenor in exchange for a picture. He called the dog Kachina, after the Hopi dolls he loved. Peggy was annoyed, but succumbed to the charms of the affable Kachina, the progenitor of a long dynasty of tiny furry dogs that would live unhousetrained around her for the rest of her life.

OLD FRIENDS
TOGETHER

Peggy planned to open "a new art center" where she would show her collection and mount exhibitions. It would also serve, she hoped, as a testing ground for undiscovered artists. In effect, it was to be the sum of her ambitions: gallery, museum, and artists' retreat. Jimmy Ernst would be her secretary, publicity agent, and jack-of-all-trades; Howard Putzel would help her find pictures and artists; Max Ernst and André Breton would be her advisers.

Jimmy Ernst recalled the ire of the Baroness Rebay, who had been monitoring Peggy's progress with undisguised animosity since Guggenheim Jeune. It had been the baroness's desire to open an art center in Paris before the war (when Peggy, too, had had a similar idea) and it appeared to her that Peggy was trailing along on her coattails, misusing the name of Guggenheim for her own vulgar commercial purposes. She was alarmed that people might confuse the baroness's own Museum of Non-Objective Art with Peggy's importunate venture. Jimmy Ernst learned through friends who worked at the Museum of Non-Objective Art that Rebay was surreptitiously calling New York real estate brokers and pressuring them into not helping Peggy. Moreover, she threatened, if "that dreadful Guggenheim girl" called her "an evil Nazi witch" one more time, she would use her influence (that is, Solomon Guggenheim) to have Max Ernst deported.

Despite the baroness's thorny interference, Peggy located a space above a grocery store at 30 West Fifty-seventh Street, a wide and sunny commercial avenue. It consisted of two lofts of square, rather ordinary rooms. Howard Putzel suggested she hire Frederick Kiesler, a diminutive (he was four foot three) Viennese architect and designer, to give her some ideas for the gallery. Kiesler, who had been in the United States since 1926, was the director of scenic design at the Juilliard School and had designed theaters, sets, houses, sculpture, and even display windows at Saks Fifth Avenue, using his unconventional concept of "design correlation." There should be no boundaries, he believed, between paintings on the wall, architecture, or sculpture, but a "continuous flow without being pinned down to a spot as if each lived in a separate prison cell." He dreamed of an "Endless House," an egg-shaped shelter where the walls would be curved and "all ends meet, and meet continuously." He hoped thereby "to unify in one structurally continuous building the visionary magic of the theatre, the cinema and sports." Kiesler's ideas were very definite, and the opportunity to design Peggy's gallery was a welcome challenge as, he later wrote provocatively, "The art museum everywhere today is often a tour de farce."

Peggy and Kiesler discussed original exhibition methods and her request that the paintings in the gallery remain unframed, a novel concept in 1942 but one that appealed to Kiesler's notions of "transparency"—the interrelatedness of art and its environment—and which he had used as far back as 1925. In a letter dated March 7, Kiesler wrote Peggy that "the development of new ideas too demand a certain time —especially if they must be most practical—and it would be neither your nor my intention to ruin this excellent chance for a new art center in New York by rushing it through." He suggested that Peggy consider opening in May, an overly optimistic projection, as it turned out. Peggy agreed to Kiesler's fee of six hundred dollars for general planning and design and an equal amount for detailing and supervision.

Peggy originally wished to open the museum gallery to coincide with the publication of a book about her collection, a compendium begun in her cold, cramped hotel room in Grenoble. However, the catalogue, which originally had a publication date of May 15, and the gallery refurbishing took longer than she expected, and it made little sense to inaugurate a gallery at the end of New York's art season when every gallery in the city closes and every critic goes to the beach. Peggy resigned herself to an opening sometime the following fall, and entertained herself meanwhile with the catalogue and the completion of her collection.

Peggy hoped to open the gallery with as thorough a sample of modern masters as possible. Using Read's list, revised by Marcel Duchamp and Nellie van Doesburg in Paris, she went around the city with Ernst and Breton and Putzel to buy art. In New York Peggy found "millions of things," as she put it, including Duchamp's 1911 *Sad Young Man on a Train,* for four thousand dollars, an early Cubist Picasso, *The Poet,* as well as his 1914 *Lacerba*, two de Chiricos, various Mirós, including the 1939 *Seated Woman II,* a Malevich that she received in trade from the Museum of Modern Art for an Ernst, a charcoal-and-gouache drawing on paper by Mondrian, and works by Archipenko, Calder, Giacometti, Klee, Lipchitz, Ozenfant, and Tanguy. She added American artists cautiously, buying one piece by John Ferren. She did not really start to collect American art until she opened her gallery and began, as she had done in London, to acquire works from her shows. With each acquisition, Peggy rushed to the publisher, Inez Ferren, the painter's wife, to include that work in her catalogue.

Peggy asked Breton, who was using his mellifluous voice as an announcer for the Voice of America, to cast his critical eye over the catalogue. He did not hesitate to pronounce his judgment: *"Désastroux."* It was just a boring list, a packing crate of artists' names and works. With his years of experience editing Surrealist journals, Breton came up with the idea of taking a photograph of each artist's eyes and placing the pictures over a statement by or about the artist, thereby making the point that it is not how the world is, but how the artist views it, that is important.

Breton went faithfully to the MOMA library (resolutely asking the very American elevator boy for the *quatrième étage*), to hunt out material for the anthology. In back issues of Surrealist magazines and in catalogues he found biographical information and statements about the artists. From the library archives or the private photo albums of his friends he culled photographs in which the eyes were prominent. Jimmy Ernst was assigned to help produce the catalogue and he used his prewar experience in Germany, where he had worked as a typesetter, to great advantage.

Peggy already had a preface written by Jean Arp on Abstract/Concrete art to which Breton added a much longer one of his own, outlining the "great physico-mental stream of *Surrealism*" and its ongoing glory in automatism. It took so long for Laurence Vail to translate Breton's fourteen-page introduction that the catalogue had to be delayed. To be impartial, Breton also included a short piece by Piet Mondrian on abstract art, and for good measure assembled an appendix of additional material: the manifesto of Futurist painters, the Realistic manifesto, Max Ernst's *Inspiration to Order,* and an article by Ben Nicholson on abstract art. Max, with whom Breton was delighted to have made amends after their 1938 feud, designed the cover, an interwoven maze of—what else?

—birds, and Laurence Vail invented the title, *Art of This Century,* which further incensed the Baroness Rebay because of its similarity to "Art of Tomorrow," the name she had given to the Museum of Non-Objective Art.

Breton's intervention elevated Peggy's mundane list of acquisitions to a lively, first-rate document of abstract and Surrealist art, heavily illustrated with black-and-white photographs of works in Peggy's collection (and of various bushy eyebrows). The catalogue, dedicated to John Holms, displayed the characteristic messianic enthusiasm of the Surrealist magazines and, thanks to Laurence, offered in English translation the writing of Breton and others heretofore available only in French. It made people long to see the gallery whose contents it so enticingly previewed.

With so many Surrealists in New York, it was natural that there would be a new wave of Surrealist activity in America. In fact, transplantation to virgin soil gave the Surrealist movement a second life. In Europe, undermined by the feuding and animosities of 1938, it had degenerated into the affectation of a few middle-aged *enfants terribles.* In New York, it regained its freshness.

Before the war, there had been a certain amount of interaction between the European Surrealists and New York artists. Many of the people Peggy entertained at Hale House had been reading about her in the *London Bulletin* since 1938. French magazines such as *Minotaure* or *Cahiers d'Art* were sold at book shops like the Wakefield or the Gotham. Even if not all Americans could read the language, they at least could look at the pictures and glimpse the latest developments in art.

The first Surrealist exhibition in America, called "Newer Super-Realism," was held at the Wadsworth Atheneum in Hartford, Connecticut, in 1931. Julien Levy had shown the Surrealists since 1932 in his Madison Avenue gallery and in 1936 had published an anthology, *Surrealism,* which offered English translations of many of the movement's wilder excursions. Alfred Barr, the director of the Museum of Modern Art, visited Europe, saw the 1936 Surrealist exhibition in London, and later that year, over the objections of his trustees, mounted the tremendously successful show "Fantastic Art, Dada and Surrealism," which was accompanied by a lively catalogue presenting the work of Ernst, Tanguy, Dali, and Masson to an enthusiastic public.

In November 1941, MOMA began a two-month exhibition of the works of Miró and of Dali, who was already well known in the United States as a result of the antics (most recently for his exhibit at the 1939/40 New York World's Fair, in which several bare-breasted mermaids swam about in an aquarium) that had earned him an official excommunication by Breton from the Surrealists and the anagrammatic sobriquet "Avida Dollars." The exhibition presented the two aspects of Surrealist painting—the abstract automatism of Miró and the dream imagery of Dali—to a New York audience. James Thrall Soby wrote the first comprehensive catalogue in English of Dali's work and James Johnson Sweeney wrote one on Miró.

Surrealist magazines sprang up in New York. Charles Henri Ford, a former correspondent for the *London Bulletin* and editor of *Blues,* started in 1940 with his friend Parker Tyler a little magazine called *View,* subtitled "through the eyes of poets." It was a Surrealist literary art journal dedicated to the new and exciting in which appeared ecstatic Surrealist prose and announcements of exhibitions and gallery shows, advertisements for art schools, bookstores, and painting suppliers. Not the least Surrealistic aspect of the magazine was the unexpected advertisements—White Shoulders perfume for an evening of lights and shadows or Golden Arrow Face Powder—obtained with the help of Marcel Duchamp, whose friend Enrico Donati ran an advertising agency. Physically, the review was very beautiful, since artists donated their work, which was laid out assiduously by Tyler in the midst of jangling phones and chattering visitors in the small offices *View* had right off Fifth Avenue over the Stork Club.

In the spring of 1942, *View* dedicated a full issue to Max Ernst, a flattering homage to the painter. Included were material by Henry Miller, Julien Levy, and Ernst himself, illustrations of his works, and a photograph by Berenice Abbott of Ernst seated majestically in the Victorian chair, his long, tapered fingers splayed like bird claws. Ernst was also photographed on the terrace at Hale House surrounded by kachina dolls of all sizes and shapes, dressed in his sheepskin coat, looking like an androgynous shaman. In the same issue, Ernst's original collages were advertised for twenty-five dollars by Julien Levy. And Peggy took an ad to promote the mail-order sales of her catalogue, *An Anthology of Non-Realistic Art 1910–1942,* at the price of three dollars and to announce the opening in the fall of her art center, "a research studio for new ideas of the creative effort." John Bernard Myers, then a young man in Buffalo, N.Y., preaching Surrealism in the local cafeteria, saw that Ernst issue, his first glimpse of *View,* and wrote, "It is not possible to describe the thrill that passed through me."

André Breton hated *View,* in large part because it was not his, and because his monumental biases got in the way. David Hare remembered, "He was full of prejudices—he wouldn't eat eggs. He was against gays of any sort, and he didn't like Charles Henri Ford's *View* because of the gays. He was against any sort of homosexuality."

Breton pulled together a rival magazine, *VVV,* devoted to *his* brand of heterosexual Surrealism, for which he wanted to recruit an American editor. "At first he wanted Lionel Abel," said David Hare, whom Breton eventually chose, "but he had a girl friend, and Breton felt he wouldn't be a good editor if he was going out to meet her. Motherwell he didn't like. Then me, who mostly worried about getting it out and organized."

VVV was a bit more "scientific" in its format than *View,* but it appealed to the same audience and had many of the same contributors. Max Ernst designed its first cover and served as an adviser, spending much of the spring and summer helping Breton prepare the premier issue. Marcel Duchamp helped, too, when he finally arrived in America from France in June 1942, the month *VVV* was launched. The review only lasted three issues—one of its problems being that it carried untranslated articles and captions in French, as Breton did not see the magazine as American, but rather as an organ to disseminate French literature in the United States.

VVV had articles on the evil eye, Indian cosmetics, mythology by Claude Lévi-Strauss. A "Twin-Touch-Test," a sort of collage contest created by Frederick Kiesler with a little help from Duchamp, provided a bit of real wire mesh; the reader was challenged to clap the mesh between his hands and rub until he could answer the question: "Is it an unusual feeling of touch?" in one hundred words or less. The lucky author of the best analysis would receive a year's worth of *VVV* free.

Breton, so used to leading a band of enraptured disciples, tried to re-create his Parisian milieu in New York. But the Old Guard Surrealists, now men in their fifties, had grown tired. Moving to a new country had disoriented many. They all deplored the weather and the hectic pace of life. Breton's wife left him for the much younger editor of *VVV,* David Hare, and he spent his dinner hours at Larré, a French restaurant on West Fifty-sixth Street, longing for the bistros of Paris. Breton perversely persisted, said Ernst, "in thinking everything not French is imbécile." Few of the Surrealists spoke English well, and Breton stubbornly refused to learn it, fearing it would somehow jeopardize his classical written French. In truth, "Breton never wanted to learn English," Pierre Matisse believed, "because he had absolutely no talent for languages." And Hedda Sterne suggested that all the Surrealists "preferred to have others take the trouble to understand them—they had an arrogance."

In New York the group began to dissolve. With no street life it was difficult to see one another. (But once when Ernst did manage to run into Yves Tanguy, Tanguy was wearing a very familiar sweater. According to Bridget Tichenor, Peggy gave all her lovers "the same sweater—no sleeves, V-necked, reversible, and from the cheapest possible store. When Yves met Max and both were wearing the same identical sweater they each exploded, *'C'est pas possible!'* ")

Financially, times were tough. Breton "did not have any money," said Ethel Baziotes, "and he dropped fifty pounds in weight."

All the Surrealists did very poorly. After a while there was somehow the secret feeling that they were not liked. All of these men were very learned and educated, and the Americans had a lot of learning, too, but they didn't know about black magic and . . . magical rites. It was just enough to make the Americans feel uncomfortable. They did so poorly, the Surrealists, they just didn't sell. Max Ernst felt he was really abandoned. Jimmy said his father was so miserable there was no interest in his work. Americans felt they weren't plastic enough, that they were too literary. The Surrealists had a lot of psychological painting. They weren't so much interested in the brush as they were in the idea and it bothered the Americans.

The Americans also did not take to Breton's "autocratic and priest-like condescensions." Fundamentally, Breton misunderstood America. "For the Surrealists," explained Hedda Sterne, "the greatest compliment was to say, it was *sensationnel.* They were completely and totally political. Art was useful as a means of influencing society. Whereas in the United States, no such thing" was really needed, felt Sterne. They became not only the "rebel without a cause," but the "rebel without an audience."

Old quarrels were resurrected, gripes revived, hatchets exhumed. Pierre Matisse organized an exhibition in March 1942 called "Artists in Exile," bringing together many of the old friends: Masson, Ernst, Breton, Ossip Zadkine, Eugene Berman. "I got all these people to the studio," chuckled Matisse, "for the 'Artists in Exile' show, and while [the photographer fixed] his camera all these people who hated each other were walking around trying not to greet each other. Breton didn't like Mondrian; Léger didn't like Chagall; Chagall and Ernst didn't like each other. They all wound up in the picture next to the one they liked the least." The Surrealists hated the abstractionists; the Cubists hated the Surrealists.

They all hated Dali, "because he was so bent on money and he had a fascist bent." As stated by Becky Reis,

Ernst once refused to shake hands with Dali, because Dali had made a drawing in which a Nazi plane downed an American plane. . . . Lipchitz had passed it displayed in the window at Knoedler's [New York art gallery], and mentioned it to a columnist who wrote it up and it [was removed from] Knoedler's window. Max said that while walking the dog he had curbed the dog and when he looked up there was Dali with extended hand. Max said: "I don't shake the hand of a fascist." Whereupon Dali protested, "I am not a fascist. I am only an opportunist."

Despite their infighting, the Surrealists were the most active, cohesive, and influential coterie of exiled artists in New York. Pierre Matisse reflected that the Surrealists formed a very animated group that injected new ideas, provocative ideas, into a field that was stagnant: "I daresay, there are a great many American artists who even today, at the height of their *célébrité,* admit their influence. It was the challenge of ideas that created a tremendous movement. Surrealism was not so well known to the general public, but not so among the artists. It was the *possibilité* of American artists meeting them."

The Surrealists were very sociable and were seen about town (Breton swept in, kissed the ladies' hands, bowed) by the younger American painters, who, even if they never said a word personally to the Europeans, were awed by their presence. Some Americans like David Hare, Robert Motherwell, and William Baziotes penetrated the Surrealist enclaves, and some Europeans—most notably Marcel Duchamp and Kurt Seligmann, who did not share the arrogance of a Breton—were accessible and easygoing. And then there were emissaries pollinating the two worlds, like Kiesler or Jimmy Ernst, who would spend his days around Peggy, his father, and their friends, and then go downtown in the evenings to report on their activities to his circle of acquaintances.

"The artists in exile," said Sidney Janis, "Léger, Mondrian, got around, came to parties. The Americans were very much interested in the Europeans and they went too." "We saw [the European Surrealists]," recalled Ethel Baziotes, "personally and saw them at their homes after the parties. They were so brilliant. Breton may have spoken fifteen minutes with you, but that fifteen minutes would last the rest of your life." John Bernard Myers thought of his first encounter with Breton as "a religious experience."

The painter Theodoros Stamos, who saw the Surrealists as "all very elegant" Europeans, observed,

> The fact that they were here was an influence. It didn't have to affect you directly. . . . I don't think things would have been the same [if the Surrealists had not come here]. I know they were an influence on Rothko, on me, on Clyfford Still. Baziotes was all Surrealist. . . . There was a war and the Americans were doing primitive Surrealism—a little bit of Miró, a little bit of Tanguy—and then, the whole idea of war—no exhibitions, no pictures coming. It made artists, certain artists, think about pulling your own guts out and painting it themselves. . . . Look at the pictures, look at the immediate change of Rothko's pictures. . . . I think Breton is the main influence. . . . It was the Surrealists in the forties. *View, VVV.*

The art critic Clement Greenberg disagreed, however, arguing that the American school of Abstract Expressionism, which emerged after the war,

> would have happened anyhow. [Surrealism] helped. . . . The artists saw all these people: Léger, Chagall, Mondrian [the Surrealists], but . . . they were terrible snobs. Breton was a kind of pure man. . . . The Americans were too grubby. He couldn't talk English. Masson kept away from everything, lived in Connecticut. . . . There was an anti-French tendency underway. . . . This was going to happen anyhow, and it did. The Surrealist influence has become exaggerated. I went to Europe the first time in 1939, before the war, and I remember being shocked at the French, who had not seen Klee and knew little about Miró, nothing about Kandinsky, and Matisse had had it. We saw more good contemporary art in New York: Miró, Matisse, Klee, Kandinsky. . . . We saw a lot more than the French did. . . . [The Americans] continued the school of Paris here, rather than repudiate it. . . . Picasso, Miró, Matisse were the main influences.

May Tabak Rosenberg, the critic Harold Rosenberg's widow, agreed with Greenberg that too much has been made of the Surrealist influence on American artists. Nevertheless, she said, "they had introduced a whole series of amazing values that were not art values, but art-political values, about which Americans were very naïve. They set themselves up as exclusive, whereas American avant-garde artists were held together like a fraternity. . . . They didn't know about millionaires." They soon learned, however, "that one had to be more exclusive. You don't invite all your pals when a collector comes around."

Still, "there is a secret resistance to admit the role of the Surrealists" in the emergence of the New York School, said Ethel Baziotes. "They are critical. It wouldn't have happened in the same way. Always, from the beginning, they weren't given credit and it would not have happened in such a brilliant way. Peggy was the real catalyst. They were like very cultivated brothers and fathers. The Surrealists were a little perverse, but it wasn't taken in the right spirit." Pierre Matisse, the art dealer, summed it up when he said, "Without the war, without the Surrealists in New York, the American contemporary school would have been very different."

Matta, born Roberto Sebastian Matta Echaurren, a young Chilean Surrealist, had been in New York since 1939 and had struck up friendships with a number of American painters. In contrast to Breton, the darkly handsome Matta spoke English and had no trouble communicating with the American painters he was eagerly meeting. "I found," he said, "that they were absolutely ignorant of European ideas," an ignorance he determined to remedy. "They knew nothing about Rimbaud or Apollinaire, and they were just copying the outward forms of Picasso and Miró. I started to invite them in to my place once a week to talk about the ideas *behind* modern painting." Matta was a great admirer of Duchamp and transmitted his ideas of chance and metamorphosis. More important, Matta explained Breton's principle of "psychic automatism," in which the hand is guided by an inner impulse and the unconscious is given free rein. Automatism came as a revelation to many painters still struggling to digest the rigid spatial complexities of Cubism, some twenty-odd years after its invention.

Matta organized evenings of Surrealist experimentations, games, and automatic drawing. William Baziotes and his wife, Ethel, Jackson Pollock, Lee Krasner, and Robert Motherwell all experimented with automatism together under Matta's guidance. As Virgil Thomson remarked, "The subconscious is our wellspring of inspiration. Some need to use a pump. Others have only to cap a gusher." (The Americans, said Onslow-Ford, who lectured on automatism at the New School, changed the flavor of automatism and used it to favor the technical side of the act of painting or drawing—the brushstroke, the gesture, the texture and speed of execution—whereas Breton had meant for it to illustrate the unconscious world of dreams and visions.)

Matta wanted to branch out from the traditional Surrealist orthodoxy and liberate it. In particular, he wanted to wrest Surrealism away from the exclusive control of Breton, who mistrusted and resented Matta's "upstart" activities. Matta lost no opportunity for showing up his elders as stodgy old men with rigid ideas. Yet it was whispered that what Matta really wanted was to become himself the Breton of American Surrealism, the American "Pope."

Matta presented himself as one of the more abstract Surrealists and created interior landscapes and mazelike illusionistic spaces. (Breton disliked pure abstraction. To him the linear paintings of Mondrian were devoid of humanity.) Matta's form of Surrealism was attractive to the younger painters, who were unpersuaded by the pictorially academic and literal side of Surrealist art represented by the melting watches of Salvador Dali or the bowler-hatted gentlemen of René Magritte. These pictures, while provocative, had nothing new to say about the act of painting itself, as the technique used to paint them was fairly traditional. Surrealism itself pointed in another direction—to the biomorphic abstractions of Joan Miró and André Masson. The Mirós in the Museum of Modern Art's exhibition staggered the Americans by their use of personal and bizarre organic forms and sensuous color in a shallow,

Cubist space. Masson, living quietly in Connecticut, incorporated sand and textures in his swirls of undulating color. And there was Max Ernst, who had also produced abstract works using chance and gesture, forever experimenting with technique—drips, *frottage, décalcomie*—to force inspiration.

Surrealism was still a call to arms. It embraced a contempt for the established and a passion for the new—values inherited from Dada. Surrealism remained a style of life, an attitude, a way of looking at the world. Any approach was valid; anything could be art. Unlike other great movements in the history of art, the Surrealists never proposed a *style* of painting. Nothing could be more different stylistically than a Tanguy from a Masson. How different Surrealism was from Cubism, whereas an early Picasso is virtually indistinguishable from a Braque. Later on, when American painters emerged as the Abstract Expressionists, the same diversity would hold true within that group, too. "My husband hated to be lumped together," said Ethel Baziotes. "Even Picasso said there are no schools, only artists."

SUMMER IN THE CITY

In July 1942, while Peggy remained behind to testify on behalf of Nellie van Doesburg at her immigration hearing, Max and Pegeen went to Wellfleet, Massachusetts, a town popular with artists on Cape Cod where Matta had a house, to look for a place to spend the summer. Max, Pegeen, and Matta formed a curious trio, the adolescent Pegeen dreaming of sex and the two older men, of youth. Jimmy Ernst believed that both men became Pegeen's lovers.

The house that Max and Pegeen rented horrified Peggy when she finally arrived in Wellfleet. Considering it woefully inadequate, she immediately rented another in Provincetown. Yet no sooner had Peggy and Max relocated than the FBI arrived to investigate Ernst as an enemy alien and possible spy. He was whisked away and questioned, particularly about Matta, who was also suspected of being a spy, and then released, only to be continually harassed while he stayed in Provincetown. The harassment came to a close when the Boston district attorney sent Ernst back to New York, where Bernard Reis was able to clear up the problem with the Bureau of Enemy Aliens.

Peggy and Max's contretemps with the FBI occasioned a certain amount of merriment in Wellfleet. "She and Max," recounted Mary McCarthy, who met Peggy for the first time in Wellfleet, "rented a house and didn't like it, apparently, and jumped the contract. The story was that the landlady, Mrs. Freeman, was furious, and she denounced Max to the F.B.I., who then picked him up. . . . The house was in Wellfleet, and it is unlikely that Mrs. Freeman denounced him. Locally, in Wellfleet, there was some indignation and some laughter that summer because of it. Peggy must have skipped paying or something."

As a result of Ernst's immigration travails, the couple resigned themselves to a hot and humid summer back in New York. Their change of plans was a great disappointment to Sindbad, who had been using Hale House for his trysts (and to Jimmy Ernst, who also expected to bring his girl friend to the house). Rupert Barneby overheard Peggy talking with the recalcitrant Sindbad. "Sindbad was a most ill-favored young man—horrid to look at. He had only one thought in mind—a girl. He had to have it. He spoke to his mother with total disrespect, the way you wouldn't talk to a maid."

In reality, Hale House was already somewhat congested that summer. Marcel Duchamp had been living there since June, when he had arrived from occupied France. Before leaving France, Duchamp had taken all the materials for his *Boîte-en-Valise* to Marseilles by posing as a cheese merchant making repeated trips back and forth by train from Paris. The *Boîte,* a leather box shaped like a briefcase, contained sixty-nine faithful miniature reproductions of Duchamp's life's work: the scandalous urinal, the *Large Glass,* the readymades, and paintings—even a tiny flask of Paris air—all painstakingly assembled. As a favor, Peggy let him include his material for the *Boîte-en-Valise* with the shipment from France of her collection. "That's the only thing I ever helped him in," Peggy said.

It never occurred to Peggy to help Duchamp out with money, even though he had very little of it. "Neither André Breton nor Marcel Duchamp nor I," wrote Frederick Kiesler, "had more money than to pay for carfare, a sandwich, or telephone calls." According to David Hare, "Peggy never helped anybody who didn't ask her. She never volunteered to help, and Marcel never asked her." Instead, Peggy felt free to offhandedly ask him to "get me some cigarettes."

In New York, Duchamp liked to stay home, a quiet, polite, and unobtrusive presence. Ensconced at Peggy's, he became, to a younger generation of painters, the "great priest" whose nod, whose taste meant a great deal. "When I went to Europe all these people congratulated me," Hedda Sterne recalled, "because Duchamp had said I wasn't bad, in French: *Pas mal,* and I was supposed to be terribly complimented." To Rupert Barneby, Duchamp appeared a "pompous pundit. He felt he was so marvelous, and he would play chess and tell people off." And to Lillian Kiesler, Kiesler's widow, the quality that stood out was his indifference. "He didn't give a goddam."

By contrast to André Breton, Duchamp fared better with his American counterparts. Duchamp liked New York; he understood America. "Duchamp wasn't so snobby and he was homier," said Ethel Baziotes. "He was more willing to do practical things like hanging pictures. . . . Breton would never do that. Duchamp didn't mind wearing old clothes and having a bowl of soup for dinner, but that's no reason to overemphasize his influence. The other man, Breton, was more Olympian in his tastes. He had a grand personality and the Americans didn't like that. The Americans always favor the homy." Breton was too severe. He never laughed; he only half-smiled. "His whole life was his baby, Surrealism. He was always quarreling if people were not doing what he felt they should do." Breton counted heads to see who was still in and who was out of his party. And although aloof, even Duchamp was careful not to displease Breton. "Duchamp's emphasis was misplaced," said Ethel, who added, quoting Edgar Allan Poe, "The Americans favor talent over genius."

With Duchamp underfoot, Peggy suddenly realized that she had secretly lusted for him since her days in Paris as a young matron. But with her husband flinging bottles around Montparnasse, Peggy claimed she thought "it better not to add to the general confusion." In New York, however, Max was becoming less and less interested in her and Duchamp was available. On Peggy's birthday, August 26, she and Max gave a big party attended by William Saroyan, Gypsy Rose Lee, and altogether, in Peggy's view, "too many stars." During the party, Duchamp pulled her aside and gave her a kiss. With this encouragement, on another night, Peggy appeared in a transparent silk coat wearing nothing underneath—for Duchamp's benefit. But it was Max who grabbed her and gave her a few sobering swats, while Duchamp looked on, filling his pipe, with his customary detachment. Eventually, Peggy managed to seduce Duchamp, or so she said.

"If Marcel were alive," said his stepson, Paul Matisse, "he would neither confirm nor deny. He felt that to say no was the same thing as to say yes." David Hare could not believe Duchamp could have had an affair with anyone as unattractive as Peggy, with that "dyed black hair, absolutely black" and all that "makeup, so badly put on." Many others shared his low assessment of Peggy's looks: "She was ugly," said Theodoros Stamos bluntly, "very ugly." And she did not have a nose, exclaimed Stamos, "she had an eggplant!" Her face was often blotchy with red patches and her nose was more prominent than ever. Bridget Tichenor asserted, "Ugly?? Peggy? She was not *croyable!* Her nose was like this," she explained enthusiastically, grabbing a rust-colored zinnia, "in texture and color. It was like a sponge." And Jean Hélion, Peggy's future son-in-law, observed, "She was remarkably ugly, in such a pleasant way."

But whereas David Hare was distressed at the very *idea* of a liaison between Duchamp and Peggy, Hare's former wife, Jacqueline Lamba, pointed out that Duchamp's taste was broad and that he "liked a lot of different types of women. . . . He didn't mind if they were ugly."

Peggy's sister Hazel, who was in and out of New York after the death of her husband Charles McKinley, never believed Peggy's claim to an affair with Duchamp. "Peggy imagined a lot, especially if they were famous." On the other hand, Hazel herself was treated to an unusual experience with Duchamp: "I went out with Marcel, and he spent the evening cutting my nails and toenails. I think it's a great privilege having my nails and toenails pedicured by Marcel Duchamp." Apropos of Hazel, Hedda Sterne laughed when she recalled: "I talked once to Duchamp and I said, 'Hazel is crazy. She killed her children.' And Duchamp said, 'That doesn't make her crazy. Peggy is the crazy one. Don't you see she never finishes a sentence?' "

John Cage, then a young composer with ambitious ideas, also arrived that summer at Peggy's doorstep with his wife, Xenia. Cage had met Max the previous spring when the latter went to Chicago for an exhibition of his work. A native Californian, Cage was in Chicago working on the score of a radio show for CBS, called "Columbia Workshop." Max casually suggested to Cage that he come see him if he were ever in New York. Cage packed up his wife and his possessions and boarded a bus to the Port Authority Bus Terminal.

By the time they arrived in New York, he and Xenia had twenty-five cents between them, and Cage hazarded five cents on a telephone call to Max, with whom he expected to be lodging. Max, answering the phone, could not seem to place Cage, but asked anyway, "Are you thirsty? Come over on Monday for a drink." When Cage told his wife of this turn of events, Xenia reminded him that they could not possibly stay in New York with only twenty cents in their pockets and urged him to call again. "It was Xenia who said to me we had everything to gain and nothing to lose," recalled Cage. "When I called back, Max said: 'It's you! We've been waiting for you for weeks.' " Cage added, "My suspicion is that between the first and the second call he talked to Peggy and [recalled his cavalier invitation]."

John and Xenia were given a guest room on the ground floor and were introduced to Peggy. "I saw a person very friendly and very open, at the very center of the art world," said Cage of his first impression of her. "It seemed to me she was like an open sesame. She was full of plans. The meetings with Kiesler were frequent. It was very exciting. I came from the west and had read about all these people and here I was seeing the people I had read about. It was an astonishing moment. Peggy had the keys to the whole art world. Even though there was something unattractive, one forgot that in the brilliance of everything else. She was lively, fun."

Xenia and John settled in for a protracted stay at Hale House, while John set about trying to make his mark on the art world. At Peggy's house he was introduced to it full blast. "It was like Grand Central Station for artists. People enjoyed Peggy . . . enjoyed the affluence in the environment. She was not reticent about having ideas," said Cage. "She was not at all boring."

In the heat of a New York City summer, the behavior at Hale House became increasingly bizarre. Peggy continued entertaining and one night after a party, Max, Xenia, Marcel Duchamp, and John Cage decided to play a game, the object of which was to see how detached the players could remain. They all four undressed while Peggy, Kiesler, and his first wife, Steffie, watched. Kiesler was impressed by Duchamp's obsessive neatness. As he took off his garments, each one down to his socks was meticulously folded—even his tie was rolled. Max was the first to lose, as he became visibly excited over Xenia. "One could always tell if Max were excited about a woman," wrote Peggy. "His eyes would nearly pop out of his head with desire, like Harpo Marx's." In this situation, even more definitive signs of interest were apparent. Then, "there was the time," Cage recalled, "the four of us traded partners and I went to bed with Peggy and Max with Xenia. . . . Peggy had a kind of sense of humor about things other people would consider serious." If Peggy and Duchamp had indeed had an affair, thought Cage, it was "surprising in that they didn't stay together. He was always with wealthy women, and always faithful, once he connected."

John Cage's tenure at Hale House ended in tears when Cage told Peggy that he would be giving a concert of his percussion music at the Museum of Modern Art. Rather than being delighted for him, Peggy was outraged. She had wanted to have a Cage concert to celebrate the opening of her gallery and had offered to underwrite the transporting of his instruments from Chicago to New York. She was furious that Cage would consider giving a concert at a rival institution, and refused to lend her support.

Cage was caught in a vise. He had discovered that establishing himself in the city was more difficult than he had anticipated.

I had been active in the West Coast and Seattle. I thought I'd be received with open arms in New York. CBS had no work for me. . . . I had the idea of doing music for radio using sound effects in a musical way. . . . None of those doors opened. . . . Meanwhile, I was playing recordings for anyone who would listen. . . . The next thing practical, I decided to give a percussion concert. Through Virgil Thomson and Lincoln Kirstein the concert at the MOMA was arranged. . . . I was delighted, and I told Peggy—it must have been at a meal—and she responded, "In that case, there won't be a concert at the gallery, because I won't pay to bring the instruments."

Cage had no money of his own to ship his instruments to New York for a concert anywhere. "I simply burst into tears and got up and went to the room where Marcel sat in a rocking chair, smoking a pipe. He just peacefully continued rocking without saying a word, and after a while, I stopped. I didn't think it was so bad. Marcel had an Oriental way of behaving."

Shortly after this incident, Peggy told John and Xenia that she and Max were leaving Hale House and that the Cages would have to leave, too. "It was foolish of us to believe we could stay there indefinitely," Cage recalled. The Cages found a home for the summer with the mythologist Joseph Campbell and his dancer wife, Jean Erdmann. Erdmann was about to perform with the choreographer Merce Cunningham in Bennington, Vermont, and in exchange for his lodgings, Cage wrote a score for a Cunningham duo, *Credo in Us,* thus beginning his long personal and professional association with Cunningham. (Cage and Peggy eventually became friends again, but he was more wary thereafter.)

The climax of the summer was Gypsy Rose Lee's wedding to the actor Alexander Kirkland at midnight on the last Sunday in August. The ceremony took place at the stripper's Highland Mills, New York, farmhouse. Peggy and Max attended the wedding lost in a crowd of burlesque queens, actors, writers, and reporters, who watched the bride march down the aisle dressed all in black with a headpiece of purple and green grapes designed by the painter Tchelitchew. She was quoted as feeling like "an Aztec virgin being prepared for the sacrifice." To Peggy's annoyance, a picture of Max, gaily sipping champagne and snuggled beside pretty Pat Sanchez, the rich young daughter of a Cuban sugar planter, appeared in *Life* magazine. Peggy was also displeased to discover that Max had given Gypsy a painting as a wedding present a few nights earlier at Peggy's own birthday party, and she nagged Jimmy Ernst to send Gypsy a bill.

PART VII

ART OF THIS CENTURY

ISMS RAMPANT!

The autumn was filled with preparations for Peggy's gallery, to be called —like the catalogue—Art of This Century. Frederick Kiesler had been working madly on the space since the previous March and had prophesied to Peggy that one day her gallery would be known not for her artworks but for his design. The tiny, balding Kiesler, always very talkative, was especially so about the interior architecture he was creating for Peggy. To date he had had many brilliant ideas but few opportunities to see them realized. "He was very short, very sure of himself, and had nothing to show for it," said Jean Hélion, who met him in 1932. Although he was a master draftsman, portraitist, sculptor, and architect, Kiesler considered himself primarily an impresario, an impresario of genius.

But little personal problems began to crop up as the meetings between Peggy and Kiesler became more and more frequent. He was spending too much money, said Peggy, and they began to quarrel about expenses. Kiesler had grandiose ideas for Art of This Century; it was to be a statement of "design correlation" used to "break down the physical and mental barriers which separate people from the art they live with, working toward a unity of vision and fact as prevailed in primitive times." Pictures would interact with their environment, walls would curve, nothing would be static. Of course, it would cost money; but money was what Peggy had, and what did she have it for if not to spend it? Kiesler's original estimate of the cost had been forty-five hundred dollars plus a twelve-hundred-dollar fee for himself for planning and supervision. The project, Peggy pointed out, was actually costing closer to seven thousand. (Jimmy Ernst suspected that Kiesler's original estimate had been unrealistically low to appeal to Peggy's notorious sense of thrift and to guarantee him the commission.) The materials that Kiesler was ordering for the gallery were scarce and, therefore, expensive commodities during the war—linen, fluorescent lighting fixtures, oak floors. Kiesler did not skimp in the slightest and Peggy was furious. Kiesler begged Jimmy (unsuccessfully) to hide the invoices that were rapidly stacking up from Peggy, at least for a while.

"Peggy was avaricious to the point of comedy," said David Hare. "She always quarreled about money . . . the kind of person who goes from place to place looking for the cheapest bottle of milk and who argues about who pays for the coffee. But Kiesler *was* difficult." Kiesler was tyrannical and quick to take offense. His world consisted of friends and "frenemies." Dorothy Miller, who dealt with Kiesler while curating a show at the Museum of Modern Art, exclaimed,

> Kiesler—what a pest! I somehow undertook to put him in "15 Americans," but I only wanted to include one sculpture. . . . He would call me every morning—"I have a new piece," and try to get me to come to see it. His aim was to have the sculpture surrounded by other of his things on the walls. I wanted just the sculpture alone. I would come home exhausted and my husband would say, "You've been Kieseled again." He had a pesky, pesky personality.

And Becky Reis found Kiesler "very witty, a real *Spitzbuber* (a German word for someone who does naughty and frightening little things)."

The tiny Kiesler had an eye for the ladies and would arrive at a gathering and kiss every woman's hand, European-style. Hedda Sterne laughed as she recalled, "Once he came to a party of mine, and I had a friend who was six foot four, and he went straight to her." But he was democratically fond of *all* women—tall, short, or in between; "he had a penchant for *everybody*," smiled Jean Hélion. Becky Reis added that "he had mistresses wherever he could find them." Kiesler was "fun," exclaimed the painter Charles Seliger. "He was enthusiastic; he promoted people in the gallery. He said, 'Seliger, what the trouble with you is you are giving them too much. Ten percent would be enough.'"

By October, Peggy's gallery was nearly ready. "Kiesler picked out everything," said Peggy, from the color of the floors to the shape of the rooms. He worked frantically to finish the gallery before a large-scale exhibition of Surrealist work, scheduled to take place in early October, opened. Kiesler did not want anything to steal the thunder from his innovative designs for Art of This Century. But Elsa Schiaparelli (the dress designer who upended a felt shoe to wear on her head and appliquéd Dali-designed red-satin lips on her suits) had approached Peggy with the idea of a Surrealist exhibition as a benefit to aid French prisoners of war and children. Peggy pledged her support, but passed Schiaparelli along to André Breton who, delighted with the idea of a big Surrealist exhibition in New York, enlisted the help of his old cronies Max Ernst and Marcel Duchamp.

This "First Papers of Surrealism" show (the title being a play on an immigrant's first papers) opened on October 14, less than a week before the inauguration of Peggy's gallery, and ran through November 7, 1942. (Kiesler and Peggy consoled themselves that Art of This Century was so special that nothing on earth could diminish its impact.) As the distinguished and elegantly dressed opening-night public arrived for an auction of Surrealist works at the Whitelaw Reid mansion on New York's Madison Avenue they ran into two miles of string wound by Duchamp around pillars and columns inside the house. (Duchamp had bought sixteen miles of it, reasoning that "it would have been fatal to run short.") The effect was of a gigantic spider's web through which Surrealist pictures and objects could barely be seen. Moreover, the unmistakable cacophony of children noisily playing came from the maze. Duchamp had cornered Sidney Janis's eleven-year-old son the night before, telling him: "Get some friends together and I'll send taxis for you. . . . And pay no attention to anyone. Just play all evening." Boys, some armed with football helmets, scrimmaged around the hall in dirty sneakers, while little girls skipped rope and played hopscotch and jacks. The "whole ballroom, in fact," noted one observer, "looked like a public playground." The guests were encouraged to join in the games and by evening's end grown women were skipping rope and men in tails were throwing football passes. Enigmatically, the mastermind, Duchamp, was nowhere to be seen, following his long-standing tradition of disappearing on his opening nights.

Through the twine and the fly balls, the truly diligent art lovers could glimpse works by Picasso, Klee, Miró, Masson, Ernst, Seligmann, Magritte, and Matta as well as the works of lesser-known young Americans, showing for the first time with the European artists—Motherwell, Baziotes, David Hare, Joseph Cornell, and Jimmy Ernst. Breton, once again, presented Surrealism as an attitude by including artists who had long resisted the honor of being inducted into his fraternity, like Picasso and Klee. Pictures of Superman and Father Divine and cartoons by William Steig punctuated the exhibition. Sidney Janis wrote a foreword for the catalogue in which he praised the Surrealist spirit, "This communion, a sort of festive ceremonial dedicated to the imagination."

The critic from *Art News* was delighted to observe one woman and her umbrella become tangled in the chichi maze of twine. Peggy headed the list of sponsors, but was doubly miffed, both because the show was so outrageous and because the pictures she had lent to the exhibition were not properly identified.

Almost a week later, on October 20, Art of This Century was officially ushered into existence. The opening-night exhibition of Peggy's collection of European art was staged as a benefit for the American Red Cross and proved to be just as much an event as the umbrella-catching Surrealist show had been. It was the kind of exhibition that Peggy had hoped to present with Herbert Read in London, covering every nonrealistic movement after 1910. The real innovation, however, was in Kiesler's staging. Until almost the last minute, no one had any idea of what Kiesler had done, not even Max, who was only allowed to see it two days before the opening.

Kiesler had transformed the mundane, dingy loft space into a recreation park of modern art, full of gadgets, inventions, protrusions, serpentine walls, roaring sounds, and even light shows. "What a showman he was!" exclaimed Seliger approvingly. Kiesler had divided Art of This Century into four galleries and made everything in them flexible and changeable, so that like stage sets they could be dismantled in thirty minutes. The Abstract/Cubist gallery had movable walls made of stretched deep-blue canvas, laced to the floors and ceilings like giant undulating sails. The floors were painted turquoise, Peggy's favorite color. Unframed pictures "swaying in space" at eye level were actually mounted on triangular floor-to-ceiling rope pulleys resembling cat's cradles. The gallery had the effect of being "like a large cubistic painting."

The Surrealist gallery beyond was a long, narrow, cavernous room with panels of curved gumwood attached to black walls and ceilings, from which protruded paintings mounted on cantilevered arms that could be moved to whatever angle the visitor fancied. Periodically the recorded roar of a train reverberated through the womblike gallery and every three and a half seconds concealed lighting eerily shone first on one then the other side, pulsating "like blood," said Kiesler. The elaborately plotted spotlighting drove people crazy. Pierre Matisse, who saw the gallery in its early days, said, "The light went on in the other side . . . just at the moment you wanted to see something better." Eventually it was abandoned as the light show gave off more headaches than illumination.

In the center of the Surrealist gallery, and throughout Art of This Century, were Kiesler's specially designed amoeboid chairs, four designs in all—a rocker, two recliners, and a seven-way unit—made of ash, on which rested Peggy's sculptures and from which also protruded pictures mounted on the gripping end of baseball bats (sawed off by Kiesler and a carpenter in a garage in the Bronx to save time and money). The chairs, in unexpected colors—puce, yellow, red, maroon, blue, black, and white —were varifunctional and could be laid on any of their linoleum-upholstered sides for use as seating, sculpture pedestals, coffee tables, lecterns, hatracks, room dividers, or, stacked side by side, as sofas. Kiesler envisioned at least eighteen uses for his seven-way chair, or "correalist tool," as he called it. To further eliminate the problem of museum fatigue, collapsible blue canvas benches with and without backs were also put at the disposal of the public.

In a passageway, a whirring machine called a paternoster triggered by an invisible light beam brought into view a series of Klee paintings on a conveyer belt. "You put your finger on a button," Peggy explained, "and a Klee came. Then you pushed another button and another Klee came. There were about nine on the thing." Opposite the Klees was a large spiral wheel next to a peephole. When the wheel was rotated, the viewer saw through the tiny aperture fourteen reproductions of Duchamp's life's works, from his *Boîte-en-Valise,* a tribute to Duchamp, whose ideas Kiesler greatly admired. In another corner was a shadowbox. When the spectator put his face to the viewer and lifted a lever, seven black concave mirrors reflected him as he looked at a pupillike diaphragm imprinted with a signed portrait of André Breton, which then dilated to reveal Breton's poem/object, *Portrait of Actor A. B.* swinging into place ("to facilitate the co-reality of fact and vision"). The Kinetic gallery and its gadgets were quickly dubbed "Coney Island," complete with peepshow and penny arcade.

Last, there was one somewhat conventional space, the Daylight gallery along the Fifty-seventh Street side of the building where Peggy proposed to show new artists. The room boasted white walls and soft, diffused light produced by a large screen in front of the windows made of ninon, a sort of sturdy chiffon, most typically seen as lingerie. Whatever did not fit on the walls or on the chairs Peggy could show on rolling easellike storage stands, pyramidical plywood constructions devised by Kiesler. For example, a comfortably seated customer could leaf through folders of art done by children or the insane—always offered as a counterpoint to the exhibition on view—and then replace them inside Kiesler's portable painting bins.

On opening night, women wearing Chinese robes and dangling

giant sculptural bracelets and men jabbering in French, drinks in hand, swerved to avoid paintings jutting out into the room or suspended in midair. Peggy greeted her guests, who each paid one dollar to get in, in a white dress, her eyes bright, her hair solid black, her lips a smudge of scarlet. From one ear dangled the tiny pink oval desert landscape Tanguy had made for her, and on the other, a huge wire mobile by Alexander Calder, to represent, she liked to say, her impartiality between abstract and Surrealist art.

Peggy and Jimmy had shrewdly arranged a press preview of Art of This Century and practically every major New York paper and art publication carried a banner headline on the new gallery. "Surrealist Circus!" was one response. "Isms Rampant," shrieked *Newsweek,* "Peggy Guggenheim's Dream World Goes Abstract, Cubist and Generally Non-Real." Henry McBride at *The New York Sun* said, "My eyes have never bulged further from their sockets than at this show."

Edward Alden Jewell, the art critic for *The New York Times* (Peggy secretly called him her "jewel"), was "filled with a sense of wonders never ceasing." He wrote, "In this rebel arrangement art moves out into the open. Sometimes, thus liberated, it looks faintly menacing—as if in the end it might prove that the spectator would be fixed to the wall and the art would stroll around making comments, sweet or sour as the case might be." Peggy responded by taking an ad in *View* quoting Jewell and announcing: "WE *will* DO JUST THAT—SWEET or SOUR AS THE CASE *will* BE."

Art of This Century was irreverent, full of fun, and a smashing success. People could not only touch these paintings, but even move them around, tilt them, handle them. Staggeringly different from any gallery ever seen before, Art of This Century was certainly worlds away from the blue-chip galleries such as Knoedler or Wildenstein that exhibited their paintings elaborately gilt-framed in hushed velvet rooms. Nor was it anything like the stark, dour, proletarian-style worker-galleries of the Depression. "It was talked about and criticized," said Sidney Janis. "Mostly, people hated what Kiesler did. Artists and their close friends liked it, but the audience of beginning collectors and collectors didn't." Julien Levy, who was in the army reserve at the time, was frankly envious. "I had spent years trying to do what Peggy did with a snap. Peggy suddenly appeared and she showed Ernst, after I had been showing him for years. . . . She made a big impression, got here at a time when everything was ready to burst. Art of This Century was a big, expensive job, and she did it all on her own, a modern museum." The net effect was that swarms of people crowded into the gallery to see just what all the fuss was about.

GALLERY LIFE

Peggy was delighted with her success. Although she had a tiny office tucked behind the ultramarine-blue sails, she was too excited to sit in it for long. She bobbed her head, put her hand up to fidget with her neck, crumpled Kleenexes, and applied great smears of deep red lipstick every few minutes. She had to be everywhere looking at everything that went on and could not resist moving her desk right next to the entrance, where some gallery-goers mistook her for the receptionist. As time went on, she would ask people while she leaned against the doorway, "And what did you think of the paintings?" If they did not seem to understand them, she would shrug her shoulders—"Come back again in fifty years" —and begin again with the next person.

David Hare, who was among the first visitors to Art of This Century, recalled,

> If the gallery were here today, more people, I expect, would see it as a *happening.* . . . Now her gallery would be thought too fussy, not minimal enough. Nobody knew what it was. It was dusty, dirty in the corner. There were papers on the floor. It looked like a hock shop. It was more real than galleries today. It was too homey, in a way, more like a European gallery. The walls had spots, odd nails

sticking out. It didn't look like a hospital. It looked more like a personal collection. Today it would be considered crowded and not very large.

"Duchamp's reproductions were very small," continued Hare, making a circle of his index finger and thumb. "The wheel would be set up and then in about six months it would begin to squeak, the paint chip; it would be fixed, but it was like somebody's home." Peggy ran the gallery as she ran her life, and it was, admitted Pierre Matisse, a "little sloppy."

It was so much like home that visitors were confused. What was for sale and what was part of the owner's collection? Peggy's intention was to sell Ernst's paintings for him and to sell the work of young discoveries, but certainly not her treasures.

The informality helped make Peggy's gallery a meeting place for artists, especially those European artists feeling a little homesick and eager for companionship. Breton would stop by, or Mondrian, or, if he felt dispirited at home, Ernst. To each one, she would say, "I have something very interesting to show you." American artists also would visit. Where else could they see such an eclectic collection of modern art? And if they were in luck, Peggy would introduce them to her European friends. In addition, an occasional Seligman or Guggenheim would sneak in to see just who this outrageous cousin was.

So many people came to visit that soon after the gallery opened, Peggy decided to help defray her overhead by charging admission, an astonishing and unheard-of thing in those days for a gallery or museum. She loved to stay by the door and collect the twenty-five cents herself, which went into a large fishbowl or tambourine. Hedda Sterne dropped by to pick Peggy up for lunch and saw Peggy happily reach into the bowl, full of nickels and dimes, to pick up a handful before going out. Peggy was vigilant lest anyone escape without paying. Sidney Janis came by to see the gallery and Peggy announced her new policy. "I guess I better give you a quarter, then," he said and was genuinely shocked when "she took it!" Jimmy Ernst, who continued to act as Peggy's assistant in the gallery, recalled collecting money from people during Peggy's long, European-style lunch break and waving his poor artist friends in for free. One day Peggy surreptitiously waited in the lobby to count people as they came in, checking the indicator over the elevator to see who stopped at the seventh floor. After lunch, "she came up without a word, counted the quarters in the tambourine, and announced that we were two dollars and seventy-five cents short," stating with authority that "there were eleven people who did not pay!"

Whatever people thought, Peggy adored collecting admission. "I loved that," she admitted. "It was absolutely ridiculous, of course."

When she was chided for it by Laurence, she would say "I can't give up this business of peddling a little."

Peggy also happily sold copies of her catalogue, *Art of This Century,* and Jimmy Ernst looked on as Peggy's Aunt Irene Guggenheim, who braved the wrath of the Baroness Hilla Rebay to visit Peggy's bastion, thanked Peggy profusely in the mistaken belief that she had been gifted a catalogue, only to have Peggy ask her for "three dollars, please."

Eventually, Peggy reluctantly gave up collecting admission. Howard Putzel, who acted as Peggy's unofficial counselor, curator, and guide in the gallery, "made me stop," she said. But few people who saw it could forget the sight of Peggy by the door with her hand stretched out.

As her relationship with Ernst became increasingly remote, Peggy was happy to have a place to go every morning and to stay all day. Jean Hélion observed, "She found a favorable something to love, and she loved it until the end." The gallery opened its doors at 10:00 A.M. and Peggy would arrive shortly after eleven (never having been an early riser) and would stay until after 6:00 P.M. Max would wait until Peggy was safely out of the house before coming downstairs to make himself breakfast. All day he would be left alone to fend for himself, which, given Peggy's inattentive and frugal housekeeping, could sometimes be a highly creative endeavor. When she came home in the evening, she went on and on about how much money she had collected, sitting on her bed counting nickels, dimes, and quarters.

Under the spell of her Surrealist advisers, Breton, Ernst, and the unofficial Surrealist, Duchamp, Peggy proceeded at first more or less as she had in London, with a Surrealist bias. She followed up her opening exhibition with a show of objects by Marcel Duchamp, Laurence Vail, and Joseph Cornell scheduled for December and the Christmas season. Duchamp exhibited his *Boîte-en-Valise,* in a multiple limited edition. Laurence Vail presented his "bottles," amusing leftovers from his drinking bouts, which he covered in tiny images cut out from glossy magazine advertisements. (As testimony to her onetime affection for him, Peggy kept one of Vail's bottles in her bedroom until the end of her life.)

A little-known American eccentric living on Utopia Parkway in Queens with his mother, Joseph Cornell was represented by his Surrealist-inspired "objects." These magical boxes, dioramas of the unconscious, were full of evocative scraps of everyday life—pills, sequins, marbles, cocktail glasses. Peggy hoped that the public would buy the objects as Christmas presents, and she herself gave away Cornell boxes to a lucky few. A reviewer labeled it "the weirdest show in town. . . . It's all surrealist, pretentious and silly in the extreme."

Duchamp once suggested to Peggy the idea of a show exclusively by women artists and Peggy decided its time had come. Buffie Johnson, who eventually exhibited in the show, claimed that it was her idea. "I had talked with [Howard] Putzel about women being neglected in the arts, and we talked about doing a show, and I knew his influence with Peggy and said, why don't you try and get her interested. He talked to Peggy and Max and Max thought it would be a good idea, so Peggy thought it would be a good idea."

The concept of a women's show appealed to Peggy because of its daring. The bohemian world of art had room for women as mistresses or models but not as serious artists in their own right. Some women painters toiled in the shadows of well-known husbands or lovers and sacrificed their own opportunities to the careers of the men. Others simply couldn't get their work shown. Even Peggy was hostile to women, doubtless out of competitiveness and jealousy. "Peggy hung her pans on a Sophie Täuber," said Hedda Sterne, who also showed in Peggy's exhibition. "Her generation, or even my generation were mean towards women; when a woman was exceptional she wanted to be the only exceptional one." Buffie Johnson thought Peggy "was not unpleasant at all. Women—they weren't very useful to her. I don't think she was particularly [hostile]. . . . People had to amuse her or be useful in some sort of way."

(In later years, ironically, Peggy was thought of as a forerunner of women's liberation for her unconventional behavior and her shows featuring women artists, but she dismissed that notion. "I seem to have been. . . . But I'm not a women's liberationist—at least, I hate the exaggerated, overdone way it goes on nowadays. I certainly believe in all the things they want and stand for, but I think they're making too much of a fuss over it. They seem to be trying to do the world over in woman's own image. . . . It would be going from one tyranny to another.")

The exhibition of women artists was scheduled for the month of January. A jury was set up, European-style, consisting of Breton, Ernst, Duchamp, Putzel, Sweeney, Soby, Peggy, and Jimmy Ernst, to select the women artists for the show. The judges chose pieces by Leonora Carrington, Leonor Fini, Buffie Johnson, Meret Oppenheim, Irene Rice-Pereira, Kay Sage, Hedda Sterne, Frida Kahlo, and Louise Nevelson as well as works by such unlikely participants as Gypsy Rose Lee (she submitted a collage self-portrait with seashells and a picture of her body topped with a dog's head, tearing down a runway), Peggy's sister Hazel, Xenia Cage, Djuna Barnes, and two paintings by a young painter called Dorothea Tanning.

The show was titled "31 Women," and later Peggy often joked that the exhibition should have been kept to only thirty. Somehow, Max was designated to make the final selections directly from the studios of the women artists. Several times during the period of these selections (which in some cases apparently "required" more than one visit), Peggy observed to Jimmy, "Max is very, very happy. . . . It will be a very exciting show." Ernst encouraged the rumor that he had managed to seduce all thirty-one artists. "Of course not," Peggy remarked. "Most of them weren't seducible anyhow. They weren't attractive enough to be seducible."

Max had encountered Dorothea Tanning the year before at Julien Levy's doorstep—literally—and then later at a party given in her honor by Levy, who thought "Max would be interested in her paintings and give her a boost." Max was taken by much more than her paintings. Dorothea was young, still in her twenties, lively, beautiful, and "very, very female." She had dark brown hair and dazzling blue eyes. All in all, "Tanning was very gorgeous," exclaimed John Bernard Myers. In addition, she showed real talent as a painter and, as Peggy snidely observed, "He was always interested in women who painted."

When Max arrived at Tanning's studio to make his selection for Peggy's show he was confronted by *Birthday,* a self-portrait of Dorothea, in which she posed herself in front of a series of open doors, bare-breasted and sporting a skirt of thorns. Ernst could resist neither the portrait (this painting would one day hang in the stairway of Jimmy Ernst's house, where his children could point to it and say proudly—if inaccurately—"That's Grandma!") nor its painter.

Dorothea was thrilled to meet the reigning star among Surrealist painters. She had begun painting as a child and by the age of eight decided to become a painter. She arrived in New York from her native Illinois just in time to see the huge Surrealist exhibition at the Museum of Modern Art in 1936, and was inspired to paint in that style. She had wanted to meet Max Ernst for a long time and had even gone to Paris in 1939 with a letter of introduction to him which because of the war she was unable to deliver. Now she had the famous painter, lonely and restless in his marriage to Peggy, at her feet while her own husband was conveniently away in the navy. Their meeting was a *coup de foudre,* a thunderbolt. Each was prepared to fall in love with the other.

Peggy suspected something from the beginning. "Dorothea Tanning was living next door to me, and at first the accusations were that I was the 'one,'" said Buffie Johnson, in a reference to the *1* in "31 Women." Buffie recalled Tanning at the time as "self-important . . . beautiful in a cheap way, very kind of Hollywood starlet, very ordinary kind of looks. She tried to look very Surreal, but it didn't go together." And Peggy simply "couldn't understand why Max fell for her. It seemed absolutely incredible, because Leonora Carrington was so marvelous, I could understand that perfectly, really, that he fell in love with her, and after that I couldn't understand how he could fall in love with Dorothea." Peggy considered Tanning vulgar and embarrassingly pushy. She couldn't stand the fact that she was from the Midwest. And no, "she wasn't breathtakingly beautiful. I never saw that anyhow." Peggy was very distressed when she intercepted a note for Max from Dorothea in which Dorothea had included a mass of blue silk and referred to it as a lock of her hair.

All of forty-four-year-old Peggy's insecurities about her looks came pouring out when this young woman snatched Ernst away from her. "I never really had him," Peggy admitted, "and I was made nervous by that and trying to play up to him. I just had the fear that he didn't really like me, because I wasn't the kind of person he liked. He liked stupid, beautiful young girls and people who weren't so genteel or refined. He really liked sort of common young girls. But Leonora wasn't at all common. Leonora was very refined."

Everything Peggy did backfired. She took away Ernst's keys to the house, only to wonder if she had sent him into Dorothea's arms. She tried to make him jealous with tales of her infidelities, first with Duchamp and then, when Mary Reynolds arrived from Europe and put an end to the affair, with a series of one-night stands. She slept with whoever was available—John Cage, Sidney Janis—hoping that Ernst would find her desirable if others did. "Peggy was jealous of Dorothea and did it to compensate," said Janis, who observed, "Peggy was very democratic about her favors."

Peggy became more and more argumentative and irritable, giving vent to the frustrations of her life with Ernst. She would make grating, disagreeable comments and dinners would end with plates crashing and someone rushing out of the room. She used Laurence Vail, who moved in with her for a while when he broke his leg skiing and couldn't negotiate the stairs in his own home, as a foil, confiding in him all her troubles and making cutting remarks about Ernst. "She was horrible to Max," said her sister Hazel. "She did everything she could to humiliate him. Laurence was staying with her and she'd say, 'Oh, Laurence, go out and get me some whiskey. You're the only one who can speak English.' " Consequently, Max wanted to see her as little as possible. He confided in his friend Julien Levy. "Max said that Peggy was getting more and more impossible, that he was getting sick of her and that Dorothea *was* juicy."

Dorothea was bubbly and wide-eyed and fanciful. She loved to dress up, wear makeup, have a good time. A story circulated that once when she was invited to a very proper and formal ladies' lunch, Dorothea arrived in a silk dress, which upon closer inspection revealed a nipple discreetly peeking through a cutout circle. Dorothea, justly proud of her beautiful breasts, was amused when all the women pretended to notice nothing at all strange. (John Myers described a party Tanning gave years later in which "she decorated the whole place with fallen leaves she had gathered in Central Park. It gave everyone the giggles.")

Ernst confided to Jimmy that he had made a mistake in letting Peggy believe he loved her. He was grateful to Peggy for rescuing him at a low point in his life, but no one besides Peggy believed that Ernst was in love with her—and even Peggy did not really believe it. Peggy warned that she would commit suicide if he left her. He insisted he only wanted to have a fling with Dorothea, that if Peggy let him go to Arizona with her, he would come back a new man.

Peggy poured her heart out to Howard Putzel, whom she felt free to call at all hours of the day or night. "The things that are going on!" Putzel would tell his friend Buffie Johnson. Putzel would invite Peggy to concerts and recitals or take her to the opera, but returning home, Peggy "ran into the perfidy of Max Ernst and Dorothea and Howard was terribly upset about it all."

At first Ernst would spend a few days with Dorothea and come home again, even telling Peggy the details of his life with Tanning. But before long, Max was coming back to Hale House only to paint. "He used his studio all the time," explained Peggy indignantly. "That annoyed me very much. He just came to use the studio. Everything was quite a nerve about that affair." Marcel Duchamp did his best to console Peggy, but sweet as he was, she felt he "behaved more like a nurse than a lover." Pegeen tried to intervene with Ernst; even Emily Coleman tried her hand at getting them back together, but nothing worked.

In desperation, Peggy went to see André Breton and asked him if he would analyze her, as she thought he was "some kind of a psychiatrist." But Breton simply suggested, "Why don't you marry Duchamp?" pointing out that he was not qualified to advise her. "After Max she became unstable," noted Ethel Baziotes.

> She was under treatment with doctors and she wasn't sleeping. She was crying all the time. Her eyes were always red, her nose all swollen. She was so hurt by this. I think he was the only man she really loved. I have real sympathy for that. I think she loved him, his reputation, and he was extremely handsome. She felt that she was really catching someone important. She had a mind like that, you know, somehow, for important people. I think she really did love him as much as she was able. He was physically for her. She really felt he had a lot of iron in him, and I think he dominated her. I know he dominated, and it probably had never happened to her before.

It was doubly difficult for Peggy, because in the tiny art world in which they moved, she would run into Dorothea, her hair dyed turquoise, her blouse or skirt decorated with little pictures of Max—an idea she took from Ernst himself, who always dressed his girl friends. Peggy got her revenge by writing about the affair, while it was still warm, in her memoirs, calling Dorothea "pretentious, boring, stupid, vulgar and dressed in the worst possible taste."

The spectacle of a woman disporting herself with a German national while her naval officer husband was fighting for his country caused Max and Dorothea a great deal of trouble. They were given the cold shoulder by those people in New York to whom Peggy showed copies of her manuscript well in advance of publication. Jimmy Ernst was also given an early look at the manuscript, but termed Peggy's treatment of Max petty and vindictive and an "act of self flagellation" that would hurt Peggy just as much as it would Ernst. When Peggy's autobiography appeared in 1946, Ernst and Dorothea decided to move to Arizona. "The climate in Arizona will be better for Dorothea's health," Max explained, "and maybe they will leave us in peace there." Nevertheless, they could not get away from the climate of hostility fed by Peggy's bitter book. "They were pursued even there," wrote Jimmy Ernst, "by the scandal sheets and newsmagazines with stories elaborated from Peggy's now published book. The New York art world, museums, galleries and all, treated the couple as 'non-persons.' " Ernst and Dorothea both had difficulty selling their paintings, and there were times when the two had barely enough money to eat.

Hurtful as it was, it finally dawned on Peggy that it was all "very simple. Max just wasn't in love with me. He was in love with Leonora Carrington, terribly, and then afterwards he fell in love with Dorothea Tanning, and I was sort of sandwiched in between and never loved, I think."

THE SPRING SALON

Peggy's personal life might be in turmoil, but at least she had the gallery to distract her and keep her mind off Max and Dorothea Tanning. In February, the French painter Jean Hélion was to have a show of his pictures at Art of This Century. Before the war, Hélion had been a founder with Theo van Doesburg of the Abstraction-Création group in Paris and had produced a name for himself with his distinctive abstractions of cylindrical forms. Peggy had met Hélion as a young soldier in Paris, and since then Hélion had suffered a series of adventures. He had been taken prisoner by the Germans and detained in Pomerania and then in Stettin, but had managed to escape the German camps and make his way to the United States, where he had left a wife and young son in Virginia. Hélion chronicled his experiences in a book published in 1943, *They Shall Not Have Me,* which received a great deal of publicity. When Peggy offered him a show of his prewar abstract paintings, Hélion readily assented.

Ernst, who had known Hélion in Europe, helped hang the exhibition, and Hélion could not help but notice the tension between his patron and her husband. "What went on between them," he said, "I don't know." The opening on February 8, 1943, was staged as a benefit for the Fighting French Relief, and Hélion gave a talk on his escape from the Nazi prison camp. James Johnson Sweeney wrote a catalogue in which he hailed Hélion as a "leader of the youngest generation" of French painters. More than a hundred people crowded into the gallery to hear Hélion, and afterward Peggy had a party at Hale House, where "it was wild and very gay, plenty of drinks, plenty of people," said Hélion. "Most of the vernissage crowd were there—Charles Henri Ford, John Cage, Merce Cunningham, Baziotes, Motherwell." Peggy's parties were always a mix of the great and amusing with Duchamp, Breton, Mondrian, and Kurt Seligmann frequently present. Pegeen mingled with the guests, an old hand by now at her mother's parties. It was the first time that Hélion had set eyes on Pegeen, a lissome student of seventeen. Although at thirty-nine he was considerably older, he was instantly attracted to her.

"Pegeen was very young, with long blond hair, a bit wild." recalled Hélion. "Peggy and Pegeen had difficulties together. There was a sort of row between them all the time." Hélion observed that Pegeen seemed unhappy, out of place, her face sad, her eyes always worried. He later grew to believe that "Pegeen suffered a good deal because of her mother. . . . I always had the feeling that Peggy had feelings, but she couldn't show them. . . . Pegeen admired her mother enormously. Pegeen was very unstable. She could be very sweet, but not always." Pegeen had picked up a bit of her mother's challenging conversational style and sarcasm, but none of her armor.

In March, Peggy had an exhibition called "15 Early 15 Late Paintings," by Braque, Chagall, Dali, de Chirico, Duchamp, Ernst, Gris, Kandinsky, Klee, Léger, Masson, Miró, Mondrian, Picasso, and Tanguy. The exhibition was hastily assembled, as the show originally slated for that month—one of covers designed for *VVV*—was canceled as a result of a falling-out with Breton over whether or not Peggy should have to pay for an advertisement in *VVV*. Given her huge support of the Surrealists, Peggy argued she should get one ad for free. Breton countered that he himself "had sacrificed to truth, beauty and art" and so should she. In the middle of the fray, Pegeen called the Surrealists *mesquin* (cheap). The formal Breton was incensed that a young girl should so dare to affront him and blamed Peggy for this lapse of protocol. Consequently, a new show had to be arranged within forty-eight hours.

As her relationship with Max drew to a close and her new problems with Breton emerged, it seemed that Peggy also started to drift away from the influence of her Surrealist friends; after Ernst's exit from Peggy's life they came around Hale House less frequently.

Peggy was now more receptive to other voices—American ones such as those of Howard Putzel, Alfred Barr, James Johnson Sweeney. When Art of This Century opened, Peggy hoped that it would become a "center where artists will be welcome and where they can feel that they are cooperating in establishing a research laboratory for new ideas." Moreover, she said, the gallery would serve its purpose "only if it succeeds in serving the future instead of recording the past." In the spring of 1943, Peggy scheduled two shows that were aimed at unearthing new talent.

Several young artists friendly with Matta were tempted to try their hand at a collage and *papiers collés* exhibit to be held April 16 through May 15. Taking out their paste pots and scissors, these artists snipped and glued—working together in some cases—collages for Peggy's show. Ad Reinhardt, David Hare, William Baziotes, Robert Motherwell, and a fellow whose name was misspelled in the catalogue as Jackson "Polloch" were exhibiting for the first time at Art of This Century.

Peggy installed these younger talents alongside works by Max Ernst, Kurt Schwitters, George Grosz, Francis Picabia, and Juan Gris and leavened them with collages by Laurence Vail and Gypsy Rose Lee. It was a thrill for a young painter to see his work alongside the European masters. And even if he had to hang next to Gypsy Rose Lee, hadn't Julien Levy shown Walt Disney's studio?

From the beginning, Peggy had announced her intention of holding at Art of This Century "a yearly salon of young artists creating in America and elsewhere," an idea of Herbert Read's for their projected London museum. Now, advertisements were placed in the art magazines soliciting recent work by artists under the age of thirty-six. A jury was selected, consisting of Duchamp, Mondrian (who was always gracious and approachable and, like Duchamp, selflessly receptive to younger painters), Alfred Barr, James Johnson Sweeney, James Thrall Soby, Howard Putzel, and Peggy. (Max Ernst and André Breton, who had served on Peggy's earlier jury, were conspicuously absent from this one.) Jimmy Ernst, uneasy at continuing with Peggy under the circumstances of his father's defection, quit his job in the gallery but came to help nevertheless.

Word of the spring salon traveled fast in the downtown studios, and young artists were eager to show with Peggy. As had been the case in London, the New York art world barely existed. And if the following for art was small, the audience for *modern* art was minuscule. It was a community, according to David Hare, of "maybe one hundred contemporary and modern painters and sculptors," swelled somewhat by critics, writers, poets, dealers, actors, and singers. Paintings went from one gallery to another in search of buyers, and dealers passed the few paying collectors around to one another. "There were maybe," said Sidney Janis, "a dozen galleries in all of New York, and a dozen picture framers who worked with them. You could go to the most wonderful exhibition and there would be two or three people there. Uptown, there were the old-timers—Wildenstein, Knoedler's. Today, there are maybe six hundred galleries."

The fact that the art world was so small made it very difficult for an American artist to show his work, since the handful of galleries showing modern art in New York were oriented predominantly toward European art. Pierre Matisse or Valentine Dudensing or Paul Rosenberg, Peggy's rivals on Fifty-seventh Street, sold the likes of Kandinsky, Klee, Max Beckmann, Picasso, Braque, and only a handful of American artists. Those gallery owners, who like so many of the artists found themselves in exile in America from the Nazis (such as Kurt Valentin at the Buchholz Gallery, Karl Nierendorf from Cologne, or J. B. Neumann of the New Art Circle), carried with them the European bias against American art and continued exhibiting their European compatriots. Even the American Julien Levy, whose gallery was by some accounts the most interesting of them, established his reputation showing the European Surrealists—Ernst, Dali, Tanguy—with the occasional inclusion of an American Surrealist such as Joseph Cornell. American painters were relegated to second-class status and left to founder in a few pioneer galleries.

All through May, artists carried their canvases up from studios in the Village to 30 West Fifty-seventh Street. Matta, who still hoped to become the American Breton, had his feelers out for artists of promise and suggested to Baziotes and Motherwell that they bring along Jackson Pollock. Pollock had recently been included in a gigantic exposition in support of the war effort held at the Metropolitan Museum of Art titled "Artists for Victory," and was regarded in the small circles of "downtown" artists as someone to watch.

Born in Cody, Wyoming, but raised in Arizona and California, the thirty-one-year-old Pollock had been in New York since 1930, where he had studied at the Art Students League. There he found an early mentor in Thomas Hart Benton, under whose influence Pollock experimented with Social Realism. During this time he shared an apartment with his two brothers, Charles and Sanford, and supported his painting by working at various unskilled odd jobs. But poverty had been a fact of life as far back as he could remember; he had been so poor that he could not even afford to go to his father's funeral. During the Depression, his finances sank even lower and he stole food from pushcart vendors. When the Federal Art Project of the Works Progress Administration was established in 1935 to employ artists and get them off the breadlines, he signed up for the easel division and began working intermittently, first for $103.40 a month and later for $95.44. Every two months he was required to submit a painting. All told he produced about fifty paintings for the WPA.

Withdrawn, mercurial, troubled, and alcoholic, Pollock let his paintings speak for him, much like Duchamp and Ernst, a violent language that failed him in real life. Pollock projected the moodiness of a caged animal and looked like a "pessimistic cowhand or a pugilist seriously considering quitting the ring." A tip was missing from his right index finger and his hands were so sensitive that it was sometimes painful for him to touch things.

Pollock was influenced by Picasso's Analytic Cubism to start painting in an abstract mode, and by 1936 his work had begun to show an original sensibility. Pollock was brought to the attention of the art establishment in 1941 when John Graham, an influential painter and critic, included Pollock in an exhibition of American and French painting at the MacMillen gallery. Pollock's *Birth,* a Picasso-like tangle of swirls and lines, hung alongside works by Picasso himself, Braque, Pierre Bonnard, and Matisse. And then there were the other Americans—Stuart Davis, Walt Kuhn, and a young woman named Lee Krasner.

Krasner (née Lenore Krassner) was the daughter of Russian Jewish immigrants who had settled in Brooklyn and ran a grocery store. At thirteen she decided to become a painter and studied variously at the Women's Art School of Cooper Union and the National Academy of Design. She was just a year younger than Pollock but had been painting in an abstract modern vein before him. She met Pollock at a loft party, when he stepped all over her feet in an attempt to dance, but it was not until Graham included both of them in his show that any real relationship developed. Krasner was far from a classic beauty, but "Lee," said Hedda Sterne, "when she was young had a very good figure, and she was very successful and attractive to men." When she learned that Pollock lived just around the corner from her, she went right over to visit him. Soon she had cleared a place for herself in Pollock's tiny Eighth Street studio. The two made a strange pair: she articulate, urban, cooking gefilte fish for Passover; he a hungover, untamed child of the prairies. Nevertheless, they maintained a workable, if stormy, relationship for many years.

Between 1937 and 1940, Lee had been a prize student of Hans Hofmann, a German emigré painter who had settled in America in 1932 when he was already fifty-two years old and in 1933 had established an art school on Madison Avenue. (Lee caused quite an impression on her first day there, arriving in black fishnet stockings, high-heeled shoes, and a tight black skirt.) Hofmann knew Picasso and Braque, the Delaunays, and Matisse. Hofmann also knew the Surrealists but he likened them to the devil—anti-art, anti-aesthetic, anti-Cubist. He was primarily drawn to a search for a spiritual ideal and to Kandinsky's lyrical and mystical colors. Hofmann's own abstractions were more spontaneous than Kandinsky's; he let his colors run into each other and dripped paint in layers on wood. In lectures and in class, he acquainted his students with European modernism and instilled a dynamic sense of the canvas as a meeting ground for what he called the "push and pull" of color, form, and space. Some tones, he explained, have the effect of pulling the viewer into the picture, whereas others seem to jump off the canvas and practically hit the onlooker in the face. By manipulating them in the right way, the painter could create, much as the Cubists had, a shallow, abstract space electrified by the pull of one color and the push of another. Hofmann's school became known as the "Temple of Cubism." (Remarkably, his students had never seen Hofmann's work until Peggy gave him his first one-man show in 1944. Until then, he had been esteemed primarily as a teacher.) Krasner introduced Pollock to Hofmann and he attended some of Hofmann's lectures but refused to study with him. Remarking on Hofmann's predilection at that time for starting a painting from nature, Pollock announced, "I am nature."

Krasner also introduced Pollock to her many artist friends "downtown," and to Sidney Janis, who was collecting material for his 1944 book *Abstract and Surrealist Art in America*. Janis liked to take credit for discovering Pollock, because he included a color reproduction of Pollock's *The She-Wolf* under the Surrealist section of the book. "When doing my book," he related, "forty-one, forty-two, I saw Hans Hofmann and said I wanted to get in touch with some of his better students. So, he sent me to Lee Krasner." After looking at her work, Krasner, said Janis,

> asked me if I knew Pollock. I said no, so she took me over to see him. He was working in an Orozco vein. I was impressed, so I sent a photographer over to photograph his work. I called Pollock both abstract and expressionist in my book—the first time the terms were used together. When I told Hans Hofmann later, "I have come from a neighbor of yours—Jackson Pollock," Hofmann said, "Never heard of him." Lee Krasner was the only one who knew Pollock.

When the entries—including Pollock's—were finally assembled for the spring salon jury, Peggy was surprised by the quantity and quality of new art being produced in New York. Mondrian was the first member of the jury to join her in the gallery the day of the selection. He wanted to take his time and see everything. (Mondrian, who had the first one-man show of his career in America at the age of seventy, never lost his look of a kindly professor. He wore a homburg, double-breasted suits, suede shoes, horn-rimmed glasses, and narrow ties. He even stuttered a bit. He invited Peggy to his studio to hear boogie-woogie music, where she watched him as he flitted funny little pieces of colored paper over his canvas and asked her where to put them.)

As Peggy and Mondrian waited for the other jury members to arrive, Peggy began to set out the works around the gallery. She noticed Mondrian looking at a picture in the corner—one submitted by Pollock. "Pretty awful, isn't it?" she asked. "That's not painting, is it?" Mondrian made no reply, but stood staring. Peggy continued, "There is absolutely no discipline at all. This young man has serious problems . . . and painting is one of them. I don't think he's going to be included . . . and that is embarrassing because Putzel and Matta think very highly of him."

When he finally spoke, Mondrian told Peggy that it was the most exciting painting he had seen—in Europe or New York—in a very long time. "You must watch this man." Peggy was stunned. But, she said, "You can't be serious. You can't compare this and the way you paint." "So, don't compare this," he replied. "The way I paint and the way I think are two different things."

Jimmy Ernst, who witnessed this scene, admired the way Peggy could learn. "She was willing to listen, she was willing to be told, she was willing to see. . . . You know, there was nothing phony about it. And it *was* shocking to see those paintings." Peggy herself said, "I took advice from none but the best. . . . Many people buy the best advice, but then they don't heed it. I listened, how I listened! That's how I finally became my own expert—at least, I knew enough to manage on my own." After Mondrian's remarks, Peggy took aside each member of the jury as he arrived and led him over to the Pollock, a dynamic oil on canvas called *Stenographic Figure.* "Let me show you something very, very interesting." Yet Duchamp did not much like it and Breton, when he came to visit, remained unconvinced. Neither one ever understood Pollock. Lee Krasner observed, "Vail, and the whole outgoing group, were furious at her for taking on someone like Pollock."

"The Spring Salon for Young Artists" was held from May 18 to June 26, 1943. Some thirty artists under the age of thirty-six exhibited their work, the great majority unknown to the public or the press. Jackson Pollock, Ad Reinhardt, William Baziotes, Robert Motherwell, and Matta were among the exhibitors. Two main currents were apparent in the paintings of these young artists exhibiting at Peggy's gallery, abstraction and a new brand of abstract Surrealism, raw and unpolished, going beyond "the Freudian dream catalogue." "Despite a faint air of the haphazard," wrote Robert Coates when he reviewed the exhibition for *The New Yorker,* "about the hanging and a certain amount of deadwood in the paintings, the new show at Art of This Century . . . deserves your attention." Coates went on to add, "A good share of the work is amateurish. . . . But in Jackson Pollock's abstract 'Painting,' with its curious reminiscences of both Matisse and Miró, we have a real discovery."

Pollock was the star of the show. At the urging of Howard Putzel, Peggy went down to Pollock's studio to look at more of his work. Putzel, who was wildly enthusiastic about Pollock, wanted Peggy to give him a contract, so that he could leave his low-paying custodial job doing installations and carpentry at, ironically, Peggy's uncle Solomon's museum, where Hilla Rebay had a number of artists on staff as receptionists, photographers, watchmen, or technicians and where Pollock stood out as a loner.

Lee Krasner's first impression of Peggy on the occasion of her coming to look at Pollock's pictures soured her subsequent opinion of her. Because of a misunderstanding, neither Pollock nor Lee was home when Peggy arrived at the appointed hour. "Something went amok with the timing," said Krasner, "because the fact is we got back to the apartment after our coffee and we met Peggy leaving the building in a total rage." Peggy was fuming and the distraught Krasner and Pollock had to cajole her into retracing her steps to take a look at Pollock's paintings. "She walked back up the stairs and into the studio," Krasner related, "and there were paintings of mine hanging on the wall. She started ranting—'Who's L.K.? Who's L.K.? I did not come up here to look at L.K.'s paintings!' " Krasner fell to thinking, "What a bitch."

After this unsettling encounter, Peggy was prevailed upon by Putzel to give Pollock a one-man show in the fall, and at Putzel's continued insistence and Matta's urging, Peggy agreed to provide the painter with a modest one-year contract so that he could quit his job. If more than twenty-seven hundred dollars' worth of pictures was sold in the first year (allowing a one-third commission to Peggy), Pollock was to receive a hundred and fifty dollars a month and a settlement at the end of the year; if a sum less than twenty-seven hundred a year were to be realized, Peggy was to receive Pollock pictures to make up the difference. In effect, for a hundred fifty dollars a month, or eighteen hundred dollars a year, Peggy was to receive Pollock's entire output of paintings for that year. (Nevertheless, Peggy's contract with Pollock was a rarity in the art world of the 1940s. "There wasn't very much subsidy, in those days," said Betty Parsons, who represented Pollock in later years. Clement Greenberg observed, "The contracts were utterly unique for that generation of artists. . . . [John] Marin, Milton Avery might have contracts. [But generally] it wasn't done and dealers wouldn't buy. . . . They got 'Europeanized' towards the end of the fifties, where dealers felt they had to give artists money.") At Putzel's behest as well, Peggy commissioned Pollock to do a mural-size canvas for the entrance hall of a new apartment that she had rented when her lease at Hale House expired. Putzel was curious to see whether a larger scale would release the force contained in Pollock's smaller paintings.

Lee Krasner believed that "Howard Putzel really got Jackson his contract. Surely Peggy made the gesture, but the fact is I doubt that there ever would have been a contract without Howard. Howard was at our house every night, and he told Jackson what to do, and how to behave. Otherwise, I doubt it would have happened. The whole thing was based on our friendship with Putzel."

Pollock was excited by the possibilities that he now saw before him: a one-man exhibition at a prestigious gallery and money in his pocket. Peggy's spring salon was a big step for Pollock. He wrote his brother Charles toward the end of July 1943:

Things really broke with the showing of that painting [*Stenographic Figure*]. I had a pretty good mention in the *Nation*—I have a year's contract with The Art of This Century and a large painting to do for Peggy Guggenheim's house, 8'11 ½" x 19'9". With no strings as to what or how I paint it. I am going to paint it in oil on canvas. They are giving me a show Nov. 16 and I want to have the painting finished for the show. I've had to tear out the partition between the front and middle room to get the damned thing up. I have it stretched now. It looks pretty big, but exciting as all hell.

LIFE IN THE DUPLEX

Max Ernst had left Peggy so shaken and so alone that she, in desperation, fell madly in love with an English intellectual named Kenneth Macpherson. Peggy had always been taken with Englishmen; there was something in their cool reserve that undid her. She adored reading Henry James over and over again and dreamed of being a romantic heroine carried off by some handsome English lord. In fact, to marry an English noble was the fantasy of many young women of her generation. Had not her own cousin Eleanor married the Earl of Castle-Stewart? In Macpherson she foolishly envisioned the fulfillment of those daydreams. She had met Macpherson through Ernst. He was one of the individuals whom the Museum of Modern Art had prevailed upon to write an affidavit in support of Ernst's admission to the United States. Ernst called him up to thank him for his support and invited him over to see the collection and to meet Peggy. Not long after Max began his affair with Dorothea Tanning that winter of 1943, Peggy ran into Macpherson again at the opera, and this time, sorely in need of comfort and kindness, Peggy felt what she labeled a "peculiar current" between them—peculiar indeed, as Macpherson was not interested in women and made no bones about his homosexuality.

Nevertheless, Macpherson was involved in a marriage of convenience to the English poet Bryher (whose real name was Winifred Ellerman), the daughter of an English shipping magnate, Sir John Ellerman. To keep her parents distracted from her lesbian relationship with the poet Hilda Doolittle—known as H.D.—and to gain a measure of independence, Bryher first married the American Robert McAlmon, who had been a friend of the Vails in their Paris days. When Bryher singled him out, McAlmon was scratching out a living in New York's Greenwich Village. With Bryher's generous support, McAlmon, a talented writer himself, went to Montparnasse and made his mark as the publisher of the Contact Press. When she tired of McAlmon's drinking bouts and surly moods, Bryher dismissed him with a substantial divorce settlement, and married Kenneth Macpherson in 1927. Young Macpherson had been having an "affair" with H.D., beginning when he was twenty-four and she forty. He thus became an amiable appendage to Bryher and H.D.'s lesbian twosome. With his new wealth, Macpherson produced films and started a magazine devoted to film as art called *Close-Up.* Ultimately, Bryher and H.D. became disillusioned with him—and would come to agree he was a "nasty bit." Macpherson was beautiful but narcissistic, charming but spoiled, and rich—as long as he remained married to Bryher. During the war he came to New York, leaving Bryher in Europe, although he remained legally married to her until 1947.

He absolutely dazzled Peggy. Tall, with wavy reddish-blond hair, to Peggy he seemed handsome, rich, and elegant. She was fascinated by his marriage to Bryher ("You can imagine what it was like, can't you?") and Bryher's unconventional relationship with H.D. Other women's lesbian relationships always intrigued Peggy. And Bryher (and therefore Macpherson) was *really* rich. When he died, Sir John Ellerman had left close to eight hundred million dollars, of which Bryher had inherited a substantial portion. It was a relief for Peggy to be involved with someone whom she did not suspect was after her for her money, a doubt that had plagued her through some of her earlier relationships. Peggy could even overlook the fact that Macpherson did not desire her sexually, as long as he continued to speak to her with that English accent.

She fell hopelessly in love with him, after her schoolgirl fashion, and imagined that he represented the height of English taste and erudition. As an example of his search for *le mot juste,* Peggy noted that Macpherson hated the word *fairy* and much preferred the use of *Athenian*—a term that came into use in Peggy's circle. Fastidious about his dress, Macpherson owned countless suits tailored to perfection and matching the exact blue of his eyes. Peggy did not mind that he was also "very much made up with Max Factor's cosmetics, and his hair was bleached too blond. In his bathroom," she chronicled in her memoirs, "which was more like a star's dressing room than anything else, were every kind of makeup and the most expensive perfumes from Paris. He showed me how to fix my hair. He knew how to do it much better than I did." (That hair of hers certainly begged for help. Black as it was, "in a certain light it would look kind of orange—a strange orange glow—from the dye in those days," said Rupert Barneby. "She wasn't very careful about doing it, so occasionally one saw a gray line.") Macpherson also knew a great deal about women's fashion and style. In sum, Peggy portrayed Kenneth Macpherson less as a lover than as a girl friend.

Love-struck, Peggy set out on a course of self-improvement to impress Macpherson. She began listening to Bach, went shopping for fashionable clothes, and tried to pull herself together in a more appealing way. "She really flipped for him," said Lee Krasner. "She went all out, changed her whole style of dressing, bought clothes, furs." Evidently, it came not a moment too soon. "When we knew her," said Ethel Baziotes, "she had very little interest in clothes. She had the wrong haircut, the wrong clothes." "To describe her to you," said Hedda Sterne of Peggy's attire, "I start with the bottom and go up. She had kind of sneakers on with rolled down socks, no stockings, unshaved legs and a very short sable coat. She was never bourgeois—totally unconventional."

Peggy needed a few lessons in makeup, which by all accounts she could have been applying with a broom. "She was never a genius with makeup," said Lee Krasner. Two black, round pencil lines made do for eyebrows, and the quick swipes of the lipstick she loved (and was always running out to buy) finished her maquillage. Yet "Peggy's lipstick was always cockeyed," said Krasner. "She looked like one of de Kooning's women." To Rupert Barneby, "She looked like a hag. Her clothes were absolutely awful. She wore bizarre earrings sometimes in the evening, and an enormous great fur coat, gray. She looked absolutely grotesque in that." When Hazel came to visit her (as she did once Peggy's marriage to Ernst broke up), "Hazel always wore satin, even in the middle of the day, and she had her décolletage cut so it just covered the nipple. So, side by side Peggy and Hazel were an absolutely grotesque couple of sisters."

Even though Peggy cared intensely about how she looked during this phase of her relationship with Macpherson, her attempts to improve her style were hopeless, since her taste was innately eccentric and she had no idea (that is, no good idea) how to complement her person. Adding to the problem of taste was the fact that she could not bring herself to pay the price for good-quality clothes. Instead, she bought her furs at the Ritz Thrift Shop, secondhand. And even though she admired pretty, well-made shoes, for her own she shopped at mass outlets like Kitty Kelly's. "She was very tight," explained Ethel Baziotes. Then again, Peggy paid for a painting what Barbara Hutton would have lavished on a dress.

As Peggy got older, her clothes became ever more bizarre, stiff, and armorial, with bold designs in questionable colors. She painted her fingernails and toenails with odd lacquers—at one point sporting silver toenails. She was fond of strange upturned sandals and big papier-mâché butterfly sunglasses. She seemed to like hiding behind props of one sort or another. "I suppose," said Barneby, "it must have been because of her nose."

Macpherson rewarded Peggy's efforts with kindness. He was used to sexually ambiguous rich women and knew how to maneuver around them. He liked having a mother figure. His own mother had been extremely overbearing and, it was said, enjoyed seducing his school chums. Peggy mistook his elegant manners and good breeding as signs of love, but he remained firmly homosexual. She, nevertheless, threw herself at him and perhaps managed to seduce him once, when "Kenneth simply did it out of kindness," said Barneby, who knew him well, "and on a magnum of champagne—I can't conceive of him doing it any other way."

Macpherson was a real friend to Peggy and immediately pointed out to her the pitfalls of her continuing relationship with Ernst, who still used his studio at Hale House to paint while openly living with Tanning. Macpherson insisted that Peggy draw up a separation agreement outlining the responsibilities of each party. Having plenty of money of his own, he empathized with Peggy's financial insecurities.

Peggy was keenly concerned about the pictures she believed Ernst owed her. This occasioned a great many disagreements with the artist, who deeply resented Peggy's appropriating his paintings. "Max said it was disgusting," stated Julien Levy. "She claimed she had bought clothes for him, and she said he owed her his paintings, because she had kept him. She was both generous and stingy." In addition, Peggy and Ernst squabbled over the dog, Kachina. Both wanted her and couldn't come to an agreement. Max finally just sneaked into the house and kidnapped her. Eventually, Ernst and Peggy reached an accommodation. Peggy bought two of Kachina's offspring and Max was forced to find another studio and take himself, Dorothea, and Kachina elsewhere.

Peggy now spent as much time as she could with Macpherson. "I was with Kenneth an awful lot once we got involved," she stated. "You can have an affair, you know, without sex, like a real, real affair, without sex. Once in a while sex, maybe one time, certainly not often."

Impulsively, Peggy and Macpherson decided to share a house. Macpherson complained that his present apartment was too small and Peggy leaped at the chance to suggest that they look for a place together. Realizing that they could never truly live together, they resolved to search for an apartment that would afford each one a measure of privacy. Meanwhile, Peggy looked forward to spending the summer in Connecticut near Laurence and his daughters. She had grown closer to her former husband over time and they constituted a sort of family now.

Laurence rented a house for himself and the girls on Candlewood Lake. Peggy wanted to rent the house adjacent to it, but the community was a restricted one where lake frontage was not rented or sold to Jews, so that a Guggenheim could not sign a lease. Consequently, Peggy found as a stand-in the very young avant-garde composer and writer Paul Bowles and his no-less-talented wife, Jane, who herself was Jewish.

Peggy had gotten to know Bowles through Jimmy Ernst. At one point, Peggy had decided to produce contemporary music (to get back at John Cage, perhaps) under her own label, "Art of This Century Recordings," and to begin with an unknown early Bowles flute sonata. "It was Paul Bowles' idea at the beginning of the war," explained Robert Fizdale, who along with his partner, Arthur Gold, played on this first and only album,

> and Peggy had opened Art of This Century, and Paul suggested she do something about the new music, albums with beautiful covers of music by composers that were unknown or that had never recorded much, and he asked us to play. We were still students and were delighted at the idea. The first album was a flute [and piano] sonata played by René Le Roy [with Georges Reeve on piano] and on the other side were two Mexican dances, *Sayula* [El Indio] and *El Bejuco*. It had a beautiful bright yellow cover with a line drawing by Max Ernst and only one hundred copies were printed. It was very exciting for us, because we were still students, kids. We were thrilled. We had no idea that we should be paid. She gave us each a copy. When we later told her we had misplaced them, she said she would give it to us in her will.

Peggy never did give Gold and Fizdale the album in her will, but the recordings, in their Ernst sleeves, were one more item she stacked on her desk by the door of the gallery and happily peddled to whoever she could. She regretted only having made a hundred copies. It was, she said, "a great mistake. We could have sold many more."

Paul and Jane Bowles became good friends of Peggy, and Paul obligingly went down to lower Broadway to sign the lease on the Connecticut house under the name of Mr. and Mrs. Bowles. Consequently, Peggy was addressed throughout the month of August as "Mrs. Bowles" by well-meaning local merchants. Laurence's daughters once again had the mixed pleasure of Peggy's quips and unconventional behavior, and Apple Vail recalled being unable to go down to the water that summer without finding Peggy at all hours of the day on the shore sprawled spreadeagle, sunbathing in the nude. Peggy was proud, with good reason, of her "excellent body" which looked to Hedda Sterne "like a de Chirico—lean, firm, and well preserved."

Laurence himself continued to behave toward his daughters in an incestuous manner. He treated Apple practically as his wife. "He was very sad sexually," concluded his younger daughter Clover. "He used to talk a lot to me about sex. He used to lie in bed with me every night, 'cuddling,' he called it. He told me he had a small penis, and that's why his wives had left him. He talked about his wives. He used to insist that I have baths with him."

Next door, Peggy enjoyed playing house for a while. Macpherson came to stay for three weeks and Peggy was happy puttering around and making plans for a new life with him. "We spent that summer, you know, together," she said, "settled in a way."

In the fall Peggy moved with Macpherson into a duplex in a double brownstone at 155 East Sixty-first Street. It consisted of two full floors which, although connected by an impressive winding staircase, could easily be used as separate apartments. (Sharing a kitchen posed no problem, as Macpherson rarely used one, and Peggy never kept much in hers.) The walls were covered with pictures and a brightly colored mobile by Calder hung from the ceiling in the living room. Laurence's new girl friend, Jean Connolly, who also had lived next door to Laurence in Connecticut, moved in with Peggy, and often shared a bed with her hostess.

Peggy continued to give big parties, only now Macpherson's friends mingled with the crowd. "Peggy's house was pandemonium," stated Julien Levy (whom Peggy had not forgiven for having introduced Max to Dorothea), "particularly with Macpherson's fairies around. The crowds got muddled. Peggy might be having a quiet evening at home, and there would be a noise, and Peggy would knock on the door and go to the party." The reverse was also true. "They were all interesting, fun people," added Levy, "and they tumbled into each other's parties." Lee Krasner and Jackson Pollock, Peggy's new protégé, formed part of the scene. "Jean Connolly, Dwight Ripley, Matta, Duchamp were around a great deal. They were at all the parties," said Krasner. They were "all 4F," snickered Sindbad. "Pollock, Motherwell, Baziotes." Baby-faced but open-eyed, Sindbad was in the army, stationed at Drew Field near Tampa, Florida. "My mother," he said, "didn't know there was a war on. If they," meaning all her artistic friends, "hadn't seen me in uniform, they wouldn't have known I was in the army. All those people behaved as if there were no war."

"I was shy in those days," Peggy mused. "I must have been. Yes, I guess I always was very shy, 'cause I used to hate to walk into a restaurant. . . . Oh, I did like them," she said in reference to parties full of people, "I liked them very much. I guess, I drank a lot and I was less shy. This sounds crazy. I think I went to bed every night in New York drunk . . . but I never had a hangover."

"Once," Lee Krasner remembered, "Peggy had been invited with Howard Putzel to our place, and I made a meatloaf, and they both raved about it." Peggy liked the meatloaf so much, she asked Lee for the recipe. "And shortly Peggy got hold of me and asked us to dinner for a few people at her house, but would I come earlier and see if she did the meatloaf the right way." Upon arriving at Peggy's, the astonished Lee discovered

> it was a party for fifty people. The two maids were there peeling potatoes, and she had a huge amount of meat in the kitchen. I could not multiply the recipe for so many people. We both got tight making the meatloaf. We just opened the closet doors and put in everything in the closet. There were a lot of mashed potatoes. Matta, Duchamp, an awful lot of other people were there. Meatloaf, mashed potatoes, and endive salad. It was not exactly what you'd call a catered situation.

Lee found Peggy "kookie. Sex always seemed to dominate [her conversation]; she tried to slant things that way." Krasner recounted an episode that quite appalled her. "Once when I was staying at Peggy's the phone rang, and it was Hazel, who said: 'Go tell Peggy I must talk to her. I'm in terrible pain.' I found Peggy in one of the guest rooms and gave her the message. Peggy said: 'Go tell her she fucks too much.' " (No one could accuse Hazel of being overly delicate, either. One acquaintance recalled, "Hazel and I had the same dentist in New York, on West Twenty-third Street, and she walked in with a tire. She dropped the tire on a sofa, sat on it, and said, 'I've got piles.' ")

The sisters continued being competitive and jealous of each other. Peggy was always embarrassed by Hazel and discouraged her friends from seeking her out. Peggy enjoyed irritating Hazel and Hazel in turn goaded Peggy, particularly about Kay Boyle, who Hazel maintained was *so* nice. "When my husband died," Hazel said, "she wrote me a note. She just had a child, was in the hospital. I thought it was so nice, I called her up to thank her, and Peggy said, 'You know, that's a long-distance call. Please pay me back.' " Rupert Barneby sympathized with Hazel. "Hazel would get a check every month, I suppose, and would cash it and put the money in her purse, and one day, when she was staying with Peggy, she put her bag on a radiator, and it fell behind and was lost, and Peggy wouldn't lend her anything. . . . So, Hazel would have to ask for a dollar here and a dollar there. . . . The loss of the money was not so bad as the fact that Peggy thought she was so careless that she should suffer for it."

During this time, Peggy was more than ever surrounded by homosexuals. Peggy's gay court had bothered Ernst and Breton. As Sindbad told it, they "were around because no one else was around; most everyone else was drafted. Only those that were too old, or queens, or 4F, or married" remained behind. Moreover, homosexual men "were more likely to put up with a middle-aged woman who they didn't have to perform with," explained David Hare. "She would try and persuade them to have a love affair. Male homosexuals like the idea of a woman being interested in them."

But Peggy "went to bed with everyone," stated Dorothy Miller. "She tried awfully hard to go to bed with Alfred Barr." According to Lee Krasner, "she went after every male that was there." It left Peggy with little energy for anything else, "she was so busy wanting to sleep with everything in pants." And not only in pants. "She was sexually aggressive," said Hedda Sterne. "She said to me, 'I tried women, but I didn't like it. It didn't give me any pleasure.' She had to try *everything.*"

Peggy considered "fucking" a tonic for all ailments. If her maid was out of sorts, she'd say, "She doesn't get enough fucking." If a cat wailed, she'd say the same thing. But, as with any drug, there were those who overdosed, she thought, like her sister Hazel. "What Peggy *said* was shocking," declared Hedda Sterne. "She had an obsession—she was man-mad. . . . It ran in the family."

"I had so many odd people," Peggy joyfully admitted. "I used to have so many people when I lived in that flat with Kenneth. I can't even remember their names now. I had a Frenchman, a Viscount somebody. I can't remember his name. And I had an Irishman who was very amusing. I can't remember his name either. . . . I had a man who made pottery in the north of New York, who I went up to visit once, who gave me beautiful dishes, and I bought beautiful dishes from him, but I can't remember any of their names. They weren't that important. I think I was almost a nymphomaniac. . . . I don't think I was especially attracted. I just think I wanted to make love. . . . I think I was very sexy," Peggy went on. "I think I always felt very sexual. My son said I was not a nymphomaniac. He said it's perfectly normal for women to want to make love as much as men. He objected to my saying I was a nymphomaniac. Just a question of being oversexed, probably."

Of Peggy's detached pursuit of love, the writer John Richardson remarked, "She had a homosexual approach to sex. She was around them so much, she picked up the one-night stands." She was like Nancy Cunard, he said, who was famous for calling in her maid to ask about her husband, the butler, "Does Osgood fuck? Good. Send him up. I need one." Eleanor Perenyi found women like Peggy, Nancy Cunard, and Caresse Crosby of a type—"she-wolves. . . . They wanted to be out of society and into the art world."

Peggy talked so much and so blatantly about her sexual obsessions that stories—true or wildly exaggerated—circulated about her insatiable appetites. "There were grisly stories," said Rupert Barneby, "that she liked to have the dogs go down on her." It was rumored that she met Macpherson when he asked to borrow her dog for a love session and she said, "Not without me." Tanya Stern thought Peggy "straightforward and indelicate, rather vulgar . . . sitting in her museum with her hand out. . . . She was capable of making love with the window cleaner watching." Like Catherine the Great, who gave each of her lovers a handsome stipend, Peggy was falsely credited with giving her lovers all sorts of boons. Mary McCarthy believed, "She supported everyone she'd slept with and everyone who'd slept with anyone she'd slept with."

Later, Peggy admitted she went with so many men because "I was lonely and I didn't like to be alone. I wanted to *feel* something." Peggy was a "sad, lonely person," thought David Hare. "Her life was all parties but not all gay." Ethel Baziotes recalled watching Peggy one evening: "Leonard Bernstein was performing a play with Maria Motherwell in it. Peggy wore a Spanish mantilla, and she kept looking around [expectantly] at everyone and I felt she was looking for somebody to fall in love with. I really liked that about her."

Peggy loved attention. She reacted with almost childish enthusiasm if anyone did her a kindness. The smallest gestures touched her. David Hare remembered, "I often used to go out to lunch with her and because of my own hangups—I was brought up to pay for a woman—I always paid for lunch. Years later, Peggy told me I was the only one who ever took her to lunch. She saw it as personal attention."

But "affair after affair of hers is a Fantasyland," scoffed Lee Krasner. "She has a fantasy of her sexiness." The way she chased after homosexuals, even, illustrated, said Theodoros Stamos, that "she didn't want to get the picture. It was a whole perverse world. It was a fantasy and at the same time for real, the gallery, the pictures were for real, but within all that it was a fantasy." Sidney Janis also thought Peggy invented many of her affairs, "She really believed it after the fact."

Peggy used the word *affair* rather loosely to describe her encounters. "An affair," said Eleanor Perenyi, "in any proper sense, is a relationship that goes beyond a pretty obvious connection." Peggy desperately needed to believe her beddings were more than they were, yet "she had not much of an idea of what an affair is. Peggy really wanted to feel loved," said David Hare, "and money doesn't help to feel it. She was living her whole life as an abstraction, never knowing anybody, never feeling she was one of two people against the world, and she couldn't understand that feeling. Little affairs seemed to be all she had. I don't think Peggy was capable of love. She never had any friends or real lovers. She didn't know what it's about."

Hare was invited to spend a weekend with Peggy in Connecticut. It was obvious to him that she expected the two of them to go to bed together, but when Hare said no, "she went to her own room. She got drunk and went to sleep. The next morning, she asked me if we had gone to bed the night before."

Ormond de Kay had the dubious distinction of being picked up by Peggy "and some old crone friend of hers" when he was a twenty-one-year-old naval officer. He was dining with a date, Eileen McVeigh, at the Balkan Armenian restaurant on New York's East Twenty-seventh Street the night before he was set to sail for the battle zone. De Kay had noticed a table with "three rather elderly women and a couple of wispy youths —not in uniform—and I had noticed, through my tears, a kind of woman looking over this direction. The minute Eileen disappeared to go off to the ladies' room the waiter came over and asked me to join this group. So, I went over. (I had poured out my self-pity and was ready for something different.)" When his date returned from the ladies' room, Ormond was happily relocated at Peggy's table and beckoned her to join him. He found Peggy "somewhat dumpy. I remember the face of her companion better—very striking face, long, rectangular, elongated, high cheekbones, intense staring eyes. She was wearing lots of wooden beads. I was wondering what I was supposed to do. I was rather hoping I was expected to perform sexually."

Eventually this odd party piled into

a couple of taxis and went over to Peggy's apartment. I had the particular recollection that Peggy and the other lady did not welcome Eileen—that they wanted to detach me from her. New York was a kind of funny place during the war. There was an acute man shortage, and you were in danger from attacks and seductions. When we got up there to the apartment, somebody put some records on. I think partial disrobing took place. I think I was encouraged to take my jumper off. The youths were taking their tops off, their jackets and shirts off, and I was rather looking forward to making love to this old bag of bones, when along came Eileen and marched me off.

More scandalous than picking up young men—complete strangers —in restaurants was that Peggy encouraged Pegeen, still in high school, to go out on double dates with her and have affairs of her own. As Yvonne Hagen recalled, "Laurence thought Peggy during the war drove her into the arms of lovers. She would bring soldiers home and force them on Pegeen. . . . Peggy was really out of her head with her children." Jimmy Ernst believed that Peggy even included Pegeen in three-way encounters.

This was a disturbing atmosphere for Pegeen, who was recognized even by Peggy to have been "always a very unhappy girl and terribly neurotic. I don't know, I think she had a maybe nervous inheritance from my [Seligman] grandmother, Rosa, who was very, very, peculiar." To John Bernard Myers, "Pegeen had a frozen face, but she could be charming. She was a waif, a lost child, who'd never grow up. There was obviously something wrong."

Although Peggy loved Pegeen, she had no idea how to be maternal. She treated her daughter as a friend, which meant talking about her affairs and maintaining an unrealistic vision of Pegeen as a beautiful goddess of love whom no man could resist. As a young woman, Pegeen was far more attractive physically than her mother and more successful with men. What was a fantasy for Peggy—a wild, promiscuous, bohemian life with famous lovers—became for Pegeen a reality. "Pegeen was very bohemian," Sidney Janis observed, "had a casual attitude toward sex in a prepermissive society. . . . She knew the score probably by the time she was twelve. At fifteen or sixteen she was a woman."

Pegeen was "hell-bent on passionate romance every moment," observed Yvonne Hagen. "She was different from Peggy counting off her lovers. With Pegeen it was a real sort of dramatic thing—Stendhal." (Indeed, when Pegeen's first son was born, she named him Fabrice, after Stendhal's hero.) Artists she met at her mother's parties like Matta and Rufino Tamayo became her friends. "During that period," recalled her stepsister Bobbie Cowling, "Pegeen was having a wild love life. She'd say: 'Tamayo's always late.' 'Oh! Tamayo hasn't come tonight.' " Pegeen told her friend Eileen Geist that it was Tamayo who bought her the white dress that she graduated from high school in. Peggy was too busy to bother. Peggy was "cold and irresponsible," said Yvonne Hagen. "That's her trouble. She was a one-upmanship sort of lady. She told me she'd had seventeen abortions—'Oh! It's nothing. Absolutely nothing.' "

In the summer of 1943, Pegeen was seventeen and went to Mexico alone. By October she still had not come back. She had been picked up by Errol Flynn and had stayed with him aboard his yacht docked in Acapulco Bay. Next she fell in love with a young man from Acapulco, who dove from cliffs by torchlight for tourist pennies. Pegeen moved in with him and his family, preferring to sleep in a *petate* in their one-room dirt-floor hut with chickens and dogs wandering around rather than return to New York and the life she led with Peggy. Alarmed, Leonora Carrington had sent the Reises, whose daughter Barbara had been with Pegeen, a telegram warning them that Pegeen had fallen in with a bad element in Mexico. Laurence especially was thrown into in a state of tremendous agitation, fearing Pegeen would marry the diver—or worse. Frantic telephone calls were placed to Mexico in an effort to locate Pegeen. Laurence was convinced that she needed rescuing (as much from Peggy as from the diver), but Pegeen craved the warmth and affection she had found in the Mexican family and was loath to give up her Mexican without a struggle. She refused to come home or even contact her parents. She insisted that she wanted to marry the diver and that he was the love of her life. Peggy just shrugged her shoulders.

Finally, Laurence went to Mexico and collected his daughter. According to Apple Vail, "He found her there in a little cabin in the corner, sick, with the boy's mother." Pegeen had contracted a venereal disease. But Laurence, who at times could be astonishingly self-involved, treated this situation calmly. "Laurence should be given more credit," said Yvonne Hagen, "for saving his daughter."

Unrepentant and miserable, Pegeen returned to New York, appearing on Peggy's doorstep in the middle of the night, forlornly clutching one tiny suitcase. She was confused by Peggy's relationship with Kenneth Macpherson and sarcastically called him "father." No sooner had Pegeen returned than she began having hysterical arguments with Peggy. Pegeen wanted to go back to Mexico and marry her diver. Then, "Pegeen just walked out of her house one day," recalled Betty Parsons, "and Peggy never gave her any money." Parsons and Arshile Gorky were running an art class at the time. "Pegeen called me up and said 'I'm stony broke. Can you hire me as a body model?' We hired her. She had a beautiful body, but Peggy should never have let her get to that point." Peggy and Pegeen could not continue to live in the same house. "We got on very badly," said Peggy. "and I think, at a certain time, she wouldn't even speak to me, and then, well, she went to live on Hudson Street." It was decided that Pegeen would move into her own apartment, really nothing more than a tiny whitewashed studio with red brick floors in Greenwich Village, to reestablish some sort of peace between mother and daughter.

Laurence asked the painter Jean Hélion, who had met Pegeen the year before, to talk to Pegeen, and before long Hélion was sharing the studio with her. Peggy and Laurence were delighted, as they saw in the older, more mature Hélion a stabilizing influence on their uncontrollable daughter. Hélion was charming, "very bright, a real intellectual," and as Laurence was desperate to get "Pegeen out of the clutches of Peggy," he urged Hélion to marry Pegeen. Hélion was receptive to the idea. "Pegeen was a waiflike creature," observed Laurence's friend Jimmy Stern, and "the Guggenheim money and background were quite appealing to Hélion." Unfortunately, Hélion was not altogether free. As Stern put it, "Hélion had left an unfinished picture in Virginia," referring to the fact that the artist had first to divorce his long-suffering wife.

(His wife, who came from a conventional Virginia family, had a rare and incapacitating eye disease. Her family fully expected that when Hélion returned from the war he would return to this young woman, left to fend for herself and their son alone. But after he was freed from the German prison camp, he began openly having an affair with Pegeen. And, according to Maria Jolas, "many years later, when his son saw him, he wouldn't speak to him. Then, I don't know how the divorce took place. Poor Pegeen's marriage was a rather sad and murky affair to begin with.")

Pegeen and Hélion were married in Peggy's apartment by a woman judge. "I was so pleased he married her," said Peggy, "because she was such a problem, Pegeen, at that time. It was a great relief. She was terribly unhappy because she wanted to go back to Mexico and marry that diver, and she wasn't talking to me and God knows what else." For the moment everyone seemed content. But as Sindbad observed, Peggy "was very happy when Hélion married Pegeen, and then she did everything she could to wreck the marriage."

After the wedding, Peggy and Pegeen got along somewhat better. "I adored her. We were like lovers," Peggy said, her remarkable blue eyes filling with tears. "She was like my mother." Peggy went on, "We used to go to parties in New York and meet and get in a corner and ignore everybody else." "Those children," observed Pierre Matisse, "had a pretty bad time . . . never knew the milk of human kindness."

SHOOTING STAR

Whenever Peggy was asked to name her greatest accomplishment, she would inevitably answer, Jackson Pollock, "by far my most honorable achievement." Her collection was "my second achievement." Peggy was the first to give Pollock a one-man show and the first to give him a measure of financial security, which allowed him to dedicate himself full-time to his painting. Said Lee Krasner, "She was an important moment, no matter what her motivations were. That moment, a major moment, she is there. There is no way of removing that. Peggy was there before Betty Parsons, that's a fact, that's what happened. In spite of the fact that I can't stand her, it's a fact."

Peggy opened her second season at Art of This Century with an exhibition of de Chirico's early works, borrowed from museums and private collections. But the new sensation of the season was to be the young Jackson Pollock.

Pollock was the first painter of his generation of American abstract artists to bring America into the mainstream of the international tradition.

For generations, Paris was the undisputed center of the art world, the city whose dealers and painters set the pace for everyone else. But as the twentieth century wore on and America entered the age of technology, the influence traffic was not always one-way. The Surrealists, for example, were wildly enamored of American movies. Charlie Chaplin, Buster Keaton, Mack Sennett, the slapstick comedies of the Marx Brothers. Mickey Mouse, Donald Duck, and the American comic strip influenced Picasso while he was painting *Guernica.* Moreover, Europeans such as Duchamp and Picabia—the darlings of New York's literati during World War I—had taken back to Paris a love of bridges, plumbing, and neon lights.

American collectors bought the avant-garde art that Europe was producing and rejecting, and, like Duchamp's patrons Katherine Dreier and Walter Arensberg, and Peggy herself, actively proselytized for the cause of modern art. Even the indefatigable Baroness Rebay, despite her posturing, had presented the groundbreaking work of Kandinsky and Klee to a New York audience.

In plastic terms, the problem facing Pollock and other American painters was how to combine the lessons of Cubism (its shallow, purely pictorial space, its densely organized, geometric subject matter) with the more human perspective, filtering through from Surrealism, that embraced chance, accident, and forced inspiration as revelatory aspects of the unconscious. To leaven that with the geometric grid of Mondrian, the mystical abstractions of Kandinsky, or the flat, pure color of Matisse was a challenge.

By 1943, Pollock had experimented with automatism and was painting what could be called an abstract Surrealism of organic forms. It was the ideas of Surrealism that appealed to Pollock. The varied techniques of Surrealist painting, like Max Ernst's oscillating can, were alternatives to conventional painting with brush and palette. And the Surrealists' reverence for the psyche and its secrets, their interest in myths and symbols, spoke to Pollock, who had undergone psychoanalysis in an effort to treat his alcoholism and wildly shifting moods. "The fact that good European moderns are now here," Pollock said in an interview, "is very important, for they bring with them an understanding of the problems of modern painting. I am particularly impressed with their concept of the source of art being the Unconscious." On another occasion, he added, the "source of my paintings is the Unconscious."

Of the Surrealists, Pollock had the greatest affinity for the work of André Masson. "Look at early Pollock," suggested Hedda Sterne, "and then look at Masson, and it is totally derived from Masson." In translating his "automatic" drawings from paper and ink to canvas and paint, Masson found the repeated loading and reloading of his brush cumbersome and disruptive. He experimented by squeezing the paint directly out of the tube onto the canvas. In America, during the war, he painted deeply erotic, organic canvases full of undulating lines and rhythms, with subtle contrasts of bright colors and textures achieved by mixing sand into the paint. Clement Greenberg later wrote of Masson, "He is still the most seminal of all painters, not excepting Miró, in the generation after Picasso's. He, more than anyone else, anticipated the new abstract painting." (Years later, finding Masson at an exhibition of Jackson Pollock's work in Switzerland, a friend asked him, "What are you doing so far from home?" To which Masson answered, "I come to pay homage to the master.")

Pollock spent the summer of 1943 in feverish preparation for his first one-man show at Art of This Century, producing fourteen paintings (fifteen were shown in total) in a burst of productivity. The show was scheduled for November 9–27, with a cocktail reception on November 8. Peggy rarely saw Pollock and dealt mostly with Lee Krasner, as she found the taciturn painter too difficult to talk to. Lee and Peggy formed a symbiotic and often tense relationship as each tried to assert her claim on Pollock. "They were fighting over the same guy," observed the artist Charles Seliger. "He needed wifely protection."

Lee Krasner was commandeered by Peggy to stuff and address envelopes and help fold the twelve hundred catalogues announcing the Pollock opening. "She was always penny-pinching," Lee complained of Peggy. "I made a mistake on three envelopes. When she got back she bawled the hell out of me for the nine cents I was wasting." Lee was further irritated when Peggy first saw Pollock's *The She-Wolf,* a mutiteated wolf overworked with a maze of savage lines and swirls. "She asked me, in all seriousness, if I posed for it. You see, she had the kind of knowledge about art which felt that if something is there someone must have posed for it. I said, 'Of course I did.'"

As people arrived for the Pollock vernissage, they sensed that here was a discovery to reckon with, a strange, original talent. Indeed, if Pollock had learned anything in those evenings with Matta, he had learned to spill out emotions in an automatism of rhythms, gestures, and pulsations uniquely his own. Included in this first show were paintings with totemic titles, like *The She-Wolf, Male and Female, The Guardians of the Secret, The Moon-Woman Cuts the Circle, The Mad Moon Woman, Stenographic Figure* (the picture he had entered in the spring salon, which remained unsold in the fall), as well as gouaches and drawings. They were energetic, evocative, primitive. Sometimes a figure could be seen shrouded in the background. In their lack of polish and bold use of loaded brushes oozing black and blood-red paint, they were the antithesis of European Surrealist painting, which tended to have a surface slickness. It appeared as though Pollock were painting his soul. And indeed he once said, "Painting is self-discovery. Every good artist paints what he is."

"Pollock's talent is volcanic. It has fire. It is unpredictable. It is undisciplined. It spills itself out in a mineral prodigality not yet crystal-lized. It is lavish, explosive, untidy," wrote James Johnson Sweeney in the catalogue for the exhibition. *Art Digest* exclaimed, "We like all this. Pollock is out a-questing and he goes hell-bent at each canvas. Mostly big surfaces, not two sizes the same. Youthfully confident, he does not even title some of these painted puzzles . . . plenty of whirl and swirl." Clement Greenberg, writing in *The Nation,* found Pollock "young and full of energy," his titles "pretentious," his color "muddy" but called his smaller works "among the strongest abstract paintings I have yet seen by an American."

More than anything else it was the violence that impressed the viewers of Pollock's first show. "Pollock unnerves me," reacted art historian Ethel Schwabacher, who worked with Betty Parsons at one time. "At his retrospective show I had to leave. Either the guy is too sick. I just couldn't take it. . . . I thought he was impotent. This thing he does, circling in arcs, never getting anywhere."

"Any new art," observed Holger Cahill, who was briefly director of MOMA as well as head of the federal WPA Project,

> that comes along has to have in it, as Gertrude Stein has said, an element of ugliness. It's like a child being born. It is usually a very ugly little lump of flesh. The same is true with art and not only the artist, but also the revealer, like Peggy Guggenheim. . . . There is something outrageous, something violent, something vulgar, some-thing in bad taste in American life. If you can take that and transcend it in some way, that is a very important thing. I think that Peggy Guggenheim helped these artists in that way. She agreed to show them and in Jackson Pollock's work you realize that there is this transcendence toward beauty out of this violent and in some ways outrageous painting.

The public wrote obscenities in her guest book, but Peggy realized that she had stumbled onto something great. She took on Pollock with a messianic fervor. She thought of him as her "spiritual offspring." Lee Krasner credited Peggy's genetic inheritance for her promotion of Pol-lock. "She had a tiny touch of Meyer Guggenheim, a kind of shrewdness, and she knew how to use it." As to the business side of her relationship with Pollock, since Peggy had contracted to give the painter a hundred and fifty dollars a month, she was determined to sell as many pictures as she could. She managed to sell the *Guardians of the Secret* to the San Francisco Museum and other paintings to Kenneth Macpherson, Joseph Hirshhorn, and Edward Root. She sold *The She-Wolf* to the Museum of Modern Art. "Then, she was marvelous about that picture," said Krasner.

The MOMA put a reserve on it of six hundred and fifty dollars. Sidney Janis, Meyer Schapiro, Iris Ringe were the advisory commit- tee and they wanted *The She-Wolf.* So Janis went to Peggy to see if she would lower the price. He said they couldn't afford more than six hundred dollars. Would she drop the price to four hundred and fifty? She said, without first calling Pollock, "Go tell them to tell my Aunt [Mrs. Simon Guggenheim] to make up the difference." Then *The She-Wolf* was reproduced in a Sweeney article and Peggy sent us a telegram: "Congratulations," because the MOMA had decided to buy it at full price. Another dealer would have insisted we drop the price to get into the museum.

Peggy never was able to sell a Pollock for more than a thousand dollars, "but I did sell them all the time . . . not very much, but a little bit. People always bought a little bit." Pollock himself did little to promote the sales. In fact, Peggy preferred that he stay away. "He didn't help me sell his pictures at all 'cause he was so drunk all the time."

Although Pollock was glad for the opportunity to devote himself to his painting, he chafed under the arrangement with Peggy. "I am getting $150 a month from the gallery," he wrote his brother, "which just about doesn't meet the bills. I will have to sell alot of work thru the year to get it above $150." "Pollock was very angry on this contract sort of thing," said Lee Krasner. "He was grateful for the chance to do the mural, he was appreciative, but she wanted him in her bedroom every night to prove it." In truth, Peggy lured Pollock into her bedroom only once, "when Lee was away somewhere, which was very unsuccessful, and he threw his drawers out the window." "It is always a difficult relationship," observed Eleanor Perenyi, "between artists and the would-be patron. There's always that bad feeling. There's a natural resentment and not necessarily deserved. Pollock was one case in which she selflessly gave."

During the course of the show, and at all of Pollock's subsequent shows at Art of This Century, Krasner kept a vigil in the gallery. "Lee was always there," said David Hare, "in the gallery when Peggy couldn't be bothered coming in. Lee and Peggy are quite alike. They would quarrel, be friends again, then quarrel some more. They got to be good friends. Quarreled about what the paintings should sell for. Lee used to sit there every day while Jackson showed." Krasner, a major painter in her own right, was so dedicated to Pollock that she allowed her career to take second place to his and was content to paint in what- ever part of the studio he did not use, to the consternation of those who believed she was the greater talent.

Pollock was supposed to finish the mural for Peggy's duplex to coincide with his one-man exhibition at Art of This Century, but the size of the painting, almost nine feet by nineteen, was too enormous. As he had written his brother, he had to tear down a wall in his tiny studio to make room for it. For weeks he stared at the empty canvas, unable to paint a single stroke. Finally, he was seized with a furious inspiration and began painting in a syncopated rhythm of curved black lines and gray-green swirls, a cross between painting and drawing that sprawled all over the canvas and seemed to have no beginning and no end. It was the largest picture he had done to date and the very size of it was liberating. When Clement Greenberg saw the mural soon after its completion, he was more convinced than ever of Pollock's stature ("the strongest painter of his generation and perhaps the greatest one to appear since Miró"). Robert Motherwell believed that the painting of the mural, its scale and allover calligraphy, was a pivotal moment in Pollock's art.

Duchamp, who was actively unsympathetic to Pollock's work, had had the good sense to suggest that the mural be done on canvas, rather than directly on the wall, so that it could be removed. When David Hare and Duchamp, who had been entrusted with the painting's installation in Peggy's foyer, tried to hang it, they found it was too large. "It missed the wall. Peggy wanted us to tack it up, but it missed by eight inches, so we cut eight inches off from the end. Duchamp said that in this type of painting it wasn't needed. We told Jackson, who didn't care." Once installed, the painting proved a conversation piece. Some people positively loathed it. "Kenneth," recalled Lee Krasner, "hated the mural, and his friends used to write 'shit' and what-not on it."

To show what he thought of Peggy's friends, just after the mural was hung and while Laurence's girl friend Jean Connolly was having a party, Pollock, who had been calling Peggy hysterically on the phone every ten minutes about the placement of the mural, showed up drunk and naked and proceeded to urinate in the fireplace. As Lee put it, "Jackson peeing in the fireplace was his way of saying 'screw you,' his comment on the party." Pollock was a mean drunk, but Hedda Sterne perceived a Surrealist method to his madness. "He was obnoxious in certain places," she said. Yet "I would meet him at the Novollas, they had small children, and he would drink, but he had no rapport with the Pollock who tore down tablecloths, goosed women, peed in fireplaces. I remember he told all kinds of beautiful stories. I'm sure he did it on purpose—to *épater les bourgeois.*"

Pollock was not the only one relieving himself in public. Krasner had occasion to witness bizarre behavior in the streets of New York on the part of Peggy herself. "Once," she recounted, "we were going to visit a woman, a moviemaker, I can't remember her name, but Peggy started saying, 'I've got to pee. I can't wait.' I asked her if we weren't almost there, but she said, 'I can't wait.' She bolted out of the cab, and she stood over a manhole, picked up her skirt, and peed. I was left stunned."

Pollock's mural was not shown to the public until his second show at Art of This Century in March–April, 1945. For opening day, March 19, Peggy's home was opened to the public so that the mural could be viewed. When Peggy left New York some years later, she gave the mural, which she felt was too large to take with her, to the University of Iowa—a gesture she lived to regret. "I tried to get it back again," she said. "I offered them a Braque instead and they replied, 'We prefer American art.' "

In time, Peggy had so many Pollocks that she gave quite a few of them away. "I never would have had space for them all." The Art Museum of Omaha, the Tel Aviv Museum in Israel, the National Gallery of Art in Rome were all beneficiaries of Peggy's largesse with Pollocks, especially after she discovered the tax-deductible contribution. Jimmy Ernst liked to tell the story of how Peggy gave him and his bride a Pollock, *Red Composition,* as a wedding present. His wife-to-be was none too impressed with the gift, suspecting Peggy's well-known frugality. As she and Jimmy were very poor, she said to him, "We don't need any more paintings. What we need is a can opener." Years later, when Jimmy sold this Pollock for the then magnificent sum of three thousand dollars, he came back to his wife and said, "Here's your can opener." Pollock himself was impressed with the prices his pictures commanded. "I remember," said Hedda Sterne, "when Pollock sold a picture for four thousand dollars he said, 'I just sold my first picture for four thousand dollars. Imagine, my picture selling for the price of a Cadillac!' "

THE MAN
BEHIND THE SCENE

Peggy liked to schedule Christmas shows that offered what she thought of as "gift items," like Cornell's boxes and Vail's bottles, hoping gallery-goers could pick up a stocking-stuffer or two. Jackson Pollock's first show was followed by a Christmas exhibition of "Natural Insane Surrealist Art." Pieces of driftwood, petrified tree roots, and jawbones competed with the drawings and watercolors of Joseph Cornell, the stabiles of Alexander Calder, and pictures by Ernst, Tanguy, Matta, Masson, Motherwell, and Miró. Also included were artworks by inmates of various European insane asylums, at least one of whom was an engraver one hundred years old. (The question was raised "whether the insane work isn't rather saner than some of the surrealist items.")

During 1944, Peggy began to show more American artists and continued to juxtapose these with the work of established Europeans. In her group show of April 1944, for example, she hung Kandinsky, Léger, Dali, and Braque next to Motherwell, Rothko, Pollock, and Hare. Not only did these gestures boost American confidence, but they also exposed the recent work of the Europeans to their New World counterparts. In February 1944 Peggy had exhibited her old friend Jean Arp. The range of Arp's work—twenty-seven pieces dating from 1915 to 1940—impressed New Yorkers, used to seeing only one or two Arps at a time in museums, and his oeuvre was looked upon with a "kindliness and respect" inconceivable just ten years before. In the course of her gallery's career, Peggy also gave retrospective shows to Duchamp, de Chirico, Giacometti, Wolfgang Paalen, Hans Richter, and Theo van Doesburg, and included Schwitters, Grosz, Gris, Chagall, Miró, Mondrian, Picasso, Tanguy, Matta, Picabia, and many others in larger group exhibitions.

Peggy's judgments about whom to showcase were often founded on her uncanny intuition for talent. For more than twenty years she had sought out and surrounded herself with people of genius. Peggy had an eye for quality in people and in paintings. "She had the advantage of having artist friends who helped her choose. . . . She had a feeling as to what might be good. . . . Whether she gave you a show depended on whether she liked you or not. . . . It was like a family, intramural relationship, always," said David Hare. When a reporter once asked how Peggy judged a painter or his painting, she was quoted as replying, "This too is simple: a good painting has originality and a bad one simply repeats the ideas of others. A purely instinctive approach makes me feel the quality. When I started to collect, I strived for historical survey and not necessarily for pictures I liked. After getting the past settled, I started to buy things I liked. The points for judging modern art are originality in a deep sense, intensity, color, composition and poetry—a poem one can either see or imagine." Clement Greenberg said of Peggy, "Her taste . . . was often erratic and unsure. But she had a flair for life, a sort of smell for life that made her recognize vitality and conviction in a picture. It was surer ground in selecting the new than taste."

Peggy continued her policy of holding salons for young artists and advertising in the art press for new talent. She held a spring salon in 1944, followed by an autumn salon in 1945. Occasionally, artists walked in off the street and Peggy would usually be willing to take a look. "In New York, I discovered some people I regretted afterwards. I had a lot of very bad shows."

One show Peggy particularly remembered as "crazy" was an exhibition of photographs and commentaries called "The Negro in American Life." "That had nothing to do with art. That was Mr. [John] Becker, who I had an affair with, and he wanted me to do that, and I did it to please him. I guess it was crazy. But Mrs. Roosevelt came to that show. That was very amusing. . . . She came and I had a friend called George Barker who came up with her in the elevator and rushed into the gallery and began imitating her, [but she was right behind him] and she could have heard him imitating her, and he said he didn't know what to do. We didn't know who she was at first, and he didn't know . . . whether to embrace her or shake hands with her. . . . She was very nice. She didn't seem to mind that he mimicked her." Peggy tried to show Eleanor

Roosevelt some modern art, and the First Lady reluctantly looked at a Calder, "but she wouldn't look at other things. She walked out of the gallery backward like a crab so she wouldn't need to look at anything, and she had a lady-in-waiting with her who tried to make her look at things, but she wouldn't. Said she didn't know anything about modern art and the next day she wrote an article in the paper and talked about 'Art in This Country' instead of 'Art of This Century.' "

Peggy could be brave and pioneering in her selection, partly because, for all her penny-pinching, she didn't really care if she sold a painting. "I never sold very much, you know," said Peggy. "No. Very, very little." After all, she did not need the gallery to live and ran it primarily for her own amusement—she liked the life, the parties, the "fun thing." Betty Parsons recalled, "She got into endless controversies with critics, dealers. She was hostile to the general public, very indifferent, which is not good for business if you are trying to sell pictures. . . . She cared, all right, about quite a few people, but she was indifferent to the public, not a good saleswoman." "Well," Peggy admitted, "I wasn't very businesslike. I wasn't commercial." Instead, Peggy was a personality—someone who knew artists and who had a great collection. "And she was frightfully lucky," said Rupert Barneby. "If she'd come to America ten years later, she would have been showing soup cans."

Peggy credited men like Alfred Barr and James Johnson Sweeney as her primary influences during those whirlwind days of the 1940s. "I adored Barr; I worshiped Barr," Peggy exclaimed. "I adored Sweeney." Peggy was mesmerized by Alfred Barr in the same way that she had revered Herbert Read, as a paternal figure. In fact, as the director of the Museum of Modern Art, he held in New York the same position that Peggy had hoped to establish for Herbert Read in London. Credited with making MOMA the vital cultural institution it had become, Barr was as adept at coping with the vagaries of patrons and trustees as he was at presenting novel and successful exhibitions to the general public.

When Barr served on Peggy's juries, he pointed out to her artists who impressed him. In the collage show, Barr called Robert Motherwell to Peggy's attention and acquired Motherwell's collage elegy, *Pancho Villa, Dead and Alive,* for the museum. "Barr and Soby took her very seriously," according to Barr's assistant, Dorothy Miller. "She was passionately interested and had the money to make a go of it. There were so many small and impoverished galleries and only a few who had money."

But neither Barr nor Sweeney found pictures for her. Peggy was supported in her efforts for Pollock and in finding new talent by her friend Howard Putzel, who had eagerly replaced Jimmy Ernst as secretary, assistant, and general adviser in the gallery. Putzel had an unerring sensibility, "a sense of taste and quality," said Betty Parsons. If he saw a picture he loved, he absolutely had to possess it—whether he could afford it or not. "He was one of the first customers to buy a Gorky," Julien Levy recalled. "He paid twenty dollars a month, but he simply had to have the picture." As a dealer, Putzel's conviction was contagious. "I had a great admiration for him," said Betty Parsons. "If Peggy liked something, he would bolster her up. He was a very fine adviser."

Putzel cut a colorful figure around New York art circles. Nervous, friendly, a great talker, clasping his big cigarette holder and thrusting it into the air, he loved going to parties and stammering to a critic or an influential dealer about his latest discovery. He was "owl-like," said Charles Seliger, "had thin hair, absolutely slicked into place, round glasses. His clothes were askew. He adored the image of Hugh Walpole —crumpled but very rich." Theodoros Stamos remembered Putzel with a perennially red face "like a beet, from booze," popping sourball candies into his mouth from a big glass jar. "His fingers, I don't know if he bit his nails, or what, but they looked like twigs. They didn't look like fingers any more. They looked like Surrealist twigs."

Putzel loved to eat and could not resist the gourmet food that settled about his middle and complicated his numerous physical problems: thyroid and heart trouble, epilepsy, and an irresistible urge for too many martinis. Although highly intelligent, educated, and well read, Putzel had speech difficulties that made him appear inarticulate. "He stuttered but could recite *Finnegans Wake* from memory," according to Seliger. But suddenly, "in the middle of a sentence, he would stop," said Buffie Johnson. "And then, he'd come to. Peculiar, dead silences of half a minute. . . . I've learned since then that is peculiar to people who have the *grand mal* [epilepsy]."

Putzel's overbearing mother added to his problems. "His mother was a harridan," said Julien Levy. "She was a horror. Putzel was an epileptic, and his mother was angry at him for being sick and would say he was an 'insane and embarrassing nuisance.'" She treated her son with contempt and allowed him to live a hand-to-mouth existence while she maintained a luxurious suite at the Plaza.

Putzel's relationship with Peggy was equally problematic. She paid him the barest minimum and liked to remind him in public that she was the boss holding the purse strings. Putzel was her escort, confidant, shoulder to cry on, but his laundry bills were none of her concern. Whatever frustrations accumulated during the day ("and Peggy was always," in Buffie Johnson's view, "ill humored . . . always complaining about anything, everything, the most trivial unimportant, insignificant things. She was not a contented, happy person") Peggy took out on Putzel, who felt like a whipping boy. If he did not give her one hundred percent of his attention, Peggy resented it. If he got a telephone call at the gallery, she was jealous. Peggy accused him of trying to steal her gallery. "Putzel was a fat, poor, middle-aged homosexual," remarked Sindbad of his mother's adviser. "She treated him like a slave."

Putzel complained to Krasner and Pollock, at whose house he frequently ate, "I don't know how I can face another day." "I don't know if I can continue working there." To Buffie Johnson, Peggy and Putzel "sounded like husband-and-wife kind of bitching. . . . I had no doubt that she was very unpleasant and difficult, but there he was—staying. . . . That was his life. It was so important to him to be dealing in pictures and around pictures and around the people who made pictures. . . . She liked to devil him. She liked to devil everybody. She wasn't going to do anything easily."

Under Putzel's influence, Peggy gave first one-man shows to artists who would later become internationally known but were then obscure painters whom few understood and even fewer valued. At Lee Krasner's insistence, Putzel went with Peggy to see Hans Hofmann's pictures. Putzel strongly urged Peggy to give Hofmann a show, which she did in March–April 1944, but she was not completely won over. "Although she admitted he had sold," Krasner said, "she was convinced he gave the gallery a bad image and she never gave him another show."

Putzel proselytized for his friend Mark Rothko, a painter born Marcus Rothkowitz in Russia, who had arrived in the United States as a young child. Rothko went from a period of doing expressionistic subway scenes to experimenting, like so many other painters of his generation, with an abstract Surrealism of biomorphic forms and squiggles floating in a shallow space. "Mark Rothko never had any gallery," recalled Buffie Johnson. "I was introduced to him by Ruth Ford, whose [acting] coach, Sophie Rosenstein, had a nephew who painted—Mark Rothko. . . . I was just coming up and into the art world. . . . I wasn't going to meet the nephew that paints." When Johnson finally met Rothko, she asked him, "What kind of painting do you do?" Whereupon "he took a spiral-bound notebook, five by seven, out of his breast pocket and began to show me these gouaches. . . . I said 'Where do you show?' He said, 'I don't have a gallery,' . . . and I said, 'You ought to be in Peggy Guggenheim's gallery, and if you're in New York, I'll see if I can arrange something' . . . and I did so through Howard Putzel."

Along with Motherwell and Pollock, Rothko exhibited in a group show held in April 1944 with Dali, Braque, Léger, Kandinsky, Tanguy, and others. Peggy did not much like Rothko's work, but Putzel convinced her to give him his first one-man show in January 1945. "Peggy hated Rothko," said Lee Krasner, "and wouldn't give him a show, so Howard took down all the paintings in his apartment and hung it solidly with Rothko, and invited people to cocktails, including Peggy. She had already said no to a Rothko show, but seeing all the Rothkos and listening to everyone talk about them resulted in Peggy giving him a show."

There were occasions when Peggy put her foot down, and not even Putzel could dissuade her. She refused to give Adolph Gottlieb, included in her autumn 1945 salon, a solo show, no matter how hard Putzel pushed. She wouldn't give contracts to Baziotes or to Motherwell, the two other stars besides Pollock to emerge from the spring salon. She had all she could handle affording Pollock, and moreover, she said, she might at any minute give up her gallery.

Putzel was always receptive to young painters. Charles Seliger was one such artist who arrived at Art of This Century and caught Putzel's eye. "I had no connections from France, from Surrealism, from friendship, from anything. I was simply a fellow who had lived with a divorced parent all his life," said Seliger.

> Painting was always there. I drew portraits of famous people and got them to autograph them. I had a collection of about a thousand. I was sixteen or seventeen, painting, moving about with mother. . . . I came to New York and saw a *Time* magazine article on the opening of Peggy Guggenheim's gallery and I saw in the picture, behind a desk, Jimmy Ernst. So, I went into the city and to Art of This Century and I recognized Jimmy Ernst and asked, "Aren't you Jimmy Ernst?" and he said, "I'm leaving here. I don't like it. . . ." I had submitted a painting to the spring salon, but it was not accepted and I went to pick it up and a very strange man, with round glasses, was there saying it was very good. . . . Putzel treated me like some sort of a jewel, protected me. . . . He would show my drawings to Jewell and the [other] critics at cocktails. He got me a strange commission to design the windows for Saks, caused a furor of sorts. Breton saw it and so did Peggy. The following day, Putzel said, "Don't get upset. They've moved something in your window, but don't do the same thing that Dali did."

William Baziotes had his first one-man show, with only two weeks' notice, in October 1944, when Alberto Giacometti's exhibition, scheduled to open the season, was postponed. Baziotes was one of the few Americans whom the European Surrealists tolerated, and along with Motherwell and Pollock he experimented with automatism. His paintings of the early 1940s display the influence of both Matta and Masson, charged with his own luminous color. Baziotes and his wife, Ethel, were very excited when Peggy proposed to look at Baziotes's paintings. Ethel recalled, "We were very poor, had no furniture, and my husband went out and bought a chair in which she sat for an hour and it broke." Seeing the straits Baziotes was in, Ethel added, Peggy "gave him Sindbad's clothes."

The Baziotes show was followed in October and November by the paintings, *papiers collés,* and drawings of another gifted young artist, Robert Motherwell. Motherwell occasionally gave lectures on painting at Art of This Century, as Peggy considered him "very intellectual." Along with Baziotes, Motherwell was one of the Americans who socialized with the Surrealists and he, too, was impressed by their ideas. The technique of automatism freed him to paint more spontaneously and emotionally, and he balanced this against the sense of composition and structure imposed by Cubism. Motherwell was particularly taken with Freud's theory of the death wish in light of the feverish rush to war of the 1940s and was drawn to themes of conflict and destruction. As a consequence of Peggy's refusal to give Motherwell and Baziotes contracts, however, the two soon defected from her gallery in favor of Sam Kootz, an up-and-coming rival art dealer, who lured them away by making promises of contracts he later had trouble keeping. Jealous of Peggy's commitment to Pollock rather than themselves, Baziotes and Motherwell felt she had left them in the lurch to sink or swim.

David Hare's was the third one-man show in succession during Peggy's 1944 fall season. He had published a well-received portfolio of photographs of American Indians before turning his eye to Surrealist sculpture, working almost exclusively in plaster or plastic cement and wire. "She didn't know why she gave a certain show," said David Hare of Peggy. "It was quite instinctive. The first show she gave me, she came down to my Tenth Street studio, arrived a bit drunk and lay down on the sofa resting on one elbow. I kept trying to get her to see the sculpture. She was half asleep and quite drunk, but as she left she said, 'I'll give you a show.' The next day, she called up and said, 'I don't remember what your sculpture looked like. Did I tell you I'd give you a show?' When I said yes, she said, 'Well, then, I guess I will.' "

Between Rothko's first show and Jackson Pollock's second, Peggy showed the collage bottles of Laurence Vail. "I hear he now makes bottles," said a friend. "He used to empty them in the old days."

Nell Blaine felt discovered by Howard Putzel and exhibited at Art of This Century in "The Women," a group show reminiscent of that fateful one that had put Dorothea Tanning into Max Ernst's life and taken him out of Peggy's. "Well, I had no husband to lose anymore," said Peggy, "so it wasn't dangerous. . . . I liked the idea, I guess," she went on, "and I knew so many women painters." The exhibition ran from June 12 to July 7, 1945, a "throwaway date," as Peggy less than graciously commented to another exhibitor, Buffie Johnson. Lee Krasner was invited to join but declined, although her name appeared on the catalogue invitation. She felt insulted that Peggy had only asked her to exhibit in what was, in her eyes, a minor group show. Peggy's sister Hazel also felt insulted when she was purposely excluded from "The

Women." In the exhibition were works by Kay Sage, Jacqueline Lamba, Ronnie Elliot, Xenia Cage, Barbara Reis, Irene Rice-Pereira, and Pegeen.

Howard Putzel had left his mark on the 1944/45 season in which Peggy showed so many of his own personal discoveries, but the tensions of working with Peggy had already proved too much for him. Although he continued to advise her, he left her employ shortly after the Hofmann show in 1944 to set up his own gallery. Kenneth Macpherson, for whom Putzel had been finding pictures at reasonable prices, offered to back the gallery and give Putzel a chance to work on his own. The double perfidy of Putzel's and Macpherson's defections stung Peggy, who feared that many of her artists would follow Putzel. "She resented his going," observed Eleanor Perenyi, who worked with Julien Levy for a while. "Yelled and screamed. She was a totally self-absorbed, self-obsessed, manipulative person."

But Putzel's gallery, called the 67 Gallery, located at 67 West Fifty-seventh Street, lasted only one season. It opened in the fall with the ballet designs of Eugene Berman, while Peggy was showing Putzel's enthusiasms, Motherwell and Baziotes. In December there was an exhibition of "40 American Moderns," including Milton Avery, Alexander Calder, Joseph Cornell, Adolph Gottlieb, David Hare, Hans Hofmann, Matta, and Jackson Pollock. In January Buffie Johnson exhibited.

Putzel went on to show two painters Peggy never liked, Adolph Gottlieb and Hans Hofmann. Putzel sensed that in the work of the artists he was showcasing and other American artists something new was emerging, something that had not yet been defined. It was Surrealist, but not doctrinaire Surrealist. It used automatism, but not as a tool to reveal the unconscious. Gestures, spillings, accidents were incorporated in a technical and pictorial way. It was abstract, but it was not hard-line and geometrical. It was emotional, expressionistic, mystical. Putzel called it, for lack of anything better, the *new metamorphism.* But what was it?

This was the question Putzel posed in his last exhibition: "A Problem for Critics," which ran from May through July 1945. In it he showed Krasner, Rothko, Masson, Pollock, Pousette-Dart, Seliger, Tamayo, Gorky, and Gottlieb next to Miró, Arp, and Picasso. Howard Putzel, said Charles Seliger, "had his eye right on where it was. . . . It was a fantastic feeling being in a room with all those Pollocks, all those Rothkos." "Classification is extraneous to art," wrote Putzel. "Possibly classification leads to clarification. . . . I hope that some art critic, museum official or someone will find as pertinent a first syllable which may be applied to the new 'ism.' "

Putzel's show occasioned a lively debate. Maude Riley, the critic for *Art Digest,* wrote, "Reader, don't leave that ism dangling! Here's your chance, if ever there was one, to call modern painting that name you've had in mind for it." And Emily Genauer in the *World Telegram* scoffed, "really, we have plenty of problems as it is."

Robert Coates of *The New Yorker* believed that

> a new school of painting is developing in this country. It is small as yet, no bigger than a baby's fist, but it is noticeable if you get around the galleries much. It partakes a little of Surrealism and still more of Expressionism. . . . One can make out bits of Hans Arp and Joan Miró floating in it, together with large chunks of Picasso. . . . It is more emotional than logical in expression, and you may not like it (I don't either, entirely), but it can't escape attention.

"There is no question," wrote Clement Greenberg in *The Nation,* "that Mr. Putzel has hold of something here."

Putzel did not live to see the movement he tried to define finally labeled "Abstract Expressionism" by some, "Action Painting" by others. Soon after his gallery closed for the season, Putzel suffered a fatal heart attack. He was alone in the gallery on a Sunday shortly before his forty-seventh birthday planning his next season. Putzel had been under a great deal of pressure and despondent, because Kenneth Macpherson had refused to advance him any more money to run the gallery and he could not afford to go on alone. A terrible businessman (he would sell a painting for twenty-five dollars and then put it in a fifty-dollar frame), he kept his financial affairs and records a jumble of confused paperwork. Help from Peggy was out of the question, but he had been raising money wherever he could. Walter Chrysler gave him some, but it was not enough. He had even given up his apartment and started living in the gallery, sleeping on a folding cot he kept in the bathroom and sending out for coffee and brioches from the Plaza.

Peggy was convinced that Putzel committed suicide, because he had no money. At the time, Peggy was out on Long Island sharing a house with David Hare and Jacqueline Lamba in Hampton Bays. (Many of the European artists gravitated toward eastern Long Island in the summer, where they continued playing Surrealist truth games while sitting on the dunes. Hare recalled Peggy was a good sport and fun to have around, but when it came time to pay the bills, out came her pencil and paper. "She insisted on splitting the grocery bills to the last cent—to the last *mill.*") Peggy could not forgive Putzel—even in death—enough to drive the two hours to his funeral. "We weren't together, anymore, by that time," she said by way of explanation. "I was very upset that he left me. I don't think I was terribly upset when he died. But I had a sort of vision. He came to me and said: 'Don't give up your work. You must keep on with your work. Don't give up the gallery whatever you do.'"

THE 1945 SEASON

Many of Howard Putzel's protégés exhibited in the autumn salon at Art of This Century, opening the 1945 season on October 6: William Baziotes, Julian Beck (who went on to fame as founder of the Living Theater), Willem de Kooning, Adolph Gottlieb, Jim Davis, John Ferren, David Hare, Lee Hersch, Peter Busa, Robert de Niro (the father of the actor), Jerome Kamrowski, Robert Motherwell, Jackson Pollock, Richard Pousette-Dart, Mark Rothko, and Clyfford Still—a virtual who's who of postwar American art. "My chief function," wrote Peggy to Herbert Read in London, "seems to be to find and give unknown artists a chance, and I have quite a few who are really worthwhile. . . . [Jackson Pollock] is, I think, the best of all these new young people, and may sometime be as well known as Miró. I support him, and Sweeney and I have in a measure got him very well started. His painting is rather wild and frightening and difficult to sell. Motherwell, on the contrary, is much weaker, and his taste is so perfect that he sells much more readily."

Charles Seliger was left without a gallery after Howard Putzel's death, and Peggy agreed to give him his first one-man show. Accordingly, he had his debut at Art of This Century in October 1945. Peggy personally picked up Seliger's paintings. "She came with a big touring car; it had a big back seat and front, and she drove—erratically is putting it mild—and picked up the pictures at Kootz and took them back to her gallery." Peggy liked to joke that Seliger, who was still in his teens, was one of her "war babies," as she called her wartime discoveries, and once said to him, "Of all my artists, Jackson Pollock was the greatest, and you were the nicest." Seliger, who had the ability to imitate handwriting, amused himself by addressing his catalogue invitations "in the handwriting of the person receiving it. Some thought it extremely funny, but Max Ernst didn't." Original works of art were so inexpensive throughout the 1940s that Seliger's drawings and paintings sold for twenty-five dollars.

André Breton visited Seliger's show, as did Jean-Paul Sartre. "Sartre," recalled Seliger, "looked like a cloth cutter. Cuffs and shirt sticking out of his overcoat. He showed up at the gallery and remarked that my work had 'exquisite tracery.'" Peggy, standing around in her funny clothes, did her best to encourage Sartre to write something about Seliger. When she liked people, as she did Seliger, she tried to push them forward with motherly concern. Nevertheless, Seliger found Peggy, the person, elusive. "She keeps you slightly on edge."

Seliger as a teenager was already a pro when Clyfford Still asked him to "show me the ropes." A native of North Dakota who grew up in Canada, Still had arrived in New York's Greenwich Village that summer, and Rothko, whom he knew from California, was so impressed by his dark, mystical pictures that he insisted Peggy go see them. Rothko saw in Still's heroic canvases a mythic motif common to the "small band of Myth Makers" who exhibited at Peggy's gallery. Peggy wrote Read, "there is a melancholy, almost a tragic sense incorporated in the paintings which makes them seem particularly near to me now." She included Still in the autumn salon and promised him a one-man show in February and March 1946 (Rothko wrote an admiring introduction for the catalogue). Clyfford Still was always grateful to Peggy for this chance, which came when he was already forty-four years old.

Still was as powerful a personality as he was a painter. Idiosyncratic, opinionated, restless, Still had his wife copy each of his paintings as a miniature oil so they all could be buried in a time capsule in the Mojave Desert. He could talk for hours about baseball or the prairies of his youth with a beguiling eloquence. A "strange man," said Peggy. "Oh, he'd sit in the gallery all day long. It was simply terrible when we had the show, so it was very embarrassing to sell things, or not to sell them, because he was there all day long, never left." Later on, he refused to have a dealer and blamed the gallery personnel at Art of This Century for giving his paintings titles for "their own amusement" and convenience in identifying them. He subsequently changed to numbers and dates. Peggy's *Jamais* was one of the few paintings to have retained the original title.

One of Peggy's innovations was the double one-man show. In this way she could showcase two artists at once. For example, Lee Hersch and Ted Bradley followed Seliger in November. "It is a new policy I have endeavoured to establish here, Peggy wrote Herbert Read, "but it only works for unknown artists. The others all object to showing in company."

Peggy kept up her correspondence with Read and apprised him of her discoveries. She wrote him about Hare, Seliger, and about Clyfford Still. "He works on large canvases, and isolates his forms dramatically against large solid, or merely suggested backgrounds. The forms evolve perhaps from Miró, and are in the line of Picasso, but again the feeling is distinctly new." These missives, which have the flavor of press releases, were often penned by the latest of Peggy's colorful assistants in the gallery, Marius Bewley, later a distinguished professor of English literature at Fordham University.

Bewley had come to Peggy's attention through Emily Coleman. Bewley reminded Peggy of a priest with a phony English accent. Peggy so adored anything (even ersatz) English that, on impulse, she asked him to work with her. For a while their arrangement went remarkably well. They were both mad about dogs. Max had agreed to sell Peggy two of Kachina's puppies, which she called Emily and White Angel and referred to as her "little babies." Peggy talked so much about them that she gushed, "I feel like a grandmother finding the perfections of her children in her grandchildren."

Besides being a dog lover and a fluent writer, Bewley was a brilliant talker. When he did not manage to sell pictures to others, he bought some himself. To the adolescent Seliger, to see and hear Bewley trilling, "Dear boy, oh, dear boy," was to be reminded of "an English don, always in black with an umbrella, like Edward Everett Horton." Julien Levy described him as "a very high-keyed homosexual with some slight talent and very hard up, very fluttery."

It was not long before Peggy was having the same difficulties with Bewley that she had had with Putzel: high expectations, meager remunerations, and many, many recriminations. After one year, and just in time to preserve his relationship with Peggy as her "darling Marius," Bewley quit to pursue a Ph.D. at Columbia. Peggy never successfully replaced Putzel or Bewley, and had to make do with a disappointing young man who couldn't type or even answer the phone and who preferred to avoid the gallery completely by walking Peggy's dogs.

Peggy's interest in homosexuals did not end with Macpherson, and when he shut her out of his life, Peggy began what John Bernard Myers described as an "opera booth" relationship with Dwight Ripley. Neither Peggy nor Ripley took the affair seriously, Ripley least of the two. Ripley came from a distinguished American "old money" family. "They were burghers in Connecticut," explained his great friend Rupert Barneby, and Ripley had studied at Harrow. Peggy could not resist his erudition, aristocratic manners, and, yes, English accent. Ripley was a gifted dilettante—botanist, linguist, poet. He occasionally painted, and Peggy included him in a group show with Seliger, John Goodwin, David Hill, and the future dress designer Kenneth Scott.

Peggy went around with Ripley for a time, introducing him as her "fiancé" and fantasizing about a relationship between them. "She was always vocally in love with someone. I know how hollow it was with Dwight," said Barneby. "It was all done in a deliberately shocking way . . . outrageous—look how weird I can be, how far out." Periodically, Ripley helped her hang shows (even though Peggy herself had an excellent eye for placement), and was persuaded to buy Pollocks from her. But it all ended rather suddenly one evening. "She fell abruptly out of love with Dwight," related Barneby. "He was staying at her house at East Sixty-first and she'd gone out to some party, and Dwight came back in a cab with a very handsome driver, and Peggy found them in bed together."

In October 1945, an enormous *bal masqué* was given by Alice de Lamar in her barn in Weston, Connecticut, to celebrate the fifth anniversary of *View*. The painter Pavel Tchelitchew decorated the place with huge stalks of corn and wheat. All the guests arrived in elaborate and fanciful costumes. Two drunken gentlemen rolled in habited as nuns. Marius Bewley staggered about as a black-robed British judge, his curly wig lurching from side to side. John Bernard Myers came as Alfred de Musset, crowned by a laurel wreath. Charles Henri Ford and Parker Tyler presented themselves as leaf children. An entire North Pole contingent waltzed in, each member dressed as Santa Claus. Peggy decided to be "old fashioned and wore an eighteenth century slightly Pietro Longhi dress," with a wide skirt and train draped over her arm, a tricornered hat on the back of her head. Looking like an owl in costume, she jitterbugged until five in the morning, as the hoops of her dress swooped up to reveal that she had absolutely nothing on underneath. "She never wore any underwear," explained John Bernard Myers.

Notwithstanding the personal failures, lost connections, and disappointments, during the next two years, from the fall of 1945 until Art of This Century closed in May 1947, Peggy gave first one-man shows to an impressive list of painters who would one day be known as the New York School. It was in Peggy's gallery that Lee Hersch, Clyfford Still, Peter Busa, Robert de Niro, Virginia Admiral, and Richard Pousette-Dart had their debuts. In the group shows appeared Louise Nevelson, Hedda Sterne, Ad Reinhardt, Nell Blaine, Jimmy Ernst, Adolph Gottlieb, Joseph Cornell, Dorothea Tanning, Alexander Calder, Kay Sage, Willem de Kooning, and many other young hopefuls. "Abstract Expressionism," Peggy said with good reason, "began in my gallery. . . . You couldn't explain it. It was like a sudden burst of flame." "What happened, rather," wrote Clement Greenberg in explaining the genesis of Abstract Expressionism, "was that a certain cluster of challenges was encountered, separately yet almost simultaneously, by six or seven painters who had their first one-man shows at Peggy Guggenheim's Art of This Century gallery in New York between 1943 and 1946."

Peggy's gallery had become a catalyst for many painters who could rub elbows there with established European masters or meet a museum director who might possibly buy their work or a critic who just might champion them. And there was Peggy, affable if she liked someone, ready to introduce one painter to another, eager to communicate her enthusiasms. "Actually," Peggy allowed, "anyone who came into the gallery could meet Rothko or Motherwell or Baziotes, if they happened to be there." Not only did Peggy introduce the foreigners to the Americans and the Americans to each other, but where else could a painter go to *see* the latest Pollocks, Hofmanns, or Bazioteses? Rothko met Motherwell for the first time while hanging his show. Greenberg recalled how impressed Pollock had been by the one-woman show in 1946 of a grandmother from Brooklyn, Janet Sobel, in whose pictures tiny images sprawled all over the surface. And Baziotes, riding in the elevator with Pollock and Seliger, said to the younger painter, "Charlie, move away. Jackson's going to influence you."

Other women dealers existed at the time, but none with Peggy's social flair. For Charles Seliger, "her gallery was the most exciting, original experience for any young artist to come across. . . . There is not a gallery yet that can touch that one."

Peggy's encouragement of artists was not limited to shows in her gallery. For her bedroom Peggy commissioned a jingling, swirling, hammered-silver headboard decorated with fish and strange underwater fauna by the sculptor Alexander Calder. Peggy resented the price, as silver was the only material Calder could find during the war, but she adored his creation and loved to wake up in it blanketed by her maribou coverlet and fluffy dogs. Hans Richter approached her for a loan to film *Dreams That Money Can Buy,* a full-color Surrealist fantasy that he had begun in 1944 (under the aegis of Art of This Century Productions), which featured, among others, Max Ernst and his red velvet chair. For one sequence, "The Nude Descending a Staircase," Peggy lent her sweeping spiral staircase with the proviso that Richter and his cast and crew be out of the house by six, at which time she expected guests for dinner. Predictably, however, at 6 P.M., just as four nudes were descending the staircase, Peggy walked in with her astonished dinner guests. She stared at one of the nudes—recognized her as Jimmy Ernst's girl friend —and calmly demanded: "And what are *you* doing here?"

Once in a while, to keep the gallery going, Peggy had to dip into her capital or sacrifice something from her personal collection. "Every time I needed money," she recalled, "I sold something, and usually something that was a great mistake. And then they would all turn up in either my uncle's museum or in the Museum of Modern Art, and that makes me feel even worse." She sold a 1936 Kandinsky, *Dominant Curb,* for two thousand dollars to the dealer Karl Nierendorf (who then resold it to her uncle Solomon), which she very much regretted later, a 1913 Delaunay, a 1921 Picasso *Still Life,* several Brauners, a Laurens sculpture, and one of Schwitters's *Merz* collages. What she didn't sell or give away was sometimes stolen, like those Klees on the revolving machine that Kiesler invented. Finally, the plundered paternoster began to look like a manicured hand with two or three nails chipped off. That's when "the worst of all happened," sputtered Peggy. "I decided to sell the ones that were still left, and just keep one or two for myself, and when I went out of the room to make a telephone call, someone stole another one. I decided to sell the rest of them because there was no use keeping them there, but I put Arp on the wheel and even that was stolen." Their loss was not a monumental financial burden. "No," confessed Peggy. "I paid $100 for them."

As part of her never-ending effort to economize, keep the gallery open, and support Pollock, Peggy decided, without remorse, to cut off Laurence Vail's allowance, which he had been receiving since their divorce. "He didn't like it at all," said Peggy unperturbed. "I remember when she did that," reminisced Apple Vail, "and my father said, 'Well, she's not going to continue my allowance. Of course, it's her right . . . but she could have warned me a little.' "

Every season, after his first one-man show in 1943, Peggy mounted a Pollock exhibition. He was the only painter for whom she did this. Partially it was her obligation to give him one hundred and fifty dollars a month, which she raised in 1946 to three hundred a month at the insistence of yet another boyfriend, Bill Davis, who was a collector and great admirer of Pollock's work.

Lee Krasner and Jackson Pollock had found in 1945 a small but affordable farm in the Springs, Long Island. It consisted of five acres and a barn, which could easily be converted into a studio for Pollock. It would allow Pollock to work on a scale hitherto impossible in his cramped Eighth Street studio and get him out into the open air and quieter life of eastern Long Island, where Krasner hoped he would drink less. Unfortunately, they did not have the money for the down payment of two thousand dollars out of the total price of five thousand. Would Peggy possibly help them? Lee went to see Peggy every day about the matter. Remarking that Krasner was "tough and very ugly," Peggy said that she found her persuasive powers very powerful: "When she wanted something she got it, by God! She came and bothered me every morning when I was sick in bed with mononucleosis. She wanted to borrow two thousand dollars to buy the house in Long Island. . . . I simply didn't have the money, but I gave it to her in the end, she bothered me so much." (Once, when they needed money, Peggy snidely remarked to Pollock, "Why don't you send Lee out to work?")

Peggy agreed to advance the couple the money to buy the house on condition that the contract with Pollock be renegotiated. Peggy would lend Lee and Jackson the two thousand dollars, deducting fifty dollars from the three hundred a month that she would give them for two years until the loan was paid off. For good measure, Peggy required paintings as collateral: "The three paintings put up," said Lee, "were *Totem Lesson I, Totem Lesson II,* and *Pasiphaë,*" which would revert back to Krasner and Pollock when the loan was repaid. In addition, two thirds of the price of any pictures already in the possession of Art of This Century, if sold, would be applied toward the repayment of the loan, the other one third being the gallery's commission. In return for the remaining two hundred and fifty dollars a month that she promised the painter, Peggy was to receive all works of art produced by Pollock save for one painting a year for the duration of the contract. Those pictures already in Lee's possession were carefully itemized. Bill Davis drew up a contract to this effect for the period beginning March 15, 1946, and running until March 15, 1948, which Peggy and Pollock signed on February 19, 1946. In the end the Pollocks paid back the loan in full, offering a painting to cover the unpaid balance, perhaps the most expensive two-thousand-dollar loan in history.

Before moving to the Springs permanently in the fall of 1945, Lee and Jackson decided to get married. Pollock insisted on a church wedding. May Tabak Rosenberg, who was to be a witness, recalled that it was not easy to find a church that would marry them. "I first went to the church on my corner," she said.

It had gone very High Episcopalian and it would not marry them, because she was Jewish and he Methodist. . . . Rabbis didn't want to marry them. I'd never run into this. We'd arrived at a stalemate. Then somebody told me that the Dutch Reformed Church had a minister who was liberal. I called him up and he said, "Yes." I asked, "Are you sure?" He said, "Yes." I called back and asked if Lee needed to wear a hat. . . . We ran around looking for a hat, then the three of us went to the church. Another witness was needed so a cleaning woman was called in. . . . It was a beautiful ceremony. The minister spoke about . . . beauties in faith. . . . It was a lovely simple ceremony. Quite wonderful. Then we left and I took them to breakfast or brunch. We were ecstatic.

The only sour note was sounded by Pollock's dealer and patron. As a special honor, the couple had asked Peggy to be a witness, "because the wedding was to be in the afternoon," said Krasner, "and we thought, 'Who would be available?' Most men would probably be working. So we thought, May Tabak and Peggy. We called May who was delighted, and we called Peggy Guggenheim, who said, 'Why are you getting married? Aren't you married enough?' She said she couldn't come because she had a luncheon. She certainly didn't want to attend the wedding."

Peggy did not much like Pollock himself. "No," she said. "I couldn't like him very much. He was too far removed. Too drunk." Peggy admitted that she had not attended the wedding because she so resented Krasner for pressuring her to lend them the two thousand dollars for the house in the Springs: "I didn't have the money. I don't know how I managed to get it for them. But I really didn't want to give it to them. Lee forced me to give it to them. . . . But it was very nice of them to ask me in a way. It showed their recognition of me." To the Pollocks, Peggy would not admit her irritation.

OUT OF HER HEAD

Peggy worked on her autobiography during the summer of 1944 while lying on the beach at Fire Island. The Dial Press had asked her to write her story for them, although it was a task she had begun on her own as far back as 1923. A literary career had always appealed to her—she admired writers above all other artists. Peggy's memory was expansive, and when she finally sat down to work at her ancient portable typewriter, the only things she could not remember clearly were exactly which stories she had promised never to reveal. She claimed, "I have no memory. I always say to my friends, 'Don't tell me anything you don't want repeated. I just can't remember not to.'"

Writing her autobiography gave Peggy the perfect opportunity to settle old scores. In her book, *Out of This Century,* a play on the name of her gallery, she gave vent to her frustrated pride, her spite. She took revenge on Max Ernst and Dorothea Tanning, on her parents, on the Guggenheims and Seligmans—the crazy aunts and uncles—on Laurence Vail and Kay Boyle. She dwelt with loving and disproportionate tenderness on those she felt truly had appreciated her—her sister Benita and John Holms, who died before he had a chance to leave her. "I wept a lot," she said, while writing about those lost loves. "Nothing," she added, weeping again, "upsets me more than my memoirs." But still, she remembered what she wanted and forgot the rest—the loneliness, the random lovers, the affairs with women, the sexual insecurities. Instead, she presented herself as a woman of infinite allure with famous lovers trailing after her. People who betrayed her, like Howard Putzel, who had dared leave the gallery, she downplayed. And while she told of affairs, abortions, and arguments that others would have done their best to hide, she never mentioned the episode of Hazel and her babies. Written in a style that was chatty and rambling, her memoirs were Peggy speaking, quipping one-liners, being amusing. There was little introspection, no elaboration, and people were presented as anecdotes. Facts were heaped one upon the other in a breathless chronicle.

Afraid of libel suits, Peggy decided to use fictitious names, all of which were transparently obvious: Laurence Vail became "Florenz Dale," his sister Clotilde, "Odile," Douglas Garman, "Sherman," Samuel Beckett, "Oblomov," and Roland Penrose, "Donald Wrenclose." Duchamp she called "Luigi," and Giorgio Joyce was "Anthony." Kay Boyle was "Ray Soil," Leonora Carrington she christened "Beatrice," Kay Sage she dubbed the "Princess," Dorothea Tanning became "Annacia Tinning," Macpherson she called "Quentin." No one who had the slightest acquaintance with Peggy or her world was fooled for a second. "Peggy's memoir," said Hedda Sterne, "caused a lot of trouble. She would sleep with a married man and then his wife would find out about it in the book. She wanted to prove to the world that she had all the lovers she wanted."

After Peggy turned her book in, she complained, "The copy editor had a very dull little mind which reacted to my fantasies by trying to turn them all into clichés or omitting them." And then Peggy spent five weeks in "complete hysteria" trying to set her manuscript to rights. Peggy wanted Laurence to help her edit the book even though he would not be spared in it. In fact, she enlisted all the help she could get. She begged Lee Krasner to go over the manuscript with her, which Krasner obligingly did for hours. She asked Jimmy Ernst his opinion. Mary McCarthy read it, and her dog chewed it up. Eventually, a wide circle of friends were well acquainted with the revelations of Peggy's life and loves.

When the book was published in March 1946, on the brittle paper that was the only kind available as a result of the war, and with a bold yellow and black dust jacket designed by Jackson Pollock, it caused a sensation.

"Out of My Head," suggested Aaron Bohrod in the Chicago *Sunday Tribune*, would have been a more appropriate title for her autobiography, "considering the nymphomaniacal revelations and other mad doings related in the book." "Flat and witless as a harmonica rendition of the *Liebestod*," said *Time*. "When Peggy Guggenheim's autobiography, *Out of This Century*, appears later this month," wrote Harry Hansen in the New York *World-Telegram,* "a lot of men mentioned in it will wish they were disguised as non-objective art." Ten days later, the same reviewer added, "The more I read this type of writing, the more I begin to understand the social and artistic usefulness of restraint."

As to the book's literary merits, Elizabeth Hardwick, writing in *The Nation,* commented on the "astonishing lack of sensibility," the "limited vocabulary, and the primitive style"; it appeared to her "an unconsciously comic imitation of a first-grade reader." Nevertheless, reported *Art Digest,* Peggy's tome of "Boudoir Bohemia" could be seen under every arm on Fifty-seventh Street, as the art world tried to figure out who was who. Wags said Peggy was being sued by two artists for *not* mentioning them.

Out in the Springs, Lee Krasner received a copy of the book in the mail. "She had me edit *Out of This Century* . . . and when it arrived it was dedicated 'to Jackson.' She invited me to have dinner with her, and her book had just come out. I didn't say a word about it and finally, she couldn't take it and said, 'You saw the book? I suppose you're thinking I could have done better to have gotten on the analyst's couch rather than write the book?' 'Yes, I do,' I said, thinking what I always thought when I looked at her, 'You bitch.' "

Peggy also sent a copy of the book to Herbert Read, and from the Yale University Art Gallery he wrote back: "You have outrivalled Rousseau and Casanova. . . . I found it quite fascinating as a document—an historical document—and it is only the lack of introspection and self analysis which prevents it from being a human psychological document (masterpiece?) like *Nightwood.*"

Peggy sat in the Putnam Bookstore on East Fifty-seventh Street, almost next door to the gallery, signing copies of her by-now-infamous opus. At the gallery, Peggy pushed the memoirs, keeping vigil at her desk with a stack of books by her side. Whenever a friend came through the door, she would exclaim, "You've got to buy my book. That'll be two dollars." Rumor had it that Peggy's family, particularly the Guggenheims, were so outraged by Peggy's kiss-and-tell-all revelations that they bought up all the copies to keep it off the bookshelves. "I don't see why they should have been so upset," said Peggy. "I didn't say anything awful about the Guggenheims, only about the Seligmans." In truth, said Peggy, "only six thousand copies of *Out of This Century* were printed. It sold well, but the publisher refused to bring it out again."

To Peggy's delight, the book did what she wanted it to do: shock. Pierre Matisse found the reaction on Fifty-seventh Street to her book "very mixed. It must have rubbed some people wrong. She doesn't care about anything." By its omissions and lack of reflection, *Out of This Century* presented a picture of Peggy as a strident, coarse woman, who was labeled by the press as "an urge on wheels" in quest of an "orgasm a day." When they met her, people who knew her only through her book were surprised to find a mild-mannered, shy woman who listened attentively and spoke in a quiet voice. Her real achievements, the establishment of a first-rate art collection and her collaboration with men of genius, were depicted as secondary to the pursuit of love in climates hot and cold. "She is so touchingly ridiculous in her own books," observed Maria Jolas, echoing the feeling of several others who thought Peggy put her worst foot forward (when she could get it out of her mouth). Yet the book was a testament to an attitude and way of life, and more than anything else she did, it established Peggy as a legend.

Peggy had to share some of the limelight with Max Ernst, who appeared on the same page as the review of her book in *Newsweek*. He had won a three-thousand-dollar first prize in a contest sponsored by the producers of a movie based on the Guy de Maupassant story, *Bel Ami or the History of a Scoundrel.* Max's picture *The Temptation of St. Anthony,* depicting the tortured saint in a bright-red, lobsterlike suit, won over Salvador Dali's entry. It seemed fitting that Peggy's photograph on the opposite page as that of her lost husband showed her in a petulant pose, mouth downturned, hair center-parted and pulled back, huge earrings dangling from her ears. Alongside her stood Pegeen with her long, sorrowful Vail face. The three together made the page a Surrealist family portrait.

Ernst and Clement Greenberg came to blows partly as a result of Peggy's book. Greenberg had encouraged Peggy to write it, pointing out that "everything in it was public knowledge." Still, Max was annoyed. Not only did the book cause him and Dorothea a great deal of grief, but Greenberg added insult to injury by writing a piece in *The Nation* saying that there was no comparison between Ernst's sculpture and his "diabetic, prematurely worm-eaten pictures." Coincidentally, Max and Greenberg found themselves at the same party, "full of art types, critics, painters." Pierre Matisse said, "Max, with his usual, aggressive, Surrealist attitude, after the book was published went up to him and asked: 'You are Clement Greenberg?' " According to Mary McCarthy, Greenberg's onetime girl friend, "There was a big, heavy, junky round ashtray on a low table, and Max Ernst picked up this heavy ashtray and inverted it on Greenberg's head. His position was so absurd—ashes and cigarette butts falling down his head—it was cruel and sadistic of Ernst. His paintings were cruel but I had never seen that in him." "Max was sitting on a sofa," continued Pierre Matisse, "and Clement Greenberg comes in and says: 'You are Max Ernst?' Wham! They start to fight."

Hitler's entry into the vast frozen plains of Russia had proved to be the death knell of the Third Reich. The Allies liberated Paris in August

1944. By January 1945, the Russians were in Cracow and German troops were retreating toward the Reich. By March, General Patton had crossed the Rhine. As the Allies advanced on Berlin, Hitler committed suicide in his bunker on May 1, five years after he began his bloody offensive on the west. The unconditional surrender of Germany in a little red schoolhouse in Reims, France, was announced to jubilant crowds six days later, as thousands piled into New York's Times Square blowing horns, cheering, and dancing, while confetti fell and loudspeakers blared the news. In July 1945, the four Allied powers met in Potsdam to discuss the partition of Germany and the disposition of Eastern Europe. With the dropping of the first atomic bomb on Japan in August, the war in the Pacific was finally over. For Peggy, the end of the war that had been relegated to the back of her mind meant a time of decision. She had never intended to stay in New York permanently. "She always told us," said Robert Motherwell of Peggy's departure from New York, "she belonged to Hemingway's generation and would go back to Europe when the war was over."

There was very little to keep Peggy in New York. Although her work might justify the sacrifice, she really had no one to share her life. Sindbad was in Paris acting as an interpreter with the army. Pegeen and Hélion returned to France in April after her first one-woman show at Art of This Century in March 1946. (Peggy boasted to Read that her daughter was blossoming forth as a rival to her painter husband. "Her work is delightfully fresh and primitive and quite original.") Laurence Vail married Jean Connolly, and the couple left for France in June. "They both hated America," said Yvonne Hagen of Peggy and Laurence, "the old fashioned America, not the America of today, after the war. Hated an America that had disappeared, but they didn't know it."

With the liberation of Paris, the Surrealists and other artists in exile began their exodus back to Europe. In America they had been uncomfortable aliens. Julien Levy closed his gallery. Charles Henri Ford announced the end of *View*. André Breton went back to Paris. Those who did not return to Europe scattered. Max Ernst went to Arizona with Dorothea Tanning, who soon became his fourth and last wife. (Others suffered from a shift in influence, like Matta, excommunicated by Breton for going to bed with Gorky's wife when the painter was dying of cancer.) The Americans felt abandoned, forgotten, left to fend for themselves. For Peggy, it seemed that the art world had irrevocably changed. The influence of the Surrealists, Peggy's spiritual fathers, had begun to wane. As grisly evidence of Hitler's atrocities filtered out of Germany, grown men playing Surrealist games lost their appeal. Words like *alienation* and *nothingness* were cropping up in conversation in place of psychoanalytic and Jungian jargon. Jean-Paul Sartre lectured at Carnegie

Hall in March 1946. It seemed to John Bernard Myers that the exodus of artists was not merely physical but the conclusion of a way of thinking and living that would never be the same again.

Peggy was at loose ends, alone in the apartment, going to movies or concerts by herself. In the aftermath of her scandalous autobiography, she was afraid she would be unwelcome in England. She had written about Humphrey Jennings pursuing her, about Roland Penrose shackling her to the bedpost, about Llewelyn's baby, about Douglas Garman's Communism. Moreover, she had her two dogs, and in Britain they would be quarantined. "I hate America so much," Peggy wrote to Read, "but I am scared to come back to Europe for the moment. I have become rather spoiled by the materialistic side of American life, as it offers nothing else one concentrates very much on that aspect."

During the summer of 1946, Peggy left for Europe to see her children and think about her future. She had not yet decided to return for good. "I wanted to go back to England," Peggy said, "to settle my affairs, because I'd left everything there in a dreadful mess. I left an enormous chest in my house in Petersfield, and I had to go down and get a wall opened to get it out again. And also I'd left a set of silver I inherited from my mother, an enormous, enormous tea set in a jewelry shop in Petersfield to be sold and I didn't know what had happened to it and I went back and I had no receipt or anything for it and I got it back again."

Peggy went first to Paris, where she left her two dogs with "Mamselle" Hoffman, her mother's ever-faithful retainer, and saw Sindbad and Pegeen. Peggy found Paris after the war totally changed and the cafés full of people she didn't know. The Paris of her youth had disappeared. Everything was extremely expensive, with food and housing both in short supply. People ate mostly beans and potatoes. Gone was the great interest in Surrealism that had pervaded Peggy's life there. The Surrealists themselves, tired, dispirited, middle-aged men, unable to make ends meet, had lost their cohesion. Only Breton continued dauntless, mounting an international exhibition, "Surrealism in 1947," at the Galerie Maeght, for which Duchamp designed the black velvet catalogue cover (a lifelike, foam rubber breast, with the words "Please touch" on it), and Kiesler did the installation. But Sartre had already declared that the Surrealist revolution was abstract and ineffective. A new breed of angry young man was taking over, hard-boiled, pragmatic, existentialist, unconnected by inclination or anything else to Peggy and her world. Still, as she sat at a tiny table on the terrace of a café, the saucers of her drinks piled in front of her, Peggy was thrilled to be back. "Isn't it marvelous?" she called out to an acquaintance passing by. "Isn't it wonderful?"

Installed at the Regina-Lutetia, little toilet bottles and jars of cream spread out on the bureau, Peggy was still uncertain where to go. "Peggy was rattling around not knowing what to do with herself," said Mary McCarthy, who ran into Peggy quite by accident. McCarthy was stopping in Paris on her way to Venice with her husband, Bowden Broadwater. Peggy was trying to decide whether to go to London, "and we persuaded her to come along with us." Peggy was easy to convince. She liked being with friends younger than herself and the Broadwaters were a good twenty years her junior. The idea of going to Venice delighted her. She loved Venice, she had always loved it. London, bombed out and dreary, could wait. As McCarthy wrote of the character she based on Peggy in her story "The Cicerone" (which eventually appeared in her anthology *Cast a Cold Eye*), she did

> not lack courage. She had learned how to say good-bye and to look ahead for the next thing. Paris, she quickly decided, was beautiful but done for, a shell from which the life had retreated out into the suburbs where a few old friends still persisted, a shell now inhabited by an alien existentialist gossip, and an alien troupe of young men who cadged drinks from her in languid boredom and made love only to each other. Her trip to Italy, therefore, had the character of a farewell and a new beginning.

Peggy left for Italy with Mary, Bowden, and their friend Carmen Angleton by train. Rail travel after the war was an adventure in itself—schedules were meaningless and trains fell apart. The four friends, bearing a mountain of bags, boxes, suitcases, and a picnic lunch, met at the station.

Weighed down with baggage, they had the luxury of a compartment to themselves. It was on the train that Peggy conceived the idea of going back to Venice to live. "The idea," said McCarthy, "clearly took hold of her. She said she would sell her whole collection if she could get one Giorgione." Venice made perfect sense to Peggy. There was nothing for her in Paris, London was out of the question, and Italy was said to be the least devastated of the European countries. In Venice she could start afresh, look for a palazzo on the Grand Canal, and finally establish her long-dreamed-of museum.

Peggy's reverie was cut short in Dijon, where her party was asked to disembark because of mechanical problems with the train. Unfortunately, they also had to take off the train the unwieldy packages, bags, and paraphernalia that they had brought along. "We got off at Dijon," Mary McCarthy remembered, with the lunch which we'd eaten part of and Carmen carrying a Charvé hat box with a pearl-gray homburg in it for her father. I had a little bag full of Elizabeth Arden skin lotion. . . . We got off at the empty platform and Peggy, being the most capable, found a porter and we [laughed when we] heard her saying *"coucher?" "coucher?"* [but she was only] asking for a place to sleep [not someone to sleep with]. He counseled her to stay on the platform until the next train. At about four a train came through absolutely jammed with people, so we pressed together with the damn lunch and Carmen's father's hat box and landed right in front of the toilets. The smells were atrocious. People were throwing up and everyone was very grateful for my Elizabeth Arden skin lotion which was passed around. . . . We got as far as the Swiss border and they put us off that train and we got on a Swiss hard-board train, divine, partly open.

From the excruciating ride spent standing most of the way, Carmen Angleton's feet had become so swollen that her sandals had to be cut off.

When they got to Lausanne, another complication arose. Mary McCarthy, who had been ill since she left New York, realized that she had a bad case of mononucleosis and could not go on. "We called a doctor," she recalled,

and Peggy began to flirt with him every time he came. The nurse was there; she gave her the evil eye. Peggy took things in hand, and instead of going on to Venice, stayed with me. She remembered she had had a baby in Lausanne, and Peggy called her *accoucheur,* who sent a doctor for me. He got us moved to a pension in Ouchy and Peggy stayed and Peggy used to go to the beach with Bowden and take her neat little swimming bag. And then she departed and went off to Venice.

Peggy had been in Venice for some time, inspecting palazzos, before Mary McCarthy was well enough to continue the trip with her husband and join her. "She had met an old White Russian who was going to sell her his palazzo, but he had to guarantee to die within two years. . . . The deal fell through." On the train to Venice the Broadwaters met an Italian who seemed to be following the same itinerary, retracing Lord Byron's footsteps, from Lausanne to Milan to Florence and then on to Venice.

Peggy met the Broadwaters at the train station in a gondola. She was tanned the color of a chestnut. The Broadwaters observed, as they eyed Peggy across the gondola, that, compared to themselves, who were merely tourists, Peggy was an "explorer." Extravagantly Italianate in her "snood and sandals, her bright glass-bead jewelry, her angora sweater, and shoulder-strap leather handbag," she wore these "in the manner of a uniform that announced her mobility in action and her support of the native products." They introduced Peggy to the Italian they had met on the train, but Peggy paid scant attention as he tagged along other than to casually ask him for the names and addresses of the good restaurants in Venice. Yet she wound up rather matter-of-factly in bed with him.

McCarthy's experiences with Peggy during that first summer after the war were fictionalized in "The Cicerone." Explained McCarthy, "The cicerone is a male figure, a guide or companion, somebody who shows you around and who is looking for some gain." In the tale, Peggy is identified as Polly Herkimer Grabbe, a flower-bulb heiress, "middlingly but authentically rich," an impresario of modern architecture and collector of husbands. Although Miss Grabbe's intelligence was flighty, "her estimates were sharp; no contractor or husband had ever padded a bill on her; she always put on her glasses to add up a dinner check. Men, it was true, had injured her, and movements had left her flat, but these misadventures she had cheerfully added to her capital. An indefatigable Narcissa, she adapted herself spryly to comedy when she perceived that the world was smiling; she was always the second to laugh at a pratfall of her spirit."

Miss Grabbe had been traveling through Europe taking in the sights. "Sexual intercourse, someone had taught her, was a quick transaction with the beautiful, and she proceeded to make love, whenever she travelled, as ingenuously as she trotted into a cathedral: men were a continental commodity of which one naturally took advantage, along with the wine and the olives, the bitter coffee and the crusty bread." In the McCarthy story, Miss Grabbe, who is looking for a palazzo in Venice, lets Mr. Sciarappa, as the Italian is called, accompany her and a young couple about town. Eventually she goes to bed with him, describing the experience in detached detail the morning after to the young couple, propped up in bed with hot water bottles—one of which is actually a douche bag she uses to hide her liras—on all sides, using the confession as a "species of feminine hygiene, to disinfect her spirit of any lingering touch of the man."

"The story," said its author, "is all true." At first Peggy did not know what to make of it. "I read the story to her," said McCarthy, "in my apartment, and she was on the sofa. She may have nodded. She behaved very well about it. But later they listen to what their friends say. When I read her the story, I left out her neck wrinkles like a travelling bag, and her name, Miss Grabbe. That name was mean," McCarthy admitted, "I had intended another name, but the publisher felt it was too close to the name of a socialite, that another one would be better. . . . Later, I regretted it."

Peggy admitted to a friend that Mary McCarthy had indeed "read it to me, but I had mononucleosis and fell fast asleep. I never heard a word. Later, I was furious."

FAREWELL FIFTY-SEVENTH STREET

When Peggy returned to New York in the fall, she discovered that her apartment, which she had sublet to some friends for the summer, was under siege. She had let them have it at her cost, she said, "the rent, just nothing extra, just, you know, to have it covered. When I came back, they wouldn't move out." Peggy rented another apartment from a "disgusting man" who wrote about bridge. She was convinced that he cheated her. "He rented me an apartment for about five times the rent it should have been. . . . He charged me five hundred dollars a month for an apartment of two rooms."

Macpherson, too, was joining the exodus back to Europe, and Peggy had definitely decided to move to Venice. She let it be known that she would close her gallery and fulfill commitments only through the following spring. Her decision was surprising to some observers. "It puzzled us," said Dorothy Miller. "Venice then was just a beautiful backwater." It seemed to Clement Greenberg that there was an edge of disillusionment in Peggy's leaving. "The last time I saw Peggy in this country she was disappointed. . . . She felt she had launched something," but it was not until considerably later that the artists Peggy showcased were appreciated. "She gave up in 1947 and it's only after 1950 that Rothko, [Pollock, Still, and the others] start to become known." Her son-in-law, Jean Hélion, thought Peggy very clever in going to Venice. "Peggy could be a queen in Venice. It suited her and her pictures very well. In New York or Paris, she could not be the first person, as she was in Venice, to show modern art."

Many of Peggy's discoveries, like Still, Rothko, Baziotes, and Motherwell, had already defected to Sam Kootz or to Betty Parsons. Ethel Baziotes recalled the misgivings with which the artists had begun to view Peggy's commitment, the impetuousness of some of her choices, her showing Pegeen and her inclusion of Gypsy Rose Lee and Hazel in group exhibitions. "The gallery became a plaything. The artists were uneasy."

The most important thing on Peggy's mind was finding another gallery for Jackson Pollock. She called all her rivals up and down Fifty-seventh Street, but there were no takers. Pollock was still misunderstood and difficult to sell. Greenberg said, "He was notorious, but he wasn't selling until 1949." Peggy called Pierre Matisse, who didn't bite. "She tried to get me into it," said Matisse. "She berated me about not being interested in Pollock. My impression was that I could have had him directly without passing through her." Sam Kootz, who took over Baziotes and Motherwell, did not want to deal with a drunk. Kurt Valentin didn't believe in Pollock. Julien Levy was closing his gallery. Finally, but not until May 1947, Peggy convinced Betty Parsons, who had recently started a gallery of her own, to take Pollock over. "She was subsidizing him," said Parsons, "and she called me up and I said, 'I'm crazy about him.'"

Peggy would have preferred to give Pollock over to a dealer who could cover all her obligations to the painter, but Parsons said she could not afford Peggy's payments to Pollock. As a result, Peggy proposed to continue paying Pollock his monthly stipend, receiving all his output, save for one picture a year, until February 15, 1948, if Parsons would give him a one-man show and forward to Peggy the profits from any sales at prices set by Peggy. Parsons was to hold any paintings produced by Pollock during this period to sell as she deemed fit, on Peggy's behalf, retaining a dealer's commission. James Johnson Sweeney was to act as Peggy's representative to check on sales and see that Pollock fulfilled his end of the bargain. Peggy had a contract drawn up to this effect.

While Peggy was in Venice looking for a palazzo, Pollock was preparing for his fourth one-man show at Art of This Century, which took place in January–February 1947. He had spent a year in the Springs and that summer moved his studio into his barn. The open space was liberating to him. Instead of working in a cramped bedroom, he had the entire barn floor to work on and circulate around. He no longer stretched his canvas, a procedure whereby an artist prepares a piece of canvas on a wooden frame, but rather unrolled it from a bolt onto the floor. "My painting," he said in a statement in the review *Possibilities,* "does not come from the easel. I hardly ever stretch my canvas before painting. I prefer to tack the unstretched canvas to the hard wall or the floor. I need the resistance of a hard surface." He worked feverishly, a cigarette dangling from the corner of his mouth, for his last show with Peggy and managed to produce fifteen paintings, divided into two series, that he called, in honor of his Long Island home, "Accabonac Creek" and "Sounds in the Grass." He always waited until the last minute before a show to title his pictures and then solicited associations from his wife and friends—a device learned from the Surrealists—so that quite often the title had nothing to do with the actual content of the picture. For example, the 1943 *Pasiphaë* had started out as *Moby Dick,* but Peggy didn't like the title. James Johnson Sweeney, who had accompanied Peggy to Pollock's studio to view his work, suggested *Pasiphaë.* Pollock said, "Who the hell is Pasiphaë?" Sweeney explained that she was the queen of Crete, wife of King Minos, who was fated to fall in love with a bull and give birth to the Minotaur. When Sweeney explained the story, Pollock liked it enough to switch the title.

Clement Greenberg hailed this fourth show as the best since Pollock's first. Something was resolving itself in these paintings. They were the final stage in a process of "veiling the image." They were bigger and the paint on them was freer, looser. In a picture such as *Eyes in the Heat,* with its surface thickly impastoed, one could see little eyes, but they were part of an overall design. Cubism, with its underlying geometric grid, had posed a problem. The image tended to float in the center, leaving the edges bare. Pollock, in his mural for Peggy, had already envisioned a technique whereby the image would be pulled to the corners, making the entire surface of the canvas of uniform visual intensity. Whereas even in a Miró or a Kandinsky, forms and figures could be distinguished from the background, or ground, of a painting, here there were no distinctions; forms were not modeled, figure and ground were one, the illusion of space purely optical.

Sometime in late 1946 and 1947, in his barn in the Springs, Pollock began to pour and drip paint on his canvases. He found it liberating not to stop and reload his brush, to be able to continue in a rushing stream of color, as swirls and loops of liquid paint, dripped and poured at random, welled all over the picture surface, in an improvisation as rhythmic and syncopated as the jazz music he adored and listened to for hours at a time. Cigarette butts, spent matches, thumbtacks, spills, even shoe prints were left as part of the overall effect. Here was the *objet trouvé* of the Surrealist, the *Merz* collage of the Dadaist, the "canned chance" of Duchamp, or as the art historian Rudi Blesh saw it, "a violent Duchamp, not gravely accepting the 'laws of chance,' but flinging the door open to chaos." The paintings were revelatory of an inner compulsion, but they were plastic, even beautiful. "Everything that had been amorphous, contingent on circumstances, and unstable in advanced painting suddenly came into focus in his art." Or as de Kooning put it: "Every so often, a painter has to destroy painting. Cézanne did it. Picasso did it with Cubism. Then Pollock did it. He busted our idea of a picture all to hell. Then there could be *new* paintings again."

Pollock began to pour enamel and aluminum paint, the same kind used for cars. At first, in pictures such as *Galaxy,* he dripped paint to overwork images that had begun as eyes or limbs or figures, a process that had taken him through his first shows at Peggy's gallery. But soon the image emerged totally and freely from the spontaneous flow of the paint itself. Others had dripped paint before—Max Ernst with his paint-can construction, who liked to claim that Pollock derived his drip technique from him, and Hans Hofmann—but what was fresh and new was the synthesis Pollock achieved of Cubist space and a gestural abstraction derived from Surrealism in which the painting and the image were one, creating the "first significant change in pictorial space since Cubism." In place of the violent, dark, tortured images of the early 1940s came lyrical, soaring, ever-larger abstractions, which by their very size pulled the viewer into experiencing them. "My painting," Pollock said in a Hans Namuth film of him at work, "is direct. I usually paint on the floor. I enjoy working on a large canvas. I feel more at home, more at ease in a big area. . . . This way I can walk around it, work from all four sides and be *in* the painting. . . . I want to express my feelings rather than illustrate them." The richness of association was so great that Pollock's pictures worked on many levels. With these astonishing pictures he signed his name in history.

All through 1947, Pollock's breakthrough paintings found their way into the Peggy Guggenheim collection. Few people bought them; they were too radical, too new. Even Peggy did not realize what had fallen into her hands. "In the end, Peggy was in the gallery every day, begging people to buy a Pollock," said Sidney Janis, who would eventually be Pollock's dealer.

When Betty Parsons agreed to take over Pollock in May 1947, Peggy could relax. She had done all she could, in her own mind, for the painter. After that he would no longer be her concern. "The first show I gave him," Parsons said of the January 1948 exhibition, "he was still under subsidy from Peggy Guggenheim, so I gave her that money, and then he was with me." However, Parsons saw that with the end of the contract, and of the two hundred and fifty dollars a month that Krasner and Pollock depended on, the Pollocks would be in bad shape. Betty herself felt she did not have the money to subsidize Pollock. The January show at Parsons', the first show of exclusively poured paintings, did not sell well at all. Only two pictures changed hands. Most people came away feeling that their dog or cat could have done better. (Peggy's sister Hazel recalled an incident that illustrates the general public's attitude toward Pollock. "Peggy once left Pollock with me," said Hazel, "at the Chelsea Hotel, saying she couldn't take him to lunch with her. Pollock was so drunk, he vomited all over the carpet. . . . Years later, the manager asked me if I didn't have a Pollock to sell. I told him to cut himself a piece of the carpet.")

Betty Parsons wrote Peggy, who was by then in Venice, of the Pollocks' terrible financial situation, suggesting that Peggy forgo her profits on one of the pictures that Parsons' had sold from the show and allow the Pollocks to replace it with a future work. Peggy agreed to that, but did not offer any further help. "She appeared to care very much," said Parsons about Peggy's attitude toward Pollock, "but she just disappeared. Either she was childish or inhuman." It is a myth, concluded John Bernard Myers, "that Peggy supported Pollock. She exploited, gouged Pollock. Shameful."

Although Peggy believed that Pollock was one of the greatest artists of the century, she did not concern herself with whether he had anything to eat. Out in the Springs he would trade a painting for a grocery bill, but that did not always work. Krasner was very bitter: "The idea of her dedication to Pollock was fanciful. When she was off, she left him high and dry—that was her great dedication. When other galleries would not take over the contract, she said bye-bye, hope you can swim." As the poet John Goodwin observed, "People were disappointed, because people expected too much from Peggy." In Peggy's mind she had done the most she could, and to outsiders her efforts even appeared "heroic."

Before closing the gallery Peggy had a retrospective memorial exhibition of the paintings of Morris Hirshfield, followed by a one-man show for Richard Pousette-Dart, and then a show of David Hare's sculpture. The final exhibition was dedicated to Theo van Doesburg, arranged by Nellie, who at last had made it to America and impressed Mary McCarthy by wearing "something like an ice-pack on her head, a turban." It seemed fitting that for the end of Art of This Century Peggy and Nellie van Doesburg should be together, as Nellie had helped search for and find many of Peggy's best pieces. Nellie, observed McCarthy, "was one of the people she was good to. I felt she owed something to Nellie."

The gallery closed on May 31, 1947. Peggy did not shed a tear. She was too fatigued. "I'd always wanted to come back to Europe. I never meant to stay in America. I got exhausted in the gallery 'cause my secretary couldn't even type. I had to do everything myself. If I went out for a meal then some museum director came and said I was never there. I got fed up. Everything got to be too much."

All that remained was for Peggy to dismantle Kiesler's fabulous creations: the curved gumwood walls, the wheels, the peepshows, and the multifunction chairs. "Everyone came to the gallery," Peggy said, "and bought one, and I sold them, one by one. . . . Poor Kiesler. I didn't even keep one for him. Wasn't that mean? I sold them all." Sidney Janis, whose gallery was three doors away, bought one of the chairs for about three dollars. Charles Seliger managed to sell the round walls to the Franklin Simon department store, where he was working, "to the display department. I think she got about seven hundred dollars." He also helped her throw out some of the pictures she did not want to be burdened with, "a lot of Jimmy Ernsts." Max Ernst would occasionally come around to see how the dismantling was coming along, and "they'd be cordial. He'd come with the little dogs."

The closing of Art of This Century signaled the end of an era. Never again would American artists strain to hear the bon mots of an André Breton or feel themselves second-class provincials. With America's emergence as a superpower in a world devastated by war, New York would assume its position as the undisputed center of the art world. Perhaps it all would have happened anyway, but without Peggy's gallery to serve as a meeting and exhibition space, without her support of America's leading painters, without the parties at her apartment where she mixed European greats and up-and-coming New Yorkers, Surrealists and Abstractionists, baseball players and strippers, it would not have been the same. "No one has ever forgotten that marvelous place where sculptures hung in mid-air and paintings leaped out at you on invisible arms from the walls, where miniature pictures revolved in peepshow cabinets, where Marcel Duchamp displayed his life's work in a suitcase, tables became chairs, and chairs became pedestals."

PART VIII

THE BOHEMIAN
OF VENICE

VENICE

Venice had emerged from the war relatively unscathed. The city was still a pink-dusted fairy tale, its world of gondoliers and canals an improbable illusion. Shops there were full and the Italians, unlike the French, who had been hungry for five years as their farms fed the Reich, remained lively.

When Peggy first arrived in Venice the previous summer, she knew no one. "I felt," she said, "very much alone." Moving into a hotel, she began reacquainting herself with the Venice she had known as a young woman. She took her meals by herself in restaurants, and at one she asked the patron where she could meet artists. Peggy was directed to a restaurant near St. Mark's Square, the Al Angelo, where the two or three modern artists living in Venice frequently ate, since they were allowed liberal credit by its proprietor, Renato Carrain. One drawing bought an artist three days of meals.

Peggy wrote down the name of one of these painters, Vedova, on a matchbook and set off in search of the Al Angelo. She found the place and the artist seated at a table. She went over to him and saying nothing handed him the matchbook, which bore the words, "Vedova, artist." Emilio Vedova looked up from his plate to see an extravagantly dressed, unnaturally black-haired woman, deeply tanned, with shiny blue eyes.

The woman sat down next to him and began speaking terrible Italian and a rapid mixture of French and English. She seemed to Vedova altogether fantastic. Giuseppe Santomaso, another young painter who ate at the Al Angelo, came over to see who this woman was. She seemed to have arrived from another planet. Santomaso said, "Oh, yes. Gugge, Guggehem, Guggenheim! *La grande collezionista Americana!*" The young men had heard of Peggy, her famous collection, her uncle Solomon's museum, her gallery. The tall and bearded Vedova and his friend Santomaso were enthusiastic about her coming to live in Venice—what a boon to Venice's handful of modern artists!—and they spent hours sitting at the Café Florian, its small, round tables spilling out onto St. Mark's Square, chatting with Peggy about her plans, making themselves understood in Italian through much flailing of hands.

Peggy took to eating all her meals at the Al Angelo for a while; "It was like my family." She would arrive in strange red or green dresses, always open in some way, with many clanking bracelets, her large earrings, and shawls, and always accompanied by her dogs. She impressed Vedova as totally original. Even with her big nose, "She was a *buona màcchina del amore.*" Peggy said she wanted to buy a palazzo, and it did not take long for an informal network of concierges, artists, and waiters to become ersatz real estate agents.

In November 1947 Laurence Vail and Jean Connolly appeared and took Peggy to Capri. From that island, where she decided to rent the Villa Smeraldo, high on a cliff, for the winter months, Peggy wrote Clement Greenberg happily, "I do not in the least regret having left New York. . . . The only thing I miss is buying pictures. In fact I dreamt I was back in New York spending all the money of a trust I just have broken on a painting. That dream must have been inspired by seeing Baziotes get the Chicago prize. It was very gratifying to me even if it wasn't Pollock."

Kenneth Macpherson had bought a house on Capri and Peggy momentarily enjoyed a return to "old times," chasing after the few available men in a resort known for its attraction for homosexuals. In Capri, Peggy told Greenberg, "people do mad things and no one can be held responsible for their actions. . . . There is an intense social and sexual life in Capri. One need never be alone for five minutes." By her own account, Peggy had a "very, very sexy life in Capri, quite mad," meeting "all kinds of people I never knew before, all new people." She had a "very unpleasant experience with a fairy boy friend who tried to commit suicide with a sleeping draught" and dropped his lit cigarette on the bed. "It was all about a boy whom we shared and who was not worth the trouble." Pegeen visited her mother for ten days with her infant son, Fabrice, and even she, according to Peggy, was "astounded by the crazy life one leads here, but was delighted by the beauty of the place. It really is a dream. But of course all the people are crazy and as they do nothing they are completely demoralized." In the joy of the moment, Peggy wrote Charles Seliger, "My only ambition is to remain in Italy forever. I don't even wish to go to Paris anymore. I can't tell you how marvelous it is here. A sort of paradise on earth. I never miss New York for a second."

By the spring of 1948, Peggy was back in Venice. She had rented an apartment for the summer in the Palazzo Barbaro on the Grand Canal, famous because Henry James had lived on its top, bookcase-lined floor while writing *The Wings of the Dove.* Venice had always been a magnet for writers and artists, who found its magical vistas endlessly alluring. Even in the summer, when the city was most crowded with tourists, one could swim and sun at the Lido, or on the rocks beyond the lagoon, and at the same time enjoy a stimulating urban environment. It was sun just as Peggy liked it—civilized and well groomed.

Theodoros Stamos came through Venice with his friend the poet Robert Price and ran into Peggy in St. Mark's Square. Peggy had dinner with the young men, who brought with them a big bunch of flowers. Stamos remembered, "Bob said, 'I find Venice very sexy.' And she got very excited. 'How do you mean?' Bob said, 'The whole idea of water. The gondolas.' It was like a come-on. That was the beginning of it." The trio ended in bed together, with Peggy holding out "the promise of an Ernst."

Bernard Reis, the art world's accountant, and his wife, Becky, arrived from New York. They brought with them a male Lhasa Apso for Peggy's "girls," who Peggy complained in letter after letter were "misbehaving terribly" with various boxers and fox terriers and giving birth to "horrible canine grandchildren." Peggy dubbed the new arrival Peccora, Italian for little sheep, and although the dog acclimated himself well to his Venetian home, it took him some time to stop mistaking the sofas for fire hydrants. Peggy was so grateful to the Reises, however, that she gave them Pollock's *Cathedral* as a Christmas present. Peggy and Reis talked about breaking one of her trusts so that she could buy a palazzo.

The Canadian photographer Roloff Beny remembered meeting Peggy that summer at the Palazzo Barbaro. "I read *Out of This Century,*" he said, "in the University of Iowa, where I was a scholarship student, and I decided to meet her. When I was in Greece I felt I had to go to Italy and find that woman." Between Beny and Peggy there was an instant sympathy and the two remained friends until the end of her life. Dramatically dressed all in black, Beny became a frequent guest at her palazzo. (Some said that Beny was so adoring he patterned himself after Peggy in every way—including the cheapness.) He stayed with Peggy at the Barbaro, where he threw lilacs all over the room and saved one of the dogs by plunging into the canal after it. "The dogs slept all around her in baskets. There were dogs everywhere. I got up in the middle of the night," he recalled, "and stepped into one of the baskets the dogs slept in, and it was full of pipi."

Sindbad also visited Venice with his new wife, the former Jacqueline Ventadour, Pegeen's school chum and Peggy's traveling companion out of France during the war. The two had met again in Paris, where Sindbad had been stationed and then demobilized, and where Jacqueline worked as an interpreter. The couple had had a son, Clovis, born in 1946.

Peggy always claimed that she felt closer to Pegeen than to Sindbad with whom she had no tastes in common, remarking, "I have nothing to say to him." Jacqueline Ventadour, who remembers Peggy as a good mother-in-law, thought "Peggy was destructive of Sindbad, and of Pegeen as well, but not more so than Laurence. . . . A family gathering was a pick-all." There were many occasions when Jacqueline herself rushed away from the endless needling at the dinner table in tears, finding the Vail sarcasm unbearable.

No longer a child, without any special talents, Sindbad didn't know what to do with his life. "He certainly never wanted to be a painter, my God," said Peggy. "He's almost anti-painting, but a writer, yes." It was entirely possible, Peggy conceded, that Sindbad felt overpowered by his egocentric and forceful parents. To please his mother, Sindbad started a magazine in Paris, *Points,* for unknown writers under the age of thirty-five. For a while, Sindbad kept *Points* alive, going about Paris in his car to distribute it. But he would say, half in disgust, "I'm not an intellectual." He much preferred cricket and billiards. The magazine was short-lived, and, eventually, Sindbad became a real estate broker and then an insurance agent, despite his mother's thinly disguised disdain.

Peggy had not yet found a permanent home and spent all her time looking for one, but she had been offered the opportunity to exhibit her collection (which sat, boxed and crated in a New York warehouse) at the Twenty-fourth Venice Biennale to take place that summer. Inaugurated in 1895, the Biennale was a biannual, international exhibition of contemporary art, in which each participating country had a pavilion—something like a world's fair of the art world. During the war, the pavilions on the Biennale Fair Grounds near the Lido had stood derelict. In 1948 the Biennale was officially to recommence and Santomaso approached the secretary-general of the Biennale, Rodolfo Pallucchini, with the idea of showing Peggy's pictures. At the time, Greece was involved in hostilities and its pavilion was vacant. Why not show Peggy's avant-garde collection and the work of new American talents there? It would be inspirational, he argued, for modern Italian painters, kept ignorant by the Fascists of developments around the world. Even though Pallucchini had very little interest in modern art, preferring the Italian Renaissance, he invited Peggy to show her collection in the vacant Greek pavilion.

Peggy was concerned that her collection was not representative enough. She asked Greenberg, "Is my small collection of modern painters good enough to be shown in the Biennale summer show? . . . There are so many people missing in my collection that I feel ought to be included somehow. I mean Graves and David Smith and Toby [sic] and some others. . . . Maybe I should have a Diller or a Glarner or a Xeron [sic]. Who do you think is eminently missing?" She wrote to Seliger asking him to send her biographies of Motherwell, Virginia Admiral, Hedda Sterne, Hofmann, Pousette-Dart, Still, Rothko, Hare, Busa, Ralph Nelson.

Insecure or not, Peggy was delighted to be honored in this fashion. It was the first official recognition of her achievement. To exhibit alongside entire countries was for Peggy a great thrill, and she loved to dwell on the fact that the Biennale guide listed pavilions for Poland, Romania, Great Britain, France, Holland, and Guggenheim. "I felt," she wrote, "as though I were a new European country."

The Biennale ran from June 6 to September 30, 1948. Peggy's collection arrived safely from New York and her paintings were hung in the small pavilion, refurbished for the occasion by the Italian architect Carlo Scarpa. Because it was the first Biennale since the war, it was attended by all manner of Italian and foreign dignitaries, not to mention journalists and an international crowd of dealers, collectors, and pleasure-seekers. The president of Italy, Luigi Einaudi, was carried in the Venetian state gondola to the Biennale grounds on the edge of Venice to open the event. He visited Peggy's pavilion last, and Peggy, very chic and simple, her black hair cut short and wavy, wearing enormous daisy earrings, greeted the president under the Calder mobile, which dominated the exhibit. Looking around the president asked her, "Where is your collection?" And Peggy had to say, "Right here."

Visitors liked to push the huge Calder, which was hung low right in the middle of the entrance, and watch its twiglike arms swing. (It narrowly escaped being thrown out in its dismantled form, mistaken for discarded packing bands.) Peggy's dogs, scampering about the exhibits and wagging their tails in the hopes of a handout, added a homey touch. A tiny black catalogue, badly translated into Italian, accompanied *La Collezione Peggy Guggenheim,* and Peggy's pavilion, full of contemporary American art as well as her historical collection, was by far the most sensational of all. By comparison, the other thirteen pavilions lacked immediacy and seemed to present only "official art." Europeans had not seen so much modern American painting in one place before. Willy-nilly, Peggy had become the ambassador of the new American art in Europe, introducing Pollock, Baziotes, Rothko, Motherwell, and Still to a foreign audience who one day would be wild for American art.

For a moment Peggy felt as she had in New York—at the center of a vital and lively art world. "It was wonderful. It was marvelous," she exclaimed, "in the beginning. . . . Everybody came—all the dealers and all the artists and all the collectors. My life changed, of course, when I came here completely, but I didn't feel that I'd left the art world, no." Every two years, with each successive Biennale, Peggy acted as a hostess, inviting art people from all over the world to drinks, and buying a piece or two from the visiting dealers. It did not take long, however, for Peggy to become disenchanted with the Biennale itself. "I had absolutely nothing to do with the Biennale ever, after my show, except I lent them some pictures once for their shows. And after that they always wanted to borrow from me, and I said, no, I couldn't lend them anymore, I had my own gallery here. And then the director, the president of the Biennale, got very angry with me and he said after all they'd done for me, I should be more grateful, and I said I had done just as much for them, that I had the most successful show in the Biennale and they shouldn't think they'd done me a favor at all. And then he had my name struck off the list of people to be invited to the opening, because he was so angry with me."

The 1948 Biennale brought Peggy a great deal of attention and publicity, so much so that she decided to hire a Venetian assistant, Vittorio Carrain, one of the owners of the Al Angelo restaurant and hotel. Carrain helped her keep the press at bay and deal with the notoriety the show occasioned. After the close of the Biennale, Peggy received an invitation to exhibit the collection in Turin, which was withdrawn at the last minute by the city council which claimed that it was *"arte degenerata"*—which Carrain pointed out was the same as Hitler's phrase. Instead the paintings went to the Palazzo Strozzi in Florence, where they were shown in three separate installments: Cubist, Surrealist, and New Artists, in February, March, and April, 1949. Cleverly, Peggy let the Strozzi prepare an excellent Italian catalogue of her collection, which was to serve as the model for her own catalogue.

In Florence, Peggy stayed with her new friend Roloff Beny. Together he and Peggy went to a great many parties. At one, "I looked all over for Peggy and I finally found her under the table with Count Orsini. She didn't come home that night and the next day she telephoned that she needed a day outfit—she had on her Fortuny dress—her black eyebrow pencil, and her lipstick. I put these things in a basket and, for delicacy's sake, covered them with daisies." An acquaintance of theirs, Elise Cabot, astonished by the number of works in the Strozzi and observing Peggy's ardent social life, remarked: "How did Peggy ever find the time to paint all those paintings?" From Florence, the collection traveled to Milan's Palazzo Reale in the early spring.

For those first two years in Italy, Peggy was "very busy having shows all over." She kept the pictures moving, because she had discovered that her collection, brought to Italy at the expense of the Biennale, was unavailable to her without the imposition of a large entrance tax. Only a few pictures at any one time were allowed her for personal use. She hesitated over what to do. She certainly did not want to pay the full duty. To no effect she tried offering the Italian government a posthumous gift of the collection. The impasse was a particular shame, because Peggy had finally found her dream palazzo on the Grand Canal.

Begun in 1748, the Palazzo Venier dei Leoni was the only "unfinished" palazzo on the Dorso Duro side of the Grand Canal. It was near the Salute, and just opposite the Prefetura, or the Venetian city hall (whose workers always knew summer had arrived when they saw Peggy sprawled nude on the roof). It had been intended as a grand counterpart to the opulent Sansorino Palace across the canal, but when Napoleon invaded, construction was arrested at the first story, which had been designed as a long ballroom. It was subsequently called the *Palazzo non Finito.* Wide and white, covered by green vines, with broad terraced steps leading to the edge of the canal, it gave the appearance of a noble ruin. The palazzo boasted one of the largest gardens in Venice, shaded by ancient cedar, elm, magnolia, and acacia trees, which Peggy thought was perfect for the dogs.

Originally, the palazzo had belonged to the Veniers, a family of doges, who were supposed to have kept lions, the symbol of Venice's patron saint, in the garden and had decorated the facade of the house with eighteen lion's heads. In the nineteenth century, the palazzo fell into the hands of the exotic Marquessa Casati, supposedly a gift from her lover, Gabriele D'Annunzio. Luisa Casati, who liked to dress up in masquerade and rim her eyes in kohl, kept parrots, leopards, and black panthers in the garden and draped herself in a live (but drugged) boa constrictor, while "D'Annunzio lived across the canal with La Duse," the actress and rival of Sarah Bernhardt, Eleonora Duse. Famous for her elaborate parties, the Marquessa on one occasion took over St. Mark's Square, placing around it on columns beautiful youths, "naked and gilded and bearing flaming torches." Unfortunately one of the gilded youths suffocated to death under all the paint and the Marquessa was forced, rather hastily, to leave Venice. The Casati let the palazzo run down and Peggy marveled that any of it was left by the time it passed to the Viscountess Castlerosse, who installed six mammoth black marble bathrooms and central heating. Finally, Peggy bought it for about sixty thousand dollars (twenty-one thousand pounds) during the Christmas season of 1948, negotiating the sale with the Viscountess's brother.

Since it was unfinished and not considered a Venetian landmark, Peggy was allowed to make improvements without much of a fuss. She redid the garden in the English manner with grass growing between flagstones; goldfish swam within a byzantine wellhead encircled by stone pillars and covered in iron latticework. She also added a Renaissance "folly" and a massive square, thronelike stone seat that she loved to pose in.

She replaced the palazzo's flat roof, installed some plumbing, and stripped away the heavily stuccoed interior, until what remained was a series of simple, boxy rooms with bare granite floors. Her bedroom, overlooking the canal, she had painted pale turquoise, her favorite color, and installed her silver Calder headboard. On either side of the bed she pinned up her collection of unusual earrings, including one pair that commemorated Fulton's steamboat and another that once had belonged to Sarah Bernhardt. On one wall hung the Lenbach portrait of herself and Benita, and on the mantel, under a smoky Venetian mirror, Laurence Vail's bottles were neatly arrayed. Peggy had a spacious double sitting room, painted a dark blue and decorated in 1950s bohemia, with white plastic leatherette couches and furry black-and-white rugs. In the rectangular dining room, on the garden side of the palazzo, she placed the heavy Venetian chest and narrow table, rescued from Yew Tree Cottage, that she had bought with Laurence twenty years before. Over the windows were black iron vines and beyond them, the russet colors of Venice itself. When she moved into her palazzo on the Grand Canal in early 1949, Peggy was labeled "La Dogaressa" by the Venetians, who could not conceive of an ordinary mortal so ensconced.

She never wanted to be reminded of America and would not even permit nasturtiums, which grew so well in Venice, in her house, because they had been plentiful on the Jersey shore of her childhood. Peggy preferred to cultivate English roses. "I sent her a lot of roses," said Sir Norman Reid, the director of the Tate Gallery, "and thereafter, I used to go there and prune them. Strangely, they did very well in Venice."

Peggy chose "a wonderful turquoise blue" and white for her palazzo's identifying candy-cane posts in the canal, each Venetian family having a different color combination, "but the blue was very hard to reproduce. Finally, in the end, they got painted quite a different color and I didn't do anything about it, because it was too complicated, but they used to be a wonderful sort of turquoise blue." Peggy had her gondoliers dress all in white with a turquoise sash to match the blue of the posts and of her eyes.

A steady stream of guests made their way to the Palazzo Venier dei Leoni, even though for most of her first summer there Peggy fought off a recurring case of mononucleosis that she attributed to her having donated so much blood to the Red Cross during the war. Nellie van Doesburg arrived, extravagant as ever, as well as Pegeen, Matta, Tchelitchew, the Antoine Pevsners, and Giacometti and his wife. Mary Reynolds came for two weeks with Charles Henri Ford, nervous lest Peggy and Ford fight over his mention in her memoirs. Reynolds found the palazzo pretty and Peggy very sweet, her house full of waifs and strays. Immediately, Peggy started asking Mary Reynolds what she should do about Djuna Barnes, still in New York and still dependent on Peggy's checks.

In order to keep her houseguests amused, Peggy felt compelled to entertain "thousands of other people" at parties that ended late at night with someone diving into the canal or with another rolling up the carpet to dance. "My house," Peggy complained in a letter to Seliger, "instead of a museum is a sort of non-profit-making hotel. I have four guest rooms so you can imagine what happens." At the end of the first summer, Peggy found herself very busy trying to undo the ravages of the thirty-four houseguests she had entertained. Santomaso, who was one of the few Italians to visit Peggy's house regularly, recalled the palazzo as "the only place in Venice that's really international." Peggy liked to have her guests sign a guest book and over the years her books overflowed with famous autographs and drawings, as everyone coming through Venice wanted to meet the eccentric legend and see her palazzo by the water.

The stream of visitors was augmented by an ever-increasing dog population. Eventually, more than fifty-seven puppies were born in the palazzo, most of which Peggy gave away. She always kept seven or so at home, giving them names like Baby, Cappuccino, Pegeen, Madame Butterfly, Foglia, Toro, and Sable. When Peggy did not feel like dealing with a litter, the dogs could be seen wearing chastity belts.

Guests had to fight with curled-up pups for space on the sofas, or would look down to see a dog begging for some of whatever they were eating. Meals al fresco were followed with scraps flung out for the dogs. Roloff Beny wrote in her guest book: "26 Pollocks and 32 dogs copulating under the bed." Piers Paul Read, just a boy when he went with his father, Herbert Read, to visit Peggy, recalled, "She had a lot of gassy little dogs. One of them was called Sir Herbert because she thought my father ought to have a knighthood before he actually got one. . . . And these dogs used to do little messes in our bedroom." Peggy and her troop of long-haired Lhasa Apsos became a familiar sight in Venice. She often claimed that she was happiest with her dogs and preferred them to people. "They're almost human," she said, and she let her life be governed by them. David Kalstone, who met Peggy years later, remembered that she "would have to take them along for dinner, so there were very few restaurants you could go with her. Usually dives which would allow the poochies, and she would like to go nearby so she wouldn't tire the dogs. She was always very concerned about them."

Peggy so loved her dogs that when she ordered her shiny black gondola, which was to be the last private gondola in Venice, she insisted that it be decorated with Lhasa Apso heads. The Venetian gondola makers had never seen Lhasa Apsos, however, so the heads came out looking like the ubiquitous and more familiar lions.

When summer was over and the early winter chill set in, before setting off for Capri once again, Peggy enjoyed being left alone to plant her garden and walk with her dogs about the empty rooms and frigid corridors. She felt as though she were back at Yew Tree Cottage. (In fact, anyplace that was cold and dank reminded her of Yew Tree Cottage.) All Peggy had for heat was the fire in the living room and a few useless electric heaters, which went off three times a week with the electric current; the bedrooms were freezing.

Happy though she was, Peggy was frustrated by the status of her collection in Italy. The Biennale let her borrow some of her sculptures for an exhibition in her garden during the summer of 1949. "The show was a great success," Peggy wrote to Charles Seliger, "as it gave all the curious people a chance to get into my palace. They even started wandering down the corridors and into the kitchen and bedroom, where they are not supposed to come, and I had to rope off the private apartments. The public were supposed to walk from the garden into the entrance hall and from there down to the terrace on the Grand Canal . . . but that of course did not satisfy them at all."

Peggy also kept busy trying to arrange a one-man show for Pollock in Paris, but the French were not yet ready for him. Peggy had introduced Pollock to Europe at the 1948 Biennale, where she exhibited six of his paintings. In July–August 1950, Peggy mounted an exhibition of her Pollock paintings, twenty-three in all, at the Correr museum, opposite the cathedral of St. Mark. At night the show was lit up and the pictures looked strangely alive when viewed from the square below. It was Pollock's first European exhibition. "This show sent all the Venetian painters mad with excitement," wrote Peggy to Clement Greenberg. *Time* magazine called it "Chaos, Damn It," and inaccurately stated that Pollock had come to Italy for the event. Pollock cabled them: "NO CHAOS DAMN IT."

Thereafter, Peggy organized an exhibition in the Palazzo Giustinian for her son-in-law, Jean Hélion, who came to Venice along with Pegeen. Peggy was so discouraged by the complications at customs of getting Hélion's pictures into Italy, as well as by an endless series of disasters (topped by a rainstorm that caused the crimson banner waving over the entrance to pour red dye on passersby), that she forswore importing another show.

Peggy's dream, however, was to have her own museum. "This was supposed to be," said Peggy, "like the Jacquesmart André collection in Paris. It's beautiful. It's the same kind of building. It's a one story building. It's very low, and very white and very wide. But they have only Renaissance paintings. They didn't have anything modern." But without access to her collection, her hope would be impossible. For a while, letters went back and forth to various cabinet ministers who promised to help, but nothing came of it. The only solution was to have the paintings leave Italy and to bring them back at a lower valuation. Exhibitions were planned in Amsterdam at the Stedelijk Museum in January 1951, from which the collection traveled to Brussels and its Palais des Beaux Arts, and then in the spring to Zurich's Kunsthaus, whence it was to return to Italy. "It was very easy," after all, Peggy declared. "I didn't have to pay the duty because they were brought in at four o'clock in the morning—an Alpine pass. These very stupid, sleepy *douaniers,* who didn't know what it was all about, let them come in for I think $1000."

LIFE WITH TARZAN

Finally, in 1951, Peggy's palazzo was opened to the public as a museum. The entire interior was covered with modern pictures and sculptures extending even into the bathrooms (where visitors viewed Peggy's wet stockings along with the art). In the entrance hall hung the Calder mobile, which hit many a guest physically in the eye. On a pebble-glass table lay Giacometti's *Woman with Her Throat Cut,* and Picasso's *Les Baigneuses,* Peggy's favorite picture, loomed over it. In the dark dining room she hung her amber-toned Cubists: Braque, Duchamp's *Sad Young Man on a Train,* Picasso's *The Poet,* Juan Gris. The courtyard was turned into a sculpture garden featuring Brancusi's two *Birds.* On the white marble terrace overlooking the Grand Canal Peggy had already installed a 1948 Marino Marini bronze horse and rider, nearly six feet high, *The Angel of the Citadel.* The rider, flaunting an erect phallus, greeted visitors and passing gondolas with head thrown back and outstretched arms. The sculptor cautiously insisted that the upright organ not be interpreted as a sexual symbol but rather as an expression of general ecstasy on the part of the young man. In any event, the erection could be unscrewed and once, Peggy wrote to Seliger, "in honor of the visit of 20 nuns, who came to watch a procession on the Grand Canal of an Itinerant Virgin, my secretary removed the phallus without consulting me. I'm sure he was right judging from the faces of the visitors to the show, whom I can watch from my study." There were times, though, when Peggy forgot to remove the member and suffered acute embarrassment, as when the Duchess of Kent's parents visited. Eventually, the rider became permanently ecstatic after some prankster stole the phallus and a new one was soldered on.

Visitors were allowed to see the collection on Mondays, Wednesdays, and Fridays from three to five in the afternoon. In the beginning, Peggy let the tourists walk around the private rooms, but soon she issued heavy, old-fashioned iron keys with distinguishing colored-silk tassels and warned her houseguests to lock their doors and to watch out for the sandal-clad throngs in Bermuda shorts who snooped in every doorway. Sometimes a bleary guest, looking for a cup of coffee, forgot and wandered out into the exhibition spaces in his pajamas or less. Peggy would repair to the roof, where she sunbathed until it was all clear downstairs. "On the days the Palazzo was open to the public," recounted Robert Fizdale of one visit, "she'd say you had two choices. Either you can go off to the roof and have a sun bath or you can lock yourself up in your room and be sure to lock the door from the inside so they don't steal the key for the silk tassel. The first Wednesday or whenever it was the public came in, I chose to go up on the roof with Peggy, and it was very hot. Peggy was wearing a red and white, diagonally striped silk dress, and I said, 'You look like a candy cane.' And she told me, 'You can lick me if you want.'"

In time, Peggy decided to close off the sitting rooms from public view so that she could use them undisturbed. Having been criticized for doing so in New York, she decided against charging admission, but to make money, sold catalogues of the collection, which—purposely—was otherwise poorly identified. Commandeered to be museum curators as well as to sell catalogues, the servants kept vigil to make sure that no one made off with an Arp or a Mondrian. As it had been in New York, Peggy's happiest moment came at the end of the day when she spilled out over her bed, which was covered in pink maribou feathers, all the money they had collected.

Pegeen's marriage to Hélion was floundering, in large measure because Peggy had decided that she no longer liked Hélion's (now figurative) pictures and, therefore, that he was not important enough. She encouraged Pegeen to leave him and have other affairs. But Hélion anchored Pegeen; the perfect father figure, Hélion was protective, charming. The couple had two sons, Fabrice and David. They had a lovely apartment in Paris, decorated in quilted satin, where Pegeen gave beautiful dinner parties and seemed to have the home life and family that she had been seeking. "She was very happy with him," said Pegeen's friend Eileen Geist Finletter, "very secure. Peggy just said, 'Oh! It's boring.' "

Peggy loved to talk about sex to Pegeen, and if she saw that it upset her, she continued all the more. "Once," recounted Eileen Finletter, "Pegeen and I had tea with Peggy at the Pont Royal." In contrast to her mother, Pegeen did not have indiscriminate sex, but was always falling madly in love, so Peggy said, "I don't know why you younger people take this sort of thing so seriously. It's just like having a cup of tea." On her visits to Venice, Pegeen had affairs at her mother's house with Peggy's full endorsement. In 1951 Pegeen had a relationship with a Milanese antiques dealer, and afterward Hélion was desperately upset by Peggy's mischievous invitations. While still married to Hélion, Pegeen had a third son, Nicolas, born in Paris in 1952, by her Milanese lover.

In August 1951 Pegeen and Hélion were in Venice visiting Peggy. Evidently they had an argument, and after coming home from the theater Pegeen, restless all evening, drinking a great deal of whiskey, went into one of Peggy's big black bathrooms and slit both her wrists. She was saved just in time by Hélion, who rushed her to the hospital by motorboat. "I prevented Pegeen five times from committing suicide," said Hélion. Soon after the incident, Hélion left for Paris and Pegeen spent more and more time in Venice.

Pegeen painted naïve, childlike scenes, in primary colors, of women flatly outlined against squiggly Venetian landscapes or seascapes of happy family outings that were reminiscent of Hélion's work at the time. Usually there appeared in her paintings one very black-haired woman with huge, dangling earrings and one blond woman. Sometimes, milk spurted out of their bare breasts. Since she was proud of Pegeen's painting, Peggy let her have a studio in the basement and decided to start a sales gallery in the museum, from which she could sell Pegeen's paintings and possibly those of talented young Italian artists. A painter from Feltre by the name of Tancredi came to Peggy's attention as one of the most talented of the new generation. "I thought he was wonderful. Oh, he was marvelous," gushed Peggy. "Tancredi did beautiful gouaches." He also did oils and lacquer on paper, in dreamy colors. But Tancredi was so poor that his teeth were black and discolored from lack of care, and he ate in return for painting *frutta i latte* signs. Peggy offered him a tiny room in her basement next to Pegeen's studio and seventy-five dollars a month, hoping to do for him what she had done for Pollock. Indeed she called him her "Venetian Pollock." However, she soon found that Tancredi, who spoke in trances, was too unstable even for her. "He was so difficult, and so complicated, his character was so crazy."

Soon, Pegeen and Tancredi's passionate affair was the talk of all of Venice. Part of the gossip in Venice was that mother and daughter were both having affairs with Tancredi. The suggestion made Peggy furious.

Nothing could be further from the truth, she insisted. "Absolutely not. I never thought of him for a second in that way. He didn't even attract me. He was a protégé, pure and simple, like Pollock." Moreover, added Peggy as to the alleged ménage à trois, "I alone know about this affair, which I was supposed to have had with Tancredi. The whole thing is a complete lie and completely made up. Why should I hide one affair when I tell about all the others?" Sindbad added, "I know for a fact she didn't have an affair with Tancredi. He wasn't interested in a fifty-five-year-old woman, and he couldn't get it up." In addition, it wasn't long before Peggy began saying of Tancredi that he was a bore, too, and referring to Pegeen's love life as her "stupid affairs."

Peggy's museum became one of Venice's tourist attractions, publicized by her book and by the numerous articles written about her, the *ultima dogaressa,* who was always receptive to visiting journalists. Laurence Vail accused her of having a mania about publicity. "Fifty per cent of the people who come here," she said, "genuinely want to see my collection, the others to meet what they consider a celebrity." She never knew who would ring up with a letter of introduction from a friend, or simply walk through the gate. Her white leather guest books in time read like an encyclopedia of twentieth-century arts. Harold Acton, Stephen Spender, Elsa Schiaparelli, Alfred Barr, Herbert Read, Isamu Noguchi, Paul Bowles, Virgil Thomson, Henry Moore, Lucia Chase, Stella Adler, Somerset Maugham, and Marlon Brando, were among those who made their way to the Palazzo Venier dei Leoni in the early years after the opening of the museum.

The tiny terror, Truman Capote, arrived unannounced one summer day. "He just walked in," said Peggy. "I met him in my entrance hall." Peggy found the young, fey Capote with his high-pitched voice and air of a spoiled boy genius intriguing. Soon he was visiting her on a regular basis, as he spent his first winter in Europe in Venice, realizing what it really means to be cold. At one point he spent six weeks with her. He repaid Peggy's hospitality by including her in his unfinished novel, *Answered Prayers.* He was more charitable toward Peggy than he was to many, asserting that he might have married her, despite their thirty-year age difference, "her habit of rattling her false teeth and even though she did rather look like a long-haired Bert Lahr." Peggy was sanguine about Capote's observations. "He said so many stupid things about me," she shrugged. "He said I had all false teeth, which isn't true. He said he would have married me, imagine, and took it for granted that I'd marry him. . . . He wasn't nearly so mean to me as he was to most people. He was terrible to most people."

As popular an attraction as she was in their city, Peggy never felt really welcomed by the Venetians themselves, particularly the Venetian aristocracy, who imagined that wild parties and orgies went on late into the night at her palazzo. "There was a dancer," Peggy recounted, "he was called Count Medina, and he did a dance naked with candles. It was very beautiful, really wonderful, I mean he wasn't completely naked, but he was more or less naked, and he danced with candles. Maybe that's the kind of thing the aristocracy considered wild."

The Venetians—especially all the old dogaressas—were too conservative to understand Peggy, particularly her freewheeling and self-broadcast sexual notions, not to mention her daughter's. Stories abounded of Peggy sleeping with gondoliers or taking them to Harry's Bar. According to John Hohnsbeen, who would become Peggy's last assistant, "When Peggy arrived in Venice, Elsie Gozzi, née MacNeil in the Midwest, who runs the Fortuny factory, said to her: 'We Venetians will never accept you.' Peggy never forgave her, wouldn't speak to her even if they were in the same elevator."

The Italians did not comprehend Peggy's collection either; it seemed to them somehow pornographic. "Venice had a grand history," observed Santomaso. "It died in the eighteenth century, and [Peggy's collection was] too recent to consider. That people would love this recent art" seemed to the Venetians impossible. Michael Wishart, who knew Peggy from her days with Douglas Garman, said, "Peggy, by their standards, was a highbrow, let's face it. She had people of genius staying with her. They," meaning all the contessas and dogaressas, "are so vulgar, really."

Peggy kept saying it didn't matter to her. "I felt they were terribly boring. They just played canasta and bridge all the time and gossiped, and I didn't want to know them. I don't suppose they wanted to know me either." Nevertheless, Peggy's romantic illusions were crushed. "She wanted to shock," observed Wishart, "and be accepted as an enfant terrible, but she didn't realize she was the enfant *too* terrible."

In the summer of 1951, Peggy began a relationship with a man twenty-three years younger than herself, an extremely good-looking Italian of dubious reputation named Raoul Gregoritch. Peggy liked to say that he was Venetian, but in reality he was from Mestre, a small industrial community outside of Venice. Raoul came from a family of magistrates but had had trouble with the law. "He was in prison," Peggy explained. "Well, it's a crazy story. He was in the Underground, you know, against Fascism, and he was in a sort of company, people he had, and after the war was over, he felt he had to go on supporting these people because they had no money. So they used to go out and do sort of banditry on the road, and then, one night, in Venice, they went into a man's house and they wanted to get some papers or something or other, and that was what he was arrested for, and people afterwards said

he'd killed the man, but it wasn't true. He hadn't killed anybody at all.
. . . No, this man who was not killed, he died long afterwards. He was
in prison for breaking into this man's house with his companions, a sort
of bandit." Or burglar.

Dark-haired and movie-star handsome, Raoul looked like a gigolo
and one, moreover, who seemed suspiciously homosexual. He looked,
thought the astonished Sindbad, "like Tarzan. He was two years older
than me!" Raoul was terribly impressed by Peggy, the American mil-
lionairess, and Peggy was besotted with her young lover. "Raoul," said
John Hohnsbeen, "was a gorgeous Italian stud. She kept him and he kept
her. The Italians are very practical about money." It was certainly not
an arrangement that would further Peggy's cause with the aristocratic
Venetians. No true dogaressa would countenance at her table a former
convict and a gigolo. Observed Maria Theresa Rubin, a member of
Venice's aristocracy, "In the fifties and also in the sixties, Venice was way
behind. The *dolce vita* was at the end of the fifties, in Rome, but here,
it was more moralistic. People of her age had a different mentality. Now,
that has changed, thanks God." "Raoul," said John Richardson, "was
bad news, really bad news. He was like something out of Tennessee
Williams—*The Roman Spring of Mrs. Stone.*"

No intellectual, Raoul was little more than a garage mechanic,
although his father was a judge, a "poor judge," as Peggy said. For a
while he sold animal feed in the Tyrol, and Peggy would accompany him
on his rounds to veterinarians and farmers. Peggy spent most of their first
winter together waiting in the car. "It was crazy," she gushed, "my
winter, absolutely mad. I was madly in love with him. It was ridiculous."
The affection seemed to be somewhat reciprocated. "Raoul," said Michael Wishart, "slightly idolized her. . . . A gigolo can love a person. She
spoiled him. She bought him a car." It was as far as Peggy was concerned
a perfect relationship. Raoul was unobtrusive, uncomplicated, totally
uninterested in art or in anything else for that matter, except cars, and
spoke only Italian. And he was so good-looking. When he wasn't selling
grain, they could sun together on her roof or motor out to the rocks
beyond the lagoon and swim. Guests to her palazzo grew accustomed to
seeing the quiet, good-natured Raoul, smiling sheepishly, although he
often felt inferior to Peggy's illustrious friends and sometimes sulked.
Peggy treasured a photograph she had of Herbert Read and Raoul
holding Sir Herbert the dog.

When Jane Bouché Strong arrived to visit Peggy in Venice, she was
told by a voice on the telephone to take the *vaporetto* to the Accademia,
where she would be met by Peggy's manservant. She was given a pink
room on the canal with a tall four-poster bed embedded with shells and
made up with pink silk sheets. She was amused by the silver starfish

faucets in the black marble bathroom and by the long-handled clothes hangers in the very high closets. Sprinkled about were "little turds, from *i cani disobbedientes.*" She was advised to lock up her jewelry in case a tourist found it on visitors' days. Strong found Peggy more settled and happier than when she had last seen her in New York, and she had lost none of her animation or nervous energy. Peggy "had a throaty, beautiful laugh. She would say: 'It's such a bore to lie in the sun to get a suntan. There should be an atomic blast.' " Raoul impressed Strong as a "very tall, handsome, and toothsome man, ingenuous." When they motored out to the rocks near the lighthouse in the mornings to sun, the muscular Raoul seemed a "regular porpoise in the water," totally at home in his element. Lunches were had in the palazzo, but, "Well, we have leftovers again today," was the vacation's most quoted refrain. In the evenings, the women would all wear lovely white dresses. At night, Peggy refused to eat at Harry's Bar, an institution in Venice, either because Raoul would not or could not go. Strong would go instead with Pegeen, who with her baby son Nicolas was also staying with Peggy. "Pegeen was having a wonderful time, living the most sybaritic life," and "Peggy kept giving Pegeen lots of money to buy oodles of clothes. Everyone was having a good time." In Venice, Strong learned, they called Peggy behind her back "the dirty woman."

Peggy spent three years with Raoul. She did not seem to mind that he still had other girl friends, and one in particular, who kept calling him. Being Peggy's lover made Raoul even more attractive to other women. Raoul wanted to marry her, Peggy insisted, but she had no need to get married, "and certainly not to him, anyhow." Eventually, Raoul decided to go into business and asked Peggy to buy him some cars "so he could go into the auto hire business," she explained. "So, I gave him the money to buy three cars. . . . He rented them in Venice to people who wanted to go out in the country."

Unwittingly, Peggy sowed the seeds for Raoul's destruction. During the Regatta Storica of 1954—an annual September pageant of decorated floats and gondolas on the Grand Canal, for which Peggy liked to give a party on her terrace—Raoul was killed instantly in one of his cars as he unsuccessfully swerved to avoid a motorcyclist. It was no surprise to those who knew how fast he drove or sensed the streak of violence just under the surface. Before he died, Peggy and Raoul had quarreled over changing her car for a racer and they did not speak for seven weeks. "I suppose," Peggy wrote Herbert Read just after the accident, "those who live by the sword die by the sword. I'm probably using this quotation all wrong, but you know what I mean." Raoul was only thirty-three years old, even younger, thought Peggy, than John Holms was when he died. Peggy was distraught. She had been so lonely without Raoul and began to think that she should have married him, or even died instead of him. Raoul's funeral, a lengthy procession of black-draped gondolas to Venice's funerary island, depressed her. "I don't think," Peggy wrote Djuna, "I'll ever love anyone again; I hope and pray not."

Raoul was Peggy's last boyfriend, or what she would consider her last real love affair. After Raoul, Peggy's life, for all the scandal it conjured up, consisted of a series of disconnected encounters. "I used to have," she sighed, "British naval officers and people like that." But as she wrote Becky Reis, "the navy moves on."

Surprisingly, after years of neglect by the public, Max Ernst won the 1954 painting prize at the twenty-seventh Venice Biennale and was invited to show his works there. The wild-eyed Surrealists had become members of the art establishment. Jean Arp, whom Peggy had not seen since the war, also won that year for sculpture and Joan Miró won the prize for drawing. The Biennale marked a turning point in the career of Ernst, who returned to Paris from America in 1953. It also earned him André Breton's indignation and a final excommunication from the Surrealists (who termed the Biennale the Banale) for, in Ernst's words, selling his "soul to the Vatican, my integrity to the merchants of Venice." Max, Dorothea Tanning, and the dog Kachina paid a nostalgic visit to Peggy. After all the trouble her memoirs had caused them, "they decided," said Peggy coyly, "to forgive me." Peggy entertained Max and her onetime rival, and insisted that she no longer loathed Dorothea as she had in New York. Her love affair with Max Ernst was all over, a thing of the past. What was the point of being jealous? "We had a tender reconciliation," Peggy wrote Djuna, "which means a great deal to him, as he's so sentimental and German, but to me it was only a social event. I feel quite cold to him now, but he was very sweet." Peggy was as gracious as she could be, but managed to spill a glass of red wine over Dorothea. Ironically, Victor Brauner was staying with Peggy at the time and the group around the lunch table brought back memories of Marseilles in 1940. Ernst wrote in Peggy's guest book: "Peace for ever, *un vrai ami est revenue*, for ever, *contre signé* darling Peggy, Max." And Tanning cooed, *"Tou-tou d'affection."* But for her part, Peggy never forgave Ernst for leaving her: "He's been so unpleasant," she once said, "I've decided I feel very unfriendly towards him."

THE GOLDEN AGE

Venice, with its romantic lagoons and fabulous salons hidden behind ancient exteriors made possible an extravagant life. Glamorous and exciting, alluring to socialites, movie stars, dress designers, and English aristocrats alike, Venice was experiencing in the 1950s what the painter Robert Brady, who lived there between 1953 and 1959, called the "last golden epoch," when people still kept up their palazzos, had liveried servants and balls." Charles de Bestegui took over the entire Gritti Palace Hotel for his lavishly famous eighteenth-century *bal à Venise*. The old families—the Volpis, the Cicognas—were very grand and arrogant, with their opulent houses lined in tooled leather and *piani nobiles* of stuccoed angels. In addition, there was the literary, artistic, cosmopolitan set that came to Venice in the summer, which included people like Nancy Mitford, Ruth Ford and Zachary Scott, Valentina Schlee, Caresse Crosby, Helena Rubinstein, Somerset Maugham. There was always someone interesting passing through, stopping at Peggy's palazzo for a drink or a meal: Cyril Connolly, Roland Penrose, Francis Steegmuller, Giacometti, Cocteau, and old friends from New York like Clement Greenberg, Becky and Bernard Reis, Buffie Johnson, and Mary McCarthy, who signed Peggy's guest book, "To a huge, gay forgiving heart." It was an enchanted world of midnight swims, languorous gondola rides, lunch parties at the Lido. If Peggy was not always invited to some of the older, grander houses in Venice, life had its consolations.

Peggy loved the international titles, the beautiful, famous, and rich people who came through Venice. Ever the Anglophile, she was particularly impressed by English titles, and had the improbable fantasy of marrying Martin Wilson, whose brother Peter was the head of Sotheby's, because he had a title. She adored being invited to the British Embassy and listening to those "divine" accents. The parties were constant. "I used to think," she said, "they were the breath of life, essential."

Peggy became more and more extravagant in her dress and affectations. (For a while she went around in a carriage pulled by mules.) "Everyone gets exotic in Venice," she said. "It's a sort of dream world. Everything floats. I want to live as I like and do what I want. In Venice you can do anything." Peggy, who each year dyed her hair a deeper, darker black, was still proud of her slim figure. In summer she went barelegged and wore upturned sandals appropriate to a seraglio. She had clothes made out of Indian saris or Aztec-inspired dresses with mirror inserts, and for very special occasions, she wore her favorite dress—some said her favorite possession—a champagne-colored Fortuny, a pillar of tiny Grecian pleats. Michael Wishart remembered Peggy swooping by in a voluminous green gauze dress, a Calder mobile hanging from each earlobe.

Peggy enjoyed entertaining, serving drinks or dinner to friends and glittering arrivals from abroad. "She gave wonderful dinner parties, very glamorous and beautiful, a mixture of Venetian society and artists," said Pegeen's friend Eileen Finletter. "Yes, Venetian society rejected her, but certain ones, the kind who travelled, the few who did, were there. . . . I loved her chocolate chicken and chocolate soufflé. She was a very good hostess, very charming. . . . We were glad to be invited." Said Robert Brady, "Every year, before November, she would call and say Thanksgiving was coming . . . and she would plan weeks ahead a real turkey dinner."

Some dinner guests complained that there was never enough wine or that the food was uneven. Mary McCarthy found that "she served cheap wine. The food could be good, but quite often depended on the cook." The less charitable suggested that the food was a function of how grand Peggy perceived the guest of honor to be. Wishart thought Peggy "the incarnation of generosity. Peggy was criticized for being cheap by many of the people who constantly accepted her hospitality, because the food was simple, but of course, she didn't want fifty sycophantic faggots for lunch every day." Certainly her parties were not wild, said McCarthy, "rather the reverse, rather dull. . . . She always had hangers-on—not really the greatest accessories to a party."

Peggy was desperate to have Bernard Berenson come to her house.

"She was just possessed with the idea," recalled Mary McCarthy, who had met Berenson in the fall of 1955. "And she said, 'Look, you tell him that I guarantee to turn my pictures to the wall, hang sheets over them if he'll come.' He didn't that time, but somehow they met, and he asked her quite impertinently: 'To whom will you leave these pictures?' 'To you, Mr. Berenson.' "

To Brady, who became Peggy's friend and "cavalier," in her late fifties Peggy was still "marvelously wild. She loved to dance, jazz, fox-trot, from the twenties and forties, together dancing with a fling to it. She loved to drink, good food." Her only flaw, Brady found, was her persistent and well-known tightness, skimping here and there, sitting in semidarkness, giving the servants cheaper, whole-wheat bread, going through extraordinary inconvenience to save a penny. Christina Thoresby recollected how, "many years ago, we went out on a ride in the gondola, and we went to the other side of Venice where there is a Standa," an inexpensive Italian department store, "and she got off and came back with her arms full of lavatory papers saying: 'These are quite good enough for my houseguests.' She took the trouble to go clear across Venice to get them cheaper." Wishart, who once traveled to Capri with her, remembered Peggy going from one restaurant to another. "She'd say: 'Are you sure there's not a cheaper one? But there's another block,' " and reminded him a week later that he still owed her his half of the bus fare.

True to form, Peggy also was capable of spontaneous acts of personal generosity. In 1956 Mary McCarthy was to go to Padua, about an hour's drive from Venice, but McCarthy recently had had an experience in a car of bumping into a child, which had totally unnerved her, and she did not want to drive. She had arranged for a friend, Tony Bauer, the former editor of *Art in America,* to drive her, but at the last minute he reneged.

> The last night of my stay I came to dinner, and Peggy said: "I've decided I'm going to drive you to Padua. I remember the ending of your last book." (*A Changed Life,* where the heroine dies in a car.) It was no treat, but she did it, and she did it very gamely. Part of her pleasure was in excoriating Tony Bauer for being unfeeling. I think she might have even said something to him when she saw him . . . and then she got on the train and went back, having driven my car. I have never, never forgotten this and have loved her ever since.

Even approaching sixty, Peggy retained a beguiling little-girl quality. According to Robert Brady, "She was madly curious." She once took the tourists' *scenata* with him, just so she could hear her own palazzo pointed out. "She just loved it . . . loved it like a child." Peggy was especially fascinated by personal relations. In the 1960s, when the manager of the rock group the Who, well known for his dissipations, bought the Palazzo Dario next door (thought to carry a curse, because everyone who lived in it seemed to die mysteriously), Peggy asked of her houseguests: "Would you mind if we ask Lambert to dinner?"

Peggy was especially intrigued by other rich or famous women. She was "fascinated by Barbara Hutton," said Hutton's friend Robert Brady, "dying to meet her. . . . Barbara was a genuine beauty, the only one of the heiresses that could be a movie star, and she was not Jewish." Peggy was terribly curious about Violet Trefusis, a fact that drew her to historian Peter Lauritzen. She would ask out of curiosity "the most outrageous questions, out of the blue." Years later, Peggy entertained Lillian Hellman at dinner, and David Kalstone, also a guest that evening, noticed Peggy's intense fascination with Hellman's age. "She tried," he said, "with many indirect questions to get it out of her." Peggy could also be endearingly innocent. "In jest, a friend had addressed a post card to Rabbi Lillian Hellman, which card was on my desk and Peggy obviously saw it, for later she remarked, 'Is Lillian Hellman really a rabbi?' " When confronted with a bagel, Peggy asked, "Oh! What are these?" Peggy's ideal woman was, improbably, Jacqueline Kennedy. Peggy and Pegeen gushed adoringly, "She is our dream."

Peggy spent most of the year in Venice, opening her museum in the spring and keeping it open until the fall. When the amusing summer visitors were gone, there was always a moment of wistfulness as she realized the damp, gray winter was coming. But then she would go to Paris—only a train ride away—to spend Christmas with Laurence and to see Sindbad and Pegeen. Or she would go on exotic trips. In 1955, on her way to India, Peggy stopped off to see Paul Bowles, living on his own island in Ceylon, telling a journalist en route that she was sick of Western art and was "looking for geniuses in the East."

Paolo Barozzi, a Venetian acquaintance, went to Greece with her.

One day I bumped into Peggy, and she asked: "Would you like to come to Greece? I have a spare ticket. But you have to take care of your expenses." She was very direct. . . . So we went to Greece and in Athens became acquainted with all the beats. Alan Ansen, who was a great friend of Jack Kerouac and Gregory Corso. I think I met Burroughs once, so I was introduced to these people. We met Jean Genet, the playwright, and he had the reputation of being a kleptomaniac and I had a friend who was also a kleptomaniac, and we organized for the two kleptomaniacs to meet. It was fabulous. Peggy was my university.

If Peggy missed the excitement of Art of This Century, she did not admit it, although every once in a while she felt a pang as she saw her old protégés gaining recognition without her. Peggy did feel resentful that pictures she had sold for practically nothing were now selling for thousands. Venice was beautiful, but artistically little was happening there. To believe that what happened in New York in the 1940s could be transferred to a sleepy, if glittering, backwater was a fundamental misjudgment. In Venice she could be a queen, but queen of a very small kingdom.

Jackson Pollock was the subject of a photographic essay in *Life* magazine, which posed the question, "Is He the Greatest Living Painter in the United States?" As Pollock gained recognition, Peggy saw her own role in his career go unheralded. She complained that he and Lee Krasner were ungrateful to her, that they did not write to her, did not send her announcements of his activities or clippings of his reviews. She wrote Charles Seliger, "I gathered Pollock was becoming very important in America. It certainly is due to me and Lee, but he is so ungrateful that they never even answer letters nor thot [sic] to send me *Life* magazine which I finally received from Betty [Parsons] upon request."

After his contract with Betty Parsons ran out in 1952, Pollock signed up with Sidney Janis, one of the first of a new generation of more professional and more aggressive dealers. He was included in the vastly influential traveling show organized by Dorothy Miller at the Museum of Modern Art in 1952, "15 Americans," and had an exhibition in Paris at the Studio Paul Facchetti. Pollock was gaining renown and nowhere could Peggy find references to her role in his career. Despite the fact that she had not lifted a finger to help the Pollocks financially after she left New York, during which time they suffered great hardship, Peggy was annoyed. "It is a great pity," she wrote Clement Greenberg, "that Lee never sees to it that the facts of Pollocks exhibitions are put straight."

Beginning in 1954, after more than a decade of remarkable fecundity, Pollock suffered a period of inactivity brought on partly by the success of his poured paintings and a desire to do something new. Between 1950 and 1953 Pollock interspersed the large, sweeping lyrical swirls that had become his trademark with primarily black paintings that expressed his inner anguish. Pollock had used heavy black lines before, but now he returned to figuration, drawing heads and faces by pouring enamel paint onto unprimed canvas, which stained the fabric and had the effect of integrating the image and the surface—a technique that presaged the work of younger painters such as Helen Frankenthaler, Kenneth Noland, and Morris Louis, who let their colors run and soak into raw canvas. If Pollock had chosen to veil his imagery before, now he let it surface, giving vent to the obsessions that were always there— men, women, sex. Pollock did not know where each work would lead him; he simply unrolled a piece of canvas on the floor and attacked it from all sides, holding a can of paint and conjuring images with flat wooden sticks and dried brushes. When he was finished, he cut the canvas where he pleased. But his public wanted more swirls and drips, not big black paintings of women. (Pollock had traded two of his black-and-white canvases to the art dealer Martha Jackson for a green Oldsmobile.)

Pollock started drinking heavily once again and sank into severe depression. His marriage to Lee Krasner suffered. In 1956 he began an affair with a high school student named Ruth Kligman, who later wrote a book called *Love Affair* about their short-lived romance. "So, she got fucked," shrugged Krasner cynically. "Once." But in the summer of 1956, Lee planned a trip to Europe as a trial separation to see, she said, if Jackson could pull himself together.

This was to be Krasner's first trip to Europe and she planned a stop in Venice, taking it for granted that Peggy would be glad to see her. "When I went to Europe, everyone here knew what the schedule would be. I was going to Paris first, then Venice, then London. When I arrived in Paris, on the second day I was there, I ran into the Gimpels, whom I was going to visit, and who said: 'You must come to Menèrbes [in the South of France] and then you'll go on to Peggy.' " Once in the Midi, Krasner went on, "I hadn't gotten in touch with Peggy, so I asked Charles to call her. She had a fit, and said 'No, I can't receive her.' I said to tell her that I didn't want to stay with her, but just to find me a place to stay, and she said, no, that everything in Venice was booked solid. The Gimpels, Douglas Cooper, said it was impossible, it couldn't be." Lee's friends in Europe were flabbergasted by Peggy's behavior. All her New York friends assumed that she would be staying with Peggy; in fact, it was there that they phoned her to break the news that Pollock had died August 11 at the age of forty-four in a car accident.

Pollock had crashed head-on into the trees off Fireplace Road in the Springs. His green Oldsmobile overturned and he died instantly. Ruth Kligman was injured, and a girl friend of hers, also in the car, was killed. Clement Greenberg sought to tell Peggy first and have her break the news to Krasner. "I told someone in Paris to tell Peggy and the story got back she said, So what?" In fact, Peggy was relieved that Krasner had not been with her when Pollock died and admitted as much to Greenberg. As to the death of the painter she considered the greatest since Picasso, Peggy said, "I didn't give a damn." However, according to Krasner, Peggy did eventually write her a "lovely note, saying that she knew Jackson wouldn't have gotten anywhere without me."

Peggy, who could be generous and gracious in some instances, could be callous and cruel in others. Guitou Knoop, an artist who knew

Peggy, remembered that "I called up from a phone booth in Venice. I was dizzy, very sick, just off a ship where I'd been given a pill and some whiskey, and the combination was terrible. I said: 'Peggy, I'm very sick. Can you help me find a place to stay while this wears off?' and she said: 'Sorry, but I have no time for sick people,' and hung up." In general, those people who found Peggy most generous or got along best with her were those who needed her the least.

Her children needed her more than most other people. In 1955, Sindbad's marriage to Jacqueline Ventadour finally came apart. They were not getting along well and Sindbad was doing too much drinking. Nobody had really paid attention to how much Jacqueline admired her brother-in-law, Jean Hélion, until it became obvious that Hélion and Jacqueline were very much in love and wanted to be married. Hélion was drained, physically and emotionally, from living with Pegeen, whose mental illness was becoming more and more apparent. Said Peggy matter-of-factly, "Pegeen and Sindbad neglected their husbands and wives badly and naturally Hélion and Jacqueline got together." Sindbad became depressed and gave up his literary magazine. (After a period of despondency, Sindbad met and married Peggy Angela Yeomans in 1957, but Peggy couldn't be bothered to meet the bride or go to the wedding.)

Pegeen, who had believed that her husband would go on forever forgiving her flagrant infidelities, was shattered. Her affair with Tancredi was winding down. He was becoming too crazy (he followed her to Paris and beat her up) and Pegeen could not make up her mind whether to break with him while still carrying on an affair with another artist, Takis. Tancredi fell out with Peggy, saying that she was cannibalizing his professional and emotional life and threatening to sue her for artistic domination, and became the protégé of Beatrice Monte, a Milanese art dealer. He finally married a Swedish woman with whom he had two children, and moved to Rome, where he committed suicide in 1964 by flinging himself into the Tiber. "He was mad, oh, completely mad," Peggy exclaimed. "I met him in the street one day, and he was so strange, and so queer he hardly knew me, and his mother had been in a loony bin."

Pegeen came to Venice with four-year-old Nicolas and stayed with her mother for a year, after which she found an apartment of her own, the first of several. Peggy hoped that Pegeen would choose an aristocrat for her next fling. But instead of finding a duke, Pegeen began a stormy relationship with a New Realist painter, Ralph Rumney, whom Peggy detested on sight.

Rumney, the son of the Vicar of Wakefield, was bright and quite literate, but not exactly the Englishman Peggy had in mind. He was a man with an unpredictable temper. At parties, people would steer clear of him, and he was never popular with Pegeen's family or friends.

Pegeen's stepsister, Bobbie Cowling, called him a "horror," an "extremely weak, neurotic person. . . . I always disliked Ralph." Her husband John found him a "complete caricature of a ridiculous Englishman."

Peggy made Pegeen's life miserable because of Rumney. She refused to see him or have him in her house and complained about him to all her friends. Even after Pegeen had a son by Rumney, born in 1958 (named Sandro, he was listed in Venetian archives as the son of "an unknown mother," so that he could take his father's name), Peggy continued to despise Rumney, refusing even to visit Pegeen in the hospital. Then, to make matters worse, shortly after the birth, when Pegeen's divorce from Hélion became final, she "married this awful creature whom I couldn't stand," Peggy complained, "whom I absolutely loathed and . . . that sort of broke up our relationship, because I wouldn't see him and then she wouldn't see me for ages."

Pegeen moved back to Paris in 1959 with Rumney, who felt the atmosphere there would be better for his painting. To avoid confrontations, Pegeen rented an apartment in Venice, where she could stay with her husband and go by herself to visit her mother.

THE BARCHESSA

Peggy continued buying art, including works by Tancredi, his fellow Italian Edmondo Bacci, and the painters Bill Congdon and Alan Davie. The palazzo became crowded as little by little the art encroached upon the available space, until there was none left. There were pictures in the halls, in the bathrooms, in the basement. Eventually, even the laundry room and the servants' quarters below were taken over as galleries, so that visitors walking up the steps of the museum could see the household washing being done outside in a huge vat. A Milanese architect, Enrico Peressutti, was called in at one point to design a superelevation on pilasters, meant to hover over the palazzo, but Peggy realized that the Belle Arti would never allow such a creation, so she abandoned the project. Peggy did have a pavilion, called a *barchessa,* designed to run at a ninety-degree angle to the palazzo overlooking the sculpture garden. The one-story white structure had large glass doors opening onto a covered walkway framed by six arches. Eventually it housed Peggy's Surrealist collection and one wall of Max Ernsts.

Peggy also decided to change the dark-blue walls of her sitting room to white. As work progressed on the *barchessa* and the surrounding garden, which had been left in a state of weedy neglect for years, Peggy was delighted with the presence of the strapping workmen. Nellie van

Doesburg was staying with Peggy, and John Richardson, in Venice at the time, found Nellie and Peggy both "very excited by the attractive young workmen. Each one was vying with the other, saying, 'Keep your hands off Guido.' It was very amusing to watch two aging nymphomaniacs making passes." When the work was finished, Peggy invited the young men to a celebration at a nearby restaurant at the end of which they all signed her guest book in wobbly script and Peggy added, "This is the nicest night of my life in Venice 1946–1958, Peggy Guggenheim."

For all Peggy's and Nellie's chasing after young men, their relationship toward each other remained unusually intimate. "Once Nellie passed out at Arthur Jeffress's," an art dealer who had a house in Venice, "and Peggy poured Cognac on her private parts to wake her up," declared an onlooker.

In 1951 Laurence Vail's third wife, Jean Connolly, died of cancer, and Laurence looked to Peggy once again for continuity. During the early 1950s he had several exhibitions of his collage bottles in Venice and was a frequent guest of his former wife. Laurence had not changed over the years. He remained the irrepressible, charming bohemian. "He couldn't settle down to anything," said Clement Greenberg. "He was not an alcoholic, but he was a big boozer. I saw him in Paris," sometime in the late fifties, "and there he was in the bars with the latest generation of artists."

Clover Vail was introduced to a whole range of experience tagging along with Laurence. "I spent so many drunken nights with my father in Venice. Late one night, he loses the key to Peggy's house and he tries to push me over the wall, and some police officers scuttle us away. . . . We end up sitting in a bar and some Algerians pick us up and take us to a whorehouse, where we spend the night. The next day, he gets up all fluttery when he realizes where I've spent the night and tells me to get up and get dressed. It was scary, too."

Clover was uneasy at Peggy's house.

I was scared of Peggy, actually. Once she called me into her bedroom to give me a book, one of those books on Venice where the pictures stick up. She jumped out of bed completely nude to reach the book and the butler came in and she stood there nude discussing with him what to have for lunch. She always went around with hardly any clothes on. She had a crocheted dress with holes in it. You could see her body underneath.

One afternoon, I was put in one of the bedrooms to take a nap . . . and I opened the bathroom, which also opened on the other side, and I saw a naked young man huddled there. . . . I was so frightened . . . I remembered moaning and groaning. I got on all fours and crawled in under a vanity table. I was so afraid of seeing that man again. I didn't want to go to dinner. Finally, I went and kept my head down through dinner.

Clover recalled Tancredi as "the first person I ever fell in love with. I felt he, too, was this poor little wisp who fell in this destructive atmosphere. And my father was pushing me and Peggy was pushing me, and Pegeen, and I was very frightened. Fortunately I resisted. . . . There was a heightened sexual state that always seemed to be in that place. . . . I used to walk around Venice alone to get away from that place."

But for all the emphasis on sexuality, Peggy could be almost prudish about other people's behavior. "I had many fights with her," said Pegeen's eldest son, Fabrice, "about my sexual affairs. When I was twelve —I have the sentimentality of my mother—I fell in love with a Venetian girl called Manuela. She was of low-class society. . . . I needed the help of the gondolier to sneak the girl into my room. I remember my grandmother knocking furiously on the door. 'What are you doing?' " Peggy was used to a sexual banter intended to shock, but it was a Surrealist attitude, a pose. "In a way, [the Surrealists] became bourgeois themselves. You could never ask, 'Did you have an orgasm, What did he do?' " observed Arthur Gold. "She was of a curious generation, if one can ever generalize, that went through the release from Puritanism and found the young people around her much freer than she had ever meant to be." Nevertheless, Peggy was not a typical grandmother. Fabrice asked her what she liked most and Peggy answered, "To make love on the terrace." To David, Pegeen's second son, Peggy said, "The best thing is to make love in the garden."

David, however, saw through Peggy's pose. "I felt this person was very lonely. She couldn't trust people. She would ask herself, Who are they? What do they want?" She was constantly protecting herself from people by keeping them at a distance and off balance. She was the kind of person with whom one had to renew a connection every time one saw her. Ruth Ford remembered that on her visits to Venice Peggy was always gracious, very generous and kind, but "one never really felt quite at home with her. I felt in awe of her, too. You didn't quite know when she was going to be nice." Christina Thoresby, who knew her for years, had the same feeling: "You were never quite sure whether she wanted you there or not." Peggy could be ill at ease at her own party. Or, if she had too much to drink, a terrible streak of aggressiveness could burst out. She would pick fights with her guests over imagined little slights. Her grandson David Hélion added, "She could be nice and she could be mean, only it was more important for her to be in control."

Peggy was terribly concerned with the outward show of behavior. "I hate bad manners," she declared emphatically. She loathed, for example, being addressed as "Peggy" by those who barely knew her. Vestiges of her extremely "proper" upbringing in old New York cropped up when things were not quite comme il faut. No saucers under fingerbowls upset her. Vulgar gossip when not her own could annoy her. She once stopped Jane Rylands, an American living in Venice who became her great friend in later life, in midsentence, saying, "You do say the most appalling things!" On the other hand, Peggy was capable of behavior that no *grande dame* would likely indulge in. "Do you have the clap?" she asked of her friend John Goodwin. Or rushing into the bathroom even when it was occupied, lifting her skirts, exclaiming: "I can't wait. I can't wait!"

Yet almost everything she did was with an eye to its effect. Like Duchamp (and probably from Duchamp) she learned how to fan the flames of an enigmatic fame. "She knew exactly what her image was," observed her grandson Nicolas. She enjoyed talking to reporters and collected every scrap of newsprint about herself in large, overstuffed albums.

For Peggy's birthday in 1959, Alan Ansen, a wildly eccentric poet who dressed all in red (he was a friend of the Beat writers Jack Kerouac, Gregory Corso, Allen Ginsberg, and William Burroughs), dedicated a performance of his masque *Return from Greece* in honor of fellow poet James Merrill and his friend David Jackson. It was the first of three Ansen masques (with music by Frank Amey) performed in Peggy's garden. John Bernard Myers acted as master of ceremonies and Paolo Barozzi, who would soon be Peggy's secretary, had a role as "Garbage Man." Ansen played the role of "Venice." The rehearsals were more like cocktail parties punctuated by heated arguments.

"Peggy was very chintzy," remarked Myers of the experience. Merrill and Ansen made up the guest list of eighty or ninety people, "which Peggy went through and cut down to twenty-five. She pooh-poohed all the people they wanted, and passed out sandwiches—dreadful, vile, dry, icky sandwiches. The guests left in forty-five minutes. It was the kind of thing that needed more people. She picked up nine bottles out of a case Jimmy Merrill had sent her of good whiskey and she served the rest. The next year she asked Alan to do it again and she invited more people who all came in evening clothes, probably everybody staying at the Gritti or Cipriani, so she could sell her paintings." Merrill wrote in her guest book, "until next year—*or* save a bottle of Scotch!"

Peggy felt very much at home with Venice's expatriate homosexual community, who livened up the social scene. One of Peggy's best friends among them was Arthur Jeffress, who ran the Hanover Gallery in London with Erica Brausen. Jeffress, who was known for his impeccable taste and "savage mysogyny," rode around Venice in his private gondola with his gondoliers dressed in white and papal yellow. He kept a beautifully appointed house in Venice, full of lovely antiques and liveried servants, and wore a ring full of poison, which he described as his "emergency exit." A traditionalist, he chided Peggy, who appeared to him the eternal flapper, a perennial twenties girl, for her taste in modern art.

By 1962, however, the homosexual community of Venice, including the extravagant Ansen, Jeffress, and Robert Brady, was expelled by the authorities. At that time, said Peter Lauritzen, "the chief of police and the *questare* had two bêtes noirs—Communists and queers."

Ruth Ford recalled that Jeffress "had a cabaña on the Lido, and he would come every day in his gondola. . . . Arthur's cabaña was right next door to the mayor of Venice, and one day, I think . . . a lot of gossip and bitchery was going on and a lot of things were said about the mayor's wife, who overheard, and subsequently Arthur Jeffress would not be let back into Venice."

With the expulsion of so many of Peggy's friends (and Jeffress's subsequent suicide), some of the gilt came off Venetian life; the grander and more amusing parties came to an end. A pall was cast over the remaining expatriates, who never knew if they, too, might become displeasing to the local authorities. Peggy herself ran the risk of being expelled if she were too outrageous and in the end she harbored a bitterness, saying, "The Venetians don't deserve Venice."

CONFESSIONS OF
AN ART ADDICT

Something happened to Peggy in 1959. She let her hair go gray. "The moment she stopped dyeing her hair," observed Mary McCarthy, "was a watershed. It is clear she made some sort of life decision then that the hair was a sign of." Going from boot-black hair to a natural white softened Peggy's face, and her features seemed to relax. Her personality, as well, seemed to soften and become less aggressive, less strident. Although older, Peggy seemed prettier.

Peggy hated snow and cold, but that winter she went to visit Laurence in Mégève. He had managed to fall out a window ("tight in the night") the previous autumn and had hurt his head and, as Peggy phrased it, "his balls." Recovering from the accident, he found Peggy's visit touchingly sweet.

Peggy told Laurence of her intention to return to New York for the opening of the Solomon R. Guggenheim Museum. After fifteen years of work on the plans and discussions with the quixotic Baroness Rebay, who approached him for something "organic, refined, sensitive to space," Frank Lloyd Wright looked forward to the completion of his controversial, spiral cocoon for Solomon's collection of modern art. It was the culmination of Hilla Rebay's dream, a permanent museum dedicated to the kind of art that she loved, designed by one of the century's architectural geniuses, and bearing the name of the man who had made it possible. Wright wrote Hilla, "the building is built *for* you around you." And it was the architectural sensation of the year. The most avant-garde building in New York, it still sits like an enormous flying saucer fallen in among the staid apartment houses on Fifth Avenue. "It looks like a giant Mix-Master. Take it down," exclaimed Frederick Kiesler, and Peggy liked to call it "Uncle Solomon's garage."

In June 1959, two months before the scheduled opening of the museum (intended to coincide with the architect's ninetieth birthday), Frank Lloyd Wright died. Solomon had been dead since 1949 and Hilla Rebay had been replaced as director by James Johnson Sweeney. When the baroness stepped aside, she left behind a legacy of eccentricity and excess that the museum was hard pressed to live down. "I used to agree with Hilla's detractors," said the subsequent director of the museum, Thomas Messer, "but I changed my mind completely. The quality in the collection is there because of Hilla. One must give Hilla her due."

Peggy arrived in New York in April, on her way back to Venice from Mexico. She was met by her cousin Harry Guggenheim, at one time ambassador to Cuba and the elder statesman of the Guggenheim family, whom Peggy had not seen for thirty-five years. Harry was proud of the museum, but he was at the same time uneasy about—and even deeply offended by—its modernist direction. It seemed that the Guggenheims could not shake the stigma of being parvenus, and as such they often worried excessively about appearances. Because the museum was not yet open, Harry personally escorted Peggy around Wright's spiraling galleries that reminded Peggy, fresh from Mexico, of an evil serpent. It also brought to mind, as she became woozy going around the ramps, of her experience with the dictatorial Frederick Kiesler, who cared more about his architectural innovations than about the pictures that they were meant to serve.

Peggy was flattered by the attention from Harry. For years she used to say that she was not a real Guggenheim, being nowhere nearly as rich as her cousins and certainly not as rich as Harry, whose father, Daniel, had masterminded the Guggenheim brothers' rise to riches. As much as she reacted against her family, it was still on their terms that Peggy wanted to prove herself.

Peggy was almost sixty-one years old and the question of who would inherit her collection was on people's minds. She owned one of the largest and most important private collections of modern art in the world. Thomas Messer, who became director of the Guggenheim in 1961, said, "I do not know of a single collection that was as distinguished." But Peggy had not announced any definite plans for it after her death, although she liked to dangle it as a plum in front of various museum directors. In a letter, Harry referred to his hope that the collection should ultimately rest at the Solomon R. Guggenheim Museum on Fifth Avenue. But upon reflection, he concluded that its proper home was Venice and the palazzo on the Grand Canal. During Peggy's New York visit the subject was raised, of leaving the collection to the Guggenheim, and Peggy departed impressed with the family institution, its power, and its money.

Staying at the Reises' spacious New York town house, Peggy saw Lee Krasner, Jimmy Ernst, Djuna Barnes, and Charles Seliger. Zachary Scott and Ruth Ford gave a party for her. "Zachary and I used to adore to give parties," said Ruth Ford, "and at this one there were a lot of artists and people like that, and I lost sight of Peggy. I kept looking around for her, and finally there she was, sitting in the basin of the bathroom, surrounded by people."

Peggy also attended a cocktail party at the home of collector Ben Heller, where she saw Pollock's sixteen-foot-long *Blue Poles,* an allover layering of enamel and aluminum paint, with black poles shooting up from the bottom to the top. Peggy reflected that everything had changed. She found nothing to inspire her in the art of the moment and thought the art world crass and commercial. Americans, she suggested, "are ready to accept anything in the name of culture, which is now as much of an American must as eating, sleeping, lovemaking and, of course, drinking." She criticized the new breed of collectors, conjuring up "images of fat, rich millionaires trying to dodge taxes or be socially in." Going about to the galleries, what really impressed her was the prices commanded by artists whom she had sold little more than a decade earlier for a few hundred dollars. She was offered a Brancusi head for forty-five thousand dollars and remembered how she had quibbled over paying the sculptor four thousand dollars for his *Bird.* "Most painters think only of money," she claimed. "The boom has ruined art."

The art world had left her behind. She didn't understand the cool black-and-white paintings of Frank Stella, the soft hamburgers of Claes Oldenburg, Jasper Johns's bronzed beer cans and targets. Pop Art left her cold. "This whaddayacallit, phooey." Jasper Johns and Robert Rauschenberg she said she liked. "They're pre-pop," she explained. "I wanted to buy Rauschenberg's goat with a tire around it for my grandchildren," but she never did buy anything by them, even when Rauschenberg won the 1964 Venice Biennale prize for painting. As far as Peggy was concerned the twentieth century ended with Jackson Pollock. Even the worldly Duchamp was a trifle uncomfortable with the latter-day Dada of Pop Art and liked to quote Marx: Everything repeats itself, the first time as tragedy, the second as comedy.

What really inhibited Peggy was the money. She simply did not have fifty thousand dollars to spend on a painting. Robert Brady suggested that she buy primitive art instead, and while in New York Peggy acquired a number of African and Oceanic sculptures, which she subsequently perched above the bookcases in her Venetian sitting room, re-creating the atmosphere popular in the 1920s when Breton and the Surrealists collected African masks. She still bought paintings occasionally, those she understood. She bought a 1939 Picasso gouache, *Bust of a Man in a Striped Jersey,* a 1958 de Kooning, a Tamayo oil, a picture by Leonora Carrington, two sculptures by Max Ernst. As the decade wore on, she acquired a Victor Vasarely (purchased for her at auction in London by the director of the Tate, Sir Norman Reid), a Mark Tobey, a Sam Francis, and a great many Italian artists, including Piero Dorazio, Arnoldo Pomodoro, Ludovico De Luigi, Manfredo Massironi, and thirty-five sculptures by another "protégé," Edigio Constantini, who worked in blown Venetian glass and reproduced in it the works of Ernst, Miró, and others. In 1961, the artist Claire Falkenstein designed and installed a massive black iron gate encrusted with heavy multicolored glass drops for the San Gregorio entrance of Peggy's palazzo. (A picture of it subsequently graced the cover of Peggy's catalogues.)

Generally speaking, the later acquisitions in Peggy's collection are not of the same quality as those pieces that she bought with the help and advice of Duchamp or Breton or Ernst or Putzel or Nellie. After all, said Arthur Gold, "her taste was always other people's taste." "She did buy some valuable European pictures," said Thomas Messer, of Peggy's collecting in later years. "Some are knick knacks." During the 1940s in New York and Paris, Peggy had been collecting the past, pictures that had been around for twenty years.

The European paintings Peggy bought were already history when she bought them, just as Alfred Barr was doing, presenting them as novelty in New York to a public who was unaware of them. Hilla Rebay was doing the same thing buying Kandinsky. Kandinsky was not an unknown painter. There was a gap between what was established and what was known here. What happens with a number of collectors, like Peggy, Hilla, is that because they have so successfully bought the past they think they can peer into the future. In New York, Peggy was heavily advised. Peggy must be given credit for her advisors. If she found good advisors she could also have found a fool.

Moreover, said Messer, "Not everything she bought here was good. . . . America emerged as an art center after the Second World War. She did catch some of the major figures, although not always their major work. She was there when they were in formation. Nobody can foretell when they buy modern art."

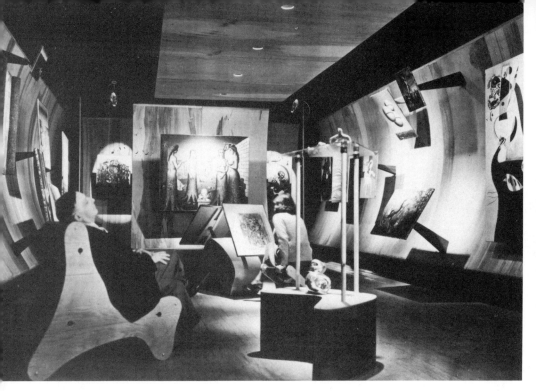

(ABOVE) *Frederick Kiesler seated in one of his seven-way chairs in the sensational Surrealist Gallery at Art of this Century, with its curved gumwood walls and paintings mounted on cantilevered arms.* (Berenice Abbott)

(BELOW) *The Abstract Gallery, with pictures suspended on rope, sinuous aquamarine canvas walls, and turquoise floors. Wassily Kandinsky's 1922* White Cross *is in the right foreground, and Antoine Pevsner's* Cross in the Form of an Anchor *is on the left pedestal.* (Berenice Abbott)

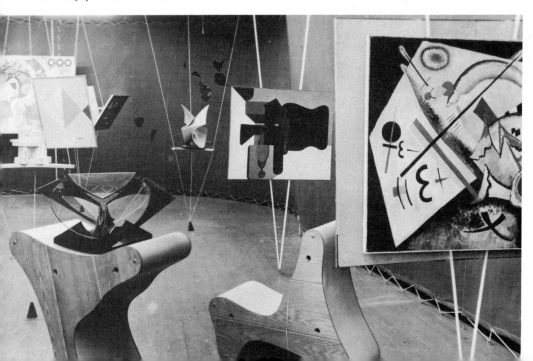

(ABOVE) *Looking through the peephole
in the Kinetic Gallery, dubbed "Coney
Island" by some reviewers who saw
Kiesler's wheel as a hokey sideshow.*

(RIGHT) *Kenneth Macpherson with whom
Peggy fell hopelessly in love.*

*(ABOVE) Peggy in front of one of
Pegeen's works
at the Daylight Gallery.*

*(LEFT) Sindbad's first wife,
Jacqueline Ventadour, holding their
firstborn, Clovis.*

(ABOVE) *Jackson Pollock and Lee Krasner in Pollock's East Hampton studio.*
(Lawrence Larkin; courtesy Guild Hall Museum, East Hampton)

(OPPOSITE) *Newlyweds Pegeen and Jean Hélion in New York.*

(ABOVE) *Peggy's uncle Solomon, Hilla Rebay, and Frank Lloyd Wright in front of a Bauer painting. (Ben Greenhaus; courtesy The Solomon R. Guggenheim Museum)*

(OPPOSITE, TOP) *Peggy at the opening of her pavilion at the 1948 Venice Biennale greeting Italian President Luigi Einaudi. The Calder mobile that children liked to swing on hangs in the foreground.*

(RIGHT) *A heefy Raoul Gregoritch lounging with Peggy's Lhasa Apsos, Emily and White Angel, on the roof terrace of the Palazzo Venier dei Leoni in Venice, 1950.*

(ABOVE) *A suntanned Peggy on the terrace overlooking the Grand Canal.*

(OPPOSITE) *Peggy and Pegeen on the steps leading to the Grand Canal with yet another litter of Lhasa Apsos. (Milton Gendel)*

Peggy in her favorite Fortuny dress on her bed with the silver headboard designed by Alexander Calder, circa 1960. (Roloff Beny; courtesy The Solomon R. Guggenheim Museum)

(*TOP, LEFT*) *Peggy and the painter Joan Miró on her roof.*

(*TOP, RIGHT*) *Peggy in the Barchessa. (Jerry Harpur)*

(*ABOVE*) *Peggy showing off her sitting room on the Grand Canal.*

(TOP) *Peggy's greatest triumph, the exhibition*
of her collection at London's prestigious
Tate Gallery. (Left to right) Roloff Beny, Peggy,
her cousin Rosemary Seligman. (Desmond O'Neill)

(BOTTOM) *Peggy, in Surrealistic glasses, looks*
through her meticulously kept scrapbook, 1971.

(OPPOSITE) *Peggy and her Brancusi bird,* Maiastra.

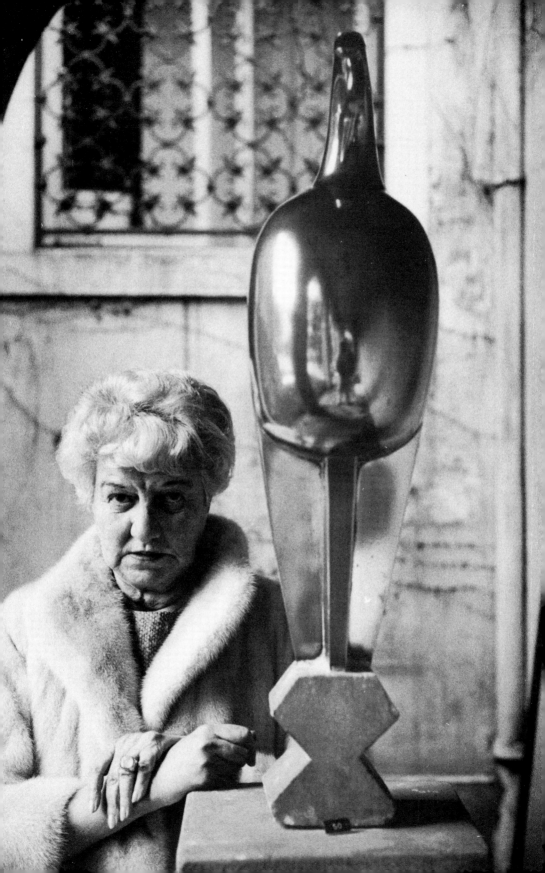

(OPPOSITE) *Peggy surrounded by treasures in the Barchessa.*

(ABOVE) *Sindbad, his second wife, Peggy Angela, and his four children, Julia, Clovis, Mark, and Carol.*

(LEFT) *John Hohnsbeen, Peggy's last curator, in his all-white apartment, circa 1955.*

Peggy's own montage of her passport photographs through the years.

In keeping with her newfound image as a graying *grande dame* of modern art, Peggy decided it was time to redo her memoirs. She had been uncomfortable with them as early as 1949, when she wrote Charles Seliger, "I am considering rewriting my book of memoirs as I have an offer to have it translated into Italian and possibly French, but in its present state I would rather throw it into the canal." Nicholas Bentley, an English friend of Peggy and a partner in the publishing house of André Deutsch, urged her to revise the book. Fourteen years had passed since *Out of This Century* initially appeared and she had a lot more to tell. Besides, she could present herself more seriously in this second book than in the first with its breathless recitation of affairs and loves. Roloff Beny captured Peggy in one of his many photographs of her, hands on her typewriter keys, laughing gaily, demurely dressed in a tailored suit that bespoke the new image she wanted to project.

Confessions of an Art Addict came out in 1960. It was *Out of This Century* brought up to date, toned down and edited, with some of the real names revealed. In it Peggy tried to emphasize her role in buying and promoting modern art. Instead of pages devoted to Laurence stepping on her stomach, or Max Ernst absconding with Dorothea Tanning, Peggy concentrated on her life as a patron. Ernst and Tanning received barely a paragraph. Unfortunately, the book was not nearly as much fun as the original, but it did bring the "Bohemian of Venice" once again to the attention of the public through the endless articles and reviews of the book as well as the personal appearances of its author. *Confessions of an Art Addict* did not give rise to the ferocious criticisms of the earlier book, but neither did it earn any kudos. It fell, rather, with a dull thud.

A line in her newly rewritten autobiography, however, eventually settled the brewing dispute between Peggy and Lee Krasner. After Jackson Pollock's untimely death his legend grew, proving once again the old adage that the best thing an artist can do for his career is to die. It was an era of brooding rebels—epitomized in the movies by Marlon Brando and James Dean—and Pollock's image as the troubled loner, a cigarette burning at the corner of his mouth, tortured by despair and the bottle, had been captured in photographs by Hans Namuth. This image of the artist as rebel promoted by an art press eager for romance became inseparable from the work itself. As the years wore on, prices for Pollock's works began to soar. Whereas during his lifetime, he never sold a picture for more than eight thousand dollars, after his death *Blue Poles,* purchased by Ben Heller for a few thousand dollars, sold for two million. Peggy watched Pollock's growing reputation with mingled pride and envy. When she left New York, she had never sold a Pollock for more than a thousand dollars, and even at that she had to cajole and argue. Now, without her, he and the other Abstract Expressionists had taken off.

It rankled Peggy that she had given away so many Pollocks—at least ten since she arrived in Italy! Rather than selling her Pollocks, Lee Krasner had kept them in a vault. That Lee, the once-starving consort to a genius, was now a millionaire infuriated Peggy. In addition, Krasner was gaining recognition as an artist in her own right, at last emerging from Pollock's shadow. (When Lee Krasner died in 1984, she left an estate valued at more than ten million dollars.)

Peggy was sure that she saw Pollocks springing up "all over the place, all the time," which should have been hers under the terms of her 1946 contract with Pollock. The contract had stipulated that Peggy was to receive "all the works of art" created by the painter during the contract's life, in exchange for three hundred dollars a month and the two-thousand-dollar loan to buy the house in the Springs. In 1957, Peggy had noticed in a traveling exhibition in Rome a 1947 drawing, *War,* that she had never seen before. Peggy began to scrutinize catalogues of Pollock exhibitions and to suspect and, indeed, hope that Krasner had kept back gouaches, studies, and notebooks, and possibly even a painting, created during the period covered by her contract with Pollock.

Finally, Peggy could bear it no longer. She went to New York in June 1961 and filed a lawsuit against Lee Krasner as executrix of the Jackson Pollock estate in Federal District Court, asking damages of one hundred and twenty-two thousand dollars and demanding all artworks in Krasner's possession dating from the contract period of March 1946 through March 1948, alleging that she was deceived and defrauded out of fifteen works of art, including oils, gouaches, ink, and crayon, owed under the terms of her contract with Pollock. Moreover, Peggy alleged, at the time of Pollock's death Lee had come into possession of artworks that were rightfully Peggy's and that Lee had retained, and that at least on one painting, *Vortex,* Krasner had falsified the date by erasing it and substituting another.

Bernard Reis, with whom Peggy stayed for four weeks, urged her to settle with Krasner out of court. Peggy had an argument with Reis over his not doing enough about her suit against Pollock, and she left in a huff to stay at a hotel. Part of her anger may have been attributable to Reis's advice that she give away Pollocks as tax deductions.

Peggy also alienated Betty Parsons. "For one week she sat in the gallery looking at the books. I was furious she thought that I would cheat her. It was outrageous. I don't know why she was so suspicious. I certainly don't think Lee ever hid a painting from her. They never really liked each other. Peggy had quite a yen for Pollock and Lee made her nervous. She was very suspicious." Parsons attributed Peggy's behavior to jealousy of the New York School, pure and simple.

Krasner said, "Her behavior sickened me. She was such a champion of Pollock that she never bought three cents' worth after she had left. Later, she couldn't believe the prices. . . . She goes into her own world and wakes up to the money the pictures are worth and the way she acts it out—she's a killer, a real killer." At issue in the case were "works of art" not exhibited in any of Pollock's annual shows and claimed by Krasner to be mostly small, in two cases, scraps, in others doodles, and in one, a Christmas card. Were it not for Pollock's posthumous fame, Lee alleged, these items would have been worthless. As far as she was concerned, Peggy had received more than a fair bargain for her investment, getting twenty-eight Pollock oils for seventy-two thousand dollars.

During this period of acrimony, Lee burst a capillary in her brain and was admitted to the hospital with a hemorrhage. Friends blamed the situation on her distress over Peggy's lawsuit. "The trial," said Krasner, "was harassing. She was a real bitch, bitch, bitch. The suit was originally against Pollock and Lee Krasner, but she changed that so it was just against *me.*"

Philip Rylands, who became the administrator of her collection, tried to explain Peggy's attitude by saying, "If she thought she had been tricked . . . she'd be ruthless in a way. I'm sure that is the way it worked with Lee Krasner and Jackson Pollock." Peggy admitted that it had not been very nice of her to sue Krasner, but, she added, "I hate Lee, if you can hate a crook. I hate her . . . millions of things turned up signed '1947,' gouache . . . I kept finding things . . . all kinds of oil paintings, all kinds of things were done in 1947." Pressed, Peggy admitted that she did not really believe that Krasner had actually hidden pictures from her: "I think they just just sold things from that year that they shouldn't have. I found things all over the place."

The suit dragged on without resolution for four years until in the end it was settled out of court. Peggy's case sank on the basis of one casual line included in *Confessions of an Art Addict.* Describing Pollock's first show with Betty Parsons, Peggy wrote about his unsold pictures, "All the rest were sent to me, according to the contract, at Venice, where I had gone to live." Charges of wrongdoing against Krasner were dropped and Peggy accepted in settlement a pair of Pollocks then worth four hundred dollars.

A TRAVELING COLLECTION

John Cage had become one of the world's leading composers of avant-garde music, influencing an entire generation of painters and poets with his ideas on chance and silence. In May 1958 he was honored by a twenty-five-year retrospective of his music in New York City's Town Hall. That summer Cage was invited to Milan, where he spent four months composing a work called *Fontana Mix* on magnetic tape. He and Peggy had long since become reconciled, and now that he was in Italy he came to see her.

Cage had become something of a television celebrity during his visit to Italy. He appeared on an Italian quiz show called *"Lascia o Raddoppia"* *(Double or Nothing),* for the last five weeks of his stay. Said John Cage,

My subject was mushrooms, and I said I would do it if they chose one book from which they formed the questions. I gave them three books, and they chose one. . . . I went to Venice with the book and studied it on the train. . . . There was only one channel for TV so the whole country enjoyed it. I became very famous. When I would go for a walk with Peggy and all her dogs, people would point to me and her and she said, "I recognize you're even more famous than I!"

Cage did very well on the program, winning six thousand dollars for answering all the questions correctly. He also played his unusual compositions for the television audience. One he called *Sounds of Venice* —sounds recorded while visiting Peggy's palazzo.

Cage remarked that "the big pleasure for me in visiting Peggy was actually being with her and walking . . . being alone with her when you could converse." Cage found Peggy always interesting and Venice, though beautiful, a curious choice for an active woman who had been so important in New York. "My impression was the basic Venetian society wasn't always really interesting. What made it so boring was that you saw the same people at lunch and then at dinner. . . . It was like an obligation, a fact of nature rather than a choice, same as in Cadaqués, when I visited Marcel [Duchamp] and Teeny."

Cage returned to Venice in 1960 with the choreographer Merce Cunningham, and Peggy gave a party for Cage, Cunningham, dancer Carolyn Brown, and pianist David Tudor in September. When in the fall of 1962 Cage was invited to go to Japan with David Tudor, Peggy went along. It was important for Peggy to find something amusing to do as winter approached. Yoko Ono, the future wife of Beatle John Lennon, acted as interpreter on the Japanese trip, and frequently she and Peggy shared a room. At that time Yoko Ono was married to a musician on the tour, but was followed everywhere by an American, Tony Cox, who crept into her room at night with Peggy's approval. Peggy, who loved nothing more than amorous adventures, said Cage, "was in on all the details of the switch from Toshi to Tony Cox." Yoko confided to Peggy that "John Cage was going to propose marriage to me but he didn't because he went back to his friend again, whom he always adored all his life, the dancer." Later on, Peggy liked to joke that she had considered marrying the composer, "but then, I thought of the electric bills" for his electronic music.

In 1962 Paolo Barozzi became Peggy's secretary. He wrote letters, translated, and gave tours of the collection to visitors. Three times a week, when the palazzo was open to the public, he was there collecting money for the catalogues or watching that no one strolled away with a picture. Peggy still maintained a sales gallery in the basement (Pegeen called it her "bargain basement"), where she dealt a few things, mostly pictures by Pegeen, Tancredi, Edmondo Bacci, and sometimes Laurence Vail. Peggy joked that her greatest expense in running it was gin—to soften up the customers. She paid Barozzi sixty thousand lira a month, the equivalent of about seventy-five dollars.

Like all of Peggy's secretaries, Barozzi found it "very difficult to be near her," although it was educational, to be sure. She had a marvelous library and famous people were constantly dropping by, but an increase in intimacy brought with it a sense of being cannibalized. No matter how much time he spent with her, she made Barozzi feel guilty if he went off without her. "That possessiveness she has," said Barozzi, "is like a sickness. She sucks you dry and gives nothing in return. She doesn't even know that she could give something. She does not have an inner life. She takes from other people. Finally," he exclaimed, after three years, "I couldn't take it anymore."

In a similar vein, the director of the Guggenheim Museum, Thomas Messer, observed of Peggy, "She only existed as a reflection of other people. The ultimate tragedy was her essential nonexistence, and because of this she needed a sense of self from other people. . . . The question of this insubstantiality made her irritating and jumpy. I was afraid of her moods. I've known her for a long time and our relationship was always tenuous."

Peggy accepted with alacrity an invitation by the Tate Gallery in London to exhibit her collection for five weeks in 1965. Behind the Tate's offer was the expectation that Peggy could be persuaded to leave her collection to them. Sir Norman Reid, the director of the Tate, who had met Peggy for the first time at the 1948 Biennale, recalled that Peggy began talking about the disposition of her collection soon after that. Publicly, Reid denied and took affront at press suggestions that the Tate was vying for the legacy of a patron so very much alive. But privately he admitted as much and Herbert Read, who soon thereafter was appointed a trustee of the Tate, joked with Peggy that he had been appointed to look after "her" interests.

The invitation from the Tate was perceived by Peggy as an enormous honor. For the first time since she opened her palazzo to the public in 1951, practically her entire collection was crated and sent out of Italy. One hundred eighty-seven pictures, sculptures, and Oceanic and primitive sculptures were sent to London. The Marini horseman remained in Venice, as Peggy deemed it unsuitable for inclusion in the exhibition. What if the queen were to visit? Out of courtesy, the Tate conservators cleaned and restored Peggy's artworks, which were beginning to show the effects of fourteen years of salty breezes off the Grand Canal.

Peggy traveled to London in, as Laurence Vail observed to his girl friend, Yvonne Hagen, "a blaze of glory as the Queen of Modern Art." The Tate made a great fuss over Peggy. "We put out the red carpet for her," said Sir Norman Reid. Indeed, for the private opening on New Year's Eve, hundreds of guests arrived to walk up the splendid steps of the Tate, red carpeted and canopied for the occasion. Peggy wore a blue velvet suit that she had bought in London, and was accompanied by Sindbad and his second wife, Peggy Vail. "The whole of London was there," said Marietta Stern, one of Peggy's friends from Venice who went to London for the occasion, "including Princess Margaret." Herbert Read, who had recently celebrated his seventieth birthday, was there, as were Hazel and Pegeen. On another evening the Tate gave Peggy a dinner party in the gallery for about twenty people. As Marietta Stern described the event, "They emptied the whole ground floor. There was a buffet with low, round tables, yellow daffodils and candles." "We borrowed splendid silver and china for it," said Reid. "And one of our guests suddenly exclaimed, 'Why it's my silver, and it's my china, and it's my butler!' " Peggy was in heaven, dressed in an ocher brocade dress made by her dressmaker in Venice.

During her visit, Peggy was besieged by interviewers and she gave journalists her opinions on Pop Art, Venice, husbands, and lovers. Dressed in a conservative tweed suit, her hair a bob with a fringe of tightly curled white bangs, Peggy, except for her sparkling silver fingernails, appeared disappointingly mundane. If she seemed Surrealistic, it was only by accident. "On one occasion," recollected Sir Norman Reid, "Peggy's hair was bright pink, by sheer mischance. Someone had brought her a red dress from Mexico. In the morning Peggy appeared with pink hair. My wife asked me if she should point it out and finally asked: 'Peggy, do you know your hair is bright pink?' She had used the Mexican dress as a towel and dried her hair with it, and it not being colorfast had dyed her hair."

Michael Glazebrook, whose job at the time was publicity director for the Tate, took Peggy around. "I was rather shocked," he remarked, "at the way everyone behaved towards Peggy Guggenheim, trying to get their hands on her collection. She was rather sulky. I did feel rather sorry for her."

The Tate devoted three large rooms and an antechamber to the collection and prepared an excellent catalogue, which later became the prototype for the catalogues that Peggy sold at her palazzo. The exhibition itself, as Peggy said, was a "terrific success" when it opened in January. It was so successful that its closing date was extended by one month from February 7 to March 7. "It is a bombshell," said one journalist, "and London is rapturous." Better than many a museum, exclaimed a Sunday newspaper. "The people were lined up all along the Thames to come into the gallery," Peggy boasted. Peggy loved seeing the bright yellow posters announcing the exhibition all over London, the city where she felt she had more friends than anywhere else. Spread out over the Tate's spacious galleries, the pictures took on a new life, appearing fantastic and striking. Peggy loved walking about the collection. "She had the touching habit," said Reid, "of coming and hearing what other people said about it."

It was the first time that Peggy's collection had been scrutinized as a whole. Peggy not only received a great deal of attention from the

British press, but in America a number of articles appeared on Peggy and her collection. To some critics the collection appeared soulless and impersonal, with an archival completeness, or predominantly strange and fantastic, with its real strength the Surrealist works. *The New York Times* quoted one art expert as saying that Peggy "has been a real influence in modern art. . . . She never had the intellectual status of Gertrude Stein but she has always had a quick unintellectual eye for interesting experiments."

Returning to the Venier dei Leoni after the heady experience of the Tate, Peggy realized the palazzo's limitations as an exhibition space. The garden, overgrown and damp, was dark and gloomy. The narrow hallways where Peggy hung works by Kandinsky, Severini, and Mondrian seemed inadequate for the pictures. The underground galleries still looked like the maids' rooms that they originally were, small and cubicular, with tiny, high, grated windows, augmented only by fluorescent lights that "squeak like mice when you turn them on" and that competed with the whirring noise from the boiler.

John Loring, the design director for Tiffany's, met Peggy around this time when she came to a party that his mother gave for her friends in Venice. There seemed to be hundreds of people about, but Peggy took an interest in the young Loring. "She was perfectly marvelous," he exclaimed. She enjoyed meeting him and thanked him profusely for including her in the party. Her parting words were, "Let's not lose each other. Of course, you're very young. You'll want to go off and find people your age. You'll go away, but you'll come back and find I am the only interesting person in this city." "And," said Loring, "she was right. There was no one of her charm, her intelligence." John Loring became very fond of Peggy. "She was all manners, politeness. Peggy was no snob. She was willing to meet anybody, go anywhere."

With the closing of the American consulate next door to Peggy in 1963, the American colony in Venice had dwindled, until Peggy could boast, "I am practically the American colony." Peggy tended to see, over and over again, the forty or so souls from the tiny Anglo-American group remaining in Venice. Christina Thoresby, one of Peggy's English friends, liked to laugh over a fiancé she and Peggy had in common—a

crazy old Count Zorzi. He used to go duck shooting with Ernest Hemingway. He was the correspondent for *Time/Life*. . . . His own mother wanted him to get married. A delegation came to see me, to ask if I would marry him. I replied: "If you had asked me ten years ago, perhaps my answer would have been different. But today it is no." However, she had made a list of other possible marriage prospects for him. The next day, his mother called up Peggy to ask her if *she* would marry him. After that Peggy would say: "Our fiancé."

Peggy impressed Thomas Schippers, the conductor, when he was in Venice. He asked Peggy, "How many husbands have you had?" "My own, or other people's?" she replied. John Goodwin stayed often with Peggy and tried to convince her that turning the lights off every five minutes was actually more expensive than leaving them on. He recalled groping his way back to his room at night in total darkness. "Once I called to say I was arriving in town with a friend, would she be able to get us a hotel room, hoping she might ask us to stay with her. But she said, '*You* can come, but your friend cannot.'" John Hohnsbeen thought, "It's the sheets she worried about. It was all right if you had someone in the same bed."

PEGEEN

Her success at the Tate encouraged Peggy to accept other offers to exhibit outside of Italy. In November 1966 Peggy was in Stockholm for the opening of her collection at the Moderna Museet. King Gustaf Adolf attended the vernissage and Peggy personally took him around the exhibition. The timing of the show proved fortunate, because several weeks earlier Venice had suffered severe flooding and the pictures, crated for shipping north, narrowly escaped immersion when the palazzo's cellar filled with water. Peggy traveled from Stockholm to Copenhagen and spent three days in the Danish capital discussing another exhibition of her collection at the Louisiana Museum for the following year. Pegeen joined her in Copenhagen and the two toured the sights together.

Peggy went to Mexico for the month of February to visit her old friend Robert Brady. She loved the sunny warmth of Mexico and the attention that she received from her adoring host. Wolf and Florine Schoenborn, rival collectors of modern art, entertained Peggy at a lunch for seventy people following a riotous costume party the night before. Peggy was having such a good time that she decided to remain an extra three weeks and went to a doctor to see if she could get a medical excuse to extend her stay without losing her prepaid round-trip excursion fare. "It was a very hot day," recalled Brady,

> and we came to the house. . . . All the mail was stacked. . . . I saw a telegram for her and she said: "Oh, my dear, you open it." I ripped it open and, I'll never forget, it said exactly: "Pegeen deceased. Come to Paris immediately. Sindbad." I turned green and faced her and she said, "Pegeen is dead." I made her a strong drink. She shed no tears. She went with the telegram into the bathroom, and she came out about ten minutes later, still not a tear. . . . I said I felt we better call Sindbad, and she said, "You can't make a collect call to Europe."

It was no easy matter to get out of Mexico. There were only two or three flights a week and they were fully booked. Brady went to Air France and explained the situation and managed to get Peggy a seat to Paris. "We still didn't know what had happened," he stated,

> but I said to Peggy: "Go back, you're on the flight in the morning." . . . [We were] still trying to get Sindbad the day after she died. I kept thinking to keep her occupied. What could she have done? She was very controlled, preoccupied with what she would find in Paris . . . very strong. We reminisced that night, had a nice dinner. I told Leopold [at Air France] that she can stay on the plane in New York to avoid the press. She got to Paris and made contact with Sindbad, wired him just before. Not a tear since the news. Leaving she said, "Thank you my dear for the last happy days of my life."

Pegeen died on March 1, 1967, at age forty-two. News of her death was not released to the press for a week, during which time the family tried to sort out the situation. Everyone knew that Pegeen had been especially troubled in the last several years. Peggy hated Pegeen's husband, Ralph Rumney, and mother and daughter went through periods when they refused to see each other. "Well," said Peggy, "I wouldn't see him, so she decided she wouldn't see me. Oh, I don't know, it went on for months. It was awful, agonizing. The whole thing. The whole situation. It was simply ghastly." John Goodwin heard the two arguing in a restaurant in Torcello, "yelling like two fishwomen. 'You took my lover!' 'You make me pay for my own meals!' The worst insults back and forth. Forty-eight hours later they were friends again. Peggy made Pegeen what she wished she could have been, but she was jealous at the same time." Pegeen complained, "Mother spends more time with her dogs than with me." And it was true that if Peggy made reference to her children and her grandchildren she meant the dogs.

Peggy manipulated both Pegeen and Sindbad with money. "She certainly gave us enough money," said Sindbad, "but she didn't teach us how to make our own." Peggy tried to help Pegeen by selling her paintings; she never forgot, however, to keep a commission for herself. Considering how much money she herself had, Peggy did give each of her children a generous allowance, which she periodically threatened to cut off. Peggy's income hovered around eighty thousand dollars a year. The children, according to Eileen Geist Finletter, got "ten to twelve thousand dollars a year income from her."

Peggy fretted that whatever amount she gave Pegeen would be gone within a week. When Pegeen wanted to buy an apartment for herself and Rumney on the Île St. Louis with a large balcony overlooking the Seine, Peggy refused to help. "It was very expensive, so Pegeen sold her Ernst to make up the difference," said Eileen Finletter. Pegeen constantly complained that she did not have enough money, that she was raising four boys, that Peggy did not come through. She was jealous of Peggy's wealth. Peggy had a beautiful sable-lined coat and Pegeen would ask, "Why can't I have a sable coat?"

"Peggy didn't care about anything much," said Buffie Johnson. "Not about her children, friends, home, lovers. Personally, I think she never gave herself to anything, and therefore she never was rewarded." Although Peggy loathed Rumney and made Pegeen suffer because of him, the kind of solid man Peggy dreamed of for her daughter, Pegeen would not have known how to talk to and would never have been attracted to.

Before her death, Pegeen's marriage to Rumney was showing signs of strain. By the end of 1966 they had decided to separate. Pegeen went up to Paris and Ralph stayed on in Venice.

In February, Rumney suddenly went up to Paris to seek a reconciliation. The filmmaker Taylor Mead, who used to hang out around La Coupole and Le Flore, saw Pegeen and Ralph loudly carrying on in various cafés for two nights in a row. They "stood out, almost too much," he said. "They really were a pair." In Le Flore, Pegeen appeared to be on drugs. "Pegeen was on everything, all kinds of stuff, yelling at the waiters, if they put something down in the wrong place. And Ralph would back her up in everything she did. At one point, I said, 'There's a wonderful tranquilizer called Nubarène,' the French Quaalude, and Ralph said, 'Oh, she has everything.' "

The next night, said Mead, "we wound up in a tourist restaurant, an anonymous restaurant because of the hysterics at the Flore. There were people at the next table, and Pegeen decided they were talking about her. She said something like 'They said I was a whore,' or 'They're talking about me,' and he immediately started shouting at them, and I said, 'Please, Pegeen, please. They're not talking about you.' I decided not to see them anymore. It was embarrassing.''

On the night she died, Pegeen had been drinking heavily and taking tranquilizers. According to Peggy, she and Ralph were arguing and talking through the night. Pegeen retired to a spare room and Ralph passed out in the bedroom. The following morning, Pegeen was found dead, lying on the floor with her arm stretched out toward the door. Half of her face was black. Ralph, who had taken Nicolas to school, found her when he came back.

Pegeen had tried to kill herself so many times (once even trying to starve herself to death) that it was natural for people to think of suicide. "Suicide. Too much to drink, pills," said Hélion. "I call that suicide." Yet she had heretofore acted with other people around to save her. This time, "Everyone was drunk," said Santomaso, who rushed to the scene when he heard the news. The technical cause of death was strangulation. She had choked on her own vomit. "Sindbad was called," said Christina Thoresby, "and Sindbad rather jumped to the conclusion that she'd committed suicide."

The French police, uninterested in pursuing the matter, held no inquest. Had Pegeen been French, perhaps their decision would have been different. Accidental drug overdose was the most obvious explanation. There was no evidence, according to both Santomaso and Sindbad, of a note scribbled in lipstick, "I hate you mother," that Pegeen was rumored to have left on the bathroom mirror.

Peggy was unshakable in the conviction, born of hatred, that Ralph Rumney had murdered Pegeen. She went so far as to suggest he could have suffocated her with a pillow or strangled her. Peggy was insisting he leave the apartment, which she had finally bought. (He suspected Peggy just really wanted to get her hands on the apartment.) Taylor Mead found Peggy's accusation ridiculous. "Ralph was incapable of anything as imaginative as murder," he said. If anyone "murdered" Pegeen, thought Hélion, it was Peggy. Peggy competed with Pegeen, but between mother and daughter there was no real contest. "How can there be when one is strong and the other weak?" asked Hélion bitterly.

Laurence Vail, who had wanted to protect Pegeen from Peggy, wrote Djuna Barnes,

> Ralph finished off Pegeen—but also Peggy is responsible. She loved Pegeen, but jealously, possessively—for over 20 years she has done all she could to break up Pegeen's relationship with whomever she was living with, husband or lover. So Pegeen had a miserable life —it was a perpetual tug of war between Peggy and the man Pegeen

was living with. Pegeen was the rope between the two. And the rope snapped.

I can't absolve Peggy. But because of Sandro [Pegeen's son by Rumney] it's up to me to be the complete hypocrite and get on with her. Peggy is out for revenge; her hostility towards Ralph seems to be stronger than her grief. And she's concerned about money—talked chiefly about money, money, money, when I saw her last. Ralph is penniless, and Peggy's main desire is that Ralph should not get a cent. This is all most sordid—sickeningly so.

Peggy felt deeply remorseful, because she thought she could have made a difference. She went over and over the circumstances of Pegeen's death. "Sindbad and Laurence once said to me," admitted Peggy, " 'You killed Pegeen,' and sometimes, I think I did. . . . I wasn't a good influence on her, wasn't good for her. We were like two sisters, friends, having lovers. She was very weak."

Clover Vail said, "You can't say where Peggy went wrong with Pegeen. Peggy was so off with Peggy . . . engrossed with herself, and like my father, rebelling against something that she never came to terms with."

Pegeen was cremated and laid to rest in a wall at the Père Lachaise cemetery in unsanctified ground. Sindbad could never forget the stench of the cremation. Peggy refused to go to Pegeen's funeral because Ralph would be there. No amount of pleading by Sindbad or his wife could dissuade her. "Not even for Sindbad's sake. She was inhumane," said Sindbad's wife, Peggy, who could not get over coming back to their house that day, where they had a "sort of wake" with Nellie van Doesburg and Laurence, and being greeted by Peggy talking on the telephone about stocks and bonds. According to Peggy Vail, Peggy said Pegeen's death was almost a relief, that she always knew it was going to happen and finally it did.

"There was no service at all," recalled Christina Thoresby. Peggy "wanted to bring back the ashes to Venice and she had two projects: to have the ashes scattered in the lagoon, or have them buried in the garden. But Venice wouldn't permit it."

After Pegeen's death, Peggy went on reviling Rumney. "Rumney was a lunatic. He was an alcoholic. He was impossible. He was hardly a human being, he was so dreadful," she said passionately. "He wound up in Paris on the French radio. God knows how anyone so drunk could be on the French radio. And then, I think, after that he went to England, and he got married again, but his wife couldn't stand him. She left him. Oh, he was dreadful, a psychopath, a drunken psychopath."

Laurence looked over his life and wrote Djuna in April 1966, "Saw Peggy who looks younger and brisker. We get on fairly well, though I have known her too long to find her funny. Looking back, I dislike Kay —the symbol of romantic hypocrisy. I love my last wife, Jeanie. The only mean thing she ever did to me was to die. But had she lived on—20 years longer, one of those familiar situations might have arisen. Well—one never knows. Good night. . . ."

The onetime golden boy, the King of Bohemia, was abdicating. Laurence himself was dying. Frail, thin, unable to eat, suffering from cancer, he had been operated on for an ulcer as well, which left him with only part of a stomach. "Hopelessness is a more satisfactory condition than hope," he wrote Djuna. "Hope keeps me going, just as an itch makes you scratch." Paris seemed grim and dreary to him, most of his friends long gone. Whenever he was depressed or nervous he liked to take a trip. In the fall of 1967 he went back to America to visit his daughter Apple, who was living in Miami and about to have a baby. He was worried that he might not see his favorite child again. In New York, Djuna found him a pale shadow, displeased with everything. Apple, who had been so close to him, saw that he wasn't laughing anymore.

Laurence survived Pegeen by one year. He died in April 1968 in the south of France, on a trip with another daughter, Kathe. He never recovered from the blow of Pegeen's death and never stopped blaming Peggy.

GUGGENHEIM TO GUGGENHEIM

Since she could no longer sell her daughter's paintings, Peggy closed her sales gallery and dedicated one of the basement rooms to Pegeen. In it she placed Pegeen's paintings, naïve and fresh, and a wall of glass figurines designed by Pegeen and executed by Edigio Constantini. She hung a mournful photograph of Pegeen and called the room Pegeen's tomb. Whenever she was depressed, Peggy would go down and commune with her daughter in this dank and clammy cell. Eventually, she could no longer bear to go downstairs. To Christina Thoresby, Peggy said, "Every time I love someone they're taken away from me."

Peggy turned to the past, trying once more to get John Holms's letters published. She wrote Djuna Barnes, who perpetually bemoaned the strangeness and deterioration of everything, "I find life also gets worse all the time, but TG, I have my health and the dogs I adore. I miss Pegeen more and more. She was my best friend. I think she wanted to be destroyed, or to die as she always chose men who were bound to do that for her (of course I do not refer to Hélion). Pegeen's children, I mean, the younger ones, are better off now without her, as the terrible life she led with that dreadful husband was ghastly for them. If only she could have left him."

Peter Lauritzen saw Peggy that fall at the reopening of the Anglican church. "She cried in the back for the whole ceremony." After Pegeen's death she was calmer, sweeter, more human. "She has no problems," said Pierre Matisse. She "has no more talons." Once, when she was asked what had changed her the most, Peggy spoke of Pegeen: "We were terribly close to one another and her death has left me quite bankrupt. Her loss and my becoming older have caused me to quiet down considerably. I am more indifferent to everything than formerly, and if you call that inner peace, maybe you're right. My life is no longer turbulent in any sense of the word, and I intend to live in Venice always. But if I were asked by young people for my advice on how to lead their lives, I would answer—to the fullest."

During Easter 1968 Peggy went on a second trip to India, this time with Roloff Beny, who was shooting one of his famous books of photographs—one he ultimately dedicated to Peggy. "He was a state guest," Peggy observed, "and I was a nothing." They traveled by car and covered forty-five hundred miles in five weeks, spending every other night in a different "terrible resthouse." Peggy waited patiently while Beny set up his shots, which often took an hour or more. "While he photographed I almost went mad!" To pass the time, Peggy sat and dispensed candies from a big jar to the countless beggar children who gathered around. The food was dreadful and the accommodations worse, but Peggy was a good sport. "In India," Beny recalled, "she never complained on the trip, but afterwards she said: 'Never again!' One night we had to sleep in a bordello, and I went to sleep with all my clothes on, but Peggy had to change into one of her filmy nightgowns and she was bitten head to toe by mosquitoes."

Peggy's world was vanishing. In October 1968 Marcel Duchamp died at age eighty-one. He had remained a shadowy figure, attending art gatherings, playing chess, being careful never to repeat himself. Ever the iconoclast, he bequeathed the task of watering his unfinished literalistic leather bride every day (as the pigskin it was made of dried out) to a relative of John Goodwin. "He left pubic hair, underarm hair, neatly, in cases. He had made tiny holes in the leather" where, according to Goodwin, presumably the well-catalogued assortment was to go. Mary Reynolds had died many years earlier. That same year Herbert Read, Peggy's "Papa," also died. Jean Arp, Victor Brauner, and Alberto Giacometti had all died in 1966. André Breton, ever the combatant, after establishing more reviews—*La Brèche, Le Surréalisme Même*—and continuing to hold forth in cafés, had organized a Surrealist exhibition, "L'Écart Absolu" (The Absolute Digression), as recently as 1965 at the Galerie de l'Oeil. He, too, finally succumbed in 1966 at seventy. Tristan Tzara, who called on Dada to piss on the world of his elders, was already dead. The wild-eyed youths of Peggy's day, the mocking provocateurs, were leaving the stage to youths in long hair and beads, who took mind-altering drugs and pursued free love. Peggy remarked wistfully to Sir Norman Reid, who used to visit Venice, "I'm afraid I'm going to live a long time and have no friends left."

Even those friends who remained alive had changed enormously. Emily Coleman, who had suffered a debilitating stroke, was monstrously fat and spoke incoherently. Djuna Barnes complained of fading powers and an aching back; typing a line or a letter had become an ordeal for her. Peggy could barely believe that they once had been bright young things together in Paris. It had been so easy to shock then; everything was taboo. "Was that us?" she wondered.

At seventy, death became Peggy's main concern—her own death, and what she would leave behind. "She is a prisoner in that house," said Paolo Barozzi. "Everything she does is for her death: like Pharaoh." Not a pyramid, but her house and her collection would be her monument. Peggy toyed with the idea of donating the collection to Venice and had made overtures in that direction, but the Venetians, unaware of the value of the prize being offered them, did not snap it up. "I thought they were crazy," Peggy explained. "Afterwards, I was very happy they didn't, because it wouldn't solve my inheritance tax problem at all, but I didn't realize that at the time, I was so stupid. But afterwards, when I found out it wouldn't have been tax free, I felt, my God, lucky I got out of this." Since she was an American citizen, Peggy's collection would have to pass to an American institution to avoid massive estate taxes. This effectively eliminated the Tate Gallery in London.

The Tate had come closer than any other museum to getting the collection, but the Tate was in no position to take on the burden of maintaining it in Venice, and expected Peggy to make some posthumous contribution towards its upkeep. Peggy realized that in the vast galleries of the Tate her collection would have been lost. Santomaso urged Peggy to keep the collection in Venice. Before he died, Peggy hashed the matter over with Laurence Vail who said that Santomaso was right. "If you leave it to the Tate, you would just have a plaque, but if you leave it to Venice, it would be like the house of Beethoven."

In 1967 Peggy managed to get into a row with the Tate, which decided the matter. "I wanted to buy a Léger," she explained, "a small Léger painting, and I wanted the director of the Tate Gallery to go and look at it in Paris and see if it was all right, and instead of that he sent his aide-de-camp, his assistant, to go and look at it. And the assistant said it was all right and the price was all right and actually it was much too expensive and I was terribly cheated. I was furious with the Tate Gallery for sending this man to look at it who said it was the right price when it was all the wrong price and I had bought it in the meantime." (John Loring believed that this 1913 Léger, *Contraste de Formes*—of questionable authenticity—cost Peggy sixty thousand dollars. It no longer appears as part of the Peggy Guggenheim Collection.)

There was no dearth of suitors for Peggy's art. The real problem was finding an institution willing to keep the collection in Venice. The industrialist Norton Simon arrived in October 1968 as an advocate for the University of California. He was somewhat annoyed when Peggy would not see him right away. "We were giving a party for Alan Ansen, who's a very Bohemian wild sort of poet, a very nice friend of mine. And then Norton Simon got very angry and said the embassy had made a special appointment for him to come, and he kept telephoning, and finally we let him come." Peggy found Simon unaffected and likable, but joked that she would only give him the pictures if he would promise to save Venice.

Each time a museum director came to Venice and told Peggy how valuable her artworks had become, Peggy cringed. "I thought what a responsibility it was to own such expensive pictures," she said. "I didn't like it at all." In discussing the ever-increasing insurance valuations and the concomitant increase in premiums, Peggy asked, "Isn't it awful?" The collection she had begun to buy with forty thousand dollars in Paris eventually was worth more than forty million.

Thomas Messer, the director of the Solomon R. Guggenheim Museum in New York, knew that there was a good chance Peggy could be persuaded to leave her collection to her uncle's museum, as Harry Guggenheim had hoped she would. It was a question of going after it. "The function of a museum director," Messer explained,

> is to attract collections for his museum. When I arrived at the Guggenheim in 1961, the question of where the Peggy Guggenheim collection would go was wide open. . . . Between 1961 and 1969, with Harry Guggenheim's encouragement, I made many trips to Venice, perhaps a half dozen, to acquaint myself with the collection . . . and eventually broached the subject of the collection for the museum. The assumption was that the Tate would get the collection. Also great interest was shown in it by the Berkeley Museum. I had certain advantages in speaking for the museum and the board. . . . I took the initiative, but also considered that I was riding on the Guggenheim horse. . . . Harry wanted it very much, but there was no unanimity on the board. . . . There were assets and liabilities, and it was Harry's firm belief that it was right [which eventually carried the day].

The Guggenheim Museum was willing to maintain the collection in Venice and was an American institution, two factors that made their interest tempting. Nevertheless, it took an active campaign of persuasion on Messer's part before Peggy could be cajoled into considering his proposition. Peggy believed herself to have been on bad terms with her uncle Solomon; she certainly loathed the Baroness Rebay and keenly felt the irony of leaving her collection to their museum. "She was always mildly suspicious of my motives" as Solomon Guggenheim's representative, said Messer. "Peggy was on her guard with me as to this whole relationship, and only in moments of personal proximity would warmth come through, and then it would be followed by an irritating letter."

Still, neither Solomon nor the baroness was around to witness Peggy's capitulation, the baroness having died in 1967. The Guggenheim name, Messer believes, was a key factor in Peggy's decision: "If we had not been the Guggenheim Museum I don't think we would have gotten the collection."

The Solomon R. Guggenheim Museum invited Peggy to exhibit her collection in New York, in the expectation that she could thus finally make up her mind to leave it to the museum. Far less excited than she had been at the Tate proposals, Peggy accepted and went to New York with the idea of settling the future of the collection. "It was like proposing to somebody who's dying to marry me," she liked to say. "And it was in the family."

Robert Fizdale recalled seeing Peggy busily at work, typing one of her inimitable letters, replete with spelling mistakes and raised *I*'s—from her rusty typewriter—to her cousin Harry. She was arranging for the forthcoming exhibition of her paintings at the Guggenheim, and "she was working it over, and she'd ask, 'Do you think I can ask them to pay for my hotel?' 'Do you think I can ask them to pay for my meals?' " Arthur Gold interjected, "She was very, very funny about that letter. She went over every nuance. She wanted it very correct." Yes, added Fizdale, "She polished it and polished it. I said it was absolutely Jamesian, and she was very pleased."

When Peggy arrived in New York for the opening of the Peggy Guggenheim Collection at the Guggenheim Museum, in January 1969, she faced the traveler's nightmare at the airport: no luggage. For twenty-four hours, she stayed in the same disheveled woolen dress, wrapped in her mink coat. Just before a dinner in her honor, she finally received the suitcase with her clothes—but not the one with her shoes. She made quite an impression that evening in a white lace dress with beige plastic knee-high boots.

One hundred twenty-five of Peggy's works had been selected by Thomas Messer to be shown in New York, accompanied by much fanfare and publicity. As Peggy had still not committed her collection, it was important to tread cautiously. Peggy was fêted on the evening of January 14 at a private black-tie dinner held in the museum offices, before the gala opening. Harry Guggenheim, old and ailing, could not personally do the honors as planned, but an assemblage of Guggenheims, headed now by Peter Lawson-Johnston, Solomon's grandson, welcomed their long-lost enfant terrible to the fold. (After producing a generation that was predominantly male, it had been the fate of the Guggenheims that the next, Peggy's, had barely any men to carry on the name.) Many of them had never met Peggy or had been too young when she left for Europe to remember more than stories about her. "There's no question," said Lawson-Johnston of Peggy's return to the flock, "that the family on this side of the Atlantic was pretty disturbed, primarily about her books." His grandfather, Solomon, was shocked by *Out of This Century,* in particular by the way Peggy wrote about her own father. "Grandpa referred to it as *Out of My Mind.* . . . [The books] were critical of the members of the family and grandfather. . . . The Guggenheims were running enterprises in this country and were concerned about their image, and she was not conservative."

At the opening were Barbara Obre, Peter's mother and Peggy's first cousin; Barbara's other son, Michael Wettach; Roger Straus, the publisher, and his brother, Oscar, both Daniel Guggenheim's grandsons; and Harry's daughter, Joan van der Maele. In addition to the family, the Justin Thannhausers, Mrs. Andrew Fuller, Bernard Reis, and Thomas Messer were invited. At the last moment, Peggy discovered that she no longer fit into the long skirt that went with the dark blue and gold tunic she intended to wear, so she wore just the top. It was the era of the miniskirt, after all. The tables in Harry's office were decorated with anemones, and a dinner of filet mignon with ice cream and black cherries for dessert and plenty of champagne was served. Peggy was impressed by the prosperity of the family and by Lawson-Johnston's good looks and patrician demeanor, although she commented, "I have . . . spent most of my life trying not to be square. Then I loved being official and loved being shown in museums. And now I'm at another stage: blasé."

After dinner, a thousand more guests passed beneath a red banner emblazoned with the golden lion of Venice to the spiraling ramps. The fountain in the middle of the gallery was painted blue and filled with live goldfish and the guests vied for Surreality with the pictures and the sculptures. "The best show is on the floor rather than the walls," said Jackie Rogers, a New York boutique owner and a show herself in a red-spangled jumpsuit and long feather boa. Ultra Violet, Andy Warhol's superstar, wandered around in a see-through green lace dress with only a red velvet band around her hips. People in sequins, outlandish copper or feather jewelry, black eye makeup, and outré costumes ogled the artworks and tried to pick the legendary Peggy Guggenheim out of the crowd. The most flamboyant and bejangled guests were guessed to be the collector, but the real Peggy, subdued and shy, kept to the background.

"When I installed the show here," Messer recalled, "the night of the opening, I took her arm and wanted to show her the collection before anyone came. She said, 'I think that Uncle Solomon is turning in his grave.' " To the press Peggy quipped, "Uncle Solomon is now dead. . . . We've reconciled." In the introduction to the catalogue for the show, Peggy wrote, "I never dreamt that the collection would be shown in my uncles museum in New York and that one day I would see it descending the ramp like the Nude descending the Staircase."

As splendid as the opening ceremonies were, Peggy felt a little let down. At the Tate she had been among friends, including Herbert Read and Pegeen and Sindbad. In New York Peggy was pretty much on her own, reacquainting herself with faces that she had not seen in years and feeling a little dazed as she circulated. Robert Brady, who accompanied her down the winding galleries, recalled that nothing was planned for her afterward, "like Maria Callas with nowhere to go for Christmas." She was never as proud of the exhibition at the Guggenheim as she had been of the earlier show at the Tate. It was always the English who were foremost in her heart.

In the upper galleries there was a concurrent Kandinsky show from the Guggenheim's permanent collection. Seeing the Kandinskys acquired by Hilla Rebay and the Abstract Expressionist works ending in a roomfull of Pollocks in Peggy's collection sharing the museum, said the art critic Barbara Rose, gave "one . . . some notion of what America owes to the patronage of the Guggenheim family." Years later, Messer was struck by the interchangeability of Peggy's and the museum's collections and "the choices made by four people: Peggy, Hilla, Sweeney, and myself. You could not tell who had chosen what. While Peggy and Hilla were antagonistic to each other, they actually were collecting the same things."

Some critics found the collection top-heavy with Surrealist works, and the Abstract Expressionist pictures that were represented tentative and disappointing. But all were in agreement that Peggy's was a remarkable achievement, a historically organized collection with spectacular works by Picasso, de Chirico, Ernst, Kandinsky, and, of course, Pollock and her "war babies"—Rothko, Still, Baziotes, Motherwell. Peggy had "created a collection," said Alfred Barr, "which is unique in its span, variety and consistent top quality. There's no one like her around now and probably won't be someone for some time."

The exhibition ran from January 16 to March 30. Peggy took the opportunity of being in the United States to visit John Goodwin in Santa Fe. With Goodwin, she visited the Navajo reservation, thinking she ought to look at the art there. Goodwin chuckled as he recalled Peggy up to her old tricks, going "around everywhere looking for a present for Becky Reis. She started with jewelry and asked how much a squash-blossom necklace was. She heard 800 dollars, and said 'No, no, no.' She went on to baskets . . . and bought one for twenty-two dollars. When she went to pay for it, she said, 'But, there is a big hole in it. I intend to give it as a present. How can I give it as a present with a big hole in it?' She bargained them down two dollars to twenty dollars.'' In Cambridge, where she saw Perry Rathbone who as director of the Boston Museum of Fine Arts, was another contender for her collection, Peggy was robbed of one hundred dollars by two teenagers who snatched her purse as she walked on the Common in the late afternoon. This left her with some trepidation about returning to New York where, she was told, crime was even worse.

Peggy was still being coy about the destination of her collection. "No one knows," she replied to one interviewer as to its disposition. It was Thomas Messer's recollection that Peggy had arrived in New York undecided as to whether to leave the collection to the museum, but that during her stay she turned to him and simply said it was fine. There was a meeting of the board of trustees and Peggy and the museum drew up an agreement, practically at the dying Harry Guggenheim's hospital bed. Peggy agreed to bequeath her collection and the palazzo to the Solomon R. Guggenheim Foundation, the legal entity that administers the museum, with the proviso that the collection remain in Venice under her name. Later on, in 1974, Peggy gave the collection and the palazzo outright to the museum, inter vivos, retaining the right to live in the palazzo and administer the collection until her death and making the Guggenheim the legal owner of the collection during her lifetime. Peggy had in 1959 established the Peggy Guggenheim Foundation for tax purposes, as the legal owner of the collection, to administer and operate it. That foundation would be dissolved (it was dissolved in 1977) and the Peggy Guggenheim collection brought under the administration of the Solomon R. Guggenheim Foundation.

"There are no terms," explained Messer of the arrangement with Peggy. "Peggy's collection is as much our collection as the things now in the museum." Until Peggy's death, however, the museum would sit back and maintain a hands-off policy, offering conservation services and advice but nothing more.

The only real problem with the arrangement, from the point of view of the museum, was the condition of the paintings. The salt air and casual upkeep had taken a toll. Visitors to the palazzo noticed huge waterbugs crawling behind the back of Mondrians and Tanguys, and Peggy's security system consisted of vigilant maids. "None of the important pictures is lost," Messer said later. "But it got to be so serious, it became a question of what would survive whom. Had she lived another ten years, the damage would have become irreparable." The Guggenheim managed to restore, added Messer, "Jackson Pollock's *Circumcision, The*

Poet by Picasso, possibly the most important and valuable painting in the collection, and Peggy went around saying we ruined the pictures, because they were not 'the same' afterwards"—they were clean.

The news of Peggy's bequest to the Guggenheim was released as the show was being dismantled in March. "I'm very happy about it," remarked Peggy of her arrangement with the museum. "I think it's a solution to all my problems. I've been worrying about it for years and now it's all settled." In Venice, Peggy "was so happy to get back and so happy to see my *barchessa* in contrast to the Guggenheim Museum in New York, I was glad," she said, "that my father had lost all this money."

TWILIGHT

Having settled the matter of the collection, Peggy returned to Venice freer. Behind her, she knew, she had the Guggenheim Museum and all its power. Marietta Stern recalled accompanying Peggy to a concert in the *cortile* of the Palazzo Ducale one evening. They were ushered to some not very good seats. "The concert had not yet begun when two very smart looking young men had obviously recognized her and asked, 'Are you Peggy Guggenheim? Come with us.' She responded, 'No!' very rudely. They just wanted to give her a better seat, but for a moment, she said, she thought they were going to kidnap her. I asked her what she would want me to do if anyone ever did, and she said, 'Phone the museum in New York.'"

Marietta was in Peggy's museum one afternoon, helping out, as friends were expected to do occasionally on public days, and overheard one member of a couple say to the other while standing in front of a painting, "Do you think that would be a good one to take?" "I told Peggy, and she went up to them and said, 'I hear you're going to steal one of my paintings.'" Peggy was not there, however, when a real burglary occurred in February 1971. She was in London, after visiting Sindbad in Paris, when Sindbad got a call from Venice saying that thieves had broken a window in the basement Pollock room and had made off with several paintings—fifteen as it turned out. Remarkably, the pictures were returned two weeks later when the chief of police discovered them hidden under a canvas tarpaulin in the mud near the railroad tracks. Peggy paid the informant who found them a reward and gave the police chief a small painting in gratitude.

That same year, in December, thieves broke in again. Only this time Peggy was asleep in the palazzo, unaware that three men in a motorboat were sawing their way through the black iron grille protecting the windows of her sitting room. The dogs had barked so many times before at nothing that Peggy paid no attention to them now, while the thieves loaded their boat, making off with sixteen paintings. Marietta Stern went over to the palazzo and found Peggy alone, unable to find someone to fix the gaping grate, "no cook to sleep there, no man, no weapon." Yet Peggy "insisted on sleeping there alone with the railings broken." These paintings, too, were recovered, after Peggy paid a nominal ransom and bought off the various new proprietors of her paintings. The Guggenheim Museum finally installed an alarm system that went off every time anyone even approached a picture too closely, and Peggy could sleep without worrying.

Peggy stopped buying pictures altogether in 1973, after she bought a Calder gouache. "Everything," she kept saying, "is so terribly expensive. I don't see anything I like anyhow." It was impossible, Peggy thought, without being a multimillionaire, to start collecting in the present day. And, on the whole, she found contemporary art "pretty lousy." Sometimes dealers would come to the palazzo hoping to tempt Peggy into buying. "Of course, I don't," she said. "They bring awful things, too."

Mornings, she spent writing letters or reading, mostly Henry James or Nancy Mitford, clutching a handkerchief, her dogs cuddled up on the white sofa next to her. Adore the dogs she did, but she spent little time grooming, bathing, or even feeding them, and they were often smelly. When one died, she added its little corpse without ceremony to the cemetery in one corner of the garden, under an engraved marble sign, "Here lie my beloved babies." Worried that she would predecease her pups, Peggy refused to acquire any more dogs. Finally, she was down to just three—Gypsy, a Shih Tzu (Peggy had bought her from an Englishwoman who walked into the palazzo one day and erroneously claimed that she had the "same dogs" as Peggy's Lhasa Apsos) and her two daughters, Hong Kong and Cellida. When Hong Kong developed cataracts, an appointment was duly made with an oculist, whose astonished nurse discovered upon being handed the four-legged creature that Hong Kong Guggenheim was a dog. "When Hong Kong died," John Hohnsbeen said, "Norman, the black butler, was digging a place for her in the mass grave where the rest of the dogs were buried, and out came

Sable. Its skull came out near Peggy's feet, but she didn't notice. She couldn't see it. She was sobbing so over the dog. Norman, being Jamaican and full of voodoo, was very impressed by the portent."

Black Norman, as he was called, was one of the many servants who came and went under Peggy's watchful eye. As Peggy was not paying him full wages, he used to say, he would only work part time and spent a great deal of the other part of the time at the municipal building researching what his rights were. As a result, Peggy got her own meals and made her own bed. Peggy's servant problems usually revolved about money. "She paid them the bare minimum on the scale," said Christina Thoresby. Peggy worried about being cheated, continuing into old age to keep scrupulous accounts in her notebook. Indeed, keeping accounts remained one of her great joys, which she attributed to "a very mathematical mind." Peggy counted every penny that she gave the housekeeper to buy groceries and kept all her money, wines, and valuables locked in the hall closet. She carried the key in a battered little straw handbag with her everywhere. Peggy insisted that the help eat from a different, less expensive stock of food than she and her guests did. John Goodwin recalled that when he dined at Peggy's house, she repeatedly asked, "Are you finished?" When he finally said yes, Peggy told him, "No, you *must* eat more. If you don't they'll eat it in the kitchen, and I already bought them their own food." The stories that circulated about her starving the help made it difficult for Peggy to attract servants into her employ. Her last couple, Izia and Roberto, simply bought their own food: if a guest smelled delicious roasting meats or sizzling omelettes it would invariably be the servants' meal.

Peggy decided that life was too expensive and she had to cut back. She got rid of her motorboat when her chauffeur quit and gave her ancient car, which never had any gas in the tank, to Sindbad's son, Clovis. The only real luxury she allowed herself was her gondola. Whereas before she had used it to go to the market and buy fruit in the morning or to do errands and shop, now she gradually decreased her gondoliers from two to one and her expeditions to a single ride in the early evening. It was always a problem to find a gondolier cheap enough and negotiations were endless. Though she herself spent only two hours in the gondola, the gondolier spent many more fitting out the boat before he could take her out and then removing even the floorboards at night to prevent theft. Yet she insisted on paying for just two hours. Once Peggy hired a medical student to avoid paying the union scale. As she put it, "All Venetians can row."

Nevertheless, long, languorous gondola rides remained for Peggy a necessity. Starting in June, weather permitting, Peggy would go out from 4:00 to 6:00 P.M. every day. She loved the feeling of floating, the sense of freedom. "You get a completely different idea of Venice if you go in a gondola," Peggy remarked. "Everything floats, yes. Don't you feel the houses are floating and everything? I think you have a tremendous sense of freedom in Venice in general, tremendous. You can wear any clothes you want and walk everywhere you want. No automobiles to run over you, no bicycles to run over you." She had written Djuna Barnes when she first bought her gondola, "I adore floating to such an extent, I can't think of anything as nice since I gave up sex, or rather, since it gave me up."

On those days when the palazzo was open, Peggy relished the attention she received from gawking tourists as she progressed down the steps to the canal and her waiting gondola. It was much better to have a friend along, and Peggy considered it a particular treat to have rambling conversations to the tune of the lapping waves and the deep-throated warning *Ahuii*'s of the gondolier. On those occasions, David Kalstone was struck by Peggy's perpetual schoolgirl interrogatory. "She has a fascinating amnesia. Everything comes to her as a total surprise. 'He did?' is her favorite remark. In her gondola she is charming. She knows every canal in Venice. She loves Henry James and rereads him because she doesn't remember. We discuss the plots of the novels and she is always astonished. 'No, he did?' 'He didn't?' "

Peggy's favorite subject matter remained sex: who liked it, who didn't, who did it, who didn't, and with how many. The dogs always came along and scampered over to the sides for a better view. Eventually, many of the canals in Venice were closed and Peggy simply circled around and around the same ones. *"Dove andiamo, signora?" "Per là,"* Peggy would say, directing her gondolier by the imperious aim of a hand. Her favorite ride was down the Grand Canal, avoiding the wake of motorboats and *vaporetti,* over to the Church of the Madonna del-'Orto, across from the funerary island, and then to the Arsenale, where the Venetians had once made their boats. Her last gondolier, Gino, large and brawny, dressed all in white down to his white sneakers, with a turquoise sash around the middle, "was the corpse collector and he sang funeral songs as they went along. He knew all the canals and homes, presumably from picking up the corpses. He loved to wander near the funerary islands." As Peggy passed, tourists would point her out to each other—"She's that famous American eccentric"—and snap her picture. Framed by two golden lions on their hind legs holding a trident, Peggy seemed quite regal, very much the *contessa,* as Gino insisted on calling her. She would say, "I'm only happy now," in the gondola, with the dogs, and a life of no event.

In 1973, Peggy's solitude was broken by John Hohnsbeen, a sociable, gregarious art dealer, who had once worked with Kurt Valentin in New York and had co-founded the Peridot Gallery, where he showed the young Philip Pearlstein. Before that, he had been a Martha Graham dancer. Hohnsbeen's career had been interrupted by a bout with tuberculosis and he spent a year at Bedford Hills (before it became a correctional institution) recovering. He liked to joke that therein lay the secret of his ever-youthful blue-eyed, blond good looks. During the 1950s Hohnsbeen maintained an all-white apartment, designed by Philip Johnson, where the only touch of color was the ice-blue of his dressing gown. Since 1961 Hohnsbeen had shuttled between Paris and Rome and had moved to Rome in 1970, seeing Peggy on her periodic visits to Roloff Beny, who kept an apartment overlooking the Tiber.

Peggy adored Hohnsbeen's wicked sense of humor and companionable nature and started staying with him in his tiny but central apartment in Rome. He seemed to know everyone and was invited to every party. They traded visits back and forth, until Peggy suggested that he become her permanent houseguest, help her with the collection from Easter until fall, and call himself its curator. The arrangement worked very well. Hohnsbeen spent seven months of the year with her and swore that his first two years with Peggy were "magical." He helped her handle the business of the collection, dealt with her correspondence, did little errands for her, accompanied her to the doctor, and generally behaved like a dutiful son. Once he even offered to go to bed with her, "but she said no." Every day the two would have lunch at a little blue-green, slatted, wooden folding table (set with her mother's elaborate Victorian silver) propped in front of the sitting room window, next to the chest where Peggy hid the catalogues and a big glass vase by Constantini with nipples of various colors protruding from it. Lunch was a spartan affair, consisting of boiled fish accompanied by Peggy's favorite tiny yellow potatoes smothered in butter. Peggy still had dinner parties in her dining room lined with paintings by Duchamp, Louis Marcoussis, Picasso, and Gris, and Hohnsbeen recalled how at dinner the same boiled fish was usually brought out, served with taste-free whipped cream. Once, when Peggy entertained the director of the Louvre museum, the ubiquitous whipped cream was inadvertently sweetened. Maria Theresa Rubin went to a great many of these dinners and recalled the alternate menu, "chicken floating in a red sauce, always the same food in fact. Really not very good. There were never more than six or seven people. She was very relaxed. She would have the vicar who died, Victor Stanley, Peter Lauritzen and his wife, Rose, Santomaso, the Rylands. She was always the same—never different—with anybody." Rubin was amused when on a visit with her son, then four or five years old, Peggy gave him a Joseph Cornell box to play with. "She didn't know what children were."

Peggy much preferred to give cocktail parties, which ended in Venice punctually at 8:30 P.M., since she could get away with serving just a few hors d'oeuvres of mashed sardines on saltines. Her son, Sindbad, who liked to eat well, remarked, "A can of sardines goes a long way with her." To which his wife added, "Especially if you don't open it." To these festivities she invited visiting celebrities and friends from the Anglo-American colony. Often Peggy was nervous introducing the guests to each other and jumbled the names or made gaffes, as when she completely forgot the name of the director Joseph Losey, who turned deep red. Her favorite guests were writers. Painters she had always found too egotistical. She adored "even lesser, minor writers" and once said, "I was much more interested in literature than I was in art. I just got into art by mistake." Unless the guest of honor was impossibly difficult, said Hohnsbeen, her "parties were invariably a great success."

Thanks to the enormous publicity surrounding her shows at the Tate and the Guggenheim and the general public acceptance and interest in modern art, tourists began to come to Peggy's palazzo in earnest. Often, she pridefully pointed out, they came to her museum even before seeing St. Mark's. On those days that the museum was open to the public, Hohnsbeen would sit at the same little blue-green table used for lunch, set out this time in front of the steps leading to the canal, and sell catalogues which, at six dollars apiece, went toward maintaining the house. Peggy estimated that they sold four thousand of them a year and that about one in every seven visitors bought one. Occasionally Peggy would sit outside herself, having learned that a potential autograph helped increase catalogue sales. She loved overhearing what people had to say about her art or her house. White-haired and simply dressed, Peggy was mistaken by some tourists for the maid. Nothing tickled her more than being asked, "When did Miss Guggenheim die?"

Having rejected her collection as not worth saving during the war, the Louvre invited her to show it in the Orangerie during the winter of 1975. For Peggy it was an endorsement well worth waiting for. "The Orangerie was a great revenge for me." After complaining that she was too old at seventy-six and too tired, Peggy did not miss going to Paris and receiving all the honors she felt were her due. "She said," recollected Arthur Gold, " 'I haven't got the strength,' but she did go and stood for twelve hours shaking hands and then drove out to Sindbad's where he had a dinner and kept it up for three more days. She was full of energy. She was like a young girl. Finally, there was the recognition she craved."

The lines for the show, which was to run for three months, from December 1974 to March 1975, gratified Peggy, as, clad in red tights and a bright blue embroidered shift, she greeted friends old and new. Tirelessly she met with journalists and reporters who found her "curiously ageless," "as direct and delightful as a sporty Miami dowager." Peggy continued to deprecate the art of the moment, exclaiming "Terrible! Shocking! Horrible!" and saying, "If I were forced to start today, I simply wouldn't know where to begin."

She went around Paris in knee-high boots on Sindbad's arm. Sindbad and his wife, Peggy, lived in a small house in Boulogne-sur-Seine, which his mother liked to complain was "the sticks." Mary McCarthy recalled seeing Peggy and her son together and thinking it a "rueful relationship." They seemed "tied together. Sindbad is much more considerate of Peggy than Peggy is of Sindbad. I can't help feeling that those children have a right to have a grudge against their mother. Sindbad is a sweet, sweet man, and if Sindbad doesn't like himself, that, he may feel, is what she did." Added McCarthy, "I don't think he had much respect for her intense selfishness, terribly self-centered self-centeredness. She is not interested in much outside that little circle."

Sindbad resembled Peggy physically, spoke with the same intonations, and shared the same mordant wit. "I'm the last Vail, Vail, Vail," he liked to say, mimicking his long-dead triple-talking grandmother, Florette—and Peggy herself, who always used expletives at least three times—"Oh no no no!" There was the same remarkable nose, the same clear blue eyes. "They are very much alike in manner," said Jane Rylands, who first met Peggy in 1973. "They love each other intensely, but they don't seem to enjoy each other's company very much. They don't find each other interesting. They're not affectionate."

Sindbad's greatest sin, in Peggy's eyes, was living a simple life, selling insurance. Cricket seemed to be his one great enthusiasm—talking about it, he blossomed. "In my parents' household," observed Clover Vail, "if you're not interesting, artistic, you were not tolerated." Sindbad was overwhelmed by the pressure of Peggy's opinions and around her he was always wary of saying the wrong thing. "Everybody felt sorry for Pegeen," said Sindbad's wife, Peggy, "but it was really Sindbad who suffered the most. He was 'square'; his wife, his children were 'square' to the cousins, Pegeen's sons even. [Peggy] was cruel and inhumane." But if Peggy had harbored great hopes for Sindbad's career, what better way could he rebel than by disappointing them?

Sindbad used to say to Jane Rylands, "My mother called me a 'pest' and a 'nuisance.' How could I like her?" It hurt Sindbad if Peggy forgot to mention him in her rambling interviews, as if he didn't exist, but he found his own way to remind her of his presence: "I'm always milking her for money," he said. "I've made her pay for having me."

At first, Peggy admitted to wild jealousy of Sindbad's lovely, blue-eyed, dark-haired second wife, also named Peggy, with whom he had two beautiful daughters. The unwelcome duplication of names only exacerbated the jealousy: Peggy was mean to her daughter-in-law for more than twenty years. "She tried everything," said Sindbad's wife, "to break up the marriage. She threw boys, women, anything at Sindbad" and encouraged Peggy Vail likewise to infidelity. Laurence added his salt to the wounds by drawing on his New England prejudices to dismiss

Peggy Vail as déclassé because she had worked at UNESCO. Later, Peggy grew to like her daughter-in-law very much and quoted Laurence, who used to say, "It's every other spouse one gets along with."

Between Peggy and her son there was a "great unfulfilled relationship," a yawning void they tried to breach, but never could. "In the last fifty-six years," Sindbad once said, "she fucked me up, bitched, and was terribly good to me."

By Easter Peggy was back in Venice, ready to open the museum again. She kept hoping for a visit from Françoise Sagan, with whom she had been very taken in Paris. Peggy was utterly fascinated by the writer's life, titillated as she was by the peccadillos of famous women. "She liked very much Françoise Sagan, and after Françoise Sagan gave her this necklace she wore it all the time. . . . And then, once, Françoise Sagan was to come to Venice to a party at Peggy's house, and Peggy was thrilled, but for some reason she never showed up, and after that Peggy stopped wearing the necklace and speaking about her," recalled Maria Theresa Rubin.

Peggy was retiring more and more from the world. "I hate it," she said about social life in Venice. "I try to avoid it as much as I can. We don't go to Italian parties, mostly English and American ones. I don't mix with the Italians very much. They bore me. You can always know what they're going to say before they do." Consequently, Peggy spent most of her time alone. "I'm a lone wolf," she acknowledged, "not at all gregarious. I used to love parties, it's true, but I don't like them anymore."

Not surprisingly, Peggy began to have health problems. She broke eight ribs when she fainted because of high blood pressure and spent seventeen days in the hospital in May 1976. Hardening of the arteries caused her painful circulatory problems, which made it difficult for her to walk. She shuffled from her bedroom to the sitting room couch, collapsed, and shuffled back to her room. The last remaining dog, Cellida, mangy, deaf, and blind, followed her around or, confused, pursued someone else. Often Peggy said she regretted not having moved to London, where it would have been easier to get about and the taxis at least ran on asphalt. When she made her way to the gondola landing for her daily ride, Gino had to lift her into the boat. She missed the turbulent days of her youth. "I wish I were young enough to have lovers," she said. Wistful and lonely, she cried when her guests left and fall approached, wondering, "What is to become of me?"

As she dozed on the couch, a book in her hand, she would review her life, analyze her actions and reactions, think about Pegeen, and ponder. When she felt she had detected a possible flaw or mistake, she would be the first to explore it. "Do you think," she would ask, "I'm terribly egotistical?"

Peggy's infirmities made it hard for her to get out of the house much, except perhaps to the Cantinone Storica restaurant around the corner. When she was asked to be interviewed by *Playboy* magazine, she told them she would love to accept "but it wouldn't be seemly at my age to appear without any clothes on."

A healthy vanity prevailed, as Peggy worried about her figure, remained proud of her legs, and tried not to eat too much. She missed being tan and spending long hours basking in the sun—so many years of exposure had produced a mild form of skin cancer and a blotchy face. But every few minutes, Peggy was still reapplying her bright red lipstick.

Her grandson Nicolas came to see her. She was fond of him because he was so handsome, and found the circumstances of his birth romantic. He produced a movie about his grandmother, her art and life, in which she appeared along with Hélion, Henry Moore, John Hohnsbeen, and Black Norman. At one point she asked Thomas Messer if Nicolas could become the curator of her collection after her death. "I responded," he said, "that if that were his interest we better take measures to qualify him. I volunteered to try to get him a scholarship—because Peggy said she could not afford to pay—at Harvard. When I had pulled whatever strings I could all interest in that was lost." When Nicolas appeared on Peggy's doorstep with a girl friend, Peggy told him they could stay in the palazzo but not eat there.

In the spring of 1978, as she approached her eightieth birthday, Peggy had a heart attack. John Hohnsbeen was with her and sobbed by her bedside, afraid of the worst. Seriously ill, Peggy nevertheless recovered and maintained that her heart did not worry her nearly so much as the arteriosclerosis that restricted her movements. She searched in vain for cures. "Nothing seems to work." Peggy thought of going to Romania or Zurich—anywhere to find relief from the debilitating pains.

For Peggy's eightieth birthday, in August 1978, there was a large celebration at the Gritti Palace Hotel. Hohnsbeen had to struggle to get her to invite her older friends. "She didn't give a damn about people." Yet Peggy got quite a kick out of it, and wore, for the first time in a long while, her Fortuny dress. Joseph Losey was asked to be toastmaster for no better reason than that he was the biggest celebrity there, and Peggy was none too pleased when he referred to her as "bawdy" and a *"jolie laide."*

Christina Thoresby recalled that "Peggy's birthday party fell on the day the Venetian, Luciani, who became Pope John Paul I, was named. When she arrived at the Gritti, via gondola, all the bells of Venice were ringing." The naming of the pope overshadowed Peggy's birthday, and she was irritated that the interview she had granted for Italian television was put off until later in the evening. After the dinner, added Thoresby, "Peggy offered a ride to me and Santomaso, who lived on her side of the canal. We walked through Peggy's palazzo to the door, and when we came out, Santomaso said, 'I feel as if I had assisted at the marriage of Peggy Guggenheim and the pope.' "

THE LAST
DOGARESSA

Peggy celebrated her eighty-first birthday, August 26, 1979, at the Cantinone Storica with David Kalstone, John Hohnsbeen, and Jane and Philip Rylands, receiving so many flowers that she had nowhere to put them all. She liked celebrating her birthday, but it aroused anxieties and made her a little churlish. Her favorite present was an almond cake that Christina Thoresby brought by during the day, which had been dreary and rainy. When she blew out the candle on her cake, Peggy remarked, "If I made a wish it would be that I'd be dead, or that I don't live to the next one." Soon thereafter, during the first week in September, she had her annual cocktail party on the terrace for the Regatta Storica, for which the Venetians prepare the whole year, and during which they dress up in costume and sail their decorated vessels up the Grand Canal. On the roof her servants Izia and Roberto were having a barbecue, and the inviting aromas distracted the guests below. Peggy, more than ever, looked the lost little girl with nowhere to hide, her right hand character-istically at her throat, pulling her collar. She studiously avoided all the guests John Hohnsbeen had cajoled her into inviting, including Alice Tully, who was moved to remark of her hostess, "Very interesting, but not very interesting."

Peggy was greatly looking forward to the reissuing of her memoirs, out of print for thirty-three years, in October 1979. Fred Licht, an art historian who lived in Venice, interceded with Universe Press, which offered to bring it out again, updated with the relevant sections of *Confessions of an Art Addict* and a new section written by Peggy. In the revised version all the pseudonyms, already exposed to some degree in *Confessions of an Art Addict,* would be changed to real names. "The truth can't hurt any of the poor dears now," said Peggy, "because they're all dead." Roland Penrose, identified as Donald Wrenclose in the 1946 edition, was reluctant to have his identity revealed, but eventually relented as long as Peggy deleted a sentence saying that he was a bad painter. However, Llewelyn flatly refused to be identified.

Universe Press added a transitional chapter, "Interlude," which surprised Peggy, joining her two books as if it were Peggy speaking and listing some of the bad reviews for *Out of This Century.* Peggy managed, in a last chapter, to cram twenty years of her life in Venice, including Pegeen's death, into thirteen matter-of-fact pages. Gore Vidal was prevailed upon to write a foreword, in which he likened Peggy to Henry James's "Daisy Miller with rather more balls." Peggy was none too delighted by the comparison, but on the whole she was very happy with the book, a well-produced and handsome volume. She was pleased by the cover photograph that Man Ray had taken in Paris of her slim and youthful self, dressed by Poiret, long cigarette holder in hand. "Isn't it beautiful?" she murmured.

As the memoirs neared publication, there was renewed interest in Peggy. *The New York Times* sent a reporter and photographer to see her, but she was confused and frightened when the interviewer arrived. For *Women's Wear Daily* she posed uncomfortably in the Fortuny dress. Marie Cosindas photographed her in the same dress, but it now seemed to wear Peggy. Peggy had become fragile and wan, her huge blue eyes pleading. For all her years of talking to reporters, she still treated each one as a social acquaintance and gave good interviews only to those she liked.

This time around, the reviews were somewhat more charitable, generally discussing Peggy's life and accomplishments before dealing with the book. Hilton Kramer in *The New York Times Book Review,* after praising Peggy's considerable achievement and observing that the "whole public history of the Abstract Expressionist movement" began in the "pioneering exhibitions" at Art of This Century, went on to say that, unfortunately, it did not follow that Peggy knew how to write. "The result is a rather chattering and disjointed book largely devoted to recounting the whims and indulgences of an American heiress." Quentin Crisp in *New York* magazine pointed out that whereas Peggy's affairs were no longer shocking, "what now so deliciously appalls is the aggression with which she hunted down her quarry." Sex and family oneupmanship seemed to be the driving motivations, added John Richardson, behind Peggy's metamorphosis from a "dizzy amateur" to a "canny impresario of the most important art movement to emerge in this country," concluding that "Peggy may have aged but, for better or worse, she has not grown up." Nevertheless, the book enjoyed its measure of success. It sold well, was excerpted in the *New York Post,* and was published in a paperback edition.

There was no question of Peggy's going to New York for the publication of her book. She was not well enough. When the last of her dogs, Cellida, practically hairless and reeking of age, died, Peggy quickly began to decline. She suffered another heart attack and never seemed to recover from a cataract operation that she had had in England the previous winter, which left her ten pounds lighter and with two pairs of thick glasses, one for reading and one for seeing, that she was careful to remove if she heard the click of a camera shutter. Even so, she was in good spirits. Her mind was as quick as ever, but her arteriosclerosis made even a short walk excruciatingly painful. Indeed, she averred, "I wish I'd died four years ago to avoid having had so much pain." In late September, John Loring took Peggy out to dinner at the Cipriani with Nicolas, his girl friend Dolly, Santomaso, and the jewelry designer Elsa Peretti. They finished late and the manager refused to let the boat be brought around to pick her up, insisting that the group walk to the back of the hotel.

"You're not going to suggest Mrs. Guggenheim walk to the back," Loring argued, making a great scene. Finally, after much debate, they walked over to the dock, and in getting into the boat, Peggy wrenched her ankle. "I just stepped forward," she said, "and there seemed to be no ground there." Peggy said nothing at first, but later admitted, "It really hurts." John Loring didn't know what to do. They "picked her up and carried her up the stairs into the house." Peggy insisted, "I'm perfectly fine. Put me on a sofa in the front hall. I really hurt my ankle. I can't walk."

X rays revealed a tiny crack in the bone of Peggy's foot. The fracture made it impossible for her to walk at all and she stayed in bed, dressed in a kimono, propped up on pillows under the glittering Calder headboard, or in an armchair fitted with casters, reading Thomas Hardy, having found the later novels of Henry James too taxing. She refused to have a nurse.

All of October slipped by and still Peggy was immobilized. She was terribly feeble and frustrated. She wanted to go to Yugoslavia to a clinic near Dubrovnik and take the cure for arteriosclerosis that Marshal Tito reputedly had had, yet her ankle would not heal. "She was always trying to get above it," said Christina Thoresby of Peggy's confinement. Peggy started thinking that if she had an operation on her foot, on a slight deformity, a bone that stuck out, that she had had for years, it would help. "Peggy was literally clutching at straws," said Thoresby. Izia and Roberto, according to Jane Rylands, found a doctor in Padua who agreed to do the operation.

On November 15, at 6:00 or 7:00 A.M., recounted Rylands, Izia and Roberto "carried her out of the palazzo, quite terrified, and put her in a boat to the car." She took with her a copy of *The Brothers Karamazov,* because it would take a long time to read. The hospital in Padua, the Camposampiero, was an hour's drive from Venice, but it was cumbersome to get out of Venice proper, as it was necessary first to take a motorboat to the garages on its outskirts. In her condition it was difficult to move Peggy at all, let alone through the canals of Venice, into a car, and then to Padua. When, finally, Peggy and the couple arrived at the Camposampiero, a large, modern, uninviting building that stood starkly in the sun, there was no doctor waiting for Peggy. At first, no one knew what Peggy had come for. Eventually, it was understood that she was there for an operation on her foot. Exhausted, she was placed in a room, but that night she suffered a pulmonary edema. Later, she said, "Isn't it lucky that I came to the hospital. Otherwise, I would have died."

Looking around, Peggy was well enough to ask, "How much is this room?" and when told it was one hundred thousand lira a night, said it was much too expensive. Peggy dismissed the private nurse and was moved to a reconverted doctor's anteroom with two other patients, a small Formica folding table along one wall, and a tiny view of the landscape from a window too high and too small to see out of. Since the trip back and forth from Venice to Padua by train was a whole-day affair, Peggy discouraged people from coming to see her. "Don't bother to come and see me, it's miles away." Jane Rylands made the trip once a week, and tried to speak with her on the telephone every day. John Hohnsbeen, who moved out of the palazzo and was living with a friend, said, "she didn't let people go see her, because she didn't want anyone to watch her die." Peggy was very concerned that Rylands not worry Sindbad. She kept saying, "Don't have Sindbad come. Please don't have Sindbad come." A month went by, and the doctor on the floor noticed that Peggy was always alone. *"La signora,"* he said, *"sempre sola, sempre sola."*

Peggy began to have doubts about the wisdom of this operation on her foot, related Rylands, so, when the doctor told her she could have it, she said, "I'm too tired. I've had a terrible night. I don't want it." She postponed it again one time after that, and again it was rescheduled. But in the end, always willing to take a chance, she went ahead with the surgery, hoping it would somehow make her well again.

Peggy kept insisting to her friends, "Oh, I'll be home before Christmas. I'll be home soon." But a few days after the operation, Peggy fell out of bed and was found the next morning asleep on the floor. It was feared that she had broken two or three ribs. Jane Rylands noticed in talking to Peggy that "her mind was wandering, her voice very weak. I decided willy-nilly that was the time for Sindbad to come and get her away from that hospital."

That day Peggy suffered a stroke that paralyzed her on one side. She couldn't talk and realized she couldn't be heard. Sindbad came to Venice the following morning. When Rylands saw Peggy, "She was terribly paralyzed on the right side. Her whole arm was covered with bruises, all black and blue. She tried to ask questions and so forth and she couldn't. The phone rang and it was Vittorio Fiorazzo [one of Peggy's oldest friends in Venice] who wanted to come up, and she said 'No, no, no.' I realized later she wanted to *know* who was on the phone." Sindbad arrived at the hospital, Rylands went on, and "when he walked into the room burst into tears, as did [my husband] Philip, which Sindbad found really touching. He never quite believed anyone loved his mother."

"The minute I saw her," said Sindbad later, "I knew she would die." Sindbad's wife Peggy described Peggy then: "Her face was contorted. She looked trapped, terribly frustrated. It seemed as if her soul were trying to say something and she couldn't. She was frustrated and gave up. It was as if her soul was trapped in this body that didn't function anymore." Her eyes blue and yearning, with all the strength left to her, "she managed to say to Sindbad, 'Please, kiss me.' "

Peggy went in and out of a coma for a week. Occasionally she would recognize Sindbad or would wake up and say hello and begin complaining. "These nurses don't have any idea what's wrong with me. They haven't a clue." On Friday, December 21, Sindbad went to visit Peggy and found her calmer. The next day, Saturday, Venice was flooded. No one went to see her. Everyone was too busy bailing out water. At the palazzo, the water missed the Pollocks in the basement by two inches. As the Rylands were getting ready to drive to Padua the following day, Sunday, December 23, the telephone rang. It was the hospital. A voice intoned, "She's dying." Philip Rylands alerted Sindbad and then phoned the hospital to ask, "What can we do?" But it was already too late. "She's dead. There's nothing you can do."

Sindbad was devastated. He had no desire to view his mother's body. "Please, no," he winced when asked. All through Christmas week he drank a great deal. Peggy had left a list of personal possessions she wanted to leave her friends and Sindbad went around personally delivering the items. Peggy gave Christina Thoresby her ranch mink coat. Jane Rylands got the Fortuny dress Peggy loved so and her sable-lined raincoat. Peggy left her pale mink coat to her sister Hazel. John Hohnsbeen received a Picasso plate. To Nicolas, she left her art books. To Roloff

Beny, she left her books on architecture. Her collection of earrings she bequeathed to Sindbad's daughters.

On January 9, 1980, Philip Rylands was the only one who went to the small cremation precinct at San Michaele, the funerary island. Sindbad insisted that no one else go. "Sindbad hated cremation," remarked Jane Rylands. "You could smell it. He saw his sister be cremated. He hated it. Then the ashes were put under lock and key, until they could be put in the garden." It wasn't until April 4, 1980, that Peggy's ashes were put to rest. There was always some typically Venetian bureaucratic muddle. Philip and Sindbad went to pick the ashes up on a sunny spring day, and they stopped to see Stravinsky's and Diaghilev's graves. They brought Peggy's ashes in a big box wrapped in newspapers, carrying it through the tiny streets of the Dorso Duro to the palazzo. Without ceremony, Peggy was placed in the garden next to her dogs, a black marble plaque on the stone wall attesting: "Here lies Peggy Guggenheim, 1898–1979." Around the small grave were planted marguerites, in honor of the name she never used, appropriately called dog daisies. "Even though Peggy was Jewish and not religious," said Christina Thoresby, "she managed to observe the Christian holidays. She died at Christmas and was buried at Easter."

A HOUSE
IS NOT A HOME

Within a day of Peggy's death, Thomas Messer was in Venice to see about safeguarding the collection. It upset Sindbad to see his mother's home become an institution overnight. Messer appointed Philip Rylands as administrator to look after the collection and the palazzo.

Peggy's will was admitted to probate in New York City in March 1980. She left, in a handwritten document, dated 1979, "all of my estate in the United States real and personal . . . to my son, Michael Sindbad Vail," whom she appointed as executor of her estate. Peggy left him four hundred thousand dollars, the money she held out of trust. Sindbad gave one hundred thousand dollars to his nephews, Pegeen's children, as he felt this would have been Pegeen's share had she been alive. Peggy made no provision in her will for her grandchildren, who were, in the case of Pegeen's sons, already receiving about two hundred thousand dollars from a generation-skipping trust set up by their great-grandmother, which would similarly devolve to Sindbad's children on his death.

"By the time I've paid lawyers' fees and other expenses," said Sindbad, "I'll be lucky to have a hundred and fifty thousand dollars. I have a trust which gives me an income of about thirty-five thousand dollars before taxes. What with bringing up two girls in France and keeping this house I'm worse off than before when the money I received was not taxed. It's being taxed retroactively now.''

Peggy had made no stipulation in her will about Djuna Barnes, whom she had been consistently supporting. Instead, she made Sindbad promise that he would continue to give Djuna three hundred dollars a month, which he did out of his own money, increasing Djuna's stipend to a thousand dollars a quarter. (Djuna died soon afterward.)

Sindbad was distressed. She "gave away her entire collection (not one picture for me) and her palace. The entire has been valued at forty million. As you can imagine I'm rather cheesed off. No one believes this and everyone thinks I'm damned rich. . . . My mother has left me with plenty of worries. Her vanity is quite revolting.''

When the dust settled, however, Sindbad discovered he had been left an additional million dollars, of which seven hundred thousand was in trust and another three hundred thousand out of it. And his nephews, Pegeen's sons, were to share a like amount. But still, whenever he was asked whether his mother had left him a painting, he would respond, "She left me only back income taxes.''

On Easter Sunday, April 6, 1980, the Peggy Guggenheim Collection officially reopened under the direction of the Solomon R. Guggenheim Museum. (John Hohnsbeen remarked that Peggy herself would have opened the week before to be sure to get all the German tourists to buy catalogues.) Peggy's friends and family, those who had not had an opportunity to pay their respects or show their bereavement, looked forward to the occasion as a memorial to Peggy. There had been no funeral, no ceremony to mourn her, and this was the first time most of them had set foot in the palazzo since her death.

Thomas Messer, Peter Lawson-Johnston, Sindbad and his wife, their daughters, Carol and Julie, and three of Pegeen's four sons, Fabrice, Nicolas, and Sandro, converged on Venice. Sindbad was upset to discover that he could not stay in the palazzo. Indeed, only a guard would be allowed to sleep there. Sindbad felt that there should be arrangements made for him to continue staying in the house. Nicolas was upset by the changes. He had been turned away at the door for arriving for the opening twenty minutes early. For them, who had seen the Venier dei Leoni as a fixture of their lives, it was a shock to realize what Peggy's ambition really meant.

The palazzo had been swept clean of Peggy's presence. There was barely a hint of the woman who had created the collection. Those who expected to see the palazzo as it had been during Peggy's lifetime were stunned. Freshly painted white, devoid of most of her furniture, save in the dining room and for the Calder headboard, the palazzo looked for the first time like what it was intended to be, a museum. The doors to the sitting room, formerly closed to protect Peggy on visiting days, were thrown open, and her bookcases, desk, and liquor chest were gone. Even her hall closet was emptied out. The pictures had taken over, as if they had waited patiently all these years to have the last say.

John Hohnsbeen, Roloff Beny, Bill Congdon, Christina Thoresby, and the Rylands were all in the garden waiting for the ceremony on the afternoon of the reopening. Thomas Messer, dressed in a pink shirt, beige jacket, and tiny bow tie, stood at the head of the stairs leading into the main entrance hall and said a few words. Peter Lawson-Johnston addressed those assembled and recalled Peggy's candor, speaking about the time at Harry's Bar when Peggy asked Sindbad's daughter Carol, not *if* the boys and girls slept together at school, but *where.* Peggy Vail in a blue-green dress and wide-brimmed floppy straw hat laughed and pointed to Carol, but Sindbad and his wife felt left out. Sindbad had not been asked to say anything. The ceremony offered none of the catharsis Peggy's friends had wished for, and only added fuel to criticisms of the takeover by the Guggenheim, which had little to do with honoring Peggy and more with the business of fund raising. It was too much like the lawyer expressing his condolences to the family of the deceased but secretly anticipating his fee.

A black-tie dinner in the palazzo was planned for that night to entertain those patrons of the Guggenheim who had donated ten thousand dollars or more and other friends of the collection. Pegeen's sons, by three different fathers, met at the Gritti Palace Hotel before going on to the dinner. Fabrice, speaking Spanish, French, and English, arrived in a top hat and tails. He kept threatening in his accented voice to make a *demonstration* against the museum, whose function he perceived was to introduce Guggenheim to Guggenheim. Nicolas was equally handsome, more Italian in his looks, with soft brown eyes, a lovely mouth, and wavy hair. Sandro, tall, gaunt, angular, with large haunted eyes, appeared young and shy. Looking at them, one could appreciate the human price Peggy had paid in creating a monument. All were unsettled and disappointed and threatened a lawsuit under Italian law, which forbade the estate of a resident passing out of the country. Enemy camps had begun forming—the family versus the museum.

Gondolas from the Gritti brought guests across the canal to the palazzo. The terrace was lit by votive candles, a beautiful sight from the canal. (Peggy would never have wasted the money.) Drinks were served in the entrance hall under the Calder mobile. Few of the assembled guests had known Peggy. Peggy Vail, wearing one of Peggy's turquoise-and-gold caftans, complained that Sindbad had not been asked to speak.

Dinner was served by candlelight in the double sitting room. Thomas Messer rose to make a few remarks. He started by expounding on the three *W*s—Work, Wisdom, and Wealth—which one diner snickered really meant Wealth, Wealth, Wealth. He was announcing with great pride that Mrs. Richard Gardiner, the wife of the then American Ambassador to Italy, had graciously consented to serve on a committee to raise funds for the Peggy Guggenheim Collection, when Sindbad's deep, gravelly, and inebriated voice resounded through the darkened rooms: "BIG DEE-AL." After dinner, Peggy Vail went around weeping and reasserting that Sindbad should have been invited to say something. Some assured her that he had made the most memorable speech of the evening.

The museum suffered from the effects of a certain degree of misunderstanding as to what would happen after Peggy's death. Thomas Messer, now technically the director of the Peggy Guggenheim Collection, explained the changes the Guggenheim made in hanging the pictures and eliminating from view some of the artifacts:

> I don't consider we inherited a historical house. Its inherent importance is negligible. What is most important now is the assurance of support from the *Commune* in Venice, accompanied by a drive among Italian banks to raise funds. It will be a first-rate museum. At the first opening, we re-hung the collection—the Mondrians couldn't be seen in the dark hall—used some of the spaces, gained two rooms. The year after, we added two more rooms. In the bedroom we added the Pegeens, the Laurence Vail screen, we put the bottles on a shelf over the window.

Messer also explained that "there was no stipulation on Pegeen. I put them in the bedroom. There should be one room where we put items separate from the collection. Pegeens would be misinterpreted. This was very much opposed. She never required, nor even discussed, the Pegeens." Moreover, Peggy had made no requirements as to her bedroom, the dining room, or anything else—only that the proceeds of a sale go to Sindbad. Peggy knew full well that the Guggenheim Museum would make administrative changes and did not much care. "The garden has become a sculpture court, which previously it was not. All the sculpture is out in front except for the Marini. . . . We are running the administration of a half-a-million-dollar operation, which should become the best modern art collection in Italy.

"The most important elements in taking over the collection," Messer went on, "were: one, the rescue of works of art and conservation, and two, public meaning: re-installation and cataloguing." Watchmen were hired, museum interns arrived, experts looked into the long-range effects of light on the paintings. "We are working toward the development of the collection in a public direction. We had to change a home into a museum." And without benefit of any endowment bequest from Peggy.

In the years since, the collection has been administered by the Guggenheim Museum in New York, and it has shed the gloom of its first reopening. It hums along smoothly, with Philip Rylands as its administrator in Venice, although the ultimate responsibility rests with New York. "We have one hundred thousand visitors each summer," says Rylands. "Peggy Guggenheim is the best collection of modern art in Italy." Now, with the palazzo clean and white and bright, visitors can actually *see* the pictures. The dining room has remained as it was, but all the other rooms, with the exception of Peggy's bedroom, have been taken over as museum spaces. In the bedroom, Peggy's Calder headboard is now encased in glass, and a Fortuny bedspread subsequently acquired by the museum decorates the bed. The entrance hall, where so many guests once hit their heads against the Calder mobile, is an information center with catalogues, posters, and other museum memorabilia available for sale. The dank and dark basement where Peggy displayed the Abstract Expressionists is closed off; the Pollocks have been brought up to the light of the main floor. The Surrealists in the *barchessa* have been reinstalled with a small de Chirico in the spot where Max Ernst's big, red, powerful *Attirement of the Bride* used to hang. The garden, once dark and overgrown with weeds, has been repaved. It is a spanking-white and efficient museum. "It's a pity," said Maria Theresa Rubin, echoing the sentiment of the museum's detractors, "they should have changed her house, the atmosphere it had. Museums are sometimes a little bit cold and it was not."

But occasionally, in the sight of the headboard that jingles and shines, in the dust and cigarette ashes in the corners, in the Pollocks, de Chiricos, and Ernsts, there is something of Peggy, who said, "I always did what I wanted," and did so to the end.

APPENDIX

EXHIBITIONS AT GUGGENHEIM JEUNE, LONDON

JANUARY 24–FEBRUARY 12, 1938: Jean Cocteau drawings, also furniture designed for *Les Chevaliers de la Table Ronde.*

FEBRUARY 18–MARCH 12, 1938: Wassily Kandinsky, paintings, watercolors, drawings, gouaches.

MARCH 18–APRIL 7, 1938: Cedric Morris, portraits.

APRIL 8–MAY 2, 1938: Contemporary sculpture, including Brancusi, Laurens, Pevsner, Duchamp-Villon, Moore, Arp, Calder, Täuber-Arp.

MAY 5–MAY 26, 1938: Geer van Velde, paintings, gouaches.

MAY 31–JUNE 18, 1938: Benno, paintings, and Rita Kernn-Larsen, Surrealist paintings.

JUNE 21–JULY 2, 1938: "Contemporary Painting and Sculpture," including Kandinsky, Picasso, Masson, de Kermadec, Borès, van Velde, P. Norman Dawson, G. L. Roux, Suzanne Roger, Laurens, Kernn-Larsen, Dali, Moore, Magritte, Ernst, Miró, Paul Nash, Penrose, Eileen Agar, Arp, Hazel King-Farlow, Edward Burra, Benno, André Beaudin, Anthony Brown, Francis Butterfield, Kokoschka Henghes.

JULY 6–16, 1938: Yves Tanguy, paintings.

SECOND SEASON

OCTOBER 14–29, 1938: Children's art.

NOVEMBER 4–26, 1938: "Collages, Papiers-Collés, and Photo-Montages," including Breton, Ernst, Braque, Arp, Duchamp, Man Ray, Laurens, Mina Loy, Picasso, Schwitters, Gris, Masson, Miró, Picabia, and others.

DECEMBER 2–23, 1938: Jill Salaman, pottery.

DECEMBER 2–23, 1938: Marie Wassilieff, paintings, sculpture, masks, portrait dolls, decorative objects.

JANUARY 10–31, 1939: G. W. Pailthorpe and R. Mednikoff, paintings, drawings.

FEBRUARY 15–MARCH 11, 1939: Wolfgang Paalen, Surrealist exhibition.

MARCH 16–APRIL 8, 1939: John Tunnard.

APRIL 14–MAY 6, 1939: Henghes, sculpture.

APRIL 14–MAY 6, 1939: Charles Howard.

MAY 11–MAY 27, 1939: "Abstract and Concrete Art."

JUNE 5–22, 1939: "André Breton Presents Mexican Art" (This catalogue is missing from Peggy's collection of exhibition catalogues, but she said there was one missing. Although Roland Penrose could not recall this show taking place, it was advertised in the *London Bulletin* no. 13 [April 15, 1939]).

JUNE 8–22, 1939: Julian Trevelyan, paintings, collages, etchings.

JUNE 8–22, 1939: S. W. Hayter's Studio 17, engravings, etchings, plaster prints.

JUNE 22, 1939: A Farewell Party, Miss Gisèle Freund will show projections of color photography of famous contemporary artists.

ART OF THIS CENTURY, NEW YORK

OCTOBER 20, 1942: Opening for benefit of American Red Cross, from 8:00 P.M. to midnight.

DECEMBER 1942: Joseph Cornell, Objects; Marcel Duchamp, *Box in a Valise;* Laurence Vail, Bottles.

JANUARY 5–31, 1943: "Exhibition by 31 Women" including Djuna Barnes, Xenia Cage, Leonora Carrington, Vera da Silva, Leonor Fini, Suzy Frelinghuysen, Valentine Hugo, Buffie Johnson, Frida Kahlo, Gypsy Rose Lee, Hazel King-Farlow, Louise Nevelson, Meret Oppenheim, Barbara Reis, Irene Rice-Pereira, Kay Sage, Hedda Sterne, Dorothea Tanning, Sophie Täuber-Arp, Pegeen Vail.

FEBRUARY 8–MARCH 6, 1943: Jean Hélion, retrospective.

MARCH 13–APRIL 10, 1943: "15 Early 15 Late Paintings" by Braque, Chagall, Dali, de Chirico, Duchamp, Ernst, Gris, Kandinsky, Klee, Léger, Masson, Miró, Mondrian, Picasso, Tanguy.

APRIL 16–MAY 15, 1943: "Collage," including Cornell, Pollock, Jacqueline Lamba, Ad Reinhardt, David Hare, Max Ernst, Jimmy Ernst, Calder, Gris, Picabia, Baziotes, Schwitters, Gypsy Rose Lee, George Grosz, Laurence Vail, Arp, Balcomb Greene.

MAY 18–JUNE 26, 1943: "Spring Salon for Young Artists," including Virginia Admiral, Baziotes, Bolotowsky, Peter Busa, Ronnie Elliot, Jimmy Ernst, Perle Fine, Morris Graves, Fannie Hillsmith, Kamrowski, Matta, Motherwell, Rice-Pereira, Pollock Reinhardt, Sekula, Sterne.

SECOND SEASON

OCTOBER 5–NOVEMBER 6, 1943: "Masterworks of Early de Chirico."

NOVEMBER 9–27, 1943: Jackson Pollock, first exhibition, paintings and drawings.

NOVEMBER 30–DECEMBER 1943: "Natural Insane Surrealist Art."

JANUARY 4–22, 1944: Irene Rice-Pereira.

FEBRUARY 1944: Jean Arp.

MARCH 7, 1944: Hans Hofmann, first exhibition, oils, gouaches, drawings.

APRIL 11, 1944: Group show, first exhibition in America, works by Braque, Dali, Hare, Hélion, Hirshfield, Kandinsky, Léger, Matta, Miró, Motherwell, Pollock, Rothko, Tanguy, Vail, Waldberg.

MAY 2–JUNE 3, 1944: Spring Salon, including Baziotes, Elliot, Hillsmith, Salemme, Motherwell, Pollock, Hare.

MAY 29–JUNE 3, 1944: "The Negro in American Life," photographic exhibit.

THIRD SEASON

OCTOBER 3–21, 1944: William Baziotes, first one-man show.

OCTOBER 24–NOVEMBER 11, 1944: Robert Motherwell, paintings, papiers collés, drawings.

NOVEMBER 14, 1944: David Hare, sculptures.

DECEMBER 12, 1944–JANUARY 6, 1945: Isabelle Waldberg, constructions, and Rudolph Ray, paintings.

JANUARY 9–FEBRUARY 4, 1945: Mark Rothko, paintings.

FEBRUARY 10–MARCH 16, 1945: "Collages on Bottles" by Laurence Vail.

FEBRUARY 10–MARCH 16, 1945: Alberto Giacometti.

MARCH 19–APRIL 14, 1945: Jackson Pollock, paintings, gouaches, drawings, March 19: mural on view at 155 East 61, from 3:00 P.M. to 6:00 P.M.

APRIL 17–MAY 12, 1945: Wolfgang Paalen.

MAY 15–JUNE 7, 1945: Alice Rahon Paalen.

JUNE 12–JULY 7, 1945: "The Women," including Virginia Admiral, Nell Blaine, Louise Bourgeois, Xenia Cage, Leonora Carrington, Ronnie Elliot, Perle Fine, Annie Harvey, Fannie Hillsmith, Leonore Krasner (listed but did not show), Jacqueline Lamba, Gypsy Rose Lee, Muriel Levy, Loren MacIver, Marjorie McKee, Dorothy Miller, Anne Neagoe, Alice Paalen, Helen Phillips, Barbara Reis, Irene Rice-Pereira, Kay Sage, Sonia Sekula, Janet Sobel, Hedda Sterne, Julia Theckla, Pegeen Vail.

FOURTH SEASON

OCTOBER 6, 1945: Autumn Salon, including William Baziotes, Julian Beck, Ted Bradley, Peter Busa, Jim Davis, Willem de Kooning, Robert de Niro, Jimmy Ernst, Manny Farber, Adolph Gottlieb, Ernest Gutman, John Ferren, Joseph Funck, David Hare, S. W. Hayter, Lee Hersch, Foster Jewell, Jerome Kamrowski, Robert Motherwell, Ralph Nelson, Jackson Pollock, Richard Pousette-Dart, Kurt Roesch, Mark Rothko, Charles Seliger, Leon Smith, Clyfford Still, Paul Wilton.

OCTOBER 30–NOVEMBER 17, 1945: Charles Seliger, first exhibition.

OCTOBER 30–NOVEMBER 17, 1945: Paul Wilton, first exhibition.

NOVEMBER 20–DECEMBER 8, 1945: Lee Hersch, paintings.

NOVEMBER 20–DECEMBER 8, 1945: Ted Bradley, paintings.

DECEMBER 11–29, 1945: "Christmas Exhibition of Gouaches."

JANUARY 2–19, 1946: Janet Sobel, paintings.

JANUARY 22–FEBRUARY 9, 1946: David Hare, sculpture.

FEBRUARY 12–MARCH 2, 1946: Clyfford Still, first exhibition.

FEBRUARY 12–MARCH 2, 1946: Pamela Bodin, five sculptures.

MARCH 9–30, 1946: Pegeen Vail, first exhibition.

MARCH 9–30, 1946: Peter Busa, paintings.

APRIL 2–20, 1946: Jackson Pollock, paintings.

APRIL 23–MAY 11, 1946: Teresa Zarnower, sixteen gouaches.

APRIL 23–MAY 11, 1946: Robert de Niro, first exhibition.

MAY 14–JUNE 1, 1946: Sonia Sekula.

FIFTH SEASON

OCTOBER 22–NOVEMBER 9, 1946: Hans Richter (1919–1946).

NOVEMBER 12–30, 1946: Rudi Blesh, paintings, 1946.

NOVEMBER 12–30, 1946: Virginia Admiral, six paintings.

DECEMBER 3–21, 1946: John Goodwin, David Hill, Dwight Ripley, Charles Seliger, Kenneth Scott.

DECEMBER 24, 1946–JANUARY 11, 1947: Marjorie McKee.

DECEMBER 24, 1946–JANUARY 11, 1947: Helen Schwinger.

JANUARY 14–FEBRUARY 7, 1947: Jackson Pollock, Sounds in the Grass (series), Accabonac Creek (series).

FEBRUARY 1–MARCH 1, 1947: Morris Hirshfield, Memorial Showing, last paintings.

MARCH 4–22, 1947: "Richard Pousette-Dart."

MARCH 25–APRIL 19, 1947: David Hare, sculpture.

APRIL 29–MAY 31, 1947: Theo van Doesburg, first American retrospective.

MAY 31, 1947: Gallery closes.

NOTES

The reader may assume that unless otherwise noted all direct quotes in the text are from a series of personal and telephone interviews conducted by the author from 1977 to 1985.

ABBREVIATIONS USED

BOOKS:
> Peggy Guggenheim, *Confessions of an Art Addict* (New York: The Macmillan Company, 1960): *CAA*
>
> Peggy Guggenheim, *Out of This Century:* Confessions of an Art Addict (New York: Universe Books, 1979): *OTC.*

PERIODICALS:
> *The New York Times: NYT*

INDIVIDUALS:
> Peggy Guggenheim interviews, July 1978; August 1979: PG.

REPOSITORIES:
> Djuna Barnes Archives, University of Maryland, College Park: DBA.
>
> Herbert Read Archives, University of Victoria Library, Victoria, B.C., Canada: HRA.
>
> Archives of American Art, Smithsonian Institution, Washington, D.C.: AAA.
>
> The New-York Historical Society, N.Y.C.: NYHS.

CHAPTER 1: FROM SELLING RAGS TO RICHES

3   "they set the tone": Stephen Birmingham, *Our Crowd* (New York: Harper & Row, 1967; reprint, New York: Berkley, 1984), p. 14.

4   "Most of the Seligman brothers": Geoffrey T. Hellman, "Sorting Out the Seligmans," *The New Yorker* (October 30, 1954), p. 39.

4   "Guggenheim Smelt Her": *OTC*, p. 2.

5   "bag around our waists": "James Seligman, 88, Tells of Early Life," *NYT*, April 14, 1912, p. 12.

5   "nail customers": George S. Hellman, *The Story of the Seligmans* (New York, 1945), p. 17, NYHS.

5   "rings, bracelets, and watches": "James Seligman, 88," p. 12.

6   "unerring instinct for profit": Gatenby Williams (William Guggenheim, pseud.) and Charles Monroe Heath, *William Guggenheim* (New York: Lone Voice Publishing, 1934), p. 32.

6   "another extremity entirely": Milton Lomask, *Seed Money: The Guggenheim Story* (New York: Farrar, Straus, 1964), p. 19.

8   "seven sticks" Guggenheim, *William Guggenheim*, p. 37.

9   "ashes which spilled": Bernard M. Baruch, *My Own Story* (New York: Henry Holt, 1957), pp. 192–93.

9   "unyielding courage": "Meyer Guggenheim, Smelter King, Dead," *NYT*, March 17, 1905, p. 9.

11   "I suggest the name Schlemiel": George S. Hellman, "Joseph Seligman, American Jew," *Publication of the American Jewish Historical Society* 41 (September 1951), p. 33.

CHAPTER 2: ECCENTRICS

12   "highly bred": Birmingham, *Our Crowd*, p. 279.

12   "tempestuous unaccountable": George Hellman, *Story of the Seligmans.*

13   "When do you think my husband": *OTC*, p. 2.

13   "Take that child away": Hazel Guggenheim McKinley interview, May 20, 1980.

13   "old gentleman clad in black": "James Seligman, 88," p. 12.

14   "a family name no doubt": Victor Bernstein interview, 1980.

14   "tired of being sick": "W. Seligman Kills Himself in a Hotel," *NYT*, February 13, 1912, p. 7.

14   "This is the only way": "Seligman Kills Wife and Himself," *NYT*, December 17, 1915, p. 9.

14   "would come to visit": Susan Miller interview, November 1979.

14   "just for a minute": ibid.

15   "Go look in the closet": ibid.

15   "I don't see why I shouldn't": Geoffrey Hellman, "Sorting Out," p. 64.

15   "helped subdue any desire": Ross Muir and Carl White, *Over the Long Term: The Story of J. & W. Seligman & Co.* (New York: J. & W. Seligman, 1964), p. 133.

15   "where the brains were supposed": Geoffrey Hellman, "Sorting Out," p. 64.

15   "wearing a flower": ibid., p. 65.

15   "a somewhat diminished estate": ibid.

16   "Whether she was stupid": Maude (Mrs. Eustace) Seligman interview, October 22, 1979.

16   "I would probably starve": Susan Miller interview, 1979.

16   "feather, feather": *OTC,* p. 49.

16   "Good morning, good morning": Eleanor Castle-Stewart telephone interview, April 28, 1979.

16   "a piece from Gertrude Stein": Harold Loeb, *The Way It Was* (New York: Criterion Books, 1959), p. 97.

16   "ranging in glitter": Lomask, *Seed Money,* p. 40.

–17

17   "make love to a woman before breakfast": ibid., p. 41.

17   "looked after by his cook": *OTC,* p. 4.

18   she sued Will: cf. "Guggenheim Hearing Ends," *NYT,* January 1, 1913, p. 17; "Guggenheim Tells Marriage Story," *NYT,* January 2, 1913, p. 6.

CHAPTER 3: THE TORMENTS OF THE DAMNED

20   "excessively lonely and sad": *OTC,* p. 8.

20   notorious psychotic: cf. Sigmund Freud, "The Psychotic Dr. Schreber," *Three Case Histories* (New York: Collier Books, 1963), pp. 103–86; and William G. Niederland, *The Schreber Case* (New York: Quadrangle Books, 1974), pp. 49–154.

20   German fairy tales: cf. Robert Darnton, *The Great Cat Massacre* (New York: Basic Books, 1984), pp. 9–74; Dr. Heinrich von Hoffmann, *Der Struwwelpeter* given to all "good" little boys and girls at Christmastime.

21   "I have no pleasant memories": *OTC,* p. 6.

22   "I adored my father": ibid., p. 10.

23   *Ausklopfer:* William G. Niederland letter to author, November 1, 1980.

23   "had the same agreeable quality": *OTC,* p. 11.

23   "I can't say much for my mother": Maude Seligman interview, 1979.

CHAPTER 4: THE *TITANIC*

26   "God himself": Walter Lord, *A Night to Remember* (New York: Holt, Rinehart & Winston, 1955), p. 50.

27   "Each day, as the voyage went on": Charles Herbert Lightoller, *Titanic and Other Ships* (London: I. Nicholson & Watson, 1935), p. 221.

27   "It was pitch dark": ibid., p. 225.

27   "nothing could have saved her": ibid.

27   "That cold, green water": ibid., p. 237.

28   more than 1,500 people drowned: (1503) Lord, *Night to Remember,* p. 172.

28   "I *know* something happened": Hazel McKinley interview, May 20, 1980.

28   "great mental agitation": "Seeking News of Lost Relatives," *NYT,* April 17, 1912, p. 1.

28   "There should have been more boats": ibid.

28   "Then she suddenly drew back": ibid.

29   "prostrated with grief": "Sent Wife Message," *NYT,* April 20, 1912, p. 9.

29   "The steward produced": ibid.

29   "stayed together": ibid.

29   "new, uneasy era": Lord, *Night to Remember,* p. 39.

30   assets of about two billion: Janice Simpson, "Founding Families: Some Guggen-

heims Carrying on Tradition of Eccentric Heirs," *The Wall Street Journal,* May 31, 1979, pp. 1, 33.

30   "My mother made eggs": Jenifer Cosgrieff interview, November 17, 1980.

31   "one gentleman in leisure": Simpson, "Founding Families," p. 1.

CHAPTER 5: ADOLESCENCE

33   "She drove the girls crazy": Jenifer Cosgrieff interview.

33   "mad about hygiene": Eleanor (Guggenheim) Castle-Stewart interview.

33   "frightfully interested in our temperatures": Hazel McKinley interview.

33   "no social life except the family": Susan Miller interview.

34   "more German than Jewish": Stephen Birmingham, "The Temple that Our Crowd Built," *New York* (April 21, 1980), p. 47.

35   "Cohn was once": Ernest Hemingway, *The Sun Also Rises* (New York: Scribners, 1926), p. 1.

35   "as an Episcopalian": Iris Love interview, March 12, 1980.

CHAPTER 6: THE SUNWISE TURN

38   "a mind to lose?": *OTC,* p. 20.

38   "tip-tilted like a flower": ibid, p. 22.

39   "completely unworthy of her": ibid., p. 21.

39   "walls painted a rich orange": Loeb, *The Way It Was,* p. 34.

39   "only a clerk": *OTC,* p. 23.

39   "Awkward as a young magpie": Loeb, *The Way It Was,* p. 36.

40   "slight which she never forgot": ibid., p. 41.

41   "I'm almost as old": Edmund Wilson, *The Twenties* (New York: Farrar, Straus & Giroux, 1975), pp. 65–66.

CHAPTER 7: OVER THERE

46   "an intoxication": Cyril Connolly, *The Evening Colonnade* (New York: Harcourt Brace Jovanovich, 1973), p. 6.

46   "we were idiotic": *OTC,* p. 25.

47   "How far shall I put it in": PG.

CHAPTER 8: THE KING OF BOHEMIA

48   "decent alcoholic drink": Harold E. Stearns, *The Street I Know* (New York: Lee Furman, 1935), p. 299.

49   "They would spend": Malcolm Cowley, *A Second Flowering: Works and Days of the Lost Generation* (New York: The Viking Press, 1973), p. 13.

49   "no problem about her identity": Maria Jolas interview, April 12, 1980.

50   "had suicidal tendencies": Sharon Cowling interview, April 12, 1980.

50   "as I love you": William Carlos Williams, *A Voyage to Pagany* (New York: New Directions, 1928, 1970), p. 33.

50   "A few Byronic figures": Matthew Josephson, *Life Among the Surrealists* (New York: Holt, Rinehart & Winston, 1962), p. 86.

51   "there was a remarkable procession": Kay Boyle and Robert McAlmon, *Being Geniuses Together* (New York: Doubleday & Co., 1968), p. 198.

51   "*other* people's fornications": Josephson, *Life Among the Surrealists,* p. 85.

51   "toes like a prow" Boyle and McAlmon, *Being Geniuses Together,* p. 204.
51   "long mane of yellow hair": Josephson, *Life Among the Surrealists,* p. 86.

CHAPTER 9: THE ROYAL WEDDING

53   "buy him a drink": Josephson, *Life Among the Surrealists,* p. 86.
53   "Every time I saw him look": *OTC,* p. 29.
54   "I scarcely know him": Stuart Gilbert, ed., *Letters of James Joyce* (New York: The Viking Press, 1957, 1966), p. 182.
54   "barelegged and be-sandaled": Loeb, *The Way It Was,* p. 120.
55   *"Old men and little birds"* ibid., p. 148.
55   "lax intestinal control": ibid., p. 149.
55   "Everything was 'my brother' ": *OTC,* p. 33.
56   "He brought me into": ibid., p. 36.
56   "I met so many people": Stanley Price, "The Mrs. Guggenheim Collection," *The NYT Magazine,* January 17, 1965, p. 17.
56   "They had the kind of nose": *OTC,* p. 28.
56   "a kind of Surrealist thing": Yvonne Hagen interview, March 15, 1980.
56   "breaking crockery and smashing": *OTC,* p. 36.
56   "little agonized screams": Malcolm Cowley interview, August 2, 1979.
57   "it spat in the eye": David Gascoyne, *A Short Survey of Surrealism* (London: Cobden-Sanderson, 1935), p. 23.
57   "You are all ASSES": Josephson, *Life Among the Surrealists,* p. 128.
57   "let loose a great volley": ibid., p. 129.
57   "For the first time": Calvin Tomkins and editors of Time-Life Books, *The World of Marcel Duchamp: 1887–1968* (New York: Time-Life Books, 1966), p. 62.
58   "as if Brancusi's egg": *OTC,* p. 38.
58   "Peggy will see": ibid., p. 49.
59   "Knock, Knock, Knock": Laurence Vail, *Murder! Murder!* (London: Peter Davies, 1931), pp. 145, 146.
59   "Cedy boy": Sindbad Vail interview, May 2, 1979.
59   "toes on view": Loeb, *The Way It Was,* p. 174.
59   "mass velocity": Malcolm Cowley, *Exile's Return* (New York: The Viking Press, 1951), p. 164.
59   plebeian carnival": ibid., p. 165.
60   "decapitated pimples": William Carlos Williams, *The Autobiography of William Carlos Williams* (New York: Random House, 1948), p. 188.
60   "An informer" Loeb, *The Way It Was,* p. 177.
60   "and assault the proprietor": Cowley, *Exile's Return,* p. 165.
60   "raincoat which he never removed": ibid.
60   "Harold Loeb, looking on": ibid.
60   "with his look of a dog": ibid., p. 166.
60   *"Quel Salaud":* ibid., p. 167.
61   "In any case": Boyle and McAlmon, *Being Geniuses Together,* p. 38.

CHAPTER 10: PROMISCUOUS

62   "you could have sworn": Stearns, *The Street I Know,* p. 300.
62   "Paris had a quality": *NYT,* November 16, 1980.
62   "making love on my bed": *OTC,* p. 48.
63   "dirty Jew": ibid., p. 49.

64   "If I were to add up": ibid., p. 51.

64   "first name for fertility": Laurence Vail letter to to Eleanor ("Fitzi") Fitzgerald, 1925, collection of Apple Vail.

65   "a great, big blustering": Maria Jolas interview, April 12, 1980.

65   "Let's go home to the Lutetia": Laurence Vail, "Here Goes" (unpublished memoirs), collection of Sindbad Vail; in the interest of clarity I have substituted the real names for Vail's pseudonyms: John Holms for Jacobeaus and Peggy for Pigeon throughout.

65   "her total unconcern": Apple Vail interview, February 13, 1980.

65   "only once in twenty thousand years": PG.

65   "constant and furious rebellion": Clover Vail interview, November 19, 1979.

65   "there was a blankness": Apple Vail interview, February 13, 1980.

65   "They were completely empty": Williams, *Autobiography,* pp. 220–21.

66   "The younger folk": Sisley Huddleston, *Paris Salons, Cafés, Studios* (New York: Blue Ribbon Books, 1928), p. 81.

68   "We lived in a house": Yvonne Hagen interview, March 15, 1980.

68   *"always* disagree": Apple Vail interview, February 13, 1980.

68   "rich Jews": Laurence Vail letter to Eleanor ("Fitzi") Fitzgerald, January 3, 1929, collection of Apple Vail.

68   "mad Guggenheim women": Laurence Vail to Eleanor ("Fitzi") Fitzgerald, December 7, 1928, collection of Apple Vail.

68   "Oh, you bloody idiot": Sharon Cowling interview.

68   "She knew nothing": Vail, "Here Goes."

69   "marvelous way of making you interested": Yvonne Hagen interview.

69   "Can you imagine?": Apple Vail interview.

CHAPTER 11: A ROLLS-ROYCE ON THE BLINK

71   "a distinct talent": Boyle and McAlmon, *Being Geniuses Together,* p. 163.

72   "Try some of this": Julien Levy, *Memoir of an Art Gallery* (New York: G.P. Putnam's Sons, 1977), p. 34.

72   "In those days": Josephson, *Life Among the Surrealists,* pp. 315–16.

73   "She was always a city girl": Vail, "Here Goes."

73   "I felt I had": *OTC,* p. 74.

73   "Don't take yourself seriously": Apple Vail interview.

73   "squat, with feet turned outwards": John Glassco, *Memoirs of Montparnasse* (Toronto and New York: Oxford University Press, 1970), p. 17.

74   almost motherly: Boyle and McAlmon, *Being Geniuses Together,* p. 225.

74   "cynically betrayed": Glassco, *Memoirs of Montparnasse,* p. 17.

74   "bitter old woman": Samuel Putnam, *Paris Was Our Mistress: Memoirs of a Lost and Found Generation* (New York: The Viking Press, 1947), p. 87.

74   similarly slighted: Aaron Bohrod, "Surrealism and Sex à la Guggenheim," *Chicago Sunday Tribune,* March 31, 1946.

74   "Jewish cordon bleu": *OTC,* p. 79.

74   do better writing a cookbook: ibid.

75   "Pink Whiskers": Laurence Vail letter to Eleanor Fitgerald, January 3, 1929, collection of Apple Vail.

76   "a spectacle of herself": *OTC,* p. 82.

76   "whipping boy": PG.

76   "feeds on other people's": Laurence Vail letter to Eleanor ("Fitzi") Fitzgerald, December 7, 1928, collection of Apple Vail.

76 "Suddenly, I surprise": ibid.
76 "mature man": Laurence Vail letter to Eleanor ("Fitzi") Fitzgerald, December 7, 1928.
76 "dressing briskly, as she always": Vail, "Here Goes."
76 "ruminating the details": ibid.
77 "I can't go": ibid.
77 "Don't know if I'll come back": ibid.
77 "No one could fall": ibid.

CHAPTER 12: MEDEA

78 "No, I'll be all right": Audrey (Mrs. Cornelius Ruxton) Love interview, June 27, 1979.
79 "You mustn't be upset": ibid.
79 "Why would she choose me?": Jenifer Cosgrieff interview, November 17, 1980.
79 "the murderess": Virgil Thomson interview, 1979.
79 "I shall have to prove": Laurence Vail letter to Eleanor Fitzgerald, December 7, 1928.
79 "until they met her": Buffie Johnson interview, May 16, 1979.
80 "Hazel killed": Jenifer Cosgrieff interview.
80 "looked like her mother": Susan Miller interview, November 1979.
80 "nervous breakdown": Jenifer Cosgrieff interview.
80 sent the . . . Loves a . . . candelabra: ibid.
81 "It has nothing to do with me": PG.
81 "spoke to the Englishman's family": Susan Miller interview.
81 "Did mother ever tell you?": Jenifer Cosgrieff interview.
81 "let the waters close": Maria Jolas interview.

CHAPTER 13: FINIS

82 "Something dreadful is happening": Vail, "Here Goes."
82 "His woman told": Laurence Vail letter to Eleanor Fitzgerald, December 7, 1928.
82 "She was always a fool": Vail, "Here Goes."
83 "most unceremoniously": Laurence Vail to Eleanor Fitzgerald, January 3, 1929, collection of Apple Vail.
83 "I was the bridesmaid": Vail, "Here Goes."
84 carnation in the buttonhole: Boyle and McAlmon, *Being Geniuses Together*, p. 263.
84 "of-the-world": ibid., p. 293.
84 "but then Raymond": ibid., p. 274.
85 "rolled in a blanket": Caresse Crosby, *The Passionate Years* (London: Alvin Redman, 1955), p. 248.
85 "I'll sit between you": Boyle and McAlmon, *Being Geniuses Together*, p. 325.
85 Harry Crosby . . . reported seeing them: Harry Crosby, *Shadows of the Sun: The Diaries of Harry Crosby*, ed. Edward Germain (Santa Barbara, Calif.: Black Sparrow Press, 1977), p. 227.
85 "color of moss": C. Crosby, *The Passionate Years*, p. 248.
85 "frightened of you": *OTC*, p. 145.

86 "clicking of a busy Underwood": C. Crosby, *The Passionate Years,* pp. 302–303.

86 "any one of them": Apple Vail interview.

CHAPTER 14: HANGOVER HALL

91 "That enchanted country": Edmund Wilson, *Memoirs of Hecate County* (Boston: Nonpareil Books, 1980, p. 438.

92 "little skyscraper": *OTC,* p. 105.

93 "financial status": Alec Waugh, *My Brother Evelyn and Other Portraits* (New York: Farrar, Straus & Giroux, 1967), p. 77.

93 "You drink": Vail, "Here Goes."

93 "instructed her, daily": William Gerhardie, *Resurrection*(New York: Harcourt, Brace, 1934), p. 177.

95 "rather rococo": *OTC,* p. 114.

95 "looking for a night": Wilson, *The Twenties,* p. 109.

95 "You've got the money": PG.

96 "never felt you really liked": Peggy Guggenheim letter to Djuna Barnes, November 29, 1967, DBA.

96 "Emily was very strange": Sindbad Vail letter to author, October 14, 1980.

97 "blue, purple, and green": Paul Bowles, *Without Stopping* (London: Peter Owen, 1972), p. 167.

97 "I had such a happy": *OTC,* p. 121.

98 "If I had had any sense": ibid., p. 125.

CHAPTER 15: YEW TREE COTTAGE

99 son of a country doctor: Walter Chancellor Garman.

100 "old tweed suit": Michael Wishart, *High Diver* (London: Quartet Books, 1977, 1978), p. 5.

100 "father Wishart in Heaven": ibid., p. 13.

103 "like Sir Galahad": *OTC,* p. 152.

103 call her a Trotskyite!: ibid., p. 153.

103 "more and more Communist": PG.

104 Peggy remembered the sheets: Michael Wishart interview, September 29, 1982.

105 "I think my life is over": *OTC,* p. 158.

CHAPTER 16: A CHANGE OF LIFE

107 "I never knew": Virgil Thomson interview.

108 to "promote the advancement": Lomask, *Seed Money,* p. 248; cf. "Guggenheim's Modern Art Foundation," *Art News* 35 (September 18, 1937), pp. 16, 23.

109 "like a lazy echo": Rudi Blesh, *Modern Art USA* (New York: Alfred A. Knopf, 1956), p. 216.

109 "crazily in love": Lomask, *Seed Money,* p. 175.

109 "Always Bauer": ibid., p. 176.

109 "a genius, the greatest": Hilla Rebay, press releases, writings, and other miscellaneous pieces on file at the Museum of Modern Art, New York.

110 "Home of the Spiritual": Lomask, *Seed Money,* p. 177.

110 "Rubbish!": ibid., p. 171.

110   "streetwalker and a spy": "Hilla Rebay Dies; Artist, Curator," *NYT,* September 28, 1967.

110   "Heil Hilla": *NYT,* December 8, 1942.

110   philanthropists and patrons: see Harvey O'Conner, *The Guggenheims* (New York: Covici Friede, 1937).

111   "plausible pedants": Joan Lewisohn Crowell interview, December 12, 1979.

111   "immodest fashion": "Hilla Rebay Dies."

112   Bore house: *OTC,* p. 251.

112   "mystic double-talk": "Hilla Rebay Dies."

CHAPTER 17: THE GALLERY AND THE BACHELOR

114   "a true liaison": Pierre Cabanne, *Dialogues with Marcel Duchamp* (New York: The Viking Press, 1967, 1971), p. 68.

115   "I liked that face": Calvin Tomkins, *The World of Marcel Duchamp,* p. 78.

115   "It is characteristic of the guilty": Robert Lebel, *Marcel Duchamp* (New York: Grove Press, 1959), p. 1.

115   "not exactly Cubism": Belle Krasne, "A Marcel Duchamp Profile," *Art Digest* 26, no. 8 (January 15, 1952), p. 11.

115   *bête comme un peintre:* cf. Arturo Schwarz, *The Complete Works of Marcel Duchamp* (2d ed., New York: Harry N. Abrams, 1970), p. 19.

116   "not considered proper to call a painting": ibid., p. 16 n. 2.

116   "On the day before": ibid., n. 3.

116   "through with the world of the artists": ibid.

117   "I always had a horror": Winthrop Sargeant, "Dada's Daddy," *Life* 32, no. 17 (April 28, 1952), p. 111.

117   "a social milieu": Cabanne, *Dialogues with Marcel Duchamp,* p. 32.

118   submitted four works: *The Armory Show in Retrospect: 1913–1963* (New York, Munson-Williams-Proctor Institute and Henry Street Settlement, 1963) lists these four; Tomkins, *The World of Marcel Duchamp* includes *Sad Young Man on a Train.*

118   "most stupidly ugly": Blesh, *Modern Art USA,* p. 51.

118   "explosion in a lumber yard": ibid., p. 54.

118   "most famous 'woman' ": ibid., p. 54.

118   "happy idea": Michel Sanouillet and Elmer Peterson, eds., *The Essential Writings of Marcel Duchamp* (London: Thames & Hudson, 1975), p. 141.

119   "Columbus Day": Marcel Duchamp, "Statement," *The Armory Show in Retrospect,* p. 93.

119   "smiling composure": Tomkins, *The World of Marcel Duchamp,* p. 37.

119   "nothing but antipathy": Schwarz, *The Complete Works of Marcel Duchamp,* p. 20.

119   "tiny peephole": Blesh, *Modern Art USA,* p. 33.

119   "brightest stars": Tomkins, *The World of Marcel Duchamp,* p. 38.

120   "leaving some unwanted debris": Man Ray, *Self Portrait,* p. 68.

120   six-dollar entrance fee: Man Ray writes it was two dollars, ibid., p. 70.

120   "plumbing and her bridges": Tomkins, *The World of Marcel Duchamp,* p. 39.

120   "did not discuss functional plumbing": Blesh, *Modern Art USA,* p. 78.

120   "a dreadful revolutionary": *Art and Artists* (London) 1, no. 4 (July 1966),
–21   Special issue on Duchamp, p. 10.

121   "attention is so completely absorbed by chess": Schwarz, *The Complete Works of Marcel Duchamp,* p. 58.

121   "better than to change religion": Tomkins, *The World of Marcel Duchamp*, p. 79.

121   "designing an aeroplane": Hans Richter, *DADA Art and Anti-Art* (New York and London: Oxford University Press, 1965, 1978), p. 94.

121   "My capital is my time": Sargeant, "Dada's Daddy," pp. 110–11.

121   "dinner with Knoedler": *Art and Artists* (London), pp. 33, 35.

121   "I sensed the danger": Cabanne, *Dialogues with Marcel Duchamp*, p. 106.

121   "disarming courtesy and polished charm": Sargeant, "Dada's Daddy," p. 108.

122   "Société Anonyme": Man Ray, *Self Portrait*, p. 89.

123   "paper wrapping for the stand": ibid., p. 96.

123   Dreier was . . . an early fascist: Lillian Kiesler interview, April 24, 1985.

123   "doing it for friendship": Cabanne, *Dialogues with Marcel Duchamp*, p. 58.

123   "The artist exists only if": ibid., p. 70.

123   "The game is never over": *Art and Artists* (London), p. 10.

123   "One mustn't give a F——": ibid., p. 11.

CHAPTER 18: A GREEN-EYED OBLOMOV

124   "He had to educate me completely": *CAA*, p. 47.

125   received in the manner of a royal *levée:* Levy, *Memoir of an Art Gallery*, p. 167.

125   "The odor was extremely pleasant": *OTC*, p. 165.

126   "the office boy's revenge": Richard Ellmann, *James Joyce* (New York, London, Toronto: Oxford University Press, 1959, 1977), p. 684.

126   "He has talent": Richard Ellmann, ed., *Letters of James Joyce* (New York: The Viking Press, 1966), vol. 3, p. 316.

126   "engaged in conversations": Ellmann, *James Joyce*, p. 661.

126   "I don't love anyone": ibid.

126   "almost always": ibid., p. 685.

127   "enjoyed spending": Sylvia Beach, *Shakespeare and Company* (New York: Harcourt, Brace & Company, 1956), pp. 196–97.

127   "pinpoint precision": Nancy Cunard, *These Were the Hours* (Carbondale and Edwardsville: Southern Illinois University Press, 1969), p. 112.

127   "very tall and slim": ibid.

127   "We soon found ourselves": *OTC*, p. 163.

127   "Thank you": ibid.

128   "our day as it was a living thing": ibid.

128   "making love . . . without brandy": ibid., p. 164.

128   Beckett's stabbing incident: Deirdre Bair, *Samuel Beckett* (New York: Harcourt
-29   Brace Jovanovich, 1978), pp. 277–78.

129   *"Je vous en pris":* PG.

CHAPTER 19: "LA JEUNE"

130   pubic hair: *Confessions*, p. 49.

131   "I have a horror": Cabanne, *Dialogues with Marcel Duchamp*, p. 82.

131   "to try and get a bit of gaiety": *Art and Artists* (London) (July 1966), p. 9.

132   "The jeune concerned is Peggy": Noel Thompson, *Daily Sketch*, January 1938.

132   "I really know nothing": Ellmann, *Letters of James Joyce*, vol. 3, p. 419.

133   "stream-of-consciousness symphonies": Blesh, *Modern Art USA*, p. 63.

134   "so jolly and charming": *OTC*, p. 168.

134 "the most daringly original minds": Morley Callaghan, *That Summer in Paris* (New York: Coward-McCann, 1963), p. 142.

134 "everybody adored him and detested her": *OTC*, p. 168.

134 regretted she had not bought all: *CAA*, p. 52.

134 "looked like a businessman": PG.

135 "Kandinsky claimed": *CAA*, p. 52.

135 "known for great art": *OTC*, p. 171.

135 "You will soon find": ibid.

135 precisely how Morris: *Sunday Times* (London), March 27, 1938.

135 "in any Surrealist": *OTC*, p. 171.

136 "quite idiotic": "Tate Gallery Director Will Admit Sculptures Duty Free After All," *Evening Standard,* March 28, 1938.

136 "the sort of stuff": *The New Statesman and Nation,* March 26, 1938.

136 "It's difficult to know": "What He Says Goes Back," *Daily Express,* March 22, 1938.

136 "He is not": ibid.

136 "Herr Hitler painted water-colours": "Sculptures Under a Ban," *Daily Telegraph,* March 24, 1938.

137 "crowing like a rooster": Roland Penrose interview, September 14, 1979.

CHAPTER 20: MY HEART BELONGS TO DADA

141 "stuffed birds and withered": James Thrall Soby, *Arp* (New York: Doubleday/ The Museum of Modern Art, 1958), p. 7.

141 "was no good for me": Josephson, *Life Among the Surrealists,* p. 180.

142 "manhattan there are tubs": Gascoyne, *Short Survey of Surrealism,* p. 27.

143 "I was there": ibid., p. 23.

143 Janco saying dada: H. H. Arnason, *History of Modern Art* (rev. and enl. ed., New York: Harry Abrams, 1977), p. 307.

143 "to be subversive": Georges Hugnet, "Dada and Surrealism," *The Bulletin of the Museum of Modern Art* 4, nos. 2–3 (November–December 1936), essay too late for inclusion in first edition of Alfred H. Barr, *Fantastic Art, Dada and Surrealism,* p. 3.

143 "Logic is always false": Tristan Tzara, *Seven Dada Manifestos,* trans. Barbara Wright (London: John Calder, 1977), p. 11.

143 "a dossier of human imbecility": ibid., p. 77.

143 "ring up your family": ibid., pp. 23–24.

143 "neither bedroom slippers nor": ibid., p. 1.

143 "We spit on humanity": ibid.

144 "spread like a spot of oil": Hugnet, "Dada and Surrealism," p. 4.

144 "the whole immense *Sweinerei*": Uwe M. Schneede, *Max Ernst* (New York: Praeger Publishers, 1973), p. 16.

144 "Dada was the sickness of the world": Hugnet, "Dada and Surrealism," p. 3.

144 "lovable and fantastically comic": Josephson, *Life Among the Surrealists,* p. 180.

144 "dyed-in-the-wool Dadaist": ibid., p. 183.
–45

145 "In nature . . . a broken twig": Patrick Waldberg, *Surrealism* (Cleveland: The World Publishing Co., 1962), p. 46.

145 "bearing his name ARP": Man Ray, *Self Portrait,* p. 244.

146   "It was an important period": Henry Moore in Nicolas Hélion, co-producer, *Peggy Guggenheim: La Ultima Dogaressa,* film (1977).

146   "borrowed my little Henry Moore": PG letter to Herbert Read (November 12, 1945), HRA.

CHAPTER 21: A NEW VICE: SURREALISM

149   "wished to destroy the hoaxes of reason": Arp quoted in William S. Rubin, *Dada, Surrealism, and Their Heritage* (New York: The Museum of Modern Art, 1968), p. 12.

149   "We were intentionally irrational": *Art and Artists* (London) (July 1966), p. 33.

149   "organized pranks": Hugnet, "Dada and Surrealism," p. 17.

149   "the need was felt for new": Julien Levy, *Surrealism* (New York: The Black Sun Press, 1936; reprint ed., New York: Arno Press, 1968), p. 11.

149   "serviceable as a purgative": "Eleven Europeans in America," *The Museum of Modern Art Bulletin* 13, nos. 4–5 (1946), p. 20.

150   "A new vice": Louis Aragon, *Le Paysan de Paris* (1924) in Maurice Nadeau, *The History of Surrealism,* trans. Richard Howard (New York: The Macmillan Company, 1965), p. 39.

150   "psychic automatism": André Breton, "Manifesto of Surrealism," p. 26.

150   "only the marvelous is beautiful": ibid., p. 14.

150   "life pure, naked, raw": Nadeau, *History of Surrealism,* p. 98.

150   "to explode the social order": Luis Buñuel, *My Last Sigh* (New York: Alfred A. Knopf, 1983), p. 107.

150   "set free the imagination of love": Gascoyne, *Short Survey of Surrealism,* p. 2.

150   reclaimed his primitive instincts: Paul Éluard, *La Révolution Surréaliste* no. 8 (December 1926).

150   "existence of the enormous illogical world": Gascoyne, *Short Survey of Surrealism,* p. 3.

151   Is Suicide a Solution?: *La Révolution Surréaliste* no. 1 (December 1, 1924), p. 2; a question of great interest to Breton since the suicide of Jacques Vaché.

151   "Suicide is an act": *La Révolution Surréaliste* no. 2 (January 15, 1925), p. 8. Author's translation.

151   "sprayed with perfume": Levy, *Memoir of an Art Gallery,* p. 170.

151   seemed incredible: Buñuel, *My Last Sigh,* p. 102.

151   "For twenty-five years": Nadeau, *History of Surrealism,* p. 95.

151   "single meaning: pederastic": Gascoyne, *Short Survey of Surrealism,* p. 70.

152   flung his napkin: Roger Shattuck, *The Banquet Years* (New York: Vintage Books, 1955, 1968), pp. 359–60.

152   *"Vive l'Allemagne!":* ibid.

152   "like a woman": Nadeau, *History of Surrealism,* p. 86.

152   "an imposing *chef d'école":* Josephson, *Life Among the Surrealists,* p. 117.

152   *"there* was a governess": Bridget Tichenor interview, November 1980.

152   "most hateful being": Malcolm Haslam, *The Real World of the Surrealists* (New York: Rizzoli, 1978), p. 41.

152   *"Qu'est-ce que c'est ce pédé?":* Bridget Tichenor interview, November 1980.

152   "age of Lautréamont": Nadeau, *History of Surrealism,* p. 121.

153   "things that were taboo": Belle Krasne, "A Marcel Duchamp Profile," pp. 11, 24.

153   Without the language barriers: cf. Anna Balakian, *Surrealism* (New York: E. P. Dutton, 1970).

154   "immense carnivorous flower": Hugnet, "Dada and Surrealism," p. 25.

154   "undeniable ingenuity in staging": André Breton, "Genesis and Perspective of Surrealism," preface to Peggy Guggenheim, ed., *Art of This Century* (New York: Art of This Century, 1942), p. 24.

154   "encounter of two explorers": Roland Penrose, *Scrap Book 1900–1981* (New York: Rizzoli, 1981), p. 56.

155   "a passionate speech in French": ibid., p. 60.

155   "brought to the surface": ibid., p. 62.

155   "Do not judge": Marcel Marcel, ed., *The Autobiography of Surrealism* (New York: The Viking Press, 1980), p. 364.

156   "pettiness and ignorance": ibid., p. 370.

156   "highest point in the graph": André Breton, in Herbert Read, ed., *Surrealism* (London: Faber & Faber, 1936), p. 95.

157   "was rather good": *OTC,* p. 178.

157   "We had a united front": ibid., p. 177.

157   "devoted to 'fancy religions' ": *The Times* (London), May 1938.

158   "She is very slim": *Daily Express,* January 1938, p. 5.

158   "She had the sort of personality": Stanley Price, "The Mrs. Guggenheim Collection," *The NYT Magazine,* January 17, 1965, p. 16.

158   "lots of people": PG.

159   "gay little Flamand": *OTC,* p. 178.

CHAPTER 22: A SAILOR FROM BRITTANY

161   "Like at least one other": "Plenty of Pictures," *The Yorkshire Post,* May 5, 1938.

161   "all because I loved Beckett": *OTC,* p. 176.

161   "listlessly in his apartment": ibid., p. 178.

163   "I took a pencil": Julien Levy, "Tanguy Connecticut Sage," *ARTnews* 53, no. 5 (September 1954), p. 27.

163   "belongs to the domain": Waldberg, *Surrealism* p. 78.

164   "light into nasturtium": André Breton, *Yves Tanguy,* trans. Bravig Imbs (New York: Pierre Matisse Editions, 1946), p. 84.

164   "What Is Surrealism?": *London Bulletin* nos. 4–5 (July 1938; reprint ed., New York: Arno Press, 1969), p. 38.

164   "tchk-tchk tk": Levy, *Memoir of an Art Gallery,* p. 248.

165   "La Noisette": *OTC,* p. 181.

165   "creator of the most tragic": Gascoyne, *Short Survey of Surrealism,* p. 75.

165   "astonished reality": Hugnet, "Dada and Surrealism," p. 25.

166   "I expect nothing": James Thrall Soby, *Yves Tanguy* (New York: The Museum of Modern Art, 1955), p. 19.

166   "Tanguy found himself rich": *OTC,* p. 182.

CHAPTER 23: STRANGE ILLUSIONS

168   *Towards an Independent Revolutionary Art: London Bulletin* no. 6 (October 1938); English translation, no. 7 (December 1938/ January 1939).

168   "seems to have failed": Parker Tyler, "American Letter," *London Bulletin* no. 11 (March 1939), p. 18.

169   "I needed a father": *OTC,* p. 188.

CHAPTER 24: THE SECOND SEASON

171 "very excitingly far beyond": Hugh Porteus, "Art News," *New English Weekly* (November 24, 1938).

172 "He had one eccentricity": *OTC,* p. 191.

172 "was a painter": PG.

172 "He looked like": PG, *Out of This Century* (New York: The Dial Press, 1946), p. 220.

173 "pink ones": "Wonderful London," *Daily Sketch* (December 5, 1938).

173 "With few exceptions": *London Bulletin* no. 10 (February 1939), p. 23.

174 "the bangs of the dictators": *London Bulletin* no. 11 (March 1939), p. 13.

175 "Don't be silly": Julian Trevelyan, "John Tunnard," *London Bulletin* no. 12 (March 15, 1939), pp. 9–10.

175 "like lightning: "Acrobatic Artist," *Daily Sketch,* February 18, 1938.

175 –76 "if I was losing that money": *OTC,* p. 196.

176 "arch highbrow": *Evening Standard,* May 23, 1939.

176 "he looked like a prime minister": *OTC,* p. 198.

177 "I think that was": Steven M. L. Aronson, "Piers Paul Read, A Married Man," *Interview* 10, no. 6 (June 1980), pp. 40–42.

177 "would have been on her guard": Benedict Read interview, April 30, 1979.

177 "open the eyes": *London Bulletin* no. 14 (May 1, 1939), p. 2; editor's disclaimer, p. 22.

178 eliminating meaning, history, humanity: cf. Levy, *Surrealism,* pp. 9–10.

178 "byzantism, escapism": Herbert Read, "An Art of Pure Form," *London Bulletin* no. 14 (May 1, 1939), p. 9.

CHAPTER 25: A DARWINIAN DILEMMA

180 "skillful in technique": Raymond Mortimer, "Notes on Current Shows," *New Statesman and Nation,* June 17, 1939.

180 married to a member of the Darwin family: Roland Penrose interview, September 14, 1979.

180 Freund and her projector: Gisèle Freund, *Gisèle Freund, Photographer,* trans. John Shepley (New York: Harry N. Abrams, 1985), p. 164.

181 "baby Marlene Dietrich": "Wonderful London," *Daily Sketch* (Manchester edition), June 24, 1939.

181 "always be jeune": Winefride Wilson, "Critic's Column," *The Tablet* (January 23, 1965), p. 103.

181 "full of wonderful ideas": *Folio '65,* PG Scrapbooks.

182 "most adorable": PG.

182 "Women are so boring": *OTC,* p. 200.

CHAPTER 26: THE PHONY WAR

187 a plot: Bair, *Samuel Beckett*, p. 299.

188 "I did not know": *OTC,* p. 203.

188 "we were told that Cannes": ibid.

189 "met a few of the people": ibid., p. 204.

190 "in a complete state of collapse" ibid., p. 205.

190 "Take a look": Tom Shachtman, *The Phony War* (New York: Harper & Row, 1982), p. 93.

191   "I have no war aims": William L. Shirer, *The Nightmare Years* (Boston and Toronto: Little, Brown, 1984), p. 459.

191   "We were all safe": Mary Jayne Gold, *Crossroads Marseilles 1940* (New York: Doubleday & Co., 1980), p. 40.

191   "people were tentatively picking up": A. J. Liebling, *Liebling Abroad* (New York: Playboy Press, 1981), p. 33.

192   "You cannot keep": ibid., pp. 37–38.

CHAPTER 27: A PICTURE A DAY

194   "movie people": Charles Seliger interview, March 31, 1979.

195   "no more than observed them": Williams, *Autobiography,* p. 197.

195   "project for a Bird": Nicolas and Elena Calas, *The Peggy Guggenheim Collection of Modern Art* (New York: Harry N. Abrams, 1967), p. 90.

195   "a true form ought to": James Thrall Soby, *Modern Art and the New Past* (Norman: University of Oklahoma Press, 1957), p. 94.

195   "his own famous cuisine": Williams, *Autobiography,* p. 188.

195   "Like a gnome": Loeb, *The Way It Was,* p. 152.

195   "shaved after each meal": ibid., pp. 151–52.

195   "He loved me very much": *OTC,* p. 211.

195   "every one was wrapped": Sidney Janis, "Of Brancusi, Mondrian and Paris in the 30's," *NYT,* December 19, 1982, p. 35.

196   "Nothing could have been easier": PG, "Introduction," *Works from the Peggy Guggenheim Foundation* (New York: Solomon R. Guggenheim Museum, 1969).

196   for three hundred: prices are from Bernard Reis's Accountant's Report for Art of This Century, December 31, 1942, Bernard Reis Papers, AAA.

196   "My initial investment": "Venerable Bohemian of Venice," *Life* 58 (June 18, 1965), pp. 101–106.

197   "little Greek heads": *OTC,* p. 215.

197   "like an imprisoned lion": ibid., pp. 214–15.

197   "vaguely crustacean": William S. Rubin, *Dada and Surrealist Art* (New York: Harry N. Abrams, 1968), p. 252.

197   "from earliest childhood": ibid., p. 251 n. 169.

197   "exactly like a painting": *OTC,* p. 215.

197   "but rude remarks": Hilton Kramer, "20th-Century Masters Dominate Guggenheim Collection," *NYT,* January 16, 1969, p. 44.

198   "Lingerie is on": Jimmy Ernst, *A Not-So-Still Life* (New York: St. Martin's/Marek, 1984), p. 213.

198   "deviate the movement": Joan M. Lukach, *Hilla Rebay* (New York: George Braziller, 1983), p. 131.

198   "I think Peggy": ibid., p. 132.

198   "full of pessimism": Shachtman, *The Phony War,* p. 161.

198   "The first year": Gold, *Crossroads Marseilles,* p. ix.

199   "I walked into Léger's studio": *OTC,* p. 218.

199   *"Finie la drôle"*: Liebling, *Liebling Abroad,* p. 60.

199   "The Germans gained": Gold, *Crossroads Marseilles,* p. 43.

200   "We have been defeated": Shachtman, *The Phony War,* p. 211.

200   *"Aucune"*: ibid., p. 215.

200   "indecent to think of anything": *OTC,* p. 218.

201   "seemed to concentrate": Liebling, *Liebling Abroad,* p. 65.

201   "People got thin worrying": ibid.

201   "Every day somebody said good-bye": ibid.

202   "It is really incomprehensible": *OTC,* p. 220.

202   mock Pulitzer Prize: "The Happy Days," *NYT,* May 26, 1946.

202   "possibly the strangest assortment": Liebling, *Liebling Abroad,* pp. 80–81.

203   "There wasn't much left": *OTC,* p. 220.

203   wept with rage: Kay Boyle, *Primer for Combat* (New York: Simon & Schuster, 1942), p. 22.

203   "No dream is worse": *London Bulletin* nos. 18–20 (June 1940), p. 1.

CHAPTER 28: THE *BOCHES*

204   "The intruders": Gold, *Crossroads Marseilles,* p. 144.

205   "extraordinary run": ibid.

205   "Mother seeks baby": Varian Fry, *Surrender on Demand* (New York: Random House, 1945), p. 20.

206   "Isn't life boring?": Apple Vail interview, February 13, 1980.

207   "state of *traumatisme*": Sharon (Bobbie) Cowling interview, April 12, 1980.

CHAPTER 29: THE EMERGENCY RESCUE COMMITTEE

214   "old magazines, colored paper": Fry, *Surrender on Demand,* p. 117.

214   *"Le terrible crétin":* ibid.

215   "Living in Grenoble": *OTC,* p. 228.

216   "I have not, meanwhile, forgot:" André Breton letter to PG, August 13, 1965, PG collection.

216   "intense, emotional": Fry, *Surrender on Demand,* p. 185.

216   "One slept on bricks": Patrick Waldberg, *Max Ernst* (Paris: Jean-Jacques Pauvert, 1958), p. 331. Author's translation.

217   "I wept for several hours": Leonora Carrington, "Down Below," *VVV* no. 4 (February, 1944), p. 70.

218   "Take a walk": Jimmy Ernst interview, November 1977.

218   "Why couldn't you": ibid.

218   acquired some of: Angelica Zander Rudenstine, *Peggy Guggenheim Collection, Venice* (New York: Harry N. Abrams and Solomon R. Guggenheim Foundation, 1958), cites New York, 1941, as the acquisition date. It is likely that the transaction occurred in France, but that payment was deferred and made in New York.

219   "seduced by the painter": Waldberg, *Max Ernst,* p. 340.

CHAPTER 30: DADAMAX ERNST

221   *"Seeing* was my chief preoccupation": Gaston Diehl, *Max Ernst,* trans. Eileen Hennessy (New York: Crown Publishers, 1973), p. 18.

221   "dangerous confusion": Max Ernst, "Some Data on the Youth of M.E. as Told by Himself," *View* ser. 2, no. 1 (April 1942), p. 30. Special issue on Max Ernst.

221   "a phallic symbol": Julien Levy interview, February 22, 1979.

221   "all forms of study": Diane Waldman, *Max Ernst* (New York: Solomon R. Guggenheim Museum, 1975), p. 16.

222   "Ironhead": Julien Levy, "The Children Outside and the Children Inside," *View* ser. 2, no. 1 (April 1942), p. 27.

222 "triumph of Dada": Hugnet, "Dada and Surrealism,"

222 "My curse upon you": Uwe M. Schneede, *Max Ernst* (New York: Praeger
-23 Publishers, 1973), p. 25.

223 "crazy with resentment": John Russell, *Max Ernst: Life and Work* (New York:
Harry N. Abrams, 1967), p. 60.

223 density of association: Lucy R. Lippard, "Dada into Surrealism (Notes on Max
Ernst as Proto-Surrealist)," *Artforum* 5, no. 1 (September 1966), p. 10. Special
issue on Surrealism.

224 "Good sense and logic": Russell, *Max Ernst*, p. 64.

224 "pregnant rather than a calm silence": Rubin, *Dada and Surrealist Art*, p. 131.

225 "Well I love Max": Josephson, *Life Among the Surrealists*, p. 179.

225 "altogether of an extraordinary male beauty": ibid., p. 177.

225 "Love is the great enemy": Russell, *Max Ernst*, p. 108.

226 "crazy little darling": Levy, *Memoir of an Art Gallery*, p. 172.

226 "stage-jeweled coronets": ibid., p. 171.

226 "Blue feathers and tinsel dust": ibid.

226 fly was open: Arthur Gold interview, 1982.

226 "made a startling effect": Robert Fizdale interview, 1982.

CHAPTER 31: THE UGLY DUCKLING AND THE SWAN

229 "When, where, and why": *OTC,* p. 231.

229 "To Leonora": ibid.

231 "Insult to German Womanhood": Schneede, *Max Ernst.*

232 "Oh, that is nothing": *OTC,* p. 234.

CHAPTER 32: EXIT MARSEILLES

233 "I spoke that day": Waldberg, *Max Ernst,* p. 342.

234 "You know your papers": ibid.

235 "I have found Leonora": *OTC,* p. 237.

235 "getting a dirty deal": ibid.

236 "No one knew": ibid., p. 241.
-37

237 *"La jolie robe"*: Vail, "Here Goes."

237 "like some mute and faithful animal": ibid.

237 "When we went swimming": ibid.

238 "I used to have a Guggenheim": Jimmy Ernst interview.

238 "He was ashamed to arrive": *OTC,* p. 238.

CHAPTER 33: ELLIS ISLAND

244 "kept vomiting": *OTC,* p. 245.

244 "while old cities crumble": unidentified photograph and caption, 1941, PG
Scrapbooks.

244 "Hello, Jimmy": J. Ernst, *A Not-So-Still Life,* p. 201.

244 "You must be Jimmy": ibid., p. 200.

244 "The anxiety-ridden eyes": ibid.

245 "unnaturally bulbous nose": ibid.

245 "From hearing this": Levy, *Memoir of an Art Gallery,* p. 254.

246   "Will you let me": J. Ernst, *A Not-So-Still Life,* p. 204.

246   "Sophisticated . . . people": ibid., p. 205.

247   "I don't think I'm likely": Laurence Vail letter to Djuna Barnes, August 3, 1941, DBA.

247   "deep in domestic smash up": Laurence Vail letter to Eleanor Fitzgerald, July 26, 1941.

249   "driving back across Arizona": Jimmy Ernst, "The Artist Speaks," *Art in America* 56 (November 1968), pp. 54–64.

250   "At night it is very gay": PG letter to Djuna Barnes, September 12, 1941, DBA.

CHAPTER 34: HALE HOUSE

251   "echo of people appreciating": Sidney Janis, "School of Paris Comes to U.S.," *Decision* 2, nos. 5–6 (November–December 1941), p. 91.

254   "treasure hunt": J. Ernst, *A Not-So-Still Life,* p. 221.

254   "he believed all the advertisements": Levy, *Memoir of an Art Gallery,* p. 188.

256   "whose lack of affectation": J. Ernst, *A Not-So-Still Life,* p. 211.

256   "we were partying all the time": Louise Nevelson and Diana MacKown, *Dawns and Dusks* (New York: Charles Scribner's & Sons, 1976), p. 97.

257   "always good food": Rebecca Reis interview, February 12, 1979.

257   "It was amazing the respect": ibid.

CHAPTER 35: MARRIAGE

258   "living in sin with an enemy alien": *OTC,* p. 263.

259   "Oh, marriage is so bourgeois": Rebecca Reis interview.

260   "In Paris at six-o'clock": "Eleven Europeans in America," *The Museum of Modern Art Bulletin* 13, nos. 4–5 (1946).

260   "like a radio": Russell, *Max Ernst,* p. 136.

260   "a difficult character": Max Ernst, "Beyond Painting," p. 19.
–61

261   "three reasons why I love Max": *OTC,* p. 282.

261   "ferocious glee": Levy, *Memoir of an Art Gallery,* p. 270.

261   "composed himself perfectly": ibid., p. 129.

262   "Ugh! Peggy": David Hare interview, February 26, 1979.

262   "he was born *dépaysé*": Henry Miller, "Another Bright Messenger," *View* ser. 2, no. 1 (April 1942), p. 17.

262   "magic ingenuity": Julien Levy, "A Summer in Long Island," *Homage to Max Ernst* (New York: Tudor Publishing, 1971), p. 62.

262   "abstracted, distant sharpness": Levy, *Memoir of an Art Gallery,* p. 271.

263   Various American painters saw these works: Waldman, *Max Ernst,* p. 54, cautions that the relation between Ernst's drips and Pollock were probably not direct, although Ernst always said Pollock got the drips from him. Cf. Alain Jouffroy, "Max Ernst: Ma peinture et mes procédes sont des jeux d'enfants," *Arts* (Paris) no. 756 (January 6–12, 1960), p. 8.

263   depicts Max's . . . relationship with Leonora: Lucy Flint, *Handbook: The Peggy Guggenheim Collection* (New York: The Solomon R. Guggenheim Foundation, 1983), for a more detailed discussion of the iconography of this and other pictures in the collection, see Rudenstine, *Peggy Guggenheim Collection, Venice.*

CHAPTER 36: OLD FRIENDS TOGETHER

265 "a new art center": *View* (April 1942).

265 "that dreadful Guggenheim girl": J. Ernst, *A Not-So-Still Life,* p. 224.

266 "continuous flow without being pinned down": Frederick Kiesler, *Inside the Endless House* (New York: Simon & Schuster, 1966), p. 262.

266 "all ends meet, and meet continuously": ibid., p. 566.

266 "structurally continuous building": Frederick Kiesler, "Design Correlation," *VVV* nos. 2–3 (March 1943).

266 "tour de farce": Kiesler, *Inside the Endless House,* p. 95.

266 unframed pictures: Dore Ashton sees the influence of James Johnson Sweeney in promoting the unframed picture, *The New York School* (New York: The Viking Press, 1973).

266 notions of "transparency": Lillian Kiesler interview, April 24, 1985.

266 "the development of new ideas": Frederick Kiesler letter to PG, March 7, 1942, Charles Seliger collection. The original plans (March 7, 1942) included an auditorium with facilities for musical evenings and a removable seating capacity of 150 people, as well as storage, office, and spaces for permanent, changing, and loan exhibitions. Kiesler hoped to be done with the main work by May 1, 1942.

267 In New York Peggy found: cf. Grace Glueck, "Paintings Descending a Ramp," *The NYT Magazine,* January 19, 1969, p. 37; J. Ernst, *A Not-So-Still Life,* p. 225; PG, "Introduction," *Works from the Peggy Guggenheim Foundation; The Peggy Guggenheim Collection* (Venice: The Peggy Guggenheim Foundation, 1965); Rudenstine, *Peggy Guggenheim Collection, Venice.*

267 "great physico-mental stream": André Breton, "Genesis and Perspective of Surrealism," *Art of This Century,* ed. PG, p. 26.

269 "Avida Dollars": Rubin, *Dada and Surrealist Art.*

269 advertisements . . . obtained with the help: John Bernard Myers, *Tracking the Marvelous* (New York: Random House, 1983), p. 34.

269 *View* offices: started out at 360 East Fifty-fifth Street and moved to 1 East Fifty-third.

269 Max Ernst issue: *View* ser. 2, no. 1 (April 1942).

269 "a research studio": ibid.

269 "the thrill that passed through me": Myers, *Tracking the Marvelous,* p. 7.

270 to disseminate French literature: David Hare interview, February 26, 1979.

270 "Twin-Touch-Test": *VVV* nos. 2–3 (March 1943).

270 deplored the weather: "Eleven Europeans in America," *The Museum of Modern Art Bulletin* (1946).

270 "everything not French": ibid.

271 "autocratic and priestlike": J. Ernst, "The Artist Speaks," p. 58.

271 "he was so bent on money": Rebecca Reis interview, February 12, 1979.

272 "a religious experience": Myers, *Tracking the Marvelous,* p. 32.

274 "they were absolutely ignorant": Tomkins, *The World of Marcel Duchamp,* p. 156.

274 Matta organized evenings: Lee Krasner interview, April 19, 1979.

274 "only to cap a gusher": Virgil Thomson, "Answers to Questions," *Possibilities* (Winter 1947/48).

274 changed the flavor: Gordon Onslow-Ford letter to Hermione Benhaim, March 29, 1966, Howard Putzel papers, AAA.

274 showing up his elders: Sidney Simon, "Concerning the Beginnings of the New

York School: 1939–43 (an interview with Robert Motherwell, January 1967)," *Art International* 2, no. 6 (Summer 1967).

274   disliked pure abstraction: It should be noted that in New York Breton championed the organic abstractions of Arshile Gorky, hailed the automatism of Masson, and denounced the retrograde technique of Dali. Cf. "Genesis and Perspective of Surrealism," although he was said to favor illusionistic renderings of oneiric images.

CHAPTER 37: SUMMER IN THE CITY

276   Jimmy Ernst believed: Barbara Goldsmith interview, 1984.

277   "Neither André Breton nor Marcel Duchamp": Kiesler, *Inside the Endless House,* p. 194.

277   "get me some cigarettes": Lee Krasner interview.

277   "great priest": Charles Seliger interview, March 31, 1979.

278   he understood America: Hedda Sterne interview, June 26, 1982.

278   he only half-smiled: John Bernard Myers interview, September 27, 1978.

278   "His whole life was his baby, Surrealism": David Hare interview, February 26, 1979.

278   "too many stars": *OTC,* p. 271.

279   "Are you thirsty?": John Cage interview, November 14, 1979.

280   Kiesler was impressed by Duchamp's obsessive neatness: Lillian Kiesler interview.

281   "Aztec virgin": "Hovick-Kirkland, Miss Gypsy Rose Lee, author, weds Broadway actor," *Life* 13, no. 11 (September 14, 1942), pp. 41–44.

281   nagged Jimmy Ernst to send Gypsy a bill: J. Ernst, *A Not-So-Still Life,* p. 224.

CHAPTER 38: ISMS RAMPANT!

285   "break down the physical and mental barriers": Kiesler, "Design Correlation," p. 76.

286   original estimate of the cost: Frederick Kiesler letter to PG, March 7, 1942, Charles Seliger collection.

286   Jimmy Ernst suspected: J. Ernst, *A Not-So-Still Life,* p. 229.

286   friends and "frenemies": Kiesler, *Inside the Endless House,* p. 265.

287   to aid French prisoners: The Coordinating Council of French Relief Societies.

287   "fatal to run short": Blesh, *Modern Art USA,* p. 200.

287   "Get some friends": ibid., p. 201.

288   "festive ceremonial dedicated to the imagination": *First Papers of Surrealism: October 14–November 7, 1942* (New York: Coordinating Council of French Relief Societies).

288   one woman and her umbrella become tangled: "The Passing Shows," *Art News* 41, no. 12 (November 1–14, 1942), p. 24.

288   could be dismantled in thirty minutes: Lillian Kiesler interview.

288   "swaying in space": Pierre Matisse interview, May 29, 1979.

288   "like a large cubistic painting": "Isms Rampant: Peggy Guggenheim's Dream World Goes Abstract, Cubist and Generally Non-Real," *Newsweek* (November 2, 1942), p. 66.

288   "like blood": ibid.

289   four designs in all: Lillian Kiesler interview; in Kiesler's notes on the gallery

he lists three types of mobile seats: folding, rocker, and seven-way unit, but there were four amoeboid designs.

289   sawed off by Kiesler and a carpenter: Cynthia Goodman, "Frederick Kiesler: Designs for Peggy Guggenheim's Art of This Century Gallery," *Arts* (June 1977), p. 93.

289   unexpected colors: list of colors from PG.

289   eighteen uses for his seven-way chair: Kiesler, "Design Correlation," p. 76.

289   "to facilitate the co-reality": ibid., p. 79.

290   "Surrealist Circus!": Klaus Mann, *American Mercury* (February 1943).

290   "Isms Rampant": *Newsweek* (November 2, 1942).

290   "never bulged further": Henry McBride, "New Gallery Ideas," *The New York Sun,* October 23, 1942.

290   "wonders never ceasing": Edward Alden Jewell, "In the Realm of Art," *NYT,* October 25, 1942, sec. 8, p. 9.

290   "WE *will* DO": *View* ser. 2, no. 4 (January 1943), p. 54.

CHAPTER 39: GALLERY LIFE

291   "And what did you think": Michael Georges-Michael, *From Renoir to Picasso: Artists in Action* (Boston: Houghton Mifflin, 1957), p. 139.

292   "I have something very interesting": Jimmy Ernst interview, November 1977.

292   "she came up without a word": ibid.

293   "I can't give up this business": Rebecca Reis interview, February 12, 1979.

293   "the weirdest show in town": *New York World-Telegram,* December 19, 1942.

294   "I'm not a women's liberationist": Alan Levy, "Peggy Guggenheim: Venice's Last Duchess," *Art News* 74 (April 1975), pp. 57–58.

295   "Max is very, very happy": J. Ernst, *A Not-So-Still Life,* p. 236.

295   "very, very female": Catherine Viviano interview, March 1979.

295   "He was always interested": *OTC,* p. 280.

295   "That's Grandma!": J. Ernst, "The Artist Speaks," *Art in America,* p. 60.

296   nipple discreetly peeking through: Arthur Gold and Robert Fizdale interview, 1982.

297   "The things that are going on!": Buffie Johnson interview, May 16, 1979.

297   "behaved more like a nurse": *OTC,* p. 282.

297   "some kind of a psychiatrist": PG.

298   "pretentious, boring, stupid": *OTC,* p. 280.

298   "act of self flagellation": J. Ernst, *A Not-So-Still Life,* p. 252.

298   "The climate in Arizona": ibid.

298   "They were pursued even there": ibid., pp. 252–53.

CHAPTER 40: THE SPRING SALON

300   "leader of the youngest generation": James Johnson Sweeney, catalogue introduction, Hélion (New York: Art of This Century, February 1943).

300   "sacrificed to truth": *OTC,* p. 282.

301   "establishing a research laboratory for new ideas": Jewell, "In the Realm of Art," p. 9.

301   "serving the future": ibid.

301   "a yearly salon": ibid.

302   "Artists for Victory": opened on December 7, 1942, at the Metropolitan Museum of Art, displaying nearly fifteen hundred works by living artists includ-

ing Aaron Bohrod, Lyonel Feininger, Mardsen Hartley, Charles Howard, Jack Levine, and Mark Tobey.

302   had been so poor: Francis V. O'Connor, *Jackson Pollock* (New York: The Museum of Modern Art, 1967).

303   "pessimistic cowhand": Blesh, *Modern Art USA,* p. 253.

303   tip was missing from his right index finger: Francis V. O'Connor and Eugene V. Thaw, *Jackson Pollock: A Catalogue Raisonné of Paintings, Drawings, and Other Works* (New Haven and London: Yale University Press, 1978), vol. 4, p. 274.

303   met Pollock at a loft party: Lee Krasner interview, April 19, 1979.

303   arriving in black: Lillian Kiesler interview.

303   likened them to the devil: ibid.

304   "I am nature": O'Connor, *Jackson Pollock,* p. 26.

305   "Pretty awful, isn't it?": J. Ernst, *A Not-So-Still Life,* p. 241.

305   "You must watch this man": Lee Krasner interview.

305   "You can't be serious": Jimmy Ernst interview.

305   "I took advice from none but the best": A. Levy, "Venice's Last Duchess," p. 57.

305   "Let me show you": Jimmy Ernst interview.

305   among the exhibitors: as were Fanny Hillsmith, Irene Rice-Pereira, Ralph Rosenberg, Perle Fine, C. Dilworth.

305   "the Freudian dream catalogue": J. Ernst, *A Not-So-Still Life,* p. 196.

305   "Despite a faint air": Robert M. Coates, "The Art Galleries: from Moscow to Harlem," *The New Yorker* (May 29, 1943), p. 49.

307   "Things really broke": O'Connor, *Jackson Pollock,* p. 28.

CHAPTER 41: LIFE IN THE DUPLEX

308   "peculiar current": *OTC,* p. 287.

309   "nasty bit": Barbara Guest, *Herself Defined: The Poet H.D. and Her World* (New York: Doubleday, 1984) p. 180.

309   "very much made up": *OTC,* p. 292.

319   "very bright, a real intellectual": Sidney Janis interview, February 28, 1979.

319   "out of the clutches": Yvonne Hagen interview, March 15, 1980.

CHAPTER 42: SHOOTING STAR

321   "my most honorable achievement": Henry Ehrlich, "Peggy Guggenheim's Art Comes to America," *Look* 33 (February 4, 1969), p. 37.

321   "my second achievement": PG.

322   "The fact that good European moderns": "Jackson Pollock," *Arts and Architecture* 61, no. 2 (February 1944), p. 14. O'Connor, "Jackson Pollock," p. 32, reprinted in Ellen H. Johnson, ed., *American Artists on Art from 1940 to 1980* (New York: Harper & Row, 1982), pp. 1–4.

322   "source of my paintings": Sam Hunter, "Jackson Pollock: The Maze and the Minotaur," *New World Writing* (New York: New American Library, 1956), p. 178.

323   "the most seminal of all painters": Clement Greenberg, *Art and Culture* (Boston: Beacon Press, 1961), p. 126.

323   "What are you doing": Laura de Coppet and Alan Jones, *The Art Dealers* (New York: Clarkson N. Potter, 1984), p. 36.

323   "Painting is self-discovery": Selden Rodman, *Conversations with Artists* (New York: Devin-Adair, 1957), p. 82.

323   "Pollock's talent is volcanic": James Johnson Sweeney, *Jackson Pollock* (New
-24   York: Art of This Century, November 9–27, 1943).

324   "We like all this": *Art Digest* (November 15, 1943).

324   "among the strongest abstract paintings": Clement Greenberg, "Art," *The
Nation* (November 27, 1943), p. 621.

324   "Any new art": *Holger Cahill Memoirs* (interviewed by Joan Pring, 1957),
Columbia University Oral History Research Office, Section on Art Movements: Abstract Expressionism Since 1943, pp. 561–62.

325   "I am getting $150": O'Connor and Thaw, *Catalogue Raisonné*, vol. 4, p. 233.

325   "when Lee was away": PG.

326   "the strongest painter": Clement Greenberg, "Art," *The Nation* (April 7,
1945), p. 397.

326   "It missed the wall": David Hare interview, February 26, 1979.

327   "I tried to get it back": Christopher Andreae, "One Painting a Day," *Christian
Science Monitor,* February 4, 1969.

327   "I never would have had space": ibid.

327   "We don't need any more paintings": Jimmy Ernst interview.

CHAPTER 43: THE MAN BEHIND THE SCENE

328   "whether the insane work": Howard Devree, "A Reviewer's Notes," *NYT,*
December 5, 1943, p. xii.

329   "kindliness and respect": Maude Riley, "Fifty-seventh Street in Review," *Art
Digest* 18, no. 10 (February 15, 1944), p. 20.

329   "This too is simple": *Daily American,* November 17–18, 1974.

329   "Her taste . . . was often erratic": Aline B. Saarinen, *The Proud Possessors* (New
York: Random House, 1958), p. 337.

330   "fun thing": David Hare interview, February 26, 1979.

332   "I don't know": Lee Krasner interview.

333   only two weeks' notice: PG letter to William Baziotes, September 13, 1944,
Baziotes Papers, AAA.

334   left them in the lurch: Robert Motherwell letter to William Baziotes, 1945,
Baziotes Papers, AAA.

334   "I hear he now": *Laurence Vail* (New York: Art of This Century, March 16,
1945).

334   Nell Blaine felt discovered: Nell Blaine interviewed by Anne Skillion (March
15, 1979), Columbia University Oral History Research Office.

335   finding pictures at reasonable prices: Howard Putzel papers, AAA.

335   "Possibly classification leads to clarification": Howard Putzel, *A Problem for
Critics* (New York: 67 Gallery, 1945), Charles Seliger collection.

335   "don't leave that ism dangling": Maude Riley, "Insufficient Evidence," *Art
Digest* (June 1, 1945).

336   "we have plenty of problems": Emily Genauer quoted in Edward Alden Jewell,
"Toward Abstract or Away?" *NYT,* July 1, 1945.

336   "a new school of painting": Robert Coates, "The Art Galleries," *The New
Yorker* 21, no. 15 (May 26, 1945), p. 68.

336   "There is no question": Clement Greenberg, "Art," *The Nation* (June 9,
1945).

336   terrible businessman: Charles Seliger interview, March 31, 1979.

336   sleeping on a folding cot: ibid.

CHAPTER 44: THE 1945 SEASON

337   "My chief function": PG letter to Herbert Read, November 12, 1945, HRA.

337   "She came with a big touring car": Charles Seliger interview.

338   "you were the nicest": ibid.

338   "show me the ropes": ibid.

338   "small band of Myth Makers": Mark Rothko, *Clyfford Still,* catalogue introduction (New York: Art of This Century, 1946); and Dore Ashton, *About Rothko* (New York: Oxford University Press, 1983), pp. 93–94.

338   "there is a melancholy": PG letter to Herbert Read, February 2, 1946, HRA.

338   had his wife copy each of his paintings: Douglas MacAgy interview, 1968.

338   could talk . . . about baseball: Dorothy Miller in *Holger Cahill Memoirs,* Columbia Oral History, pp. 578–79.

339   "it only works for unknown artists": PG letter to Herbert Read, November 12, 1945, HRA.

339   "He works on large canvases": PG letter to Herbert Read, February 2, 1946, HRA.

339   "I feel like a grandmother": PG letter to Herbert Read, November 12, 1945, HRA.

340   *bal masqué:* cf. Myers, *Tracking the Marvelous,* p. 49.

340   "old fashioned and wore": PG letter to Herbert Read, November 12, 1945, HRA.

340   "began in my gallery": "Poor Peg's Treasure," *Time* 85 (January 22, 1965),
–41   p. 52.

341   "What happened, rather": Greenberg, *Art and Culture,* p. 212.

341   "Charlie, move away": Charles Seliger interview, March 31, 1979.

341   "And what are *you* doing here": Peggy's clippings scrapbook beginning 1948 (March 1948), PG collection. Author's translation.

342   "Every time I needed money": Andreae, "One Painting a Day."

342   Kandinsky: sales information in Bernard Reis, "Accountant's Report for Art of This Century for the year ending December 31, 1945," Bernard Reis Papers, AAA.

343   "Why don't you send Lee out": Lee Krasner interview, April 19, 1979.

343   Pollock's contract with Peggy: a copy of which is appended to *Peggy Guggenheim* v. *Lee Krasner Pollock,* executrix of the Jackson Pollock Estate, U.S. District Court, S.D.N.Y., 61 Civ. Action No. 2034 (filed June 8, 1961); also included in correspondence file 1960–1964, Bernard Reis Papers, AAA.

CHAPTER 45: OUT OF HER HEAD

345   summer of 1944: *OTC* states 1945 in a chapter not written by Peggy, but Peggy recalled writing it on Fire Island, which would make it summer 1944 not 1945; "Peggy in Abstract," *Newsweek* 27 (March 25, 1946), p. 98, also says she wrote it on Fire Island, summer 1945, but it is likely she started it the summer before and completed it in 1945.

345   "I have no memory": *OTC,* p. 1.

346   fictitious names: all names from Peggy Guggenheim, *Out of This Century* (New York: Dial Press, 1946).

346   "The copy editor had a very dull": PG to Herbert Read, November 12, 1945, HRA.

346   "complete hysteria": ibid.

346   "Out of My Head": Bohrod, "Surrealism and Sex à la Guggenheim."

346   "Flat and witless": "Temptations of Peggy," *Time* 47 (March 25, 1946), p. 57.

346   "wish they were disguised": Harry Hansen, *World-Telegram,* March 15, 1946.
–47

347   "The more I read": Harry Hansen, "The First Reader: Art and A Guggenheim," *World-Telegram,* March 26, 1946.

347   "astonishing lack of sensibility": Elizabeth Hardwick, *The Nation* (April 6, 1946), p. 405.

347   "Boudoir Bohemia": *Art Digest* (April 15, 1946).

347   Wags said Peggy was being sued: *Art Digest* (May 15, 1946).

347   "You have outrivalled Rousseau": Herbert Read letter to PG, February 28, 1946, PG collection.

347   "You've got to buy": Robert Fizdale interview, 1982.

347   "an urge on wheels": Florence Haxton Bullock, "Stripped Down to Sex," *New York Herald Tribune Weekly Book Review,* April 28, 1946.

347   "orgasm a day": Malcolm Cowley interview, August 2, 1979.
–48

348   "diabetic, prematurely worm-eaten pictures": Clement Greenberg, "Art," *The Nation* (April 7, 1945), p. 398.

348   "full of art types": Mary McCarthy interview, September 12, 1979.

349   "She always told us": "The Last Duchess," *Time* (December 16, 1957), p. 76.

349   "delightfully fresh": PG letter to Herbert Read, November 12, 1945.

349   Words like *alienation:* Myers, *Tracking the Marvelous,* p. 70.

350   it seemed to John Bernard Myers: ibid.

350   "I hate America": PG to Herbert Read, February 2, 1946, HRA.

351   "not lack courage": Mary McCarthy, "The Cicerone," *Cast a Cold Eye* (New York: Harcourt, Brace & World, 1950), pp. 114–15.

353   "snood and sandals": ibid., p. 110.

353   "middlingly but authentically rich": ibid., p. 105.

353   "her estimates were sharp": ibid., pp. 107–108.

353   "Sexual intercourse": ibid., p. 113.

353   "species of feminine hygiene": ibid., p. 124.

354   "read it to me": David Kalstone interview, September 28, 1978.

CHAPTER 46: FAREWELL FIFTY-SEVENTH STREET

356   deal with a drunk: B. H. Friedman, *Jackson Pollock: Energy Made Visible* (New York: McGraw-Hill Book Co., 1972), p. 115.

357   "My painting": Jackson Pollock, "My painting," *Possibilities* (Winter 1947/48), p. 79.

357   "Who the hell is Pasiphaë?": William Rubin, "Pollock as Jungian Illustrator: The Limits of Psychological Criticism," *Art in America* 67, no. 8 (December 1979), p. 74.

357   "a violent Duchamp": Blesh, *Modern Art USA,* p. 254.

358   "Everything that had been amorphous": Hunter, "Jackson Pollock," p. 180.

358   "Every so often": Blesh, *Modern Art USA,* pp. 253–54.

358   image emerged . . . from the spontaneous flow: Rubin, "Pollock as Jungian Illustrator," p. 83.

358   "first significant change": Barbara Rose, *American Art Since 1900* (New York: Praeger, 1967; rev. ed. 1975), p. 150.

358   "My painting": O'Connor and Thaw, *Catalogue Raisonné,* vol. 4, p. 262.

360   "they'd be cordial": Charles Seliger interview.
360   "that marvelous place": Blesh, *Modern Art USA,* p. 208.

CHAPTER 47: VENICE

363   handed him the matchbook: PG and Emilio Vedova interview, July 20, 1978.
364   "Oh, yes. Gugge": Giuseppe Santomaso interview, September 9, 1979.
364   "I do not in the least regret": PG letter to Clement Greenberg, December 2, 1947, AAA.
364   "people do mad things": ibid.
364   "It was all": PG to Bernard Reis, December 11, 1947, AAA.
364   "astounded by the crazy life": PG letter to Charles Seliger February 24, 1948,
-65   Charles Seliger Collection.
365   "My only ambtition": ibid.
366   "I have nothing to say to him": Christina Thoresby interview, August 29, 1979.
367   "Is my small collection": PG to Clement Greenberg, December 2, 1947, AAA.
367   "I were a new European country": *OTC,* p. 329.
369   "How did Peggy": Roloff Beny interview, September 6, 1979.
369   *Palazzo non Finito:* Wishart, *High Diver,* p. 92.
369   The palazzo boasted: Nicholas Bentley, "Two Venetian Palaces: The Palazzo Venier dei Leoni," *House and Garden* (September 1958), p. 52.
369   "D'Annunzio lived across the canal": Maria Kozslik Donovan, "An American in Venice," *Holiday* 56 (January 1975), p. 58.
369   "naked and gilded": Wishart, *High Diver,* p. 92.
369   "forced, rather hastily, to leave": ibid.
371   "thousands of other people": PG letter to Charles Seliger, November 11, 1949, Charles Seliger Collection.
371   "a lot of gassy little dogs": Steven M. L. Aronson, "Piers Paul Read, A Married Man," *Interview* 10, no. 6 (June 1980), pp. 40–42.
372   "The show was a great success": PG letter to Charles Seliger, November 11, 1949, Charles Seliger Collection.
372   "This show sent all the Venetian": PG letter to Clement Greenberg, 1958, AAA.
372   "Chaos, Damn It": *Time* 56, no. 21 (November 20, 1950), pp. 70–71.
372   "NO CHAOS": "Letters," *Time* 56, no. 24 (December 11, 1950), p. 10.

CHAPTER 48: LIFE WITH TARZAN

374   visitors viewed Peggy's wet stockings: Robert Quinlan interview, 1984.
374   "in honor of the visit of 20 nuns": PG letter to Charles Seliger, November 11, 1949, Charles Seliger Collection.
375   when the Duchess of Kent's: PG letter to Herbert Read, June 6, 1961, HRA.
376   "Oh! It's boring": Eileen Finletter interview, June 13, 1979.
377   "Fifty per cent of the people": "Venerable Bohemian of Venice," *Life* 58 (June 18, 1965), pp. 101–106.
377   "her habit of rattling her false teeth": Truman Capote, "Unspoiled Monsters," *Esquire* 85, no. 5 (May 1976), p. 126.
380   "little turds": Jane Bouché Strong interview, March 1980.
380   "Pegeen was having": ibid.
380   was killed instantly . . . as he . . . swerved: PG letter to Djuna Barnes, October 25, 1954, DBA.

380 "those who live by the sword": PG postcard to Herbert Read, undated, HRA.

381 "I don't think": PG letter to Djuna Barnes, October 25, 1954, DBA.

381 "the navy moves on": PG letter to Becky Reis, March 9 (year not given), Bernard Reis Papers, AAA.

381 "soul to the Vatican": Georges Bataille, *Max Ernst* (Paris: Éditions d'Art Gonthier-Seghers, 1959), p. 28. Author's translation.

381 "We had a tender reconciliation": PG letter to Djuna Barnes, October 25, 1954, DBA.

381 "He's been so unpleasant": *International Herald Tribune,* December 3, 1974.

CHAPTER 49: THE GOLDEN AGE

383 "I used to think": Price, "The Mrs. Guggenheim Collection," p. 79.

383 "It's a sort of dream world": "The Last Duchess," *Time,* p. 76.

383 voluminous green gauze dress: Wishart, *High Diver,* p. 91.

385 "Would you mind": Arthur Gold interview, 1982.

385 "Oh! What are these?": Jane Rylands interview, July 22, 1978.

385 "She is our dream": Sharon Cowling interview, April 12, 1980.

386 "Is He the Greatest": "Is He the Greatest Living Painter in the United States?" *Life* 27 (August 8, 1949), pp. 42–44.

386 "I gathered Pollock was becoming": PG letter to Charles Seliger, November 11, 1949, Charles Seliger Collection.

386 "It is a great pity": PG to Clement Greenberg, February 12, 1958, AAA.

387 "So, she got fucked": John Bernard Myers interview, September 27, 1978.

388 threatening to sue her for artistic domination: "The Last Duchess," *Time,* p. 76.

CHAPTER 50: THE BARCHESSA

393 "You do say": Jane Rylands interview, July 22, 1978.

393 "Do you have": John Goodwin interview.

393 "I can't wait": PG

393 "savage mysogyny": Wishart, *High Diver,* p. 94.

394 white and papal yellow: ibid., p. 174.

394 the *questare:* the civil government.

394 "The Venetians don't deserve": David Kalstone interview, September 28, 1978.

CHAPTER 51: CONFESSIONS OF AN ART ADDICT

395 "tight in the night": PG letter to Bernard Reis, October 20, 1958, Bernard Reis Papers, AAA.

395 "organic, refined, sensitive": Lukach, *Hilla Rebay,* p. 184.

396 "the building is built": ibid., p. 200.

396 "like a giant Mix-Master": Kiesler, *Inside the Endless House,* p. 197.

397 "ready to accept anything in the name of culture": *Daily American,* November 17–18, 1974.

397 "images of fat, rich millionaires": "Venerable Bohemian of Venice," *Life* p. 102.

397 "Most painters think only of money": ibid., p. 103.

397 "This whaddayacallit": "Poor Peg's Treasure," *Time* 85 (January 22, 1965), p. 52.

397   "They're pre-pop": ibid., p. 55.

397   liked to quote Marx: Hedda Sterne interview, June 26, 1982.

398   purchased for her . . . by the director: Sir Norman Reid interview, May 1, 1979.

399   "I am considering rewriting my book": PG letter to Charles Seliger, November 11, 1949, Charles Seliger Collection.

399   inseparable from the work itself: cf. Barbara Rose, "Hans Namuth's Photographs and the Jackson Pollock Myth: Part One: Media Impact and the Failure of Criticism," and "Part Two: Number 29, 1950'," *Arts* 53, no. 7 (March 1979), pp. 112–19. Special issue on Jackson Pollock.

399   never sold a picture for more than eight thousand dollars: de Coppet and Jones, *The Art Dealers,* p. 39.

399   never sold a Pollock for more than a thousand: PG; in Bernard Reis's Accountant's Reports for Art of This Century, Bernard Reis Papers, AAA, the highest price that appears for a Pollock is $740 paid by Mrs. Gates Lloyd.

400   "all the works of art": a copy of the contract is annexed as an exhibit in *Peggy Guggenheim* v. *Lee Krasner,* U.S. District Court, S.D.N.Y., Civ. No. 61, 2034 (1961).

400   lawsuit against Lee Krasner: ibid.

400   The works PG alleged at issue listed in Plaintiff's Answer to Interrogatories, pp. 4–5, filed January 10, 1962, in *Guggenheim* v. *Krasner* were *Composition* (1946), *Shimmering Image* (1947), *War* (1947), *White Horizontal* (1941–47) *Eyes in the Heat II* (1947), *Pittura* (1947), *Ink and Colored Pencil* (1947), *Drawing #39* (1946), *Drawing #40* (1946), *Drawing #41* (1946), *Drawing #44* (1947), *#128, Sunscape* (1946), *Equine Series II* (1946), *Vortex* (1947), *Free Form* (1946).

401   "All the rest were sent": *CAA,* p. 109.

CHAPTER 52: A TRAVELING COLLECTION

403   "I thought of the electric bills": Robert Fizdale interview, 1982.

403   "bargain basement": PG letter to Bernard Reis, undated, Bernard Reis Papers, AAA.

404   took affront at press suggestions: Neville Wallis, "Art at the Tate," *The Spectator* (January 15, 1965).

405   "It is a bombshell": "Poor Peg's Treasure," *Time,* p. 52.

406   "has been a real influence in modern art": "Art Collector and Patron: Peggy Guggenheim," *NYT,* December 31, 1964.

406   "squeak like mice": Edwin Mullins, *Weekend Telegraph*, January 1, 1965, PG Scrapbooks.

406   "I am practically": Robert C. Doty, "Whither the Gondola," *NYT*, May 22, 1965, pp. 24–25.

407   "How many husbands have you had?": Robert Fizdale and Arthur Gold interview, 1982.

CHAPTER 53: PEGEEN

411   found dead, lying on the floor with her arm stretched out: Giuseppe Santomaso interview, September 9, 1979.

411   Half of her face was black: Christina Thoresby interview, August 29, 1979.

411   even trying to starve herself: Eileen Finletter interview, June 13, 1979.

411 to get her hands on the apartment: Taylor Mead interview, November, 6, 1980.

412 "I can't absolve Peggy": Lawrence Vail letter to Djuna Barnes, March 31, 1967, DBA.

412 in unsanctified ground: Christina Thoresby interview, August 29, 1979.

412 "Saw Peggy who looks younger": Laurence Vail letter to Djuna Barnes, April
-13 12, 1966, DBA

413 "Hopelessness is a more satisfactory condition": Laurence Vail letter to Djuna Barnes, December 31, 1966, DBA.

CHAPTER 54: GUGGENHEIM TO GUGGENHEIM

414 "I find life also gets worse": PG to Djuna Barnes, November 29, 1967, DBA.

415 "We were terribly close": Felicia Warburg Roosevelt, *Doers and Dowagers* (New York: Doubleday & Co., 1975), p. 218.

415 "He was a state guest": PG to Djuna Barnes, April 16, 1968, DBA.

415 leather bride: the once virgin bride is totally debauched and lying wantonly on a bed of leaves, titled *Given: 1. The Waterfall/ 2. The Illuminating Gas*, in the Philadelphia Museum of Art.

416 "If you leave it to the Tate": Giuseppe Santomaso interview, September 9, 1979.

419 "I have . . . spent most of my life": Roberta Brandes Gratz, "The Art of Being Peggy," *New York Post Weekend Magazine*, January 18, 1969, p. 25.

419 "The best show": Angela Taylor, "At the Guggenheim, Party for Cousin Peggy and Her Art," *NYT*, January 16, 1969, p. L4.

420 "Uncle Solomon is now dead": David L. Shirey, "Peggy's Back in Town," *Newsweek* 73 (January 27, 1969), p. 70.

420 "I never dreamt": PG, "Introduction," *Works from the Peggy Guggenheim Foundation* (New York: The Solomon R. Guggenheim Museum, 1969), exhibition catalogue.

420 "one . . . some notion": Barbara Rose, "The Taste of the Guggenheims," *Vogue* 153 (April 1, 1969), p. 152.

420 "created a collection": Shirey, "Peggy's Back in Town," p. 70.

421 "No one knows": Grace Glueck, "Paintings Descending a Ramp," *NYT Magazine,* January 19, 1969, p. 45.

422 "I'm very happy about it": Richard F. Shepard, "Peggy Guggenheim Entrusts Art Here," *NYT,* March 25, 1969, p. 42.

CHAPTER 55: TWILIGHT

425 he would only work part time: Nicolas Hélion, co-producer, *Peggy Guggenheim: La Ultima Dogaressa* (1977) film.

425 "All Venetians can row": Edmund White interview, August 29, 1978.

426 "I adore floating": PG letter to Djuna Barnes, October 3, 1956, DBA.

426 "was the corpse collector": David Kalstone interview, September 28, 1978.

426 "I'm only happy now": ibid.

427 and call himself its curator: John Hohnsbeen, "The Last of the Last Dogaressa: Memories of Peggy Guggenheim in Venice."

428 adored "even lesser, minor writers": John Hohnsbeen interview, 1979.

428 "I was much more interested in literature": Mario Amaya, "Peggy Guggenheim," *Interview* (November 1979).

428   "parties were invariably": Hohnsbeen, "The Last of the Last Dogaressa."

428   "When did Miss Guggenheim die?": ibid.

428   "curiously ageless": Donovan, "An American in Venice," p. 58.

428   "as a sporty Miami dowager": Levy, "Venice's Last Duchess," p. 57.

428   "Terrible! Shocking!": ibid., p. 58.

428   "If I were forced to start": ibid.

429   "the sticks": Sindbad Vail interviews: September 13, 1979; Venice, April 1980; New York, 1980.

429   "I'm the last Vail": Jane Rylands interview, July 1978.

429   talking about it, he blossomed: Eileen Finletter interview, June 13, 1979.

430   "great unfulfilled relationship": Jane Rylands interview, July 1978.

430   "She liked very much Françoise Sagan": Maria Theresa Rubin de Cervin interview, September 23, 1982.

430   "I hate it": Joan Juliet Buck, "Eye View: An American in Venice," *Women's Wear Daily,* September 29, 1974.

431   "Do you think": Jane Rylands interview, July 1978.

431   but not eat there: John Hohnsbeen interview, March 27, 1979.

431   "bawdy": Joseph Losey letter to author, February 16, 1981.

CHAPTER 56: THE LAST DOGARESSA

433   "Very interesting": John Hohnsbeen interview, September 1979.

434   "The truth can't hurt": "Notes on People: Peggy Guggenheim Names the Last Poor Dears," *NYT,* September 16, 1979.

434   "Daisy Miller with rather more balls": Gore Vidal, "Foreword, *OTC,* p. xiii.

434   "whole public history": Hilton Kramer, "Glamorous Characters, Expensive Settings," *The NYT Book Review,* December 23, 1979, p. 4.

434   "The result is": ibid.

434   "what now so deliciously appalls": Quentin Crisp, "The Collector," *New York* (November 26, 1979), p. 86.

435   "canny impresario": John Richardson, "La Dogaressa," *New York Review of Books,* November 22, 1979, p. 18.

435   "Peggy may have aged": ibid., p. 20.

435   "I just stepped forward": Amaya, "Peggy Guggenheim," p. 42.

435   "picked her up": John Loring interview, June 1984.

436   "Isn't it lucky": Jane Rylands interview, April 9, 1980.

436   "How much is this": George Smith interview, April 1980.

436   "Don't bother to come": Christina Thoresby interview, April 8, 1980.

436   "Don't have Sindbad come": Jane Rylands interview, April 9, 1980.

436   "Oh, I'll be home": Christina Thoresby interview, April 8, 1980.

437   "These nurses don't have any idea": Jane Rylands interview, April 9, 1980.

437   "She's dying": ibid.

437   he drank a great deal: Christina Thoresby interview, April 8, 1980.

CHAPTER 57: A HOUSE IS NOT A HOME

439   "By the time": Sindbad Vail letter to author, September 22, 1980.

440   "gave away her entire collection": ibid.

440   "She left me only back income taxes": Sindbad Vail interview, November 17, 1984.

INDEX